T0389596

The Italian Yearbook of International Law

The Italian Yearbook of International Law

VOLUME 30

The titles published in this series are listed at *brill.com/iyil*

The Italian Yearbook of International Law Volume XXX (2020)

BRILL

NIJHOFF

LEIDEN | BOSTON

Typeface for the Latin, Greek, and Cyrillic scripts: "Brill". See and download: brill.com/brill-typeface.

ISSN 0391-5107
E-ISBN 2211-6133
ISBN 978-90-04-50821-7 (hardback)

Editorial assistance for this volume has been provided by Anthony Wenton. Manuscripts, books for review and correspondence may be sent to THE ITALIAN YEARBOOK OF INTERNATIONAL LAW - Prof. Daniele Amoroso, Dipartimento di Giurisprudenza, University of Cagliari, Via Nicolodi 102, 09123 Cagliari (Italy) and/or by e-mail to italianyearbook@gmail.com.

Each article submitted with a view to publication in the IYIL is subject to peer-review by two anonymous referees.

CONTENTS

Symposium
CITIES AND INTERNATIONAL LAW

Focus
THE ENRICA LEXIE AWARD

ARTICLES

PRACTICE OF INTERNATIONAL COURTS AND TRIBUNALS

ITALIAN PRACTICE RELATING TO INTERNATIONAL LAW

JUDICIAL DECISIONS
(edited by *Daniele Amoroso* and *Andrea Caligiuri*)

DIPLOMATIC AND PARLIAMENTARY PRACTICE
(edited by *Pietro Gargiulo, Marco Pertile* and *Paolo Turrini*)

BIBLIOGRAPHIES

GIULIO BARTOLINI (ed.), *A History of International Law in Italy*, Oxford, Oxford University Press, 2020 *(Giorgio Sacerdoti)*; GABRIELA A. OANTA, *La sucesión de Estados en las Organizaciones internacionales: Examen de la práctica internacional*, Barcelona, J.M. Bosch editor, 2020 *(Alessandra Lanciotti)*; SERENA FORLATI, MAKANE MOÏSE MBENGUE and BRIAN MCGARRY (eds.), *The Gabčíkovo-Nagymaros Judgment and Its Contribution to the Development of International Law*, Leiden/Boston, Brill Nijhoff, 2020 *(Dario Piselli)*; EMMANUEL H.D. DE GROOF, *State Renaissance for Peace: Transitional Governance under International Law*, Cambridge, Cambridge University Press, 2020, pp. 395 – EMMANUEL H.D. DE GROOF and MICHA WIEBUSCH (eds.), *International Law and Transitional Governance: Critical Perspectives*, Abingdon, Routledge, 2020 *(William Underwood)*; ROBERTO VIRZO, *La confisca nell'azione internazionale di contrasto ad attività criminali* (Confiscation in International Action against Crime), Napoli, Edizioni Scientifiche Italiane, 2020 *(Serena Forlati)*.

LIST OF ABBREVIATIONS

Periodicals[*]

AFDI	Annuaire Français de Droit International
AJIL	American Journal of International Law
ASIL	American Society of International Law Proceedings
AVR	Archiv des Völkerrecht
BISD	GATT – Basic Instruments and Selected Documents
BYIL	British Yearbook of International Law
CI	La Comunità Internazionale
CJIL	Chinese Journal of International Law
CML Rev.	Common Market Law Review
Columbia JTL	Columbia Journal of Transnational Law
Cornell ILJ	Cornell International Law Journal
CS	Comunicazioni e Studi
CYIL	Canadian Yearbook of International Law
DCI	Diritto del Commercio Internazionale
DCSI	Diritto Comunitario e degli Scambi Internazionali
DPCE	Diritto Pubblico Comparato ed Europeo
DUDI	Diritti Umani e Diritto Internazionale
DUE	Il Diritto dell'Unione Europea
ECLR	European Competition Law Review
ECR	European Court Reports
EdD	Enciclopedia del Diritto
EG	Enciclopedia Giuridica (Treccani)
EHRR	European Human Rights Reports
EJIL	European Journal of International Law
EL Rev.	European Law Review
ETS	European Treaty Series
Foro It.	Foro Italiano
Giur. Cost.	Giurisprudenza Costituzionale
Giur. It.	Giurisprudenza Italiana
GU	Gazzetta Ufficiale della Repubblica Italiana
GYIL	German Yearbook of International Law
Harvard ILJ	Harvard International Law Journal
HRLJ	Human Rights Law Journal
ICJ Pleadings	International Court of Justice, Pleadings, Oral Arguments, Documents

---

[*] The present list covers only the most frequently cited periodicals.

ICJ Reports	International Court of Justice, Reports of Judgments, Advisory Opinions and Orders
ICLQ	International and Comparative Law Quarterly
IJCP	International Journal of Cultural Property
ILDC	International Law in Domestic Courts
ILM	International Legal Materials
ILR	International Law Reports
Int. Lawyer	International Lawyer
IOLR	International Organizations Law Review
IRRC	International Review of the Red Cross
IYIL	Italian Yearbook of International Law
JDI	Journal du Droit International
JICJ	Journal of International Criminal Justice
JIEL	Journal of International Economic Law
JWT	Journal of World Trade
Leiden JIL	Leiden Journal of International Law
Max Planck UNYB	Max Planck Yearbook of United Nations Law
NILR	Netherlands International Law Review
NYIL	Netherlands Yearbook of International Law
OIDU	Ordine Internazionale e Diritti Umani
OJ EC	Official Journal of the European Communities
OJ EU	Official Journal of the European Union
PCIJ Series	Permanent Court of International Justice, Series
QIL	Questions of International Law
RBDI	Revue Belge de Droit International
RCADI	Recueil des Cours de l'Académie de Droit International de La Haye/Collected Courses of the Hague Academy of International Law
RCGI	Rivista della Cooperazione Giuridica Internazionale
RDI	Rivista di Diritto Internazionale
RDIPP	Rivista di Diritto Internazionale Privato e Processuale
RECIEL	Review of European Community and International Environmental Law/ Review of European, Comparative and International Environmental Law
RGA	Rivista Giuridica dell'Ambiente
RGDIP	Revue Générale de Droit International Public
RIDPC	Rivista Italiana di Diritto Pubblico Comunitario
RMUE	Revue du Marché Unique Européen
RTDH	Revue Trimestrielle des Droits de l'Homme
Schw. ZIER	Schweizerische Zeitschrift für Internationales und Europäisches Recht
Texas ILJ	Texas International Law Journal
UNTS	United Nations Treaty Series
Yale JIL	Yale Journal of International Law
YEL	Yearbook of European Law

YIEL	Yearbook of International Environmental Law
YIHL	Yearbook of International Humanitarian Law
YILC/ACDI	Yearbook of the International Law Commission/ Annuaire de la Commission du droit international
ZAÖRV	Zeitschrift für Ausländisches Öffentliches Recht und Völkerrecht

Italian legal acts

Law	Legge (Act of Parliament)
DL	Decreto Legge (Decree-Law) (Decree adopted by the Government in case of extreme urgency which has the same, albeit provisional, effect of a Law, and which must be approved by the Parliament within 60 days. On the contrary, it looses its legal effect)
D.Lgs.	Decreto Legislativo (Legislative Decree) (Decree adopted by the Government upon delegation by the Parliament)
DPR	Decreto del Presidente della Repubblica (Decree of the President of the Republic)
DPCM	Decreto Presidente del Consiglio dei Ministri (Decree of the President of the Council of Ministers or Prime Minister)
DM	Decreto Ministeriale (Ministerial Decree)
Reg.	Regolamento (Administrative Regulation)

ITALIAN COURTS

Tribunale	Court of First Instance
Corte d'Appello	Court of Appeals
Corte di Cassazione	Court of Cassation
TAR	Regional Administrative Tribunal
Consiglio di Stato	Council of State (Supreme Administrative Court)
Corte Costituzionale	Constitutional Court

THIRTY VOLUMES ON: GENESIS, DEVELOPMENT AND PROSPECTS OF THE ITALIAN YEARBOOK OF INTERNATIONAL LAW

RICCARDO PAVONI[*]

Abstract

On the occasion of its 30th Anniversary Volume, the genesis, evolution and prospects of the Italian Yearbook of International Law (IYIL) are set out in the present piece. After sketching the main stages of development from its creation to the current volume, consideration is given to the dynamic scholarly and historical context which favoured the emergence of the IYIL in the 1970s. Notwithstanding several precursors, a rising number of competitors and a growing reliance on internet-based services by international law researchers and practitioners, it is submitted that the IYIL was born out of, and continues to appear as, a distinctive experience in the Italian legal publishing environment.

Keywords: State practice; Italian scholarship; Positivism; international law-making process; international law journals; online publishing.

1. BIRTH, DISAPPEARANCE AND RESURRECTION

The Italian Yearbook of International Law (IYIL) was founded in 1975 by Francesco Capotorti, Benedetto Conforti and Luigi Ferrari Bravo, who may certainly be included in the restricted list of the most renowned Italian international and European law scholars of the last century. Sadly, all of them have now passed away, after Conforti and Ferrari Bravo died – only a few days from one another – in the early weeks of 2016.[1] They left behind an enormous intellectual legacy which the current Editors of the IYIL are striving to honour.

---

[*] Of the Board of Editors. This piece updates and reviews an article originally published in NYIL, Vol. 50, 2019, p. 195 ff. I am gratefully indebted to the members of the IYIL Board of Editors for their invaluable suggestions and comments on prior versions of this work.

[1] Capotorti died in 2002; for an overview of his contribution to international law scholarship and a full bibliography of his works, see STARACE, "Francesco Capotorti", RDI, 2003, p. 152 ff. For tributes and bibliographies relating to Conforti and Ferrari Bravo, see FRANCIONI, "Ricordo di Benedetto Conforti", RDI, 2016, p. 493 ff.; IOVANE, "Benedetto Conforti", IYIL, 2015, p. 3 ff.; PISILLO MAZZESCHI, "Benedetto Conforti, innovatore della cultura giuridica internazionalistica. Laudatio", Studi senesi, 2016, p. 792 ff.; CATALDI, "Il contributo di Benedetto Conforti al diritto internazionale del mare", RDI, 2017, p. 98 ff.; PISILLO MAZZESCHI, "Benedetto Conforti ed il suo contributo scientifico in materia di diritti umani", DUDI, 2016, p. 277 ff.; RAIMONDI, "Benedetto Conforti prima Commissario poi Giudice dei diritti umani a Strasburgo", *ibid.*, p. 287 ff.; GIARDINA, "Benedetto Conforti (1930-2016)", RDIPP, 2016, p. 748 ff.; TESAURO, "In ricordo di Benedetto Conforti", OIDU, 2016, p. 163 ff.; NESI, "Ricordo di Luigi Ferrari Bravo", RDI, 2016, p. 857 ff.; SACERDOTI, "Luigi Ferrari

IYIL, Vol. 30 (2020), pp. 1-14
ISSN 0391-5107

The IYIL was born with the mission of communicating and disseminating, within a larger international audience, the Italian scholarship and practice in the field of public international law. This was done with the awareness and pride that such scholarship and practice had a significant and enduring relevance for the discipline.[2] The IYIL was originally published by Editoriale Scientifica, a well-known publisher in Naples, particularly active in the area of international law. It represented a breakthrough in Italian academic publishing, for at least two reasons. First, the IYIL was intended to only cover issues of public international law, thus deviating from the well-entrenched and persistent Italian tradition of periodicals (and scholars) dealing with both public and private international law.[3] Secondly, and most importantly, it was the first ever Italian international law periodical entirely written in English.[4] Although in line with a growing trend of the 1970s,[5] the choice of English for the national yearbook of international law was particularly innovative in the Italian context. It broke with a deep-rooted habit in Italian scholarship. When at the time Italian scholars wanted to express themselves in a foreign language, either orally or in writing, they were almost invariably using French. Contributions in English from Italian authors were exceptional, and these exceptions normally involved works translated from – and frequently already published in – Italian.

Yet the choice of English would prove to be a lasting challenge for the IYIL. It is safe to observe that the main reason for the termination of the first series of the IYIL in 1996[6] had to do with overwhelming problems associated with the *full* translation into English of an increasing amount of documentation relating to Italian practice, especially judicial decisions, as well as of – occasionally – schol-

---

Bravo", IYIL, 2015, p. 13 ff.; CAGGIANO and TRIGGIANI, "In ricordo di Luigi Ferrari Bravo", Studi sull'integrazione europea, 2016, p. 7 ff.; TRIGGIANI, "In ricordo di Luigi Ferrari Bravo", OIDU, 2016, p. 165 ff. See also the various contributions in NESI and GARGIULO (eds.), *Luigi Ferrari Bravo. Il diritto internazionale come professione*, Napoli, 2015, and in *Benedetto Conforti and Luigi Ferrari Bravo. From Naples to Strasbourg and Beyond: An Extraordinary Journey*, Napoli, 2018.

[2] See "Foreword", IYIL, 1975, p. vii ff., p. viii.

[3] *Ibid.*, p. vii. In the same context, the Editors made clear that contributions on European law would be considered only insofar as they dealt with aspects relevant to public international law, *ibid.*, pp. vii-viii.

[4] Even today, the IYIL essentially remains the only Italian international law periodical fully written in English. The thriving e-journal *QIL-Questions of International Law*, established in May 2014 by a group of Italian scholars, publishes in English, but it occasionally features contributions in French. Its present Editor-in-Chief is Maurizio Arcari; see: <www.qil-qdi.org/about-us>. Invariably written in English is *The Global Community: Yearbook of International Law and Jurisprudence*, a yearbook published since 2001 (currently by Oxford University Press) which contains doctrine, as well as summaries and excerpts of *international* judicial practice. As its title and the composition of its boards indicate, this publication vindicates a "global" identity; however, it has a firm connection with Italy, since it was created at the University of Salerno, where it continues to be based under the general editorship of Giuliana Ziccardi Capaldo.

[5] DE LA RASILLA, "A Very Short History of International Law Journals (1869-2018)", EJIL, 2018, p. 137 ff., p. 166.

[6] See *infra* in this Section.

arly contributions. Translations were also a challenge to the overall quality of the IYIL, as underlined in a lengthy note in the Canadian Yearbook of International Law reviewing the first two volumes of the IYIL.[7]

The first series of the IYIL was relatively short-lived. It consisted of eight volumes unevenly published between 1975 and 1996. The production process went smoothly only for the first three volumes – i.e. Vol. I (1975), Vol. II (1976), and Vol. III (1977) – which duly covered one year of practice each and were released in a timely manner. As to doctrine, these volumes included many cutting-edge articles written by established and emerging Italian scholars. These articles engaged with a variety of areas of international law, such as the law of the sea,[8] the law of treaties,[9] the rights of minorities,[10] the law of armed conflict,[11] international law in domestic legal systems,[12] and the history and theory of international law.[13]

The following two volumes – i.e. Vol. IV (1978-1979) and Vol. V (1980-1981) – showed the first symptoms of a looming crisis, since they each covered two years of Italian practice and were published less punctually. The Editors reacted to this situation with a change of publisher. Giuffrè (now Giuffrè Francis Lefebvre), a company based in Milan with a prestigious pedigree in the field of legal science and practice, managed to publish Vol. VI (1985) in 1986 and Vol. VII (1986-1987) in 1988, whereas Vol. VIII (1988-1992) had to wait until 1996 to see the light. Crucially, Vol. VIII did not contain a doctrinal section. It was just made up of some 400 pages of Italian practice, plus a bibliographical index of literature on international law published in Italy from 1987 to 1992. This volume

---

[7] IANNI, "The Italian Yearbook of International Law", CYIL, 1978, p. 342 ff., p. 358 (underscoring that "[i]n an undertaking of this nature dependent as it is upon translation services, infelicities of phrase and minor errors are bound to creep in", and concluding however that "by and large these examples are rare" and that "in this regard, Volume 2 is an improvement over Volume I").

[8] See e.g., CONFORTI, "Does Freedom of the Seas Still Exist?", IYIL, 1975, p. 3 ff.; GIULIANO, "The Regime of Straits in General International Law", ibid., p. 16 ff.; FRANCIONI, "Criminal Jurisdiction over Foreign Merchant Vessels in Territorial Waters: A New Analysis", ibid., p. 27 ff.; TREVES, "Devices to Facilitate Consensus: The Experience of the Law of the Sea Conference", IYIL, 1976, p. 39 ff.

[9] GAJA, "Reservations to Treaties and the Newly Independent States", IYIL, 1975, p. 52 ff.; CAGGIANO, "The ILC Draft on the Succession of States in Respect of Treaties: A Critical Appraisal", ibid., p. 69 ff.; NAPOLETANO, "Some Remarks on Treaties and Third States under the Vienna Convention on the Law of Treaties", IYIL, 1977, p. 75 ff.

[10] CAPOTORTI, "The Protection of Minorities under Multilateral Agreements on Human Rights", IYIL, 1976, p. 3 ff.

[11] See especially, RONZITTI, "Wars of National Liberation – A Legal Definition", IYIL, 1975, p. 192 ff.

[12] CASSESE, "Parliamentary Control of Treaty-Making in Italy", IYIL, 1976, p. 165 ff.; CONDORELLI, "Acts of the Italian Government in International Matters before Domestic Courts", ibid., p. 178 ff.; SACERDOTI, "Application of G.A.T.T. by Domestic Courts: European and Italian Case Law", ibid., p. 224 ff.; SPERDUTI, "Dualism and Monism. A Confrontation to Be Overcome", IYIL, 1977, p. 31 ff.

[13] See especially, AGO, "Pluralism and the Origins of the International Community", IYIL, 1977, p. 3 ff.

opened with a sombre preface where the Editors informed the readership about unexpected and persistent (yet unspecified) difficulties that had prevented the production of the IYIL in the previous years.[14] They announced, however, their decision to release the considerable amount of Italian practice which had meanwhile been collected, in order to avoid its obsolescence.[15] The preface ended on a wishful note, i.e., that the publication of the volume had to be regarded "as a sign of the Board of Editors' intention to keep the initiative alive, hoping the Yearbook can once again be published regularly in the near future".[16]

Volume VIII marked an irreversible crisis for the first series of the IYIL. At the same time, it became clear that, in order to fulfil the wish expressed in the preface to that volume, radical innovations had to be introduced, starting from the Board of Editors, the publisher, and – to a certain extent – the structure and contents of the IYIL. Under the leadership of Conforti and Ferrari Bravo, these innovations were soon planned and implemented, thus leading to the resurrection of the IYIL, which opened its second series with Vol. IX (1999), released in 2000. Since then, twenty-two volumes have been published at regular intervals, i.e. from Vol. IX (1999) to the current Vol. XXX (2020).

In the last volumes of the first series, the number of members of the Board of Editors had surged to sixteen[17] and there was no explicitly designated editor- or editors-in-chief[18] with primary responsibility for the realization of the project. This formula proved unsuccessful. Evidently, a certain lack of cohesiveness and unity of purpose among the Editors gradually undermined the viability of the IYIL.[19] By contrast, at the time of refoundation, a restricted Board of Editors made up of five scholars with different academic affiliations and diversified scientific expertise was established: Conforti and Ferrari Bravo were joined by Francesco Francioni, Natalino Ronzitti and Giorgio Sacerdoti.

Simultaneously, Conforti and Ferrari Bravo played another trump card when they identified Francioni as the General Editor of the "new" IYIL, a position which he uninterruptedly held for more than fifteen years,[20] that is, until 2016 when Massimo Iovane took over from Vol. XXV (2015) up to Vol. XXVII (2017).[21] Francioni's general editorship proved pivotal in consistently and effectively securing the planning, production and publication of the second series

---

[14] "Preface", IYIL, 1988-1992, p. xi.

[15] *Ibid.*

[16] *Ibid.*

[17] In addition to Capotorti, Conforti and Ferrari Bravo, these were Antonio Cassese, Luigi Condorelli, Laura Forlati, Francesco Francioni, Giorgio Gaja, Andrea Giardina, Riccardo Luzzatto, Paolo Picone, Natalino Ronzitti, Vincenzo Starace, Antonio Tizzano, Tullio Treves and Ugo Villani.

[18] Plausibly, the roles then played by Capotorti, Conforti and Ferrari Bravo were to be the intellectual leaders, motivators and general supervisors of the IYIL, rather than editors-in-chief *stricto sensu*.

[19] FRANCIONI, *cit. supra* note 1, p. 499.

[20] See FRANCIONI, "Foreword: On My Way Out", IYIL, 2015, p. xxi.

[21] On the introduction of a rotating system for the position of General Editor, see *infra* Section 3.

of the IYIL. His skilful coordination of complex research networks and editorial projects, his perfect (mother tongue-like) English, his impressive and exponentially growing[22] web of international affiliations, contacts and colleagues – coupled with pragmatism, endless scientific curiosity and proverbial intuitions about expanding areas and future directions of international law – have translated into invaluable assets for the "new" IYIL. In turn, I was honoured and thrilled when, as a young law graduate from Siena and Oxford with just a couple of articles on my CV, I was asked by Francioni to take responsibility for the editorial matters and overall organizational aspects of a new series of the IYIL.[23] Concurrently, each member of the Board was entrusted with the general supervision of a research team in charge of drafting one of the four sections making up the part of the IYIL devoted to the Italian practice of international law.[24] While for obvious reasons I refrain from expressing specific comments on the scientific value of the volumes of the past twenty-two years, it is fair to note that the foregoing editorial set-up achieved a reasonable and effective balance between centralization and decentralization in the production of the IYIL, as well as a well-defined division of responsibilities.

In 1999, digital advances in academic publishing were rapidly emerging and the associated market was fast-changing and increasingly global. It was crystal clear to the Editors that a non-Italian, international publisher had to be identified, one that would make state-of-the-art technologies available and secure worldwide distribution of the IYIL. Under the guidance of Francioni, a deal was struck with then Kluwer Law International which published Vols. IX-XI. Following the restructuring of that publisher, all subsequent volumes of the new series have been released by the publishing house Brill, under the imprint Martinus Nijhoff (Vols. XII-XXII) and – lately – Brill Nijhoff (Vols. XXIII-XXX).

Comparatively less radical innovations involved the structure and contents of the second series of the IYIL vis-à-vis the first series. The second series was still made up of three essential parts. The first part was devoted to doctrinal contributions, but with a more definite distinction between "articles" *stricto sensu* and "notes and comments", as well as a growing preference for "focus"[25] or "symposium"[26] sections zooming in on topical issues of international law. The

---

[22] A key factor in this regard was Francioni's appointment – in 2003 – to the prestigious Chair of International Law and Human Rights at the European University Institute in Florence. He had previously held the Chair of International Law at the Faculty of Law of the University of Siena since 1980.

[23] Since then, I have consecutively held the positions of Assistant Editor (Vols. IX-XIV), Associate Editor (Vols. XV-XXIV), and member of the Board of Editors (from Vol. XXV on).

[24] Conforti, Ferrari Bravo, Ronzitti and Sacerdoti were put in charge of, respectively, Italian judicial decisions, diplomatic and parliamentary practice, treaty practice, and legislation.

[25] See e.g., "The ICJ Judgment in *Jurisdictional Immunities of the State (Germany v. Italy: Greece Intervening)*", IYIL, 2011, p. 133 ff., with contributions by CONFORTI, PAVONI, ESPÓSITO, and SOSSAI.

[26] See e.g., "International Law in Italian Courts: Ten Years of Jurisprudence", IYIL, 2009, p. 1 ff., collecting a set of contributions arising from a symposium held on 8 April 2010 at the

second and third parts respectively covered Italian practice and bibliographies, including an Italian bibliographical index of international law and a gradually expanding book review section. A crucial change, however, was implemented with regard to Italian practice. This part would no longer contain full translations of Italian documentation, as it would henceforth feature concise personal accounts and reports on the relevant manifestations of practice. Translations would be exceptional (that is, only for key passages of – *inter alia* – a judicial decision or parliamentary speech) and would be taken care of by the individual authors. It is clear that such innovation has greatly eased the editorial process, while perhaps making this part of the IYIL more attractive.[27]

Before reverting to the recent evolution of the IYIL, it is apposite to take a step back and consider its genesis in more detail.

2.   BACKGROUND AND CONTEXT

2.1.   *Historical and scholarly environment*

Given the present space constraints, this is definitely not the right context in which to engage in comprehensive reflections on the place of the IYIL within the thorny discussion about Italian methodologies and schools of thought in the area of international law.[28] I will therefore confine myself to a few general observa-

---

European University Institute and organized by Francesco Francioni; "The Future of the ECHR System", IYIL, 2010, p. 1 ff., featuring a variety of topical pieces by leading experts – including several judges – on the law of the European Convention on Human Rights, which were first presented at a symposium held in April 2011 at the Higher Education School of the University of Napoli "L'Orientale" on the island of Procida and organized by Giuseppe Cataldi.

[27] See *infra* Section 3 for current prospects of this part of the IYIL. Significantly, the Editors of the new series expressed their hope that a selective approach to Italian practice "may stimulate interest in the original sources of Italian legal culture, and, indirectly, in the Italian language itself", see "Foreword", IYIL, 1999, p. vii.

[28] For thoughtful accounts and exhaustive references, see BARTOLINI (ed.), *A History of International Law in Italy*, Oxford, 2020; PALCHETTI, "International Law and National Perspective in a Time of Globalization: The Persistence of a National Identity in Italian Scholarship of International Law", KFG Working Paper Series, No. 20, November 2018; MESSINEO, "Is There an Italian Conception of International Law?", Cambridge Journal of International and Comparative Law, 2013, p. 879 ff.; SALERNO, "L'influenza di Santi Romano sulla dottrina e la prassi italiana di diritto internazionale", RDI, 2018, p. 357 ff.; ID., "L'affermazione del positivismo giuridico nella scuola internazionalista italiana: il ruolo di Anzilotti e Perassi", RDI, 2012, p. 29 ff.; ID., "La *Rivista* e gli studi di diritto internazionale nel periodo 1906-1943", RDI, 2007, p. 305 ff.; CANNIZZARO, "La doctrine italienne et le développement du droit international dans l'après-guerre: entre continuité et discontinuité", AFDI, 2004, p. 1 ff. For a less recent, yet excellent and illuminating contribution, see CASSESE, "Diritto internazionale", in BONANATE (ed.), *Studi internazionali*, Torino, 1990, p. 113 ff. In 2017, the full text of this pioneering manuscript was retrieved from the Antonio Cassese fond of Villa Salviati's historical archives of the European Union at the European University Institute. It has lately been edited and published by Micaela Frulli, one of Cassese's pupils, see CASSESE, *Il diritto internazionale in Italia*, Bologna, 2021.

tions, which obviously do not render justice to the impressive intellectual heritage represented by outstanding scholars such as – just to mention a few – Anzilotti, Quadri, Morelli, Ago and Sperduti, or to that of their succeeding generations.

First, the IYIL adventure set off in a climate of profound renewal in Italian international law scholarship. Indeed, the 1970s are commonly regarded[29] as the turning point for the gradual shift from an "old" Positivism – championed by Italian scholars since the beginning of the 20th century and frequently translating into a mechanical, aseptic and overly theoretical approach – to a "modern" or "inductive" Positivism increasingly focused on a meticulous analysis of practice and open to the examination of the socio-economic foundations of the law. Certainly, the original Editors of the IYIL perceived themselves as key players in this movement towards an overhaul of the positivist method in Italy. In their Foreword to Vol. I (1975), they pointed out that "articles and comments relating to present and actual situations will have priority over studies of a predominantly theoretical nature",[30] and that "this should also help to confute the belief that Italian doctrine on international law has a leaning towards abstract subjects (a belief which, today at least, is incorrect)".[31]

Secondly, this attitude was in line with the choice of English as *the* language of the IYIL. Clearly, the style of various Italian authors – with their elaborate theoretical disquisitions, doctrinal quarrels, endless sentences and footnotes – was utterly inconsistent with the short propositions, pragmatic statements, and practical mindset associated with the use of legal English and with a vast share of the Anglo-American tradition of international law scholarship.

Thirdly, the founders of the IYIL were no doubt protagonists of the modernization of international law studies in Italy that gathered speed in the 1970s, as is best epitomized by the publication of the first editions of Ferrari Bravo's and Conforti's textbooks in those years. Ferrari Bravo released his *Lezioni di diritto internazionale* in 1974, a volume characterized by the attention paid to the historical, diplomatic and political dimensions of international law concepts and institutions.[32] In 1976, Conforti inaugurated what was to become the leading textbook of international law[33] in Italian universities for decades.[34] The style, purpose

---

[29] CASSESE, "Diritto internazionale", *cit. supra* note 28, pp. 124-136; CANNIZZARO, *cit. supra* note 28, p. 9. The evolution of Ago's thought and method is also insightful in this respect, see ZICCARDI, "Il diritto internazionale nell'insegnamento di Roberto Ago", RDI, 1995, p. 305 ff., pp. 315-316; CASSESE, "Diritto internazionale", *cit. supra* note 28, p. 122.

[30] "Foreword", *cit. supra* note 2, p. viii.

[31] *Ibid.* On this belief, see also CASSESE, "Diritto internazionale", *cit. supra* note 28, pp. 114 and 145-147.

[32] FERRARI BRAVO, *Lezioni di diritto internazionale*, Napoli, 1974. See the positive remarks by CASSESE, "Diritto internazionale", *cit. supra* note 28, pp. 135 and 137-138.

[33] CONFORTI, *Appunti dalle lezioni di diritto internazionale*, Napoli, 1976. This textbook, later renamed *Diritto internazionale* and translated into various languages, has now been published in its 12th edition, with updates, revisions and co-authorship by Massimo Iovane, see CONFORTI and IOVANE, *Diritto internazionale*, 12th ed., Napoli, 2021.

[34] Cf. FRANCIONI, *cit. supra* note 1, p. 498 (referring to Conforti's textbook as an evergreen and exceptional manual). In a review to the 7th edition (dated 2006) of this textbook, Bruno Simma, after summing up its remarkable qualities, concluded that they "explain why

and structure of this manual – kept essentially intact throughout its succeeding editions – perfectly corresponded with the foregoing manifesto of the original Editors of the IYIL. It was permeated by extreme clarity, incisive analysis and a clever combination of methods.[35] Yet the hallmark of the textbook was its "domestic approach", according to which international law was examined and explained through the lens of its application by domestic legal operators, chiefly domestic courts. In his moving *mémoire* of Conforti, Massimo Iovane neatly recalls the origins and purposes of this pioneering perspective:[36] it was meant by Conforti as a reaction to the widespread criticism coming from several colleagues who would pompously announce that, after all, international law was not positive law, but a blend of law, politics, sociology, and whatever else pleases one; actually, an area of studies especially useful to the general *cultural* education of students and researchers, and not primarily for people aspiring to become skilled *lawyers*. In order to debunk such a myth, Conforti saw fit to show how international law was bound to become practical and effective due to its increasing use by domestic authorities operating as agents of the international community. Thus, the renewal of the positivist method was also intended as a means to ensuring the survival of Positivism as a viable framework for engaging with international law. The multitude of largely theoretical, deductive and abstract works which had mushroomed in Italian scholarship in the wake of orthodox Positivism was evidently throwing itself to the just mentioned "academic wolves".

Fourthly, and finally, the expanding practice-oriented approach to international law, especially in a pre-digital era such as the 1970s, could successfully be undertaken by scholars with a deep knowledge of international law-making processes and their interaction with domestic legal orders, accompanied by a well-trained capacity to research and supervise research of endless archival materials, law reports and official documents. The founders of the IYIL were surely in that position. Capotorti had already published, for instance, several analytic commentaries on Italian judicial practice of international law.[37] As said, Conforti, after digging through hundreds of United Nations documents for his 1968 monograph,[38] was increasingly concentrating on domestic judicial practice, a predilection which led to the publication of authoritative collections of case law[39] and to Conforti's appointment as Rapporteur of the Institut de droit international on the "Activities of National Judges and the International Relations of

---

in Italian universities the name Conforti is frequently used as synonymous with international law", SIMMA, IYIL, 2006, p. 447 ff., p. 450.

[35] SIMMA (*cit. supra* note 34, p. 447) considers Conforti's approach as a bold, yet successful, blend of realism and Kelsen's Pure Theory of Law. On this combination of methods in Conforti's scholarship, see also the insightful remarks by IOVANE, *cit. supra* note 1, pp. 7-9, and PISILLO MAZZESCHI, "Benedetto Conforti, innovatore", *cit. supra* note 1, pp. 793-795.

[36] See IOVANE, *cit. supra* note 1, p. 6.

[37] See e.g., CAPOTORTI, "Problemi di diritto internazionale nella giurisprudenza italiana recente. Parte terza: anno 1952", CS, 1953, p. 387 ff.

[38] CONFORTI, *La funzione dell'accordo nel sistema delle Nazioni Unite*, Padova, 1968.

[39] PICONE and CONFORTI, *La giurisprudenza italiana di diritto internazionale pubblico. Repertorio 1960-1987*, Napoli, 1988.

their State".[40] In turn, on the heels of his growing involvement in Italian delegations to international forums,[41] Ferrari Bravo was nurturing a keen interest in the diplomatic practice of States and its multiple manifestations. A key achievement in that regard was his leadership of a research network that engaged in the systematic collection of Italian diplomatic documents relevant to international law from the years 1887-1918, which resulted in the monumental second series of *La prassi italiana di diritto internazionale*.[42] Eventually, this insider, profound knowledge of the variety of expressions of diplomatic practice, their historical significance and their place in the customary law-making process was one of the highlights of Ferrari Bravo's insightful course at the Hague Academy.[43]

2.2. Precursors

The IYIL was established at a time – the 1970s – when a veritable "gold rush" to State practice, especially judicial practice, was taking place among and within the various Italian "schools" of international law, as reflected in the pertinent publications and existing periodicals. In that pre-digital era, this scholarly competition about the best way to collect, select and systematize Italian judicial decisions relevant to (public and private) international law invariably resulted in bulky and partly overlapping volumes.[44] Perhaps more than scientific works *stricto sensu*, these volumes were conceived as useful professional tools to be constantly consulted by domestic courts and lawyers, thus giving them (and their

---

[40] See e.g., CONFORTI, "Final Report", Annuaire de l'Institut de droit international, Vol. 65-I, 1993, p. 428 ff.

[41] This increasing and relentless experience in international affairs led to Ferrari Bravo's appointment as the Legal Adviser at Italy's Permanent Missions to the United Nations (first in New York, 1981-1984, then in Geneva, 1984-1985) and, subsequently, as the Head of the Legal Service (*Servizio del Contenzioso Diplomatico*) of the Italian Ministry of Foreign Affairs (1985-1994).

[42] In introducing the series, Roberto Ago, who was co-Editor-in-Chief with Riccardo Monaco, singled out and praised Ferrari Bravo for his work and ascribed to him the principal credit for the realization of the *oeuvre*: AGO, "Foreword", in *La prassi italiana di diritto internazionale. Seconda serie (1887-1918), Vol. I*, Dobbs Ferry, 1979, p. xiii ff., p. xiv. See SACERDOTI, "Luigi Ferrari Bravo", *cit. supra* note 1, p. 16; NESI, "Ricordo", *cit. supra* note 1, pp. 858-859.

[43] FERRARI BRAVO, "Méthodes de recherche de la coutume internationale dans la pratique des Etats", RCADI, Vol. 192, 1985-III, p. 233 ff.

[44] The project *La giurisprudenza italiana in materia internazionale*, aimed at collecting the Italian jurisprudence relevant to (private and public) international law as from 1861, resulted in seventeen volumes published between 1973 and 1997; see e.g., LAMBERTI ZANARDI, LUZZATTO, SACERDOTI, and SANTA MARIA, *La giurisprudenza di diritto internazionale, Vol. I (1861-1875), Vol. II (1876-1890)*, Napoli, 1973, reviewed by DUINTJER TEBBENS, Nederlands Tijdschrift voor Internationaal Recht, 1974, p. 359 ff. See also GAJA, *Decisioni della Corte costituzionale in materia internazionale*, Milano, 1966; STARACE and DE CARO, *La giurisprudenza costituzionale in materia internazionale*, Napoli, 1977; PICONE and CONFORTI, *cit. supra* note 39. For similar initiatives relating to treaty practice, see CASSESE, "Diritto internazionale", *cit. supra* note 28, p. 131.

authors) high visibility. Yet they were bound to be examined only by readers with knowledge of the Italian language, as their clear limitation was that both jurisprudence and related commentaries and indexes were published, indeed, in Italian.

Around the same period of time, a few Italian periodicals also regularly included extensive sections on Italian practice relating to international law. The prestigious quarterly *Rivista di diritto internazionale* has always reproduced relevant Italian judicial decisions and legislation, as well as information on treaties binding upon Italy, in dedicated parts.

To a certain extent, the same holds true for periodicals intended as annual publications, which are, in fact, the Italian precursors of the IYIL. *Comunicazioni e studi*, a yearbook founded at the University of Milan in 1942 by Ago, subsequently developed with the help of other prominent scholars – especially Giuliano and Ziccardi – and irregularly published until 2007 for a total of twenty-three volumes, was characterized by a peculiar technique. It normally featured – *inter alia* and with the exception of the latest volumes – lengthy critical surveys on the Italian jurisprudence of international law, rather than *verbatim* reproductions of the individual decisions.[45] This model is comparable to the IYIL's current approach to Italian practice, save for the use of English and much shorter case reports in the IYIL.

Even though they have now gone extinct, three further annuals should be noted. The first was *Jus Gentium: annuario italiano di diritto internazionale*, which appeared in 1938 and was marked by a robust propagandistic outlook in favour of the Fascist regime.[46] However, this yearbook did not contain any materials on Italian practice, with the exception of a few selected treaties binding upon Italy. Moreover, it was a transient experiment,[47] which resulted in four volumes only, published between 1938 and 1942.[48]

Another precursor of the IYIL was *Diritto internazionale*, a periodical founded in 1937[49] and originally directed by Giorgio Balladore Pallieri.[50] It prima-

---

[45] See e.g., CAPOTORTI, *cit. supra* note 37, and, more recently, GRANDI and FUMAGALLI, "I problemi di diritto internazionale nella giurisprudenza italiana (1976-1980)", CS, 1985, p. 855 ff.

[46] Oddly, the first volume (Vol. I (1938)) did not provide any information about the Editors of this yearbook and their programme of work, as noted by a bewildered reviewer in the AJIL, see RIESENFELD, AJIL, 1938, p. 871 ff. According to a study dating back to those years, the General Editor of *Jus Gentium* was Pietro La Terza, see GIANNINI, "Il diritto internazionale in Italia (1851-1948)", Rivista di studi politici internazionali, 1948, p. 377 ff., p. 389.

[47] After World War II, it was renamed *Jus Gentium: diritto delle relazioni internazionali* and in this guise twelve volumes were published between 1949 and 1985.

[48] See BARTOLINI, "The Impact of Fascism on the Italian Doctrine of International Law", Journal of the History of International Law, 2012, p. 237 ff., p. 282; ID., "Le leggi razziali e la dottrina italiana di diritto internazionale", in RESTA and ZENO-ZENCOVICH (eds.), *Le leggi razziali: passato/presente*, Roma, 2015, p. 55 ff., pp. 60-61; INGRAVALLO, "The Formation of International Law Journals in Italy: Their Role in the Discipline", in BARTOLINI, *cit. supra* note 28, p. 190 ff., pp. 203-204; DE LA RASILLA, *cit. supra* note 5, pp. 152-153.

[49] On the genesis of this periodical and its pre-World War II attitude towards the Fascist regime, see BARTOLINI, "The Impact of Fascism", *cit. supra* note 48, pp. 281-282; INGRAVALLO, *cit. supra* note 48, pp. 204 and 209-210.

[50] The number of editors-in-chief progressively increased in the following years. At the time of the periodical's disappearance in 1974, these were Balladore Pallieri, Giuseppe

rily pursued an informative and documentary function,[51] given that its bulk was constituted by a systematic collection of Italian judicial, legislative and treaty practice relating to private and public international law, as well as a meticulous account of developments of international concern, multilateral treaties and decisions by the International Court of Justice. Yet Italian practice was again exclusively published in its original language with no explanatory notes or summaries in English (or French). In addition, this periodical had an especially troubled history. Its publication was first interrupted after the release of five volumes between 1938 and 1942. It was relaunched as *Annali di diritto internazionale* after World War II with an essentially unchanged purpose and structure.[52] Under this guise five further volumes were produced between 1951 and 1957, before another break led to the resumption of the initial name *Diritto internazionale* and the transformation into a quarterly journal. The latter was released from 1959 to 1974, when it definitively disappeared upon decision of the institution[53] which had sponsored its publication until then.[54]

Finally, mention must be made of the *Annuario di diritto internazionale*, created in 1965 and directed by Rolando Quadri. This yearbook contained doctrine, bibliographies, book reviews and the text of selected treaties, whereas Italian practice was not considered. All such materials were, with a few exceptions, published in Italian. The exclusion of Italian practice was probably due to a desire to avoid competition and duplication with *Diritto internazionale*,[55] which – as previously indicated – was overwhelmingly devoted to the collection of that practice and, as from 1959,[56] featured Quadri as one of its Editors-in-Chief. Unfortunately, the *Annuario* lasted for three volumes only, respectively dated 1965, 1966 and 1967-1968, and published between 1966 and 1970.[57] It is safe to assume that the disappearance of this yearbook was a matter of deep regret for Quadri and, as such, played a significant role in the genesis of the IYIL and its resurrection towards the end of the 1990s. Conforti and Ferrari Bravo were pupils of Quadri and were part of the editorial staff of the *Annuario*. Therefore, their unbending

---

Biscottini, Giorgio Cansacchi, Rodolfo De Nova, Rolando Quadri and Giancarlo Venturini.

[51] See the unauthored foreword to the first volume, Diritto internazionale, 1937, p. ix ff.

[52] See the unauthored foreword in Annali di diritto internazionale, 1949, p. v. For a brief notice welcoming the resumption of publication of this periodical, see KUNZ, AJIL, 1952, p. 144 ff.

[53] That is, the *Istituto per gli studi di politica internazionale* (ISPI) in Milan.

[54] See the foreword to the last issue (published in March 1974) by DE NOVA, Diritto internazionale, 1971, p. iii.

[55] At any rate, this failure to consider Italian practice by a periodical which – though not presenting itself as a national yearbook – had been created, based and edited in Italy, was quite controversial. See indeed the criticism expressed on this point in a review of the third and final volume (1967-1968) of the *Annuario* by BARDONNET, Revue internationale de droit comparé, 1971, p. 661 ff., p. 662.

[56] As said, in 1959 *Diritto internazionale* became a quarterly journal. It is thus easy to speculate that Quadri decided to step in with "his own" yearbook, which would be in direct competition with the other remaining Italian yearbook, *Comunicazioni e studi*.

[57] A plausible reason for its termination were financial hurdles, see INGRAVALLO, *cit. supra* note 48, p. 211.

determination to establish the IYIL in the 1970s and to resume its publication in the 1990s may also be regarded as a means of making up for the failure of that periodical. The first volume of the IYIL appeared in December 1975, just a few months before Quadri died in April 1976.[58] It is poignant to think about two of Quadri's most beloved pupils handing him Vol. I of the IYIL, thereby easing the hardship he was experiencing in the last weeks of his life.

To sum up, the IYIL emerged from this fragmented, frequently overlapping and inaccessible-to-non-Italian-speakers publishing environment, with the ambition to become an authoritative reference – entirely written in English and covering only public international law – for cutting-edge Italian scholarship, as well as reports and documentation on Italian practice.

3. DEVELOPMENT AND CHALLENGES AHEAD

Upon publication of its 30th Anniversary Volume, a few considerations about the evolution and future prospects of the IYIL seem apposite. I will particularly refer to the transformation of the governing bodies of the IYIL and to the impact of online publishing on substantive matters.

The IYIL is currently experiencing a new phase of its development, which started with the release of Vol. XXV (2015) in 2016, a few months after the deaths of Conforti and Ferrari Bravo. In October 2015, the five original Editors of the second series agreed on a substantial overhaul of the IYIL governing bodies. First, upon Francioni's resignation from his long-standing mandate, they introduced a rotating system for the position of General Editor, pursuant to which the latter would periodically change following the publication of a given number of volumes under her/his leadership. Accordingly, Massimo Iovane was General Editor for three volumes, i.e. from Vol. XXV (2015) to Vol. XXVII (2017), before being succeeded by Giuseppe Nesi. Secondly, the size of the Board of Editors was doubled and consisted of ten members, including – for the first time – two renowned non-Italian scholars.[59] Thirdly, the Editorial Committee was also renovated and enlarged.[60] Last but not least, Daniele Amoroso was appointed as Associate Editor, i.e. the position – midway between the Board and the Editorial

---

[58] A brief tribute to Quadri by the Board of Editors was published in the second volume of the IYIL, see "In memoriam – Rolando Quadri", IYIL, 1976, p. 299 ff. For an excellent overview and insightful reflections on Quadri's contribution to the science of international law, see CONFORTI, "L'opera di Rolando Quadri", RDI, 1978, p. 5 ff.

[59] That is, Pierre-Marie Dupuy and Nigel White. Dupuy has lately resigned from his position. Following recent decisions by the Editors, there are currently twelve members of the Board of Editors. In addition to Francioni, Ronzitti and Sacerdoti, they are Pia Acconci, Giuseppe Cataldi, Pietro Gargiulo, Marco Gestri, Massimo Iovane, Marina Mancini, Giuseppe Nesi, Riccardo Pavoni and Nigel White.

[60] The Editorial Committee has been reshuffled in the ensuing years, so that it now includes the following eleven members: Giulio Bartolini, Leonardo Borlini, Andrea Caligiuri, Alessandro Chechi, Serena Forlati, Federico Lenzerini, Raffaella Nigro, Marco Pertile, Elena Sciso, Paolo Turrini and Valentina Vadi.

Committee – which I had previously held for many years and which performs a key function of coordination and organization of the whole editorial process.

A rotating system for the position of editor-in-chief is a rare occurrence in Italian legal periodicals. Its introduction by the original Editors of the second series evidently aimed at boosting dynamism and pluralism in the production of the IYIL. It is too early to assess whether such innovation lived up to those expectations. Undeniably, it is somewhat in tension with the pursuit of a stable and consistent editorial policy which a long-term mandate as General Editor may certainly facilitate. However, much will depend on the continued willingness of the Board's members to operate in a cohesive manner with the exclusive purpose of maintaining the standard which the IYIL has gained in the past decades. As to the steady enlargement of the Board and the Editorial Committee, what seems important is that the appointment of any new member should be motivated by the necessity for the IYIL to avail itself of the specific expertise and skills of the scholar in question, and accordingly assign her/him precise responsibilities. In this regard, the appointment of Marco Gestri as Book Review Editor starting from Vol. XXII (2012) constitutes a successful model.

With respect to substantive matters, we have seen that – similarly to many other national yearbooks – the IYIL was created with a fundamental mission of collecting and disseminating Italian practice of international law, duly excerpted and commented upon in English. Yet, upon resumption of publication in 2000, digital technologies were fast developing and within a few years, together with the expansion and increasing centrality of the Internet, they dramatically trans-formed the techniques for researching materials and instruments pertaining to State practice relevant to international law. Since then, the World Wide Web has largely supplanted hard copies of yearbooks as the *locus* for finding and studying the *primary* materials constituting State practice. The growing reliance on the Internet and online publishing by researchers has also signified the end of the monopoly of the IYIL over the systematic *English* coverage of Italian practice. A number of online services and platforms aimed at collecting and reviewing domestic practice have indeed been created.

Mention must be made of at least three online tools. The first is "Italy's Diplomatic and Parliamentary Practice on International Law", a website launched in 2014 at the University of Trento which contains English excerpts of Italian diplomatic and parliamentary documents, as well as brief introductions thereto.[61] The second is "Italy and International Law", a bilingual – Italian and English – online publication started in 2014 under the aegis of the Institute for International Legal Studies of the National Research Council of Italy. It publishes *inter alia* the text of, and commentaries on, Italian judicial decisions and legislation relevant

---

[61] See: <https://italyspractice.info>. The founder and Editor-in-Chief is Marco Pertile. The website includes materials dating from March 2011. It should be noted that this website is basically run by the same scholars who are in charge of the section on Diplomatic and Parliamentary Practice of the IYIL. For the purposes of the IYIL, the materials published on-line are further selected, revised and elaborated upon. Therefore, this website may be regarded as a sort of spin-off of that section of the IYIL.

to international law.[62] Finally, a third (non-Italian) online tool are the "Oxford Reports on International Law in Domestic Courts" (ILDC), an impressive service providing original text, headnotes, and selected English translations of thousands of judicial decisions – mostly from 2000 on – from about seventy jurisdictions, including Italy.[63]

Whither the IYIL mission in the face of this constant proliferation of "competitors"? Should the IYIL revisit its original agenda and accordingly put a stop to, or at least play down, its emphasis on domestic practice? I would firmly answer in the negative: if the IYIL wants to retain a distinct identity among the plethora of existing and emerging periodicals, it should maintain a robust focus on Italian practice of international law and scholarship relating thereto. This conviction also stems from the traditional and persistent richness of that practice, which has never been a peripheral phenomenon in Italy.

Of course, this is not incompatible with the idea that the structure and contents of the IYIL should be continuously reviewed and reshaped. In recent years, several changes have already been operationalized. Thus, the section on Judicial Decisions now contains contributions increasingly resembling short doctrinal comments with their own title, rather than mere case notes.[64] A comparable evolution can be observed in the section on Diplomatic and Parliamentary Practice.[65] Along the same lines, the meticulous reproduction of the list of agreements to which Italy is a party has in fact been abolished as from Vol. XXVI (2016) and replaced with insightful pieces on the most significant treaty practice.[66]

Plausibly, the future achievements of the IYIL will be closely dependent on its capacity to reinvent the treatment of Italian practice relating to international law. Following the lead taken by other national yearbooks,[67] this process may unfold through a progressive integration of the analysis of practice into the doctrinal sections of the IYIL. In this regard, preference might well be given to contributions which display innovative and analytic approaches to the study of domestic practice, for instance through its contextualization within the history and theories of international law.

---

[62] See: <http://www.larassegna.isgi.cnr.it/en/homepage>. The current Editors-in-Chief are Giuseppe Palmisano and Ornella Ferrajolo. The time span covered so far is the years 2012-2017.

[63] See: <https://opil.ouplaw.com/page/ILDC/oxford-reports-on-international-law-in-domestic-courts>. The current Editors-in-Chief are André Nollkamper (co-founder with Erika de Wet) and August Reinisch. I have been coordinating the work of Italian reporters for some fifteen years, on the assumption that there would be no duplication with the IYIL section on Judicial Decisions. This is indeed the case, since the format of headnotes in ILDC and that of case notes in the IYIL is very dissimilar, the latter being much more elaborated.

[64] See e.g. IYIL, 2017, p. 427 ff., and IYIL, 2018, p. 455 ff.

[65] See e.g. IYIL, 2017, p. 465 ff., and IYIL, 2018, p. 505 ff.

[66] See e.g., RONZITTI, "The Agreement between France and Italy on the Delimitation of Maritime Frontiers", IYIL, 2016, p. 617 ff.; MANCINI, "The Memorandum of Understanding between Italy and UNESCO on the Italian 'Unite4Heritage' Task Force", *ibid.*, p. 624 ff.

[67] Reference is especially made to the section on German Practice inaugurated by the German Yearbook of International Law since its Vol. 52, see GIEGERICH and PROELSS, "Foreword from the Editors", GYIL, 2009, p. 635.

Symposium
CITIES AND INTERNATIONAL LAW

THE SHIFTING STATUS OF CITIES IN INTERNATIONAL LAW? A REVIEW, SEVERAL QUESTIONS AND A STRAIGHT ANSWER

Giuseppe Nesi*

Dear Mayors, the international community is changing, and cities are more important than ever. I believe in a future for the United Nations based on an inclusive, networked multilateralism that links national governments, civil society, businesses and cities with global and regional organizations, trading blocs and financial institutions.**

Abstract

Witnessing the sometimes confusing and often nebulous debate on the position of cities in international law, one could wonder what cities are and what they do in contemporary international law. One could also wonder whether allowing cities to actively participate in the formation and implementation of international norms, and to contribute to international multilateral negotiations on issues of global concern such as sustainable development, climate change or human rights, does really imply a change in their status in international law. In this contribution, the reasons why cities are not subjects of international law, or better, why cities and local authorities still matter in international law because they are part of a State, are systematically assessed. Specific attention is paid to the status and role of transnational city networks. Before concluding, this article makes some final comments on the prospects for cities and transnational city networks in international law.

Keywords: cities; international legal personality; transnational city networks; subnational diplomacy.

1. Introductory Remarks

In November 2019, the Board of Editors and the Editorial Committee of the Italian Yearbook of International Law decided to devote the 2020 Symposium to the topic "Cities and International Law". Those who proposed this topic emphasized its growing interest in light of the role of cities in crucial fields of in-

---

* Of the Board of Editors.
** UN Secretary-General Antonio Guterres opening remarks to meeting with leading mayors supported by C40 Cities, "Advancing a Carbon-Neutral, Resilient Recovery for Cities and Nations", New York, 16 April 2021.

ternational law such as, to name a few, climate change, human rights, migration, cultural heritage, sustainable development, economic cooperation, health, security, and foreign policy. In recent years, international associations and institutions have been quite active in organizing meetings and conferences on cities and international law, while efforts to systematize this topic have been conducted through specialized articles, books and research projects.[1] However, no one could have predicted that the 2019 meeting would be the last gathering in person of the Italian Yearbook of International Law Board of Editors and its Editorial Committee before the eruption of the COVID-19 pandemic that is still afflicting us all. The pandemic is having profound consequences across the globe. However, while every corner of the world is touched by this pandemic, its devastating consequences have been even more damaging in densely populated urban areas, where the pandemic allegedly originated. COVID-19 obliged us to discontinue our habit of meeting at the end of the year to present the new volume of the Italian Yearbook of International Law and to hold the symposium at which participants introduce their papers for the next volume, in order to collect opinions and advice on what they have written. However, what was happening all over the world confirmed that *cities and international law* was a timely topic for our symposium.

The legal status of cities in international law and the legal impact of transnational city networks (TCNs) on the law of international organizations appeared to be inter-linked and particularly worthy of attention. The place of cities and their legal status under international law is fundamental, but this does not mean it has been consistently addressed in the literature. It seems undeniable that in recent

---

[1] The proliferation of initiatives, research projects, books and articles on the topic in recent times is really impressive. Among the relevant research projects on cities and international law, see "Les villes et le droit international", available at: <http://vdicil.org/>, launched in June 2016. On this project see BEAUDOUIN, *Droit international des villes*, Paris, 2021. Moreover, the International Law Association launched, in May 2017, a study group on Cities and International Law (see: <https://www.ila-hq.org/index.php/component/easyblog/new-ila-study-group?Itemid=347>), co-chaired by Aust and Nijman (more information is available at: <https://www.jura.fu-berlin.de/en/forschung/fuels/Projects/ILA-Study-Group-on-the-Role-of-Cities-in-International-Law/index.html>). Together with this study group, the T.M.C. Asser Institute for International and European Law organized a workshop in March 2019, and further initiatives followed such as the closing plenary of the American Society of International Law Meeting, in June 2020, entitled "Cities and other sub-national entities: what promise do they hold for international law?", now available in ASIL, 2020, p. 359 ff., with contributions, among others, by AUST and NIJMAN. A special issue of the Journal of Legal Pluralism and Unofficial Law was recently (2019) devoted to "Cities and the contestation of human rights between the global and the local", available at: <https://www.tandfonline.com/toc/rjlp20/51/2?nav=tocList>. A very important and all-encompassing volume on various aspects of cities and international law is forthcoming. In introducing the volume, the editors underline that "it marks the coming into existence of an actual research field which takes stock of the varying roles that cities play in and for international law" (AUST and NIJMAN, "The Emerging Roles of Cities in International Law – Introductory Remarks on Practice, Scholarship and the Handbook", in AUST and NIJMAN (eds.), *Research Handbook on Cities and International Law*, Cheltenham, 2021). The volume's introduction is available at: <https://papers.ssrn.com/sol3/papers.cfm?abstract_id=3739922>.

times the role of cities and TCNs in international law and international relations has significantly increased. This change is witnessed by both the active participation of cities and TCNs in international fora where issues of local, regional, national and international concern are debated, negotiated and decided upon, and the increasing development of huge networks of cities and local authorities that negotiate themes that are crucial for cities and urban conglomerations but also of international concern. In several cases, cities and local authorities have called upon States to implement international obligations and commitments deriving from international law – whether from treaties, customary law or, quite often, "soft law" instruments. On certain occasions, however, cities have gone further by deciding to act against the position that their States take in international law matters; such as, the incorporation in cities' deliberations of international conventions that have not been ratified by their States, or the decision to implement international conventions notwithstanding the withdrawal of their States from those conventions, as happened recently in many cities in the United States with regard to the 2015 Paris Agreement on Climate Change. Some authors derive from these facts the idea that a new era has begun in which cities and local authorities have acquired a new status that cannot be ignored by international law.[2]

The interest of cities in participating in international meetings and international legal debates and their aspiration to build up relations with cities in other States and have their voice heard at the international level is not completely new. At the beginning of the last century, international associations of cities were created even before the first universal intergovernmental organization was established and they were vocal in the international arena, but this phenomenon remained isolated.[3] At that time, the attitudes of cities towards international law did not have a follow-up in their participation in international negotiations, and the phenomenon did not attract the attention that has been recently dedicated, *inter alia*, by international law scholars to the role of cities in international law and its potential effects.[4] Those who look at cities as protagonists of international relations do not hesitate to affirm that cities fill a gap in representativeness and democracy in an international system characterized by the alleged lack of effec-

---

[2] *Ex multis*, more recently, DURMUS, "Cities and International Law: Legally Invisible or Rising Soft-power Actors?", in FERNÁNDEZ DE LOSADA and GALCERAN-VERCHER (eds.), *Cities in Global Governance. From Multilateralism to Multistakeholderism?*, Barcelona, 2021, p. 45 ff., and other contributions by various scholars in the same volume.

[3] On the creation of the Union internationale des villes, in 1913, see United Cities and Local Government (UCLG), Centenary of the International Municipal Movement, 2013, available at: <https://www.uclg.org/en/centenary>.

[4] NIJMAN, "Renaissance of the City as Global Actor: The Role of Foreign Policy and International Law Practices in the Construction of Cities as Global Actors", in HELLMANN, FARMHEIR and VEC (eds.), *The Transformation of Foreign Policy: Drawing and Managing Boundaries from Antiquities to the Present*, Oxford, 2016, p. 210 ff.; AUST, "Shining Cities on the Hill? The Global City, Climate Change and International Law", EJIL, 2015, p. 255 ff.; OOMEN and BAUMGÄRTEL, "Frontier Cities: The Rise of Local Authorities as an Opportunity for International Human Rights Law", EJIL, 2018, p. 607 ff.; OOMEN and DURMUS, "Cities and Plural Understandings of Human Rights: Agents, Actors, Arenas", The Journal of Legal Pluralism and Unofficial Law, 2019, p. 141 ff.

tiveness and legitimacy of States. In this regard, the phrase by the then Mayor of New York, Michael Bloomberg, that "while States talk, cities act" has become a mantra.[5]

These elements put the issue of cities in international law, "a topic which is still at the margin of the international law discourse",[6] in a context in which even the most sceptical (and positivist) international lawyer cannot ignore that something (new) is happening and the issue cannot be underestimated. The traditional, maybe realist, view that cities do not have any standing in international law since they are simply administrative units of States does not seem to be satisfactory to some.[7] By contrast, some authors have gone as far as to speak about cities as

---

[5] The reasons supporting this position have been presented and developed in BARBER, *If Mayors Rule the World. Dysfunctional Nations, Rising Cities*, Yale, 2013. See also: EMANUEL, "The New City States. How Local Governments Make Foreign Policy", Foreign Affairs, 21 February 2020, available at: <https://www.foreignaffairs.com/articles/2020-02-21/new-city-states>, who writes that "as national governments become weak, paralyzed, and dysfunctional, cities and their mayors have filled the vacuum"; and "nation-states do not reflect the future. Rather, they are in a state of atrophy and decline". To conclude that "cities offer disaffected citizens a different approach. They have become places where function has replaced dysfunction, intimacy has replaced distance, and immediacy has replaced dithering". Along the same lines, LIN, *Governing Climate Change: Global Cities and Transnational Lawmaking*, Cambridge, 2018, esp. p. 106. Since 2016, Michael Bloomberg has been the UN's special envoy for cities and climate change and his mandate has been renewed in 2021. In 2016, he played a key role in setting up the Covenant of Mayors for Climate and Energy, which unites 10,500 cities, populated by almost one billion people, from 200 countries in the fight against climate change (see: <https://www.globalcovenantofmayors.org/>). It unites several earlier initiatives like the C40 Climate Leadership group, the International Council for Local Environmental Initiatives, Climate Alliance, Energy Cities, Eurocities and UCLG. For an all-encompassing and updated list of transnational cities networks and a description of their activities and interactions at the international level, see SWINEY, "The Urbanization of International Law and International Relations: The Rising Soft Power of Cities in Global Governance", Michigan Journal of International Law, 2020, p. 227 ff. (esp. pp. 243-256).

[6] AUST, "The Shifting Role of Cities in the Global Climate Change Regime: From Paris to Pittsburgh and Back?", RECIEL, 2019, p. 58 ff. See also RIEGNER, "International Institutions and the City", in AUST and DU PLESSIS (eds.), *The Globalization of Urban Governance: Legal Perspectives on Sustainable Goal 11*, New York, 2019, p. 38 ff., who wrote that "despite their increasing significance, relations between international institutions and cities are still an unusual topic for legal research. While international lawyers have accepted international organizations as legal subjects and significant actors, cities are still treated primarily as subnational entities mediated by their nation states. Likewise, local government lawyers have traditionally paid little attention to cities' international relations. More recently, however, this dualist framework has been challenged by legal scholars who argue that an 'international local government law', or a 'law of the global city' is emerging".

[7] The fact that cities are considered part of the State in international law is what emerged (*a contrario*) during a meeting whose proceedings (with contributions by Albert, Coulée, Crawford and Mauguin, Daillier, Dominicé, Jos, Mauguin, Pellet, Ruiz Fabri, Sorel, Tchikaya and Thouvenin) were published by the Société Française pour le Droit International: *Les collectivités territoriales non-étatiques dans le système juridique international*, Paris, 2002. It is meaningful that in the introductory report, although the diversification of actors "et dans une certaine mesure des sujets de droit international" is recognized, cities were not included among these new actors that are listed as "les organisations non gouvernamentales, les sociétés transnationales, les organisations internationales, les individus et les collectivités territoriales

subjects of international law.[8] Others emphasize the impact of changes that are happening, and argue that this may lead to cities becoming international legal persons, or maybe that even the concept of legal persons has to be reviewed in contemporary international law and cities will fit into this modified category.[9] Expressions such as "actors", "international legal authorities", "non-party stakeholders", "multi-stakeholders" or "agents" have been more frequently used to describe today's standing of cities in international relations and international law.[10] For some scholars, "the domestic legal relationship between cities and their states is itself a proper subject of international legal relationship" and this has led to the development of topics such as *international local government law*.[11]

Witnessing this sometimes confusing and often nebulous debate on the position of cities in international law, one could wonder what cities are and what they do in contemporary international law.[12] One could also wonder whether allowing cities to actively participate in the formation and implementation of international norms, as well as admitting their active contribution – as cities or transnational city networks – in international multilateral negotiations on issues of global concern, do really imply a change in their status in international law and in the relationship between cities, States and international organizations. Finally, one could wonder "how" (this author would rather say "whether") "international law is transformed through the growing role of cities".[13]

All the articles in the present Symposium offer insightful contributions to the debate and provide thorough analysis on several, relevant aspects of the impact of cities on contemporary international law in different fields such as climate change, cultural heritage, sustainable development, human rights, and the relationship between cities and the countryside.[14] In the following pages I will review (and try to better understand) the different positions on the role of cities

---

non-étatiques" (Jos, "Collectivités territoriales non-étatiques et système juridique international dans le contexte de la mondialisation", *ibid.*, p. 9 ff.).

[8] BODIFORD, "Cities in International Law: Reclaiming Rights as Global Custom", City University of New York Law Review, 2020, p. 1 ff.

[9] BLANK, "International Legal Personality/Subjectivity of Cities", in AUST and NIJMAN (eds.), *cit. supra* note 1.

[10] BLANK, "The City and the World", Columbia JTL, 2006, p. 868 ff.; FRUG and BARRON, "International Local Government Law", The Urban Lawyer, 2006, p. 1 ff.; NIJMAN, "The Future of the City and the International Law of the Future", in MULLER et al. (eds.), *The Law of the Future and the Future of Law*, Oslo, 2011, p. 213 ff.; AUST, *cit. supra* note 4, p. 255 ff.; ID., "Cities as International Legal Authorities – Remarks on Recent Developments and Possible Future Trends of Research", Journal of Comparative Urban Law and Policy, 2020, p. 82 ff.; HERRSCHEL and NEWMAN, *Cities as International Actors: Urban and Regional Governance beyond the Nation State*, London, 2017.

[11] FRUG and BARRON, *cit. supra* note 10, pp. 13 and 22.

[12] For a confirmation of this state of affairs as regards the global climate change regime (but the observation holds true also for other international law regimes), Aust affirms that "cities and their networks blur considerably the established boundary between public and private actors" (AUST, *cit. supra* note 6, p. 59).

[13] AUST and NIJMAN, *cit. supra* note 1.

[14] See, in the present Symposium, the articles by BAKKER, FRANCIONI, LITWIN, LIXINSKI, MARTINEZ and PAVONI.

in contemporary international law with regard to the basic concepts of international legal personality and looking at the participation of cities in international relations.[15] I will examine (and briefly comment upon) some of the most recent doctrinal efforts to reconsider the status of cities in international law. In doing so, I will focus mainly on observations related to the incremental participation of cities in international affairs in recent years and the conclusions to be derived therefrom on the international legal standing of cities (Section 2). Then, the reasons why cities are not subjects of international law, or better, why in international law cities and local authorities still matter but only because they are part of a State, will be systematically assessed and, consequently, attention will be devoted also to the rise of transnational city networks in international law (Section 3). Some final remarks will be made on the prospects for cities, transnational city networks and States on the international scene (Section 4).

2. A REVIEW OF THE DIFFERENT POSITIONS ON THE STATUS OF CITIES IN INTERNATIONAL LAW

As recalled above, in recent years, cities have been the subject of several studies by legal scholars, in both national and international law, and in other disciplines such as international relations, sociology, geography, demography, economics, politics and urban studies. Among these disciplines, in order to better understand the role of cities, local authorities and transnational city networks in contemporary international law it may be useful to first refer to a recent sociological study, or rather a study by two sociologists of human rights, that tackle (and criticize) the position of international law scholars towards the role of cities.

Oomen and Baumgärtel have noticed that recent behaviour of States and city representatives in international negotiations in the field of human rights indicates that, while States appear in crisis or unable to reach decisions, cities and local authorities have "increasingly asserted themselves as an alternative with greater legitimacy and more hands-on impact, and they are recognized as such by policymakers, scholars and international and regional organizations alike".[16] While social science scholars paid attention to this practice, the same did not happen

---

[15] I cannot embark on an in-depth perusal of issues of international legal personality in international law, which is out of the scope of this brief article. For a seminal, classical study on legal personality and international law see ARANGIO-RUIZ, *Diritto internazionale e personalità giuridica*, Bologna, 1972. See also ACQUAVIVA, "Subjects of International Law: A Power Based Analysis", Vanderbilt Journal of Transnational Law, 2005, p. 345 ff. With reference also to the issue of international legal personality in relation to cities: NIJMAN, *The Concept of International Legal Personality: An Inquiry into the History and Theory of International Law*, Den Haag, 2004; PORTMANN, *Legal Personality in International Law*, Cambridge, 2010, pp. 48-49. With specific regard to the issue of the alleged international legal personality of cities, see SOSSAI, "Invisibility of Cities in Classical International Law", in AUST and NIJMAN (eds.), *cit. supra* note 1; and BLANK, "International Legal Personality/Subjectivity of Cities", *ibid.*

[16] OOMEN and BAUMGÄRTEL, *cit. supra* note 4, p. 608.

with regard to international lawyers who were more focused on "how to integrate local authorities into static conventional frameworks firmly based on the premise of State sovereignty".[17] In other words, according to these authors, international law scholars show a certain interest in the activities of cities on the international scene, but they do so only in order to preserve the current state of affairs and the basics of their discipline, and not to acknowledge the alleged enhanced force of local authorities in international negotiations, including as a form of civil society network, as has been seen in the field of climate change and the negotiations that led to the Paris Agreement of 2015, as well as its follow-up, with the creation of huge networks of cities.

The "sins" of international law scholars in addressing the relationship between local authorities and States are first that they "have so far followed a predictable pattern that […] is predisposed to accommodate rather than challenge conventional frameworks";[18] secondly, international law scholars have "sought to assess the relevance of these processes using established categories of international law".[19] As to the latter, Oomen and Baumgärtel stress that, in their opinion, the attempt was not successful since it ended up stressing the key role of domestic law in defining the competence of the local authorities and concluding that local authorities only make a "modest" contribution to the development of international law.[20]

In the field of international responsibility, for example, they take note that according to Crawford and Mauguin "the prospect of bypassing the State is simply impractical".[21] Consequently, according to Oomen and Baumgärtel, international law scholars have tried to get around these difficulties by not addressing the "challenging issue of legal subjecthood right away", but rather refocusing "on cities as the object of international norms", and by stressing that cities' activities "may count as 'soft law instruments with some degree of international normativity'".[22]

It is clear that these attempts by international law scholars at answering some of the questions concerning the role of cities in contemporary international law are aimed at circumventing those questions rather than answering them, as recognized by the same authors cited here.[23] The failure to directly engage with the

---

[17] *Ibid.*

[18] *Ibid.*, p. 611. After a perusal of some of the most important contributions by legal scholars (Blank, Frug and Barron, Porras, Aust) to the debate, the authors conclude that on this point "these works join the chorus of social science scholarship that describes a close and almost dialectical relationship between global and local actors".

[19] *Ibid.*, p. 612.

[20] *Ibid.*

[21] CRAWFORD and MAUGUIN, "Collectivités territoriales non-étatiques et droit international de la responsabilité", in Société Française pour le Droit International, *cit. supra* note 7, p. 157 ff.

[22] OOMEN and BAUMGÄRTEL, *cit. supra* note 4, p. 612. This last assertion is made citing the conclusions reached by NIJMAN, *cit. supra* note 10, p. 225.

[23] OOMEN and BAUMGÄRTEL, *cit. supra* note 4, p. 613. According to Oomen and Baumgärtel "international law scholarship on local authorities has come quite a long way from its modest beginnings. A genuine interest exists to understand the rise of cities and other 'localities' and

issue at a more fundamental level stems from concerns put forward by other authors and recalled in the same article: from those who think that elevating the status of cities and local authorities would lead to a world even more "unmanageable" than the current one; to those who warn about the intention of cities to affirm a more neo-liberal call for privatization; to those who have reservations about cities' networks since they "reproduce hierarchies known from the State system"; or, finally, to those who warn against the "premature rejection and 'demonization' of the State, which could have detrimental political consequences [...]".[24] The conclusion of Oomen and Baumgärtel is that, as regards international law scholars, they "have not so far shown the audacity to dream about 'new horizons of possibility'".[25]

Recent international relations studies have emphasized that in the last two decades cities have been entering the international political arena, notwithstanding some institutional, legal and political obstacles. According to those studies, cities have been acting on the international scene as independent actors from the States to which they belong and have been able to shape and influence international negotiations. They have done so through different strategies, including: (1) coalescing together to form large networks, which engage in city or "glocal" (globalized-local) diplomacy; (2) allying with well-connected and well-resourced international organizations; (3) gaining inclusion in UN multilateral agendas; (4) mirroring state-based coalitions and their high-profile events; (5) harnessing the language of international law (especially international human rights and environmental law) to advance agendas at odds with their national counterparts; and (6) adopting resolutions, declarations, and voluntarily self-policed commitments – *global law* – that look strikingly similar to state-made international law.[26]

The conclusion is that "using these six strategies, cities are piercing the states-only veil of international politics in ways arguably not seen in the post-Westphalian era".[27]

Looking at the standing acquired by cities on the international plane, one cannot but agree with this last observation. The fact that in the last two decades cities and their mayors have been able to construct solid inter-city alliances such as ICLEI-Local Governments for Sustainability, C40, Climate Leadership Forum, Metropolitan Mayors Caucus, the World Organization of United Cities and Local Governments (UCLG), International Union of Local Authorities (IULA), Mayors' Organizations, World Federation of United Cities (WFUC), World Urban Forum, Global Metro City, and the Glocal Forum, and that through those alliances they have been able to participate actively in inter-

---

to integrate them into the discipline". However, they think that "the combined emphasis on cities as 'objects' of international law, the prevalence of 'soft law' and the potential problems of their increased relevance precludes a more fundamental engagement with the topic that could [...] make a real contribution to the further development of international law". Along the same lines, see OOMEN and DURMUS, *cit. supra* note 4.

[24] OOMEN and BAUMGÄRTEL, *cit. supra* note 4, pp. 612-613.

[25] *Ibid.*, p. 629.

[26] SWINEY, *cit. supra* note 5, esp. p. 229.

[27] *Ibid.*, p. 230.

governmental negotiations and make their voice heard on these occasions, is true beyond any doubt.[28] However, the description of the ways and means ("the strategies") used by cities to obtain these results does not necessarily imply that by doing so cities can be considered more than "actors" or that they become subjects of international law. Actually, what cities have been able to do with regard to their standing in international relations does not differ (too much) from what other alleged international "actors" have been able to do and to achieve in what I would call the "intergovernmental plus arena", i.e. intergovernmental negotiations open to participants other than States. Reference is made here to what coalitions of NGOs do in many fields, ranging from climate change to international criminal justice. More specifically, with regard to the latter, the establishment of the International Criminal Court (ICC) would not have been possible without the constant presence and activity of the Coalition for the establishment of the ICC (CICC), an association of more than 2,500 NGOs that participated in all the phases of the negotiations that led to the establishment of the ICC and is still very active in this field.[29] However, no one even thinks that by so doing the CICC has become a subject of international law, although it is clear that it has been, and still is, a "pervasive" actor in promoting international criminal justice.[30]

Even more perplexities arise from a recent attempt to illustrate, now from a legal point of view, alleged changes in the international legal status of cities by one of the "pioneers" of international law scholarly studies on cities. After declaring the insufficiencies of what he calls the "intuitive approaches" to the question (those who reject international subjectivity/personality for cities and those who think that what matters is how cities function in reality, not whether

---

[28] All these TCNs have their own websites and it does not seem worthwhile citing them here since they are easily accessible. The scholarly contributions, from different disciplines, to the issue of TCNs are countless. For interesting observations on the role of cities' networks and updated references to their activities in a specific field such as climate change mitigation it seems useful to refer, by way of example, to HEIKKINEN et al., "Transnational Municipal Networks and Climate Change Adaptation: A Study of 377 Cities", Journal of Cleaner Production, 2020, available at: <https://doi.org/10.1016/j.jclepro.2020.120474>. Another interesting example is the role of ICLEI on "urban biodiversity", on which see FRANTZESKAKI et al., "The Multiple Roles of ICLEI: Intermediating to Innovate Urban Biodiversity Governance", Ecological Economics, 2019, available at: <https://doi.org/10.1016/j.ecolecon.2019.06.005>. The outcome of this research is that ICLEI fulfils three role patterns: knowledge role (educator and integrator); relational role (connector and mediator); and game-changing role (pathbreaker and co-creator). And the authors conclude that "ICLEI and other transnational city networks orchestrate information flows and knowledge aggregation at cross levels, resulting in more effectively knowledge integration in cities and advancing agenda on urban biodiversity". See also BAKKER's article in this Volume, esp. section 3.
[29] See: <https://www.coalitionfortheicc.org/>.
[30] TRAMONTANA, "The Participation of NGOs in the Dynamics of International Law-Making", in ARCARI and BALMOND (eds.), Diversification des acteurs et dynamique normative en droit international, Napoli, 2013, p. 123 ff. On the participation of NGOs in international negotiations concerning international criminal justice, see the papers contained in TREVES et al. (eds.), Civil Society, International Courts and Compliance Bodies, The Hague, 2005, pp. 105-146.

they are conceptualized as subjects/persons), Blank "calls into question the denial of cities' status in international law pointing to their growing importance
as central actors on the international legal plane".[31] According to Blank, cities
are "becoming crucial actors" and are allegedly involved in international dispute
settlement procedures, even if he admits that "this involvement still requires the
consent of their state". Furthermore, other changes in the position of cities in the
field of foreign relations and in the formation of global networks would lead one
to "call into question the rigid definition of what it means to be a 'subject/person'
of the law, and the theory of the international legal system, that lies behind it".[32]
Following this reasoning, Blank states that cities "are where international agreements are translated into real policies, and they are the ones that decide what
international rights and obligations actually mean", and "where more authentic
and participatory democracy is exercised". The deep involvement of cities in
the international sphere and their connection with international institutions indicates that cities, "although relying on their state's agreement to perform these
activities, are operating 'as if' they were international legal persons".[33] This final
statement indicates that in real terms cities are not international legal persons.
In explaining why cities should have international legal personality (i.e. they
do not have it yet), and why this is desirable, the same author argues that cities'
international legal personality would not replace that of States, "but would rather
complement it". One could question whether this is any different than saying
that cities, *per se*, do not possess international legal personality. However, in
his opinion cities would be much better than States in promoting participatory
democracy, combating populism, promoting cultural, religious, ethnic and linguistic pluralism, as well as economic efficiency, and in countering executive
overreach through a different and more consistent "separation of powers".[34] Each
one of these arguments would deserve several comments, although comments
and criticisms are honestly presented by the same author (in the same text). As a
concluding remark, he states that:

> even if facilitating institutions such as the UN cannot be adapted
> to a world with thousands or even millions of international legal
> subjects, we can certainly think of an international law where cit-
> ies are legal persons who bear international legal duties, who are
> capable of entering international agreements, and who are making
> international legal claims.[35]

---

[31] BLANK, *cit. supra* note 9. He founds his conviction on several studies aimed at emphasizing the enhanced role of cities in "protecting" and shaping international legal norms, developing international networks and even engaging in foreign relations, especially in certain areas
such as sustainability and climate change, human rights, immigration, and gender equality.
[32] *Ibid.*, Section II.
[33] *Ibid.*
[34] *Ibid*, Section III.
[35] *Ibid.*, Section IV.

It seems that this assessment refers, maybe, to the international law of the future; it remains to be explained whether it is compatible with institutions and norms of contemporary international law.

Another attempt to single out the role acquired by cities in contemporary international law through their impressive participation in international negotiations was conducted by one of the most authoritative international law scholars on the topic, Helmut Aust, when he looked into what has recently happened in the field of climate change.[36] In view of the difficulties arising in intergovernmental negotiations on this issue after Rio and Kyoto, cities and TCNs were very critical of States for the stalemate that preceded the conclusion of the Paris Agreement in 2015. The accusation that States only talked while cities acted was particularly harsh. The conclusion of the Agreement and its rapid entry into force in 2016 have demonstrated, according to Aust, that those criticisms were premature and that States still play a crucial and irreplaceable role in concluding international treaties. At the same time, looking at the complex content of the Agreement, it emerges that while States have kept their prerogatives in treaty-making power, cities are called upon to implement the Agreement, and strengthen their position at the international level. Therefore, after Paris, "no longer can it be argued that the inter-State system is dysfunctional [...]. But the importance of the subnational level for this part of global governance can no longer be denied".[37] And Aust concludes that:

> the growing role of cities in global governance – and increasingly also in international law – adds another layer of complexity to our understanding of these fields. This complexity is owed not least to the dual character of cities when they act at the international level. They remain State organs and hence represent to a certain extent their respective State. At the same time, the field of climate change governance exemplifies that cities frequently act globally precisely in order to pursue a policy which sets them apart from their home State.[38]

Although this position provides a possible answer to the request for clarification of the role of cities in international law (by restating that they are part of their States), it seems to introduce a sort of schizophrenia by cities, which are part of their respective State but also able to run against it globally.[39] However, one could also say that if cities criticize their central governments – whether it happens at the international or at the domestic level – these criticisms do not change the cities' nature as subnational units of the States to which they belong.

---

[36] AUST, *cit. supra* note 6, p. 57 ff.

[37] *Ibid.*, p. 65.

[38] *Ibid.*, p. 66.

[39] Aust recognizes that "it is time for international law to openly acknowledge this development and accommodate these practices in its fundamental doctrines. As of now, this process has only just begun" (*ibid.*).

Interesting observations have been presented by Aust also with reference to TCNs and their place in international law. In this regard, he recalls that in recent times TCNs have shown dynamic attitudes in global affairs and "aim to establish themselves in a broader way as part of the relevant governance structure".[40] In order to explain what is happening, it is recalled that the city networks believe that they are efficient while States are dysfunctional; that cities are pragmatic and problem-solving; and that cities have democratic legitimacy, being the closest to the people. The reactions of international law to this development are, according to Aust, twofold: according to a traditional, positivist approach, city networks are not dealing with international law, cities are not subjects of international law and do not contribute to the formation of international law; on the other side, those who enthusiastically support a sort of progressive approach to the issue ("a contourless global law mindset") would "welcome all activities of cities with open arms, stipulating that all boundaries between domestic and international law, between hard and soft law have collapsed".[41] According to Aust, "the former approach is as uninspiring and lacking imagination as the latter is falling short of law's fundamental objective to provide for normative guidance [...]".[42] Quite interestingly, he proposes a third way, inspired by the "works on transnational networks of civil servants, the global administrative law literature and recent work on 'informal international law-making'." However, this approach also does not seem to be satisfactory if Aust concludes that:

> whether this turn to informality maintains flexibility and could thus help to turn cooperation between cities into a productive laboratory for societal change, it can also mean that existing power structures are reproduced on a different level.[43]

In a further attempt to respond to "the traditional absence of cities from international law", the same author has recently proposed including cities among the international legal authorities which, according to Aust, "seems to imply that international law is recognizing the authority of a given entity", with the very important caveat that "the concept of authority goes beyond mere subjectivity".[44] Thus, in order to qualify cities as international legal authorities the first issue is

---

[40] AUST, "'Good Urban Citizen'", in HOHMANN and JOYCE (eds.), *International Law's Objects*, Oxford, 2018, p. 229 ff.

[41] This criticism has been reiterated by Aust (and du Plessis) on another occasion when they spoke about "global governance literature, which is often more interested in informal processes, international relations and political workings than in concrete questions of architecture of governance and the functioning of existing and future domestic and international law" (AUST and DU PLESSIS, "Summary of Observations and Pointers for Future Research", in AUST and DU PLESSIS (eds.), *cit. supra* note 6, p. 273 ff.

[42] AUST, "'Good Urban Citizen'", *cit. supra* note 40, pp. 229-230.

[43] *Ibid.*, p. 230.

[44] AUST, "Cities as International Legal Authorities – Remarks on Recent Developments and Possible Future Trends of Research", Journal of Comparative Urban Law and Policy, 2020, p. 82 ff., esp. p. 82.

to ascertain whether any rule of international law recognizes some regulatory power to cities; and then on which basis this authority is constituted.[45] It follows that cities would be "a most peculiar form of international legal authority as the ground for their authority is hybrid: it follows from both international and domestic law"; furthermore, the position of cities and global networks of cities in international law is equated to that of international organizations. However, it is recognized that, because of the traditional view that international law is an inter-State law, cities are not listed among the subjects of international law in international law textbooks. A bottom-up process and a top-down phenomenon would indicate, according to Aust, that "this state of affairs is gradually changing". The bottom-up process would amount to the global activities of cities and the active participation of cities and their associations in international meetings: this would imply that cities and their associations are today "relevant actors, addressing a governance gap created by the allegedly ineffective structures of the traditional system of inter-state diplomacy". On the other side, and this is defined as the top-down process, States and international organizations "increasingly recognize that cities and subnational authorities are relevant actors and could thus be understood as international legal authorities".[46] These processes are "complementary and jointly contribute to the shaping of an international legal authority for cities". Aust affirms that this authority will develop "in the sense that States increasingly recognize the global aspects of local matters", and would agree to cities going beyond their national competences in view of the achievement of their objectives.[47] Therefore, a parallel is made with the theory of implied powers in the law of international organizations. Aust does not hide the difficulties of this theoretical construction and admits that the field of global city cooperation is still a "laboratory for experimentation" and that this field "will increasingly call for robust comparative law endeavors in order to understand more fully the framework conditions under which cities can implement their international legal authority".[48]

Another commendable effort to describe the role of cities and TCNs in contemporary international law has been recently made by Durmus by looking, once again, at the international engagement of cities in various fields of international concern.[49] In this regard, phenomena such as the "pluralization of actors without established legal personality engaging in practices traditionally reserved for states", and the preference for non-binding international norms "created through multistakeholder governance processes rather than binding treaties signed by states only" would imply "a move from multilateralism – referring to an inter-

---

[45] *Ibid.*

[46] *Ibid.*, pp. 83-84. According to Aust this assertion is based on three "pillars": a) international law increasingly calls on the local level directly; b) cities are important for the enforcement of agreed upon international norms; c) States have set up international agreements regulating transboundary cooperation among subnational authorities (*ibid.*, pp. 85-86).

[47] *Ibid.*, p. 86.

[48] *Ibid.*

[49] DURMUS, *cit. supra* note 2, p. 46.

state governance system – towards multistakeholderism – referring to a system of norm generation and governance that involves many actors relevant to a subject matter".[50]

In particular, Durmus noted the engagement of cities and TCNs in international matters usually managed by States and the creation of institutions where local authorities engage, as such, in international law and global governance. This engagement paves the way to the formal recognition of cities and TCNs as actors in international law, "regardless of whether it takes a long time for any formal change of status to occur – if it occurs at all".[51] According to Durmus, the observation of the modalities through which, in the last thirty years, cities and TCNs have interacted with international organizations may contribute to "a recognition of a limited kind of legal personality", and this would amount for cities and TCNs to a recognition "if not as a 'non-state actor' then as 'stakeholders' in the multi-stakeholder processes of global governance".[52]

Durmus concludes that, while the novel, crucial role of cities and TCNs in international negotiations and more generally in contemporary international law should be recognized, cities and TCNs are not to be considered, *as such*, subjects of international law.

Finally, Bodiford has recently stated that, although "cities' status in international law remains ambiguous, they are in a twilight zone in international law between sovereign and not sovereign".[53] Furthermore, that on the basis of their participation and the active role played in international negotiations, cities "are becoming emergent actors and subjects of international law".[54] In view of the direct engagement of cities in areas such as environment, transportation, housing, water, and planning, Bodiford argues that cities should even be considered "sovereign actors". This strong support for "subjectivity" and "sovereignty" of cities in international law seems to collide with the exclusivity (monopoly) of States in foreign policy with regard to the example of the conclusion of agreements between cities belonging to different States. Leaving aside the fact that this

---

[50] *Ibid.*, p. 45.

[51] *Ibid.* According to Durmus, "[i]f cities, collectively, are seeking formal recognition of their role and status in international law, they are on exactly the right path, both in seeking a seat at the table in state-centric processes and in organising and convening with their peers to engage in international law and governance matters without reservations and concerns about whether or not they are 'permitted' by international law to do so (as 'subjects' or holders of international legal personality). The recognition of new players in the game, whether by progressive or more conservative observers or by existing players, does not come about by such permission but by a retroactive recognition of accumulated evidence showing a new de facto reality".

[52] *Ibid.*, p. 50. Those modalities are synthesized as: "seeking to take part in international law-making, seeking to have their role and responsibility with regards to norms recognized, voluntarily reporting their compliance with international norms, seeking official accreditation, acquiring an actual body in the United Nations system dedicated to them, establishing their role strongly enough for United Nations organs to invite them to deliberations (such as the Habitat III Conference) that involve the development of international norms".

[53] BODIFORD, *cit. supra* note 8, pp. 1-2.

[54] *Ibid.*, p. 22.

type of agreement is concluded between sub-national territorial entities (i.e. by sub-entities of different States) in the framework of constitutional and legislative provisions, it is acknowledged that "the agreements which cities make with each other fall outside the scope of sovereign foreign policy".[55]

Lastly, underlining the differences between cities and "rural hinterlands" and claiming an alleged superiority of cities, Bodiford assigns to cities a central role between State and rural periphery. He argues that cities should, on the one hand, "challenge the parochial interest of a nation or a region" and, on the other, should conclude "an agreement which encompasses a patchwork of the world's cities with the world's highest GDP" in order to "drag even the greatest geo-political troglodytes kicking and screaming into the twenty-first century."[56] I admit that it is unclear to me what the connection between this affirmation and the alleged subjectivity of cities in international law is.

Although I do not always see the rationale of some of these doctrinal reconstructions of the role of cities and cities' associations in contemporary international law, the attempts at attributing to them a sort of legal personality/subjectivity based mainly on the observation that these entities are participating, as such, in international negotiations and have been recognized as active contributors in shaping and implementing international law (norms) cannot be underestimated. The openness shown by States and international organizations to the participation of cities and TCNs in international negotiations is also noteworthy. Finally, the fact that local authorities are called upon, in some areas of international concern, to replace States' inability or unwillingness to act or even to counter their own States' position regarding international obligations or commitments is something that deserves attention.

However, one could wonder whether these elements suffice to pave the way to a paradigm shift towards the recognition of cities' and TCNs' subjecthood in international law, and thus to encourage the insertion of cities among the (emerging) subjects of international law in future textbooks.

3. CITIES AND TRANSNATIONAL CITIES NETWORKS IN CONTEMPORARY INTERNATIONAL LAW

The opinions expressed by scholars on the alleged international legal personality/subjectivity of cities in international law, as previously reviewed, have something in common: the position of cities in international law has deeply changed in the last 30 years and cities are today unanimously acknowledged as "actors" that participate in international negotiations, when issues concerning their areas of competence are at stake. The reasons why cities decide to participate actively in international negotiations are diverse, ranging from the desire to be directly involved in debates and deliberations on issues of global and local

---

[55] *Ibid.*, p. 25.
[56] *Ibid.*, p. 31. On the relationship between cities and the countryside, see the contributions to this Symposium by FRANCIONI and LITWIN.

concern, to an alleged lack of representativeness and inability of central governments to address those same issues. Thus, cities have been able to "sit at the table" and to affirm their crucial role, especially on these issues. Cities have almost
always participated at the international level through TCNs which, legally speaking – as I will clarify later on –, are different from cities as such in contemporary
international law.

This practice has allowed cities to be better informed, to share relevant international experiences and to make their voice heard at the international level, as
well as to improve their local governance on issues of global concern. All these
elements surely contribute to the recognition of cities and local authorities as being among the protagonists of international relations together with other entities
such as NGOs and multinationals, although with some important "constitutional"
differences since cities and local authorities are public, territorial entities within
nation States. However, this does not imply that they are, as such, subject of international law, a qualification pertaining to the State to which they belong.

Without commenting further upon the various opinions and reconstructions
made by scholars on this issue, let us be clear: to be a subject of international law
still means to have international rights and duties, to participate in the formation
of international customary and conventional norms, to be held responsible for
internationally wrongful acts. Do cities, as such, possess these features? First,
cities – in the absence of a uniform definition in international law and considering
the difficulties arising when international law scholars attempt to devise one – are
part of the State to which they belong. Being territorial units of their own State
implies that international law is relevant for cities qua part of their State. Thus,
the practice of cities and local authorities contributes as a manifestation of their
nation State's practice to the formation of customary international law,[57] while
they also give their contribution to the formation of treaties by attending and
influencing the outcome of international negotiations (although they do not ratify
international treaties, according to the Vienna Convention on the Law of Treaties)
if their participation is allowed or acquiesced to by States and intergovernmental

---

[57] International Law Commission, Draft Conclusions on identification of customary international law, with commentaries, 2018. I refer namely to Conclusion No. 5, labelled "Conduct
of the State as State practice": "State practice consists of conduct of the State, whether in the
exercise of its executive, legislative, judicial or other functions". In the Commentary (p. 2) it
is specified that: "[t]o qualify as State practice, the conduct in question must be 'of the State'.
The conduct of any State organ is to be considered conduct of that State, whether the organ
exercises legislative, executive, judicial or any other functions, whatever position it holds in
the organization of the State, and whatever its character as an organ of the central government
or of a *territorial unit of the State*. An organ includes any person or entity that has that status
in accordance with the internal law of the State; the conduct of a person or entity otherwise
empowered by the law of the State to exercise elements of governmental authority is also
conduct 'of the State', provided the person or entity is acting in that capacity in the particular
instance" (emphasis added). Many years ago, one of the founders of this Yearbook referred
to the relevance of administrative practice in the formation of customary international law
(FERRARI BRAVO, "Méthodes de recherche de la coutume internationale dans la pratiques des
Etats", RCADI, Vol. 192, 1985-III, p. 233 ff., esp. pp. 282-283).

organizations.[58] In the field of responsibility for internationally wrongful acts, if the acts or omissions of cities amount to violations of international obligations, those acts or omissions are attributable to their State, according to the Articles on the Responsibility of States for Internationally Wrongful Acts and to practice.[59] Thus, one cannot but agree with one of the authors who is more convinced about the "rising role" of cities in international law when she writes that:

> [...] cities remain disconnected from black letter international law except through the intermediation of States, and no amount of creative lawyering or interpretive gymnastics can change that fact, at least so long as the current international legal framework remains in place.[60]

We could maybe discuss whether "the current international legal framework" is still viable or something has changed or will change in the short run. And one could consider various attempts at widening the definition of international law, including a "global law variant" (even if the word "variant" is quite frightening in these pandemic times) according to which "these formal categories are obviously much less important".[61] But this is not the aim of this contribution, which, rather than foreseeing the international law of the future, attempts to clarify what is the status of cities in contemporary international law. In this regard, it seems that all those who have studied this issue, notwithstanding some attempts at making further steps towards new approaches, get to the same conclusion: cities matter at the international level because they are part of the States to which they belong, as is the case with all the various branches of the nation State according to international law. This also implies that since cities contribute to shape, through various means and in different forms, the position of States when the latter are

---

[58] On the uncertain legal qualification of certain types of contracts concluded between cities and international agencies, see RIEGNER, *cit. supra* note 6, pp. 44-47.

[59] According to Aust, "Shining Cities", *cit. supra* note 4, p. 267: "[f]rom an international law perspective [...], cities (understood as municipalities) have a particular non-status in international legal discourse. This is partly owed to the fact that they are state organs when they act internationally. As such, they are not granted the status of subjects of international law and thus lack the capability to create international law in the traditional sense. However, *their actions are attributable to the state*. Violations of international law committed by the local levels of government thus generate state responsibility under Article 4 of the 2001 International Law Commission Articles on State Responsibility" (emphasis added). On this specific issue, see also the interesting observations by SOSSAI, *cit. supra* note 15. For international jurisprudence, even before the adoption of the ILC Draft Articles just recalled, see *Elettronica Sicula S.p.A. (ELSI) (United States of America v. Italy)*, Judgment of 20 July 1989, ICJ Reports 1989, p. 15 ff., where the United States invoked the responsibility of Italy for an alleged internationally wrongful act arising from a decision made by the Mayor of Palermo (esp. paras. 105 and 129). A very in-depth reconstruction of the evolution of the concept of attribution within the ILC works and beyond, is available in ARANGIO-RUIZ, *State Responsibility Revisited. The Factual Nature of the Attribution of Conduct to the State*, Milano, 2017.

[60] SWINEY, *cit. supra* note 5, p. 243.

[61] AUST, "Cities in International Law – From Outsiders to Insiders?", ASIL, 2020, p. 368 ff., p. 369.

called upon to express their positions at the international level, they are having, and rightly so, "a seat at the table" as "actors", "stakeholders", "participants", "agents"...

Defining the standing of the associations of cities or transnational city (or municipal) networks in contemporary international law is, in my opinion, a different issue than defining the standing of cities. As cities are parts of their nation State, and the international subjectivity of the latter is not debated, when cities decide to "act" on the international scene they do it in different ways, ranging from participating in international activities to belonging to TCNs that have been established for different reasons and attend, as associations of cities and local authorities, international meetings.[62] One could also say that TCNs rather than cities as such are today the "real" representative of cities in the world of international relations since cities express their positions at the international level mainly through the TCNs.

While in international law cities are "invisible actors" since they are part of the nation State, TCNs can be defined as non-State actors similar to NGOs and other entities that participate in international relations but without being subjects of international law, thus not possessing international legal personality, and similar to – *mutatis mutandis* – other associations of "public" entities of different States such as the Inter-Parliamentary Union, an international (yet, not intergovernmental) organization of national parliaments.[63]

In conclusion, TCNs, "as innovative forms of governance [...] not losing touch with the established realities of international politics and governance",[64] are surely an expression of the common interests of cities and local authorities, and represent such interests in international negotiations. They do so on different topics and in different ways, implementing the decisions of their members. Participating in international negotiations, TCNs have shown that they are able to influence the content of international law instruments in fields such as environmental protection and human rights, and are able also to shape behaviour in these

---

[62] HERRSCHEL and NEWMAN, *cit. supra* note 10, p. 3: "[o]ver the past twenty years or so, there has been rapid growth of city and regional networks as new vehicles to protect and promote local and regional interests in a globalising, yet politically still largely state-centric, world. As a consequence, nation states and their territories come into sharper focus, as their borders lose the function of protecting and maintaining an image of a sovereign, cohesive entity in the international arena. Instead, the picture is becoming more detailed and differentiated, with a growing number of sub-national entities, cities, city-regions and regions, becoming more visible in their own right, either individually, or collectively as networks, by, more or less tentatively, stepping out of the territorial canvas and hierarchical institutional hegemony of the state. Prominent and well-known cities, and those regions with a strong sense of identity and often a quest for more autonomy, have been the most enthusiastic, as they began to be represented beyond state borders by high-profile city mayors and some regional leaders with political courage and agency. While some have ventured out individually with confidence, such as the mayors of the main 'global cities', others have invested time and resources in networking with like-minded others, and with the United Nations (UN) and other IOs, to gain the necessary capacity and desired impact which, individually, they felt lacking".

[63] On the Inter-Parliamentary Union (IPU), see: <https://www.ipu.org/>.

[64] AUST, "Shining Cities", *cit. supra* note 4, p. 275.

and other issues. They have been doing so as mediators of cities' interests but not as subjects of international law.

4. CONCLUDING REMARKS

The role of cities and TCNs in contemporary international law does not depend on whether a "traditional" or "progressive" approach to international law is adopted,[65] or whether one is sympathetic to one international law school of thought or another.[66] At a time when international liberalism and multilateralism are under attack, international lawyers – while being open to any argumentation aimed at improving a better understanding of the features of international law – should reject any selective approach as regard to the basics of international law that could result in a further weakening of the system.[67] And this holds true also for the alleged subjectivity of cities. Acknowledging cities' international legal subjectivity would imply, *inter alia*, a tremendous proliferation of international subjects that would result in an untenable situation as regards not only international law but also the essential features of international institutions, as has also been observed by the supporters of such acknowledgment.[68] Furthermore, one could wonder whether being subjects of international law would add anything to cities' capability to participate in international relations and to have an impact on relevant aspects of international law. Here too, the right answer is given by the

---

[65] AUST, "Cities in International Law", *cit. supra* note 61, p. 369. In posing crucial questions regarding the impact of cities on changes in international law and on the role (outsiders or insiders) of cities in the international legal process, Aust states that "the answer to these questions depends very much on your definition of international law". According to a traditional, formal definition of international law, "cities simply remain part of the state, they are state organs". Aust then writes that in his view cities "are both: part of the state and potentially non-state actors", but he does not delve into detail on this. However, he adds that "this duality makes them much more intriguing and complicated entities than your average non-state actor in international law [...]. *I would be careful to put too much emphasis on the non-state actor prism.* Being a non-state actor also means that you have to face less legitimacy concerns – you can more or less choose your own constituency. Public actors are different – they are defined by their competences, can only act within these boundaries and can and should be held to account whether they fulfill the functions they are supposed to fulfill" (emphasis added).

[66] DURMUS, *cit. supra* note 2, p. 81. In her essay, this author, criticizing the "positivist vision", takes a stance in favour of the "New" New Haven School of International Law. These "pluralist scholars [who] have long recognized the power of actors and types of norms not contemplated by 'official' international law [...] argue that law's power comes not only from coercion and enforcement capacity, but above all from persuasion by the actors who advocate for them, including by those *within* the State" (emphasis in the original).

[67] On the difficulties of international liberalism and multilateralism see, more recently, KOSKENNIEMI, *International Law and the Far Right: Reflections on Law and Cynicism*, Fourth Annual T.M.C. Asser Lecture, Den Haag, 2019, esp. p. 3 ff.

[68] BLANK, *cit. supra* note 9.

supporters of cities' subjectivity who do not attach so much importance to this issue.[69]

Finally, recent developments such as the fast ratification and entry into force of the Paris Agreement on Climate Change, notwithstanding the withdrawal (now in turn withdrawn by the Biden administration) of the United States, have shown that, despite their flaws and sometimes well-deserved criticisms, nation States remain at the centre of international cooperation.[70] Are we sure that if we replace States with cities and local authorities as subjects of international law this will lead to increased representativeness, accountability, efficiency, and democratic decision-making in international relations?[71] Cities and local authorities can certainly contribute, through inter-city cooperation and through a better dialogue with their central authorities, to find new ways to improve decision-making by States, founded on citizens' interests.[72] In this context one should look at cities as "actors" and "honest brokers" of the future in a world that, especially in certain activities affecting humankind, should reflect on the prospects of a "networked multilateralism" in some crucial fields of international as well as domestic law.[73] If this result is achieved, one could say that cities have had a true impact on international law or even that they have transformed it.

---

[69] DURMUS, *cit. supra* note 2, p. 45. See also LIXINSKI's contribution to this Symposium, Sections 1 and 6.

[70] On the crisis of nation States and the role of international law, see the interesting observations by CONDORELLI, "Crisi dello Stato e diritto internazionale: simul stabunt simul cadent?", Ars interpretandi, 2011, p. 172 ff. (esp. p. 179).

[71] More recently, KATZ COGAN, "International Organizations and Cities", in AUST and NIJMAN (eds.), *cit. supra* note 1, section IV.

[72] On how the "virtuous circle" of subnational diplomacy and the nation State in foreign and domestic policy is working in different fields and could work in the future, see GARCETTI and HACHIGIAN, "Cities Are Transforming US Foreign Policy. Biden Would Do Well to Work with Them", Foreign Affairs, 29 December 2020, available at: <https://www.foreignaffairs.com/articles/united-states/2020-12-29/cities-are-transforming-us-foreign-policy>. In more general terms, Beaudoin affirms that "the examination of the relations between cities and states from a legal point of view supports the observation that their interests and strengths are so intertwined that neither have interest in weakening the other too much, and the state remains the only entity not submitted to a higher legal authority" (BEAUDOIN, "Sovereignty", in AUST and NIJMAN (eds.), *cit. supra* note 1, section IV). See also the articles by PAVONI (section 1) and by BAKKER (concluding remarks) in this Symposium.

[73] These are the words recently used by the UN Secretary-General, Antonio Guterres, in his speech that was recalled at the beginning of this article and is available at: <https://www.un.org/sg/en/content/sg/speeches/2021-04-16/remarks-meeting-leading-mayors-supported-c40-cities>.

PARADOXES OF VISIBILITY AND PRESERVATION: CULTURAL HERITAGE LAW AND THE MAKING OF THE CITY AS AN INTERNATIONAL LEGAL CATEGORY

LUCAS LIXINSKI[*]

Abstract

The push for cities to be a part of international legal governance processes is tied to the promise of bridging international law's democratic deficit. However, the exercise of cities' personality in international law can end up replicating many of the same democratic deficits with which international law is usually charged. Therefore, cities as agents may be an unsatisfactory way of addressing international law's democratic deficits. Instead, cities as objects can raise the visibility of cities and the local communities that live therein, but without giving agency to a State actor. This visibility can then pave the way for communities themselves to be directly involved in international legal governance processes. This article uses the example of international heritage law, where cities are very significantly represented in international heritage lists and even a specific instrument (the 2011 Recommendation on the Historic Urban Landscape) to showcase the limitations and possibilities of the project of cities in international law. I argue that there is a paradox of visibility and agency that permeates international legal possibilities for cities, and placing the city simultaneously in the registers of object and subject ultimately defers the central question of community involvement in international law on global public goods.

Keywords: cities in international law; cultural heritage; UNESCO; visibility; expert rule; agency.

1. INTRODUCTION

There is an emerging body of literature on cities in international law, led by Helmut Aust and others,[1] and to which this volume contributes and responds. Among the key questions that preoccupy this literature are the status and visibility of the city as an international legal category. Much of the effort in this

---

[*] Professor, Faculty of Law and Justice, UNSW Sydney.

[1] See, e.g., AUST, "Shining Cities on the Hill? The Global City, Climate Change, and International Law", EJIL, 2015, p. 255 ff.; AUST and DU PLESSIS (eds.), *The Globalisation of Urban Governance: Legal Perspectives on Sustainable Development Goal 11*, Abingdon, 2019, p. 3 ff.; and AUST and NIJMAN (eds.), *Elgar Research Handbook on International Law and Cities*, Cheltenham, forthcoming.

IYIL, Vol. 30 (2020), pp. 37-57
ISSN 0391-5107

body of literature focuses on the role of modernity and the global (or "glocal")[2] city, emphasizing the role of larger metropolitan centres and their contribution to international legal debates and governance.[3] In this sense, the role of the city in international law is one of participating in or even driving the futures of governance; it is a prospective, forward-looking, role, and one in which the city is recognized, emancipated, and transformed.[4] The city, closer to the citizenry, is hailed as a means of bridging the democratic deficit in international law, and as proxies for more participatory and community-based international legal governance.[5]

Heritage studies also engaged with the matter of cities with renewed interest,[6] but there is relatively little analysis of the possibilities and impacts of heritage law on cities.[7] International heritage law, conversely, engages with the past. To be sure, it is an engagement with the past in the present for the benefit of a future,[8] but much of the work of preservation seeks to constrain the future to preserve features of the past. In that way, the built heritage of a city is ruled by international law not as a feature of forward-looking emancipation, but as the maintenance of a past that serves an agenda that is primarily national (nationalist heritage) and global (the heritage of humankind), and only incidentally local.[9] International heritage law, instead of elevating the city's international agency, constrains it. The heritage city is not an agent, it is an object of regulation that serves a separate agenda. And yet, the visibility that cities can acquire through heritage processes is second to none in international governance regimes,[10] and many cities may

---

[2] The merger of the words "global" and "local", the term indicates the intertwining of globalization forces with localized forces. For a discussion in the context of cities, see BRENNER, "Global Cities, Glocal States: Global City Formation and State Territorial Restructuring in Contemporary Europe", Review of International Political Economy, 1998, p. 1 ff.

[3] See, e.g., RIEGNER, "International Institutions and the City: Towards a Comparative Law of Glocal Governance", in AUST and DU PLESSIS (eds.), cit. supra note 1, p. 38 ff.

[4] AUST, cit. supra note 1.

[5] RIEGNER, cit. supra note 3.

[6] See, e.g., DE CESARI and DIMOVA, "Heritage, Gentrification, Participation: Remaking Urban Landscapes in the Name of Culture and Historic Preservation", International Journal of Heritage Studies, 2019, p. 863 ff.; DIMOVA, "Elusive Centres of a Balkan City: Skopje between Undesirable and Reluctant Heritage", International Journal of Heritage Studies, 2019, p. 958 ff.; GONZALEZ MARTINEZ, "From Verifiable Authenticity to Verisimilar Interventions: Xintiandi, Fuxing SOHO, and the Alternatives to Built Heritage Conservation in Shanghai", International Journal of Heritage Studies, 2019, p. 1055 ff.

[7] HAANPÄÄ, PUOLAMÄKI, and KARHUNEN, "Local Conservation and Perceptions of Heritage in Old Rauma World Heritage Site", International Journal of Heritage Studies, 2019, p. 837 ff., p. 838. Cf. SADOWSKI, "Urban Cultural Heritage: Managing and Preserving a Local Global Common in the Twenty-first Century", Journal of Heritage Management, 2017, p. 125 ff.

[8] LIXINSKI, International Heritage Law for Communities: Exclusion and Re-Imagination, Oxford, 2019, pp. 106-107.

[9] For a collection of essays, see KOHL and FAWCETT (eds.), Nationalism, Politics, and the Practice of Archaeology, Cambridge, 1995.

[10] Remarks by Kishore Rao, Director of the UNESCO World Heritage Center, at the 55th Meeting of the UNWTO Commission for Europe and Seminar on Tourism on World Heritage Sites: Challenges and Opportunities, available at: <http://europe.unwto.org/event/55th-

seek to build on that status to free themselves from the national level as a mediator of their agency before international bodies.

Therefore, and considering that the United Nations Educational, Scientific and Cultural Organization (UNESCO) was "the first United Nations agency to address issues related to the urban landscape at a global scale",[11] international heritage law and processes can serve as a roundabout way to enhance the international agency of cities through visibility. In doing so, the process of increasing the agency of cities as international legal subjects, by first going through the version of city as an object, can be a smoother, more acceptable transition to creating new subjects of international law both within and beyond the nation-State.

Further, calls for community inclusion in international heritage legal regimes[12] can both contribute to and complicate the relationship of cities and international (heritage) law. On the one hand, a key reason for including cities in international legal processes is that the city can act as a proxy for the community, a place where democracy is more directly connected to the people on the ground. Doing so resolves difficult issues of identifying a community and who gets to speak on its behalf. On the other hand, cities are still governmental entities, and therefore sit rather uneasily as between full-fledged direct participation by communities, and the same State-centric representative processes that critics of international heritage law have taken issue with.

Therefore, what does the status of heritage city mean for the promise of the city as an emancipator of local agency in international law? I argue in this article that looking at the city in international law through the lenses of cultural heritage processes reveals a paradox: emancipating the city may create a separation barrier between the city and its constituents that, instead of alleviating, may in fact repeat the alienation of communities from international legal governance projects. On the one hand, the city is made an object of international legal regulation; on the other, the same objectification of the city is a platform for its claiming of certain elements of agency that attempt to turn it into a subject. But the city becoming a subject may get in the way of it accomplishing certain of its objectives in international law, namely, bridging the field's democratic deficit.

The visibility of heritage city status, nonetheless, can be very welcome and strategically useful for emancipating community governance of cultural heritage (and other global public goods, like the environment).[13] Heritage cities, even though they are the object of international legal governance, can still achieve the same ultimate goal of the city as a subject of international law: to promote local

---

meeting-unwto-commission-europe-and-seminar-tourism-world-heritage-sites-challenges-and-o>.

[11] UNESCO Executive Board, Implementation of Standard-Setting Instruments Part IV – Application of the 2011 Recommendation on the Historic Urban Landscape, Including a Glossary of Definitions, UN Doc. 197 EX/20 (2015), para. 17.

[12] LIXINSKI, *International Heritage Law*, cit. *supra* note 8.

[13] FRANCIONI, "Public and Private in the International Protection of Global Cultural Goods", EJIL, 2012, p. 719 ff.

and glocal agency over the effects of international legal processes on people on the ground.

If the emancipation of the city as a subject of international law is not strictly required for it achieving its goals in international law, then one can think more creatively both within and beyond the project of the literature on cities in international law. That is to say, if cities as objects of international law can achieve similar objectives as cities as subjects, then it is easier for this body of literature to achieve one of its key objectives, which is to promote the emancipation of local communities and their input on the ways in which international legal regimes affect them.

In order to pursue this thesis, the article proceeds in five additional sections. Section 2 describes the context of heritage cities in international law, with some emphasis on the 1972 World Heritage Convention,[14] and primarily on the 2011 Recommendation on the Historic Urban Landscape (HUL Recommendation),[15] highlighting the ways in which cities operate as objects of international heritage law. Section 3 focuses on the ways in which international heritage law engages with sub-State entities more broadly, so as to underscore the possibilities of direct and indirect agency, or the city as a subject of international heritage law. Section 4 teases out the key issues of agency and personality of the city, while Section 5 adds the perspective of community, rather than city, governance. Section 6 concludes.

2.   HERITAGE CITIES AND INTERNATIONAL LAW

The United Nations Sustainable Development Goals (SDGs) include cities in its list, as SDG 11: "Make cities and human settlements inclusive, safe, resilient and sustainable."[16] It is noteworthy, according to Aust and du Plessis, for at least three reasons: "First, it is the only actor-specific goal among the SDGs, which otherwise focus on concrete questions [and it] stands out insofar as it addresses a particular level of governance. Secondly, it states an internationally agreed vision for good urban governance. Thirdly, [it] bridges global and local levels of governance".[17]

In fleshing out these goals, target 11.4 discusses the need to strengthen efforts to safeguard cultural and natural heritage.[18] The key indicator of success in relation to that target are the expenditure per capita on preservation, measured

---

[14] Convention concerning the Protection of the World Cultural and Natural Heritage, 23 November 1972, entered into force 15 December 1975 (WHC).

[15] Recommendation on the Historic Urban Landscape, including a glossary of definitions, 10 November 2011.

[16] United Nations Sustainable Development Goals, available at: <https://sustainabledevelopment.un.org/>, Goal 11.

[17] AUST and DU PLESSIS, "Introduction: The Globalisation of Urban Governance – Legal Perspectives on Sustainable Development Goal 11", in AUST AND DU PLESSIS (eds.), *cit. supra* note 1, p. 3 ff., p. 4.

[18] United Nations Sustainable Development Goals, Target 11.4.

against type of heritage, type of expenditure or private funding, and, key for present purposes, the level of government making the expenditure. National, regional, and local or municipal governments are to have their performance measured in this area,[19] meaning that the city's heritage is tied to its regional and national roles as well.

The inclusion of the city in the SDGs is hailed as an important moment in the literature on international law and the city, for bridging across different levels of government,[20] and for its potential to be a tool for cities to push back against the local impacts of neoliberalism.[21] Nonetheless, as far as heritage is concerned, despite the mentions in the SDG texts, heritage is not mentioned in any of the four annual implementation reports so far (2016-2019), meaning it remains low priority in the broader UN-led or global governance conversation about cities in international law. That silence is a missed opportunity to focus on an area of international law that has long engaged with cities, but may also contribute to keeping the status of the heritage city as an object at bay, while attempting to privilege the city as a subject.

Whatever the reasons for this omission so far in the SDGs space, international heritage instruments and regimes themselves have a lot to say about cities and their importance. As of 2019, over 70% of cultural heritage properties on the World Heritage List set out under the 1972 World Heritage Convention were "either located in urban areas or have urban areas within their nominated areas".[22] Much of the activity in the implementation of the World Heritage Convention has to do with urban spaces, which create frequent and significant issues of management and safeguarding. World Heritage cities have even come together and formed an association, further discussed in Section 4 below. Reconciling urban development and heritage safeguarding is the most recurring challenge.[23] In the words of the World Heritage Centre, the "main recurring factors affecting the properties are inadequate management plans, need for housing, and inadequate legal frameworks".[24]

Because of this challenge, UNESCO developed a new standard-setting instrument, to replace the 1976 Nairobi Recommendation concerning the Safeguarding and Contemporary Role of Historic Areas.[25] This instrument, the Recommendation on the Historic Urban Landscape, notes that "historic urban

---

[19] *Ibid.*, Indicator 11.4.1.
[20] AUST and DU PLESSIS, *cit. supra* note 17, p. 4.
[21] NIJMAN, "The Urban Pushback: International Law as an Instrument of Cities", ASIL 2019, p. 119 ff., p. 122.
[22] UNESCO World Heritage Centre, The UNESCO Recommendation on the Historic Urban Landscape: Report of the Second Consultation on its Implementation by Member States, March 2019, para. 3.
[23] For some case studies, see DOEMPKE (ed.), *The UNESCO World Heritage and the Role of Civil Society: Proceedings of the International Conference Bonn 2015*, World Heritage Watch, 2016, p. 85 ff. (examining Saint Petersburg, Lhasa, Aleppo and Mozambique Island).
[24] UNESCO World Heritage Centre, *cit. supra* note 22, para. 3.
[25] HENDILI, "Walled Cities, Open Societies: Managing Historic Walls in Urban World Heritage Properties", 26-28 January 2017, slides 1-23 (presentation on file).

areas are among the most abundant and diverse manifestations of our common cultural heritage, shaped by generations and constituting a key testimony to humankind's endeavours and aspirations through space and time".[26] This instrument is key for our purposes, since it directly addresses cities in international standard-setting.

The preparation of this Recommendation responds directly to the 2005 Vienna Memorandum, which answers to the need to integrate heritage considerations in contemporary architecture and urban design plans.[27] The Vienna Memorandum calls for the integration of interdisciplinary teams and approaches, as well as public consultation, into decision-making about heritage management in urban settings.[28]

Prompted by this Memorandum, the UNESCO World Heritage Committee and Centre started considering in earnest the desirability and feasibility of a new instrument. The more significant threats to urban heritage were noted as the "growing pressure of urbanization", "tensions between globalization and local development", "incompatible new development" "unsustainable tourism", and "environmental degradation including climate change", which affect a large number of world heritage properties outside the urban context as well.[29] On the latter, it is worth noting that cities have organized as purported subjects of international governance perhaps most prominently around climate change issues, as Aust notes.[30]

In relation to the tensions among globalization, development,[31] and urban heritage, drafters noted that changes to urban historic areas such as housing for larger populations, "high-rise iconic buildings, projects related to hydroelectricity, energy resource and industrial developments as well as waste disposal, are all increasing in scale and might have detrimental and irreversible effects on the historic city's physical and visual integrity, as well as on their social and cultural values".[32] This view of challenges ignores also the ways in which these same "threats" can help alleviate identity tensions in many cities, particularly through the construction of iconic buildings, which can help elevate the city and local identity in relation to a national polity that resists the autonomy of cities and their inhabitants. Specifically, in Bilbao and Barcelona, in Spain, the construction of

---

[26] Recommendation on the Historic Urban Landscape, *cit. supra* note 15, Preamble.

[27] UNESCO World Heritage Committee, Vienna Memorandum on "World Heritage and Contemporary Architecture – Managing the Historic Urban Landscape" and Decision 29 COM 5D (prepared for the fifteenth session of the General Assembly of States Parties to the Convention Concerning the Protection of the World Cultural and Natural Heritage), UN Doc. WHC-05/15.GA/INF.7 (2005), para. 29.

[28] *Ibid.*, para. 28

[29] UNESCO Executive Board, Preliminary Study on the Technical and Legal Aspects Relating to the Desirability of a Standard-Setting Instrument on the Conservation of the Historic Urban Landscape, UN Doc. 181 EX/29 (2009), paras. 12-17.

[30] AUST, *cit. supra* note 1.

[31] For an example, see LENAERTS, "Visitor Experience and Interpretation at Luang Prabang World Heritage Site", in KING (ed.), *UNESCO in Southeast Asia: World Heritage Sites in Comparative Perspective*, Copenhagen, 2016, p. 54 ff., p. 58.

[32] UNESCO Executive Board, *cit. supra* note 29, para. 14.

iconic buildings has been helpful in elevating their international status, and there-fore help these cities' quest for greater autonomy and accommodation in relation to the national Spanish government.[33]

The preparatory documents that culminated in the HUL Recommendation point out the pressure coming from development, and note that "conditions have changed and historic cities are now subject to development pressures and chal-lenges that were not fully understood at the time of adoption of the last UNESCO Recommendation on urban sites more than thirty years ago, in 1976 […]".[34] These documents also note the changing role of cities, and how actors external to them – tourism and urban development firms – correspond for much of these pres-sures.[35] In other words, non-local stakeholders are seen as a threat to the integrity of the local heritage, and cities as the passive victims or objects of their action.[36] This type of reasoning, aligned with much UNESCO thinking that focuses on external threats to heritage, sharpens the focus on local levels of governance as the ideal means to safeguard heritage, and therefore elevates the importance of cities as the loci for local governance.

Even though the initial impetus for the HUL Recommendation is a response to World Heritage cities, the drafting history makes it clear that "the proposed standard-setting document would not be specific to World Heritage cities, but broadened to all historic cities".[37] While trying to structure the new instrument, however, early consultation with Member States showed engagement with the Vienna Memorandum was "premature", and the strategy fell back on the World Heritage Convention's tenets, which focus on authenticity, integrity, and Outstanding Universal Value, via the idea of landscape.[38] The idea of landscape evolved in the urban context beyond its usual consideration in international law,[39] however, to better integrate the intangible elements of heritage, that is, the as-sociative ideas of how people experience, live in, and ultimately modify the site to remain connected to it, and keep their cultural identities alive and ever-evolv-

---

[33] See SKLAIR, "Iconic Architecture and Urban, National, and Global Identities", in DAVIS and DE DUREN (eds.), *Cities & Sovereignty: Identity Politics in Urban Spaces*, Bloomington, 2011, p. 179 ff.; and DEL CERRO SANTAMARÍA, "Sovereignty, Nationalism, and Globalization in Bilbao and the Basque Country", in DAVIS AND DE DUREN (eds.), *ibid.*, p. 85 ff.

[34] UNESCO World Heritage Committee, Report on the development of a revised Recommendation on the conservation of Historic Urban Landscapes (prepared for the sixteenth session of the General Assembly of States Parties to the Convention Concerning the Protection of the World Cultural and Natural Heritage), UN Doc. WHC-07/16.GA/11 (2007), para. 1.

[35] *Ibid.*, para. 7.

[36] UNESCO Director-General, A New International Instrument: The Proposed UNESCO Recommendation on the Historic Urban Landscape (HUL) – Preliminary Report, UN Doc. CL/3940 (2010), p. 1.

[37] UNESCO World Heritage Committee, *cit. supra* note 34, para. 11.

[38] UNESCO World Heritage Committee, Proposal for the preparation of a new recommendation relating to Historic Urban Landscapes, UN Doc. WHC-08/32.COM/7.2 (2008), para. 6.

[39] For an in-depth discussion of landscapes in international law, see STRECKER, *Landscape Protection in International Law*, Oxford, 2018.

ing.[40] The effect of the urban landscape conversation is to "challenge the legacy of twentieth century approaches".[41]

It must be noted that, for its many conceptual gains, the HUL Recommendation was drafted with relatively little input from cities themselves. One exception is the Organization of World Heritage Cities, one of "the partner organizations and institutions that are part of the ad hoc Working Group on Historic Urban landscapes".[42] This organization was also invited to the expert meeting after the first draft by the Director-General,[43] which essentially finalized the Recommendation. No cities were directly involved in the preparation of this instrument, which speaks directly to heritage cities being the object, rather than the subject, of heritage law-making.

Instead, the Recommendation focuses on the State, and only after that, on community governance. Preparatory documents were clear in this respect, with the UNESCO Executive Board highlighting that a "Recommendation on the conservation of the Historic Urban Landscape would therefore be the proper instrument to regulate at the international level a set of principles and policies that States would integrate and apply at national level, adapting it to their own traditions, discipline and practice".[44] Note that States are the addressees of the instrument, and not cities themselves. Cities are the object of the law, not the subjects making or implementing it.

In relation to community governance, it was not in the original draft prepared by the Director-General, which focused on the input of the private (corporate) sector and corporate social responsibility for safeguarding urban heritage.[45] Subsequent discussions leading to the adopted draft eliminated the reference to the role of corporations, and included the reference to local government and communities. The final stage of the preparation of the HUL Recommendation addressed "relevant local authorities" directly in its proposed resolution recommending the adoption of the Recommendation, and includes participatory planning and stakeholder consultations as key elements of local government involvement.[46] Therefore, even when cities are addressed, their role is to bring together local communities through more direct participatory democracy elements. The draft of this meeting, in which 55 member States (plus Curaçao) and 18 partner organizations (anything from the World Bank to non-governmental

---

[40] UNESCO World Heritage Committee, *cit. supra* note 38, para. 7.

[41] *Ibid.*

[42] *Ibid.*, para. 13.

[43] UNESCO Executive Board, Invitations to the Intergovernmental Meeting of Experts (Category II) Related to a Draft Recommendation on the Conservation of the Historic Urban Landscape, UN Doc. 185 EX/46 (2010).

[44] UNESCO Executive Board, *cit. supra* note 29, para. 29.

[45] UNESCO Director-General, *cit. supra* note 36, para. 37 of the Director-General's draft.

[46] UNESCO General Conference, Proposals Concerning the Desirability of a Standard-Setting Instrument on Historic Urban Landscapes, UN Doc. 36 C/23 (2011), para. 12 (draft resolution, para. 5).

organizations) participated,[47] was adopted without changes by the UNESCO Conference.[48]

The HUL Recommendation, as the drafting history suggests, does not say much about the city's status in international law, or its agency. Rather, the city is for the most part the heritage upon whom the safeguarding approach is to be applied, primarily by States. The Recommendation speaks of the importance of the "Historic Urban Landscape Approach" addressing "the policy, governance and management concerns involving a variety of stakeholders, including local, national, regional, international, public and private actors in the urban development process".[49] Further, the approach "learns from the traditions and perceptions of local communities, while respecting the values of the national and international communities".[50] In other words, international heritage law bears on the city much like on other domains of heritage: the city is a unit of analysis that lacks agency. The Recommendation is about cities, rather than addressed to cities. Even the provision that fleshes out "the responsibilities of the different stakeholders" only focuses on States, "public and private stakeholders", international organizations, and non-governmental organizations.[51] Cities presumably can fall under the category of a public stakeholder, but it is telling that they are not explicitly mentioned in this part of the Recommendation except to say that "local authorities should prepare urban development plans taking into account the area's values".[52]

Another exception in the text of the Recommendation is a reference to all levels of government working together "local, regional, national/federal [governments], – aware of their responsibility – should contribute to the definition, elaboration, implementation and assessment of urban heritage conservation policies. These policies should be based on a participatory approach by all stakeholders and coordinated from both the institutional and sectorial viewpoints".[53] Even in this text, the city is only an intermediary to getting to participatory processes outside of representative government. Lastly, there is a duty to promote "multinational cooperation between local authorities",[54] but there are no specific directives on how to accomplish that mandate in the Recommendation, and implementation

---

[47] UNESCO General Conference, Proposals Concerning the Desirability of a Standard-Setting Instrument on Historic Urban Landscapes – Addendum, UN Doc. 36 C/23 Add. (2011).

[48] UNESCO General Conference, Proposals Concerning the Desirability of a Standard-Setting Instrument on Historic Urban Landscapes – Annex: The Draft text of the new proposed Recommendation on the Historic Urban Landscape, as adopted on 27 May 2011 at the Intergovernmental Meeting of Experts on the Historic Urban Landscape (category II) at UNESCO Headquarters, including a Glossary of Definitions, UN Doc. 36 C/23 (2011).

[49] Recommendation on the Historic Urban Landscape, *cit. supra* note 15, para. 6.

[50] *Ibid.*, para. 13.

[51] *Ibid.*, para. 22.

[52] *Ibid.*, para. 22(a).

[53] *Ibid.*, paras. 22-23.

[54] *Ibid.*, para. 29.

to date has been fraught with little to no information-sharing across the majority of States implementing the Recommendation.[55]

Communities, rather than cities, are the non-nation actor of choice. The Recommendation clearly identifies "the main stakeholders: communities, decision-makers, and professionals and managers".[56] Note the absence of cities, or government in general, from this provision. The tools for implementing the Historic Urban Landscape Approach mention communities, rather than cities, as part of civic engagement and legal and regulatory systems.[57] Therefore, the text of the Recommendation does little to give agency to cities, beyond acknowledging the need for international cooperation among cities, and the importance of cities contributing to the formulation of policies alongside other levels of government, but guided by broader participatory approaches. It is the non-State actor that takes centre stage, and the city is the stage itself.

The implementation of the HUL Recommendation has for the most part been carried out by the World Heritage Centre under the World Heritage Convention. In its first years, the implementation looked primarily at Africa, Arab States, and Latin America and the Caribbean, which are generally under-represented regions on the World Heritage List.[58] Therefore, even if trying to be a separate instrument, the gravitational pull of the World Heritage Convention, and with it the background assumption that States are the primary and only addresses of international law, was irresistible, and affects the ways in which the city is placed in international heritage law. Importantly, States themselves engage with the Recommendation in reference to cities that are or contain World Heritage sites.[59]

The text continues to be addressed at States as the responsible governmental entity in the implementation phase,[60] a solution that, while understandable from the perspective of formal rules of international law, also closes down the space for cities to engage with this instrument at the international level. The first meeting on implementation, held in Rio de Janeiro, Brazil, was composed of experts drawn from UNESCO electoral groups (therefore, States), as well as ICOMOS and ICCROM as expert NGOs. No one representing cities specifically was present at this meeting.[61]

---

[55] UNESCO Executive Board, Implementation of Standard-Setting Instruments Part V – Implementation of the 2011 Recommendation on the Historic Urban Landscape, Including a Glossary of Definitions – Consolidated Report on the Implementation of the Recommendation, UN Doc. 206 EX/25.V (2019), para. 17.

[56] *Ibid.*, para. 25.

[57] *Ibid.*, para. 24.

[58] UNESCO General Conference, Report on the Implementation by Member States of the 2011 Recommendation on the Historic Urban Landscape, Including a Glossary of Definitions, UN Doc. 38 C/71 (2015), para. 5.

[59] UNESCO Executive Board, *cit. supra* note 55, para. 7.

[60] UNESCO Executive Board, Implementation of Standard-Setting Instruments Part IV – Application of the 2011 Recommendation on the Historic Urban Landscape, Including a Glossary of Definitions, UN Doc. 197 EX/20 (2015), para. 1.

[61] *Ibid.*, para. 5.

The implementation phase refers to SDG priorities such as climate change and poverty reduction,[62] and the consultation undertaken via a questionnaire with States in 2018 tied the Recommendation's implementation directly to SDG 11.4.[63] States are keen to connect the Recommendation to the SDGs, and UNESCO seems willing to help make that connection,[64] even if, as noted above, the SDGs themselves are less engaged with the heritage aspects of the goal. But this questionnaire still frames cities as for the most part an object, or at most a secondary actor. Questions on the status of heritage law bypass the possibility of city-level legislation,[65] and a series of questions is directed instead at involving local communities and neighbourhoods directly, sometimes suggesting the desirability of a direct connection between local communities and national ministries, therefore bypassing the city government.[66]

This consultation resulted in responses from 55 Member States,[67] with UNESCO making a visible effort to link the Recommendation's implementation to the SDGs.[68] Crucially, too, the report on the questionnaire highlights that States believe UNESCO should be doing more to engage directly with local governments "while maintaining linkages with the national level".[69] Therefore, it may be that in future years the city will receive a greater status in this international standard-setting instrument's implementation. At present, however, the focus remains on communities as the means to implement the Recommendation, and alongside the recommendation to include cities is the recommendation to strengthen the participation of local communities in decision-making processes.[70]

Therefore, existing international law that specifically addresses city heritage for the most part treats cities as a regulatory object, rather than an agent. The implementation phase of the HUL Recommendation suggests an appetite for more direct integration of the city as an actor, which shows promise. At the same time, however, the implementation points at the importance of greater direct involvement of communities as the local stakeholder of choice, which is in

---

[62] UNESCO Executive Board, Implementation of Standard-Setting Instruments Part IV – Application of the 2011 Recommendation on the Historic Urban Landscape, Including a Glossary of Definitions, UN Doc. 197 EX/20 (2015), para. 17.

[63] UNESCO Director-General, Second consultation on the implementation of the 2011 Recommendation on the Historic Urban Landscape, UN Doc. CL/4233 (2018), attached questionnaire, question 29.

[64] UNESCO Executive Board, cit. supra note 55, para. 8.

[65] UNESCO Director-General, cit. supra note 63, question 11.

[66] Ibid., questions 1.15/no. 48 (asks about local communities), 3.3/no. 67 (about the direct involvement of neighbourhoods), and 3.11/no. 90 (suggesting that national ministries engage directly with local communities).

[67] UNESCO General Conference, Consolidated Report on the Implementation by Member States of the 2011 Recommendation on the Historic Urban Landscape, UN Doc. 40 C/37 (2019), para. 4.

[68] Ibid., para. 5.

[69] Ibid.; and UNESCO World Heritage Centre, cit. supra note 22, paras. 78 and 80.

[70] UNESCO Executive Board, cit. supra note 55, para. 12; and UNESCO World Heritage Centre, cit. supra note 22, para. 51.

line with movements elsewhere in international heritage law.[71] Further, a key obstacle to the inclusion of cities as actors is their standing in international law, which is complicated in State-centric organizations like UNESCO. The next section focuses on the question of how to facilitate, from a formal perspective, the participation of cities as subjects in international law, through examining the engagement of sub-State entities with international heritage law.

3. INTERNATIONAL LAW AND SUB-STATE ENTITIES: HERITAGE ENTANGLEMENTS

The (possible) engagements of sub-State entities with international treaties speak directly to the question of personality and agency of cities, and are therefore relevant to thinking through the city's status in international law. Scholars have focused on examples like the "ratification" of the United Nations Convention on the Elimination of All Forms of Discrimination Against Women (CEDAW)[72] by the city of San Francisco in the United States to convey the message that, even if only informally, the engagement of cities with international law instruments can have important effects for both international law (entrenchment) and cities (increased recognition and possible formal capacity in international law).[73] It is also a type of deformalization of international law.[74]

The proper recognition of cities as subjects of international law via this route is subject to an important caveat: it is excluded from the Vienna Convention on the Law of Treaties, which only focuses on treaties entered into by States.[75] The Vienna Convention treats cities as State organs, which is the traditional position in international law, as further evidenced by cities being treated as State organs for the purposes of the international rules on State responsibility.[76] That said, sub-State entities routinely enter into treaties, particularly in areas like the

---

[71] Some of these pushes are mapped in LIXINSKI, *International Heritage Law*, *cit. supra* note 8.

[72] Convention on the Elimination of All Forms of Discrimination Against Women, 18 December 1979, entered into force 3 December 1981 (CEDAW).

[73] As discussed by KNOP, "International Law and the Disaggregated Democratic State: Two Case Studies on Women's Human Rights and the United States", in CHARTERS and KNIGHT (eds.), *We, the People(s): Participation in Governance*, Wellington, 2011, p. 127 ff.

[74] NIJMAN, *cit. supra* note 21, p. 119.

[75] Vienna Convention on the Law of Treaties, 23 May 1969, entered into force 27 January 1980 (VCLT). Art. 27 (Internal Law and Observance of Treaties): "A party may not invoke the provisions of its internal law as justification for its failure to perform a treaty. [...]". See also Art. 29 (Territorial Scope of Treaties): "Unless a different intention appears from the treaty or is otherwise established, a treaty is binding upon each party in respect of its entire territory". To be sure, one of the ILC drafts of the VCLT allowed sub-federal entities to enter into treaties as long as authorized by the federal state. The ILC commentary recognized that international law did not prohibit sub-federal entities from having the power to conclude treaties. The provision was dropped after lobbying by Canada and other countries. For a discussion, see CYR, *Canadian Federalism and Treaty Powers: Organic Constitutionalism at Work*, Bern, 2009, pp. 155-157.

[76] International Law Commission, Articles on Responsibility of States for Internationally Wrongful Acts, 2001, Art. 4(1).

management of shared transboundary natural resources when speaking of sub-State entities at a country's borders, or even more broadly in areas of exclusive legislative competence of those sub-State entities under domestic federalism arrangements.[77] For cities, this engagement with treaties includes the engagement with international financial institutions like the World Bank for loans and the financing of development projects within those cities.[78] There is an extensive history of cities engaging directly with foreign affairs,[79] and, even in the UN era, and argument has been made for a customary international legal rule of cities' engagement with treaties outside of the Vienna Convention. In Brazil, "cities' para-diplomatic activities have been supported by the Brazilian Foreign Ministry. Similarly, international norms of local law have been recognized constitutionally in South Africa".[80] Plus, like the case of San Francisco and CEDAW shows, cities and other sub-State entities engage with international law to counter the reluctance of central national authorities to do it.

For formal engagement with international law, which would be the highest level of recognition of cities in international law, there is the question of authorization by the central national government to engage with treaties. The foreign affairs competence in different domestic constitutions, as well as the larger body of foreign affairs law as a sub-branch of international law, would bear on this scenario.[81] These rules would, among other things, necessitate constitutional status for cities, an issue that the literature on cities in international law notes but does not explore.[82] Although a reality in countries like Brazil,[83] conferring constitutional status to cities is still very much a live and undecided issue in constitutional law in countries like Australia.[84] As Bodiford put it, "cities occupy what could be described as an intermediate place of mixed quasi-sovereignty that puts them in a twilight zone in international law between sovereign and not sovereign".[85] Therefore, even if cities were to formally engage with international law, under existing rules this engagement, while on the surface a recognition of

---

[77] For a more detailed discussion, see LIXINSKI, "Trialogical Subsidiarity in International and Comparative Law: Engagement with International Treaties by Sub-State Entities as Resistance or Innovation", CYIL, 2018, p. 1 ff.

[78] RIEGNER, *cit. supra* note 3, p. 43.

[79] BODIFORD, "Cities in International Law: Reclaiming Rights as Global Custom", City University of New York Law Review, 2020, p. 1 ff., pp. 36-37.

[80] *Ibid.*, p. 23.

[81] See generally BRADLEY (ed.), *The Oxford Handbook of Comparative Foreign Relations Law*, Oxford, 2019.

[82] AUST, *cit. supra* note 1, p. 267.

[83] Constitution of the Federative Republic of Brazil, 5 October 1988, Art. 18: "A organização político-administrativa da República Federativa do Brasil compreende a União, os Estados, o Distrito Federal e os Municípios, todos autônomos, nos termos desta Constituição" (The political-administrative organization of the Federative Republic of Brazil comprises the Union, States, the Federal District, and Municipalities, all autonomous, in the terms of this Constitution).

[84] WILLIAMS and MCGARRITY, "Recognition of Local Government in the Commonwealth Constitution", Public Law Review, 2010, p. 164 ff.

[85] BODIFORD, *cit. supra* note 79, p. 2 (footnote omitted).

international personality to cities, would mean upon closer examination a mediated international personality, contingent upon a license by the national State, which falls short of full international recognition.

Further, because of different constructions of the foreign affairs power in domestic legal systems, the formal engagement with international instruments can actually be used to take powers away from cities, as in the example of the approach to foreign affairs federalism of countries like Australia. There, as in other countries, foreign affairs are the exclusive competence of the national central government, and the internationalization of a legal competence can shift the legislative power away from sub-State entities to the federal level.[86] Therefore, it is not just international law that needs to make way for cities, there is also a pressing need for the revision or clarification of domestic legal arrangements that can both pave the way for city participation in foreign affairs and prevent its co-option by the central level.

The informal engagement with international treaties and instruments like the HUL Recommendation, on the other hand, would be unmediated agency, but would fall short of full international legal personality, precisely because of the lack of formal recognition. That said, there is a strong case for cities to be more proactive in engaging with international heritage law, because of the opening created by the implementation of the HUL Recommendation, which, as discussed in the previous section, openly calls for more direct engagement of cities in the implementation process. The participation of a network of cities in the drafting of the Recommendation, as discussed above, is a promising starting point for informal engagement, which reflects other informal networks of cities in international legal governance. These networks tend to concentrate on topics of international human rights and environmental law, which are global public goods, and therefore international heritage law would be easily accommodated within the spirit of existing networks.[87]

Underlying both modalities is the principle of subsidiarity, an integral part of the literature on cities and international law,[88] which in the law dictates that certain areas of legal competence are best addressed locally over nationally. As I discussed elsewhere, the principle plays dual roles whether one speaks of the subsidiarity of local to national, or domestic to international. There are good reasons, however, particularly in the realm of cultural heritage law, to break that separation that requires the mediation of the State, and to speak of more plural forms of subsidiarity.[89] Thinking about subsidiarity also brings into relief the role

---

[86] For a detailed discussion of Australia and a comparison with other countries, see LIXINSKI, "Trialogical Subsidiarity", *cit. supra* note 77; and BRADLEY (ed.), *cit. supra* note 81.

[87] NIJMAN, *cit. supra* note 21, p. 120.

[88] MARCENKO, "Cities and International Law", The Global City – The Role of Law Then and Now, 1 March 2019, available at: <https://www.asser.nl/global-city/news-and-events/cities-and-international-law/>.

[89] LIXINSKI, "Trialogical Subsidiarity", *cit. supra* note 77.

of sovereignty, and ultimately the challenge that cities pose to static and binary registers of the concept.[90]

Whether formal or informal, and beyond the risk of idealization of cities that recurs in the literature,[91] the engagement of cities with international law, leveraged by subsidiarity, is an important tool for the exercise of agency. Why is this type of recognition of agency and legal personality so important for the discussion of cities in international law? These factors are a given in the literature that pushes for the status of cities in international law, but the underlying rationale and stakes of these objectives deserves unpacking to see if, in relation to the HUL Recommendation and cities in international heritage law, the purposes of the push for recognition and agency can be met through other means. The next section scrutinizes the literature on cities in international law to attempt to distil its underlying purposes.

4. AGENCY AND PERSONALITY

The preceding sections suggest that, as it stands, international law's relationship with cities, seen through the lenses of cultural heritage regimes, is dual. On the one hand, the city is an object of international cultural heritage law. The city is itself heritage, rather than an actor within it; it is object, rather than subject. The uneasiness of the city as object becomes particularly apparent when cities are used as elements of broader national (and international) political strategies, like what happens with the city of Jerusalem, a World Heritage site, and often at the centre of disputes around Israeli-Palestinian-Middle Eastern relations. On the other hand, there is international legal practice to suggest that the city can in fact be a subject and part of international law, both as a maker of norms (like the – albeit limited – input of cities in the drafting of the HUL Recommendation), and as its addressee of certain norms in the HUL Recommendation, with a push for greater inclusion of cities directly in its implementation. This recognition as a subject, maker and addressee, is nevertheless mediated by the national or central State, and therefore rather limited. The city achieves visibility in international law through both of these pathways, but ultimately control rests with the national State.

The push for cities in international law, both via scholarship and societies like the International Law Association,[92] seeks to challenge this situation, and elevate the city. Much of this push focuses particularly on the "global city", defined as cities that are key for the organization of the global economy, where key finance and specialized service firms establish themselves, sites of production of material items and ideas, and markets for products and innovations. The global

---

[90] BODIFORD, *cit. supra* note 79, p. 5.

[91] NIJMAN, *cit. supra* note 21, p. 122.

[92] International Law Association, Study Group: Role of Cities in International Law, available at: <https://www.ila-hq.org/index.php/component/easyblog/new-ila-study-group?Itemid=347>.

city becomes a strategic site for understanding how social orders are reconfigured and in flux.[93] This definition is highly anchored in the dynamism of the global city, which would seemingly put it at odds with the idea of heritage, often conceived as safeguarding a static past. As noted above in the discussion of the HUL Recommendation, however, urban heritage is valued for its intangible relationships, which are necessarily constantly evolving and themselves affected by and affecting the social orders that are their mainspring and ultimate focus.

The engagement with heritage processes both domestically and internationally blurs the lines between global and local, however, which renders the global city a site for the performance of international legal normativity in often unacknowledged ways. Reigner discusses an important example of this broader normative engagement looking specifically at the World Heritage-listed city of Florence. He notes a dispute in 2016 between McDonalds and Florence, through which McDonalds was denied a permit to operate in the historic city centre. The refusal was based on local laws that required that operating restaurants serve typical Tuscan food. While seemingly a conflict between a global corporation and a local government, in fact Florentine laws were justified at least in part by the HUL Recommendation, to help preserve the city's status as a World Heritage site. "The global and the local thus co-constitute each other in a process that is best described by the concept of glocalisation, which can explain simultaneous tendencies of convergence and divergence and avoids politically charged dichotomies of global vs local".[94]

Further, this story showcases the invisible influence of international law on cities, and can broaden the category of global (or glocal) city to include those sites that, while not necessarily major finance hubs, are still deeply affected by the interaction of global and local orders. This definition is less elitist, and therefore more democratic and in line with the aspiration of cities in international law to connect international law to sub-State entities. It can also better account for the pervasiveness of cities as an international legal phenomenon. Further, the focus on cities can help resolve intra-national identity-based conflicts,[95] even if sometimes the city's ethnic diversity can also be co-opted into national projects.[96]

Historically, cities have aggregated in international associations, particularly under the umbrella of the League of Nations (and, as Aust points out, one of the driving forces behind the League).[97] There is a rich colonial history of cities being used as means of creating and controlling centres of colonial life, and therefore locals across a territory being subjugated by the foreign elites that moved from the imperial centres to colonial cities.[98] Nevertheless, cities in the Global South

---

[93] AUST, *cit. supra* note 1, p. 256.

[94] RIEGNER, *cit. supra* note 3, p. 54.

[95] For a collection of essays, see DAVIS and DE DUREN (eds.), *cit. supra* note 33.

[96] KINOSSIAN, "Post-Socialist Transition and Remaking the City: Political Construction of Heritage in Tatarstan", Europe-Asia Studies, 2012, p. 879 ff., p. 882.

[97] AUST, *cit. supra* note 1, p. 259.

[98] ESLAVA and HILL, "Cities, Post-Coloniality and International Law", in AUST and NIJMAN (eds), *cit. supra* note 1, p. 1 (manuscript on file).

have transformed into important sites for the contestation of central national authority as well as both the entrenchment and contestation of the influence of international governance projects,[99] while "maintaining the local as a space in which alternative worlds can flourish".[100] The emancipation of the city in international law is a challenge to a traditional model of international relations that sees States as monolithic entities. And it pursues a clear objective, in the words of Aust:

> the emergence of cities on the international level is a further blow to the traditional billiard ball model in which states are styled as self-contained unitary actors. The outer profile of the state becomes more variegated when cities start to act on the global level. In a positive light, this can be seen as a form of the vertical separation of powers, making the state more responsive to the needs of local communities and the people living in them. It could also be seen as a further variation of the division of competences in federal systems, where it is not uncommon that the federal units conduct a foreign policy of their own, albeit usually within certain confines defined by the federal constitution. In a more negative light, this trend could be seen as a harbinger of fragmentation, or even disintegration of the state which might lose its capability of maintaining a unified and coherent foreign policy.[101]

This quote is relevant in exposing the objectives of cities as a part of international law. While the discussions on federalism and separation of powers have already been noted above, it is crucial to highlight how they anchor a key objective, namely, "making the state more responsive to the needs of local communities and the people living in them".[102] Therefore, the project of cities in international law seeks to elevate the city not for its own sake, but as a means to elevate the needs and aspirations of local communities. Cities are nevertheless mediated by democratic processes, even if Aust suggests that their representative nature creates less of a separation than other types of representative democracy, suggesting that "cities can be understood as a particular form of non-state actors in international law: they are parts of states, but also bring their own political identity to the international level which transcends this characteristic of belonging to 'the state'".[103]

Key thinkers in this space admit that it is hard to define the role of cities in relation to positive law, and suggest that the answer lies in looser forms of governance like associations of cities.[104] Within international heritage processes, one noteworthy development is the Organization of World Heritage Cities

---

[99] *Ibid.*, p. 17.
[100] *Ibid.*, p. 18.
[101] AUST, *cit. supra* note 1, p. 268 (footnotes omitted).
[102] *Ibid.*
[103] *Ibid.*, p. 269.
[104] *Ibid.*, p. 273.

(OWHC).[105] This network, created in 1993, connects over 300 cities in the world that have a World Heritage site within their boundaries. Its main objectives are to "favor the implementation of the World Heritage Convention; to encourage co-operation and the exchange of information and expertise on matters of conservation and management of urban heritage; [and] to develop a sense of solidarity among its member cities".[106] It characterizes itself as an NGO, and has eight Regional Secretariats to ensure its reach across the entire world.

The engagement of these cities with international law processes happens primarily through the institutional arrangements of international institutions, as noted above. In the case of World Heritage cities, the engagement is with UNESCO more broadly, and, within it, the World Heritage Centre. The network's engagement has the effect of externalizing the effects of instruments like the World Heritage Convention, and rendering it effective not only as a matter of international legal obligations of States, but also as part of the very localized practice of different levels of government, thereby entrenching international institutional law in local and everyday life.[107] Further, UNESCO's action specifically in relation to cities creates incentives for conformity with international standards, and generates "governance by information", which "can amount to an exercise of international public authority", as long as it is justified by an international legal framework like the WHC, and, to a lesser extent, the HUL Recommendation.[108]

At the same time, however, this engagement is largely tamed and bounded, as international heritage norms can be used not to elevate, but instead to try and quash local democratic processes. The World Heritage cities of Dresden (Germany), Liverpool (United Kingdom), and Vienna (Austria) are key examples, where the World Heritage Committee vehemently opposed local development projects that had been democratically approved, because they would in their view clash with WHC requirements. In the case of Dresden, the conflict between UNESCO and that city escalated to the point of it being the second site ever to be deleted from the World Heritage List.[109] Liverpool became the third in 2001, with local reactions oscillating between lamenting the deletion because of the status associated with list status, to welcoming it because it freed the city to pursue its own development choices. Therefore, the visibility the city gains is not all emancipation, it also means becoming bound to an international legal governance process that the city has less chance to influence directly.

Networks such as OWHC participate in the implementation of instruments like the HUL Recommendation with the status of NGOs, and thus filter the direct agency of its constituent cities. Were cities to achieve more formalized recognition as direct actors, or even for the network as a whole to participate in fuller

---

[105] Organization of World Heritage Cities, "Introduction and Mission", available at: <https://www.ovpm.org/>.

[106] Ibid.

[107] RIEGNER, cit. supra note 3, p. 43.

[108] Ibid., pp. 46-47.

[109] CASINI, "Cultural Sites between Nationhood and Mankind", in BENVENISTI and NOLTE (eds.), Community Interests across International Law, Oxford, 2018, p. 177 ff., pp. 180-181.

terms, the recognition might become a double-edged sword, as it "might eat up the central factor of legitimacy that city networks rely on: their alleged flexibility as opposed to the more traditional forms of international cooperation".[110] Therefore, cities would just become another governmental form in international law, and distance themselves from the communities they represent, losing their appeal that largely derives from subsidiarity.

The project of engagement of cities in international law is not without its critics, but also finds plenty of support. Despite the risks of reinforcing colonial patterns of domination in the name of a neutral international legal order, there are potentials for cities to tap into international legal governance projects to promote objectives that subvert the expectations and internal power hierarchies of nation-States. The purpose of cities in international law, however, is guided by subsidiarity, and the promise of articulating the needs and aspirations of communities. If cities are successful in their process to achieve recognition in international law and governance, they may lose touch with this key objective. Loose associations across history and today have not thus far crossed the line, because they have not received formal recognition. Current organizations like the OWHC operate like international NGOs, and in doing so create a further barrier of mediation between the voices of communities they purport to act on behalf of and international legal processes. So, the NGO form in many ways replaces the national State, replicating its filtering effects without adding additional agency.

If the objective is to include communities, what would it mean for cities, treated either as objects or mediated agents, to be bypassed altogether? Could simply the inclusion of the communities that live in these cities in international legal governance processes achieve the same objectives? The next section surveys these possibilities with specific regard to international heritage legal regimes and processes.

5. COMMUNITY GOVERNANCE

Using cities instead of communities in international legal governance processes may be a roundabout way of including community governance, a professed key goal of the literature on cities in international law. That said, this inclusion resolves a crucial issue of community engagement: the identification of the community and who gets to speak on its behalf. There is a significant colonial baggage to the notion of community,[111] much like there is a baggage to the use of cities, as discussed above. That said, using cities as proxies for communities only defers the issue of community engagement by adding another governmental layer,[112] even if it plays well to an international legal order that is reluctant to engage with non-State actors.[113]

---

[110] AUST, *cit. supra* note 1, p. 275.

[111] LIXINSKI, *International Heritage Law, cit. supra* note 8, pp. 94-101.

[112] HAANPÄÄ, PUOLAMÄKI and KARHUNEN, *cit. supra* note 7, p. 851.

[113] MATTHEWS et al., "Heritage and Cultural Healing: Iraq in a Post-Daesh Era", International Journal of Heritage Studies, 2020, p. 120 ff., p. 122.

Further, in the event of communities whose interests do not map onto cities' geographic boundaries or political interests, they are excluded from these possibilities. Key examples are indigenous or other minority communities, and also economically disenfranchised groups like those living in shantytowns or Rio de Janeiro's favelas.[114] Urban communities of these sorts are not always the majority in any specific urban space, and in fact tend to be minorities within cities, meaning that they are inadequately represented in city government decisions. Also, a significant proportion of these communities are not urban, and would therefore be excluded from a participation model that focused on cities and urban heritage (which, as seen above, is a large part, but not the totality, of heritage sites under UNESCO regimes). Therefore, the promise of cities as agents, however cleancut to the extent the city is an easily graspable unit of analysis, can undermine the (comparatively messy) potentials of the human dimension of international (heritage) law.[115]

The boundedness of cities to international heritage processes can assist communities whose interests do not align with cities, since the incidence of international heritage norms can "allow foreign actors – or even domestic actors who do not share local or national communities' interests – to monitor and to act against states' policies that may affect the preservation of cultural heritage".[116]

That said, the international paradigm for the safeguarding of heritage cities is still largely Eurocentric, and does not successfully take into account the subaltern views of vulnerable communities.[117] The shift to intangible heritage goes a long way in addressing that gap,[118] but, as seen above, the WHC still exerts a strong influence on the implementation of the HUL Recommendation, and its embrace of intangible values, while promising, is still rather incipient, and based on legal frameworks that "are stuck in out-of-date understandings, partly even induced by colonial governments which themselves have been replaced a long time ago".[119] And attempts to negotiate the WHC with intangible values in community-led urban heritage safeguarding have led to confusion and frustration.[120]

To include the community, instead of the city, also pluralizes governance in more impactful ways, as it pierces the veil of bureaucratic expertise that often

---

[114] SIMON and BRAATHEN, "Collective Heritage and Urban Politics: An Uncertain Future for the Living Culture of Rio de Janeiro?", International Journal of Heritage Studies, 2019, p. 380 ff., p. 390.

[115] On the human dimension of international law generally, see CASSESE, *The Human Dimension of International Law: Selected Papers of Antonio Cassese* (GAETA and ZAPPALÀ eds.), Oxford, 2008. On international heritage law specifically, see FRANCIONI, "The Human Dimension of International Cultural Heritage Law: An Introduction", EJIL, 2011, p. 9 ff. Calling for the human dimension of international heritage law in a specific context, see MATTHEWS et al., *cit. supra* note 113, p. 121.

[116] CASINI, *cit. supra* note 109, p. 186.

[117] SANDHOLZ, *Urban Centres in Asia and Latin America: Heritage and Identities in Changing Urban Landscapes*, Cham, 2016, p. 4.

[118] *Ibid.*, pp. 88-89.

[119] *Ibid.*, pp. 324-325.

[120] HAANPÄÄ, PUOLAMÄKI and KARHUNEN, *cit. supra* note 7, p. 839.

separates communities from decision-making,[121] and that would be replicated in the elevation of the city in international law. Seen as a commons,[122] the city, and particularly heritage cities, are best governed by communities, and therefore the international governance that affects them should also be affected by communities directly. Admittedly, it is difficult, if not impossible, to sidestep government (whether city or national) in the governance of heritage or other similar goods,[123] but that realization makes the case for cities to work alongside, and not instead of, communities.

6. CONCLUDING REMARKS

However imperfect, communities can reach the project of democratizing international law more effectively than cities. International heritage law seems to support this view, with the inclusion of communities as potential subjects in recent reforms and projects for future reform, whereas cities are for the most part still objects of regulation. To be sure, there is still great potential in the elevation of cities, but its emancipation should not create a separation barrier between the city as an international legal entity and the populations it is meant to represent. The project for the inclusion of cities in international legal governance processes is meritorious, but international heritage law also shows its limitations with respect to what the city can actually be in international legal governance: an object, or at most a member of an NGO with limited powers. Participation as a non-State actor is still mediated by the NGO form, much like participation as part of a State, but without the decision-making powers that come alongside being part of the State. Therefore, it is an imperfect means for cities to accomplish the purported goal of bridging the democratic deficit in international law, and to trade one layer of mediation for another is insufficient. If the ultimate objective is to pluralize international legal governance projects, and allow communities a seat at the table, then that seat should be given directly to communities.

---

[121] MUNDOLI, UNNIKRISHNAN and NAGENDRA, "Urban Commons of the Global South: Using multiple frames to illuminate complexity", in HUDSON et al. (eds.), *Routledge Handbook of the Study of the Commons*, Abingdon, 2019, p. 220 ff., p. 221.

[122] FOSTER and IAIONE, "Ostrom in the City: Design Principles and Practices for the Urban Commons", in HUDSON et al. (eds.), *cit. supra* note 121, p. 235 ff., p. 235.

[123] *Ibid.*, p. 239.

SUSTAINABLE DEVELOPMENT AS A CORNERSTONE OF CITIES' ENGAGEMENT WITH INTERNATIONAL LAW

Riccardo Pavoni*

Abstract

Sustainable development may safely be regarded as a cornerstone of cities' engagement with international law, an engagement which is certainly bound to increase in the time of COVID-19. This article revisits the historical trajectory of cities' and local governments' participation in sustainable development processes. It particularly focuses on the contemporary involvement of cities and their transnational networks in the United Nations 2030 Agenda for Sustainable Development and associated Sustainable Development Goals. Subsidiarity and public participation are fully discussed as conceptual underpinnings of cities' growing role in the pursuit of sustainability. The article concludes that, as long as cities continue to demonstrate leadership and innovation in advancing cutting-edge solutions to problems of sustainability as a result of mechanisms that secure the meaningful participation of the communities of people concerned, their place in the global partnership for sustainable development will inevitably become ever more prominent.

Keywords: cities; local governments; transnational city networks; 2030 Agenda for Sustainable Development; SDG 11; subsidiarity; decentralization; public participation.

1. Introductory Remarks: Cities and Sustainable Development in the Time of Covid-19

The socio-economic devastation brought about by the ongoing COVID-19 pandemic has irrupted into the world scene at a time when sustainable development may safely be regarded as a cornerstone of cities' engagement with international law.

Historically, the emergence of sustainable development as a key tenet of contemporary international law- and policy-making processes has occurred in parallel with the recognition of the role of cities and other subnational governments in its pursuit. It is in this area that, starting from the late 1980s, local governments and their transnational networks have most significantly been addressed by international legal instruments and involved in the pertinent global forums. And unsurprisingly, it is in the same area that activities aimed at shaping and implement-

---

* Of the Board of Editors.

IYIL, Vol. 30 (2020), pp. 59-79
ISSN 0391-5107

ing international norms and standards have increasingly been carried out by local governments *as* de facto *independent agents* of the international community, rather than as mere political subdivisions of the territorial States. This trajectory has, so far, culminated with the inclusion of an urban Sustainable Development Goal (SDG 11) in the 2030 Agenda for Sustainable Development,[1] adopted by the UN General Assembly in 2015, and with the concurrent full integration of local governments in the Agenda's follow-up and review mechanisms.

Crucially, this embracing of cities by sustainable development processes (and vice versa)[2] has momentous consequences for the former's ability to participate in and/or exert influence within a wealth of global and regional organizations, forums and initiatives, thereby increasingly contributing to the formulation and application of international law. Indeed, the social, economic and environmental dimensions characterizing the concept of sustainable development intersect with a variety of fields of international law, such as environmental and climate protection, human rights, development assistance and cooperation, financial regulation, trade, and foreign investments. Sustainable development has thus become a key prism or compass for explaining cities' growing permeation of the texture and structure of international law.[3]

Yet, sustainable development is not simply relied on by cities as an instrumentally convenient umbrella term paving the way for their involvement in a rising number of international law-making processes. The pursuit of sustainable development requires actions and measures in policy areas that traditionally are, to a lesser or greater extent, within the scope of chief competencies of local governments, such as, to name a few, urban planning, public transportation and traffic regulation, waste management, energy and water infrastructures, affordable housing and other social welfare schemes, health, education, culture, disaster prevention and resilience.[4]

The current COVID-19 pandemic is unlikely to undermine or dilute cities' commitment to sustainable development. Cities are undeniably the epicentre and ground zero of the pandemic with an estimated 90% of all reported COVID-19 cases and hundreds of millions of urban dwellers at risk of falling into poverty as

---

[1] Transforming Our World: The 2030 Agenda for Sustainable Development, UN Doc. A/RES/70/1 (2015).

[2] See, seminally, PORRAS, "The City and International Law: In Pursuit of Sustainable Development", Fordham Urban Law Journal, 2009, p. 537 ff.

[3] Against that backdrop, cities' prominent role in climate law and policy may also be regarded as a sort of natural spin-off of their engagement with sustainable development law- and policy-making processes at large, rather than the most significant example of cities' acceptance as international actors, cf. AUST and NIJMAN, "The Emerging Roles of Cities in International Law – Introductory Remarks on Practice, Scholarship and the Handbook", in AUST and NIJMAN (eds.), *Research Handbook on International Law and Cities*, Cheltenham, 2021, forthcoming. See also DUPUY and VIÑUALES, *International Environmental Law*, 2nd ed., Cambridge, 2018, pp. 36-38. On cities and climate change, see the contribution to this Symposium by BAKKER.

[4] See generally, SACHS, *The Age of Sustainable Development*, New York, 2015, pp. 355-391.

a result.[5] Yet this fact should not determine a return to unsustainable pathways, justified by the imperative of the economic recovery. To the contrary, cities' leaders and their transnational networks are seemingly well aware that the root causes of zoonotic diseases such as COVID-19 lie with the increasing encroachment on natural habitats, ecosystems and biodiversity by human activities.[6] We are therefore witnessing an epochal health emergency which gives cities a unique chance to prioritize environmental sustainability, for instance by making full use of scientific and technological knowledge for "delegating back to nature",[7] while continuing to strive for the indispensable reduction of social iniquities and inequalities. If then the only appropriate way forward is a green, just, inclusive and resilient recovery,[8] there is no doubt that cities and local governments will exponentially increase their engagement with sustainable development policies and their stature within associated global processes and forums. Against that background, it is certainly telling – yet unsurprising – that one of the three key areas of action on cities and COVID-19 identified by the UN Secretary-General as an integral part of the UN Comprehensive Response to the pandemic precisely consists in strengthening the capacities of local governments.[9]

---

[5] UN Secretary-General, "Policy Brief: COVID-19 in an Urban World", July 2020, available at: <https://unsdg.un.org/sites/default/files/2020-07/sg_policy_brief_covid_urban_world.pdf>, pp. 2 and 22.

[6] See the visionary and outstanding work of scientific journalism by QUAMMEN, *Spillover: Animal Infections and the Next Human Pandemic*, New York, 2012. See also the report by WWF Italy, "Pandemie, l'effetto boomerang della distruzione degli ecosistemi", March 2020, available at: <https://www.wwf.it/pandanews/ambiente/pandemie-leffetto-boomerang-della-distruzione-degli-ecosistemi>, and lately, the authoritative assessment, analysis and recommendations by the Intergovernmental Science-Policy Platform on Biodiversity and Ecosystem Services (IPBES), "Workshop Report on Biodiversity and Pandemics", October 2020, available at: <https://ipbes.net/pandemics>.

[7] SASSEN, *Cities in a World Economy*, 5th ed., Thousand Oaks, 2019, pp. 300-303. As examples of applications caught by the notion of delegating back to nature, the distinguished urban sociologist mentions self-healing concrete in the building industry and bioreactor landfills turning waste into "landfill gas" for use in carbon sequestration and fuel generation, *ibid.*, p. 301. In Sassen's thinking, delegating back to nature must be kept clearly distinct from an unrealistic return to nature, i.e. to an ancestor-like way of life, *ibid.* Such words sound particularly instructive in the time of the COVID-19 emergency, which has provoked a controversial "big escape" from city centres of affluent households relocating in the countryside. That "big escape" may also directly run against sustainable development ("migration away from cities could undermine vital efforts to achieve the Sustainable Development Goals", UN Secretary-General, *cit. supra* note 5, p. 4; "[t]he correlation that is often implied between COVID-19 and compact urban development is misleading and can encourage de-densification and sprawl", *ibid.*, p. 23).

[8] UN Secretary-Generali, *cit. supra* note 5, pp. 21-28. See also C40 Mayors' Agenda for a Green and Just Recovery, launched on 15 July 2020 by the C40 Global Mayors COVID-19 Recovery Task Force. This Task Force, currently chaired by the Mayor of Milan, was created in April 2020 by C40 Cities, the well-known transnational network of 97 cities (mostly megacities) particularly active in the area of climate action.

[9] UN Secretary-General, *cit. supra* note 5, pp. 15-19. "Tackling inequalities and development deficits" and "[p]ursuing a resilient, inclusive and green economic recovery" represent the other two priority areas of action envisaged by the Secretary-General.

In this contribution, I have no hesitation in accepting that the expanding role of cities and other subnational governments for the advancement of the project of sustainable development is a vital addition to the contemporary landscape of international law and global governance. Pragmatically, it is by now clear that, without the proactive involvement of cities, that project is bound to fail or at least stagnate. Moreover, the robust conceptual bases traditionally militating in favour of local governments' contribution to the creation and enforcement of international law, namely subsidiarity and public participation, are enhanced in the area of environmental sustainability and social justice.

Yet local governments' engagement with sustainable development should be kept under constant review in order to make sure, for instance, that the cities and city networks which are most visibly accepted by States and international organizations as key partners in the pertinent processes exhibit strong credentials of representativeness, accountability and democratic decision-making.[10] This also implies that those cities and networks, far from promoting parochially urban agendas, should be champions of a leadership vision which in fact defends the common good, including the interests of human groups, such as rural and other non-urban communities,[11] whose activities are crucial to urban resilience, but who are certainly being less represented and influential in the forums where sustainable development deliberations take place.

Section 2 revisits the historical trajectory of cities' and local governments' participation in sustainable development processes, whereas Section 3 examines their current engagement with the 2030 Agenda and associated Sustainable Development Goals (SDGs). Section 4 discusses subsidiarity and public participation as conceptual underpinnings of cities' growing role in the pursuit of sustainable development. A few conclusive remarks follow.

2. GENESIS AND EVOLUTION OF CITIES' ENGAGEMENT WITH SUSTAINABLE DEVELOPMENT: A FEW MILESTONES

Cities and local governments were already identified as key partners of States and international organizations in their efforts towards sustainable development by the landmark 1987 Brundtland Report.[12] Chapter 9 of the Report, entitled "The Urban Challenge", made clear that issues of sustainable urbanization were key to the (then) novel imperative of sustainable development. Even though the

---

[10] As duly underlined by AUBY, "Mega-Cities, Glocalisation and the Law of the Future", in MULLER et al. (eds.), *The Law of the Future and the Future of Law*, Oslo, 2011, p. 203 ff., pp. 210-211.

[11] On the urban-rural interface, see the contributions to this Symposium by FRANCIONI and LITWIN.

[12] Report of the World Commission on Environment and Development, "Our Common Future", UN Doc. A/42/427 (1987), Annex. See BULKELEY and BETSILL, "Rethinking Sustainable Cities: Multilevel Governance and the 'Urban' Challenge", Environmental Politics, 2005, p. 42 ff., pp. 43-44.

Report mostly focused on the "urban crisis"[13] in developing countries and did not directly address local governments, it nonetheless urged States and relevant international organizations to take actions aimed at empowering cities and other local authorities in the field of sustainable development policies.[14]

On the heels of pioneering initiatives pursued by a few United States (US) and Canadian cities, the leading global association of cities devoted to sustainable development, ICLEI-Local Governments for Sustainability,[15] was founded in September 1990. ICLEI has since evolved into an impressive global network of more than 1750 local and regional governments from all continents. It is currently active in over 100 countries and has experts in more than 20 offices worldwide.[16] Although a host of other transnational city networks – both global and regional – have progressively added a more or less pronounced sustainable development dimension to their activities, ICLEI's work in this area stands out. In its 30 years of existence, ICLEI's role has been pivotal to assisting local governments in the formulation of policies informed by sustainable development requirements and to channelling their related interests and perspectives into global processes and institutions. It would suffice here to mention that ICLEI constitutes the only local government association that is accredited as observer at the three so-called Rio Conventions, that is the UN Framework Convention on Climate Change (UNFCCC), the Convention on Biological Diversity (CBD), and the UN Convention to Combat Desertification (UNCCD).

Agenda 21,[17] the key programme of action arising from the 1992 UN Conference on Environment and Development (UNCED), was the veritable turning point for local governments' engagement with sustainable development. First, Chapter 7 of the Agenda was about sustainable human settlement development and *directly* addressed also cities and other local authorities, thus urging strategies and measures *directly* from them. Thus, Agenda 21 called on *all* cities to develop plans aimed at countering their severe sustainable development problems[18] and to reinforce cooperation among themselves under the aegis of associations such as ICLEI,[19] whereas *individual* cities were directed to, *inter alia*, institutionalize participatory approaches to sustainable urban development, strengthen the capacities of their local governing bodies to deal more effectively with urban growth challenges, devise environmentally sound and culturally sen-

---

[13] "Our Common Future", *cit. supra* note 12, Ch. 9, para. 23.

[14] *Ibid.*, paras. 33-39 and 64-68.

[15] Its inaugural conference, the World Congress of Local Governments for a Sustainable Future, was held at the UN in New York. For more detail, see: <https://icleiusa.org/iclei-at-30>. The network was initially named the International Council for Local Environmental Initiatives. In 2003, its current name was approved by its membership so as to better reflect the network's mandate to engage with sustainability issues, rather than environmental issues *stricto sensu*.

[16] ICLEI's World Secretariat is presently located in Bonn.

[17] Report of the United Nations Conference on Environment and Development, UN Doc. A/CONF.151/26/Rev.1 (Vol. 1), Resolution 1, Annex 2: Agenda 21.

[18] *Ibid.*, para. 7.20.

[19] *Ibid.*, para. 7.21.

sitive tourism programmes, and mobilize resources for local environmental quality initiatives.[20] Secondly, Chapter 28 of Agenda 21 crucially singled out local governments as one of nine "major groups"[21] whose participation was deemed indispensable for the follow-up and implementation processes of the objectives and commitments laid down therein. A rationale echoing the principle of subsidiarity[22] underpinned that decision: "[a]s the level of governance closest to the people, [local authorities] play a vital role in educating, mobilizing and responding to the public to promote sustainable development".[23] Most significantly, all local governments were urged to develop a "Local Agenda 21" (LA21) through a multi-stakeholder participatory process with their respective populations, that is a local action plan adapting the global sustainable development targets and commitments to local needs and conditions.[24]

Under the guidance of their transnational networks and supported by key international institutions, such as UNDP, UN-Habitat and UNEP, cities enthusiastically embraced this LA21 mandate, to the extent that the resulting LA21 movement may certainly be regarded as one of the main successes of UNCED. Over the years, thousands of local sustainability strategies were devised and operationalized by a constantly growing number of local authorities. According to ICLEI surveys,[25] in 1997, LA21 activities were taking place in more than 1800 local governments in 64 States, and in 2002 those figures had rocketed to 6400 local governments in 113 States. Ten years later, in 2012, while it appeared impossible to calculate the precise number of (then) existing LA21 activities, ICLEI's Secretary General reasonably maintained that about 10000 local governments worldwide had put in place actions and policies under the LA21 banner or equivalent local sustainability processes.[26]

Whereas European cities were the driving force[27] behind the initial spread of the LA21 movement and accounted for the overwhelming majority of LA21

---

[20] *Ibid.*, para. 7.20. See also *ibid.*, para. 7.74.

[21] The other major groups were women, children and youth, indigenous people, non-governmental organizations, workers and their trade unions, business and industry, the scientific and technological community, and farmers. See *ibid.*, Chapters 24-27 and 29-32.

[22] See *infra* Section 4.

[23] Agenda 21, *cit. supra* note 17, para. 28.1.

[24] *Ibid.*, paras. 28(2)(a) and 28(3). See NIJMAN, "The Future of the City and the International Law of the Future", in MULLER et al. (eds.), *cit. supra* note 10, p. 213 ff., p. 219 (referring however to the LA21 process as a crucial step in the engagement of cities' with international environmental law, rather than the law of sustainable development at large).

[25] "Local Sustainability 2012: Taking Stock and Moving Forward. Global Review", 2012, available at: <https://www.local2030.org/library/227/Local-Sustainability-2012-study.pdf>, pp. 12-14.

[26] *Ibid.*, p. 3.

[27] In the wake of UNCED, thousands of European local governments started to convene in periodic gatherings known as the European Conferences on Sustainable Cities and Towns. The first of these conferences was held in 1994 in the city of Aalborg and resulted in the adoption of the Aalborg Charter of European Cities and Towns Towards Sustainability. Signed by over 3000 local authorities from more than 40 countries, the Aalborg Charter (Part III) committed the signatories to develop Local Agendas 21 through participatory processes and on the basis of a set of sustainability principles and actions (set out in Part I of the Charter). The Aalborg

initiatives, the following years have witnessed a staggering expansion of the movement in all corners of the planet, with several examples of newly-created or enhanced best practices of local sustainability coming from countries in the developing world and Global South, such as from Curitiba[28] (Brazil) or Kampala (Uganda).[29]

While the LA21 movement was underway, the involvement of cities and their networks in key global processes relevant to sustainable development grew exponentially. Two telling examples relate to biodiversity protection and disaster risk management. In the area of biodiversity, the participation of cities and their networks in the activities of the CBD and its bodies was boosted when, in 2008, on the heels of formal recognition by the CBD Conference of the Parties (COP) of the vital role of local governments in the implementation of the CBD,[30] a multi-stakeholder Global Partnership on Cities and Biodiversity was launched. It was facilitated by the CBD Secretariat and composed of representatives of local governments, multilateral organizations, NGOs, the private sector and academia. It became the key platform for the formulation of policies, standards and targets relating to urban biodiversity. In 2010, this process received further impetus with the adoption of a Plan of Action on Subnational Governments, Cities and Other Local Authorities for Biodiversity by CBD COP-10 in Nagoya.[31] Local governments gave input and advice on the drafting of the Plan and were invited to contribute to its implementation "in coordination with their national Governments".[32]

As to disaster risk, an area increasingly important for sustainable development,[33] local governments and their networks have been key partners of a major top-down initiative – the Making Cities Resilient (MCR) Campaign – launched in 2010 and concluded in 2020 under the leadership of the UN Office for Disaster Risk Reduction (UNDRR).[34] The MCR Campaign has had a significant positive impact on raising awareness and building capacities of local governments in the field of urban disaster resilience. It developed a 10-point checklist[35] – the so-called Ten Essentials for Making Cities Resilient – intended to steer city actions and policies in planning and decision-making related to disaster risk. More than 4300 cities signed up to the Campaign and endorsed the Ten

---

Charter (Part II) launched the European Sustainable Cities and Towns Campaign which remains the largest bottom-up movement arising from the LA21 mandate of Agenda 21. See: <https://sustainablecities.eu>.

[28] "Local Sustainability 2012", *cit. supra* note 25, p. 30.

[29] *Ibid.*, p. 68.

[30] CBD COP-9, Decision IX/28, "Promoting Engagement of Cities and Local Authorities", Doc. UNEP/CBD/COP/DEC/IX/28 (9 October 2008).

[31] CBD COP-10, Decision X/22, "Plan of Action on Subnational Governments, Cities and Other Local Authorities for Biodiversity", Doc. UNEP/CBD/COP/DEC/X/22 (29 October 2010).

[32] *Ibid.*, para. 3.

[33] See especially Targets 11.5 and 11.b of SDG 11.

[34] Formerly, UN International Strategy for Disaster Reduction (UNISDR).

[35] See: <https://www.unisdr.org/campaign/resilientcities/toolkit/article/the-ten-essentials-for-making-cities-resilient>.

Essentials. Thus, the Campaign has rightly been hailed by UNDRR as one of its biggest achievements.[36]

The MCR Campaign has now been succeeded by Making Cities Resilient 2030 (MCR2030),[37] a programme which is operational from January 2021 until the end of 2030. MCR2030 was *co-created* by UNDRR and a number of key partners, including several city networks such as ICLEI, C40 Cities and United Cities and Local Governments (UCLG). Meanwhile, city networks had significantly influenced[38] the drafting of the current key international instrument on disasters, namely the Sendai Framework for Disaster Risk Reduction.[39] The Sendai Framework is replete with references to the need to empower local authorities in the field of disaster risk management. For instance, one of its global targets calls for the substantial increase in the number of countries with "national and *local* disaster risk reduction strategies",[40] and one of its guiding principles is precisely the necessity of empowering local authorities to reduce disaster risk, "including through resources, incentives and decision-making responsibilities".[41]

The 2012 UN Conference on Sustainable Development (Rio+20) was another watershed for the growing involvement of local governments in global sustainability processes. With a view to capitalizing on the achievements of the Agenda 21 mandate and ensuing LA21 movement, in the Conference outcome document "The Future We Want",[42] UN Member States reaffirmed the key role of local authorities in fostering and implementing sustainable development.[43] They accordingly committed to working more closely with such authorities and endorsed their active participation in sustainable development processes.[44] Moreover, local governments were *directly* encouraged to devise local sustainability strategies, while countries were called upon to strengthen local institutions.[45] Finally, "sustainable cities and human settlements"[46] was singled out as a major thematic

---

[36] See: <https://mcr2030.undrr.org/who-we-are/history>.

[37] See: <https://mcr2030.undrr.org>.

[38] See "Towards the New Urban Agenda: Linking with International Processes", ICLEI Briefing Sheet – Urban Issues, No. 07, available at: <https://www.local2030.org/library/252/Towards-the-New-Urban-Agenda-Linking-with-international-processes.pdf>, p. 2; Sendai Declaration of Local and Subnational Governments, "Ensuring Enhanced Resilience to Disasters in the Urban World", 17 March 2015.

[39] Adopted on 18 March 2015 at the Third UN World Conference on Disaster Risk Reduction.

[40] Para. 18(e) (emphasis added). See also para. 27(b).

[41] Para. 19(f). See also para. 27(g).

[42] The Future We Want, UN Doc. A/RES/66/288 (2012), Annex.

[43] *Ibid.*, para. 42.

[44] *Ibid.*, para. 43.

[45] *Ibid.*, para. 101.

[46] *Ibid.*, paras. 134-137 (underscoring, *inter alia*, the need to increase "the number of metropolitan regions, cities and towns that are implementing policies for sustainable urban planning and design" and "the important role of municipal governments in setting a vision for sustainable cities", para. 136, as well as the necessity of strengthening partnerships and other cooperation arrangements among cities and communities aimed at fostering sustainable development, para. 137).

issue for the pursuit of sustainable development, a move filling a glaring gap[47] in the Millennium Development Goals[48] and paving the way for the inclusion of an urban SDG in the post-2015 development agenda, i.e., what in 2015 would become the UN 2030 Agenda for Sustainable Development.

3. CITIES AND THE 2030 AGENDA FOR SUSTAINABLE DEVELOPMENT

The Rio+20 Conference made clear that cities, local governments and their networks had become a key pillar of the institutional framework for sustainable development. Importantly, they were also envisaged as participants in the work of the High-Level Political Forum on Sustainable Development (HLPF).[49] The HLPF was the crucial institutional innovation devised by the Conference with a view to closely involving an intergovernmental body composed of top State leaders (Heads of State and Government or their representatives) in the follow-up process of the post-2015 development agenda.[50] A year later, when deliberating on the organizational aspects of the HLPF, the General Assembly decided that the Forum must be open to local authorities (like any other major group) and granted them a set of procedural rights to be exercised in the context of the Forum's activities, such as the right to attend and intervene in all official meetings, to have access to official documents and information, to submit documents, and to make recommendations.[51] Local authorities were *directly* invited to "autonomously establish and maintain"[52] effective arrangements for their participation in the HLPF and follow-up actions.

On their part, local governments and local government networks promptly acted upon the Rio+20 Conference's renewed emphasis on their key role in the pursuit of sustainable development. United under a Global Task Force of Local and Regional Governments and backed by UNDP and UN-Habitat, they undertook a major consultation process aimed at shedding light on the benefits, challenges and requirements of the localization of the post-2015 development

---

[47] See COHEN, "The City is Missing in the Millennium Development Goals", Journal of Human Development and Capabilities, 2014, p. 261 ff.

[48] See, however, Declaration on Cities and Other Human Settlements in the New Millennium, UN Doc. A/RES/S-25/2 (2001). The eight Millennium Development Goals, which came to an end in 2015, largely originated from the UN Millennium Declaration, UN Doc. A/RES/55/2 (2000).

[49] The Future We Want, *cit. supra* note 42, para. 85(h).

[50] The HLPF replaced the UN Commission on Sustainable Development, which had been established in 1992. See BERNSTEIN, "The United Nations and the Governance of Sustainable Development Goals", in KANIE and BIERMANN (eds.), *Governing through Goals: Sustainable Development Goals as Governance Innovation*, Cambridge (MA), 2017, p. 214 ff., pp. 220-228.

[51] Format and Organizational Aspects of the High-Level Political Forum on Sustainable Development, UN Doc. A/RES/67/290 (2013), paras. 14-15.

[52] *Ibid.*, para. 16.

agenda. This process resulted in a 2015 report[53] which, most significantly, urged States and international institutions to endorse the inclusion of a self-standing goal on sustainable cities in that agenda.[54] Around the same period of time, an "Urban SDG Campaign"[55] had indeed been launched by the UN Sustainable Development Solutions Network (SDSN), in partnership with UN-Habitat and a number of city and local government associations. This Campaign, coupled with the advocacy work by city networks during the drafting process of the 2030 Agenda and associated SDGs,[56] translated into one of the most impactful initiatives of local governments in the context of the formulation of (formally non-binding) international law instruments.

Thus, the 2030 Agenda for Sustainable Development, approved by the General Assembly in 2015,[57] contains SDG 11 where world leaders commit to "Make cities and human settlements inclusive, safe, resilient and sustainable". It is accompanied by ten targets. Seven are thematic targets which address key challenges of sustainable urbanization, namely housing, transport, planning, heritage protection, disasters, adverse environmental impacts (with a focus on air quality and waste management), green and public spaces. Three further targets concern means of implementation, that is the reinforcement of urban-rural relations, the adoption of integrated policies, and support to least-developed countries (particularly in the area of sustainable building).

Unsurprisingly, local government networks have embraced SDG 11 enthusiastically. For instance, ICLEI characterizes the urban SDG as a "truly transformational element"[58] of the 2030 Agenda, as it is "the only goal that is location-specific at a manageable scale".[59] By contrast, scholarship is more prudent. Thus,

---

[53] "Localizing the Post-2015 Development Agenda: Dialogues on Implementation", 2015, available at: <https://www.uclg.org/sites/default/files/dialogues_on_localizing_the_post-2015_development_agenda.pdf>.

[54] *Ibid.*, p. 25.

[55] See: <http://urbansdg.org>. The Campaign was officially launched in September 2013. See also "Cities and the Sustainable Development Goals", ICLEI Briefing Sheet – Urban Issues, No. 02, available at: <https://www.local2030.org/library/232/ICLEI-Briefing-Sheets-02-Cities-and-the-Sustainable-Development-Goals.pdf>, p. 2.

[56] For further detail, see ARAJÄRVI, "Including Cities in the 2030 Agenda – A Review of the Post-2015 Process", in AUST and DU PLESSIS (eds.), *The Globalisation of Urban Governance: Legal Perspectives on Sustainable Development Goal 11*, New York, 2019, p. 17 ff.

[57] *Cit. supra* note 1. The year 2015 was fundamental to the consolidation of cities' key role also in the area of climate change. In their decision adopting the Paris Agreement, the Parties to the UNFCCC endorsed stronger climate action by all "non-Party stakeholders", including cities and other subnational authorities, welcomed the efforts of cities to address and respond to climate change, and invited them to scale up such efforts, UNFCCC COP-21, Decision 1.CP/21, "Adoption of the Paris Agreement", UN Doc. FCCC/CP/2015/10/Add.1 (2015), last preambular para. and paras. 133-134. The Paris Agreement cautiously limits itself to acknowledging the "importance of the engagements of all levels of government and various actors, in accordance with respective national legislations of Parties, in addressing climate change", penultimate preambular paragraph.

[58] "Cities and the Sustainable Development Goals", *cit. supra* note 55, p. 2.

[59] *Ibid.*

Helmut Aust and Anel du Plessis[60] underscore the vagueness, loopholes[61] and inherent contradictions[62] emerging from the text of SDG 11 and accompanying targets.[63] At any rate, their overall view is that the adoption of SDG 11 is "highly commendable"[64] and should be welcomed as it finally acknowledges the city as a "specific site for global governance in the twenty-first century".[65]

I fully subscribe to this overall view. SDG 11 is one of the most dynamic and tangible aspects of the global sustainable development agenda set in motion in 2015. It has a "democratizing potential" as it connects that agenda to the daily concerns – be they decent housing, basic services, public transport, waste, green space, air pollution etc. – of the nearly 60% of the world population currently living in urban areas. SDG 11 empowers urban residents by unlocking their opportunities to participate in local decision-making relevant to global sustainable development processes and to channel – via local governments and associated networks – the resulting local policies and practices into those processes. This may translate into a veritable transformational change, whereby sustainable development ceases to sound like an abstract discourse to the ordinary citizen.

Moreover, a focus on sustainable urbanization, not only as reflected in SDG 11 but mainstreamed into all other SDGs,[66] triggers dynamism in the implementation of the 2030 Agenda, because it brings to the fore the skills, resources and expertise of local governments and their transnational networks. In the 2030 Agenda, world leaders repeatedly confirm their pledge to fully integrate local authorities in the follow-up mechanisms that will review progress in the fulfilment of the SDGs and other Agenda commitments.[67] Crucially, local authorities (like all major groups originally identified by Agenda 21) are directly addressed

---

[60] AUST and DU PLESSIS, "Good Urban Governance as a Global Aspiration: On the Potential and Limits of SDG 11", in FRENCH and KOTZÉ (eds.), *Sustainable Development Goals: Law, Theory and Implementation*, Cheltenham, 2018, p. 201 ff.

[61] Vis-à-vis, for instance, human rights, *ibid.*, pp. 218-219.

[62] For example, with regard to the purportedly competing paradigms of the inclusive versus safe city, *ibid.*, pp. 217-218.

[63] Their commentaries, however, make clear that the SDGs and the 2030 Agenda as a whole constitute a powerful document; compare their lashing criticism of the 2016 UN New Urban Agenda, regarded as verbose, hypertrophic and thus incapable of conveying any clear message as regards cities and sustainable development, *ibid.*, pp. 214-215. The New Urban Agenda was adopted in October 2016 by the UN Conference on Housing and Sustainable Urban Development (Habitat III), and eventually endorsed by, and annexed to GA Res. 71/256 (23 December 2016).

[64] AUST and DU PLESSIS, *cit. supra* note 60, p. 214.

[65] *Ibid.*, p. 216.

[66] After all, as ICLEI puts it, a city constitutes "a microcosm of all other SDGs", see "Cities and the Sustainable Development Goals", *cit. supra* note 55, p. 2. See also "The Importance of All Sustainable Development Goals (SDGs) for Cities and Communities", ICLEI Briefing Sheet – Urban Issues, No. 04, available at: <https://www.local2030.org/library/234/ICLEI-SDGs-Briefing-Sheets-04-The-importance-of-all-Sustainable-Development-Goals-SDGs-for-cities-and-communities.pdf>. This document is interesting and instructive because it provides two examples of best practices – one coming from a city in the Global North and one from a city in the Global South – in relation to each of the 17 SDGs.

[67] Transforming Our World, *cit. supra* note 1, paras. 34, 45 and 52.

in a key passage of the Agenda, where they are called upon "to report on their contribution"[68] to the Agenda's implementation.

Against that backdrop, city networks have swiftly proceeded to align their activities with the SDG framework in order to boost its execution. For instance, as of June 2019, ICLEI had an impressive portfolio of 189 active sustainability projects involving 1983 cities and regions.[69] Such projects are being mapped according to five pathways towards sustainability – nature-based, low emission, circular, resilient, equitable and people-centred development projects – and their impact on the 17 SDGs.

Individual actions undertaken by local governments in the wake of the foregoing reporting mandate in the 2030 Agenda are also very significant. Starting in 2016, with reports from the Land of North Rhine-Westphalia (Germany) and the Generalitat Valenciana (Spain), a process recalling the LA21 movement is increasingly unfolding, whereby cities and other subnational authorities compile documents describing their progress in the implementation of the SDGs and eventually submit and present them during the annual sessions of the HLPF.

This process became more structured and institutionalized when, in 2018, a few Japanese cities (Kitakyushu, Toyama, Shimokawa) and New York City labelled their reports as "Voluntary Local Reviews" (VLRs),[70] thereby imitating the title and format of the "Voluntary National Reviews" (VNRs) used by States to report on their progress towards the achievement of the SDGs.[71] New York, in particular, took the leadership in this area, by drafting, and inviting local governments worldwide to sign on to, a Voluntary Local Review Declaration, whereby signatories undertake – in a formal yet non-binding manner – to align their existing strategies with the SDGs, set up a forum for stakeholders to share experiences relevant to the SDGs, and submit a VLR to the HLPF.[72] At the time of writing, 40 VLRs and cognate reports on the SDGs and the 2030 Agenda have been filed with the UN system.[73] Unsurprisingly, local governments from high-

---

[68] *Ibid.*, para. 89.

[69] See "How Does ICLEI Support the UN's Sustainable Development Goals?", 17 July 2019, available at: <https://icleiusa.org/how-does-iclei-support-the-uns-sustainable-development-goals>.

[70] See "State of the Voluntary Local Reviews 2020: Local Action for Global Impact in Achieving the SDGs", 2020, available at: <https://www.iges.or.jp/en/pub/vlrs-2020/en>; ABEYWARDENA, "New York City: A Case Study in Localizing the Agenda 2030", in ZEVI (ed.), *Global Cities in the Age of COVID-19: Agenda 2030 and Sustainable Development*, ISPI Dossier, 19 April 2020, available at: <https://www.ispionline.it/sites/default/files/pubblicazioni/ispi_dossier_globalcities_aprile2020.pdf>, p. 22 ff.

[71] See Transforming Our World, *cit. supra* note 1, paras. 79 and 84.

[72] The Declaration was launched in September 2019 in the context of an official session of the General Assembly. Its text is available at: <https://www1.nyc.gov/site/international/programs/voluntary-local-review-declaration.page>. As of April 2020, it had been signed by more than 60 cities and other local authorities, see ABEYWARDENA, *cit. supra* note 70, p. 24.

[73] See: <https://sdgs.un.org/topics/voluntary-local-reviews>.

income countries are leading the way,[74] but a growing number of reports are also coming from cities in the Global South and low-income countries.[75]

This burgeoning practice[76] is significant at least for two reasons. First, in a few telling cases it provides fresh evidence of implementation of sustainable development commitments by front-running local governments despite the lack of consistent parallel actions by the respective national governments.[77] The clearest example is offered by the VLRs submitted by US cities, as the US federal administration has so far not envisaged the presentation of a VNR to the UN. Secondly, the submission of local SDG reports triggers a virtuous circle of salutary competition among cities and other local authorities, whereby – be it for reasons of global reputation and visibility or more genuine attachment to the cause of sustainable development – they tend to emulate each other, engage in peer-to-peer learning,[78] and accordingly devise their sustainability plans and VLRs.

As a result, local governments are strongly encouraged to harness their policies and actions towards the fulfilment of the global sustainable development agenda, thereby remarkably contributing to the daunting challenge of implementation of the SDGs.

4. Conceptual Bases: Subsidiarity and Public Participation

The principles of subsidiarity and public participation are usually identified[79] as closely interrelated rationales underlying the steady emergence of cities and local governments as autonomous contributors to the creation and application of international law at large. At the same time, these principles constitute especially powerful conceptual bases for explaining the increasingly prominent role which,

---

[74] There are currently 17 reports from local governments in Europe, four from the US, three from Japan, and one from Australia.

[75] Especially from Latin America (five reports from local governments in Brazil, three from Mexico, two from Argentina, and one each from Bolivia and Uruguay). There is also a remarkable report from a Chinese city (Guangzhou), one from South Korea (Suwon), and one from the Philippines (Cauayán).

[76] This practice is part and parcel of a wider SDG localization framework endorsed by the UN. That framework is most significantly assisted by a platform and multi-stakeholder partnership for the SDGs named "Local2030: Localizing the SDGs", see: <https://www.local2030. org>. The platform aims at sharing tools, experiences, solutions and guides to foster SDG localization among partners. In addition to a wealth of UN agencies and local government associations, the partnership may involve a range of further stakeholders, such as representatives of national governments, the private sector, academia, civil society, research and philanthropic foundations.

[77] See NIJMAN, cit. supra note 24, pp. 221-223.

[78] This process may also well result in partnerships among cities in high-income countries, as the example of Helsinki's report, which was drafted in close collaboration with New York, shows. See ABEYWARDENA, cit. supra note 70, pp. 23-24.

[79] See ex multis, BLANK, "The City and the World", Columbia JTL, 2006, p. 868 ff., pp. 903-905; PORRAS, cit. supra note 2, pp. 550-552 and 556-559.

as spelled out in the foregoing sections, local authorities have been performing in the field of sustainable development for the past three decades.

Subsidiarity and public participation are widely recognized domestic law principles, but they have also acquired a substantial international law dimension. The principle of subsidiarity governs the articulation of competencies between different levels of government. Insofar as relevant for our purposes, it dictates that, in policy areas where local governments possess regulatory powers, the function of the central government should be subsidiary, i.e., it should intervene only when, or only to the extent that, local action is lacking, insufficient or inefficient to meet the intended objectives.

This safeguard for the powers of local governments arises from the simple consideration that local authorities constitute the level of government closest to, and most immediately representative of, their citizens. They are therefore best placed to assess the needs and interests of citizens, and are – to a greater or lesser degree – directly accountable to them in case of regulatory failures. Thus, subsidiarity is a concept intimately linked to notions of democracy and good government.[80] Accordingly, it provides a robust basis for the devolution of powers to city and other local governments and for the decentralization of public policies, including when they involve the implementation of international law norms and standards.

The principle of public participation, which is a key component of the human right to take part in the conduct of public affairs,[81] may be regarded as the other side of the equation. Participatory democracy – broken down into the three pillars of public access to information, participation in decision-making and access to justice – is at its highest when it is operationalized at the city and local level. In these contexts, public participation has at least the potential to translate into truly meaningful and effective mechanisms, as it is exercised at the level of government closest to citizens and most responsive to tangible concerns impacting on their everyday life. These considerations make a strong case for the increasing involvement of local authorities, with their participatory arrangements and structures, in law-making and law-enforcing processes relevant to international law, especially – as recalled further on – in the area of sustainable development.

These associated quests for progressive decentralization of public policies and enhancement of participatory democracy at the local level have not remained confined to domestic political struggles, as they have been increasingly endorsed at the international level.

In the area of decentralization and subsidiarity, Europe and its supranational institutions have been frontrunners. Under the aegis of the Council of Europe (CoE), and as a result of the advocacy efforts long undertaken by the CoE's

---

[80] See BLANK, *cit. supra* note 79, p. 889, emphasizing the idea of local self-government as "the best schoolhouse for democracy" (by reference to the famous book by DE TOCQUEVILLE, *De la démocratie en Amérique*, Paris, 1835/1840).

[81] Art. 21(1) of the Universal Declaration of Human Rights, UN Doc A/810 (1948); Art. 25(a) of the International Covenant on Civil and Political Rights, 16 December 1966, entered into force 23 March 1976.

Congress of Local and Regional Authorities (CLRA),[82] the European Charter of Local Self-Government was concluded in 1985. Remarkably, the Charter represents a veritable pan-European treaty as it has been ratified by all 47 Member States of the CoE.[83] Considering that "local authorities are one of the main foundations of any democratic regime",[84] this treaty obliges Contracting States to recognize the principle of local self-government in domestic legislation, possibly in the constitution.[85] Without explicitly mentioning subsidiarity, it makes clear that "[p]ublic responsibilities shall generally be exercised, in preference, by those authorities which are closest to the citizen".[86] It then mandates the attribution of a set of rights to local authorities, such as the right to dispose of adequate financial resources,[87] the right to cooperate with other local governments and belong to international local government associations,[88] and – most significantly – the right to a judicial remedy to secure respect for their powers,[89] which of course allows pertinent lawsuits against the central government. As to compliance by Contracting States, a well-structured monitoring process is carried out by a committee of the CLRA. In addition, the Charter is frequently referred to by the European Court of Human Rights (ECtHR) when cases under the European Convention on Human Rights (ECHR) involve local matters. For instance, the ECtHR recently relied on the Charter to support its finding that the failure to organize local elections in the Bosnian city of Mostar for some 12 years had violated the right of a Mostar citizen not to be discriminated against on grounds of her place of residence.[90]

In this connection, it is important to underscore that subsidiarity is also a principle of ECHR law[91] and possibly a structural principle of human rights law at large.[92] The subsidiary role of international human rights bodies vis-à-vis na-

---

[82] This CoE body has been in existence (with different names) since 1953. It is currently composed of 648 elected officials representing over 150,000 local and regional authorities in the CoE Member States.

[83] This infrequent occurrence may have been facilitated by the opting-in scheme envisaged by the Charter, which allows Contracting States to declare that they are bound only by a certain number of its substantive provisions (Art. 12). As a perusal of such declarations shows, this scheme has not undermined the basic principles and provisions of the Charter.

[84] Third preambular paragraph.

[85] Art. 2.

[86] Art. 4(3).

[87] Art. 9.

[88] Art. 10.

[89] Art. 11.

[90] *Baralija v. Bosnia and Herzegovina*, Application No. 30100/18, Judgment of 29 October 2019, para. 57 ("[t]here is no doubt that democracy is a fundamental feature of the European public order [...] and that the notion of *effective* political democracy is just as applicable to the local level as it is to the national level, bearing in mind the extent of decision making entrusted to local authorities [...] *and the proximity of the local electorate to the policies which their local politicians adopt*", emphasis added). This judgment was a determining factor for the local elections which were finally held in Mostar on 20 December 2020.

[91] A reference to this principle in the Preamble to the ECHR has been added by Protocol No. 15 amending the ECHR, 24 June 2013, entered into force 1 August 2021.

[92] CAROZZA, "Subsidiarity as a Structural Principle of International Human Rights Law", AJIL, 2003, p. 38 ff.

tional authorities (broadly understood) usually implies a rather deferential standard of review of the impugned domestic measures. What matters here is that
the rationale underlying this jurisprudence – i.e. that national authorities have
"direct democratic legitimation and are [...] in principle better placed than an international court to evaluate local needs and conditions"[93] – strongly militates in
favour of a proactive and extensive involvement of cities and local governments
in the formulation and implementation of rules and policies relating to the social
pillar of sustainable development, given its close relationship with human rights
issues. Moreover, it is telling that the same jurisprudence informs the assessment
of human rights cases concerning domestic measures which interfere with or aim
at environmental protection.[94]

The law and practice of the European Union (EU) is particularly instructive
in our context.[95] It reminds us that subsidiarity, which is now a general principle of EU law,[96] originally entered the EU legal order as a specific principle of
European environmental policy.[97] This genesis shows that environmental protection is a focus area for the application of the principle, as it is where national
and subnational subsidiarity concerns are especially likely to arise due to the
inevitable diversity of local conditions, priorities and sensibilities. As a result, the
key role of cities and local authorities in administering environmental sustainability measures – about, say, urban waste or air quality and traffic regulation – is
boosted.

---

[93] ECtHR, *Hatton and Others v. United Kingdom*, Application No. 36022/97, Grand
Chamber, Judgment of 8 July 2003, para. 97.

[94] See e.g., ECtHR, *Fadeyeva v. Russia*, Application No. 55723/00, Judgment of 9 June
2005, paras. 102 and 105.

[95] Yet practice in favour of local environmental action goes well beyond Europe. See
especially, Supreme Court of Canada, *Canada Ltée v. Hudson*, 28 June 2001, [2001] 2 S.C.R.
241. The Supreme Court upheld the competence of the Town of Hudson to ban pesticide use by
relying on the international law principle of precaution and, most significantly for current purposes, the principle of subsidiarity: "[t]he case arises in an era in which matters of governance
are often examined through the lens of the principle of subsidiarity. This is the proposition that
law-making and implementation are often best achieved at a level of government that is not
only effective, but also closest to the citizens affected and thus most responsive to their needs,
to local distinctiveness, and to population diversity", *ibid.*, p. 249, para. 3.

[96] Art. 5(3) of the Treaty on European Union (TEU). As currently formulated, this provision allows the exercise of EU powers in areas of shared competence only when the intended
objectives of a given action "cannot be sufficiently achieved by the Member States, either at
central level *or at regional and local level*" (emphasis added). See also Art. 1, second para.,
and Art. 10(3) TEU. Despite its current status as a general principle of EU law, subsidiarity
continues to play a key function in the area of the environment, as duly noted by PORCHIA, "Le
politiche dell'Unione europea in materia ambientale", in FERRARA and GALLO (eds.), *Trattato
di diritto dell'ambiente*, Milano, 2014, Vol. I, p. 153 ff., p. 156. Also, the *ex ante* political control on the observance of the principle by national parliaments of EU Member States appears
especially relevant vis-à-vis EU draft environmental legislation, *ibid.*, p. 186. See Protocol
No. 2 on the Application of the Principles of Subsidiarity and Proportionality attached to the
EU Treaties.

[97] This occurred when the 1986 Single European Act granted powers to the (then) European
Economic Community (EEC) in the field of environmental policy. Subsidiarity was set out in
Art. 130 R(4) of the Treaty Establishing the EEC.

At the same time, when the higher levels of government (a loose expression here, i.e., one which is meant to include EU institutions) are willing to legislate in the field of the environment, they may easily overcome the subsidiarity hurdle by recalling that environmental problems are, by definition, of a transboundary or even global, non-local nature. But this is not the end of the story. The logic of subsidiarity still implies here that supranational and national legislation may never exhaust the environmental competence of local authorities. The latter retain the power to adapt that legislation to their local context. Certainly, the exercise of that local power may be regarded as particularly credible and legitimate when it gives rise to environmental measures that are more protective than those passed at higher levels of government.

EU law is again illuminating. In the field of the environment, it contemplates a set of disciplines that fulfil functions equivalent to subsidiarity.[98] These disciplines essentially amount to subsidiarity by other names. They are, basically, the principle of rectification of environmental damage at source;[99] the requirement that EU environmental policy must take into account the "diversity of situations in the various regions of the Union";[100] and the power of EU Member States to derogate from EU environmental law by adopting more protective measures.[101] To illustrate the far-reaching potential of these disciplines for justifying local environmental action, it is sufficient to refer to a classic case relating to the free movement of goods in the EU. In the *Walloon Waste* decision,[102] the EU Court of Justice (CJEU) held that a prohibition by the Belgian region of Wallonia on the importation of waste from other EU Member States and from Belgian regions other than Wallonia was not discriminatory and did not therefore contravene EU free movement principles. The CJEU first found that the import ban was a genuine measure of environmental protection arising from the large-scale inflow of non-local waste which at the time was affecting Wallonia.[103] It then ruled out that non-local waste was discriminated against vis-à-vis Walloon waste, given the dissimilarity between waste produced in different areas and the connection of waste with its place of production.[104] Most significantly, it emphasized that its findings were in line with the principle that environmental damage must be remedied at source, which implied that *"it is for each region, municipality or other*

---

[98] MUNARI and SCHIANO DI PEPE, *Tutela transnazionale dell'ambiente*, Bologna, 2012, pp. 84-86 and 91-95.

[99] Art. 191(2) of the Treaty on the Functioning of the European Union (TFEU).

[100] Art. 191(2) TFEU. See also Art. 191(3) TFEU.

[101] Art. 193 TFEU. On the oscillating jurisprudence on this provision, also assessed in the light of subsidiarity, see PAVONI, "Controversial Aspects of the Interaction between International and EU Law in Environmental Matters: Direct Effect and Member States' Unilateral Measures", in MORGERA (ed.), *The External Environmental Policy of the European Union: EU and International Law Perspectives*, Cambridge, 2012, p. 347 ff., pp. 361-375. See lately, REINS, "Where Eagles Dare: How Much Further May EU Member States Go under Article 193 TFEU?", in PEETERS and ELIANTONIO (eds.), *Research Handbook on EU Environmental Law*, Cheltenham, 2020, p. 22 ff.

[102] Case C-2/90, *Commission v. Belgium*, 9 July 1992.

[103] *Ibid.*, para. 32.

[104] *Ibid.*, paras. 36.

local authority to take appropriate steps to ensure that its own waste is collected, treated and disposed of".[105]

Unsurprisingly, the replication of European legal solutions at the universal level has so far proven unfeasible. During the 1990s, UN-Habitat and a network of local governments formulated and released a draft World Charter of Local Self-Government modelled after the European Charter considered above.[106] However, its envisaged conversion into a UN treaty failed due to the opposition of a number of States.[107] Eventually, UN-Habitat and cities' associations opted for a soft law instrument which was finalized in 2007 under the title International Guidelines on Decentralisation and Strengthening of Local Authorities.[108] The Guidelines are intended to steer reforms at national level in line with localist principles of subsidiarity, autonomy, empowerment, self-government, and participatory democracy.

The same objective is pursued by another soft law instrument drafted by UN-Habitat and cities' networks which is highly significant for our purposes, given its intimate connection to sustainable urban development. These are the 2009 International Guidelines on Access to Basic Services for All.[109] Although they were understood as a follow-up action to then existing UN sustainable development processes, they clearly retain significance in the context of the current 2030 Agenda and its SDGs.[110] Through a balanced and well-defined division of responsibilities between central and local authorities, they foster the creation of transparent, effective and participatory governance frameworks in crucial areas, such as waste management, water supply and sanitation, energy, transportation, education, health, and public safety. Notably, the Guidelines[111] pay special attention to issues of environmental sustainability relevant to the provision of basic services, such as the necessity of devising measures countering pollution, climate change and the depletion of natural resources, or the requirement to adopt sustainable consumption patterns.

The preceding background allows the conclusion that decentralization and subsidiarity, if not formally binding universal rules, are at least emerging general principles of law, which corroborate the growing international status of cities, especially in areas relevant to sustainable development.

That growing status is even more firmly upheld by the principle of public participation, particularly in environmental and sustainability matters. Granted,

---

[105] *Ibid.*, para. 34 (emphasis added). In line with the principles of self-sufficiency and proximity applicable in this area, waste had accordingly to be disposed of "as close as possible to the place where it is produced, in order to limit as far as possible [its] transport", *ibid.*

[106] Initial Draft Text of the World Charter of Local Self-Government, 25 May 1998, available at: <https://www.gdrc.org/uem/mea/local-charter/charter.html>.

[107] See PORRAS, *cit. supra* note 2, pp. 562-563.

[108] Approved by UN-Habitat Governing Council Res. 21/3 (20 April 2007). These Guidelines have not been formally endorsed by the UN General Assembly.

[109] Approved by UN-Habitat Governing Council Res. 22/8 (3 April 2009).

[110] See especially Target 1.4 of SDG 1 (No Poverty) and Target 11.1 of SDG 11 (Sustainable Cities and Communities).

[111] Paras. 51-58.

here too the most significant developments have occurred at the regional level. Thus, a 2009 Protocol to the European Charter of Local Self-Government secures the right to participate in the affairs of a local authority to everyone within the jurisdiction of States Parties.[112] This right is subject to narrow exceptions and must be given effect by way of national measures establishing – in consultation with local authorities – procedures that enable public access to official documents and participation in decision-making processes.

Public participation in environmental issues has also been the subject of regional treaties, at first with the landmark 1998 Aarhus Convention, concluded under the aegis of the UN Economic Commission for Europe,[113] and lately with the 2018 Escazú Agreement, promoted by the UN Economic Commission for Latin America and the Caribbean.[114]

One should also consider that, starting from the inclusion of Principle 10 on environmental access rights in the 1992 Rio Declaration on Environment and Development, a wealth of State practice, jurisprudence, international instruments and literature seem to converge towards the consolidation of public participation as a general principle of international (environmental and sustainable development) law. Scholarship is replete with robust affirmations militating in favour of the foregoing proposition. Thus, for instance, public participation is regarded as the *most* fundamental element that the international community must support in order to meaningfully address the challenge of implementing environmental law;[115] or, put more simply, public participation may be considered as an "essential requirement"[116] of sustainable development.

---

[112] Additional Protocol to the European Charter of Local Self-Government on the Right to Participate in the Affairs of a Local Authority, 16 November 2009, entered into force 1 June 2012, Art. 1(1). This Protocol is far from achieving the same pan-European status as its parent Charter. As of 22 April 2021, it has been ratified by 20 CoE Member States.

[113] Convention on Access to Information, Public Participation in Decision-making and Access to Justice in Environmental Matters, 25 June 1998, entered into force 30 October 2001. Although formally open for accession by any State, all current States Parties are in fact members of UNECE. The number of Parties is 47, that is 46 States plus the EU. At the same time, it is chiefly important to recall that the participatory rights in the Aarhus Convention have *de facto* been incorporated into the ECHR via a creative jurisprudence of the ECtHR, please see PAVONI, "Public Interest Environmental Litigation and the European Court of Human Rights: No Love at First Sight", in LENZERINI and VRDOLJAK (eds.), *International Law for Common Goods: Normative Perspectives on Human Rights, Culture and Nature*, Oxford/Portland, 2014, p. 331 ff., pp. 353-357.

[114] Regional Agreement on Access to Information, Public Participation and Justice in Environmental Matters in Latin America and the Caribbean, 4 March 2018, entered into force 22 April 2021. As of 22 April 2021, there are 12 States Parties to the Agreement (out of 33 Latin American and Caribbean countries entitled to become parties). See OLMOS GIUPPONI, "Fostering Environmental Democracy in Latin America and the Caribbean: An Analysis of the Regional Agreement on Environmental Access Rights", RECIEL, 2019, p. 136 ff.

[115] VIÑUALES, "The Rise and Fall of Sustainable Development", RECIEL, 2013, p. 3 ff., p. 8.

[116] FRANCIONI, "Revisiting Sustainable Development in Light of General Principles of International Environmental Law", in CREMONA et al. (eds.), *Reflections on the*

Major UN instruments on sustainable development are also instructive in this context. Crucially, the Rio+20 outcome document "The Future We Want", after reiterating that "broad"[117] participatory rights are "fundamental"[118] for sustainable development, emphasizes the ability, determination and achievements of local and subnational authorities in "engaging citizens […] and providing them with relevant information"[119] as chief reasons militating in favour of the enhancement of their role in the promotion and implementation of sustainability.

Public participation is a top priority in the 2030 Agenda and associated SDGs. This is unsurprising given that the Agenda stemmed from an unprecedented participatory process and was indeed conceived as "an Agenda of the people, by the people and for the people".[120] Accordingly, its follow-up processes are meant to be "open, inclusive, participatory and transparent for all people".[121] Crucially, public participation is regarded by the Agenda as a key pillar of the rule of law and good governance,[122] including good urban governance.[123]

In short, sustainable development democracy channelled through participatory processes and structures, organized by cities and local governments with the invaluable assistance of their transnational networks, constitutes an indispensable avenue for pursuing the ambitious yet compelling goals and targets that the international community has set for the planet and humanity until 2030.

5. CONCLUSION

The foregoing account of the expanding role and stature of cities and local governments in the promotion of sustainable development should not be relied on to show that sovereign States are losing their central position in the international law system. That would be a paradoxical conclusion, in my view, given that – for all legal purposes – city governments remain subnational units of States, which must comply with the will, policy guidance and legislation of their central governments. More modestly, cities' vibrant engagement with global processes for sustainable development and with local implementation of resulting outcomes

---

Constitutionalisation of International Economic Law. Liber Amicorum for Ernst-Ulrich Petersmann, Leiden, 2014, p. 475 ff., p. 490.

[117] The Future We Want, *cit. supra* note 42, para. 43.

[118] *Ibid.*, para. 13.

[119] *Ibid.*, para. 42.

[120] Transforming Our World, *cit. supra* note 1, para. 52.

[121] *Ibid.*, para. 74(d).

[122] Target 16.7 of SDG 16 (Peace, Justice and Strong Institutions) is about ensuring "responsive, inclusive, participatory and representative decision-making *at all levels*" (emphasis added), whereas Target 16.3 envisages "equal access to justice for all". In turn, Target 16.10 contemplates "public access to information […] in accordance with national legislation and international agreements". See also SDG 6 (Clean Water and Sanitation), Target 6.b ("[s]upport and strengthen the participation of local communities in improving water and sanitation management").

[123] See especially Target 11.3 urging the enhancement of capacity for "participatory, integrated and sustainable human settlement planning management".

is testimony to a sort of spill-over effect on the international plane of the values and virtues of local self-government and autonomy as increasingly promoted, mandated and exercised domestically.

That said, the consistent recognition that cities, with their transnational networks, have turned out to be fundamental partners of States and international organizations in the pursuit of sustainable development certainly constitutes one of the most dynamic, vital and promising elements emerging from practice in this area over the past three decades.

If cities continue to demonstrate leadership and innovation in advancing cutting-edge solutions to problems of sustainability as a result of processes that secure the meaningful participation of the communities of people concerned, their place in the global partnership for sustainable development is bound to become ever more prominent.

ARE CITIES TAKING CENTER-STAGE?
THE EMERGING ROLE OF URBAN COMMUNITIES
AS "NORMATIVE GLOBAL CLIMATE ACTORS"

Christine Bakker[*]

Abstract

Cities around the world are playing an increasingly active role in global climate governance. Considering their share in global emissions on the one hand, and the direct threats they face from climate-related disasters on the other, urban communities are at the forefront of mitigation and adaptation actions. While cities generally implement such actions as part of their State's international climate commitments, they sometimes go beyond, or even against the nationally adopted policy stance. This article explores the evolving normative role of cities in relation to climate change, considering how they can contribute, both to the development of new rules of international law, and to the implementation of existing norms for climate action at the domestic level. Based on an analysis of current developments and concrete examples, the article reflects on the potentialities and constraints of cities as "normative global climate actors".

Keywords: cities; climate change; international climate law; urban climate governance; city networks; normative climate actors.

1. Introduction

Cities account for 70% of global CO2 emissions,[1] but they also face direct risks from climate-related disasters. Since 90% of the world's urban agglomerations are situated in coastal areas, most cities on Earth are at risk from climate change related flooding, or powerful storms.[2] While the international legal regime addressing climate change primarily regulates the behavior of States, cities around the globe are playing an increasingly active role in both implementing and shaping the contours of global climate governance. In all parts of the world, cities take mitigation and adaptation actions, mostly implementing national climate policies, but sometimes going beyond, or even against the laws or policies adopted by the State. Moreover, various regional and international city networks

---

[*] Visiting Lecturer, Scuola Superiore Sant'Anna, Pisa, and Visiting Research Fellow, British Institute for International and Comparative Law, London. Email: christine.bakker@alumi.eui.eu.
[1] See the data available at: <https://www.c40.org/ending-climate-change-begins-in-the-city>.
[2] *Ibid.*

IYIL, Vol. 30 (2020), pp. 81-106
ISSN 0391-5107

have been set up, promoting dialogue and enhancing cooperation among urban communities facing similar challenges.

This contribution aims to explore the evolving role of urban communities as "normative global climate actors", focusing on the question how cities can contribute to both (i) the *development of new international rules* and instruments for climate mitigation and adaptation, and to (ii) the *implementation of existing norms* of international climate law at the domestic level. To this end, the article first considers whether there is a legal basis in international climate law for a role of cities in 'multi-level climate governance', also considering the relevance of the concepts of Global Environmental Law and Transnational Environmental Law in this regard (Section 2). Then, the contribution of urban communities in the formation and implementation of international climate law is examined, including examples of ambitious climate action of cities, going beyond, or even against the nationally adopted policies, including the role of cities in emission trading, and climate litigation (Section 3). Based on this analysis, the author then offers, in Section 4, some reflections on the potentialities and constraints of urban communities as "normative global climate actors". It concludes that despite various constraints of a legal, political, and factual nature, the emerging role of cities in this field, *both* by influencing the formation of international climate law itself, *and* by developing and implementing climate laws and policies at the domestic level, may contribute to the progressive transformation of the traditional role of the State as primary subjects of international law, in favor of a more inclusive, multi-level approach.

2. INTERNATIONAL CLIMATE LAW: LEGAL BASES FOR CITY INVOLVEMENT IN MULTI-LEVEL CLIMATE GOVERNANCE

2.1. Introduction

When considering how cities are gaining recognition as "normative global climate actors", the analysis in this contribution starts from the assumption that cities, through their democratically elected municipal institutions (which will be referred to as "local government"), and in the context of the powers conferred to them in the domestic legal order, contribute to the formulation of "norms", which are either translated into legal rules or included in policy documents, and which aim to address the concrete threats that each city faces as a result of climate change. In this context, "norms" are understood in a broad sense, and can range from a city-wide climate adaptation or mitigation programme, to more specific standards or targets (e.g. in terms of emission reductions in a specific sector), which have an authoritative legal or administrative value within the urban community. When adopting or implementing such climate related norms at the *local or domestic level*, cities can be considered as "normative climate actors".

However, when cities – either represented by their mayor or by other public officers mandated by the municipal authorities – engage in efforts to *influence international political decisions and multilateral agreements*, they also adopt a role as "normative *global* climate actors". In this regard, the term "global" is used to refer to two elements of city involvement in the overall response to climate change. On the one hand, it refers to the impact that cities aspire – and progressively achieve – on the "world stage", by taking part in the international climate negotiations, aiming to directly influence the content of international climate law. On the other hand, it refers to the fact that cities are challenging the traditional inter-state dynamics of international law and policy making, and are creating new ways of interacting with each other, with States, and with multilateral institutions, not by replacing or acting on behalf of their State, but as "independent" actors in a global, multilevel context.

The question what role cities, alongside other actors such as NGOs and private actors, play in norm-creating processes at the local, national and international levels, is one of the questions addressed in the scholarly debates on "multilevel governance", and on the concepts of Global Environmental Law (GEL) and Transnational Environmental Law (TEL). Therefore, before examining the legal basis for an involvement of local governments in the formal decision-making process on the global response to climate change (Section 2.4), first a closer look will be taken at how cities can interact with different government levels in the context of 'multilevel climate governance' (2.2), and how the concepts of GEL or TEL could help to better understand, or clarify the emerging role of cities as 'normative global climate actors' (2.3).

2.2. *Multi-level climate governance and the role of cities*

The recognition of the widespread and multiple challenges that climate change poses for humankind and for societies around the globe, has led to a myriad of responses. As a result, global governance related to climate change, or "climate governance" is both "multi-level" and "multi-actor". [3] It is *multi-level,* because it operates at different levels: international, national, and sub-national. At the same time, it is *multi-actor*, since it involves, besides governmental and intergovernmental actors, also various non-state actors, both public and private. Indeed, many climate change actions require collaboration among different levels of government. For example, incentivizing public transportation usage is critical for reducing greenhouse gas emissions, but it requires coordination across regions, since transportation networks and urban agglomerations often transcend political boundaries. At the same time, "the effectiveness of many climate change programs also hinges on the ability to coordinate across political jurisdictions due to the presence of transboundary risks – such as sea level rise and storm surges – that span ecosystems and infrastructure networks". [4]

---

[3] BODANSKY, BRUNNÉE and RAJAMANI, *International Climate Change Law*, Oxford, 2017, p. 264.
[4] HUGHES, CHU and MASON (eds.), *Climate Change in Cities: Innovations in Multi-Level Governance*, Cham, 2018, p. 5.

Multi-level governance generally involves horizontal relationships (between institutions at the same hierarchical or geographical level), vertical relationships (between institutions at different levels), and diagonal relationships (between institutions at different levels in different countries).[5] In the context of climate governance, all these relationships exist. Most prominently, *horizontal relationships* exist between States, especially as part of the international climate negotiations and the agreements reached therein, including the United Nations Framework Convention on Climate Change (UNFCCC),[6] the Kyoto Protocol,[7] the Cancún Agreements,[8] and the Paris Agreement on Climate Change.[9] But horizontal interactions also occur between international institutions, for example between the UNFCCC Secretariat and the Intergovernmental Panel on Climate Change (IPCC). *Vertical relationships* in global climate governance exist both between international institutions and States, but also between States and sub-national levels.

Cities occupy a special place in this complex system. On the one hand, they are public entities, and form part of the governmental structures within a State. Therefore, they are (indirectly) bound by international agreements concluded by their State, and by laws and climate policies adopted at the national level. On the other hand, in some international climate agreements, cities are also considered as non-State actors, or "non-Party stakeholders", since they have a certain level of autonomy at the local level but cannot become Parties themselves to such international agreements.[10]

In practice, cities are involved in all the above-mentioned types of relationships, as part of their role in climate change adaptation and mitigation efforts. In particular, cities maintain *vertical relationships* with the institutions at the State level, and they generally contribute to the formulation and implementation of national climate policies. Indeed, practice shows that "vertical intergovernmental dynamics play a significant role in shaping local decision-making about climate change".[11] Moreover, *diagonal relationships* involving cities occur in the context of programmes of multilateral organizations providing direct support for local

---

[5] See BODANSKY et al., *cit. supra* note 3, pp. 260-261; OSOFSKI, "Is climate change 'international'? Litigation's Diagonal Regulatory Role", Virginia Journal of International Law, 2009, p. 585 ff.

[6] United Nations Framework Convention on Climate Change (UNFCCC), 4 June 1992, entered into force 21 March 1994.

[7] Kyoto Protocol to the UNFCCC, 11 December 1997, entered into force 16 February 2005.

[8] Decision 1/CP.16: The Cancún Agreements: Outcome of the work of the Ad-Hoc Working Group on Long-Term Cooperative Action under the Convention, 15 March 2011, UN Doc. FCCC/CP/2010/Add.1, p. 2 ff.

[9] Paris Agreement on Climate Change, Annex to Decision FCCC/CP/2015/L.9/Rev.1, 12 December 2015, ("Paris Agreement"), entered into force 4 November 2016.

[10] E.g. Cancún Agreements, *cit. supra* note 8.

[11] CHU, HUGHES, and MASON, "Conclusion: Multilevel Governance and Climate Change in cities", in HUGHES et al., *cit. supra* note 4, p. 361 ff., p. 364.

climate actions.[12] Furthermore, *horizontal relations* between cities through trans-national city networks have become an increasingly important aspect of climate governance, as will be further discussed below.[13]

2.2. *The role of cities from the perspectives of global environmental law and transnational environmental law*

According to the often-cited definition by Yang and Percival, Global Environmental Law (GEL) can be understood as "law that is international, na-tional and transnational in character all at once",[14] which encompasses the "legal principles developed by national, international and transnational environmental regulatory systems to protect the environment and manage natural resources".[15] Moreover, Morgera suggests that:

> A perspective informed by global environmental law, understood as the promotion of environmental protection through a plurality of le-gal mechanisms relying on a plurality of legal orders, thus prompts the study of environmental law at the international, regional, na-tional and *sub-national* levels as inter-related and mutually influ-encing systems.[16]

Therefore, GEL does not replace "traditional" public international law, in which States – and to some extent international organizations – are the main ac-tors; rather, it comprises, besides legal principles adopted in that context, *also* those principles and laws developed at supra-national (regional and international) levels, and at "sub-national" levels, which includes local governments, or cities. Indeed, a GEL perspective as mentioned above, "calls for an analysis of the prac-tice of non-State actors, particularly […] and *local communities* and the private sector".[17]

According to the abovementioned definition by Yang and Percival, GEL also comprises "law that is transnational in character". The term "transnational" itself

---

[12] E.g. the Global Climate City Challenge, a joint initiative of the European Investment Bank and the Global Covenant of Mayors, representing over 9,000 cities from six continents, to provide technical assistance for fast-track financing of urban climate action projects.

[13] See *infra* Section 3.

[14] YANG and PERCIVAL, "The Emergence of Global Environmental Law", Ecology Law Quarterly, 2009, p. 615 ff. On the concept of Global Environmental Law, see also KOTZÉ, "Rethinking Global Environmental Law and Governance in the Anthropocene", Journal of Energy & Natural Resources Law, 2014, p. 121 ff.; VERSCHUUREN, "Global Environmental Law", in MUSA and DE VOLDER (eds.), *Reflections on Global Law*, Leiden, 2013, p. 90 ff.

[15] *Ibid.*

[16] MORGERA, "Global Environmental Law and Comparative Legal Methods", Review of European, Comparative & International Environmental Law, 2015, p. 254 ff., p. 255 (emphasis added).

[17] *Ibid.* (emphasis added).

is also subject of an ongoing debate. While an early definition provided by Jessup is often cited, according to which transnational law comprises "all law which regulates actions or events that transcend national frontiers",[18] its exact scope and content are still unclear.[19] However, as formulated by Lin: "[t]ransnational law provides an alternative theoretical framework for analyzing how states and non-state actors are involved in making and implementing law that has effect across national boundaries".[20] Applying this to the role of cities, she affirms that "[m]aking a shift from a state-centric view of international law is necessary in order to consider the role of sub-state actors such as cities and their local governments in governing climate change at the global level".[21]

Reflecting on the difference between Transnational Environmental Law (TEL) and GEL, Morgera argues that "while both transnational law and global law serve to illuminate forms of law beyond the State, global law specifically hinges upon […] a global justification, the increasingly functional role of State sovereignty to the protection of the common interest of humanity, including […] the pursuit of global public goods".[22] However, such a "global justification" can, in her view, also be pursued through the development of norms solely by non-State actors, which include – as mentioned above – local communities.

This article does not aim to assess how the various ways in which cities contribute to global climate governance, can be considered to fall within the context of either GEL, or TEL, or both. Nevertheless, both concepts are clearly relevant for the emerging "normative" role of cities, since they precisely aim to encompass the principles and laws developed by other actors than the State. Therefore, these considerations will be kept in mind as a "conceptual lens" which may help to better understand the developing practice discussed in this contribution.

2.3. From Rio to Paris and beyond: what role for cities?

The first international convention that specifically addresses climate change, the UNFCCC, was adopted at the Rio Conference on Environment and Development in 1992. This convention acknowledges that "change in the Earth's climate is a common concern of mankind",[23] and sets out the general objectives, commitments, and guiding principles of a common response to climate change.

In this early stage, the idea of multi-level climate governance with a specific role for sub-national entities had not yet matured, and therefore no reference can

[18] JESSUP, *Transnational Law*, Yale, 1956, p. 136.
[19] See e.g. COTTERELL, "What Is Transnational Law?", Law & Social Inquiry, 2012, p. 500 ff.; CAFAGGI, *Enforcement of Transnational Regulation, Ensuring Compliance in a Global World*, Cheltenham, 2014.
[20] LIN, *Governing Climate Change: Global Cities and Transnational Lawmaking*, Cambridge, 2018, p. 22.
[21] *Ibid.*
[22] MORGERA, *cit. supra* note 16, p. 256. See also WALKER, *Intimations of Global Law*, Cambridge, 2015, pp. 18-24.
[23] UNFCCC, *cit. supra* note 6, Preamble, para. 1.

be found to the involvement of cities in this framework convention. The same is true for the subsequently adopted Kyoto Protocol.[24]

It was only in 2010, with the adoption of the Cancún Agreements, that local and sub-national governments were conferred recognition as "governmental stakeholders" within the UNFCCC regime. Indeed, the Conference of the Parties:

> *Recognizes* the need to engage a broad range of stakeholders at the global, regional, national and *local levels, be they government, including subnational and local government*, private business or civil society, including youth and persons with disability, and that gender equality and the effective participation of women and indigenous peoples are important for effective action on all aspects of climate change [...][25]

The Cancún Agreements do not specify how such engagement should be realized. It should also be noted that these agreements are *decisions* of the Conference of the Parties to the UNFCCC, which were adopted by consensus. Therefore, they constitute "soft law" instruments, which do not impose any legally binding obligations on States. However, the expression of an international consensus on this point is significant in itself, and clearly has an authoritative political weight. Five years later, in 2015, the active role of local entities was reflected in far more explicit terms in the Decision adopted at "COP 21", regarding the adoption of the Paris Agreement. In particular, the Conference of the Parties "[w]elcomes the efforts of all non-Party stakeholders to address and respond to climate change, including those of civil society, the private sector, financial institutions, *cities* and other subnational authorities".[26]

Moreover, it invites the non-Party stakeholders referred to above, "to scale up their efforts and support actions to reduce emissions and/or to build resilience and decrease vulnerability to the adverse effects of climate change".[27] The States Parties also "recognized the need to strengthen knowledge, technologies, practices and efforts of local communities and indigenous peoples related to addressing and responding to climate change [...]".[28] To this end, it was decided to establish "a platform for the exchange of experiences and sharing of best practices on mitigation and adaptation in a holistic and integrated manner".[29]

The inclusion of these statements in a decision that was adopted by the large majority of States is a clear indication of an international consensus on the recognition that cities, among other "non-Party stakeholders", should strengthen their efforts to address and respond to climate change, and to support both mitigation,

---

[24] Kyoto Protocol, *cit. supra* note 7.
[25] Decision 1/CP.16, *cit. supra* note 8, para. 7 (emphasis added).
[26] Decision 1/CP.16, *cit. supra* note 8, para. 133 (emphasis added).
[27] *Ibid.*, para. 134.
[28] *Ibid.*, para. 135.
[29] *Ibid.*

and adaptation actions. It should be noted, however, that in the text of the Paris Agreement itself, the terms "cities" or "non-Party stakeholders" are not mentioned. Nevertheless, the Paris Agreement recognizes, with respect to climate change adaptation, that this is "a global challenge faced by all with *local,* subnational, national, regional and international dimensions".[30] Moreover, Parties acknowledge that

> adaptation action *should* follow a country-driven, gender-responsive, *participatory* and fully transparent approach, taking into consideration vulnerable groups, *communities* and ecosystems, and should be based on and guided by the best available science and, as appropriate, traditional knowledge, knowledge of indigenous peoples and *local knowledge systems*, with a view to integrating adaptation into relevant socioeconomic and environmental policies and actions, where appropriate.[31]

Referring to capacity building, the Paris Agreement states that such efforts "*should* be country-driven, based on and responsive to national needs, and foster country ownership of Parties, in particular, for developing country Parties, including at the national, *subnational* and *local* levels".[32]

The way in which these provisions are formulated, in particular by using the verb "should", indicates that the States Parties did not intend to make a strong, legally binding commitment to ensure an active participation of non-Party stakeholders, including cities, in their national climate action.[33] As mentioned above, the only other statements made in the official outcome documents adopted in the international climate negotiations ("the UNFCCC process") recognizing an active role for cities and other non-Party stakeholders, are included in "soft law" documents.

It can therefore be concluded that there is no international, legally binding obligation of States to actively involve cities, as sub-national governmental entities, in the development and implementation of national climate policies. This is consistent with the traditional, and still prevailing, understanding that international law primarily regulates the behavior of States, and that the regulation of competences and responsibilities of sub-national institutions falls within the ambit of domestic law. However, as evidenced by the evolving concepts of Global Law and Transnational Law mentioned above (Section 2.3), this traditional concept of international law is increasingly challenged, both by international scholars,[34] and by evolving practice.

---

[30] Paris Agreement, *cit. supra* note 9, Art. 7(2) (emphasis added).

[31] *Ibid.*, Art. 7(5).

[32] *Ibid.*, Art. 11(2).

[33] In other provisions of the Paris Agreement, the verb "shall" is used, indicating a stronger degree of commitment, which may amount to a legally binding "obligation". On this point, see further BODANSKI, "The Legal Character of the Paris Agreement", Review of European Community and International Environmental Law, 2016, p. 142 ff.

[34] E.g. NIJMAN, "The Renaissance of the City as Global Actor. The Role of Foreign Policy and International Law Practices in the Construction of Cities as Global Actors", in FAHRMEIR,

3. CITIES' ROLE IN THE DEVELOPMENT AND IMPLEMENTATION OF INTERNATIONAL CLIMATE LAW

3.1. Introduction

Since the early years of the new Millennium, cities have become increasingly active in the global response to climate change. However, as Acuto explains, "[c]ities do not claim to be simply implementers of international climate policy; they have positioned themselves as central participants and stakeholders, in their own right, of the global climate governance effort".[35]

The role of cities has been significantly strengthened by the creation of trans-national city-networks, through which cities around the world not only share best practices and experience on concrete climate actions, but also cooperate to influence national and international policy agendas. In this section, first a brief overview of the main city-networks operating in the field of climate governance is provided (Section 3.2), before addressing the questions how cities contribute to the development of new norms of international climate law (3.3), what role they play in the implementation of existing international norms (3.4), how some cities adopt and implement ambitious climate action (3.5), and what role cities play in emission trading (3.6), and in climate change litigation (3.7).

3.2. City-networks for climate governance

There are several transnational coalitions, or networks, working in the area of climate governance. Through these networks, cities around the world facilitate the diffusion of ideas and technologies, promote solidarity and cooperation, and strengthen their voice in climate-related debates at the national and international levels. Five of these city networks operate at the international level.

3.2.1. City networks at the international level

Firstly, *C40* can today be considered as the most prominent city network that is focusing exclusively on climate change. Created in 2005, it connects 97 mega-cities around the world, representing more than 700 million citizens and 25% of the global economy.[36] "Mayors of the C40 cities are committed to delivering on the most ambitious goals of the Paris Agreement at the local level".[37] It has

---

HELLMANN and VEC (eds.), *The Transformation of Foreign Policy: Drawing and Managing Boundaries*, Oxford, 2016, p. 209 ff.; LIN, *cit. supra* note 20, pp. 8-9; AUST, "Shining Cities on the Hill? The Global City, Climate Change, and International Law", EJIL, 2015, p. 255 ff.

[35] ACUTO, "The New Climate Leaders?", Review of International Studies, 2013, p. 835 ff., p. 835.

[36] See C40's official website, available at: <https://www.c40.org/about>.

[37] *Ibid.*

established partnerships with both public and private parties,[38] and provides support to member cities through sectoral networks, technical assistance, sharing of information and practices, and cooperation.

Secondly, *Local Governments for Sustainability (ICLEI)* is a global network of more than 1,750 local and regional governments. Established in 1990 as the International Council for Local Environmental Initiatives, in 2003 it revised its name and broadened its mandate. ICLEI focuses on promoting the local implementation of the UNFCCC, the UN Convention on Biological Diversity, and the UN Convention to Combat Desertification, and of the UN policies adopted as part of "Agenda 21", including the Habitat Agenda, and the UN Sustainable Development Goals.

The third global network organization promoting urban climate governance is *United Cities and Local Government (UCLG)*. UCLG is committed to representing, defending, and amplifying the voices of local and regional governments in fostering the international agenda on sustainability. Its membership includes over 1,000 cities across 95 countries and 112 Local Government Associations (LGAs).

Fourthly, the *World Mayors Council on Climate Change (WMCCC)* was created in 2005 by the mayor of Tokyo, aiming for an enhanced recognition and involvement of Mayors in multilateral efforts addressing climate change and related issues of global sustainability. While WMCCC has actively promoted the role of local governments on the international climate agenda for several years, it currently concentrates its efforts on supporting other city networks.[39]

Finally, the *Global Covenant of Mayors for Climate and Energy (GCoM)* plays a central part in coordinating local engagement on climate change. GCoM was first launched the European Commission in 2008,[40] with the objective of engaging and supporting mayors to commit to reaching the EU climate and energy targets. In 2016 it joined forces with the US Global Compact of Mayors. With a membership of more than 10,000 local authorities, GCoM is today the largest global city coalition.[41] It provides cities with opportunities to "register, implement, and monitor their strategic action plans and make information on their efforts and results publicly available".[42] C40, ICLEI, UCLG and GCoM all have observer status with the UNFCCC.

3.2.2. City networks at the regional level

Municipal governments also cooperate at the regional level. Within Europe, *Climate Alliance* is the largest city network dedicated to climate action.[43] Created

---

[38] The World Bank, the International Council on Clean Transportation, the Clinton Foundation and the Institute for Transportation and Development.

[39] LIN, *cit. supra* note 20, p. 5.

[40] The original name was *Covenant of Mayors for Climate and Energy*. See <https://www.covenantofmayors.eu/en/>.

[41] Global Covenant of Mayors, "Our Mission", available at: <http/www.globalcovenantofmayors.org/what-is-our-mission/>.

[42] *Ibid.*

[43] Climate Alliance, "About Us", available at: <www.climatealliance.org/about-us.html>.

in 1990, it has over 1,700 members (cities, towns, districts, NGOs, and regional associated members), from 27 European States.[44] From the outset, Climate Alliance has maintained a partnership with indigenous peoples of Amazonia and supporting the protection of the rainforest is one of its stated objectives. It directly engages with EU institutions to support its members in obtaining funding for climate related projects, and also works to influence policymaking at the EU and international levels.[45]

Furthermore, *Energy Cities* is a European network of local authorities focusing on energy transition and sustainable energy. It aims to "transform European governance and legal frameworks to allow cities to fully play their part in the energy transition",[46] and to provide opportunities for its members to connect and share experiences. Also created in 1990, it currently has more than 1,000 members in 30 countries.[47] Moreover, several of the abovementioned global city networks have created regional (sub-)networks. For example, the GCoM has 10 regional sub-divisions,[48] and UCLG has 7 regional sections, including in Africa, Latin America, Asia and the Middle East.[49]

3.3. Cities' role in the development of international climate law

Since the adoption of the UNFCCC in 1992, several initiatives have been taken by mayors and city coalitions to contribute to the policy debate, and to influence its outcome. As already mentioned above,[50] the international normative framework that regulates the global response to climate change, or "international climate law", is composed of legally binding instruments (UNFCCC, Kyoto Protocol), decisions, declarations and other "soft law" instruments, and a "hybrid" instrument, combining both legally binding obligations and voluntary commitments (Paris Agreement). The impact of cities on the development of this normative framework has evolved by pursuing three objectives: (i) to foster local action against climate change, (ii) to formally recognize, engage and empower local governments in international climate action, and (iii) to influence the substance of international climate commitments.

---

[44] Including non-EU countries such as Ukraine, Georgia, Belarus, and Switzerland.

[45] Climate Alliance, "Activities", available at: <https://www.climatealliance.org/activities.html>.

[46] Energy Cities, "Our Mission", available at: <https://energy-cities.eu/vision-mission/>.

[47] Energy cities, "About", available at: < https://energy-cities.eu/members/>. Its membership includes local authorities mostly from European countries, including non-EU Member-States (e.g. Armenia, Georgia, Turkey, Switzerland), but also some non-European countries (Israel, Morocco and New Zealand)

[48] Global Covenant of Mayors, "Our Regions", available at: <https://www.globalcovenantofmayors.org/our-regions/>.

[49] UCGL, "Regional Sections", available at: <https://www.uclg.org/en/organisation/structure/uclg-sections>.

[50] *Supra*, Section 2.4.

3.3.1. Foster local action against climate change

In the first years after the adoption of the UNFCCC, advocacy efforts focused on stimulating local action as part of the global response to climate change. At the request of municipal leaders, the *Local Authorities and Municipal Authorities (LGMA) Constituency* was created, alongside business and NGO groups. Such constituencies cluster and represent non-governmental organizations admitted as observers at sessions of the UNFCCC bodies. Through the LGMA, local authorities were able to take part in the international climate negotiations, from the first meeting of the Conference of the Parties (COP) held in 1995, but only a limited number of cities participated in this process in the initial period.[51] At subsequent COPs, local and sub-national governments adopted several Declarations and Statements in order to mobilize local action for climate protection.[52]

3.3.2. Recognize, engage and empower local governments

From COP13 (Bali, 2007) onwards, local authorities stepped up their efforts to strive for their formal recognition as "non-Party Stakeholders" of the global climate regime, which was achieved with the Cancún Agreements adopted by COP16 in 2010.[53] Local governments also adopted an Agreement[54] and a Roadplan[55] for climate action at the city level. The stated mission of the Roadplan included to "engage" local governments (by involving them in the agenda setting and implementation of the global climate regime through partnerships at all levels), and to "empower" them (by enhancing their access to financial resources for local climate actions).[56] Other city initiatives are the Copenhagen World Catalogue of Local Commitment,[57] and the Mexico City Pact.[58] In the years lead-

---

[51] Cities and Regions in the UNFCCC Process, available at: <https://www.cities-and-regions.org/about-the-lgma/>.

[52] See European Committee of the Regions, "An overview of regions and cities with-in the global climate change process – a perspective for the future", 2017, available at: <https://cor.europa.eu/en/engage/studies/Documents/overview-LRA-global-climate-change-process.pdf>, p. 4.

[53] *Cit. supra* note 8.

[54] World Mayors and Local Governments Climate Protection Agreement, which calls, *inter alia*, for the reduction of greenhouse gas emissions by 60% from 1990 levels worldwide and by 80% from 1990 levels in industrialized countries by 2050.

[55] Local Government Climate Roadmap, launched in 2007 available at: <http://old.iclei.org/climate-roadmap>.

[56] *Ibid.* See also European Committee of the Regions, *cit. supra* note 52, p. 6.

[57] Adopted at COP 14 in Copenhagen (2014), it covers more than 3,000 voluntary targets for cities around the globe.

[58] Available at: <https://unfccc.int/sites/default/files/mxcpact_cccr_final.pdf>. It established a system for voluntary reporting of local GHG inventories, climate actions, commitments and targets.

ing up to the Paris Agreement, cities' "engagement" was further strengthened by the creation of the "Friends of Cities at the UNFCCC".[59]

3.3.3. *Influencing substantive climate commitments and complementarity*

Local governments and city networks have also pushed for the adoption of more ambitious goals, and for ensuring complementarity between national and sub-national policies. For example, in the context of the *Lima-Paris Action Agenda (LPAA)* adopted at COP 20 in 2014,[60] local governments pleaded for an ambitious Climate Regime, which would include local and regional actions.[61] Moreover, in the *Paris City Hall Declaration,* adopted at the Climate Summit for Local Leaders held as a side event of COP 21, close to 1,000 mayors from five continents committed themselves to "advance and *exceed* the expected goals of the 2015 Paris Agreement".[62]

Furthermore, through the LGMA Constituency within the UNFCCC, local governments and city networks successfully lobbied for including the explicit recognition of the role of cities in the global response to climate change in the Decision adopted at COP 21, and in the Paris Agreement itself.[63] Since 2015, several other initiatives have been launched, supporting collaboration between national governments, cities, and other actors, including the 2016 *Marrakech Partnership for Global Climate Action*[64] and the *Race to Zero* campaign.[65]

In recent years, city networks, together with the European Committee of the Regions,[66] strongly argued – at COPs 23 to 25 – in favor of (i) a more explicit *formal* recognition of the role of local and sub-national governments in the UNFCCC process, including in the context of the Rulebook on transparency[67] and (ii) the adoption of Locally and Regionally Determined Contributions (LRDCs) to be in-

---

[59] An informal network of national governments, created in 2013, to engage in dialogues among themselves and with city authorities to explore how local climate action can be strengthened.

[60] At the initiative of Peru, France, the UN Secretary-General and the President of the COP.

[61] See European Committee of the Regions, *cit. supra* note 52, p. 13.

[62] Paris Hall City Declaration, adopted on 4 December 2015, available at: <https://www.uclg.org/sites/default/files/climate_summit_final_declaration.pdf> (emphasis added).

[63] See *supra*, Section 2.2.

[64] Created at COP 22 in Morocco, this partnership supports implementation of the Paris Agreement by enabling collaboration between governments and cities, regions, businesses and investors.

[65] Campaign led by two "High Level Climate Champions" bringing together a coalition of 992 businesses, 449 cities, 21 regions, 505 universities and 38 of the biggest investors, aiming to achieve net zero carbon emissions by 2050 at the latest: see <https://unfccc.int/news/cities-regions-and-businesses-race-to-zero-emissions>.

[66] European Committee of the Regions, "COP25: Cities and regions show unity to boost climate action", 19 December 2019, available at: <https://cor.europa.eu/en/news/Pages/COP25-Cities-and-regions-show-unity-to-boost-climate-action-.aspx>.

[67] This rulebook was adopted at COP24 in Katowice, Poland, with a view to ensure transparency in national implementation of the NDCs.

tegrated into the national climate strategies as set out by each State Party. A new coordinated effort to work towards these goals has been launched in May 2020, in preparation of COP26, to be held in Glasgow in 2021.[68]

3.4. Cities' role in the design and implementation of nationally determined contributions (NDCs)

Another way in which cities play their part in global climate governance is by contributing to the design and implementation of national climate strategies of their own State, as included in their NDCs. These are national climate plans adopted by States Parties to the Paris Agreement, highlighting climate actions, including climate related targets, policies and measures governments aim to implement as their contribution to achieving the agreed goals. Article 4(2) of the Paris Agreement requires that "[e]ach Party shall prepare, communicate and maintain successive nationally determined contributions that it intends to achieve. Parties shall pursue domestic mitigation measures, with the aim of achieving the objectives of such contributions".

Therefore, it is a legally binding obligation for States to "prepare" such national climate plans, to "communicate" them to the competent body within the UNFCCC framework, and to "maintain" such plans, as well as to "pursue" domestic mitigation measures. At the same time, the *content* of the NDCs, their level of ambition in terms of emission reductions, and the measures to achieve the set objectives are voluntary commitments of each State. Nevertheless, States also have an obligation under international law to act with "due diligence" to fulfill their international obligations, including in the field of international environmental law. As argued by Christina Voigt in this regard, the abovementioned Article 4(2), second sentence, of the Paris Agreement "establishes a standard of conduct according to which Parties ought to do as well as they can in designing, implementing and enforcing domestic measures aiming at achieving the objective of their respective NDC".[69]

While the achievement of the NDC's objective itself is not legally binding under international law, in accordance with the standard of due diligence, "Parties are under the obligation to design measures that are necessary, meaningful and, indeed, effective to function as a means to this end".[70] Moreover, when the con-

---

[68] This initiative was launched by the Global Covenant of Mayors for Climate and Energy (GCoM) together with The Global Taskforce of Local and Regional Governments, ICLEI – Local Governments for Sustainability, United Cities and Local Governments (UCLG), UNDP, UN Environment and UN-Habitat. See "GCOM joins effort to integrate regional and local contributions into national", 28 May 2020, <https://www.globalcovenantofmayors.org/press/gcom-joins-effort-to-integrate-regional-and-local-contributions-into-national-governments-cop26-commitments/>.

[69] VOIGT, "The Paris Agreement: What is the standard of conduct for parties?", Questions of International Law, Zoom-in 26, 2016, p. 17 ff., p. 20.

[70] *Ibid.*

tent of a NDC is integrated in a national climate law, it becomes legally binding at the national level, and could be invoked before national courts.

The involvement of local governments in the preparation and implementation of NDCs varies among States. As reported by UN Habitat, "approximately two thirds of all countries have included some urban references in their submitted Nationally Determined Contributions (NDCs), but there remains much still to do".[71] The benefits of integrating the adaptation and mitigation efforts pursued by cities and other sub-national governments into the national climate strategies, or to ensure full complementarity between such efforts undertaken at all levels, have been stressed both by cities themselves,[72] and by international organizations.[73]

In this context, it has also been acknowledged that cities can play an important role in ensuring an integrated approach towards implementation of NDCs on the one hand, and the UN Sustainable Development Goals (SDGs) adopted as part of the UN 2030 Agenda for Sustainable Development [74] on the other.[75] The 2030 Agenda comprises 17 SDGs and 169 associated targets that are applicable to all countries. These goals and targets address and incorporate all three dimensions of sustainable development (the environment, economics, and society) and their linkages.[76] Considering the interrelationships between sustainable development on the one hand, and climate action included in NDCs on the other, an integrated approach in policy planning is increasingly recognized and promoted, including through development cooperation programmes, both at national and local government levels.[77] Such an integrated approach is also promoted with regard to the Sendai Framework on Disaster Reduction[78], and the Making Cities Resilient (MCR2030) initiative adopted in that context.[79]

As foreseen in the Paris Agreement, States should adopt "progressive" NDCs, every five years.[80] All Parties are requested to submit the next round of new or

---

[71] UN Habitat, "Enhancing Nationally Determined Contribution Through Urban Climate Action. A guide for incorporating urban climate action and human settlement issues into the Nationally Determined Contributions enhancement process", 2020, available at: <https://unhabitat.org/sites/default/files/2020/06/ndc_guide_19062020.pdf>.

[72] *Ibid.*

[73] UNDP, UNEP, UNEP DTU and WRI, "Implementing Nationally Determined Contributions (NDCs)", UNEP DTU Partnership Copenhagen, Denmark, 2020, p. 21; OECD, "An Integrated Approach to the Paris Climate Agreement. The Role of Cities and Regions", available at: <https://www.oecd.org/cfe/Implementing-Paris-KeyMessages.pdf>; UN Habitat, *cit. supra* note 71.

[74] UNGA Resolution, "Transforming our world: the 2030 Agenda for Sustainable Development", UN Doc. A/RES/70/1 (2015).

[75] The role of cities with regard to Sustainable Development is the subject of the contribution by PAVONI to this Symposium. On the interlinkages between implementing NDCs and SDGs including the role of cities in this respect, see UNDP et al., *cit. supra* note 73, pp. 15-25.

[76] *Ibid.*, p. 18.

[77] *Ibid.*, pp. 20-21; UN Habitat, *cit. supra* note 71.

[78] Sendai Framework for Disaster Reduction, adopted at the Third UN World Conference in Sendai, Japan, on 18 March 2015.

[79] Available at: <https://mcr2030.undrr.org>.

[80] Paris Agreement, *cit. supra* note 9, Arts. 4(3) and 4(9).

updated NDCs by 2020 and every five years thereafter, regardless of their respective implementation time frames.[81] To date, 16 States have submitted a new or updated NDC, while 129 States have stated their intention to enhance ambition or action in a new or updated NDC.[82] The submission of these new NDCs constitutes an opportunity for States to better integrate urban climate action in the national climate strategies.

The United Nations Human Settlements Programme (UN Habitat) published detailed guidance for States on how to realize such integration through a "vertically integrated approach",[83] and by ensuring multilevel stakeholder participation both in the preparation and implementation phases of the NDC. UN Habitat highlights, on the one hand, the urgency for national governments "to include more ambitious urban content in their NDCs through a structured dialogue with local and regional governments and other local stakeholders". At the same time, "it is urgent that local governments recognize the national commitment made through NDCs and align their local investments and actions towards these shared national goals".[84]

3.5. Cities' climate action going beyond or against national climate policies

Even though extreme weather events have been affecting many countries, especially in the Global South for decades, the increasing occurrence of devastating hurricanes in the Global North, also directly affecting megacities such as New Orleans and New York, has contributed to a growing sense of urgency among citizens and local governments to explore alternative, or additional responses. While many examples of "success stories" in this regard concern cities in the Global North, innovative data collection through mechanisms such as the Carbon Disclosure Project (CDP)[85] and the databases of several city networks,[86] show that such far-reaching initiatives are also increasingly taken by cities in the Global South.

---

[81] UNFCCC, "Nationally Determined Contributions (NDCs)", available at: <https://unfccc.int/process-and-meetings/the-paris-agreement/the-paris-agreement/nationally-determined-contributions-ndcs>.

[82] Climate Watch, "2020 NDC Tracker", available at: <https://www.climatewatchdata.org/2020-ndc-tracker>.

[83] UN Habitat, cit. supra note 71, p. 17.

[84] Ibid., p. 18.

[85] CDP is an international non-profit organization based in the UK, Germany and the US that helps companies, investors, cities, regions and states to disclose their environmental impacts, and which serves as a global reference point for data collection on environmental and climate policies adopted by these different actors. More information is available at: <https://www.cdp.net/en/info/about-us>.

[86] E.g. the C40 resource center, on which see <https://resourcecentre.c40.org>, or the data collected by the Global Covenant of Mayors available at: <https://www.globalcovenantofmayors.org/our-cities/>.

3.5.1. *Ambitious city-level climate action in the Global North*

Copenhagen is probably the most cited example of a city that has embarked on a highly ambitious climate action plan, aiming to become the world's first carbon-neutral city by 2025. The *CPH 2025 Climate Plan* was adopted by the City Council already in 2012, well before the Paris Agreement. Aiming to combine growth with development and increasing the quality of life for citizens while simultaneously reducing GHG emissions, Copenhagen has already achieved a 38% reduction in annual CO_2 emissions compared to 2005 levels. Most savings were achieved through increasing the share of green energy from biomass used in the city's combined heat and power plants and wind energy.[87] Copenhagen's ambitions clearly exceed the goals of the Danish government, which aims to achieve a 100% conversion to renewable energies by 2050.[88]

New York City is another "success story" in terms of city-level engagement to address climate change. One day after President Trump announced his intention to withdraw from the Paris Agreement in June 2017, Mayor de Blasio signed an Executive Order affirming New York City's commitment to reach 80% carbon neutrality by 2050.[89] Many other cities in the US are also implementing ambitious climate plans. According to the Biden Climate Plan, the current Administration will aim, as part of a renewed active global stance on climate change, to "provide every American city with 100,000 or more residents with high-quality, zero-emissions public transportation options through flexible federal investments with strong labor protections".[90]

In the United Kingdom, Manchester and London both pursue significant local climate strategies. Manchester has committed to reducing its CO_2 emissions by at least 50% during 2020-2025 down to zero by 2038 at the very latest, while striving for a city that is "progressive and equitable, thriving and sustainable, livable and low carbon, high skilled, and connected".[91] Moreover, the Mayor of London's new Environment Strategy sets out how the UK capital will transition to a zero carbon future and, together with the Mayor's Transport Strategy, sets the target for a zero emission transport network by 2050.[92] As outlined in the latter plan, "London's carbon budgets are more ambitious than the national governments".[93] Finally, in Italy, two cities were included in the 2020 Carbon

---

[87] C40, "Cities leading the way: Seven climate action plans to deliver on the Paris Agreement", available at: <https://assets.locomotive.works/sites/5ab410c8a2f42204838f797e/content_entry5ab410fb74c4833febe6c81a/5b97d05514ad66062f99bd66/files/C40_Report_Cities_leading_the_way.pdf>, p. 8.

[88] *Ibid.*

[89] *Ibid.*, p. 12.

[90] "The Biden Plan to Build a Modern, Sustainable Infrastructure and an Equitable Clean Energy Future", available at: <https://joebiden.com/clean-energy/>.

[91] Manchester Climate Change Agency, "About", available at: <https://www.manchester-climate.com>.

[92] C40, *cit. supra* note 87, p. 10. These strategies were both adopted in 2018.

[93] Mayor of London, "Zero Carbon London: A 1,5 C Compatible Plan", available at: <https://www.london.gov.uk/sites/default/files/1.5_action_plan_amended.pdf>, p. 11.

Disclosure Project's "A list" of 88 cities that are demonstrating major progress in the fight against climate change since the adoption of the Paris Agreement and in transparent reporting on their climate policies: Turin and Florence.[94]

3.5.2. *Ambitious city-level climate governance in the Global South*

Cities in the Global South are also stepping up their climate actions. In the African region, Ethiopia's capital Addis Ababa is using low-carbon building designs in a comprehensive construction programme that is moving a large population from unplanned "shanty towns" into more formal living arrangements.[95] Moreover, Cape Town has been included in the abovementioned Carbon Disclosure Project's (CDP) Cities A List of best performing global cities. Cape Town's new Climate Change Strategy and Action Plan, recognises climate change as a key risk to the economy, society and environment, but also as an opportunity through the transformation to a green economy and in seeking new ways to deliver essential services in a more inclusive, cost-effective and sustainable manner.[96]

In Latin-America, several major cities were listed by the CDP as best performers, including Buenos Aires, Mexico City, Rio de Janeiro and Recife. Mexico City was also awarded the title of Global Winner in WWF's 2019-2020 One Planet City Challenge (OPCC), by impressing the jury with "its strong leadership and ambitious plans to align the city with the 1.5°C target of Paris Agreement on climate change".[97]

Finally, among the "best practices" reported by the Asian regional division of the global Covenant of Mayors is the Malaysian capital Kuala Lumpur.[98] This city "aims to reduce the City's carbon emissions intensity of GDP by 70% by 2030, (based on the 2010 level) without compromising its vision and economic growth targets".[99] The city's Low Carbon Society Blueprint 2030 is being implemented together with "a comprehensive city-wide awareness and outreach

---

[94] "Ecco perché Torino e Firenze sono le città italiane leader nella lotta ai cambiamenti climatici", La Repubblica, 17 November 2020, available at: <https://www.repubblica.it/green-and-blue/2020/11/17/news/torino_e_firenze_le_citta_italiane_leader_nella_lotta_ai_cambiamenti_climatici-274732994/>.

[95] C40, "The Power of C40 Cities", available at: <https://www.c40.org/cities>.

[96] Democratic alliance (DA), "City receives an A for climate reporting and action", 16 November 2020, available at: <https://www.da.org.za/government/undefined/2020/11/city-receives-an-a-for-climate-reporting-and-action>. See also CDP, citing the City's Executive Mayor, Alderman Dan Plato: "Cities A-List 2020", available at: <https://www.cdp.net/en/cities/cities-scores>.

[97] World Wildlife Fund, "Mexico City stands out in WWF's One Planet City Challenge 2020", 17 August 2020, available at: <https://wwf.panda.org/?574351/Mexico-City-One-Planet-City-Challenge>.

[98] Global Covenant of Mayors for Climate and Energy – Asia, "Best Practices", 2019, available at: <https://www.asian-mayors.eu/portfolio/example-3-4-2/>.

[99] *Ibid.*

programme".[100] Other Asian cities that have been recognized by CDP as "high-performers" in their climate programmes include Hong Kong, Seoul, and several urban communities in Taiwan.[101]

These examples show that ambitious climate targets are being set and pursued by local governments around the world. All the cities mentioned above participate in one or more city networks, which provide them with opportunities for exchange of information, technologies and best practices, as well as for enhancing transparency through common reporting mechanisms.[102]

3.6. Cities' role in emission trading

Countries and regions around the world are developing emissions trading systems, or "carbon markets", as a means to place a price on greenhouse gas (GHG) emissions. Emission trading aims to contribute to economic efficiency by facilitating emission reductions where it is cheapest to achieve them. "Polluters who would find it costly to reduce their emission are allowed to buy emission allowances from polluters that can abate at lower costs".[103] While emission trading mechanisms have also been established under the Kyoto Protocol, the world's largest carbon market is the European Emissions Trading scheme (EU-ETS), covering sectors that emit over 2 billion tonnes of $CO2$ each year. Other significant examples include Korea's ETS (half a billion tonnes of $CO2$ per year) and the programme linking the emission trading schemes of California and Quebec, covers sectors emitting nearly half a billion tonnes.[104]

In Asia, several cities are implementing "local" emission trading schemes. The Tokyo Metropolitan Government Emissions Trading System (TMG ETS) was established in 2010. It is the world's first urban Cap-and-Trade Program requiring $CO2$ reductions from large commercial and industrial buildings. In terms of its effectiveness, emission data for FY2018 indicate that "on aggregate covered entities had decreased emissions by 27% below the baseline year, overachieving the 15-17% target set for the second compliance period (FY2015-FY2019)".[105]

Moreover, in China, in 2011, the National Development and Reform Commission announced a plan to develop seven official ETS pilot programs in five cities (Beijing, Shanghai, Tianjin, Chongqing and Shenzhen) and two prov-

---

[100] *Ibid.*

[101] CDP, "Cities A List 2020", available at: <https://www.cdp.net/en/cities/cities-scores>.

[102] These databases complement reporting mechanisms created at the intergovernmental level, including the global portal "Non-State Actor Zone for Climate Action (NAZCA)" set up by UN Climate.

[103] OECD, "Emission Trading Systems", available at: <https://www.oecd.org/environment/tools-evaluation/emissiontradingsystems.htm>.

[104] Climate Policy Info Hub, "The Global Rise of Emissions Trading", available at: <https://climatepolicyinfohub.eu/global-rise-emissions-trading>.

[105] International Carbon Action Partnership, "ETS Detailed Information, Japan – Tokyo Cap-and-Trade Program", available at: <https://icapcarbonaction.com/en/?option=com_etsmap&task=export&format=pdf&layout=list&systems%5B%5D=51>.

inces (Guangdong and Hubei). In 2015 all programs had entered into force, and the significant Chinese national ETS, which entered into force on 1 February 2021 and is expected to become the world's largest emission trading scheme, was informed by the experiences of these city pilot programmes.[106]

While such programs developed at the national level probably offer more "possibility of scale", well-coordinated local emission trading systems may complement State-wide efforts focusing on specific urban sectors.[107]

3.7.   Cities' role in climate change litigation

Another way for cities to influence the global response to climate change, is through climate change litigation, often also referred to as "climate litigation". Starting in the late 1980s in the US, climate litigation has increasingly been used as a way of either advancing or delaying effective action on climate change.[108] Especially since the adoption of the Paris Agreement, the number of cases brought before domestic courts – and gradually also before regional and international jurisdictions – addressing the causes and consequences of climate change has grown significantly.[109] As argued by Setzer and Byrnes, the number of climate-change related cases, and the public interest in such litigation, "ha[ve] now grown to a point where litigation is considered by many as a governance mechanism for addressing climate change".[110] While defendants in domestic climate cases have traditionally been governments, litigation is increasingly being brought against commercial operators, companies or corporations. In recent years, cities and other sub-national governments have acted as plaintiffs in several cases against major energy companies, mostly in the US, but some first cases have also been brought in other States, including France.

---

[106] Climate Policy Info Hub, "The Global Rise of Emissions Trading", available at: <https://climatepolicyinfohub.eu/global-rise-emissions-trading>; Climate Home News, "China launches world's largest carbon market for power sector" available at: < https://www.climatechange-news.com/2021/01/07/china-launches-worlds-largest-carbon-market-power-sector/>.

[107] See CLAPP et al., "Cities and Carbon Market Finance: Taking Stock of Cities' Experience with Clean Development Mechanism (CDM) and Joint Implementation (JI)", OECD and CDC Climate Research, Executive Summary, available at: <https://www.oecd.org/env/cc/46561684.pdf>, p. 8.

[108] For a comprehensive discussion on recent trends in such litigation before domestic courts in 11 countries, and of the potentialities and constraints of bringing climate change-related cases before regional and international jurisdictions, see ALOGNA, BAKKER and GAUCI, *Climate Change Litigation: Global Perspectives*, Leiden, 2021.

[109] SETZER and BYRNES, "Global trends in climate change litigation: 2020 snapshot", available at: <https://www.lse.ac.uk/granthaminstitute/wp-content/uploads/2020/07/Global-trends-in-climate-change-litigation_2020-snapshot.pdf>: "In total 1,587 cases of climate litigation have been identified as being brought between 1986 and the end of May 2020: 1,213 cases in the United States and 374 cases in 36 other countries and eight regional or international jurisdictions".

[110] *Ibid.*

In the US, since 2017 several suits were brought against companies such as Exxon Mobil, Chevron, BP, Shell and Conoco Phillips by several counties, cities, and the State of Rhode Island, seeking money damages.[111] Most of the governmental plaintiffs are situated along the Atlantic or Pacific oceans, and their cases claim that they will need to undertake major expenditures to protect against sea level rise and coastal storms. They all are based on public nuisance theories.[112] Procedural questions of standing and jurisdiction may be the biggest obstacles for these cases. "One such question – whether state or federal court is the proper forum – in a lawsuit filed by the City of Baltimore[113] has reached the US Supreme Court and will be argued in the coming term".[114]

In France, in the case *Notre Affaire à Tous and Others v. Total*, an alliance of 14 French local governments and 5 NGOs launched a complaint against energy company Total in January 2020. "The complaint is based on the 2017 French Law of Vigilance, which requires a company to produce a 'plan of vigilance' that identifies and seeks to mitigate risks to human rights, fundamental freedoms, the environment, and public health that could result directly or indirectly from the operations of the company and of the companies it controls".[115] The plaintiffs "are asking the Nanterre court to order Total, which is at the origin of around 1% of the world's greenhouse gas emissions, to recognize the risks generated by its activities and to align itself on a trajectory compatible with limiting global warming to 1.5°C".[116]

These examples demonstrate how cities have started to use available legal options to claim compensation for damages suffered as a consequence of continuous high levels of carbon emissions. By requesting courts to order major emitters to pay damages, and/or to adjust their activities based on national laws and climate science, local governments contribute to clarifying the applicable legal norms. These cases will shed light on the interpretation of legal concepts such as causality, nuisance, or due diligence in the context of climate change. Despite the differences among national legal systems, domestic courts may nevertheless refer to judgments in other jurisdictions that have dealt with similar interpretative

---

[111] E.g. *City of New York v. BP plc*, 325 F Supp 3d 466 (SDNY 2018); *City of Oakland v. BP plc*, 325 F Supp 3d 1017 (ND Cal 2018). These were both dismissed, one was reinstated on appeal, *City of Oakland v. BP plc*, 2020 WL 2702680 (9th Cir 2020), the appeal in the other case is pending. See GERRARD, "Climate Litigation in the United States: High Volume of Cases, Mostly about Statutes", in ALOGNA, BAKKER and GAUCI (eds.), *cit. supra* note 108.

[112] *Ibid.*: "Some of these cases also have claims arising under the common law theories of trespass, product defect, negligence, and failure to warm".

[113] *Mayor and City Council of Baltimore v. B.P.*, on which see <http://climatecasechart.com/case/mayor-city-council-of-baltimore-v-bp-plc/>.

[114] BRUCE, "Analysis: Climate Change Litigation Plaintiffs Have Struck Oil", Bloomberg Law Analysis, 16 November 2020, available at: <https://news.bloomberglaw.com/bloomberg-law-analysis/analysis-climate-change-litigation-plaintiffs-have-struck-oil>.

[115] SETZER and BYRNES, *cit. supra* note 109, p. 22.

[116] Sherpa, "First climate change litigation against TOTAL in France: 14 local authorities and 5 NGOs take Total to court", available at: <https://www.asso-sherpa.org/first-climate-change-litigation-against-total-in-france-14-local-authorities-and-5-ngos-take-total-to-court>.

questions. In this sense, cities' engagement in climate litigation could be seen as another way in which they can act as "normative global climate actors".

Finally, there have been some significant recent developments at the EU level with respect to the role of cities in the implementation and enforcement of environmental legislation, including in relation to the measurement of GHG emissions. In 2016, the cities of Madrid, Brussels and Paris brought actions before the EU General Court,[117] asking for the annulment of Regulation No. 646/2016, concerning emissions from light passenger and commercial vehicles (Euro 6). While the cities submitted that the Commission adopted less-demanding values than those set by the applicable Euro 6 standard and that it did not have the power to do so, the Commission challenged the admissibility of the cities' actions.[118] In December 2018, the General Court declared the case admissible on two grounds: firstly, "the applicants' legal situation is affected by the contested regulation and [...] that regulation is therefore of direct concern to them, within the meaning of the fourth paragraph of Article 263 TFEU".[119] Secondly, the Court considered that "the contested regulation is a regulatory act which does not entail implementing measures, within the meaning of that same provision [...]".[120] On the substance of the claim, the General Court concluded for a partial annulment of Regulation No. 646/2016. The Commission, together with Germany and Hungary, has appealed to the Court of Justice.[121] While the outcome of this appeal needs to be awaited, the possibility for cities, in terms of legal standing, to bring an action for annulment before the General Court, clearly confirms their role as actors on the international scene.[122]

4. POTENTIALITIES AND CONSTRAINTS FOR CITIES AS NORMATIVE GLOBAL CLIMATE ACTORS

Since the effects of climate change directly and disproportionally affect populations in urban environments,[123] cities necessarily play a leading role in climate

---

[117] EU General Court, Joined Cases T-339/16, T-352/16 and T-391/16, *Ville de Paris, Ville de Bruxelles and Ayuntamiento de Madrid v. Commission*, 13 December 2018.

[118] See TATÌ, "Cities' Legal Actions in the EU: Towards a Stronger Urban Power?", European Papers, 2019, p. 861 ff., p. 861, available at: <https://www.europeanpapers.eu/en/system/files/pdf_version/EP_EF_2020_I_007_Elisabetta_Tati_00334.pdf>.

[119] *Ville de Paris*, cit. *supra* note 117, para. 84. Art. 263(4) TFEU provides: "Any natural or legal person may, under the conditions laid down in the first and second paragraphs, institute proceedings against an act addressed to that person or which is of direct and individual concern to them, and against a regulatory act which is of direct concern to them and does not entail implementing measures".

[120] *Ibid.*

[121] Pending cases C- 177/19 P, C-178/19 P, C-178/19 P, C-179/19 P.

[122] However, in another case concerning the renewed authorization of glyphosate by the Commission, legal standing of the city of Brussels was denied both by the General Court and on appeal by the CJEU: Case T-178/18 C-352/19 P, *Région de Bruxelles-Capitale v. Commission*, 3 December 2020.

[123] C40, *cit. supra* note 1.

action at the local level. Moreover, considering the need to coordinate such climate policies and actions adopted at local, national and international levels, the participation of cities in the decision-making at the global level seems to be warranted, and is progressively – albeit still rather cautiously – recognized by States. As practice shows, there are clear opportunities for cities to further develop their role in this regard. However, several factors also hamper such aspirations, or constitute limits to their realization.

4.1. Potentialities for cities as normative global climate actors

As Craig Johnson suggested, "[i]n a context of hyper-globalization that has involved some truly revolutionary changes in communication, economic organization and human mobility, cities have acquired new forms of wealth, influence and power by developing, innovating and adopting new modes of production, consumption and exchange".[124]

Indeed, the possibilities for cities to influence the normative framework for climate action at the global level are directly related to a number of external factors, of which globalization is probably the most far-reaching. Global access to, and distribution of innovative technologies in, inter alia, the energy, transport and construction sectors greatly supports local (and national) governments' climate adaptation and mitigation efforts. Moreover, the continuous development of digital communication technologies facilitates contacts, exchange of information and transnational networking between cities.

Other external factors "that influence the position of the city within the international society of today"[125] are urbanization and decentralization. With the rapid exponential growth of cities across the world as a result of continuing migration from rural to urban areas and population growth, the governance of cities has become increasingly complex. In the context of a broader tendency within the international community, since the 1980s, to progressively provide public services at the sub-national and local levels, and to strive for more direct forms of participatory democracy, cities have actively advocated for decentralization themselves too.[126]

Facilitated – and urged – by these external factors and societal trends, urban governments have created their own opportunities for inter-city cooperation through the urban city networks as discussed above.[127] By making use of the setbacks and slow progress in the international climate negotiations at the inter-State level, the number of city networks itself, but also their membership has increased significantly in recent years. The transnational city networks not only provide a de facto opportunity for cities to influence international decision-

---

[124] JOHNSON, The Power of Cities in Global Climate Policies: Saviours, Supplicants or Agents of Change?, London, 2018, p. 152.

[125] NIJMAN, cit. supra note 34, p. 211.

[126] Ibid., pp. 218-219.

[127] Supra, Section 3.

making, and therefore the development of new international norms in the field of climate change, they explicitly consider this as one of their central functions.

Another factor that favors the further development of cities' role as normative global climate actors is the progressive recognition of the need to actively involve local and other sub-national governments in the planning and implementation of climate action, as confirmed in several COP decisions and the Paris Agreement.[128] Moreover, through the development and implementation of local emission trading schemes, cities such as Tokyo and five Chinese cities directly contribute to the achievement of the global goals of emission reductions.

Finally, the engagement of cities in climate change litigation contributes to the further clarification of legal concepts such as causality, nuisance, and due diligence in the context of climate change. In this context, the recognition of legal standing of cities before the EU General Court and the CJEU confirms the role of local governments in the enforcement of EU climate regulations.

4.2. *Constraints for cities as normative global climate actors*

Despite the factors favoring cities' normative role in the global "climate arena", various constraints may limit such a development.

Firstly, there are some *legal limitations*, both at the international, and at the domestic level. In the international legal system, the only entities that have a competence to conclude international treaties are States, and under certain conditions, international organizations. Despite the progressive recognition that non-State actors, including individuals, NGOs and corporations can have rights and obligations under international law, when it comes to the adoption of new legal norms, cities and other sub-national entities cannot be Parties to such agreements themselves. Moreover, at the domestic level, the competences of local governments are regulated in the national constitution and administrative law, and powers in the fields of foreign policy and international relations are typically concentrated at the State and/or Federal level. These constraints virtually exclude the adoption of a *formal* role of cities in the international law-making process, including in the area of international climate law. Indeed, cities' "ability to engage in multilateral processes (e.g. NAZCA) remains constrained by a Westphalian model of international order".[129] However, as practice shows, cities can nevertheless participate in this process as observers through the existing city networks and the LMGA Constituency within the UNFCCC, and such participation has resulted in the decisions as discussed above.[130]

Secondly, cities' ambition to influence the development of international climate law is also hampered by *political factors*. States are still reluctant to limit their own prerogatives in favor of sub-national entities. This is illustrated by the lack of consensus on the proposal to adopt Locally and Regionally Determined

---

[128] *Supra*, Section 2.
[129] JOHNSON, *cit. supra*, note 124, p. 148.
[130] *Ibid.*

Contributions to complement the NDCs. In practice, such reluctance may also be influenced by political differences between national governments and locally elected city administrations. With the increasing size and complexities of mega-cities, tensions may arise between "powerful Mayors" and central government representatives.

A third type of constraints is of a *factual nature,* such as those related to differences between cities in terms of their resources, and their capacities to participate in any efforts to influence international climate related decisions. Although it is precisely one of the aims of city networks to enable all cities to benefit from the cooperation and exchanges with others, smaller cities, especially in developing countries, not always have the financial means or human resources to participate even in the networks themselves.

Finally, difficulties may arise in relation to the *city networks as such.* For example, tensions can arise among stakeholders within a city as a consequence of participation in a city network. As noted by Chu, cities "must negotiate between emerging best practices and expectations from such networks with the contentious and local politics of urban climate change governance".[131]

5. CONCLUDING REMARKS

As the analysis in this contribution have shown, cities are progressively claiming a role as normative global climate actors, both by actively engaging with the international climate negotiations, in particular through a number of transnational city networks, and by developing and implementing climate laws and policies at the domestic level. But are cities actually "taking centre-stage" in the international climate negotiations, and are they becoming "normative global climate actors"?

Over the years, the coordinated efforts by local governments have resulted in an explicit recognition that cities, as "non-Party Stakeholders", should be involved in national climate action. However, to date, such recognition does not go as far as a legally binding obligation of States to include local and regional governments at all stages of the formulation and implementation of national climate programmes. Neither have States accepted the proposal to establish Locally and Regionally Determined Contributions (LRDCs), to complement the five-yearly NDCs, outlining each State's climate commitments to achieve the objectives of the Paris Agreement.

At the same time, the increasing number of cities that participate in transnational city networks such as the Global Covenant of Mayors, ICLEI and C40, and the continuously strengthened cooperation among these city networks themselves to take concerted policy stances at the international level, can no longer be ignored. External factors such as globalization, urbanization and decentralization, clearly favor a progressively independent role for cities in international

---

[131] CHU et al., *cit. supra* note 11, p. 364.

decision-making. On the other hand, legal and political constraints, as well as various "conflicts of interests" limit the scope for cities to exercise such a normative influence at the global level.

There is little doubt that States are reluctant to compromise their traditional role as the primary subjects of international law, by allowing sub-state entities to formally participate in the exercise of powers that are within their exclusive domain, such as diplomacy and the conclusion of international treaties and agreements. However, in a changing global context, and faced with unprecedented global threats such as climate change, a pragmatic, multi-level and multi-actor approach is the only reasonable pathway. Despite the slow, and still insufficiently ambitious global response to the scientifically proven threats caused by climate change, a certain recognition of the need for an "alternative approach" can be discerned. By opting for "hybrid" international agreements such as the Paris Agreement – combining legally binding commitments with voluntary national pledges – and by including "controversial" compromises rather in "soft law" instruments such as COP Decisions, States have adopted a certain pragmatism in the development of international climate law. A global response to climate change not only requires innovation in terms of renewable energy sources, transportation, and low-carbon construction; it also requires innovative approaches to the international legal order itself. In this regard, the evolving concepts of Global Environmental Law and Transnational Environmental Law, which encompass legal principles adopted at national, supra-national and sub-national levels, and recognize the role of non-State actors in the development of both legally binding and non-binding rules, could provide some guidance for future developments.

Cities will not be offered to play a *lead role* in the international climate arena in the foreseeable future, but if thousands of cities continue to coordinate their acts, their *supporting role* may be equally crucial for a successful performance.

IN THE FACE OF FINANCIALIZATION:
CITIES AND THE HUMAN RIGHT TO ADEQUATE HOUSING

Kaara Martinez[*]

Abstract

The right to housing is a human right with broad but frequently overlooked implications, particularly in the urban environment. This difficulty is heightened in the context of what is known as the "financialization of housing". Financialization involves the interconnections between global financial markets and housing, and, at the extreme, has prompted a climate in which housing is conceived less as a social good and more as a commodity. The result of the financialization turn is cities with a severe lack of affordable housing, a reality that is now a global phenomenon. This naturally leads to economic exclusions and displacements from cities, but, on a deeper level, also entails major collective consequences for the social and cultural fabric. Financialization thus threatens the right to housing in cities, particularly when the right is examined and understood in its full sense. And yet, cities have a duty to ensure the right to housing even in the face of financialization. Drawing on the jurisprudence of the Committee on Economic, Social and Cultural Rights through its individual communications procedure, the European Court of Human Rights, and domestic cases from South Africa and the United States, this paper aims to elucidate this duty of cities in the realm of housing. A substantive rather than purely procedural shape of protection for the right to housing is pushed, which deliberates the connections between housing and the wider societal context, and the implicated concerns of resources, property, and urban community. In present times, our appreciation of home as a necessary nexus of safety, comfort, and productivity has come to the fore, as have our fears around economic insecurity, forcing us to confront and closely interrogate the right to housing.

Keywords: human rights; cities; financialization of housing; community; property.

1. Introduction

One of the most pervasive challenges to the implementation of the right to housing in the twenty-first century is affordability. Through a variety of ultimately connected mechanisms, severe housing unaffordability is a marker of modern

[*] Legal Consultant, World Bank Administrative Tribunal. The views expressed in this paper are those of the author and should not be attributed to the institution for which she works. Kind thanks to Professor Francesco Francioni for the invitation to contribute to this Volume and for comments on an earlier draft of this paper.

habitation and a pronounced global phenomenon.[1] The privatization of housing services, land speculation, and commodification all contribute to the affordability crisis. Added to this, the shifting role of the State with respect to housing, away from a social good conceptualization and towards "financialization", has served to undermine the human right to housing. Increasingly, even moderate-income individuals are unable to afford urban housing and, by extension, access to urban life. In many instances, they are economically displaced from the city. Predictable gentrification patterns have developed, attacking even the middle class, with proximate social and cultural relational implications. And, homelessness has reached shocking levels in major cities. These once subtle and gradual realities of economic development in the city are now increasingly obtrusive. Worse, the affordability crisis in urban centers intersects with the discriminatory potential of housing, which has long been a recurrent policy theme particularly pertaining to women, racial and ethnic minorities, and indigenous peoples, offering up increasingly stratified and exclusionary cities.[2]

Financialization to the extreme has noticeably affected the availability and affordability of urban housing, with individual and collective losses. A controversial context proliferates in many cities where foreign investors buy and hold property as a source of wealth rather than as a place to live.[3] This environment has been supported by governments which seek to attract wealthy investors and capital through methods such as tax reductions and "golden visas".[4] The reality of this pressure – cities in which a vast portion of residential property is foreign-owned and often unoccupied, and where many struggle to afford an urban home – is at once a pedestrian and provocative form of the tensions around the need for housing in cities, the inability of individuals to fulfill that need, and the failure of the State to act to ensure the right to housing.[5] Many other manifestations of

---

[1] See UN Habitat, "Addressing the Housing Affordability Challenge: A Shared Responsibility", 31 October 2020, available at: <https://unhabitat.org/addressing-the-housing-affordability-challenge-a-shared-responsibility>.

[2] ROLNIK, "The right to adequate housing", UN Doc. A/67/286 (2012), para. 12 ("As real estate prices and rents increased and came to be financed through global instead of local financial surpluses, more households faced difficulties in accessing adequate housing in the market. Many observers have pointed to the negative impacts of housing asset dispersion on social stratification and inequality, and the uneven spatial impact of these processes within cities, regions and globally").

[3] See FARHA, Report of the Special Rapporteur on adequate housing as a component of the right to an adequate standard of living, and on the right to non-discrimination in this context, UN Doc. A/HRC/34/51 (2017), para. 15. See also SASSEN, "The Global City: Enabling Economic Intermediation and Bearing Its Costs", City & Community, 2016, p. 97 ff., pp. 104-105 ("What is different about the current phase is the scale of these investments, the vast globalizing of the destinations of these investments, and the frequent underutilization of the properties").

[4] Foreign investors can receive permanent residence or citizenship for investing a certain amount in property. FARHA, *cit. supra* note 3, paras. 23 and 25.

[5] This issue has been contested in many cities, including London. In the 2019 UK general election, for instance, the specific question of foreign investment in housing was a debated issue with Labour announcing a plan to increase taxes on foreign companies and trusts buying UK properties.

financialization can also be observed. And, these observations do not reside at the fringes of international legal discourse on rights-based market critiques. Even major human rights textbooks now discuss the right to housing in the context of the affordability crisis attributed to privatization and financialization,[6] and housing unaffordability and insecurity in cities has become a familiar topic of daily news and conversation.

This reality is only magnified and further complicated by the ongoing COVID-19 pandemic, and related economic uncertainty.[7] Most obviously, the pandemic has made the need for a home as shelter urgent.[8] Also clear, the economic impacts of the attendant unemployment crisis have made rent and mortgage payments difficult for a great many. And yet, in important respects, the pandemic has also shown the possibilities for protecting the right to housing in cities and, more pointedly, that the necessary political will to ensure the right can emerge. Governments have been creative in finding ways to temporarily protect persons living in homelessness utilizing hostels and hotel rooms, and there have been moratoria on evictions as well as other protections such as rent caps and mortgage deferrals.[9] These measures should be considered as part of a systematic and sustainable approach to pandemic recovery and rebuilding and to ensuring the right to housing, rather than simply serving to postpone the COVID-19 impact.[10] Indeed, home has proven key to the coronavirus response, and the pandemic has powerfully shown that housing is in fact central to the notion of "inclusive, safe, resilient, and sustainable" cities.[11]

Another visible even if unsettled consequence of the pandemic is a flight from urban spaces. In New York City, for example, it was reported that five percent of the population – 420,000 people – left between March and May 2020.[12] New York was especially hard hit during the first COVID-19 wave in the United States, and the pandemic's toll there in terms of spread and hospitalizations was alarming. In

---

[6] See, e.g., SAUL, KINLEY and MOWBRAY, *The International Covenant on Economic, Social and Cultural Rights: Commentary, Cases and Materials*, New York, 2014.

[7] See RAJAGOPAL, "The pandemic shows why we need to treat housing as a right", The Washington Post, available at: <https://www.washingtonpost.com/opinions/2020/05/07/pandemic-shows-why-we-need-treat-housing-right/>.

[8] This is true in terms of protection against infectious disease, but also raises issues of a more comprehensive concept of safety in the home as evidenced by the rise in domestic violence widely reported since the onset of the pandemic.

[9] There are still major concerns regarding the right to housing in the context of the ongoing pandemic and forced evictions have still been reported in many places. RAJAGOPAL, "COVID-19 and the right to adequate housing: impacts and the way forward", UN Doc. A/75/148 (2020) (discussing examples from India, South Africa, Ethiopia, France, Kenya, Brazil, and the USA, and providing an overview of the major implications).

[10] See SHARIF and RAJAGOPAL, "Opinion: Housing must be at the heart of the COVID-19 response and recovery", Devex, 30 October 2020, available at: <https://www.devex.com/news/opinion-housing-must-be-at-the-heart-of-the-covid-19-response-and-recovery-98448>.

[11] See Transforming Our World: The 2030 Agenda for Sustainable Development, UN Doc. A/RES/70/1 (2015), pp. 21-22 (Goal 11: "Make cities and human settlements inclusive, safe, resilient and sustainable").

[12] "New Yorkers who fled the virus are returning home, warily", The New York Times, 1 January 2021.

addition to virus safety concerns which prompted many to leave New York and
other cities, stay-at-home orders, remote work, and online classrooms have also
forced urban dwellers to rethink the appeal of cramped city apartments, as well
as the need for proximity to urban social and economic activity when it seemed
to slow to a halt.[13] Many have a newfound appreciation for the countryside and
for suburban space. These transitions have led to an increase in the availability
of real property in the city, and may also lead to a reduction in the cost of city
housing. For example, in 2020, rents dropped by 9 percent in New York City and
8 percent in Melbourne.[14] But without more, this fluctuation is quite likely to be
a market reprieve rather than a permanent shift towards true affordability, and
investors are continuing to count on big cities as the post-pandemic choice.[15] The
housing insecurity intensified by the pandemic was there before, and the global
affordability crisis brought on by the financialization of housing has been years
in the making.

This paper therefore considers the engagement of cities in the task of safeguarding the right to housing in the context of financialization. The argument is
a straightforward one – cities have a duty to ensure the right to housing. Local
governments cannot merely deflect their responsibilities to national or other
higher levels of government, nor can local governments simply succumb to the
pressures of global competition at the expense of protecting the right to housing. These contentions necessarily imply that, while rather easy to say, the effort
needed to ensure the right to housing is far more complex. But the consequences
of the failure to act in this direction are too disturbing, and are already manifested
in cities across the globe as seen and felt through deprivations, exclusions, and
displacements.

The paper proceeds as follows. Section 2 provides an overview of the concept of financialization and briefly introduces the scope of the right to housing.
Section 3 then discusses the duty which cities must seize to ensure the right to
housing.[16] Drawing on the jurisprudence of the Committee on Economic, Social
and Cultural Rights (CESCR) and the European Court of Human Rights (ECtHR),
as well as two national cases – one from South Africa and one from the US – this
section aims to highlight both openings for cities to engage more meaningfully

---

[13] The issue of urban exodus during the pandemic is also likely to have cultural and social
repercussions in addition to the obvious economic ones. See "Some New Yorkers don't want
the superrich to return", The New York Times, 15 April 2021 (discussing New York City and
anecdotal research which suggests that Covid-19 represented a new form of city discomfort
which some simply were not willing to endure; should these individuals return post-pandemic,
those residents who stayed may harbor resentments against those who left).

[14] "The race for space: House prices in the rich world are booming", The Economist, 10
April 2021. House prices are also down in city centers. Mirroring this, prices have risen noticeably in less populated but commutable areas outside of the megacities.

[15] See *ibid.*

[16] As a definitional matter, cities can be understood in a jurisdictional sense as local governments, which are typically the lowest level of public administration within a State. But
cities can also be understood in a more expanded socio-spatial conceptualization which takes
account of wider "non-legal" concerns such as community, culture, and history, and which
ultimately impact upon the protection of the right to housing in the urban context.

in the protection and promotion of the right to housing, and some of the potential consequences attending the financialization of housing which cities must seek to mitigate. Section 4 concludes.

2. THE FINANCIALIZATION OF HOUSING

2.1. *Financialization*

The central message advocated by the United Nations Special Rapporteur on Adequate Housing[17] at the 2016 United Nations Conference on Housing and Sustainable Urban Development, Habitat III, seemed to be the need for a "paradigm shift" with respect to housing. Specifically, then Special Rapporteur, Leilani Farha, was pointing to what has come to be known as the "financialization of housing", and was using her platform at the vicennial event to present a call to action for the international community to view housing not as a commodity or an investment asset, but rather as a human right.[18] Farha emphasized that social exclusion and stigmatization, forced evictions in the name of development, increases in homelessness, and the ostracization and "othering" of migrants and refugees all flourish in cities. In her view, these problems persist due to a failure to see them as human rights issues and to respond with a human rights paradigm. She thus called for a broad *shift*, which, as she explained, directly involves challenging the commodification of housing.

Farha's predecessor, Raquel Rolnik, also identified and cautioned of the trend towards the financialization of housing in the expertise of UN Special Rapporteur in earlier reports. In 2012, she noted:

> Housing finance is now perceived not only as a tool for promoting access to adequate housing but also as critical to the development of the financial sector, and has become a central pillar of the financial market, expanding the terrain for global capital. The deregulation, liberalization and internationalization of finance that started in the 1980s had major implications for housing and urban development. Funds for mortgage lending now derive from national and international capital markets and not solely from existing savings and retail finance. These developments have been characterized as the 'financialization' of housing.[19]

---

[17] The formal title is Special Rapporteur on adequate housing as a component of the right to an adequate standard of living, and on the right to non-discrimination in this context. The Special Rapporteur since 1 May 2020 is Balakrishnan Rajagopal.

[18] Housing, United Nations Conference on Housing and Sustainable Urban Development, Quito, Ecuador, 17 October 2016.

[19] ROLNIK, *cit. supra* note 2, para. 10.

And prior to Rolnik, Miloon Kothari in his capacity as Special Rapporteur noted in a 2005 report:

> Even where developing countries have successfully attracted a large increase in private capital flows, the rapid growth of cities typically outpaces the provision of adequate housing, resulting in an increased number of the poor living in squatter settlements with no security or civic services. This situation is further aggravated when urban authorities or private operators clear such settlements for commercial use or high-income housing. Moreover, increasing trends towards privatization of housing services and markets typically result in land speculation and the commodification of housing, land and water. The application of user fees for goods such as water, sanitation and electricity, and the repeal of land ceiling and rent control legislation further exacerbate the problem, resulting in increased marginalization of the poor.[20]

Kothari's findings were particularly focused on "developing" countries and the structural factors driving housing insecurity. Similarly, Rolnik's report discussed the challenges associated with the growth of microcredit in "developing" countries, and the proliferation of unplanned urban settlements as connected to trends in global housing finance. But in more recent years, the focus of the financialization concern from the Office of the Special Rapporteur has been much more centered on "developed" countries and on the ways commodification is resulting in a now universal affordability crisis, stratifying even the wealthiest cities.[21]

Indeed, manifestations of the commodification trend became painfully apparent during the 2008 US real estate bubble burst and sub-prime mortgage fallout, and the subsequent global financial crisis and mitigation strategies.[22] In this catastrophe, the issue of housing affordability was not simply a reaction to financial shocks, but, rather, was causally central to the crisis. And while it might be tempting to dismiss this period as a dated episode, the jarring number of foreclosures and evictions remains on record,[23] and the consequences of the crisis permeate city spaces today where the devastation of foreclosures and repossessions has

---

[20] KOTHARI, Report of the Special Rapporteur on adequate housing as a component of the right to an adequate standard of living, UN Doc. E/CN.4/2005/48 (2005), para. 25.

[21] This is not to suggest that the Office of the Special Rapporteur is not also continuing to pay close attention to vulnerable populations in "developing" countries.

[22] ROLNIK and RABINOVICH, "Late Neoliberalism: The Financialisation of Homeownership and the Housing Rights of the Poor", in NOLAN (ed.), *Economic and Social Rights after the Global Financial Crisis*, Cambridge, 2014, p. 57 ff. ("From the outset of the financial crisis, housing was converted into one of the main Keynesian strategies to recover from it"). See also JAMES, *The Creation and Destruction of Value: The Globalization Cycle*, Cambridge, 2009, pp. 98-119.

[23] For example, the Special Rapporteur reports over 13 million foreclosures in the US resulting in over 9 million evictions, half a million foreclosures resulting in 300,000 evictions

clung to the social fabric.[24] The risk of evictions due to the job and financial insecurity brought on by the COVID-19 pandemic may serve to further devastate in
a great number of cities, with similar lasting repercussions.

Of course, the developments informing this whole financialization trajectory
had been occurring long before 2008, as the excerpts above from the reports of
the Special Rapporteur and substantial research have demonstrated.[25] It is worth
briefly summarizing some of this familiar history. The modern trend towards the
commodification of housing hearkens back to the late 1970s.[26] During this time,
an important transition with respect to housing policy began to take place whereby activities once under the control of the State were shifted to the private sector
in a move supported and bolstered by neoliberal economic doctrine.[27] More specifically, this transition meant that governments were encouraged to assume the
role of "market enablers" rather than that of suppliers of affordable housing for
their populations. The dominant logic at the time was that such a policy stance
would enable the efficient functioning of housing markets rather than their dis-
tortion through State interference.[28] This logic assumed the appropriate design,
regulation, and legal and institutional framework was put in place, and promised
to achieve adequate and affordable housing for all.[29]

It is this interdependence between housing, housing policy, and financial
markets, both in terms of the increasing dominance of financial actors, practices,
and markets in the arena of housing as well as the accompanying structural developments of economies and firms, such as financial institutions, States, and households, that can be loosely described as the "financialization of housing".[30] In the
past decades during which the financialization turn has taken hold, a gradual,
parallel shift has occurred in which the conceptualization of housing as a social
good has been replaced, or at least accompanied, by a greater appreciation for
housing as a commodity. Housing has become a source and strategy for individual and household wealth and security, and housing market regulations have been
critiqued as serving to promote housing as a financial asset instead of as serving
its critical social function.[31]

---

in Spain, and almost one million foreclosures in Hungary. FARHA, *cit. supra* note 3, paras. 5
and 21.

[24] See "Using the homeless to guard empty houses", The New Yorker, available at:
<https://www.newyorker.com/magazine/2020/12/07/using-the-homeless-to-guard-empty-
houses> (Francesca Mari explores some of the consequences in Los Angeles, and argues the
housing market remains broken with housing in California becoming more expensive after
the sub-prime mortgage crisis due to the snapping up of foreclosed homes by private equity-
backed real estate funds and companies).

[25] See HARVEY, *A Brief History of Neoliberalism*, Oxford, 2005.

[26] WILLS, *Contesting World Order? Socioeconomic Rights and Global Justice Movements*,
Cambridge, 2017, pp. 27-29; ROLNIK and RABINOVICH, *cit. supra* note 22, pp. 59-60.

[27] HARVEY, *cit. supra* note 25, p. 160.

[28] ROLNIK and RABINOVICH, *cit. supra* note 22, p. 60.

[29] *Ibid.*, p. 86.

[30] AALBERS, *The Financialization of Housing: A political economy approach*, New York,
2016, p. 2.

[31] ROLNIK and RABINOVICH, *cit. supra* note 22, p. 62.

It is now well-known and extensively documented that adequate housing has not been the outcome of the market-based approach. Rather, an affordability crisis emerged, exacerbated by the hollowing out and liberalization of non-market mechanisms to allocate housing resources.[32] In view of these factors, the Office of the Special Rapporteur has taken a vigorous approach to critiquing financialization. The homepage of that Office's website states upfront, "[h]ousing has increasingly been treated as an opportunity for investment, not as a social good and fundamental human right",[33] and, in a 2017 report, Farha articulated a more scathing characterization of the financialization of housing in the wake of the commodification turn:

> the "financialization of housing" refers to structural changes in housing and financial markets and global investment whereby housing is treated as a commodity, a means of accumulating wealth and often as security for financial instruments that are traded and sold on global markets. It refers to the way capital investment in housing increasingly disconnects housing from its social function of providing a place to live in security and dignity and hence undermines the realization of housing as a human right. It refers to the way housing and financial markets are oblivious to people and communities, and the role housing plays in their well-being.[34]

Farha's reference to the role housing plays in the well-being of communities must be duly noted. In this respect, she has pushed that States are holding themselves accountable to markets and investors rather than to the needs of communities.[35] The markets, in turn, are unaccountable and therefore fail to respond to actual housing needs on the ground leading to "urban centres that become the sole preserve of those with wealth".[36] One protester against rising rents in Berlin put the position even more candidly in 2019: "There needs to be some rules here for the game – it's a city, not just open land for people to do what they want. [...] It is not something that can be completely determined by the market".[37]

Furthering the financialization critique, in March 2019, the Special Rapporteur issued a series of letters concerning large-scale housing investments in cities.[38]

---

[32] *Ibid.*, pp. 63-64 ("A significant reduction in the construction of adequate public housing for the poor and most vulnerable groups has occurred along with decreasing national budgets and available public funds for social housing").

[33] Special Rapporteur on the right to adequate housing, available at: <https://www.ohchr. org/en/issues/housing/pages/housingindex.aspx>.

[34] FARHA, *cit. supra* note 3, para 1.

[35] *Ibid.*, para. 16.

[36] *Ibid.*, para. 29.

[37] "Protesters rally against 'rental insanity' in large German cities", DW, available at: <https://www.dw.com/en/protesters-rally-against-rental-insanity-in-large-german-cities/ a-48235915>.

[38] These letters were sent jointly by the Special Rapporteur on Adequate Housing and the Working Group on the issue of human rights and transnational corporations and other business

The Blackstone Group, a giant real estate private equity firm with $136 billion of assets which had already been targeted in Farha's 2017 financialization report, received a direct communication from the Special Rapporteur, as did the governments of the Czech Republic, Denmark, Ireland, Spain, Sweden, and the United States. The letter to Blackstone is critical of its general residential real estate business model which the Special Rapporteur argues demands short-term profits. It asserts that the company plays a "dominant role [...] in financial markets through residential real estate", and outlines three particular concerns with respect to the enjoyment of the right to housing.[39] First, in the wake of the 2008 financial crisis, the letter alleges that Blackstone purchased "an extraordinary and unprecedented number of foreclosed single-family properties, which were then converted into rental accommodation".[40] According to the Special Rapporteur: "[t]his large-scale ownership has made it possible for single family rentals (SFR) to become, for the first time, an asset class and has had deleterious effects on the enjoyment of the right to housing".[41] More specifically, institutional owners of SFRs are thought to contribute to the housing affordability crisis because of a tendency to engage in undue rent increases. Second, the letter claims Blackstone has been purchasing multi-family units across the world at unprecedented rates. The letter identifies a pattern: "[a] building or several buildings are determined to be located in an undervalued area, which often means they house poor and low-income tenants. Blackstone purchases the building, undertakes repairs or refurbishment, and then increases the rents – often exorbitantly – driving existing tenants out, and replacing them with higher income tenants".[42] And third, the Special Rapporteur claims Blackstone has been "using its significant resources and political leverage to undermine domestic laws and policies that would in fact improve access to adequate housing consistent with international human rights law".[43] The letter concludes by noting that, given its leadership position in global residential real estate, Blackstone's "engagement in this discussion could help to change the global narrative around housing".[44]

Blackstone replied just three days later. Its main position was that it is in fact helping to address the undersupply of housing in major urban centers globally by contributing "to the availability of well managed rental housing by bringing

---

enterprises. See Deva and Farha, "Mandates of the Working Group on the issue of human rights and transnational corporations and other business enterprises and the Special Rapporteur on adequate housing as a component of the right to an adequate standard of living, and on the right to non-discrimination in this context", OL OTH 17/2019, 22 March 2019, available at: <https://www.ohchr.org/Documents/Issues/Housing/Financialization/OL_OTH_17_2019.pdf>.

[39] *Ibid.*
[40] *Ibid.*
[41] *Ibid.*
[42] *Ibid.*
[43] *Ibid.*
[44] *Ibid.*

significant capital and expertise to the sector".[45] For Blackstone, "the answer to affordability is to increase the supply of housing", and it sees the injection of private capital into the housing market as part of the solution to the problem of undersupply.[46] Further, any harm is to be attributed to market forces and related laws, to which Blackstone is in compliance. In this respect, the Blackstone response letter highlights its compliance with strict eviction procedures in the US context. But this defense only demonstrates the dangers of an overly procedural approach to understanding and implementing the right to housing in cities, and of failing to take into view the wider societal context and consequences of housing. To put it more precisely, Blackstone is able to use the law and legal protections as a means of absolving itself of responsibility for the far larger community effects stemming from its part in the financialization of housing.[47] This is problematic, and is intertwined with the perspectives of housing rights advocates, human rights experts, and everyday citizens who recognize that national housing sectors have become fundamentally skewed through the financialization of housing, and that this, in turn, negatively impacts the fulfillment of human needs and State human rights obligations in the realm of housing.

2.2.   The right to housing

Under international law, housing is protected principally through the right to an adequate standard of living as established in the International Bill of Rights.[48] It was first recognized in the Universal Declaration of Human Rights of 1948 (UDHR) as one of the fundamental rights to be universally protected through that landmark document. Specifically, Article 25(1) of the UDHR holds:

> Everyone has the right to a standard of living adequate for the health and well-being of himself and of his family, including food, clothing, housing and medical care and necessary social services, and the right to security in the event of unemployment, sickness, disability, widowhood, old age or lack of livelihood in circumstances beyond his control.

---

[45] The letter of 25 March 2019 is available at: <https://www.ohchr.org/Documents/Issues/Housing/Financialization/Reply_OL_OTH_17_2019.pdf>.

[46] *Ibid.*

[47] See also BIRCHALL, "Human Rights on the Altar of the Market: The Blackstone Letters and the Financialisation of Housing", Transnational Legal Theory, 2019, p. 446 ff.

[48] Universal Declaration of Human Rights, 10 December 1948, Art. 25(1); International Covenant on Economic, Social and Cultural Rights, 16 December 1966, entered into force 3 January 1976, Art. 11(1); See also, International Covenant on Civil and Political Rights, 16 December 1966, entered into force 23 March 1976, Art. 17(1) ("No one shall be subjected to arbitrary or unlawful interference with his privacy, family, home or correspondence, nor to unlawful attacks on his honour or reputation").

In 1966, the right to adequate housing became legally codified through the adoption of the International Covenant on Economic, Social and Cultural Rights (ICESCR). Article 11(1) of that instrument states:

> The States Parties to the Present Covenant recognize the right of everyone to an adequate standard of living for himself and his family, including adequate food, housing and clothing, and to the continuous improvement of living conditions. The States Parties will take appropriate steps to ensure the realization of this right, recognizing to this effect the essential importance of international co-operation based on free consent.

Housing is also recognized in national constitutions such as those of South Africa, Russia, Ecuador, and Guyana,[49] in regional treaties,[50] and in specialized human rights instruments, particularly those dealing with marginalized groups at heightened risk of discrimination.[51] The shape of protection offered by the right to housing can vary across countries and regions. In India, the right to housing has been protected by courts as a part of the constitutional right to life. In the regional human rights systems of the Americas and Africa, housing is connected to rights to property, family, and health. Protection can also vary within countries, with some cities legally enabled and politically willing to advance a right to housing for their local populations and to guard against housing deprivations more than others.[52]

Importantly, the language of the UDHR and ICESCR articulates the right to housing not as an isolated asset, but, rather, as a component of the right to an adequate standard of living. This parsing emphasizes housing's inherent and indelible connection to an appropriate quality of life. Situating the right as such allows it to be seen as a necessary component to the achievement of an adequate standard of living.[53] To use Rolnik's words: "the right to adequate housing has to

---

[49] In domestic contexts, over 50 States hold the right or associated governmental obligations in their constitutions, and many other States offer housing rights protection through legislative and policy mechanisms. SAUL, KINLEY and MOWBRAY, cit. supra note 6, p. 938. See also ELLICKSON, "The Untenable Case for an Unconditional Right to Shelter", Harvard Journal of Law & Public Policy, 1992, p. 17 ff. (for arguments against a constitutional right to shelter in the United States).

[50] See European Social Charter (Revised), 3 May 1996, entered into force 1 July 1999, Arts. 16 and 31; Convention for the Protection of Human Rights and Fundamental Freedoms, 4 November 1950, entered into force 3 September 1953, Art. 8; African Charter on the Rights and Welfare of the Child, 1 July 1990, entered into force 29 November 1999, Art. 10.

[51] See Convention on the Elimination of All Forms of Discrimination against Women, 18 December 1979, entered into force 3 September 1981, Art. 14(2)(h); Convention on the Rights of the Child, 20 November 1989, entered into force 2 September 1990, Art. 27; Convention relating to the Status of Refugees, 25 July 1951, entered into force 22 April 1954, Art. 21.

[52] For example, New York City has a right to shelter mandate. NYC Department of Homeless Services, "Shelter", available at: <https://www1.nyc.gov/site/dhs/shelter/shelter.page>.

[53] HOHMANN, The Right to Housing: Law, Concepts, Possibilities, Oxford, 2013, p. 179.

be understood as a *gateway to other rights*, it is a condition that has to be fulfilled in order to ensure the exercise of belonging in all its aspects".[54] Put another way, housing must open up and protect the prospects for life which flow through both the object and concept of dwelling space, as determined by factors such as its location and its recognition in and by society. The crucial point is that the right to housing is not simply about a physical object or structure, or "merely having a roof over one's head"; it is, instead, a right to "adequate housing".[55]

Yet discussions of political priorities frequently overshadow any talk of "right" when it comes to housing. A socio-economic right subject to progressive realization and available resources,[56] the actual implementation of this category of rights remains a continuous hurdle to both realization and, arguably more broadly, general acceptance and recognition.[57] This point is particularly resonant in the context of housing. Socio-economic rights are not only about protecting against individual grievances, but are also heavily intertwined with complex social justice matters as well as the deep structural underpinnings of harms and deprivations. They conjure up the big and broad questions and processes of systemic reforms. These are difficult affairs to manage, and the ability, willingness, and appropriateness of courts to address such matters have long been debated. While civil and political rights are widely thought to encompass compensatory remedies, which are backwards looking and which typically involve individualized damages suitable to domestic courts, socio-economic rights are seen as more demanding of positive governmental action obtained through remedies such as declarations and injunctions and as therefore complicated and limited by political enforcement processes and mechanisms.[58] Difficult tensions emerge between individual corrective justice for litigants appearing in court today, and distributive justice for the larger groups similarly affected but not yet in front of the judge.[59]

Accordingly, the deliberation of a right to housing has been deemed an issue of political consideration for domestic legislatures, rather than one of legal right

---

[54] ROLNIK, "Place, Inhabitance and Citizenship: The Right to Housing and the Right to the City in the Contemporary Urban World", International Journal of Housing Policy, 2014, p. 293 ff., p. 295.

[55] United Nations Committee on Economic, Social and Cultural Rights, General Comment No. 4: The Right to Adequate Housing (Art. 11(1) of the Covenant), (1991) E/1992/23, paras. 7-8. The seven interrelated and overlapping factors which represent a minimum for housing adequacy in the view of the Committee are: legal security of tenure; availability of services, physical materials, facilities and infrastructure; affordability; habitability; accessibility; location; and cultural adequacy.

[56] ICESCR, Art. 2(1).

[57] This reality has long stemmed from the perceived justiciability, or lack thereof, of economic, social, and cultural rights and the ability to devise meaningful remedies. For a debate of whether or not social rights should be subject to judicial enforcement, see GEARTY and MANTOUVALOU, *Debating Social Rights*, Portland, 2011.

[58] ROACH, "The Challenges of Crafting Remedies for Violations of Socio-Economic Rights", in LANGFORD (ed.), *Social Rights Jurisprudence: Emerging Trends in International and Comparative Law*, Cambridge, 2008, p. 46 ff.

[59] *Ibid.*

to be enforced and dictated by courts. The European Court of Human Rights puts it starkly:

> While it is clearly desirable that every human being has a place where he or she can live in dignity and which he or she can call home, there are unfortunately in the contracting states many persons who have no home. Whether the state provides funds to enable everyone to have a home is a matter for political not judicial decision.[60]

But courts and human rights bodies have a strong role in structuring the political and public perception and response to inadequate housing, and it is crucial, therefore, that they engage with the right. When they have, it is often in the realm of evictions. Such a focus reflects the housing/property tensions inherent in the issue of home, and the dominance of tenure security – largely understood as protection against forced evictions – in interpretations of housing as a right. Courts and human rights bodies can be seen to take a primarily and overly procedural approach to the complex, competing interests involved in these cases, focusing on rather thin procedural duties at the expense of substantive rights content and, ultimately, closing off rather than opening up deeper and needed engagement with the wider societal context.[61] Yet, looking to judicial (and quasi-judicial) practice, whilst keeping this critique in hand, offers an opportunity to explore and distill the duty of local governments to ensure the right to housing.

3. A CITY'S DUTY

3.1. International and regional perspectives: the CESCR and ECtHR

The human consequences of the financialization of housing have come to the attention of the Committee on Economic, Social and Cultural Rights through its individual communication procedure. Such communications have been possible only since 2013 with the entry into force of the Optional Protocol to the ICESCR,[62] and the work of the Committee helps illuminate the role of the State as a whole in fulfilling the right to housing under obligations of international human rights law. In particular, a few important complaints of violations of ICESCR Article 11(1) by Spain have given the CESCR the opportunity to pronounce, somewhat, on the dangers of financialization for ensuring the right to housing.

---

[60] *Chapman v. The United Kingdom*, Application No. 27238/95, Grand Chamber, Judgment of 18 January 2001, para. 99.

[61] See HOHMANN, *cit. supra* note 53, pp. 129-137 (exploring procedural interpretations of the right).

[62] Optional Protocol to the International Covenant on Economic, Social and Cultural Rights, 10 December 2008, entered into force 5 May 2013. There are currently 26 States Parties to the Optional Protocol.

In *I.D.G. v. Spain*,[63] the Committee considered a complaint alleging a violation of the right to adequate housing due to a mortgage enforcement process. Ms I.D.G. claimed that a lending institution took mortgage enforcement proceedings against her after she missed several mortgage repayments, but that she did not receive adequate notice and only became aware of the proceedings once her home was ordered auctioned. She thus claimed a lack of "access to effective and timely judicial protection, which prevented her from mounting a judicial response to the proceedings and protecting her right to housing in the courts, with the result that she now finds herself in a position of vulnerability, uncertainty and anxiety".[64] The Committee found a violation by Spain of the right to housing due to the inadequate notice given during the foreclosure process. *I.D.G.* is therefore an important result from the Committee which serves as a needed rebuke against a State on account of the right to housing. But the Committee focused on the lack of proper procedure with respect to notification, and, albeit a critical safeguard, its views did little to offer substantive protection within the broader context of the dangers of financialization for the right to housing.

Ben Djazia and Bellili v. Spain[65] dealt with access to public housing and homelessness, and involved an eviction from private rental housing on the grounds that the contract had ended between the private individuals. The central issue was whether the eviction by order of the court and the failure of the Spanish authorities to grant alternative housing constituted a violation of the right to adequate housing under Article 11(1), in view of the fact that the family in this instance was rendered homeless.[66] The Committee expounded clearly in its views that the protection of legal security of tenure "applies to persons living in rental accommodation, whether public or private; such persons should enjoy the right to housing even when the lease expires",[67] and that the protection against forced evictions carries for those in rented accommodation.[68] Thus, the State is under obligation to ensure that an eviction even in the context of a rental contract between individuals still does not violate Article 11(1).[69] The CESCR specified that any evictions should be carried out in accordance with legislation compatible with the ICESCR, and that evictions must comply with the principle of propor-

---

[63] Committee on Economic, Social and Cultural Rights, *I.D.G. v. Spain*, Communication No. 2/2014, Views adopted on 17 June 2015. It must be noted that in Spain, some 400,000 foreclosures were reported between 2007 and 2011.

[64] *Ibid.*, para. 10.2.

[65] Committee on Economic, Social and Cultural Rights, *Mohamed Ben Djazia and Naouel Bellili v. Spain*, Communication No. 5/2015, Views adopted on 20 June 2017.

[66] *Ibid.*, para. 12.7.

[67] *Ibid.*, para. 13.2.

[68] *Ibid.*, para. 13.3.

[69] See *ibid.*, para. 14.2 ("States parties do not only have the obligation to respect Covenant rights, and, it follows, to refrain from infringing them, but they also have the obligation to protect them by adopting measures to prevent the direct or indirect interference of individuals in the enjoyment of these rights. [...] Thus, although the Covenant primarily establishes rights and obligations between the State and individuals, the scope of the provisions of the Covenant extends to relations between individuals").

tionality between the legitimate objective of the eviction and the consequences for those evicted.[70]

The Committee found that Spain did indeed violate the right to housing under the Covenant. The eviction, without the Spanish authorities, including the regional Madrid authorities, guaranteeing alternative housing, and "in the absence of reasonable arguments on the part of the State party regarding all the measures taken to the maximum of its available resources", constituted a violation.[71] Importantly, the CESCR offered comment beyond procedural rhetoric, touching on structural issues raised by the communication:

> The Committee considers that States parties, with a view to rationalizing the resources of their social services, may set criteria or conditions that applicants must satisfy in order to receive social services. These conditions, however, must be reasonable and very carefully designed so as to prevent not only any stigmatization but also that the mere behavior of a person in need of alternative housing be used to justify denying his or her application. In addition, the conditions must be communicated in a transparent, timely and complete manner to the applicant. Furthermore, it should be taken into account that the lack of housing is often the result of structural problems, such as high unemployment or systemic patterns of social exclusion, which it is the responsibility of the authorities to resolve through an appropriate, timely and coordinated response, to the maximum of their available resources.[72]

The Committee was particularly concerned with Spain's characterization of the applicant in terms of his employment status and lack of a job. The language "so as to prevent not only any stigmatization but also that the mere behavior of a person in need of alternative housing be used to justify denying his or her application" is potentially very significant in understanding State duties going forward and in informing the content of local government duties. The Committee's instruction regarding stigmatization and personal behavior is a needed admonishment of the tendency for judgmental attitudes to rush in and be used as a tool of rights denial, particularly in the context of socio-economic rights often mischaracterized by skeptics as "handouts".

In *Ben Djazia and Bellili*, the Committee also expressed concern with what it characterized as the State's regression with respect to the right to housing. Crucial to this matter, Spain failed to explain and justify the fact that the regional authorities in Madrid sold part of the public housing stock to investment compa-

---

[70] *Ibid.*, para. 13.4; see also Committee on Economic, Social and Cultural Rights, *Rosario Gómez-Limón Pardo v. Spain*, Communication No. 52/2018, Views adopted on 5 March 2020, para. 8.2.

[71] *Mohamed Ben Djazia and Naouel Bellili v. Spain* case, *cit. supra* note 65, paras. 18 and 17.5.

[72] *Ibid.*, para. 17.2.

nies, even though there was a significant backlog with respect to public housing with vastly fewer housing units available than in demand.[73] As the CESCR noted: "In times of severe economic and financial crisis, all budgetary changes or adjustments affecting policies must be temporary, necessary, proportional and non-discriminatory".[74] This communication is therefore an overdue manifestation of the financialization and commodification critique propounded for many years now by the Special Rapporteurs.[75] There is already a wide academic literature on the global financial crisis and the housing impact. It is now important progress to see a rights-based decision revealing the market-based displacements and disturbing social outcomes of the crisis, and deeming a State in violation. *Ben Djazia and Bellili* shows the implications of the State in both creating and failing to respond to a situation of inadequate housing, ultimately resulting in homelessness for an entire family. And while the impacts of homelessness are multiplied for families and implicate further and serious vulnerabilities especially with respect to childhood development, it is important to see homelessness writ large through a human rights lens and to be cautious about the dangers of categorizing this housing deprivation. Such categorization might run the risk of prompting discriminatory approaches to allocating resources, if families tend to be more common in particular ethnic or class groups as opposed to others for example, and should therefore be considered carefully.

Finally, in *López Albán v. Spain*[76] the CESCR also dealt with eviction from private rental property and reiterated that States indeed have a duty to ensure the right to housing for those evicted from privately owned property.[77] The Committee acknowledged that "the lack of affordable, available housing is rooted in growing inequality and housing market speculation", and that "States parties have an obligation to resolve these structural problems through appropriate, timely and coordinated responses, to the maximum of their available resources".[78] Significantly in this instance, the Committee underscored that while State parties have a legitimate interest in protecting an owner's right to property, there is a need to distinguish "between properties belonging to individuals who need them as a home or to provide vital income and properties belonging to financial institutions [...]".[79] The Committee explained that this distinction is integral to analyzing the

---

[73] *Ibid.*, para. 17.5 ("For instance, in 2013, the Madrid Housing Institute sold 2,935 houses and other properties to a private company for €201 million, justifying the measure by a need to balance the budget").

[74] *Ibid.*, para. 17.6.

[75] See generally SIVAKUMARAN, "Beyond States and Non-State Actors: The Role of State-Empowered Entities in the Making and Shaping of International Law", Columbia Journal of Transnational Law, 2017, p. 343 ff., pp. 391-392 (discussing "softer" lawmaking processes including through the use of experts and human rights special rapporteurs).

[76] Committee on Economic, Social and Cultural Rights, *Maribel Viviana López Albán v. Spain*, Communication No. 37/2018, Views adopted on 11 October 2019.

[77] *Ibid.*, para. 9.1.

[78] *Ibid.*, para. 10.2.

[79] *Ibid.*, para. 11.5; see also Committee on Economic, Social and Cultural Rights, *Rosario Gómez-Limón Pardo v. Spain*, Communication No. 52/2018, Views adopted on 5 March 2020, para. 9.5.

proportionality of the legitimate objective of an eviction. In *López Albán* there was a legitimate objective in protecting the property right of the bank which owned the apartment, but this needed to be weighed against the consequences for those evicted from the apartment. Crucially, therefore, the Committee noted that proportionality is about both the consequences for the evicted and the owner's need for possession of the property in question.[80]

These cases from the CESCR demonstrate a growing recognition of the specific harms of financialization and the related missteps of governments with respect to ensuring the right to housing. They also keenly alert us to the inevitable intersections of the right to housing and the right to property, and the jurisprudence of the Committee naturally appears to pull in the direction of more robust protection of the former. In this respect, two cases from the European Court of Human Rights regarding the protection of property bear mention.

Casa di Cura Valle Fiorita S.r.l. v. Italy[81] involved the occupation without title of a building in Rome by a group of activists for the right to housing. In December 2012, 100 persons broke into the building and appropriated the premises. The applicant company which owned the building filed complaints with the public prosecutor, claiming violations of property rights and seeking evacuation of the property. The preliminary investigation judge ordered the evacuation of the building in August 2013. This order was not executed, and the applicant alleged violations of both Article 6 of the Convention – effective judicial protection – and Article 1 of Protocol No. 1 – right to respect of property – before the ECtHR.

In this case, it is necessary to observe the complexity of the social context during the five years of occupation of the building. In Rome, many buildings had been occupied by right to housing movements sometimes numbering in the hundreds of people. Both the Public Prosecutor and the Prefect of Rome had responded to the applicant's situation by acknowledging this context, and with specific concern for the need to preserve public order and to guarantee rehousing for the people involved. There was a contention that the financial limitations of the Municipality of Rome would have prevented relocation should the occupants be evicted, and the occupants remained as a result of these limitations. The ECtHR acknowledged that these social reasons as put forward by the Italian authorities could justify difficulties in executing the decision and could delay vacating the building, but nonetheless found it unjustified in this case.[82] The Court noted that neither a lack of resources nor a lack of alternative accommodation can, in itself, constitute an acceptable justification for the non-enforcement of a judicial decision, and held that there had been a violation of Article 6 due to the failure of the Italian authorities to take measures for more than five years to comply with the judicial decision.[83] The Court further held that there had been a violation of Article 1 of Protocol No. 1, finding that the authorities should have taken the

---

[80] *Maribel Viviana López Albán v. Spain* case, *cit. supra* note 76, para. 11.5.
[81] *Casa di Cura Valle Fiorita S.r.l. v. Italy*, Application No. 67944/13, Judgment of 13 December 2018.
[82] See *ibid.*, paras. 52 and 54.
[83] *Ibid.*, para. 54.

necessary measures to comply with the court decision after a reasonable period of time to find a satisfactory solution, given the social and public order concerns. The duration had been exceeded in this case, and the Court also took note of the fact that the applicant was still liable for costs associated with the building's occupation.

Similarly, in *Papachela and Amazon S.A. v. Greece*,[84] the ECtHR held that there had been a violation of Article 1 of Protocol No. 1 where the authorities had failed to act with respect to migrants who had occupied the applicant's hotel in Athens for more than three years. During this time period, those occupying the hotel in solidarity with the migrants illegally reconnected the electricity and water supply leading to significant bills for the applicant. The value of the property was also reduced by more than half, allegedly due to damage to the building and equipment, and the applicant was forced to sell her home to cover the relevant debts to the State. As with *Casa di Cura Valle Fiorita S.r.l*, the authorities failed to execute earlier decisions to evacuate the premises and there were complex social and policy considerations – here, public interest considerations related to the migratory influx associated with the refugee crisis at the time. The Government argued that evicting vulnerable persons from the hotel without the State having the appropriate measures in place in terms of accommodation and medical care would have resulted in economic and social disruption in Athens.[85] The ECtHR found such considerations could justify a delay, but not the total and prolonged inaction by the Greek authorities. According to the Court, after a reasonable period of time devoted to finding a satisfactory solution, the authorities should have taken the necessary measures to respect the property.[86] Inaction for more than three years in a situation with significant consequences for the applicants' property meant that the national authorities had upset the fair balance between the requirements of the general interest of the community and the imperatives of safeguarding individual rights.[87]

While these cases from the European system seem to show precedence for property rights over housing rights with respect to prolonged occupation, the factual circumstances as discussed in the judgments also call our attention to some of the difficult social and policy considerations weighed by cities. Such insights are helpful in animating the local context in which the right to housing is situated, and, by not far extension, they also serve to usefully complicate narrow understandings of property. Property, in fact, comprises public values which promote its ultimate ends.[88] These ends are often contrived as private and individualistic, but property can also entail a social function. In some national constitutions,

---

[84] *Papachela et Amazon S.A. v. Greece*, Application No. 12929/18, Judgment of 3 December 2020.
[85] *Ibid.*, paras. 53 and 57.
[86] *Ibid.*, para. 63.
[87] *Ibid.*
[88] ALEXANDER, "Property's Ends: The Publicness of Private Law Values", Iowa Law Review, 2014, p. 1257 ff. (arguing that property's ends are both public and private and consist of the inclusive and multiple values which constitute human flourishing, the normative foundation of private property).

such as Italy, such a social function of property is specifically articulated.[89] And in many Latin American countries, the idea of property's social function is also constitutionally evident and serves as a limitation to the protection of private property. In these contexts, "social function" essentially refers to the public objectives within which ownership's justification becomes located, and thus imposes affirmative obligations on owners, such as to cultivate or develop land.[90] A full, ambitious understanding of property is both directly applicable to and warranted in the contemporary urban context. The national cases turned to next illustrate this point, and lend both clarity and texture to our understanding of the role of local governments in ensuring the right to housing.

3.2. Domestic perspectives: South Africa and the United States

In *City of Johannesburg v. Blue Moonlight Properties*,[91] the South African Constitutional Court considered whether 86 people, "occupiers" of private property, were to be evicted in the interest of the full exercise of property rights by the owner, Blue Moonlight, and, if so, whether such eviction must be accompanied by an order for the City of Johannesburg to provide the occupiers with accommodation. The case therefore concerned a city's obligations with respect to the right of access to adequate housing in the South African constitution, and the constitutional allocation of powers and functions to municipalities in relation to housing and resources.

In *Blue Moonlight*, the occupiers argued that it would not be just and equitable to grant eviction if it would render them homeless. The City itself did not seek the eviction, which was in fact sought by Blue Moonlight for purposes of developing the property, but the City argued that it could not be held responsible for providing accommodation to everyone evicted by private landowners.[92] In deciding this case, the Court paid close attention to the City's obligations and conduct. It noted that the "joinder of the City as the main point of contact with the community is essential",[93] and that the duty regarding housing under section 26 of the South African Constitution falls on the local, provincial, and national spheres of government which must cooperate:[94]

---

[89] See Art. 42.

[90] ESQUIROL, "Formalizing property in Latin America", in GRAZIADEI and SMITH (eds.), *Comparative Property Law: Global Perspectives*, Northampton, 2018, p. 333 ff., p. 338 (Esquirol also discusses the notion of social function of property in the Colombian context which once provided for the "extinguishment of title" in cases of continuing breach of the social function).

[91] Constitutional Court (South Africa), *City of Johannesburg Metropolitan Municipality v. Blue Moonlight Properties 39 (PTY)Ltd*, (CCT 37/11) [2011] ZACC 33, Judgment of 1 December 2011.

[92] *Ibid.*, para. 32.

[93] *Ibid.*, para. 45.

[94] *Ibid.*, para. 42. See also Constitutional Court (South Africa), *Government of the Republic of South Africa and others v. Grootboom and others* (CCT11/00) [2000] ZACC 1, Judgment of 21 September 2000, para. 40.

> The primary duties placed on national and provincial governments
> do not absolve local governments. The Constitution places a duty
> on local governments to ensure that services are provided in a sus-
> tainable manner to the communities they govern […]. A municipal-
> ity must be attentive to housing problems in the community, plan,
> budget appropriately and co-ordinate and engage with other spheres
> of government to ensure that the needs of its community are met. Its
> duty is not simply to implement the state's housing programme at a
> local level. It must plan and carry some of the costs […].[95]

With respect to the role of local government, the Constitutional Court explained that this was an important one in the provision of housing,[96] and the
analysis in *Blue Moonlight* involved an examination of the resources and budget
of the City of Johannesburg. A crucial aspect of the City's argument was that it
could distinguish between those evicted and rendered homeless by the City, for
which the City would provide accommodation, versus those so rendered by private landowners. The Court rejected this contention, and found the City's housing policy was unconstitutional to the extent that it excluded the occupiers and
those similarly evicted by private landlords from consideration for temporary
accommodation.[97] The Constitutional Court was unimpressed by the City's failure to budget for the possibility of a need for emergency housing in the event of
eviction, and details around the City's financial resources were shady and unper-
suasive.[98] The Court noted that the City's interpretation of the National Housing
Code as neither permitting nor obliging the City to take measures to provide
emergency accommodation once it had been refused financial assistance from
the province was incorrect, and that the City had a duty to plan, budget, and finance proactively for such situations.[99] The Court held that the City was obliged
to provide temporary accommodation and ordered that it be "in a location as
near as possible to the area where the property is situated",[100] emphasizing the
importance of location to economic opportunity, a more widely evident theme
in global housing rights jurisprudence.[101] Additionally, the Constitutional Court

---

[95] *Blue Moonlight, cit. supra* note 91, footnote 49.

[96] Under Chapter 7 of the South African Constitution, which deals with the functions and
powers of local government, a municipality must "structure and manage its administration and
budgeting and planning processes to give priority to the basic needs of the community, and
to promote the social and economic development of the community": *ibid.*, para. 22 (quoting Section 153(a)). The Housing Act which gives effect to the section 26 right to housing,
"obliges municipalities, as part of the process of integrated development planning, to take all
reasonable and necessary steps within the framework of national and provincial housing legislation and policy to ensure, amongst other things, that the inhabitants of their respective areas
have access to adequate housing": *ibid.*, para. 24.

[97] *Ibid.*, para. 95.

[98] *Ibid.*, para. 73.

[99] *Ibid.*, paras. 67 and 96.

[100] *Ibid.*, para. 104.

[101] Supreme Court (India), *Olga Tellis and Others v. Bombay Municipal Corporation*, 2
Supl. SCR 51, Judgment of 10 July 1985.

recognized that Blue Moonlight could not be burdened with providing accommodation indefinitely, but still required "a degree of patience" from Blue Moonlight with respect to the City's obligation to provide alternative accommodation.[102]

The City of Johannesburg highlighted the pressures it faces in dealing with housing – an existing backlog in terms of housing, a continuous influx of people through urbanization and immigration, illegal land and building invasions, as well as issues of unemployment and poverty.[103] Such pressures are real for many cities, and it is undeniable that the housing question is often contested on the basis of resources. But city governments have a duty to ensure the right to housing and are well placed to craft and implement appropriate housing policies. They are in a position to monitor closely the needs of their local populations and to carefully investigate and balance the competing interests at stake. They also, arguably, hold more trust with their local populations than their populations may hold with the national government. This kind of trust has ramifications far beyond housing, but housing is a key element in building and maintaining such trust within local communities. The content of a city's housing policy may be reasonably based on its resources, however, the point too often glossed over is that ensuring the right to housing requires cities to fully contemplate and appreciate the social context, particularly in the era of financialization. A final case example, from the United States, elucidates this point and brings forward a crucial aspect of the financialization of housing and the role of cities, that of community.

In *Bank of America Corp. v. City of Miami*,[104] the City of Miami brought a claim under the Fair Housing Act (FHA) alleging that two banks, Bank of America and Wells Fargo, had engaged in discriminatory lending practices against African American and Latino customers. The predatory practices alleged included "excessively high interest rates, unjustified fees, teaser low-rate loans that overstated refinancing opportunities, large prepayment penalties, and – when default loomed – unjustified refusals to refinance or modify the loans".[105] The injury alleged by the City was framed both in economic and noneconomic terms. Specifically, the City claimed that the Banks' discriminatory practices resulted in disproportionately higher defaults and foreclosures for minority borrowers. This meant that foreclosures were concentrated in specific minority neighborhoods and led to reduced property values and declining property-tax revenue. Further, the City claimed that it had higher municipal expenses because, it argued, higher foreclosure rates particularly when attenuated by vacant properties leads to an increased need for police, fire, and building and code enforcement municipal services. Neighborhoods become unsafe and blighted, it was argued. In short, the City claimed injury in the form of lost tax revenue and extra municipal expenses – it lost financially because of the discriminatory lending practices on the part of the Banks.

---

[102] *Blue Moonlight, cit. supra* note 91, paras. 31, 40 and 100.

[103] *Ibid.*, para. 77.

[104] Supreme Court (United States of America), *Bank of America Corporation, et al. v. City of Miami, Florida*, 137 S. Ct. 1296 (2017).

[105] *Ibid.*, p. 3.

The Supreme Court held that the City of Miami was an "aggrieved person" and thus able to bring suit under the FHA.[106] The financial injuries claimed by the City were deemed to "fall within the zone of interest that the FHA arguably protects".[107] But on causation, the Court concluded that the lower court's holding that only foreseeability was required with respect to injuries flowing from the alleged discriminatory practices of the Banks was insufficient to establish the necessary proximate cause. Justice Breyer put it as follows:

> In the context of the FHA, foreseeability alone does not ensure the close connection that proximate cause requires. The housing market is interconnected with economic and social life. A violation of the FHA may, therefore, 'be expected to cause ripples of harm to flow' far beyond the defendant's misconduct. [...] Nothing in the statute suggests that Congress intended to provide a remedy wherever those ripples travel. And entertaining suits to recover damages for any foreseeable result of an FHA violation would risk 'massive and complex damages litigation'.
>
> Rather, proximate cause under the FHA requires 'some direct relation between the injury asserted and the injurious conduct alleged'.[108]

While the Court rightly recognizes that the housing market is interconnected with economic and social life, a potential shortcoming of the opinion is that it looks at housing in individual terms with insufficient attention to the community aspects of housing and the implications of housing discrimination for wider society. This is out of step with the history and purpose of the FHA, and with the protection of housing as a human right. The Fair Housing Act is about bringing into society those who have been historically discriminated against in a context of still ongoing societal prejudices.[109] In *Bank of America Corp.*, the injury the city faced was expressed predominantly in economic terms, but some noneconomic harms were raised as well. For instance, the City alleged that the discriminatory practices by the Banks "adversely impacted the racial composition of the city" and "impaired the City's goals to assure racial integration and desegregation".[110] The City of Miami further alleged its "longstanding and active interest in pro-

---

[106] *Ibid.*, p. 2.

[107] *Ibid.*

[108] *Ibid.*, p. 11. The US Supreme Court remanded the case, declining "to draw the precise boundaries of proximate cause under the FHA and to determine on which side of the line the City's financial injuries fall".

[109] The Fair Housing Act emerged from the US civil rights movement of the 1960s and the severe social tensions and unrest linked to long-standing racial discrimination. Under Section 804(a) of the FHA, it shall be unlawful: "To refuse to sell or rent after the making of a bona fide offer, or to refuse to negotiate for the sale or rental of, or otherwise make available or deny, a dwelling to any person because of race, color, religion, sex, familial status, or national origin".

[110] *Bank of America Corporation, cit. supra* note 104, p. 2.

moting fair housing and securing the benefits of an integrated community" were frustrated by the Banks' practices.[111]

These aspects of the City's complaints were noted but not fully addressed in the Court's opinion,[112] and, indeed, the deep injury to the city which the facts of this case bring forward is one of community. The City argued that neighborhoods stricken with urban blight require increased services and police presence which costs the municipality money. Vacant buildings depress property values and reduce the city's tax coffers. But this point must be taken a step further. The increased State presence itself in these neighborhoods can contribute to negative societal perceptions about race and ethnicity, implicating housing's more nuanced intersections with discrimination. For example, when local evening news reports on crime and violence in minority neighborhoods alongside footage of dilapidated properties it may contribute to the creation of negative perceptions about these very communities. By capturing, out of full context, the social distress caused in a particular community, this publicity stokes the kind of social tensions the FHA came about to address in the first place. These perceptions may come to feed into the complexities of achieving social inclusion in cities. Unlike others who might also be aggrieved in economic terms from the predatory lending practices against minorities – local business owners, such as restaurants for instance, which would be faced with fewer customers[113] – the city level of governance is uniquely placed to promote inclusion and integration for its residents, and to build community through housing.

This case therefore illustrates the potential social consequences of the unbridled commodification of housing. It demonstrates this consequence not just for individuals but also for entire communities in cities. The case therefore allows reflection on deeper aspects of what city space means, what it means to communities, and how private law mechanisms in housing can infringe upon and damage communities and undermine public values. For instance, the neighborhoods at issue in *Bank of America Corp.* may well have been stable communities whose members had been building up, individually and collectively, though the economic and social possibilities of owning a home and creating a neighborhood.[114] Housing understood in this way is their foothold in their community and their community's foothold in the city, that is, the urban community. For an established neighborhood community with a certain, and probably hard-earned, sense of homeostasis the removal of a portion of the community will likely create a drain on the community. This bleed is as much social and cultural as it is economic and material. Schools suffer from the depletion of the community,

---

[111] *Ibid.*

[112] The idea of community harm and its relation to the history and purpose of the FHA was, however, discussed during oral argument.

[113] *Bank of America Corporation, cit. supra* note 104, p. 8.

[114] On the extreme racial wealth gap in the United States and relations to homeownership, see, e.g., CALHOUN, "Lessons from the financial crisis: The central importance of a sustainable, affordable and inclusive housing market", Brookings, 5 September 2018, available at: <https://www.brookings.edu/research/lessons-from-the-financial-crisis-the-central-importance-of-a-sustainable-affordable-and-inclusive-housing-market/>.

public recreational spaces become more and more void, and all things that require community participation are increasingly diminished. The gutting of the
neighborhood through the foreclosure impact of financialization shows that this
process not only has a dangerous individual effect, but can be profoundly deleterious to community. *Bank of America Corp.* thus raises the issue of public law
understandings of housing and property, and the close connections to community
and to city space. It highlights the city's key responsibility for the deterioration
of its neighborhoods and their cultural erosion, and for the negative impact on
communities and the wider urban community coming from a narrow, commodi-
fied understanding of housing.

4. CONCLUSION

Cities must work to safeguard the right to housing, understood not solely as
protecting an interest in an individual good, but rather as a right with uniquely
far-reaching social and cultural implications. Much of the financialization critique deliberates the ground-level reality that the city's profit-oriented value has
been emphasized over its social function thereby producing an environment
increasingly marked by, or constantly at risk of, homelessness, economic and
cultural displacements, and socio-spatial segregation.[115] Indeed, too frequently,
cities have tended to give in to the pressures of global economic competition and
financialization which threaten the right to housing. But in reality, the claims of
those seeking to establish or maintain a home in the city can come to override
those who hold property there as purely fungible assets. This recognition appears
to have begun emanating from the jurisprudence of the Committee on Economic,
Social and Cultural Rights. It is now the task of cities, understood as local governments, to buck the extremes of financialization and step up in ensuring the
right to housing. For it is in cities, understood as pivotal social spaces, where the
consequences of not doing so will continue to be felt.

---

[115] See generally LEFEBVRE, *Writings on Cities*, Oxford, 1996.

THE URBAN-RURAL DIVIDE: SPATIAL INEQUALITIES AND BACKLASH IN THE INVESTMENT TREATY REGIME

DANIEL LITWIN[*]

Abstract

A growing literature in international law has examined the backlash against international institutions and norms and its links with the rise of nationalist parties and populism. Some of this backlash have been said to originate with populations in small towns and rural areas socioeconomically "left-behind" by economic globalization. These developments have made salient the growing economic and political polarization between urban and non-urban areas. Nevertheless, this urban-rural divide and its implications for international law have only started to be acknowledged. Aligned with these concerns, this article adopts the urban-rural divide as a geographical scale or frame to suggest a new perspective on the investment treaty regime, its backlash and reform. Outside of the particularly virulent nature of its backlash, the regime's context provides fertile ground for this frame: it is structured so that urban actors principally located in global or capital cities, such as multinational enterprises, global law firms, or national executive branches, make decisions about foreign investment projects that are often located and impact non-urban areas and populations. As this article contends, this context points to the regime's potential to impact (and address) through geographical affinities the global growth of political and economic polarization between urban and non-urban areas. The impact of these urban decisions on non-urban areas has so far principally been examined through frames that emphasize impact in terms of the "environment" or "local communities" together with calls for reforms to the regime by allocating more policy space for States. An "urban-rural" frame centers additional impacts in terms of non-urban public interest, local participation, and the distribution of resources, and queries the ability of domestic policies alone to respond to them in the pursuit of socially and economic inclusive investment.

Keywords: investment treaty regime; urban-rural divide; spatial inequalities; local communities; sustainable investment.

1. INTRODUCTION

A growing literature in international law has examined the backlash against international institutions and norms and its links with the rise of nationalist par-

[*] Researcher at the European University Institute. Former Legal Adviser at the Iran-United States Claims Tribunal and Managing Editor of the Yearbook on International Investment Law and Policy.

IYIL, Vol. 30 (2020), pp. 131-153
ISSN 0391-5107

ties and populism.[1] Some of this backlash has been said to originate with populations in small towns and rural areas socioeconomically "left-behind" by economic globalization.[2] These developments have made salient the growing economic and political polarization between urban and non-urban areas.[3] Nevertheless, this urban-rural divide and its implications for international law has only started to be acknowledged,[4] with a recent intervention noting that "the values of Paris – of the city – today have received automatic priority over those of the provincial town, left to decay economically, socially and culturally" generating "a breeding ground for resentment and right-wing reaction".[5] Aligned with these concerns, this article adopts the urban-rural divide as geographical scale or frame to suggest a new perspective on backlash in the international treaty regime (regime),[6] its vast network of international investment agreements (IIAs) for the promotion and protection of foreign investment, and investor-state dispute settlement (ISDS).

Outside of the particularly virulent nature of its backlash, the regime's context provides fertile ground for study: it is structured, as this article suggests, so that urban actors principally located in global or capital cities, such as multinational enterprises, global law firms, or national executive branches, make decisions about foreign investment projects that are often located and impact non-

---

[1] This backlash has also been understood as a "crisis", see generally KRIEGER and NOLTE, "The International Rule of Law – Rise or Decline? – Approaching Current Foundational Challenges", in KRIEGER, NOLTE and ZIMMERMANN (eds.), *The International Rule of Law: Rise or Decline?*, Oxford, 2019, p. 3 ff. See also the 2018 issue of the NYIL on "Populism and International Law".

[2] See e.g. DE DOMINICIS, DIJKSTRA, and PONTAROLLO, "The Urban-Rural Divide in Anti-EU Vote: Social, Demographic and Economic Factors Affecting the Vote for Parties Opposed to European Integration", European Commission Directorate-General for Regional and Urban Policy Working Article 05/2020, 2020.

[3] The concept of an urban-rural divide is deeply embedded in classical political economy and sociological theory. For an early exposition of this divide, see SIMMEL, "The Metropolis and Mental Life", in LIN and MELE (eds.), *The Urban Sociology Reader*, 2nd ed., London/New York, 2013, p. 23 ff. (first published 1903).

[4] For early efforts to conceptualize the place of the urban-rural divide in international law in terms of social and material context, see LITWIN, "International Lawyers and the City", in AUST and NIJMAN (eds.), *Research Handbook on Cities and International Law*, Cheltenham, forthcoming. For a similar argument about the place of this divide in international legal thinking, see KNOP, "The Hidden City in International Legal Thought", in AUST and NIJMAN (eds.), *cit. supra* note 4. See also the contribution by FRANCIONI in this Volume.

[5] KOSKENNIEMI, *International Law and the Far Right: Reflections on Law and Cynicism*, Den Haag, 2019, pp. 15-16.

[6] The backlash against the investment treaty regime is often described as a "legitimacy crisis". For a recent empirical intervention in this debate, see MARCEDDU and ORTOLANI, "What is Wrong with Investment Arbitration? Evidence From a Set of Behavioural Experiments", EJIL, 2020, p. 405 ff. See also WAIBEL et al. (eds.), *The Backlash against Investment Arbitration: Perceptions and Reality*, Alphen aan den Rijn, 2010; KULICK (ed.), *Reassertion of Control over the Investment Treaty Regime*, Cambridge, 2016. For a more critical account, see SORNARAJAH, *Resistance and Change in the International Law on Foreign Investment*, Cambridge, 2015.

urban areas and populations.[7] As this article contends, from an urban-rural frame, this context points to the regime's potential to reproduce through geographical affinities the global growth of political and economic polarization between urban and non-urban areas, but also to its potential to address them. The place and impact of these decisions on non-urban areas has so far principally been examined through frames that emphasize impact in terms of the "environment" or "local communities" together with calls for more policy space for States. The addition of an "urban-rural" frame centers additional impacts in terms of non-urban public interest, local participation, and the distribution of resources, and queries the ability of domestic policies alone to respond to them in the pursuit of socially and economically inclusive investment.

By focusing on the urban-rural divide, this article adopts a geographically scaled, bottom-up, and pluralist understanding of traditional or abstracted categories such as the unitary "State" or the "public interest". It takes an urban-rural continuum, that for present purposes it frames as a binary, as a political and economic heuristic for a socio-spatial spectrum that ranges from, the urban, that is metropolitan areas formed around large cities with densely populated areas to, the non-urban, that is the "in-between" peri-urban and towns with a rural hinterland with intermediate density areas and rural areas with thinly populated areas.[8] In short, the "urban" in this article refers to the contemporary centers of global economic power and capital accumulation, that is the metropolitan areas whose political and economic preferences increasingly differ from and create the "non-urban" or "rural",[9] that is the suburb, provincial town, and rural countryside.

This article suggests that the regime's impact on spatial inequalities, and in particular the urban-rural divide, must be better understood for the regime to address a possible source of backlash and foster more political and economic inclusion.[10] Interrogating the link between the regime and the urban-rural divide might provide an additional lens to explaining backlash against the regime, as well as contemporary sources of domestic political and social unrest.[11] This should be

---

[7] See *infra* Section 3 for an elaboration of the data on which this claim is based.

[8] For an attempt at a typology of this urban-rural continuum, see DIJKSTRA and POELMAN, "A Harmonized Definition of Cities and Rural Areas: The New Degree of Urbanisations", European Commission Regional Working Article, WP 01/2014. For an overview of different approaches to describing the categories of the "urban" and the "rural", see KRATZER and KISTER, "Rural-Urban Linkages for Sustainable Development: An Introduction", in KRATZER and KISTER (eds.), *Rural-Urban Linkages for Sustainable Development*, London/New York, 2021, p. 1 ff.

[9] The "non-urban" and the "rural" are used interchangeably in this article to describe areas that are not metropolitan.

[10] One possible approach to inclusivity, albeit using the increasingly criticized concept of "growth", is provided by the OECD's framework for "inclusive growth". See OECD, "Opportunities for all: OECD Framework for Policy Action on Inclusive Growth", 2018, available at: <https://www.oecd.org/inclusive-growth/resources/Opportunities-for-all-OECD-Framework-for-policy-action-on-inclusive-growth.pdf>.

[11] "Political economy research has analyzed the channels through which domestic geography conditions policy pressures and the ultimate effects on policy outputs. Many of these studies touch on geography without engaging it squarely. Only recently have place and space en-

of great interest to foreign investors since political and social unrest can greatly affects the economic and "social license to operate"[12] of their projects, and critically undermine in the process the regime's promise of managing and mitigating political risk.[13] Such an inquiry also has the potential to provide another level of governance to advance sustainable development and the goal of sustainable urbanization provided for in the Sustainable Developments Goals (SDGs)[14] and the UN-Habitat's Guiding Principles for Urban-Rural Linkages.[15]

In the context of the highly polarized debates about the investment treaty regime, the approach adopted in this article, inspired by new legal realism and liberal theories that focus on State-society relations and transnational linkages, attempts to overcome familiar dualisms. It moves away from the way international economic agreements and domestic social policies are usually treated separately,[16] and it is not easily situated within the "pro-state" or the "pro-investor" camp. Indeed, as discussed later in the article, the urban-rural divide has important implications for both camps. This approach also suggests a different view of the elite and unequal nature of the investment treaty regime as it invites a focus on the regime's impact on global spatial inequalities within the State,[17] without denying the impact of other factors such as technological change on these inequalities.[18] Thus, it departs from the usual focus on, for example, elite arbitrators,[19] inequali-

---

tered the literature sistematically". See CHASE, "Domestic Geography and Policy Pressures", in MARTIN (ed.), *Oxford Handbook of the Political Economy of International Trade*, Oxford, 2015, p. 316 ff., p. 316.

[12] See e.g. MARCOUX and NEWCOMBE, "Bear Creek Mining Corporation v Republic of Peru: Two Sides of a 'Social License' to Operate", ICSID Review, 2018, p. 653 ff.

[13] For the classic argument about this function, see GUZMAN, "Why LDCs Sign Treaties That Hurt Them: Explaining the Popularity of Bilateral Investment Treaties", Virginia Journal of International Law, 1998, p. 639 ff.

[14] The UN's 2030 Agenda for Sustainable Development (SDGs) provides a global goal for sustainable urbanization under Sustainable Development Goal 11 to "Make cities and human settlements inclusive, safe, resilient and sustainable". At Target 11.a of SDG 11, urban-rural linkages are addressed explicitly through the need to "support positive economic, social and environmental links between urban, peri-urban and rural areas". See also SDG 9, "Build resilient infrastructure, promote inclusive and sustainable industrialization and foster innovation".

[15] The UN's 2016 New Urban Agenda aims to foster urban-rural linkages and an integrated territorial development in order to reduce inequalities and poverty in both, so that no space, urban and rural, is left behind. One of its thematic areas is the development of governance structures that promote these linkages. See UN Habitat, "Urban-Rural Linkages: Guiding Principles and Framework for Action to Advance Integrated Territorial Development", 2019, available at: <https://unhabitat.org/sites/default/files/2020/03/url-gp-1.pdf>.

[16] On a recent intervention illuminating the problems with this separation, see SHAFFER, "How Do We Get Along? International Economic Law and the Nation-State", Michigan Law Review, 2019, p. 1229 ff.

[17] On the notion of spatial inequality and its development over the past several decades, see WEI, "Spatiality of Regional Inequality", Applied Geography, 2015, p. 1 ff.

[18] On the link between trade and technology, see SHAFFER, "Retooling Trade Agreements for Social Inclusion", University of Illinois Law Review, 2019, p. 1 ff.

[19] See e.g. PUIG, "Social Capital in the Arbitration Market", EJIL, 2014, p. 387 ff.; GRISEL, "Competition and Cooperation in International Commercial Arbitration: The Birth of a Transnational Legal Profession", Law & Society Review, 2017, p. 790 ff. An approach that

ties between developed and developing States,[20] or interpersonal inequalities.[21] It also queries a traditional expectation that domestic policies alone following efficiency benefits of economic integration on aggregate national welfare are able to bear the burden of mending and compensating this urban-rural divide and other regional inequalities.[22] Indeed, "[g]lobal and regional economic integration can lead to increases in efficiency; however, those gains may be marginal in contrast to the risks to social inclusion and democracy".[23] This article also complements recent writing on the role of cities in international law.[24] This literature has focused on the perspective of the city and characterized the increasing interventions of city networks in global governance, particularly in the area of climate change,[25] in largely positive terms, following in some ways the dominant and triumphalist narrative around cities in the field of economics.[26] It has generally not considered in a critical perspective, however, what local preferences cities were thus centering or universalizing and how they might diverge, set-aside, or not include those from non-urban areas.

This article proceeds in four parts to frame the structure, operation, backlash, and reform of the investment treaty regime from the perspective of the

---

is part of the progeny of GARTH and DEZALAY, *Dealing in Virtue: International Commercial Arbitration and the Construction of a Transnational Legal Order*, Chicago, 1996.

[20] See e.g. SORNARAJAH, *The International Law on Foreign Investment*, Cambridge, 2017. The terms "developing State" and "developed State" are not without their problems as they can be imbued with colonial overtones and associated with such notions as the "civilized" and "uncivilized".

[21] Such as economic inequalities between people. For such an approach in the investment treaty regime, see e.g. VAN HARTEN, *The Trouble with Foreign Investor Protection*, Oxford, 2020. A focus more generally popularized by PIKETTY, *Capital in the Twenty-First Century*, Harvard, 2014. For a critique of Piketty's approach for the way it overlooks the geography of capital, see JONES, "The Geographies of Capital in the Twenty-First Century: Inequality, Political Economy, and Space" in BOUSHEY et al. (eds.), *After Piketty: The Agenda for Economics and Inequality*, Harvard University Press, 2017.

[22] On this and alternative narratives, see LAMP, "How Should We Think about the Winners and Losers from Globalization? Three Narratives and Their Implications for the Redesign of International Economic Agreements", EJIL, 2020, p. 1359 ff. See also PERRONE, "The Investment Treaty Regime and Local Populations: Are the Weakest Voices Unheard?", Transnational Legal Theory, 2016, p. 383 ff. For the traditional narrative in trade, see e.g. International Monetary Fund, World Bank and WTO, "Making Trade an Engine for Growth for All: The Case for Trade and for Policies to Facilitate Adjustment", 2017, available at: <https://www.imf.org/en/Publications/Policy-Papers/Issues/2017/04/08/making-trade-an-engine-of-growth-for-all>.

[23] SHAFFER, "How Do We Get Along?", *cit. supra* note 16, p. 1236.

[24] See generally AUST and NIJMAN (eds.), *cit. supra* note 4. See also AUST, "Shining Cities on the Hill? The Global City, Climate Change, and International Law", EJIL, 2015, p. 255 ff.; OOMEN and BAUMGÄRTEL, "Frontier Cities: The Rise of Local Authorities as an Opportunity for International Human Rights Law", EJIL, 2018, p. 607 ff.; SWINEY, "The Urbanization of International Law and International Relations: The Rising Soft Power of Cities in Global Governance", Michigan Journal of International Law, 2020, p. 227 ff.

[25] See e.g. AUST, "Shining Cities", *cit. supra* note 24.

[26] See e.g. GLAESER, *Triumph of the City: How Our Greatest Invention Makes Us Richer, Smarter, Greener, Healthier, and Happier*, London, 2011.

urban-rural divide. First, it provides a brief overview of the urban-rural divide and its contemporary salience as recently developed in the social sciences. Secondly, this divide is examined in the context of the investment treaty regime by contrasting along the urban-rural divide the location of the regime's principal actors (e.g. multinational corporations, global law firms, and national executive branches) and the typical foreign investment projects. Thirdly, the article examines the predominantly State-centric responses to the backlash against the regime and the consequences of such a framing in view of the growing salience of the urban-rural divide. Fourthly, and in conclusion, the article reflects on the path ahead and the possibilities for internal and external reforms towards mending this divide.

2. THE GROWING DIVIDE IN ECONOMIC AND POLITICAL PREFERENCES BETWEEN THE URBAN AND THE RURAL

This section defines the urban-rural divide in terms of two strands of literature that have examined the important changes to urban and rural life brought about over the past decades. The first strand has studied the rise of significant political and economic polarization between the urban, the suburban and the town, and the rural. The second has focused on the so-called "winners" of economic globalization: the global cities and mega-regions that have grown exponentially in economic power over the course of the past decades and are now said to manage the global economy. The object of this section is to provide a simplified account of these two strands of literature; it does not directly engage with their field-specific controversies, vocabularies, and the epistemic stakes in which they are invariably situated. This brief exposition sets the stage for an examination of how the political and economic polarization of urban and rural life described by this literature might translate into the investment treaty regime.

The first strand of literature is part of an emerging and burgeoning body of writing across several fields of the social sciences that has examined the rise of political and economic divides around the urban and the rural over the past decades. This literature began to gain momentum in response to the urban-rural divide made salient by the 2016 United Kingdom referendum on European Union membership and the inauguration of Donald J. Trump to the presidency of the United States in 2017. It has proceeded to highlight important differences in economic and political preferences across the urban-rural divide.[27]

---

[27] For a prominent intervention, see RODRÍGUEZ-POSE, "The Revenge of the Places that Don't Matter (and What to Do About It)", Cambridge Journal of Regions, Economy and Society, 2018, p. 189 ff. See also CRAMER, *The Politics of Resentment: Rural Consciousness in Wisconsin and the Rise of Scott Walker*, Chicago, 2016; RODDEN, *Why Cities Lose: The Deep Roots of the Urban-Rural Political Divide*, New York, 2019; GORDON, "In What Sense Left Behind by Globalisation? Looking for a Less Reductionist Geography of the Populist Surge in Europe", Cambridge Journal of Regions, Economy and Society, 2018, p. 95 ff.

In terms of economic development, the empirical evidence this literature has put forward is stark. According to one account, "[l]abor force participation rates have a higher inter-regional variance in the EU and the USA than since the Great Depression of the 1930s".[28] This "divergent new geography of employment and incomes thus seems to correspond to a divergent new geography of opportunities".[29] It reverses a historical trend, at least in the United States, where "[f]rom 1940 to about 1980, variation in inter-State incomes in the USA steadily narrowed, and suburbs and metropolitan hinterlands grew more in population and incomes than inner metropolitan areas".[30] A certain dominant economic narrative supports the focus on large and dense cities as bastions of productivity,[31] since "urban density provides the clearest path from poverty to prosperity".[32] It has led to policies whose main aim has been "to move people to places where there are opportunities, not opportunities to declining areas".[33] The consequence, with these policies arguably "overestimating the capacity and willingness of individuals to move",[34] have been areas left-behind. Relying on traditional policies that have emphasized transfers and welfare,[35] these areas with few opportunities have generated serious political repercussions (e.g. the rise of nationalist parties) including a backlash against economic globalization which is often seen as a cause for wage stagnation and job loss.[36]

Thus, with economic polarization come differentiated political preferences. Differences in economic development have been shown to track political preferences too, including attitudes towards globalization.[37] The divide is said to be reflected in political divergences between urban and rural areas in countries such as France[38] and Italy.[39] In the United Kingdom, for example, studies have found that "British citizens who live in economically depressed and declining districts are

---

[28] STORPER, "Separate Worlds? Explaining the Current Wave of Regional Economic Polarization", Journal of Economic Geography, 2018, p. 247 ff.

[29] Ibid.

[30] Ibid.

[31] For an example of this view, see RODRÍGUEZ-POSE, cit. supra note 27, pp. 191-192.

[32] GLAESER, cit. supra note 26, p. 1.

[33] RODRÍGUEZ-POSE, cit. supra note 27, p. 192.

[34] Ibid., p. 201.

[35] Ibid., pp. 202-204.

[36] See AOYAMA et al., "Globalisation, Uneven Development and the North–South 'Big Switch'", Cambridge Journal of Regions, Economy and Society, 2018, p. 17 ff.

[37] See generally in the context of the EU, DE DOMINICIS, DIJKSTRA, and PONTAROLLO, cit. supra note 2.

[38] See e.g. ERIBON, Returning to Reims, Cambridge (Massachussets), 2013; IVALDI and GOMBIN, "The Front National and the Pew Politics of the Rural in France", in STRIJKER et al. (eds.), Rural Protest Groups and Populist Political Parties, Wageningen, 2015, available at: <https://halshs.archives-ouvertes.fr/halshs-01245081/document>; GUILLUY, Le crépuscule de la France d'en haut, Paris, 2016.

[39] See e.g. AGNEW and SHIN, "Spatializing Populism: Taking Politics to the People in Italy", Annals of the American Association of Geographers, 2017, p. 915 ff. For an argument about the urban roots of the populist phenomenon, see ROSSI, "The Populist Eruption and the Urban Question", Urban Geography, 2018, p. 1425 ff.

more likely to develop anti-immigrant and Eurosceptic views".[40] These findings have also been examined in more systemic ways. An emerging literature that has looked at the "geography of EU discontent" has found that EU discontent is a geography composed of "people living in a mix of stagnating and low-productivity regions – mainly rural areas and medium-sized and small cities" with their views formed "as a direct consequence of the limited opportunities and economic development prospects they face".[41] Indeed, a study of the period between 2002-2018 found a "strong and significant divide between the political outlooks of urban and rural Europe", with those living in suburbs, towns, rural areas "likely to be conservative in their orientation, dissatisfied with the functioning of democracy in their country, and less likely to trust the political system". Connecting these findings more overly with economic decline, a study of 63,417 electoral districts across all EU countries in the 2019 European Parliament elections observed that voting for an anti-EU party is considerably higher in places where there is long-term economic decline, conjoined with lower population density, and rurality.[42] Although the studies above concern mostly Western States, other studies appear to confirm the global nature of this divide, finding namely that it is most striking in Africa, Eastern Europe, and in large parts of South Asia.[43]

The increasing polarization, at least in economic terms, across the urban-rural divide is further cemented by how the economic globalization of recent decades has been closely associated with the growth of the "global city".[44] Indeed, a large literature has observed that globalization and the globalized knowledge economy has led to an important rescaling from the national territory to global cities.[45] According to one prominent account, these networked global cities now act as "highly concentrated command points in the organization of the world economy", "key locations for finance and specialized service firms", and "sites of production (not only in material terms, but also ideational terms)".[46] The result are a series of metropolitan areas that are becoming ever-more central to global economic output because of their finance and knowledge economies. Studies appear to confirm this central role in global economic output as the largest 28 mega-regions within States (combinations of multiple metropolitan areas) now account

---

[40] CARRERAS et al., "Long-Term Economic Distress, Cultural Backlash, and Support for Brexit", Comparative Political Studies, 2019, p. 1396 ff. See also GOODWIN and HEATH, "The 2016 Referendum, Brexit and the Left Behind: An Aggregate-level Analysis of the Result", The Political Quarterly, 2016, p. 323 ff.

[41] DIJKSTRA et al., "The Geography of EU Discontent", Regional Studies, 2020, p. 737 ff., p. 744.

[42] Although they also found that "density becomes irrelevant once moderately anti-European votes included in the analysis [and not just parties opposed or strongly opposed to European integration]". See ibid., p. 748.

[43] See LESSMANN and SEIDEL, "Regional Inequality, Convergence, and Its Determinants – A View from Outer Space", European Economic Review, 2017, p. 110 ff.

[44] See generally SASSEN, Cities in a World Economy, Thousand Oaks, 2018.

[45] For an overview, see CURTIS, Global Cities and Global Order, Oxford, 2016.

[46] See SASSEN, The Global City: New York, London, Tokyo, Princeton, 1991, p. 3.

for over 80 percent of global economic output,[47] evoking the spatial concentration of economic activity and income.

Of course, the concept of a neat binary between the urban and rural would oversimplify what is a fairly complex political and economic divide more akin to a continuum that can vary according to the context of each country. A number of studies have indicated that this divide is "better understood as a gradient running from inner cities to metropolitan suburbs, towns, and the countryside".[48] Similarly, it can also be thought in terms of different scales, that is "between States or provinces; between metropolitan areas and less dense areas; between bigger and smaller metropolitan areas; and between inner metropolitan areas combined with their closer suburbs and the wider hinterlands of both".[49] Furthermore, not all large dense cities can be said to be bastions of productivity. This is the case of declining industrial hubs such as Los Angeles relative to San Francisco[50] or "Detroit, St Louis or Youngstown in the US, Guyuan, Yichun or Lanzhou in China, or Dnipropetrovsk in the Ukraine".[51] Finally, this divide should not obfuscate the fact that there are deep functional linkages between urban and non-urban areas in terms of products and services, labor, and environmental relations. Indeed, "[r]ural areas have provided food and water, fossil and renewable energy, timber for houses and fibre for clothing throughout history. People commute to the cities for work or education. Livelihoods and production networks depend on the relations between rural, peri-urban and urban".[52] These clarifications, however, merely provide more granular details as to the situation of certain cities and the relationship between urban and rural areas, they generally do not dispute the overall significance and growth of political and economic polarization between the urban and the non-urban.

3. THE URBAN LOCATION OF THE REGIME'S ACTORS AND THE RURAL LOCATION OF FOREIGN INVESTMENT PROJECTS

The previous section described how the economic and political preferences of the urban and the rural diverge significantly today. This section adopts a socio-legal perspective to describe how this urban-rural divide might manifest itself through the contrasting geographical location of the investment treaty regime's principal and most powerful actors and the location of foreign investment

---

[47] See ADLER, FLORIDA, and DIAS, "Mega-Regions, Agglomeration and Economic Structure", in RATLEDGE and IFTIKHAR (eds.), *Productivity Growth in the US: The Role of Urban and Regional Action*, Cham, 2020.

[48] SCALA and JOHNSON, "Political Polarization along the Rural-Urban Continuum? The Geography of the Presidential Vote, 2000-2016", The Annals of the American Academic of Political and Social Science, 2017, p. 162 ff.

[49] See STORPER, *cit. supra* note 28, p. 248.

[50] See STORPER et al., *The Rise and Fall of Urban Economies: Lessons from San Francisco and Los Angeles*, Stanford, 2015.

[51] RODRÍGUEZ-POSE, *cit. supra* note 27, p. 192.

[52] KRATZER and KISTER, *cit. supra* note 8, p. 4.

projects.[53] This contrast exposes how these actors might be confronted to largely distinct economic and political preferences compared to the local (in many cases non-urban) communities where foreign investment projects are often located. Since decision-making processes in the regime are largely an urban phenomenon, as described below, this section suggests that the economic and political preferences of the urban are, absent any correction, at risk of being prioritized within the regime.

The principal actors in the investment treaty regime are arguably foreign investors, national governments (States), global law firms, and arbitration tribunals. States negotiate international investment agreements. These agreements allow foreign investors to bring claims against host States using investor-State arbitration, also commonly referred to as investor-State dispute settlement. From the frame of the urban-rural divide, the geographical location of the regime's most powerful actors is predominantly urban. Indeed, the negotiation of IIAs is principally left in the hands of trade negotiators and foreign relations departments within the executive branch.[54] These departments are mostly located within the urban core of capital cities. Similarly, the foreign investor is generally a multinational enterprise. Its corporate and regional headquarters, the center of gravity where decisions about foreign investments or ISDS are likely to be made, are usually located in metropolitan areas, often global cities,[55] a trend also apparent in Global South economies.[56] Finally, the global law firms that most often represent either the State or the foreign investor in investor-State arbitrations are also principally located in metropolitan areas,[57] as are actual arbitration proceedings and tribunals, with an

---

[53] Socio-legal approaches are a familiar move in the scholarship on the investment treaty regime, but they have most prominently focused on investment arbitrators. See for a representative publication, PUIG, *cit. supra* note 13. For a broader focus, see the contributions collected in HIRSCH and LANG (eds.), *Research Handbook on the Sociology of International Law*, Cheltenham, 2018.

[54] With respect to ISDS arbitrations, this can readily be observed from the list of party representatives in the documents produced over the course of investor-State arbitration proceedings, such as the first procedural order or the terms of appointment. For an account of the negotiation of IIAs by government officials, and their belief that they were merely technical agreements without understanding their implications, which resulted in the absence of public and other forms of oversight, see SKOVEGAARD POULSEN, *Bounded Rationality and Economic Diplomacy: The Politics of Investment Treaties in Developing Countries*, Cambridge, 2015, pp. 162-191.

[55] According to one account, six cities are the location of 68 multinational head offices which represents 29.2% of the total market value of the 250 largest corporations in the world. These cities are New York, London, Paris, Tokyo, Beijing, and Moscow. See RODRIGUE, *The Geography of Transport Systems*, London/New York, 2020. See also BELDERBOS, DU and GOERZEN, "Global Cities, Connectivity, and the Location Choice of MNC Regional Headquarters", Journal of Management Studies, 2017, p. 1271 ff.

[56] See generally McKinsey Global Institute, "Urban World: The Shifting Global Business Landscape", 2013, available at: <https://www.mckinsey.com/featured-insights/urbanization/urban-world-the-shifting-global-business-landscape#>.

[57] A review of the structure of leading international legal directories (by major metropolitan areas) and leading law firms is revealing of this urban-core centrism. See for instance the Chambers and Partners global arbitration ranking, available at: <https://chambers.com/

increasing number being located in arbitration centres in the business districts of global cities.[58]

As noted earlier, the metropolitan location of the investor, national governments, their lawyers and arbitration tribunals, might further serve to entrench the increasingly distinct economic and political preferences of the urban. The geographical location of these actors situates them in a context where the collective pursuit, socialization, and well-organized lobbying of the economic and political preferences of the urban is greatly facilitated. Put differently, this urban location might lead to a form of minoritarian bias, where "well-organized, discrete interests shape policy"[59] by being afforded greater participation in decision-making processes through geographical affinities. This prioritization of the urban only serves to further cement how the urban is already given an important voice to shape international agendas. Besides the outsized global economic power of mega-regions and their global cities, the local governments of cities are taking an increasingly important role in international relations, by using, for example, the language of international human rights law and environmental law,[60] and incorporating international law through urban policies and local ordinances.[61] Of course, city governments, at least in electoral democracies, are representative, and not solely driven by an issue or interest like corporate actors, which should make them more legitimate. Compared to national governments, they might bring more attention internationally to the needs of a local electorate,[62] and, as argued elsewhere, they also might bring forward a less polarized politics.[63] But in view of the growing urban-rural divide described above, and the concentration of economic power in mega-regions, which already affords the urban with an outsized voice to advance its preferences, the question remains whether the local electorate of the city is the one that is in most need of better global representation.

The metropolitan location of foreign investors or central government officials contrasts repeatedly with the non-urban location of foreign investment projects in host States. The large majority of IIAs define "investments" broadly by including "every kind of asset" owned or controlled by a foreign investor. Despite this broad material scope, in terms of geography, a significant portion of the foreign investment projects that lead to ISDS proceedings are materially located in non-urban areas. This finding is based on publicly available data compiled with re-

---

guide/global?publicationTypeGroupId=2&practiceAreaId=57&subsectionTypeId=1&locatio
nId=15649>.

[58] Such as the London Court of International Arbitration or the Singapore International Arbitration Centre.

[59] On majoritarian and minority bias in the investment treaty regime, see PUIG and SHAFFER, "Imperfect Alternatives: Institutional Choice and the Reform of Investment Law", AJIL, 2018, p. 361 ff., p. 381.

[60] The most prominent example being the C40 Climate Leadership Group. See e.g. AUST, cit. supra note 24. See also the contributions by BAKKER and NESI in this Symposium.

[61] See for examples of international treaties incorporated in this way, OOMEN and BAUMGÄRTEL, cit. supra note 24.

[62] See ibid.

[63] See SWINEY, cit. supra note 24.

spect to the quantity of investment disputes as delineated by economic sector.[64] According to data compiled by UNCTAD, close to half of ISDS arbitrations occur in the primary sector (e.g. agriculture, forestry, fishing, mining and quarrying) and in the tertiary energy provision sector (e.g. power plants, offshore wind projects). They represent 402 of a total of 1061 cases compiled by UNCTAD.[65] Similarly, in ICSID's distribution of cases by economic sector, 45% of cases are in the oil, gas & mining sector, the electric power & other sector, and the agriculture, fishing & forestry sector.[66] With the assumption that these sectors have a high likelihood of being located in non-urban areas due to their focus on natural resources, close to half of ISDS cases appear to concern projects that directly impact towns and rural areas. Of course, other economic sectors are likely to concern investments in non-urban areas too just as some of the selected economic sectors might include investments located in urban areas. Nevertheless, these economic sectors appear to be a reasonable heuristic for investments that have a high likelihood of being located in non-urban areas.

The geography of the regime's actors and foreign investment projects places the regime's decision-making process at a risk of underrepresenting the non-urban and its increasingly distinct economic and political preferences. In this context, non-urban populations, in both the Global North and the Global South, might seek to challenge the legitimacy of a regime that implicates their local resources but whose decision-making process is principally crafted and operated in distant urban areas whose prferences increasingly diverge from their own "community core values".[67] Similar challenges have been discussed in terms of, for instance, the collision of natural resource development projects and local and indigenous communities,[68] and the way the protection of foreign investor rights might pay "little attention to the questions that matter most for local populations, such as whether a target resource should be exploited or how the benefits should be distributed".[69] In the context of the urban-rural divide, the contrast between urban decision-making and non-urban impacts might feed into a general impression of political disempowerment, of being economically "left-behind" for the benefit of urbans areas. It also raises more general questions as to what economic

---

[64] The geographic data available follows familiar scales. Either it considers large regional groupings such as "Eastern Europe & Central Asia" or "South America", see ICSID, "The ICSID Caseload – Statistics", Issue 2021-1, 2021, available at: <https://icsid.worldbank.org/resources/publications/icsid-caseload-statistics>. Or it is sorted by country, see Investment Policy Hub, "Investment Dispute Settlement Navigator", available at: <https://investmentpolicy.unctad.org/investment-dispute-settlement>.

[65] As of 31 July 2020. See Investment Policy Hub, *cit. supra* note 64.

[66] See ICSID, *cit. supra* note 64.

[67] See *William Ralph Clayton, William Richard Clayton, Douglas Clayton, Daniel Clayton and Bilcon of Delaware, Inc. v. Government of Canada*, PCA Case 2009–04, Award on jurisdiction and liability of 17 March 2015, paras. 502-547.

[68] See e.g. PERRONE, "The Investment Treaty Regime", *cit. supra* note 22; COTULA and SCHRÖEDER, "Community Perspectives in Investor-State Arbitration," International Institute for Environment and Development, 2017, available at: <https://pubs.iied.org/12603iied>.

[69] PERRONE, "The Investment Treaty Regime", *cit. supra* note 22, p. 385.

and political preferences the regime as it is currently structured is or can prioritize and which are marginalized.

An objection might be raised that an assimilation between national governments and the urban ignores the democratic processes States have in place to account for non-urban concerns. Several responses can be put forward to this objection. The most fortright would point to the apparent deficiencies of these processes in view of the growing political and economic polarization between the urban and the rural across the globe, as discussed in Section 2. To be fair, States do act with respect to this polarization, and at least in Europe they have traditionally resorted to inter-regional transfers and the welfare State to support declining regions. The results of these policies, however, have been mixed and subject to critique for not bringing geographically sensitive opportunities to these areas, that is opportunities that "respond to the structural opportunities, potential and constraints of each place"[70] instead of merely sheltering populations. Furthermore, despite the existence of democratic processes to account for non-urban concerns, the growing polarization between the urban and the rural might reflect the overall weakening of the link between citizens and their representatives in modern democracies, and the related divide between local and national governments.[71] Specifically, the executive branch, particularly where trade negotiations are concerned, can in both developing and developed countries abuse its "executive monopoly" to limit its "own legal, democratic, and judicial accountability vis-à-vis citizens".[72] Indeed, in many jurisdictions, constitutional arrangements are such that matters of foreign policy find themselves at quite a distance from oversight by civil society and national parliaments beyond the process of treaty ratification.[73] This has been the case, for instance, when the implications of IIAs were not well understood.[74] And it reflects a larger trend that sees globalization lead to shifts in the internal redistribution of power in the State towards the executive.[75] Overall, this is an area that, as others have already acknowledged, requires further research as "[t]he role of investment treaties for domestic policy-making has not been subject to considerable research to date"[76] just as "questions

---

[70] RODRÍGUEZ-POSE, *cit. supra* note 27, p. 205.

[71] On this weakening link, see generally ROSANVALLON, *Counter-Democracy: Politics in an Age of Distrust*, Cambridge, 2013.

[72] For a Global North account, see e.g. PETERSMANN, "Transformative Transatlantic Free Trade Agreements without Rights and Remedies of Citizens?", JIEL, 2015, p. 579 ff. For a Global South account, see e.g. SKOVEGAARD POULSEN, *cit. supra* note 54.

[73] As demonstrated, for instance, by the opacity surrounding the negotiations of investment treaties such as the EU-Canada Comprehensive and Economic Trade Agreement (CETA) and Transatlantic Trade and Investment Partnership Agreement (TTIP) which were in large part led by government officials and risked undermining citizens' rights of participation.

[74] See SKOVEGAARD POULSEN, *cit. supra* note 54. Not only developing countries but also some developed countries that signed IIAs during this period were not aware of their implications. See generally BONNITCHA et al., *The Political Economy of the Investment Regime*, Oxford, 2017, pp. 181-206.

[75] See e.g. SASSEN, *Territory, Authority, Rights – From Medieval to Global Assemblages*, Princeton, 2006, pp. 168-179.

[76] BONNITCHA et al., *cit. supra* note 74, p. 216.

about investment treaties and democracy have received little attention in scholarship on the investment treaty regime".[77]

It might be further objected that, for international law, a link between a geographical location (i.e. the metropolitan, the town, the rural) and discrete economic and political preferences is of little significance. Yet, in addition to the way the urban-rural divide has gained significance as a determinant for economic and political polarization, in the discipline of international law, associating actors with the preferences of a powerful and geographically delimited location is a well-established heuristic. The most telling example is the State, a geographically delineated form of socio-political organization that in many realist and rational choice accounts is a unit or "black box" that advances its own distinct set of national preferences.[78] In other approaches, the State is commonly used as a heuristic to explain the variety of preferences its nationals, from international judges to international lawyers more generally, might seek to advance.[79] In a similar vein, the Third World Approaches to International Law (TWAIL) movement has long associated a specific set of preferences with geographic locations such as the Third World, the Global North, the West,[80] and these locations often do not have precise contours.[81]

4. THE STATE-CENTERED RESPONSES TO BACKLASH IN THE CONTEXT OF THE URBAN-RURAL DIVIDE

As discussed above, decision-making in the investment treaty regime occurs largely in urban areas, but foreign investment projects and their material impacts are often located in non-urban areas. This geographic divide might be a source of backlash against the investment treaty regime: it potentially undermines the participation of non-urban areas and prioritizes urban preferences. Of course, there are different reasons, factors, and beliefs behind the backlash against the regime. But the principal responses to backlash have overshadowed this divide by mostly centering discussions on giving more control to a unitary State and its corollary, the national public interest.

A principal criticism around the backlash against the investment treaty regime is the perception that the regime favors a discrete group of foreign investors

---

[77] *Ibid*, p. 236.
[78] See e.g. GOLDSMITH and POSNER, *The Limits of International Law*, Oxford, 2005.
[79] For a recent espousal of this belief by considering how different States take different approaches to international law, see ROBERTS, *Is International Law International?*, Oxford, 2018.
[80] See ESLAVA and PAHUJA, "Between Resistance and Reform: TWAIL and the Universality of International Law", Trade, Law & Development, 2011, p. 104 ff.
[81] See BIANCHI, *International Law Theories: An Inquiry into Different Ways of Thinking*, Oxford, 2016, p. 205. ("It may well be that the very notion of the 'Third World' is ill-conceived to begin with. Even if it were to be accepted as a legitimate characterization of the geographical space or geopolitical entity whose existence it presupposes, many would look at it as anachronistic or terribly imprecise").

over the preferences of host States. According to this view, ISDS or the mere threat of an investment claim (usually referred to as "regulatory chill")[82] acts to curtail the ability of States to regulate in the public interest in areas such as the environment, human rights, or cultural heritage.[83] Several responses have been put forward to this criticism, namely by the European Union which advocates an investment court system (ICS),[84] by UNCITRAL and the work of its Working Group III,[85] by a large volume of academic commentary,[86] and by States directly who have acted both as principals (e.g. renegotiating IIAs) and litigants (e.g. advancing certain interpretations of treaty provisions before arbitral tribunals).[87] Much of these discussions, however, are "focused exclusively on states and their roles in, and their expectations towards, investment disputes".[88] This State-centrism reflects not only traditional notions of State consent but also, to some extent, how antagonism in the regime now appears to be coalescing around an opposition between the contracting States to IIAs vs. the foreign investor and ISDS tribunals, rather than the familiar oppositions between developed States vs. developing States or capital-exporting States vs. capital-importing States.[89] In this context, discussions about the need for more room for "public interest" are mostly assimilated with one side of this antagonism, the preferences of a unitary State.[90] Even when there is a move beyond the State, that is, when the views

---

[82] See e.g. TIENHAARA, "Regulatory Chill and the Threat of Arbitration: A View from Political Science", in BROWN and MILES (eds.), *Evolution in Investment Treaty Law and Arbitration*, CUP, 2011, p. 606 ff.

[83] See generally WAIBEL et al (eds.), *cit. supra* note 6; KULICK (ed.), *cit. supra* note 6. See the vast literature on more specific topics, e.g. DUPUY et al. (eds.), *Human Rights in International Investment Law and Arbitration*, Oxford, 2009; TIENHAARA, *The Expropriation of Environmental Governance: Protecting Foreign Investors at the Expense of Public Policy*, Cambridge, 2009; DUPUY and VIÑUALES (eds.), *Harnessing Foreign Investment to Promote Environmental Protection: Incentives and Safeguards*, Cambridge, 2013; VADI, *Cultural Heritage in International Investment Law and Arbitration*, Cambridge, 2014.

[84] See e.g. 2016 EU-Canada Comprehensive Economic and Trade Agreement, Interinstitutional File 2016/0206 (NLE) 10973/16, 14 September 2016. Adopted in Brussels on 30 October 2016.

[85] See generally the work of the United Nations Commission on International Trade Law (UNCITRAL), Working Group III (Investor-State Dispute Settlement Reform), in particular documents A/CN.9/930/Rev.1 and its addendum A/CN.9/935, A/CN.9/964, and A/CN.9/970.

[86] For an overview see PUIG and SHAFFER, *cit. supra* note 59; ROBERTS, "Incremental, Systemic, and Paradigmatic Reform of Investor-State Arbitration", AJIL, 2018, p. 410 ff.

[87] On this principal and litigant distinction see e.g. LANGFORD, BEHN, and KRISTIAN FAUCHALD, "Backlash and State Strategies in International Investment Law", in AALBERTS and GAMMELTOFT-HANSEN (eds.), *Changing Practices of International Law*, Cambridge, 2017, p. 70 ff.

[88] MARCEDDU and ORTOLANI, *cit. supra* note 6, pp. 408-409. The State-centric framing is found in most recent volumes discussing these developments, see e.g. KULICK (ed.), *cit. supra* note 6; HINDELANG and KRAJEWSKI (eds.), *Shifting Paradigms in International Investment Law: More Balanced, Less Isolated, Increasingly Diversified*, Oxford, 2016.

[89] For this articulation, see KULICK, "Reassertion of Control: An Introduction", in KULICK (ed.), *cit. supra* note 6, p. 3 ff., p. 11.

[90] For this approach, see generally KULICK, *Global Public Interest in International Investment Law*, Cambridge, 2012. See also SCHILL and DJANIC, "Wherefore Art Thou?

of the "public" as a means to buttress the external legitimacy of the regime are discussed,[91] the "public" is rarely detailed, and certainly not to account for the possibility that public opinion might fundamentally diverge along the lines of bounded domestic spatial inequalities. Such an approach is perfectly epitomized for instance by the structure of the European Commission's Public Consultation on Investment Protection and Investor-to-State Dispute Settlement and its use of an indeterminate and geographically mute approach to the "public",[92] or by the way empirical studies in scholarship define geographical scales.[93] Yet public opinion as to whether, for example, IIAs increase foreign direct investment, might readily change if the "public" is situated in a global city or a rural area "left-behind" by globalization.[94] Indeed, this approach risks omitting a significant spectrum of views in light of the increased economic and political polarization across the urban-rural divide.

From the perspective of these discussions, much of the responses to backlash and its criticisms center around whether and how more control, policy space, or "right to regulate" should be given to States. For instance, the balance of rights and responsibilities in the investment treaty regime is being re-examined after what many see as an early development that was focused almost solely on the responsibility of host States.[95] In this vein, in the context of ISDS, a number of arbitration tribunals have shown deference to host States,[96] recognizing in the

---

Towards a Public Interest-Based Justification of International Investment Law", ICSID Review, 2018, p. 29 ff.

[91] That is its sociological or public legitimacy, see the seminal BUCHANAN and KEOHANE, "The Legitimacy of Global Governance Institutions", Ethics and International Affairs, 2006, p. 405 ff. Although legitimacy remains a concept infused with "fuzziness and indeterminacy", see e.g. CRAWFORD, "The Problems of Legitimacy-Speak", ASIL, 2004, p. 271 ff.

[92] See Public Consultation Commission, Online Public Consultation on Investment Protection and Investor-to-State Dispute Settlement (ISDS) in the Transatlantic Trade and Investment Partnership Agreement (TTIP), Staff Working Doc. (SWD) 3 final (2015).

[93] See a recent empirical study that frames geographic locations in terms of large regions such as "Europe", "North America", and "Latin America": MARCEDDU and ORTOLANI, cit. supra note 6. See also VOETEN, "Public Opinion and the Legitimacy of International Courts", Theoretical Inquiries in Law, 2013, p. 411 ff.

[94] Thus, any judgments as to the cognitive bias affecting the views of the "public" is inevitably affected by where this "public" is located. On cognitive biases and their impact on the legitimacy of international arbitration, but without accounting for these regional disparities, see STRONG, "Truth in a Post-Truth Society: How Sticky Defaults, Status Quo Bias and the Sovereign Prerogative Influence the Perceived Legitimacy of International Arbitration", University of Illinois Law Review, 2018, p. 533 ff.

[95] See HENCKELS, Proportionality and Deference in Investor-State Arbitration: Balancing Investment Protection and Regulatory Autonomy, Cambridge, 2015; HINDELANG and KRAJEWSKI (eds.), cit. supra note 88. For an earlier intervention, see KINGSBURY and SCHILL, "Public Law Concepts to Balance Investors' Rights with State Regulatory Actions in the Public Interest – The Concept of Proportionality", in SCHILL (ed.), International Investment Law and Comparative Public Law, Oxford, 2010, p. 75 ff.

[96] See e.g. Total S.A. v. Argentine Republic, ICSID Case No. ARB/04/1, Decision on Liability of 27 December 2010, paras. 114-34, para. 115 (noting that States "do not thereby relinquish their regulatory powers nor limit their responsibility to amend their legislation in

process the complex nature of democratic decision-making and the proximity of States to their populations. Although never articulated in terms of the urban-rural divide, by leaving sensitive matters of public interest in the hands of the States and its deliberative processes, this deference might be more inclusive of political and economic preferences that might otherwise be marginalized. Indeed, compared to the domestic order, the international legal order and ISDS in particular do not have processes of democratic deliberation in place that would account for local populations or contextualize them within national development goals. Or as some critical accounts have noted, ISDS might actually undermine these processes of democratic deliberation.[97]

Yet the working assumption of a unitary State and related arguments for more State control are nevertheless confronted with the "little evidence that host States will necessarily use their regulatory powers to promote and protect local communities".[98] A number of ISDS disputes arise precisely because of the tension between the State's role in attracting foreign investment and the necessity that it benefits its entire population, including local (in many cases non-urban) communities most affected by the investment.[99] As noted earlier, the executive branches of host States, particularly those deciding on matters of foreign investments, might themselves be overly exposed to urban preferences as a result of their urban location and the economic power of these areas. Decisions with significant impact on non-urban areas are often taken by the executive branch, principally from the location of urban areas, with a risk that they end up being decoupled from the political and economic realities of non-urban areas. This decoupling can have important consequences, as "official approval of an investment without prior consultation [of affected local communities] could trigger community protests, State action to address community concerns, and ultimately the investor-State dispute".[100] Unless decisions are also expressly formulated in terms of the urban-rural divide, or such commitments enshrined in treaties, the question therefore remains whether executive branch officials would use their newfound regulatory room to benefit non-urban populations, or whether they

---

order to adapt it to change and the emerging needs and requests of their people"). See generally HENCKELS, *cit. supra* note 95.

[97] For well-known critiques of ISDS in terms of democratic accountability, see e.g. VAN HARTEN, *Investment Treaty Arbitration and Public Law*, Oxford, 2007; VAN HARTEN, *Sovereign Choices, Sovereign Constraints. Judicial Restraint in Investment Treaty Arbitration*, Oxford, 2013; SCHNEIDERMAN, *Constitutionalizing Economic Globalization – International Investment Law and Democracy's Promise*, Cambridge, 2008.

[98] PERRONE, "Making Local Communities Visible: A Way to Prevent the Potentially Tragic Consequences of Foreign Investment?", in SANTOS, THOMAS and TRUBECK (eds.), *World Trade and Investment Law Reimagined. A Progressive Agenda for an Inclusive Globalization*, London, 2019, p. 171 ff., p.171.

[99] For an example of this tension, see *Copper Mesa Mining Corporation v. Republic of Ecuador*, PCA Case 2012–2, Award of 15 March 2016, paras. 1.93-94 and 1.105. See also PERRONE, "The Investment Treaty Regime", *cit. supra* note 22.

[100] For an overview of instances where such disputes took place, see COTULA and SCHRÖDER, *cit. supra* note 68, p. 3.

might, in fact, contribute to further entrenching an urban-rural divide.[101] In that
sense, the proposal by the European Union for a multilateral investment court
system as a response to backlash, that is a standing tribunal with permanently
appointed judges,[102] would appear, in the absence of any concern to foster urban-
rural diversity, to further centralize decision-making in urban centres. Unless a
wide range of procedures for accounting for non-urban preferences are put into
place, the project risks feeding into representations of ISDS as an urban-centric
initiative that is disconnected not only materially but politically and economically from non-urban concerns.

Even if all of the objections to State control were set aside, the "black box"
of the unitary State would leave unaddressed the impact of the investment treaty
regime on domestic spatial inequalities. There is a longstanding debate about
whether the conclusion of IIAs attracts foreign investment and leads to global
economic integration.[103] An eventual consensus as to the positive effect of IIAs
on investment, following the traditional narrative that economic integration benefits aggregate national welfare,[104] would nevertheless leave unresolved concerns
about its effect on spatial inequalities in terms of urban-rural development, that
is on economic integration at a scale other than that of the State. Indeed, when
the "spillover" benefits of foreign direct investment and trade more generally
are examined, it is not in terms of domestic spatial inequalities, but principally
in terms of industry, sectors, knowledge, and technology.[105] Illuminating the effect of international trade on domestic spatial inequalities, one recent study, for
instance, concluded that international trade openness "bring[s] about a significant
rise in within-country inequality across the developing world and that this impact
is greatest in the poorest countries".[106] Thus, although increase in trade "benefits
the countries involved in the process in aggregate terms, [it] is generating winning and losing regions".[107] As a starkly more critical account has suggested:
"[f]oreign investment creates an exploitative climate in the host States ensuring

---

[101] For a discussion of the allocation of policy space between the national and the international level, see the contributions collected in BIUKOVIC and POTTER (eds.), *Local Engagement
with International Economic Law and Human Rights*, Cheltenham, 2017.

[102] See European Commission, "Investment in TTIP and Beyond—The Path for Reform,
Enhancing the Right to Regulate and Moving from Current ad hoc Arbitration Towards an
Investment Court", May 2015, available at: <http://trade.ec.europa.eu/doclib/docs/2015/may/
tradoc_153408.PDF>. See generally BROWN, "A Multilateral Mechanism for the Settlement of
Investment Disputes. Some Preliminary Sketches", ICSID Review, 2017, p. 673 ff.

[103] For an early intervention, see SALACUSE and SULLIVAN, "Do BITs Really Work? An
Evaluation of Bilateral Investment Treaties and Their Grand Bargain", Harvard International
Law Journal, 2005, p. 67 ff. For a general overview, see BONNITCHA et al., *cit. supra* note 74,
pp. 155-180.

[104] See International Monetary Fund (IMF), World Bank and WTO, *cit. supra* note 22.
For this and other narratives about international economic agreements, see LAMP, *cit. supra*
note 22.

[105] See BONNITCHA et al., *cit. supra* note 74, pp. 46-50.

[106] EZCURRA and RODRIGUEZ-POSE, "Trade Openness and Spatial Inequality in Emerging
Countries", Spatial Economic Analysis, 2014, p. 162 ff.

[107] *Ibid.*

that elite and, to a lesser extent, the comprador communities they support receive benefits to the detriment of others within the State, often in particular minority communities".[108]

From the perspective of spatial inequalities within States, a narrative focused on more State control, as well as conclusive causalities between the conclusion of IIAs and increases in aggregate national welfare, is unlikely to be a sufficient basis for assuaging certain forms of backlash. Indeed, the traditional response to these forms of backlash would be that domestic social policy, following the benefits from economic cooperation, should be left to handle redistribution and adjustment policies for the "losers" of economic globalization.[109] Yet unitary State responses to backlash that do not consider the regime's uneven economic and political consequences within States might not be fully capable of assessing the extent of and the State's ability to respond to these consequences after the fact.[110] They also risk perpetuating traditional policies that have not prevented backlash, that is supporting productive capital accumulation in urban areas and providing transfers or welfare that shelter the populations of declining non-urban areas.[111] The question therefore remains how the investment treaty regime can support policies that are more socially inclusive and work towards providing opportunities to both urban and non-urban areas.

5. THE PATH AHEAD AND CONCLUDING THOUGHTS

All of the concerns discussed above raise pressing questions about how the investment treaty regime might respond to spatial inequalities along the urban-rural divide. That is, how might the regime foster greater inclusion of non-urban populations. To be clear, the point is not that the State cannot or should not be a trustee of the public interest and in light of its democratic accountability and democratic deliberation processes given discretion to respond to the urban-rural divide within its own national borders. Rather, since the investment treaty regime is allocated significant economic and regulatory power, and particularly exposed to the risk of prioritizing urban preferences as detailed earlier, it has the potential to have important impacts on the urban-rural divide.

These impacts and their distributive consequences within States might require international cooperation rather than domestic policies alone. Indeed, the UN-Habitat's Guiding Principles on Urban-Rural Linkages expressly advocates for multi-level and vertically integrated governance on spatial inequalities at the

---

[108] LINARELLI et al., *The Misery of International Law: Confrontations with Injustice in the Global Economy*, Oxford, 2017, p. 152.

[109] See International Monetary Fund, World Bank and WTO, *cit. supra* note 22.

[110] Indeed, in the context of trade, international agreements "should not be assessed solely in terms of their impact on aggregate national and global GDP (the gains from trade), but also in terms of their distributional effects and their implication for social inclusion and social stability." See SHAFFER, "Retooling Trade Agreements", *cit. supra* note 18, p. 7.

[111] On these policies, see RODRÍGUEZ-POSE, *cit. supra* note 28, pp. 202-204.

local and global scale to promote integrated territorial development.[112] Such an approach can also be cast in terms of multilevel governance or "complementarity", that is where "international processes should be structured not as substitutes but as complement to domestic processes to assure government accountability".[113] Put simply, the investment treaty regime and domestic social policies should be supportive of each other,[114] and "the goal of resource allocation efficiency should be framed in terms of optimal investment to advance social welfare, not investment protection per se".[115] This approach appears to be in the interest of foreign investors too, as the disregard of excessive polarization between urban and non-urban areas by the regime might have adverse effects on their investment if it sustains political and social unrest or prevents them from obtaining a social license to operate in the non-urban areas where their projects are located. A number of adjustments to the regime could eventually be considered so that it is more responsive to local non-urban contexts, including internal reforms through the application and interpretation of existing treaties or external reforms through treaty making. Some initial thoughts on these are provided below.

Third-party participation in ISDS through *amicus curiae* submissions might be one way to empower non-urban preferences. Arbitral tribunals have accepted a number of third-party interventions, and in many of these cases, these interventions related to concerns with respect to what are commonly labelled "local communities".[116] A number of these interventions geographically scale to non-urban areas and overlap with their preferences.[117] As described by one author, "local communities are easier to identify and more homogenous than urban groups. They share a specific locality, a common cultural identity and previous experiences of resistance and organization. This applies not only to indigenous or ethnic communities but also to small towns".[118] Framing third-party interventions in terms of the urban-rural divide could broaden the scope for what is deemed a significant interest in a dispute and its degree of impact on the public interest, all threshold issues that arbitral tribunals have considered when allowing intervention.[119] And it might lead to more meaningful investment projects that respond better to the potential, opportunities, and constraints of both urban and non-urban areas. It is difficult, however, to determine to what extent in practice these inter-

---

[112] See UN Habitat, *cit. supra* note 15. See generally KRATZER and KISTER (eds.), *cit. supra* note 8.

[113] PUIG and SHAFFER, *cit. supra* note 59, p. 362.

[114] For this argument in trade, see SHAFFER, "Retooling Trade Agreements", *cit. supra* note 18.

[115] PUIG and SHAFFER, *cit. supra* note 59, p. 373.

[116] For an overview, see COTULA and SCHRÖEDER, *cit. supra* note 68.

[117] See e.g. *Bear Creek Mining Corporation v. Republic of Peru*, ICSID Case No. ARB/14/21; *Pac Rim Cayman LLC v. Republic of El Salvador*, ICSID Case No. ARB/09/12.

[118] PERRONE, "Making Local Communities Visible", *cit. supra* note 98, p. 9.

[119] See e.g. *Pac Rim Cayman LLC v. Republic of El Salvador*, ICSID Case No. ARB/09/12, Decision on Respondent's Preliminary Objections of 2 August 2010, para. 50; *Apotex Inc v. The Government of the United States*, ICSID Case No. UNCT/10/2, Procedural Order on the Participation of the Applicant, BNM, as a Non-Disputing Party of 11 October 2011.

ventions would lead to the meaningful participation by non-urban populations.[120] Indeed, general efforts to integrate local communities' preferences through third-party participation lead to collective action problems and could potentially serve to reinforce the participation of sophisticated urban agents or activists and their preferences, as resource and expertise are required to prepare such submissions. This might explain why, for instance, several of the early ISDS cases that dealt with third-party intervention were about investments located in or around urban areas where such resources and expertise might readily be found.[121] In addition to these limits, third-party interventions are rather infrequent, and it remains unclear the extent to which the views of these interventions are taken into account in an arbitration tribunal's decision-making process.[122] Finally, the overall benefits of third-party participation at the stage of ISDS are likely to be limited; this type of third-party consultation should be undertaken throughout the entire life of the foreign investment project, that is before and after the establishment of the foreign investment,[123] to better tailor investment to local contexts and opportunities.

The regime's shift towards sustainable development provides another entry point to more inclusive urban and rural development.[124] Indeed, the UN's 2030 Agenda for Sustainable Development, and in particular Sustainable Development Goal 11 and its target 11 expressly seeks "to support positive economic, social and environmental links between urban, peri-urban and rural areas". Further guidance to that effect can be found in the UN-Habitat's Guiding Principles for Urban-Rural Linkages,[125] part of the UN's New Urban Agenda which seeks to localize the UN's 2030 Agenda for Sustainable Development.[126] In ISDS, the

---

[120] For a critical view on the opportunities for third-parties to bring concerns to ISDS, see e.g. VAN HARTEN, *Sovereign Choices*, *cit. supra* note 97.

[121] For example, the privatization of water and sewage services and electricity generation in Bolivia's third largest city, see *Aguas del Tunari v. Bolivia*, ICSID Case No. ARB/02/3. Or a concession for water distribution and waste water treatment services in the city of Buenos Aires and its surrounding municipalities *Suez, Sociedad General de Aguas de Barcelona S.A. and Vivendi Universal S.A v. Argentine Republic*, ICSID Case No. ARB/03/19.

[122] According to one author, since the first series of non-disputing party submissions in ICSID well over a decade ago, only 16 applications for non-disputing party have been made out of a total of 309 concluded cases. See BUTLER, "Non-Disputing Party Participation in ICSID Disputes: Faux Amici?", NILR, 2019, p. 143 ff., p. 172.

[123] For a focus on the period before the establishment of the investment, see generally PERRONE, "The Investment Treaty Regime", *cit. supra* note 22.

[124] See e.g. UNCTAD, IIA Issues Note No. 1, May 2018, p. 5 ("In contrast to the IIAs signed in 2000, the 2017 IIAs include a larger number of provisions explicitly referring to sustainable development issues (including by preserving the right to regulate for sustainable development-oriented policy objectives)". UNCTAD, "Investment Policy Framework for Sustainable Development", United Nations, 2012. See generally HINDELANG and KRAJEWSKI (eds.), *cit. supra* note 88. See also the Special Issue "Towards Better BITs? Making International Investment Law Responsive to Sustainable Development Objectives", Journal of World Investment & Trade, 2014. For a recent overview, see BJORKLUND, "Sustainable Development and International Investment Law", in MILES (ed.), *Research Handbook on Environment and Investment Law*, Cheltenham, 2019, p. 38 ff.

[125] See UN Habitat, *cit. supra* note 15.

[126] See generally KRATZER and KISTER (eds.), *cit. supra* note 8.

concept of sustainable development tends to regularly be interpreted with environmental protection, as investment cases with increasing frequency have raised environmental concerns.[127] Many of these cases directly affect the urban-rural divide with environmental concerns often beginning where they are first located, which appears to be often in non-urban areas.[128] Indeed, reviewing a recent list of 117 cases that have raised environmental issues,[129] and assuming that the economic sector of activity provides an indication for the location of foreign investment projects, a majority of these cases seem to concern investment projects that are located in non-urban areas.[130] Tribunals might therefore seek to be more sensitive to the way environmental issues, for example, are likely to also raise important distributive effects along the urban-rural divide. In practice, this could mean that tribunals exert greater deference to government decision-making or integrate in their proportionality balancing when a foreign investor's investment project raises environmental issues or impact local communities,[131] cognizant that important urban-rural distributive issues and their associated political and social consequences might be at stake.

The incremental and internal approach to the urban-rural divide described above might prove insufficient in light of the numerous criticisms laid at the very structure of the investment treaty regime.[132] From that perspective, balancing and deference is unlikely to provide sufficient room for public interest goals that account for the urban-rural divide and the preoccupations of non-urban populations if the entire system is seen as inherently skewed in favor of the preferences of the foreign investor. An internal approach is also unlikely to entirely address the possibility that the regime structurally favors urban economic and political preferences. Indeed, an important risk to foreign investments might now reside in the competing preferences of urban and non-urban populations.[133] These geographical issues, oft-overlooked, might require more substantive treaty-making reforms to look at how the benefits of economic integration should be distributed. That is a need, like in the trade law context, to review IIAs to "facilitate domestic

---

[127] See VIÑUALES, "Foreign Investment and the Environment in International Law: Current Trends", in MILES (ed.), *cit. supra* note 124, p. 12 ff.

[128] Take some of earliest ICSID cases which have raised environmental concerns such as *Metalclad Corp v. Mexico*, ICSID Rep. 212, 2000 or *Tecmed SA v. Mexico*, ICSID Rep. 130, 2003. Both concerned investments that occurred principally in non-urban areas. In the case of Metalclad, this was a hazardous waste disposal landfill, and in Tecmed, a landfill for hazardous toxic waste.

[129] See VIÑUALES, *cit. supra* note 127.

[130] For a typical example, see *Clayton*, Award on jurisdiction and liability, *cit. supra* note 67.

[131] See generally GRUSZCZYNSKI and WERNER (eds.), *Deference in International Courts and Tribunals: Standard of Review and Margin of Appreciation*, Oxford, 2014; HENCKELS, *cit. supra* note 95.

[132] See e.g. VAN HARTEN, *The Trouble*, *cit. supra* note 21; KOSKENNIEMI, "It's Not the Cases, It's the System", Journal of World Investment & Trade, 2017, p. 343 ff.

[133] A similar view is evoked by Nicolas Perrone in connection with local populations: see PERRONE, "The Investment Treaty Regime", *cit. supra* note 22, p. 386.

policies that serve people and societies more inclusively".[134] It remains uncertain, however, when such external reforms might be adopted and whether they are feasible at all with the current return of geopolitics. Further, the lengthy period for these reforms to take effect are unlikely to dampen the current wave of backlash and unrest. In that sense, pragmatic incremental changes to interpretive practices of the regime afford more immediate solutions, as prior ISDS decisions and their reasoning often have quasi-precedential effect on arbitration tribunals.[135] At this point, more modestly, introducing a geographical concept, the urban-rural divide, as a frame to contemporary debates about the investment treaty regime and its reform, might contribute to a better understanding of "backlash", and what it stands for. It might also contributes to a conversation about the global growth of spatial inequalities within States, and how to best promote socially and economic inclusive investment.[136] Framed in these terms, the investment treaty regime might also appear as a site of struggle between the urban and the non-urban for the distribution of resources.

---

[134] SHAFFER, "Retooling Trade Agreements", *cit. supra* note 18, p. 17.

[135] See e.g. BJORKLUND, "Investment Treaty Arbitral Decisions as *Jurisprudence Constante*", in PICKER et al. (eds.), *International Economic Law: The State and Future of the Discipline*, Oxford/Portland, 2018, p. 265 ff.

[136] On how the geography of capital is overlooked with, as an example, Thomas Piketty's work on economic inequality, see JONES, *cit. supra* note 21.

CITIES AND COUNTRYSIDE: AN INTERNATIONAL LAW PERSPECTIVE

Francesco Francioni*

Abstract

Cities, as spaces of socio-cultural organization and economic interaction among people, have always played a dominant role in the development and implementation of international law. Today, a new strand of legal scholarship focuses on cities and local communities as competitors and partners with the nation State in a new project of modernization and democratization of international law. This paper looks at this new trend against the background of the historical narrative of cities in the development of international law. At the same time, it calls attention to the fact that half of humanity still lives and works in rural areas, in the vast countryside of the world. Rural communities have been the servants of the city since the beginning of time. Today, their dignity and rights are beginning to be recognized by acts of the United Nations such as the 2007 Declaration of the Rights of Indigenous Peoples and the 2018 Declaration on the Rights of Peasants. Yet, these people remain a disadvantaged and vulnerable class. A true modernization and democratization of international law requires that we keep a balanced approach to the legal recognition of the voices and rights of urban communities and those of the people who work and live in the countryside of the world.

Keywords: cities in international law; local communities; local government; Peasant Declaration; sustainable development; rural communities.

1. Cities and the Nation State

Historically, the city has been the privileged *locus* of socio-cultural organization and economic interaction among human beings (*civitas*). It is the physical place (*urbs*) where, in different epochs, different institutions and forms of socio-political organization have found their origin and evolution. The infinite variety of modes in which this phenomenon has manifested itself in the various epochs cannot easily be placed within a clear chronological and geographical frame. The best-known historical examples of cities as hubs for the development and implementation of international law range from the ancient city States of classical Greece, to the East African cities of the pre-colonial period, the Communes and Maritime Republics of medieval Italy, the northern cities of the Hanseatic league, up to the examples of the mercantile cities of the early modern age, such

---

* Of the Board of Editors.

IYIL, Vol. 30 (2020), pp. 155-165
ISSN 0391-5107

as Amsterdam and London.[1] Each different type of city and every epoch has contributed to the formation and development of international law. The Greek city States laid down the prototypes of international treaties of alliance, peace and confederations and some minimum standards of humanitarian law of war;[2] the African cities bordering the Indian Ocean gave impulse to the formation of early rules on trade; and the Italian Maritime Republics, especially Venice, in their economic relations with the Muslim world, contributed to the development of a body of norms on diplomatic relations, and the treatment of aliens and their protection through the institution of consular relations.[3] The city of Amsterdam became the cradle of classical international law thanks to the legal opinions written by its eminent lawyer-philosopher, Hugo de Groot, on the dispute between Dutch public authorities and a private company over who should benefit from the capture of the Portuguese vessel *Santa Catarina* by the Dutch captain Jacob van Heemskerck.[4]

Cities were also the birthplace of the discipline of private international law and of the early theories concerning the choice of law applicable to legal relations connected to different cities and their different legal systems. We may recall that it was in thirteenth century Europe, at a time when university cities like Bologna were reviving the fire of civilization, that a learned group of legal scholars started to address the new emerging phenomenon of a plurality of distinct legislative and customary laws that every city was adopting and superimposing on the "common heritage" of Roman law. Which city law was applicable in disputes concerning, for example, property rights or succession between a citizen of Bologna and one of Venice? The answer was provided by the classification of the city laws into the two categories of *real statutes* and *personal statutes*, hence the name "Statutists" for the scholars who proposed this classification. The real statutes would apply only within the territory of the city. The personal statutes would instead follow the citizen outside the territory of the city and would be applicable within the territory of other cities. This formulation may sound simplistic and inadequate today, but the theories of the Statutists, developed in the context of inter-city relations, laid the foundations of modern private international law, and endured in Europe for centuries, up to the nineteenth century theories of Savigny[5] and P.S.

---

[1] For a comprehensive historical overview, see BERENGO, *L'Europa delle città. Il volto della società urbana europea tra Medio Evo ed Età moderna*, Torino, 1999; BRAUDEL, *Civilisation matérielle, économie et capitalisme (XVe–XVIIIe siècle). Le Temps du monde*, Paris, 1979, esp. Chapters II and III; ID, *La Méditerranée et le monde méditerranéen à l'époque de Philippe II*, Paris, 1949; COQUERY-VIDROVITCH, *The History of African Cities South of the Sahara: from the Origin to Colonization*, Princeton, 2005.

[2] FOCARELLI, *Introduzione storica al diritto internazionale*, Milano, 2013, p. 64 ff.

[3] AGO, "Pluralism and the Origin of the International Community", IYIL, 1977, p. 3 ff.; FERRARI BRAVO, *Lezioni di diritto internazionale*, Napoli, 1993, p. 25 ff.

[4] For a brilliant account of the events leading to the foundational writings of Hugo de Groot, see HATHAWAY and SHAPIRO, *The Internationalists: How a Radical Plan to Outlaw War Remade the World*, New York, 2017, p. 28 ff.

[5] SAVIGNY, *System des heutigen Roemitschen Rechts*, Berlin, 1849, Vol. VIII, dealing with conflict of laws.

Mancini,[6] and influenced also the development of the theories of conflict of laws in the United States.[7]

The emergence of the nation State as the centre of gravity of international law and its consolidation in the nineteenth century reduced the importance of cities as poles of socio-political aggregation, of cultural identity and of influence in international affairs. Within the logic of legal positivism and of the dual nature of the relationship between international law and the domestic legal order, cities and local government were destined to be absorbed within the latter order and to have no legal status in international law. Even the transformative phenomenon of de-colonization in the post WWII period did little to help cities and local governments regain an active role in international law. Former colonial peoples achieving their independence and realizing self-determination readily adopted the model of the sovereign nation State, in spite of the devastating effects that the model entailed in terms of displacement of local communities and the fragmentation of peoples.

2. CITIES AND GLOBALIZATION

With the onset of globalization, and as part of a post-globalization critique, a new interest has emerged in international scholarship over the revived role of cities and local communities in international relations.[8] Some of these reasons are well identified and analyzed in the specific contributions to this symposium dealing with critical issues of human rights, climate change, sustainable development, and security. But from a general point of view, it is safe to say that the very structural development of international law in the post-cold war era has determined a growing relevance of cities and local communities at the level of international relations. First, one must consider the pervasive effect of contemporary international law within the internal life of the State and its influence on what used to be matters of "domestic jurisdiction". These matters include human rights, the

---

[6] MANCINI, *Della nazionalità come fondamento del diritto delle genti: prelezione al corso di diritto internazionale e marittimo*, Torino, 1851.

[7] The importation of the Statutists' theories in the United States can be traced to the writing of LIVERMORE, legal counsel of the City of New Orleans, who wrote a *Dissertation on the Questions that Arise from the Contrariety of the Positive Law of Different States and Nations*, New Orleans, 1828 (discussed in DE NOVA, "The First American Book on Conflict of Laws", American Journal of Legal History, 1964, p. 136 ff). For a masterful reconstruction of the historical development of private international law, from the point of view of the United States, see CAVERS, *The Choice of Law Process*, Ann Arbor, 1966.

[8] See BLANK, "Localism and the New Global Legal Order", Harvard ILJ, 2006, p. 263 ff.; ID., "The City and the World", Columbia JTL, 2006, p. 875 ff; NIJMAN, "The Future of the City and the International Law of the Future", in MULLER et al. (eds.), *The Law of the Future and the Future of Law*, Oslo, 2011, p. 213 ff.; AUST, "Shining Cities on the Hill? The Global City, Climate Change and International Law", EJIL, 2015, p. 255 ff., providing a rich doctrinal analysis of current literature, mainly of socio-political science. A forthcoming book by AUST and NIJMAN (eds.), *Research Handbook on Cities and International Law*, Cheltenham, is scheduled to be published in 2021.

protection of the local environment, and the safeguarding and management of the cultural patrimony, just to mention the most important domains. Today, cities and local communities are playing an active role within these domains, both as participants in the exercise of regulatory powers by local government and as recipients of obligations arising directly from international law. This is evident in the field of human rights, where cities and local authorities are considered relevant actors in the promotion and protection of human rights.[9] At the same time, human rights courts do not hesitate to focus on the conduct of cities when determining breaches of applicable human rights treaties.[10] It is also evident in the field of European Union (EU) law, where cities have been found to have direct obligations within the multilevel regulatory system of the EU.[11] Cities are playing a relevant role also in the implementation of EU standards in areas such as air and water quality, and safe disposal of urban waste, as well as regulations on climate change mitigation. Increasingly, cities are acting in opposition to the policies of their national governments.[12]

But it is in the field of international cultural heritage law that we can find the most distinctive forms of leadership by cities and local communities. On the one hand, the listing of certain cities as World Heritage sites, under the 1972 UNESCO Convention, entails their recognition as sites of "outstanding universal value", which the international community has a shared interest in protecting.[13] At the same time, the process of inscription and maintenance of a city in the UNESCO World Cultural Heritage List may enhance the sense of autonomy and international relevance of the city with two contradictory effects. On the one hand, a World Heritage city may feel entitled to enact regulations that limit traditional economic freedoms – like freedom to provide services or freedom of movement of goods – with the commendable goal of preserving the authentic cultural qualities of the city, as required by the UNESCO Convention. At the

---

[9] See Human Rights Council, "Role of Local Government in the Promotion and Protection of Human Rights: Final Report of the Human Rights Council Advisory Committee", UN Doc. A/HRC/30/49 (2015).

[10] This is the practice of the European Court of Human Rights, even if, obviously, the international responsibility of the breach ultimately falls upon the State. See, for instance, *Oneryldiz v. Turkey*, Application No. 48939/99, Grand Chamber, Judgment of 30 November 2004, finding a breach of the right to life arising from the mismanagement by the city of Istanbul of a dangerous waste disposal site in a densely populated area, resulting in an explosion and loss of life of the inhabitants. For a critical analysis of the opportunities and pitfalls of cities as active participants in the protection of human rights, see OOMEN and BAUMGÄRTEL, "Frontier Cities: the Rise of Local Authorities as an Opportunity for International Human Rights Law", EJIL, 2018, p. 607 ff.

[11] See Case 103/88, *Fratelli Costanzo v. Comune di Milano*, ECR, 1989, 01839.

[12] See, for instance, the recent decision of the General Court concerning the joint actions undertaken by the cities of Paris, Brussels and Madrid for the partial annulment of EU Regulation 2016/646 concerning the limits on air pollution by commercial vehicles. EU General Court, Joined Cases T-339/16, T-352/16 and T-391/16, *Ville de Paris, Ville de Bruxelles and Ayuntamiento de Madrid v. Commission*, 13 December 2018. On this case see the contribution by BAKKER in this Symposium.

[13] See FRANCIONI, "World Cultural Heritage", in FRANCIONI and VRDOLJAK (eds.), *The Oxford Handbook of International Cultural Heritage Law*, Oxford, 2020, p. 250 ff.

same time, these regulations may result in the violation of other international obligations of the territorial State. An emblematic case is that of the controversial rules enacted by the municipality of Florence requiring business establishments within the area of the historic centre to use only traditional products and crafts in order to preserve the authenticity of local tradition as an integral element of the World Heritage value of the site. These regulations were challenged by private investors for their alleged incompatibility with economic freedoms.[14] At the same time, the sense of empowerment and autonomy of the local government may put the city on a route of collision with the national government and the obligations undertaken by it with international institutions. This is well exemplified by the circumstances that led to the deletion from the World Heritage List of the urban landscape of the city of Dresden. This unfortunate deletion occurred after the decision by the local authorities to proceed with the building of new infrastructure deemed by UNESCO to be incompatible with the original world heritage value of the city landscape, as recognized at the time of its inscription in the World heritage List.[15] This case demonstrates the difficulties of reconciling the legitimate claim of cities to an unimpeded exercise of their democratic prerogatives in the management of local affairs, with the need to ensure respect for the obligations undertaken by the State at international level.

3.   THE TRANSFORMATION OF THE CITY

The rising relevance of cities and local communities in international affairs is not only the result of their increasing exposure to the impact of international law, as discussed in the preceding section. It is also the result of a substantial transformation of the cities themselves in the present process of globalization. The most evident manifestation of this transformation is the rise of mega-cities. These are the very large metropolitan areas with millions of inhabitants living in huge urban sprawls that contain many different "cities": some central spaces, possibly of a historical character; business districts; residential areas, sometimes with "gated communities"; and large peripheral areas (the "*banlieues*") often degrading into slums. This type of city is the result of incessant urbanization, driven by globalization and by the promise for millions of people of leaving behind the life of

---

[14] Such municipal regulations gave rise to a dispute before local administrative courts between McDonald's and the city of Florence because of the latter's refusal to grant a licence for the opening of a new McDonald's establishment in the historic centre of the city. The refusal was justified by the fact that the location of the new restaurant was the main cathedral square, the iconic, "sacred", space in the heart of the historic centre of Florence. Now, Florence has at least three McDonald's in the centre of the city.

[15] Dresden, with its urban landscape of the Elbe Valley, had been nominated by Germany as a cultural heritage site and was deleted in 2009 after the decision by local authorities to proceed with the construction of a modern bridge over the Elbe river, rather than building an underground tunnel, as recommended by UNESCO, which would have safeguarded the integrity of the world heritage value of the urban landscape. See FRANCIONI, *cit. supra* note 13. See also the contribution by LIZINSKI in this Symposium

poverty and deprivation they have experienced in their rural homelands and in foreign countries. These modern cities depart from the traditional idea of the city as an organic and fairly homogeneous ensemble of monumental and vernacular architecture (*urbs*) that has evolved hand in hand with the development of social structures and local cultural traditions that form a collective identity and citizenry (*civitas*). This was the city idealized in the Renaissance following the humanistic principles of urban design developed by Leon Battista Alberti, and concretely applied in the construction of the "ideal" city of Pienza, now a World Heritage site in Tuscany.[16] Contemporary mega-cities, or "global cities" as they are sometimes called,[17] lack the most valuable element that characterizes the traditional city, as developed especially in the European experience, which is the cultural attachment of the population to the physical element of the city, to its territory and to the social structures that have historically evolved there and that have nourished the civic pride of its inhabitants.[18]

The process of gradual devaluation of the cultural link of the urban population with the territory of the city is further accelerated by the incessant loss of the economic, artisan and cultural activities that used to constitute the vital spark of city life and an important source of the intangible cultural heritage of the urban community. The digitalization of many economic activities and governmental functions, internet commerce, home entertainment, online information and communication services, they all contribute to the de-territorialization of city life, to the progressive loss of creative and productive activities and to the erosion of the cultural link between citizens (*civitas*) and the city (*urbs*).

Of course, the silver lining of this negative phenomenon can be the re-vitalization of cultural and artisanal traditions as a reaction to the alienating effects of globalization; efforts to provide legal protection by trade marks and names of origin to valuable local products; and increased interest in rediscovering local communities and their cultural traditions.[19] But it remains uncertain to what extent these efforts may succeed in countering the effects of the profound changes produced by globalization and in restoring the loss of integrity of the socio-cul-

---

[16] Pienza was designed in the mid 15th century by the Architect Rossellino, based on an idea developed by Pope Pius II (hence the name Pienza). The city was inscribed in the World Heritage List in 1996 as "a masterpiece of human genius" and as an "application of the humanist concept of urban design" that influenced town planning in the following centuries. Recently, the mayor of Pienza, together with the mayors of other neighbouring towns, have invoked the UNESCO World Heritage Listing to oppose the inclusion of part of their territory as a possible site for the deposit of radioactive material. See "Nucleare: sindaci Val d'Orcia, piano scorie irricevibile", ANSA, 5 January 2021, available at: <https://www.ansa.it/toscana/notizie/2021/01/05/nucleare-sindaci-val-dorcia-piano-scorie-irricevibile_f1a9e9f8-0f08-484b-8776-b500dee8df31.html>.

[17] ACUTO, *Global Cities, Governance and Diplomacy. The Urban Link*, London, 2013.

[18] To capture this intangible element, one needs only to think of the frescoes decorating the "Palazzo Pubblico" of the city of Siena, painted in the 13th century by Ambrogio Lorenzetti to celebrate the virtues of good government and the effects of bad government, as a tribute to the representative government of the city.

[19] AUBY, "Mega-cities, Glocalization and the Law of the Future", in MULLER et al. (eds.), *cit. supra* note 8, p. 203 ff.

tural fabric of the city as a social community.[20] The world-wide COVID-19 pandemic has had an extremely negative impact on cities. At the time of this writing, the pandemic has ravaged the world for over a year and produced hundreds of thousands of victims and unprecedented economic and social crisis, with still no end in sight. Cities and their urban communities have suffered the heaviest blow in this international health emergency. First, because they have been the main hot spots of contagion and of the health crisis: the pandemic started in a large metropolitan area of China with more than ten million people; it quickly spread to large cities in Europe, Asia, North America and Latin America. Second, cities have been the worst victims of the economic and social crisis caused by the pandemic. Lockdowns and severe restrictions on the movement of people have brought almost to a halt many of the typical city activities and services, which presuppose freedom of urban socialization, access to entertainment and to cultural resources, and tourism. Third, and perhaps most important, the pandemic has caused a significant exodus of productive inhabitants from the city to the countryside in search of a safer environment with less density of people and lower risk of exposure to the virus. It is impossible to know whether this last effect will be temporary or lasting. What we know is that it is facilitated by new technologies, which permit remote working; home delivery of food and almost any other products; and an increasing sense of gratification achieved by participation in virtual social relations. How and when, cities, which are now hard hit by the social and economic effects of the pandemic, will recover and will regain their historical position as poles of social, economic and cultural aggregation, as well as their role as participants in international life, is impossible to know. In this time of crisis, they have struggled to remain actors in their own right in the search for solutions at national and international level. Their voice remains relevant, especially at a time when they are asked to surrender their role to the national governments and to international organizations, the latter being indispensable institutions for navigating through the terrible storm brought about by the pandemic.

4. CITIES AND COUNTRYSIDE

This last reflection brings us to the question of the relationship between city and countryside. As already suggested by the title of this paper, the idea of increasing the relevance of cities in international law should be cultivated in parallel with the idea of increasing the role played by the world outside the city, the countryside, in the progressive development of international law. The rural world is where a majority of the population of the world has always lived and worked until recently. So, it is the responsibility of the international lawyer to ask how the people who live in this area of the world perceive the current development of international law, and to consider how their perceptions differ from those of peo-

---

[20] See on this point the reflection developed by LIXINSKI in his contribution to this Symposium and, in particular, his focus on the cultural communities rather than on the city itself.

ple in the city. In the literature on cities and international law, we often encounter the adjective "invisible"[21] to underscore (or lament) the absence of legal status and voice of cities in international relations. If this image may fit the narrative on the hidden potential of cities to participate in international affairs, the attribute of "invisibility" is even more appropriate for the world of people who live and work in rural areas, in the natural world. These people, a great part of humanity, are the farmers and the peasants (*paysans, campesinos, contadini, Bauern*) who from generation to generation have been involved in agricultural, pastoral and forestry activities; they are the indigenous peoples attached to their ancestral lands as the home of their being; they are the local communities of whatever denomination who live a life of economic subsistence in close connection with their land; they are the masses of immigrants now replacing the dwindling local manpower in agricultural works in industrialized countries; they are also the increasing number of young people who decide to leave the city and embrace a more ecological and simple life style as farmers. For all these people that we may group under the label of people working and living in rural areas, the attribute of "invisibility" is much more appropriate and just than for the people living in the cities. For centuries, these people have been the servants of the city and have hardly had any voice in historical narratives, let alone in international relations. Images of peasant life may be found in the historic centres of many old towns, especially in the sculptures adorning the medieval cathedrals of many European cities. Some of these sculptures depict Adam and Eve tilling the earth, a moving reminder of the vicissitudes and pains of peasant life since the beginning of time.[22] But apart from this biblical iconography in medieval art, the life and labour of people working in rural areas has had minimal visibility in modern times. Visual arts and literature have been interested in the countryside mostly for the representation of rural landscapes and the beauty and serenity of nature, rather than for giving visibility to the hard labour and toils, and real life of rural people. This loss of visibility in visual art corresponds to a loss of memory in historical narratives. As acutely pointed out in sociological literature, peasants and people working in rural areas have been "*une classe objet*", an object rather than a subject of history,[23] due to the prevalent attention paid to cities as centres of power and as protagonists of history. This is in striking contrast with the important role played by peasants and rural people in critical periods of modern and contemporary history. One needs only to recall the so-called "peasants' war" in Germany (*Deutscher Bauernkrieg, 1524-1526*), the most important class revolt in Europe before the French revolution (condemned by Martin Luther);[24] the peasants' movement in nineteenth

---

[21] See SOSSAI, "The Invisibility of Cities in Classic/Modern International Law", in AUST and NIJMAN (eds.), *cit. supra* note 8.

[22] A beautiful example is provided by the 14th century bas relief sculpted by Wiligelmo for the Duomo of the City of Modena, now a World Heritage site.

[23] BURDIEU, "La Paysannerie une classe objet", in *Actes de la recerce in sciences sociales*, XVII-XVIII, 1977, p. 1 ff., cited in PROSPERI, *Un Volgo disperso. Contadini d'Italia nell'Ottocento*, Torino, 2019, p. XI.

[24] BLIKLE, *The Revolution of 1525: the German Peasants War from a New Perspective*, Baltimore, 1981.

century revolutionary Italy and their contribution to the *Risorgimento*; the rural uprisings in Russia between 1826 and 1854; the critical role played by rural people in the revolutions of the twentieth century in Russia and China;[25] and today's massive revolts of Indian peasants against the opening of the country to foreign agricultural investments.[26]

Against this loss of memory and of historical visibility, it was left to cinema to provide one of the most powerful representations of peasant life in contemporary historical narratives. The 1978 film by Ermanno Olmi, *The Tree of the Wooden Clogs* (*L'albero degli zoccoli*), Palme d'Or at the 1979 Cannes Film Festival, is an extraordinary and compassionate story of the hard, real, day to day life of ordinary peasants and their families in the valleys of Lombardy at the dawn of the twentieth century. The microcosm represented on the screen, its reality and authenticity, have the value of a universal testimony of the plight and injustice suffered by the rural population as a class of people dispersed and deprived of any voice and of any right in the society of their time.

More than a century after the events narrated in this film, the question of the legal status and the rights of the large part of humanity that lives and works outside of the city in the rural areas of the world has been addressed at the international level by the adoption in 2018 of the United Nations Declaration on the Rights of Peasants and Other People Working in Rural Areas.[27] This Declaration comes just about ten years after the adoption by the General Assembly of the United Nations of the Declaration on the Rights of Indigenous Peoples.[28] What these two declarations have in common is that they address the rights and dignity of a class of people long forgotten by international law. Both Declarations are timely and important because they concern people who have become more vulnerable under the impact of irreversible changes in the socio economic structures of society brought about by globalization. This impact is especially relevant for the people working in rural areas. The capital-intensive mode of agricultural production and distribution has profoundly modified the traditional methods of food production based on the work of the peasant family and the traditional economy of subsistence.[29] Industrial agriculture relies on advanced technology, expensive machinery, large investments in selective productions, and, increasingly, on a mass of migrant workers who are now taking the place of the forgotten class

---

[25] For a critical overview, see WOLFE, *Peasant Wars in the Twentieth Century*, London, 1973.

[26] See New York Times, International Edition, 5 February 2021, p. 3.

[27] Declaration adopted by General Assembly Resolution 73/165, UN Doc. A/RES/73/165 (2018). For a comprehensive commentary on the Declaration, see ALABRESE et al. (eds.), *The United Nations Declaration on the Rights of Peasants and Other People Working in Rural Areas*, London, forthcoming.

[28] Declaration adopted by General Assembly Resolution 61/295, UN Doc. A/RES/61/295 (2007).

[29] For a critical perspective on the current trends in food production and distribution, see ELVER, Critical perspective on food systems, food crises and the future of the right to food: Report of the Special Rapporteur on the Right to Food to the Human Rights Council, 21 January 2020, UN Doc. A/HRC/43/44.

of yesteryear's peasants. The social transformation in the class of rural workers made it appropriate to adopt an expansive title for the 2018 Declaration, which includes, besides peasants, also "other people working in rural areas", who are defined in Article 1 as:

> any person engaged in artisanal or small scale agriculture, crop planting, livestock raising, pastoralism, fishing, forestry, hunting or gathering, and handicrafts related to agriculture or a related occupation in a rural area. It also applies to dependent family members of peasants [...] indigenous peoples and local communities working on the land, transient, nomadic and semi-nomadic communities, and the landless engaged in the above-mentioned activities [...] hired workers, including all migrant workers regardless of their migration status, and seasonal workers, on plantations, agricultural farms, forests and farms in aquaculture and in agro-industrial enterprise.

This is a comprehensive definition. But to fully capture the dynamic interaction between city and countryside, this definition could have included also the new growing class of people who reject the idea that urbanization is the only model of social organization capable of ensuring intellectual progress and sustainable development. These people, many of them young, believe that the future of humanity will depend on the possibility of a gradual return to work in the countryside, in contact with nature and in full observance of the principle of sustainable use of its resources, as prescribed by the Rio Declaration on Environment and Development.[30] This possibility is captured by the pioneering work of the Dutch architect Ren Koolhaas, who, after having spent much of his life planning city centres and urban areas, has now turned his attention to the importance of rural areas and to the enormous potential they offer to people who live and work there to emancipate themselves from the subordinate role they have traditionally played as "servants" of the city.[31] In the digital era, they may become protagonists of a more sustainable model of economic, social and cultural development that would certainly transcend the stereotypes of "peasants" and rural workers.

The possible evolution of the relationship between cities and communities that live and work in rural areas is important also to counterbalance the limited vision of other pseudo-progressive documents adopted by the United Nations and other organizations with regard to humanity's future in cities and mega-cities. I am referring, particularly, to the UN World Urbanization Prospect, a report as-

---

[30] See Report of the United Nations Conference of Environment and Development, 12 August 1992, UN Doc. A/CONF.151/26 (Vol.1), Annex 1.

[31] "Countryside: The Future", an exhibition about the non-urban areas around the globe that opened in February 2020 at the Guggenheim Museum in New York. See: <https://www.guggenheim.org/exhibition/countryside>.

suming that, by 2050, 70% of the world population will live in cities,[32] and the so-called Eco Modernist Manifesto for the Anthropocene, which advocates massive urbanization as the key to a more efficient use of energy and natural resources and as the only way to pursue the objective of sustainable development.[33] The severe environmental degradation caused by the increasing human concentration in large metropolises and now the planetary disaster caused by the COVID-19 pandemic are combining to bring us the perfect storm of history. The current situation reminds us of how fragile life can be in densely populated metropolitan areas, and what great potential lies in the immense expanses of rural areas, in the vast countryside of the world, not only to save lives in the event of global pandemics, but also to live a "healthy and productive life in harmony with nature" (Principle 1, Rio Declaration).

5.   CONCLUSIONS

The burgeoning scholarship on the subject of cities and international law has the merit of disclosing the enormous potential that urban communities and local governments have for an active participation in the creation of international norms and in their effective implementation in the national legal order. However, this renewed focus on cities as protagonists of international relations should not occur at the expense of the other part of humanity, the one that lives and works outside of the city in the vast rural areas of the world. This paper serves as a reminder that, while cities have been at the centre of the development of international law, rural communities and people working in rural areas have historically been the servants of the city and, until recently, a largely forgotten class of people in the narrative of international law. Today, their dignity and rights are being recognized by international law, but they still remain a disadvantaged and vulnerable class of people who are worthy of further recognition as relevant communities in the progressive development of international law. A true modernization and democratization of the international system requires that we keep a balanced approach to the legal recognition of the voices and interests of urban communities and those of the people who inhabit and work in the vast countryside of the world.

---

[32] United Nations, Department of Economic and Social Affairs, "World Population Prospects 2019", available at: <https://population.un.org/wpp/>.

[33] The Modernist Manifesto was published by a private group of scientists, intellectuals and policy makers in April 2015. It is available at: <www.ecomodernism.org>.

Focus
THE ENRICA LEXIE AWARD

THE *ENRICA LEXIE* AWARD AMID JURISDICTIONAL AND LAW OF THE SEA ISSUES

Giuseppe Cataldi*

Abstract

This article analyzes the Enrica Lexie *Arbitral Award, first of all, in relation to international law issues concerning the application of the United Nations Convention on the Law of the Sea (UNCLOS). The article then focuses on the question of the functional immunity of the two marines, from the point of view of the Tribunal's assertion of its incidental jurisdiction to deal with the matter, as well as of the Tribunal's affirmation of the existence of a customary international law rule applicable in the present case. Both conclusions appear unconvincing, also in light of the role of the two marines on board a merchant ship. In any case, the fact remains that the judgment has the merit of finally putting an end to a long-standing dispute, to the satisfaction of the two parties involved.*

Keywords: law of the sea; freedom of navigation; jurisdiction according to UNCLOS; incidental jurisdiction; functional immunity; State officials; governmental functions.

1. INTRODUCTION

The arbitral award in the *Enrica Lexie* case, issued on 21 May 2020 by a tribunal constituted pursuant to Annex VII of the United Nations Convention on the Law of the Sea (UNCLOS), addresses numerous interesting legal issues. In particular, as evidenced by the writings contained in this *Focus*, the issues that determined the solution adopted, and on which the Tribunal therefore dwelts extensively, are the existence of a customary principle on the functional immunity from foreign criminal jurisdiction of the military as State bodies, and the scope of the notion of incidental jurisdiction.

The events that caused the judicial and diplomatic dispute between Italy and India and led to the Tribunal's pronouncement are well known and will therefore not be retraced here in detail.[1] On the other hand, it must be remembered that the

---

* Of the Board of Editors. The author wishes to thank Giorgia Bevilacqua and Giuseppe Barra Caracciolo for their help.

[1] On 15 February 2012 the *Enrica Lexie*, an Italian tanker coming from Singapore and bound for Djibouti, was approached by the Indian fishing vessel *St. Antony* while it was about 20 miles off the State of Kerala in the Indian contiguous zone. The ship was carrying six Italian Navy riflemen in an anti-piracy function. Among them there were the sergeants Massimiliano Latorre and Salvatore Girone who, convinced that the *St. Antony* was about to launch a pirate attack against the *Enrica Lexie*, after having issued flash signals to the approaching vessel,

basis of the Tribunal's jurisdiction lay in UNCLOS, and was justified, according to Article 288, (1), insofar as it related to a "dispute concerning the interpretation or application of this Convention".[2] In the case in point, however, the central issue, the real and fundamental subject of the dispute, was the ascertainment of the competence to exercise jurisdiction over the matter, a problem resolved, as mentioned above, in light of the rules on immunity. Hence the use of an "enlarged" notion of incidental jurisdiction by the Tribunal, which, otherwise, would have had to declare itself not competent, since there was no need to rule under UNCLOS.

Contrary to what one might expect without having read the text of the decision, the law of the sea issues are therefore much less decisive. However, this does not mean that the decision in question does not present aspects of interest to law of the sea scholars, aspects on which we will focus in the following pages.

---

fired some shots from which resulted the death of two Indian fishermen. Induced to enter the port of Kochi by the Indian authorities, the *Enrica Lexie* was detained and the Italian sergeants were subjected to Indian criminal proceedings for the murder of the two fishermen. These events led to a long judicial and diplomatic dispute between Italy and India regarding which State should exercise criminal jurisdiction over the incident. After more than three years of fruitless negotiations, in April 2015 Italy unilaterally activated the mandatory arbitration procedure provided for by Annex VII to the UNCLOS Convention (Art. 286). It also requested, first from the International Tribunal for the Law of the Sea (ITLOS) and then from the Arbitral Tribunal, the adoption of some precautionary measures. First, pending the constitution of the Arbitral Tribunal, Italy availed itself of the possibility provided for by Art. 290(5) UNCLOS and asked the ITLOS Tribunal to issue provisional measures against India consisting in the abstention from exercising its jurisdiction over the incident and the cessation of restrictions on the personal freedom of Sergeants Girone and Latorre. ITLOS, although not accepting the Italian request, with the order of 24 August 2015, established the obligation of both States to suspend the jurisdictional proceedings in progress and to refrain from initiating new ones. This precautionary measure also pursued the objective of avoiding that the continuation or initiation of jurisdictional proceedings could jeopardize, if not frustrate, the execution of any rulings of the then constituted Arbitral Tribunal. It also had the function of preventing the extension or escalation of the dispute, in accordance with ITLOS's constant orientation on provisional measures. Having constituted the Arbitral Tribunal at the Permanent Court of Arbitration on 8 September 2015, Italy also submitted to the latter a precautionary appeal pursuant to Art. 290(1) UNCLOS in which it requested that Sergeant Girone be allowed to return to his homeland pending a final ruling. By order of 29 April 2016, the Arbitral Tribunal, noting the absence of a legal requirement justifying Girone's physical stay in India, upheld the Italian appeal and established obligations of cooperation between the States in order to preserve their respective rights. For further information and insights please refer, in addition to the articles published in this *Forum*, to the review on the International Tribunal for the Law of the Sea and other Law of the Sea jurisdictions edited in this Volume by TREVES. The issue was already dealt with in this Yearbook by RONZITTI, "The *Enrica Lexie* Incident: Law of the Sea and Immunity of State Officials Issues", IYIL, 2012, p. 3 ff.

[2] UNCLOS subjects the settlement of disputes (between States that have ratified it) relating to its interpretation and application to a mandatory regime. At the moment of ratification, as a rule, the State communicates its choice of instrument to be used for resolving disputes, selected among the various instruments proposed by the Convention itself. However, in the event of inconsistent declarations, as in the present case, the competence is attributed to an arbitral tribunal constituted in accordance with Annex VII of UNCLOS (Art. 287).

Only afterwards will we humbly but briefly allow ourselves to give our opinion also on the two main issues mentioned above.

As early as the stage of provisional measures, the Tribunal made some interesting statements relating to aspects of the law of the sea.[3] By order of 29 April 2016, the Tribunal, noting the absence of a legal requirement justifying the physical detention of one of the two Italian marines in India,[4] upheld the Italian appeal by establishing obligations of cooperation between the States in order to preserve their respective rights.[5] It is interesting to note that the Tribunal justified the precautionary measure not only by the need to prevent the dispute from escalating or spreading, but also because of "considerations of humanity" which were raised in relation to the limitation of the personal freedom of one of the two Italian marines.[6] In fact, the Tribunal, while not considering it necessary to dwell on the issue of possible violation of international human rights standards, stated that "social isolation has been recognized as a relevant factor in considering the relaxation of bail conditions" and it was therefore necessary "to give effect to the

---

[3] In fact, it is well known that, having constituted the Arbitral Tribunal at The Hague Permanent Court of Arbitration (PCA) on 8 September 2015, Italy submitted a precautionary appeal pursuant to Art. 290(1) UNCLOS in which it requested that also Sergeant Girone, one of the two "indicted" Marine riflemen (the other, Commander Latorre, was already in Italy for health reasons) could return to his homeland pending a final ruling. See Order of 29 April 2016, Request for the Prescription of Provisional Measures, PCA Case No. 2015-28. All documentation of the arbitration proceedings is available at: <www.pcacpa.org>.

[4] The interim measures ordered on 24 August 2015 by the ITLOS, which resulted in the suspension of all domestic court proceedings, were still in effect at the time. Thus, the Tribunal observed that "there would be no legal interest in Sergeant Girone's physical presence in India" and that, ultimately, "no material change would result for India" (Order, *cit. supra* note 3, para. 107). On the precautionary measures adopted by the two Courts, see VIRZO, "Le misure cautelari nell'affare dell'incidente della *Enrica Lexie*", Osservatorio Costituzionale, 2016, p. 1 ff.; PERROTTA, "Il caso *Enrica Lexie* e la tutela cautelare dei diritti individuali nelle pronunce del Tribunale internazionale per il diritto del mare e dell'*Annex VII Arbitral Tribunal*: tra *inherent powers* e *human rights approach*", Politica del diritto, 2016, p. 279 ff.; CANNONE, "L'ordinanza del Tribunale internazionale del diritto del mare sulla vicenda della *Enrica Lexie*", RDI, 2015, p. 1144 ff.; PAPANICOLOPULU, "Commento a margine dell'ordinanza del tribunale arbitrale nel caso *Enrica Lexie*", RDI, 2016, p. 763 ff.

[5] It should be noted that the Tribunal considered that the requirement of urgency of the measure, even if not expressly mentioned in Art. 290(1) UNCLOS, must be taken into account for the purposes of prescription of precautionary measures (Order, *cit. supra* note 3, para. 85). In the present case, the Tribunal wished to prevent the occurrence of a real and imminent risk of prejudice to the rights of the parties while waiting for its final decision, as this risk presented itself as "particularly pronounced".

[6] According to the Tribunal, the measures restricting the liberty of the Italian Navy rifleman, in light of the time presumably necessary for the conclusion of the arbitral proceedings and of the possible criminal trial in one of the two States, would most likely be in contrast with international human rights obligations. A significant exhortation to respect international human rights standards is also contained in the motivations of the award rendered by the Arbitral Tribunal constituted under Annex VII UNCLOS in the case of the *Arctic Sunrise Arbitration (Netherlands v. Russia)*, Award on the Merits of 14 August 2015, PCA Case No. 2014-02, para. 198.

concept of considerations of humanity".[7] These considerations of humanity came to the fore precisely because of a systematic and coordinated interpretation of the norms of the UNCLOS with the norms of general international law.[8] Systematic, because in UNCLOS there are provisions having as their object the protection of life at sea[9] and other human rights;[10] coordinated, because Article 293 UNCLOS provides that an international tribunal competent under UNCLOS may also apply other rules of international law, provided that they are not incompatible with it.[11] We agree with this evolutionary interpretation of UNCLOS, certainly in line with the value that the protection of human rights has assumed in the international order.

2. FREEDOM OF NAVIGATION. WHO VIOLATED IT?

The Tribunal then dealt with the mutual accusations of violation of freedom of navigation between the two States. First of all, with regard to the impact on the freedom of navigation of the *Enrica Lexie* of the request by the Maritime Rescue Coordination Centre in Mumbai to the master to proceed to the port of Kochi when the vessel was 38 nautical miles from the coast, it was not relevant to establish, for this purpose, the exact location of the incident or the position of the

---

[7] See Order, *cit. supra* note 3, para. 104. Interestingly, the same concerns had also been expressed by Judge Jesus in his Separate Opinion attached to the 25 August 2015 ITLOS Order in which he stated (paras. 10-11): "[t]he detencion or restriction on the movement of persons who wait excessively long to be charged with criminal offenses is, per se, a punishment without a trial" and regretted the fact that ITLOS had not taken into account "the effects on the health of the marines and their family as a result of a detention that has continued […] for three and a half years".

[8] This consideration is made by VIRZO, *cit. supra* note 4, p. 3 ff.; See also, for analogous statements, PAPANICOLOPULU, *cit. supra* note 4, pp. 773-774. More generally on the issue of interpretation of UNCLOS provisions see DEL VECCHIO and VIRZO (eds.), *Interpretation of the United Nations Convention on the Law of the Sea by International Courts and Tribunals*, Heidelberg, 2019.

[9] See Arts. 18, para. 2, and 98 UNCLOS.

[10] See, for example, Art. 73, para. 3, which affirms: "[t]his Convention shall not alter the rights and obligations of States Parties which arise from other agreements compatible with this Convention and which do not affect the enjoyment by other States Parties of their rights or the performance of their obligations under this Convention".

[11] On the applicability of international human rights standards, reference is also made to the compatibility clause included in Art. 311, para. 2, UNCLOS, according to which: "[t]his Convention shall not alter the rights and obligations of States Parties which arise from other agreements compatible with this Convention and which do not affect the enjoyment by other States Parties of their rights or the performance of their obligations under this Convention". For reference to international human rights standards, again in the case *Arctic Sunrise*, according to ITLOS (para. 198): "the Tribunal may, therefore, pursuant to Article 293, have regard to the extent necessary to rules of customary international law, including international human rights standards, not incompatible with the Convention, in order to assist it in the interpretation and application of the Convention's provisions that authorize the arrest or detention of a vessel and persons". In legal literature see TREVES, "Human Rights and the Law of the Sea", Berkeley Journal of International Law, 2010, p. 1 ff.

Italian vessel and at the same time to ascertain whether the rules on the contiguous zone or the exclusive economic zone (EEZ) should apply, since in any case the Italian vessel would have been entitled to the same freedom of navigation as on the high seas. This is in accordance with Article 33 UNCLOS, which limits the permitted grounds for affecting foreign navigation in the contiguous zone to the prevention and repression of violations of customs, fiscal, health and immigration laws, and with Articles 87(1) and 92(1), which recognize, respectively, the principles of freedom of navigation and exclusive jurisdiction of the flag State on the high seas, applicable also in the EEZ by express provision of Article 58(1)[12] and 58(2)[13]

As far as the violation of the first principle is concerned,[14] Italy supported its thesis by referring to the Indian Maritime Zones Act of 1976. This piece of legislation is still in force despite its provisions being inspired by an excessively "patrimonialistic" vision of the EEZ that is rejected by UNCLOS, which, as is known, has achieved a compromise in this regard between the developing States theories and those of industrialized countries. This vision of the EEZ, however, often recurs in the practice and legislation of Asian countries, first and foremost China.[15] The Indian conception of the contiguous zone, as revealed by the judgment of the Indian Supreme Court of 18 January 2013, again in relation to the *Enrica Lexie*'s incident, does not appear to be entirely in accordance with international law. The Supreme Court upheld the jurisdiction of India over the two marines under the Indian Penal Code, the application of which was extended by

---

[12] *The "Enrica Lexie" Incident (The Italian Republic v. The Republic of India)*, Award of 21 May 2020, PCA Case No. 2015-28, para. 308.

[13] *Ibid.*, para. 315.

[14] See Art. 87 UNCLOS ("Freedom of the high seas"), which recognizes that on the high seas States enjoy: "freedom of navigation; freedom of overflight; freedom to lay submarine cables and pipelines; freedom to construct artificial islands and other installations permitted under international law, subject to Part VI; freedom of fishing, subject to the conditions laid down in section 2; freedom of scientific research, subject to Parts VI and XIII".

[15] China has repeatedly objected, even with the use of force, to the conduct of military manoeuvers in its EEZ, for example almost ramming the US destroyer Decatur on 30 September 2018 near the Spratly Islands, occupied by China but also claimed by Malaysia, Taiwan, the Philippines, and Vietnam. Indeed, China claims to condition such operations on its consent, believing them to be a potential threat to its security, and not permitted by UNCLOS. In fact, this aspect of Chinese practice, which in any case conflicts with international practice and does not appear sustainable in the light of UNCLOS provisions, is part of a more general attempt to impose a peculiar interpretation of the institution of the EEZ. This State, in fact, manages its EEZ almost as if it represents its territorial waters, in particular in the South China Sea (or Oriental Sea, as defined by Vietnam), and this attitude is also part of China's attempt to assert its claims of exclusive control of that area, claims which are, however, disputed by other States bordering that same Sea and which in turn claim sovereignty or jurisdiction in those waters. In this regard, see FRANCKX and GAUTIER (eds.), *The Exclusive Economic Zone and the United Nations Convention on the Law of the Sea, 1982-2000: A Preliminary Assessment of State Practice*, Bruxelles, 2003; FRANCKX, "The 200-mile Limit: Between Creeping Jurisdiction and Creeping Common Heritage?", George Washington International Law Review, 2007, p. 467 ff.; BECKMAN, "The UN Convention on the Law of the Sea and the Maritime Disputes in the South China Sea", AJIL, 2013, p. 142 ff.

the Maritime Zones Act of 1976 to the contiguous zone for reasons generically defined as "of security", and as such not included among the specific matters in relation to which the coastal State is allowed to exercise its powers within 24 miles from the coast.[16] However, the Tribunal, considering the reference to the provisions of the Indian law of 1976 concerning the EEZ and the contiguous zone irrelevant to the decision, stated that the Indian request to the *Enrica Lexie*'s captain to proceed towards the port of Kochi represented an interference too abstract to constitute a violation of the freedom of navigation.[17] The hypothesis that the entry of the *Enrica Lexie* in the Indian territory had been determined by the request to cooperate in an investigation related to piracy events which then turned out to be non-existent, and the consideration that if the *Enrica Lexie* had not complied with the request it could have been accused of violation of the UNCLOS provisions which impose obligations of cooperation between States in the fight against maritime piracy, in particular of Article 100 UNCLOS read in conjunction with Article 300, was thus dismissed without too much consideration.[18]

On the other hand, the Tribunal was of a different opinion with respect to Italy's responsibility for the interference with the navigation of the *St. Antony*, the Indian fishing vessel shot at by the Italian Navy's riflemen. According to the Tribunal, the change of course which the *St. Antony* was forced to make as a consequence of the Italian military action was the responsibility of the Italian State, constituting a violation of the freedom of navigation of the said vessel pursuant to Articles 87 and 90 UNCLOS.[19] On these grounds, the Tribunal ordered Italy to pay compensation for material and moral damages caused.[20]

---

[16] Judgment of 18 January 2013 of the Federal Supreme Court of India in the case *Republic of Italy and others v. Republic of India and others*, available at: <http://www.sidi-isil.org/wp-content/uploads/2013/03/SUPREME-COURT-OF-INDIA-18.01.2013.pdf>. On the specific point see WU, "The *Enrica Lexie* Incident: Jurisdiction in the Contiguous Zone?", Cambridge International Law Journal, 19 April 2014, available at: <http://cilj.org.uk/2014/04/19/enrica-lexie-incident-jurisdiction-contiguous-zone/>.

[17] Award, *cit. supra* note 12, para. 504, in which the arbitral tribunal addresses the Italian argument according to which: "the evidence on the record permits the conclusion that, since the 'Enrica Lexie' initially had no intention of proceeding to the Indian coast, there was a 'causal effect' of India's intervention on the 'Enrica Lexie''s turn for Kochi. While such a causal effect is undeniable, in the sense that, had the MRCC not requested the 'Enrica Lexie' to proceed to Kochi, the 'Enrica Lexie' would not have changed course, such effect is too remote to amount to 'interference' with Italy's freedom of navigation".

[18] On the possible violation by the Indian authorities of the principles of good faith and friendly relations between States see AVENIA, "Una rilettura del caso Enrica Lexie e dei due fucilieri della marina militare italiana", Rivista della Cooperazione Giuridica Internazionale, 2016, p. 171 ff.

[19] Award, *cit. supra* note 12, para. 1043. On these aspects please refer to RONZITTI, "Il caso della Enrica Lexie e la sentenza arbitrale nella controversia Italia-India", RDI, 2020, p. 937 ff.

[20] Award, *cit. supra* note 12, para. 1088. In particular, the court ordered Italy to adopt measures of a satisfactory nature, such as the acknowledgement of the unlawful act, and to pay compensation for material damages relating to the killing and wounding of members of the crew of the *St. Antony* as well as for the "moral harm" suffered by the captain of the *St. Antony* and his crew. On 9 April 2021 the Indian Supreme Court declared that the case will be defini-

The reason that this finding has caused so much consternation is that the freedom of navigation was deemed to have been violated without first verifying the occurrence or not of the elements of legitimate defence. In other words, could the behaviour of the fishing boat give rise to the legitimate suspicion that it was in fact a pirate boat about to attack the *Enrica Lexie*? If the answer was positive, the interference would have been justified. It must be presumed that the Tribunal implicitly gave a negative answer to this hypothesis when it determined Italian responsibility for violation of freedom of navigation, despite the fact that the Tribunal itself has referred the merits of the legitimate defence question to the Italian courts. However, in our opinion, the fact that the Tribunal made its finding on freedom of navigation without having assessed a possible defence against liability is not acceptable.

Also with reference to the subjective attribution of the offence in question, Italy argued that no infringement could be attributed to it vis-à-vis India as the *St. Antony* was not identifiable as an Indian vessel, in that it was not flagged and was not registered in the maritime register of that country. On this point, the Tribunal correctly reaffirmed the customary principle, codified in Article 91(1) UNCLOS, that States enjoy a wide discretion in determining the criteria on which the attribution of the flag is founded and that the so-called requirement of a "genuine link" with the State (referred to in the last paragraph of Article 91(1) UNCLOS) cannot entail the consequence of third States challenging the link of nationality.[21] Therefore, since Indian legislation provides that small boats are not required to fly the flag and are exempt from registration in the maritime register, this circumstance had no weight in the assessment of the conduct attributable to Italy.[22]

3. JURISDICTION ON THE CASE ACCORDING TO UNCLOS

Moreover, the question relating to the attribution of jurisdiction over the events that occurred was, of course, primarily addressed in light of the provisions of UNCLOS. Italy, first of all, proposing an extensive interpretation, affirmed the lack of Indian jurisdiction in light of Article 97 UNCLOS, which at paragraph 1 provides that

> In the event of a collision or any other incident of navigation concerning a ship on the high seas, involving the penal or disciplinary responsibility of the master or of any other person in the service

---

tively closed once the Italian State has paid the compensation granted (100 million rupees, equal to around 1.1 million euros) into an account of the Ministry of Foreign Affairs in Delhi.

[21] On this point see RONZITTI, "Il caso della Enrica Lexie", *cit. supra* note 19, p. 948. On the issue, in general, of the attribution of the flag and of the requirement of the "genuine link", we refer to the ITLOS Judgment of 1 July 1999 in the *M/V "Saiga" (N. 2) Case (Saint Vincent and the Grenadines v. Guinea)*, ITLOS Reports, 1999, p. 10 ff., para. 63.

[22] Award, *cit. supra* note 12, paras. 1017-1035.

of the ship, no penal or disciplinary proceedings may be instituted against such person except before the judicial or administrative authorities either of the flag State or of the State of which such person is a national.

On this point, however, the Tribunal, accepting the Indian argument, held that this rule was not applicable to the case in question, since the event at issue could not be qualified as an accident of navigation, as "damage [to St. Antony] and mortal harm [to its crew] were not caused by the movement or manoeuvring of either ship", but from few shots fired at the *St. Antony*.[23] The argument had also been put forward by the Italian side before the Indian Federal Supreme Court which, in its above mentioned judgment of 18 January 2013, had expressed itself in terms quite similar to those used by the Tribunal, stating that "a homicide caused by the voluntary opening of fire cannot constitute an 'incident of navigation' within the meaning of this provision".[24]

In fact, the rule in question has a special character (otherwise it would not be possible to understand its rationale, as, at a general level, the principle codified in the already mentioned Article 92 UNCLOS applies) and finds its genesis in the famous case decided by the Permanent Court of International Justice (PCIJ) in 1927, concerning a collision between the ship *Lotus*, flying the French flag, and a Turkish steamer on the high seas with the consequent arrest, in Turkey, of the French officer held responsible for the event which caused the death of eight people.[25] The Court affirmed, on the basis of the principle of freedom of the seas, the unlawfulness of any authoritarian intervention on other nations' ships (e.g., the carrying out of police investigations, the arrest of persons, the collection of testimonies and the like, in short, all enforcement activities). However, the Court did not assert the unlawfulness of the exercise of jurisdiction (*judicial jurisdiction*) by a State within its own territory in relation to facts occurring in international waters. In order to overcome the uncertainties that the PCIJ had to remedy with its judgment, and not incidentally on a proposal by France, the International Law Commission (ILC) formulated in 1956 the rule inserted in the Geneva Convention of 1958 on the high seas and finally in Article 97 of UNCLOS. The rule is therefore applied, as correctly decided by the Tribunal, only in cases of navigation accidents occurring on the high seas. Thus, exclusive criminal juris-

---

[23] Award, *cit. supra* note 12, para. 652.

[24] *Republic of Italy and others*, *cit. supra* note 16, para. 94.

[25] Judgment of 7 September 1927, PCIJ Reports, Series A, No. 10. On the basis of the compromise between France and Turkey, the PCIJ had to decide whether Turkey, by exercising criminal jurisdiction over a foreign national for acts committed on the high seas, "had acted in violation of the principles of international law – and if so, which ones". The Court affirmed that the territoriality of the criminal law, even if it implies that no State can exercise its punitive power in the territory of another State, is not an absolute principle, as demonstrated by the fact that "all or nearly all these systems of law extend their action to offences committed outside the territory of the State which adopts them, and they do so in ways which vary from State to State. The territoriality of criminal law, therefore, is not an absolute principle of international law and by no means coincides with territorial sovereignty" (*ibid.*, p. 20).

diction is attributed to the flag State or to the national State of the authors of the incident, in cases limited to collisions and other navigation accidents such as, for example, the breaking of submarine telegraph or telephone cables, and damages however produced to ships or installations of other States. In other cases, the rule that the ship is subject to the exclusive power of the government of the flag State remains unchanged, but this is only in the sense that other States cannot perform acts of government on board and towards the ship itself.[26] By the same

---

[26] On this point please refer to CONFORTI, "In tema di giurisdizione penale per fatti commessi in acque internazionali", in *Scritti in onore di Giuseppe Tesauro*, Napoli, 2014, Vol. IV, p. 2619 ff. (in particular pp. 2624-2625). He states that: "It is known that the principle of international law applicable to criminal jurisdiction over the foreigner (jurisdiction always admitted over the citizen) is that it is exercisable always when and only when, even if it is about crimes committed in foreign territory, they present some connection with the territorial State and/or its subjects. Well, it is hard to see why this rule should not also apply when the foreign territory is… fluctuating. Moreover, even current practice, although not abundant, points in this direction. To summarize: it may be that the crime takes place entirely on a foreign ship. In this case there should be no doubt about the right of the State other than that of the flag to exercise jurisdiction if the victim is one of its nationals. In the case of an offense whose action is committed on board a foreign ship but the event occurs on board another ship and to the detriment of a national of the State to which such ship belongs, the latter has two titles to exercise jurisdiction: the nationality of the victim and the event occurring on the ship which has his nationality. This is a case of competing jurisdiction with that of the State of the flag or the national State of the perpetrator of the offence, a competition which will in fact be resolved in favour of the State in whose territory the offender is located, which will obviously be free to hand him over to one of the other States or will be obliged to hand him over if bound by an extradition treaty" (our translation from Italian). Recently, in the sense of considering accidents of navigation those caused by the movement of the ship, see MAGI, "Criminal Conduct on the High Seas: Is a General Rule on Jurisdiction to Prosecute Still Missing?", RDI, 2015, p. 79 ff., in particular pp. 89 ff. and 92. For a partially different thesis, regarding in particular the reading of Art. 92 in the sense that this rule provides for "both enforcing and prescriptive jurisdiction", and that therefore Art. 97 is redundant, see RONZITTI, "The *Enrica Lexie* Incident", *cit. supra* note 1, p. 3 ff. (14-15 in particular); ID., "La difesa contro i pirati e l'imbarco di personale militare armato sui mercantili: il caso della Enrica Lexie e la controversia Italia-India", RDI, 2013, p. 1073 ff., especially p. 1086 ff., who sets out examples of shipping accidents not requiring physical contact but which, on the one hand, seem to be oriented towards the first type of interpretation and, at the same time, raise the possibility of a more modern interpretation than the one we have called "restrictive", in order to take into account the evolution of practice and other accidents whose occurrence was unthinkable at the time of the adoption of UNCLOS. References to the possible restrictive or extensive interpretation of Art. 97 UNCLOS in light of the judgment of the Supreme Court of India of 18 January 2013, are in DEL VECCHIO, "Il ricorso all'arbitrato obbligatorio UNCLOS nella vicenda dell'*Enrica Lexie*", RDIPP, 2014, p. 259 ff., in particular p. 265. On the other hand, the individual opinion of Justice Chelameswar attached to the Indian Supreme Court's 2013 judgment that Art. 97 would not apply *ratione loci* anyway because it applies on the high seas and the incident had occurred in the EEZ appears to be unsustainable. Pursuant to Art. 58(2) UNCLOS, as already noted above, the high seas regime, and in particular Arts. 88 to 115 and "other relevant rules of international law", apply to the EEZ unless inconsistent with its regime. For greater detail on the different theories relating to Art. 97 and on the solution reached by the Tribunal on the issue see CANNONE, "L'interpretazione della espressione 'altri incidenti di navigazione' di cui all'art. 97 della Convenzione sul diritto del mare nella sentenza arbitrale del 21 maggio 2020 relativa alla vicenda della *Enrica Lexie* (*Italia* c. *India*)", Ordine internazionale e diritti umani, 2021, p. 283 ff.

token, the thesis according to which the term "navigation accident" is intended to mean exclusively an accident involving "navigation activities" due to fate and unforeseeable circumstances, and not to voluntary or intentional human acts, is confirmed by the preparatory works of Article 97,[27] and also by the formulation of another article of UNCLOS, namely Article 221(2) which, even if "for the purposes of this article", clarifies that "'maritime casualty' means a collision of vessels, stranding or other incident of navigation, or other occurrence on board a vessel or external to it resulting in material damage or imminent threat of material damage to a vessel or cargo". This interpretation, moreover, combines in a systematic way the provisions of Article 97 with those of Article 94 UNCLOS(7) providing that:

> Each State shall cause an inquiry to be held by or before a suitably qualified person or persons into every marine casualty or incident of navigation on the high seas involving a ship flying its flag and causing loss of life or serious injury to nationals of another State or serious damage to ships or installations of another State or to the marine environment. The flag State and the other State shall cooperate in the conduct of any inquiry held by that other State into any such marine casualty or incident of navigation.

As mentioned above, Italy was very insistent, both before the Indian courts and before the Tribunal, in its attempts to assert the applicability of Article 97 UNCLOS to the case at hand. The reason for this is intuitive. First of all, if this argument had been accepted by the Tribunal, the jurisdiction of the Tribunal would have been established in an incontrovertible manner, since it would have been undisputed at this point that what was at stake was a "dispute concerning the interpretation or application of this Convention", according to Article 288, paragraph 1, UNCLOS. Secondly, only the acceptance of the applicability of Article 97 could have excluded Indian jurisdiction altogether, as any other solution would have to deal, at least, with the two countries' competing theories on jurisdiction, and the Tribunal would have to determine who was entitled to exercise its jurisdiction on a priority or exclusive basis.

Having rejected the main argument of the Italian defence, the starting point was therefore that the concurring jurisdiction of the two countries should be recognized, but that, in concrete terms, it was necessary to determine the rules for its exercise in the case in question.[28] The Tribunal then assessed whether the exercise of Indian criminal jurisdiction was prevented by the duty to recognize

---

[27] See NORDQUIST et al. (eds.), *United Nations Convention on the Law of the Sea 1982: A Commentary*, Dordrecht, 1995, Vol. III, p. 167 ff.
[28] For the doctrine in favor of concurrent jurisdiction, see CONFORTI, "In tema di giurisdizione", *cit. supra* note 26, p. 2619 ff.; GUILFOYLE, "Shooting Fishermen Mistaken for Pirates: Jurisdiction, Immunity and State Responsibility", EJIL: Talk!, 2 March 2012, available at: <https://www.ejiltalk.org/shooting-fishermen-mistaken-for-pirates-jurisdiction-immunity-and-state-responsibility/>.

the immunity of the two soldiers, a thesis already supported by Italy both before the Indian internal judicial bodies and on a diplomatic level. The answer, according to the Tribunal, could not be sought in the UNCLOS itself, since the relevant rules in the Convention either concern limitations on coastal State enforcement in spaces other than those in which India had exercised its powers,[29] or, with respect to immunities, refer exclusively and specifically to warships or other ships used for non-commercial purposes.[30]

We certainly agree with these findings. At this point, however, having abandoned the "safe" ground represented by UNCLOS, before proceeding to the analysis of Italy's claim regarding the functional immunity of the Italian Marines from Indian criminal jurisdiction on the basis of customary law, the Arbitral Tribunal had first to establish whether it had jurisdiction over this specific claim.[31]

4. THE FUNCTIONAL IMMUNITY OF THE ITALIAN MARINES: AN INCIDENTAL QUESTION TO THE APPLICATION OF UNCLOS

The analysis of this procedural issue appears rather complex and controversial; specifically, in order to determine whether it was entitled to exercise jurisdiction over Italy's claim regarding the immunity *ratione materiae* of the Marines, the Tribunal had first to determine what kind of relationship existed between two different questions: whereas a first question concerned the entitlement of jurisdiction over the incident, a second question concerned the immunity of the two Italian Marines from Indian criminal jurisdiction.

The issue arose because UNCLOS tribunals, like other international specialized tribunals and courts, have a limited competence *ratione materiae* which, as already said, is limited to disputes concerning the interpretation or application of UNCLOS.[32] Consequently, the jurisdiction of UNCLOS tribunals is limited to claims based on UNCLOS provisions. Thus, the Tribunal was certainly compe-

---

[29] Award, *cit. supra* note 12, para. 798, in which the Tribunal states that these rules apply: "to the exercise of rights and duties in the territorial sea and the exclusive economic zone by coastal States, while the evidence in the present case demonstrates that India enforced its jurisdiction over the Marines only in its internal waters and on land, when the Marines were arrested and detained [...]".

[30] Award, *cit. supra* note 12, para. 799, where the Tribunal affirms: "Articles 95 and 96, also invoked by Italy, do not address the immunity of persons, namely individuals who may be described as State officials. They address, first in Article 95, the immunity of warships, and second in Article 96, the immunity of ships 'owned or operated by a State and used only on government non-commercial service' [...]".

[31] Award, *cit. supra* note 12, paras. 795-811.

[32] On the international instruments potentially available in order to solve the dispute between Italy and India, see DEL VECCHIO, "Il caso dei due Marò e i possibili strumenti di soluzione obbligatoria della controversia", in *Scritti in onore di Giuseppe Tesauro, cit. supra* note 26, Vol. IV, p. 2631 ff.; MILANO, "Il caso 'Marò': alcune considerazioni sull'utilizzo di strumenti internazionali di risoluzione delle controversie", SIDIBlog, 3 April 2013, available at: <http://www.sidiblog.org/2013/04/03/il-caso-maro-alcune-considerazioni-sullutilizzo-di-strumenti-internazionali-di-risoluzione-delle-controversi/>.

tent to deal with the first question mentioned above concerning which State had jurisdiction over the *Enrica Lexie* incident, as the respective claims were based on a number of UNCLOS provisions. Yet, in theory, the Tribunal does not seem to have had competence to deal with the second question mentioned above, concerning the immunity of the Marines, which was mainly based, as we will see, on general international law.

The exclusion of certain issues *ratione materiae* can be explained by looking at the aim of compromissory clauses included in international treaties. Their aim is to distinguish the category of disputes which fall within their scope, from those which fall outside their scope.[33] Accordingly, in the present case, claims based on rules which fall outside UNCLOS provisions should normally be excluded. Exceptionally, however, international specialized tribunals can, to an extent, have incidental jurisdiction, depending on the instrument that grants them jurisdiction.[34] The latter, therefore, potentially provided a way forward for the Arbitral Tribunal to establish its exceptional jurisdiction over the second question concerning the immunity of the two Italian Marines. In essence, the Tribunal had to decide whether the two questions concerning the jurisdiction over the incident and the immunity over the Marines could be exceptionally decided together, considering the second question incidental to the first one.

---

[33] On the role of compromissory clauses, see CANNIZZARO and BONAFÉ, "Fragmenting International Law through Compromissory Clauses? Some Remarks on the Decision of the ICJ in the Oil Platforms Case", EJIL, 2005, p. 481 ff.

[34] The term incidental jurisdiction is commonly used in doctrine to mean the jurisdiction of an international court or tribunal over an issue that would otherwise be outside the court or tribunal's jurisdiction *ratione materiae*, but that falls within the court or tribunal's jurisdiction *ratione materiae* because it is incidental to the dispute. See TZENG, "The Implicated Issue Problem: Indispensable Issues and Incidental Jurisdiction", New York University Journal of International Law & Politics, 2018, p. 447 ff. The doctrine is unambiguous in considering that international tribunals have the power to decide on certain matters external to the one over which they have jurisdiction *ratione materiae*. This would be possible in the presence of clauses in international treaties which expressly refer to external norms ("referral clauses") or when, in order to correctly interpret or apply particular provisions of the convention in question, it is necessary to have recourse to fundamental or secondary norms of general international law (such as, for example, the law of treaties or the norms of international State responsibility). This is in accordance with the principle of systemic integration laid down in Art. 31(3)(c) of the Vienna Convention on the Law of Treaties, 23 May 1969, entered into force 27 January 1980, according to which international treaties are to be interpreted taking into account any relevant rule of international law applicable in the relationship between the parties. On the requirements that UNCLOS tribunals must assess in order to determine incidental jurisdiction, see SCHATZ, "Incidental Jurisdiction in the Award in "The 'Enrica Lexie' Incident (Italy v. India) – Part I", Völkerrechtsblog, 23 July 2020, available at: <https://voelkerrechtsblog.org/de/incidental-jurisdiction-in-the-award-in-the-enrica-lexie-incident-italy-v-india-part-i/>. See also RAJU, "The Enrica Lexie Award – Some Thoughts on 'Incidental' Jurisdiction (Part II)", 22 July 2020, Opinio Juris, available at: <http://opiniojuris.org/2020/07/22/the-enrica-lexie-award-some-thoughts-on-incidental-jurisdiction-part-ii/>. On this subject see also LOVE, "Jurisdiction over Incidental Questions in International Law", ASIL, 2017, p. 316 ff.; FORTEAU, "Regulating the Competition between International Courts and Tribunals. The Role of *Ratione Materiae* Jurisdiction under Part XV of UNCLOS", The Law and Practice of International Courts and Tribunals, 2016, p. 195 ff.

At this point, it is worth noting that establishing whether an international specialised tribunal facing a multifaceted dispute can exercise an "incidental jurisdiction" over substantive matters that fall outside the scope of its principal jurisdiction is of key importance for the case of the *Enrica Lexie*, and, at the same time, of key importance for international law as such. As pointed out by Marotti in his contribution, "this question reflects the more general tension between the consensual paradigm of international jurisdiction and the need to settle disputes in a complete and – to recall the wording of the Arbitral Tribunal – 'satisfactory' way".[35]

From the above we may deduce that in order to establish its competence *ratione materiae* over the question of immunity, the Arbitral Tribunal should have demonstrated the existence in the case at hand of exceptional requirements since its competence is otherwise limited to the interpretation and application of UNCLOS provisions. In order for such a tribunal to be able to exercise incidental jurisdiction, there are two necessary requirements whose recurrence appears necessary: first, the preliminary determination of the external issue must be *indispensable* to resolving the main dispute; second, the external issue must also be *ancillary* to the main issue, since it cannot constitute the real issue of the case nor the object of the claim. These requirements have already been affirmed several times by Arbitral Tribunals established on the basis of Annex VII of UNCLOS. For example, in the decision of 18 March 2015 in the *Chagos Marine Protected Area Arbitration*,[36] and in the decision of 21 February 2020 in the dispute between Ukraine and Russia on *Coastal State Rights in the Black Sea, Sea of Azov, and Kerch Strait*.[37] Indeed, the Arbitral Tribunal in the latter decision clarified that, in order to qualify an external issue as indispensable and ancillary, it is necessary for the tribunal to first define "how the dispute before it should be characterized" and thus ascertain wherein resides "the weight of the dispute".[38] There are serious doubts that in the *Enrica Lexie* case the Arbitral Tribunal followed this approach. In addition, we would have expected solid arguments since the delicate issue of incidental competence is of crucial relevance for both the present case and for future disputes having to deal with incidental questions. Conversely, after explaining that the question of immunity is not covered by

---

[35] MAROTTI, "A Satisfactory Answer? The Enrica Lexie Award and the Jurisdiction over Incidental Questions", in this Focus. The importance of striking a fair balance between the consensual paradigm of international jurisdiction and the need to settle disputes in a complete way was underlined in the past by doctrine, see CANNIZZARO and BONAFÉ, *cit. supra* note 33, *passim*.

[36] PCA Case No. 2011-03, paras. 220-221. In this regard, please refer to SCHATZ, "Incidental Jurisdiction", *cit. supra* note 34.

[37] *Ukraine v. the Russian Federation, Dispute Concerning Coastal State Rights in the Black Sea, Sea of Azov, and Kerch Strait*, PCA Case No. 2017-06. For a commentary see SCHATZ, "The Award concerning Preliminary Objections in Ukraine v. Russia : Observations regarding the Implicated Status of Crimea and the Sea of Azov", EJIL: Talk!, 20 March 2020, available at: <https://www.ejiltalk.org/the-award-concerning-preliminary-objections-in-ukraine-v-russia-observations-regarding-the-implicated-status-of-crimea-and-the-sea-of-azov/>.

[38] See para. 194 of the decision.

any UNCLOS provisions, and after referring to only one judicial precedent,[39] together with various legal literature on the topic, the Tribunal decided that the entire dispute in the *Enrica Lexie* case addressed a number of questions relating to the interpretation and application of the UNCLOS and that all these questions could not be properly decided in the absence of any reference to the question of the immunity of the Marines.[40]

This absence of strong legal arguments is particularly difficult to understand, as pointed out by Marotti in his article, given the presence of two strong dissenting opinions. Both opinions address the architecture of the dispute itself, but from different angles; on the one hand, Dr Rao begins his analysis from the premise that there exist two distinct questions – one concerning the jurisdiction over the incident of 12 February 2012, and one concerning the immunity of the Italian officials – which in his opinion should have been separately examined; on the other hand, Judge Robinson begins from the basis that the immunity constitutes the real central question of the whole dispute and not an external one. The latter, in our view, appears a particularly convincing conclusion which deserved more attention before being rejected by the majority. According to this judge, the lack of the *ancillary* requirement is evident because the external issue of the functional immunity of the Italian riflemen not only could not be qualified as a "minor issue", but represented "the core element of the dispute [...] the real issue in the dispute between the Parties",[41] as it proved to be decisive for the attribution of jurisdiction to Italy. It is also evident that the external issue of immunity was not *necessary* in order to solve the main dispute,[42] since this could have been decided by the recognition of concurrent jurisdiction of Italy and India,[43] and therefore by the affirmation of the legitimacy of the Indian criminal jurisdiction.[44]

---

[39] *Case Concerning Certain German Interests in Polish Upper Silesia (Germany v. Poland)*, Judgment of 25 August 1925, PCIJ Reports, Series A, No. 6, p. 18 ff. (Award, *cit. supra* note 12, para. 808).

[40] See Award, *cit. supra* note 12, para. 808, in which the arbitral tribunal merely stated that the issue of functional immunity was "preliminary or incidental to the application of the Convention" and that, in the absence of its definition, it could not "provide a complete answer to the question as to which Party may exercise jurisdiction". On the point see again MAROTTI, *cit. supra* note 35.

[41] See Award, *cit. supra* note 12, Dissenting opinion of Judge Robinson, para. 81.

[42] At para. 239 the Arbitral Tribunal itself had in fact recognized that "it was conceivable that the dispute between the Parties would be decided without a determination on the question of immunity".

[43] And this on the basis of the criteria of active and passive territoriality already referred to in para. 367 which states: "the alleged offence was commenced on board the Italian vessel, 'Enrica Lexie', and completed on board the Indian vessel, 'St. Antony'. According to the territoriality principle, both Italy and India are entitled to exercise jurisdiction over the incident". Similarly, para. 839 provides that: "[p]ursuant to Article 58, paragraph 2, and Article 92, each Party has exclusive jurisdiction over their respective ship involved in the incident, namely, Italy over the 'Enrica Lexie' and India over the 'St. Antony'. The Parties therefore have concurrent jurisdiction over the incident".

[44] Award, *cit. supra* note 12, para. 840, under which: "At the same time, pursuant to the principle of objective territoriality, well established in international law, a State may assert its jurisdiction in respect of offences committed outside its territory but consummated within its

Notwithstanding the additional factor of having the two clear and well-grounded dissenting opinions, the Tribunal simply stated that the exercise of its jurisdiction over the incident could not be satisfactorily answered without addressing the question of the immunity of the Italian Marines. According to the majority of the judges, since immunity from jurisdiction "operates as an exception to an otherwise-existing right to exercise jurisdiction", such exception "forms an integral part of the Arbitral Tribunal's task to determine which Party may exercise jurisdiction over the Marines".[45]

In sum, we believe that by establishing that the question of immunity "belongs to those 'questions preliminary or incidental to the application' of the Convention", the award has probably focused on the need to solve the dispute in a complete and satisfactory way, but without taking into enough consideration the other side of the coin, regarding the consensual paradigm of international jurisdiction. We are not taking here any stance with respect to the specific choice of the Tribunal, but rather affirming that, in light of the above illustrated relevance, the analysis of this procedural question might have deserved additional attention. It has been argued that this arbitration decision represents a precedent on which to build a new concept of incidental jurisdiction, such as to overcome the traditional definition.[46] Such a reconstruction does not seem to us to be acceptable, since the application of a surprisingly broad notion of incidental jurisdiction, without respecting the requirements that have evolved from jurisprudential practice, may instead result in an unlimited expansion of the jurisdiction of international tribunals. As has been clearly stated by the ICJ, it is necessary, given the unquestionable difficulty of balancing the need to adopt a satisfactory and complete decision and the need to safeguard the will expressed by the States by signing the international treaty and the arbitration clause contained therein, that international courts "must not exceed the jurisdiction conferred upon [them] by the Parties" but at the same time "exercise that jurisdiction to its full extent".[47]

5. The Functional Immunity of the Italian Marines: A Missed Opportunity to Ascertain Customary International Law

After having determined its competence over Italy's claim regarding the functional immunity of the Italian officials from Indian criminal jurisdiction, the Arbitral Tribunal also had to assess the merit of this claim. In this respect, the Tribunal established that India must be precluded from the exercise of its crimi-

---

territory or, as stated in 1926 by the PCIJ in the S.S. 'Lotus' judgment, 'if one of the constituent elements of the offence, and more especially its effects, have taken place [in its territory]'".

[45] Award, cit. supra note 12, paras. 809-811.

[46] METHYMAKI and TAMS, "Immunities and Compromissory Clauses. Making Sense of Enrica Lexie (Part I)", EJIL: Talk!, 27 August 2020, available at: <https://www.ejiltalk.org/immunities-and-compromissory-clauses-making-sense-of-enrica-lexie-part-i/>.

[47] See Continental Shelf (Libya/Malta), Judgment of 3 June 1985, ICJ Reports 1985, p. 13 ff., para. 19.

nal jurisdiction over the Italian Marines, since the latter enjoy immunity *ratione materiae*.

The point to which we wish to draw attention, is that this clear-cut stance is based on customary international law. Namely, in the absence of a specific provision of the UNCLOS dealing with the matter of the functional immunity of State officials, the majority of the judges maintained that general international law may fill in this normative gap. Confirming the approach adopted to assess the procedural aspect, the Tribunal, in order to reach and support its conclusion on the merits of the immunity issue, simply relied on two precedents – one set by the International Criminal Tribunal for the Former Yugoslavia and one by the ICJ – and on the ILC's Draft Articles on Immunity of State Officials from Foreign Criminal Jurisdiction.[48] In addition, the Tribunal took into consideration the fact that India, in its counter-claim, had not specifically questioned the existence of a general rule of international law with respect to the immunity from criminal jurisdiction of State officials.[49]

In effect, according to unanimous legal doctrine, as well as to international and domestic jurisprudence, a provision of customary international law which accords criminal (and civil) immunity to State officials, in respect of their official acts or in respect of the acts performed in their official capacity, exists.[50] However, the existence of such norm is crystal clear only when it comes to specific categories of State officials, such as diplomatic agents, heads of governments or States, and ministries of foreign affairs.[51] Yet, with the exception of these senior and diplomatic categories of State officials, unanimity with respect to other categories of State officials is far from being reached. On the one hand, we find both ILC Rapporteurs working on a study on the functional (as well as personal) immunity of State officials from foreign criminal jurisdiction, who have expressly accepted the old theory on immunity, according to which *all* State officials have, in principle, the right to functional immunity from foreign jurisdiction regarding their official acts.[52] This study certainly deserves attention and it is not surprising that the Arbitral Tribunal took it into account. This study alone, however, cannot be considered decisive for the resolution of the dispute between Italy and India or for other more recent cases. On the other hand, indeed, we find that the rule of customary international law regarding the functional immunity of State officials

---

[48] Award, *cit. supra* note 12, paras. 843-845.

[49] Award, *cit. supra* note 12, para. 846.

[50] CONFORTI, "In tema di immunità degli organi statali stranieri", RDI, 2010, p. 5 ff.

[51] To underline the fact that these categories of State officials should enjoy the benefit of immunity from foreign jurisdiction, the doctrine refers to them as "senior members of central governments". In this respect, see, for instance, FOX and WEBB, *The Law of State Immunity*, 3rd ed., Oxford, 2015; in relation to immunity of State officials, see also AKANDE and SHAH, "Immunities of State Officials, International Crimes, and Foreign Domestic Courts", EJIL, 2010, p. 815 ff.

[52] See KOLODKIN, Second Report to the ILC on the Immunity of State Officials from Foreign Criminal Jurisdiction, UN Doc. A/CN4/631 (2010); ESCOBAR HERNÁNDEZ, Third Report to the ILC on the Immunity of State Officials from Foreign Criminal Jurisdiction, UN Doc. A/CN4/673 (2014).

from foreign criminal jurisdiction is, as said, somewhat dated and in many cases controversial. Most of contemporary international law scholars disagree about its scope of application and content.[53]

Moreover, as authoritatively affirmed in this respect: "[...] what States say at international level, [and] the statements of representatives of governments within the relevant international organs [...] are not conclusive".[54] What should rather be considered conclusive are practice and domestic case law since they represent the actual context in which State authorities demonstrate their real will to enforce international law, and, with respect to immunity, practice and domestic case law are not uniform and consistent.[55] If we cannot expect an international tribunal to

---

[53] In favour of immunity in the present case see RONZITTI, "The *Enrica Lexie* Incident", *cit. supra* note 1. On the different theories, see PISILLO MAZZESCHI, "Organi degli Stati stranieri (immunità giurisdizionale degli)", in *Enciclopedia del Diritto – Annali*, Milano, 2014, Vol. VII, p. 735 ff.; ID., "The Functional Immunity of State Officials from Foreign Jurisdiction: A Critique of the Traditional Theories", Questions of International Law, Zoom out 17 (2015), p. 3 ff.

[54] CONFORTI, "A Few Remarks on the Functional Immunity of the Organs of Foreign States", Questions of International Law, Zoom out 17 (2015), p. 69 ff. This, in our view, is also true with regard to States' responses in the ILC's work on State officials' immunity, which, on the contrary, RONZITTI (in this Focus) considers relevant.

[55] See, in the sense of the denial of functional immunity in an "automatic" manner, in addition to the judgment of the Kerala High Court in the case that concerns us (*Latorre and Others v. Union of India and Others*, 29 May 2012), for example: the judgment of the Supreme Court of Burma in the *Kovtunenko* case, 1 March 1960, ILR, Vol. 31, p. 259 ff.; the decision of the Belgian Court of Cassation in the *Sharon and Yaron* case (12 February 2003); the decision of the English High Court in the *Khurts Bat v. Investigating Judge of the Federal Court of Germany* case (Queen's Bench Division, 29 July 2011, paras. 70-100); the judgment of the Italian *Corte di Cassazione* of 24 February 2014 in the *Abu Omar* case, in which the Court states: "in this situation to consider the existence of a customary norm appears incorrect because there is no consolidated case law, there are no continuous and concordant official declarations of the States and there is no univocal doctrinal interpretation" (on this decision, and for other examples, see also NIGRO, in this Focus). It must be underlined that, on the point, the *Corte di Cassazione (Sez. I penale)* had adopted a completely opposite view in its decision in the *Lozano* case, 24 July 2008, No. 31171, IYIL, 2008, p. 346 ff., with a comment by SERRA; RDI, 2008, p. 1223 ff., in which the Court, confirming the lack of Italian jurisdiction in the well-known *Lozano/Calipari* case, (affirmed by the *Corte di Assise di Roma*, 3 January 2008, No. 21, IYIL, 2007, p. 287 ff., with a comment by SERRA) substantially moved from the assumption according to which the customary principle of immunity of the State for acts *jure imperii* implies as a "natural corollary" the immunity of its individual bodies for the same type of acts, otherwise the useful effect of the first principle would be depleted. Therefore, any act carried out by an individual-organ in the exercise of official functions delegated to it by the State, and as such explicating a sovereign activity, would be exempt from criminal judgment insofar as attributable to the State itself, unless the act in question constitutes an international crime. On the logical limits of the parallelism between the immunity of the individual-organ and the immunity of the State, see the considerations made by DE SENA and DE VITTOR, "Immunità degli Stati dalla giurisdizione e violazione di diritti dell'uomo: la sentenza della Cassazione italiana nel caso *Ferrini*", Giur. It., 2005, p. 255 ff. It should also not be forgotten that there are much more radical theses which even cast doubts on the general character of the immunity of States and the – consequent – exceptional character of the exercise of jurisdiction (in this sense, BIANCHI, "L'immunité des Etats et les violations graves des droits de l'homme: la fonction de l'interprète dans la détermination du droit international", RGDIP, 2004, p. 69

make express reference to all the domestic case law on the issue, we can expect a ruling supported by profound and significant grounds. Legal exception to general rules should always be adequately substantiated. This consideration appears even more important with reference to the subject of immunities, which affects the power of the State to exercise its jurisdiction, and therefore the fundamental right of the individual to take legal action. It is no coincidence that the development of guarantees for the protection of human rights has been accompanied by a progressive reduction in the scope of immunity. Moreover, jurisdiction in criminal matters is one of the most significant attributes of State sovereignty, almost the "hard core" of sovereignty, as evidenced, for example, by the modalities relating to the progressive construction of the European Union. In fact, criminal jurisdiction is one of the subjects which has not yet been transferred from the States to the institutions of the Union. Any hypothesis of renunciation or cession by the State in this matter, therefore, must be evaluated carefully, must be ascertained without any possibility of doubt, and above all must be interpreted restrictively. Since functional immunity entails an exception to the normal exercise of jurisdiction by the State of the forum (as well as a restriction of the right of access to a judge), the existence of the customary principle must be demonstrated rigorously and on the basis of a broad, consolidated and uniform international practice, as well as on a well demonstrated *opinio juris*.[56]

The mere attribution to the State of the act carried out by the individual as its organ does not, therefore, automatically entail the activation of functional immunity in favour of the latter. Nor can it be said that the customary norm on immunity covers all the acts performed by the individual-organ in the exercise of its functions, given that it is limited, as we know, to acts *jure imperii*. Moreover, even if an autonomous norm on functional immunity is considered to exist, its object is certainly not the indiscriminate protection of any individual-organ, for any conduct on behalf of the State.[57] At most, it aims, in fact, to provide protection from judicial interference to certain functions of the foreign State. In short, functional immunity is enjoyed, as has been said, only by those high-ranking individual-organs that normally entertain the State's relations with other subjects

---

ff., or which view the granting of immunity as a mere international courtesy (cf. the considerations of LAUTERPACHT, "The Problem of Jurisdictional Immunities of Foreign States", BYIL, 1951, p. 227 ff., and, more recently, the position of CAPLAN, "State Immunity, Human Rights, and Jus Cogens: a Critique of the Normative Hierarchy Theory", AJIL, 2003, p. 744 ff.). For more details on the issue of functional immunity see DE SENA, *Diritto internazionale e immunità funzionale degli organi statali*, Milano, 1996; FRULLI, *Immunità e crimini internazionali. L'esercizio della giurisdizione penale e civile nei confronti degli organi statali sospettati di gravi crimini internazionali*, Torino, 2007; VAN ALEBEEK, *The Immunity of States and their Officials in International Criminal Law and International Human Rights Law*, Oxford, 2008; NIGRO, *Le immunità giurisdizionali dello Stato e dei suoi organi e l'evoluzione della sovranità nel diritto internazionale*, Padova, 2018.

[56] This writer highlighted these aspects in particular in relation to the decision of the *Cassazione* in the *Lozano* case, *cit. supra* note 55. See CATALDI and SERRA, "Ordinamento italiano e corpi di spedizione all'estero, fra diritto umanitario, diritto penale e tutela dei diritti umani", DUDI, 2010, p. 141 ff.

[57] In this sense, see already DE SENA, *cit. supra* note 55, p. 52 ff. and p. 241 ff.

of international law, or by individuals exercising specific functions protected by international law only for those acts that are typically performed by the organ they embody. This is the "hard core" of the functional immunity norm. Outside this perimeter, recognition of immunity cannot be presumed, but must always be demonstrated.

Additionally, the Arbitral Tribunal took a clear-cut stance on a matter that is topical for international relations, not only for relations between Italy and India in the case at stake. In 2008, in the case *Djibouti v. France*, the ICJ was required by the Parties to determine whether questions on immunity should be decided on a case-by-case basis or on the basis of a general rule of international law.[58] The ICJ opted for the first route and left open the issue of clarifying the conditions according to which immunity from foreign jurisdiction can apply. The existence of a customary principle on the functional immunity of military personnel as State organs will therefore continue to be the subject of debate in doctrine, also because we do not believe that in this regard the Tribunal (nor the ILC to whose work the Tribunal referred[59]) has made a significant contribution to the matter with the decision under consideration, having provided no decisive argument or evidence as to the existence of such a principle. The Tribunal affirmed the existence of the customary principle by referring, as mentioned above, to only two judgments[60] one of which is not relevant,[61] while the other is susceptible to criticism because it in turn recalls irrelevant case law.[62] As regards, more specifi-

---

[58] Both submissions are available on the ICJ website, see *Certain Questions of Mutual Assistance in Criminal Matters (Djibouti v. France)*, Judgment of 4 June 2008, ICJ Reports 2008, p. 177 ff.

[59] See Award, *cit. supra* note 12, para. 849, in which the Tribunal recalls the ILC Draft Articles on Immunity of State Officials from Foreign Criminal Jurisdiction adopted in 2016.

[60] Award, *cit. supra* note 12, paras. 808 and 844, in which the Tribunal recalls, as evidence of the existence of a customary principle, the 29 October 1997 Judgment of the Appeal Chamber of the International Criminal Tribunal for the former Yugoslavia in *Prosecutor v. Tihomir Blaškic*, as well as the ICJ decision in the case *Djibouti v. France, cit. supra* note 58.

[61] It should be noted that in *Djibouti v. France*, the ICJ did not rule on Djibouti's request to recognize functional immunity to the Prosecutor of the Republic and the Head of National Security from French criminal jurisdiction, stating that the exception of immunity had not been raised before the French courts. Therefore, the dispute can in no way provide evidence of the existence of the customary principle. On the point see CONFORTI, "In tema di immunità", *cit. supra* note 50, p. 10.

[62] The International Tribunal for the former Yugoslavia in its 1997 decision in the case *Prosecutor v. Blaškić* excludes the possibility of issuing injunctions for purposes of investigation against State bodies, stating that they enjoy functional immunity under customary international law. However, this assertion is not founded on solid grounds, since the Appeals Chamber cites, in support of its thesis, four cases, among which one (US Supreme Court, *Waters v. Collot*, 2 US 247 (1796)) is very old and above all does not concern immunity from criminal jurisdiction but rather immunity from civil jurisdiction, therefore is not very significant. The other cases cited (*McLeod, Eichmann* and *Rainbow Warrior*) tend to disprove, rather than confirm, this thesis. In fact, *McLeod* was tried by the Supreme Court of New York for the burning of the ship *Caroline* (*People v. McLeod*, 6 July 1841, Wendell's Law Reports, 1840-1841, p. 483 ff.) and, similarly, the two secret agents of the French Government were tried before the District Court of Auckland, New Zealand, for having blown up the ship *Rainbow Warrior* (Judgment of 4 November 1985). *Adolf Eichmann* (in ILR, Vol. 36, pp. 277-342) is not

cally, the immunity of military personnel abroad, it should be noted that the rules on jurisdiction over the latter are for the most part the subject of a conventional discipline, since they are set out in Status of Forces Agreements (SOFAs), which are based on the model of the agreement concluded within NATO in London in 1951. The practice of States to resort to conventional forms of protection must be interpreted as evidence of States' lack of conviction regarding the existence of a customary rule on the functional immunity of military personnel abroad, the existence of which would clearly make the conclusion of such agreements superfluous.[63]

Even if we accept that there is a rule of general international law which confers functional immunity on military personnel, there are still a number of questions concerning the applicability of this (alleged) rule of general international law to the marines in the *Enrica Lexie* case. While there is no doubt that the two soldiers were organs of the State,[64] in our opinion, contrary to the Tribunal's finding that the two marines were acting "in the exercise of their official functions",[65]

---

relevant for the purpose of recognizing the existence of the customary principle because first of all it was a case of judging international crimes; in this dispute, moreover, the Court rejected the exceptions of lack of jurisdiction and tried and condemned *Eichmann*. Among other things, it should be noted that the arguments used to challenge the jurisdiction of the Court referred not to functional immunity, but to the different doctrine of the "act of State" (*Eichmann*'s actions were carried out in Germany and in execution of decrees of its government, attributable only to the German State, and foreign judges could not judge on such acts because they were carried out by a foreign State on its territory).

[63] The relationship of treaties with custom is one of exception to the rule. States, in order to derogate from a general rule, or in order to fill a gap in the general law, will put in place conventional rules. If the spread of agreements, with repetition of identical rules, is significant, it is believed that this circumstance may be sufficient to prove the existence of a customary rule, at least *in statu nascendi*. The proliferation of bilateral agreements between the sending State and the territorial State on the status of participants in multinational forces (SOFA) is undeniable. But it is precisely the continued, persistent proliferation of these treaties which, in our opinion, further confirms that the rule invoked by the Court does not exist, at least not for the time being. For further details on these aspects, please refer to CATALDI and SERRA, *cit. supra* note 56, p. 153 ff.

[64] According to the definition contained in Art. 4 of the Draft Articles on the Responsibility of States for Internationally Wrongful Acts, what matters for the attribution of the status of State organ is the qualification of such subject under domestic law, as well as the fact that this subject has the power to represent the State or act on behalf of the latter in all those matters in which the latter exercises sovereign prerogatives. In the case of the two military personnel involved, there is no doubt that they were State organs as they were riflemen of the Italian Navy, and therefore a branch of the armed forces which, pursuant to Art. 110 of the Code of Military Order (Legislative Decree No. 66 of 15 March 2010) "constitutes the operational maritime component of the State's military defence". In addition, Law No. 130 of 2011 assigned to the Chief and members of the Navy embarked in anti-piracy function on commercial ships, respectively the roles of officer and judicial police officer for the repression of piracy offences under Arts. 1135 and 1136 of the Navigation Code. See Draft Articles on the Responsibility of States for Internationally Wrongful Acts, with commentary, YILC, 2001, Vol. II, Part Two, p. 40. On this point, with reference to the case in question, see BUSCO and FONTANELLI, "Questioni di giurisdizione e immunità nella vicenda dell'Enrica Lexie, alla luce del diritto internazionale", Diritto penale contemporaneo, 2013, p. 40 ff.

[65] Award, *cit. supra* note 12, para. 862.

the presence of the marines on the *Enrica Lexie* was not justified by the need to protect State functions, but by the need to defend that specific commercial vessel from possible pirate attacks.[66] The *Enrica Lexie* was not a military ship authorized to repress piracy under Article 110 UNCLOS, nor was there any international anti-piracy cooperation coordinated by the United Nations or specifically established between Italy and India.[67] It should also be noted that the presence of military personnel on the Italian tanker was at the expense of the shipowner and not on the basis of an international agreement or a resolution of the Security Council,[68] but on the basis of domestic Italian Law No. 130 of 2011[69] and the agreement that the Ministry of Defence and the private confederation of Italian shipowners *Confitarma* concluded on 11 October 2011.[70] The hypothesis would have been quite different if the Italian State (and not individual ship owners) had decided to enlist military personnel on board all ships flying the Italian flag in piracy-prone areas. Only in this case could it be assumed, without any need of further demonstration, that the State was exercising its sovereign functions.[71] Therefore, even if we admit the existence of the customary principle of func-

---

[66] In the same sense, see NIGRO, in this Focus. As expressly stated in Art. 5(6-*ter*) of Law No 130 of 2011, the use of military protection units may in no way entail additional costs for the State.

[67] The point is underlined by FOCARELLI, *Trattato di diritto internazionale*, 2015, p. 754 ff.

[68] As is well known, the Security Council has dealt with the repression of international piracy in particular with reference to events taking place off the coast of Somalia. It is worth remembering especially Resolution No. 1814 of 15 May 2008 with which the Security Council asked States to act in agreement with the Somali government to protect ships and humanitarian aid to Somalia, and Resolution 1851 of 16 December 2008 with which States are authorized to enter Somali territorial waters and adopt "all necessary means to repress acts of piracy and armed robbery" (para. 6). On the international actions against piracy, see GUILFOYLE (ed.), *Modern Piracy: Legal Challenges and Responses*, Cheltenham, 2013; KOUTRAKOS and SKORDAS (eds.), *The Law and Practice of Piracy at Sea: European and International Perspectives*, Oxford, 2014; DEL CHICCA, *La pirateria marittima*, Torino, 2016; BEVILACQUA, *Criminalità e sicurezza in alto mare*, Napoli, 2017.

[69] As already mentioned, this law authorized the presence of armed personnel on board commercial ships. In this regard, please refer to BEVILACQUA, "Counter Piracy Armed Services, The Italian System and the Search for Clarity on the Use of Force at Sea", IYIL, 2012, p. 50 ff.; RICCIUTELLI, "La recente normativa sulle misure di contrasto alla pirateria marittima", The Italian Maritime Journal, 2011, p. 2 ff.; RONZITTI, "Un passo avanti per la tutela delle navi italiane ma troppa cautela nella legge di conversione", Guida al diritto – Il Sole 24 Ore, No. 43, 2011, p. 54 ff.; HARLOW, "Soldiers at Sea: The Legality and Policy Implications of Using Military Security Teams to Combat Piracy", Southern California Interdisciplinary Law Journal, 2012, p. 561 ff.; TONDINI, "Impiego di NMP e guardie giurate in funzione antipirateria", Rivista marittima, 2013, p. 32 ff.

[70] The text of the agreement is available at: <http://www.unife.it/giurisprudenza/giurisprudenza/studiare/diritti-umani-conflitti-armati/materiale-da-archiviare/dudu-2013/salerno/A_101011_Protocollo_Difesa_CONFITARMA_UG.pdf>.

[71] Different opinions have been sustained in doctrine in this regard. See in particular: RONZITTI, "The *Enrica Lexie* Incident", *cit. supra* note 1; EBOLI and PIERINI, "Coastal State Jurisdiction Over Vessel Protection Detachments and Immunity Issues: The *Enrica Lexie* Case", Revue de droit militaire et de droit de la guerre, 2012, p. 117 ff.; CARELLA, *Il caso dei "marò" e il diritto internazionale*, Bari, 2013.

tional immunity as relied on by the majority of the judges, it is our opinion that such principle was not automatically applicable to the case at hand, since the two Marines, although exercising the typical functions connected to the security of the ship and its crew, were acting on behalf of private subjects and not on behalf of the Italian State. Therefore, also on this point, the Tribunal should have set out a more thorough and well-argued motivation.[72]

6.   CONCLUDING REMARKS

The decision commented on here has the undoubted merit of putting an end to a long-standing dispute between the two States, leaving both of them satisfied, all things considered, with the result obtained. Italy has seen the recognition of the principle of functional immunity from criminal jurisdiction of its two soldiers, with the consequence that it does not have to return them to India and can instead prosecute them at home. The Government of New Delhi, for its part, obtained the Tribunal's decision confirming Italy's violation of the freedom of navigation on the high seas, with the consequent obligation to pay compensation for damages.

However, with all due respect to the Tribunal, with a 406-page judgment, dissenting opinions included, it was reasonable to expect more convincing and detailed arguments on the individual points decided. In fact, on the one hand, the Arbitration Tribunal treated as incidental an issue that was perhaps not so incidental, and, on the other hand, it acknowledged the existence and application of the customary rule on the functional immunity of military personnel without giving adequate reasons. In this regard, let us reiterate what has already been said above, namely that the adoption of an expanded notion of incidental jurisdiction lends itself to an unlimited extension of the jurisdiction of international courts and that the recognition of the existence and applicability of functional immunity must be adequately proven, as it involves a derogation from the normal criteria of attribution of jurisdiction as well as a restriction of the fundamental right of access to justice, provided by national and supranational systems of protection of human rights. The need to reach a compromise between the Parties in an equitable spirit has therefore prevailed over a strict application of the law. It remains only to take note of it.

---

[72] In the same sense, see in particular the Dissenting Opinion of Judge Patrick Robinson (paras. 63-70).

A SATISFACTORY ANSWER? THE *ENRICA LEXIE* AWARD AND THE JURISDICTION OVER INCIDENTAL QUESTIONS

Loris Marotti[*]

Abstract

This article situates the Enrica Lexie *award's stance on the Tribunal's jurisdiction over the marines' immunity within the broader debate on the scope of the jurisdiction of international courts and tribunals over incidental questions. After illustrating the Tribunal's approach to the question at hand, the paper appraises those instances where an international tribunal with limited jurisdiction can decide issues and apply rules that are "external" to its principal jurisdiction. It then focuses on the question of the jurisdiction over incidental issues, which is the most debated avenue for an international tribunal to engage with substantive matters falling outside the scope of the tribunal's ratione materiae jurisdiction. Finally, the Tribunal's approach in the* Enrica Lexie *award is critically assessed against the above debate. It is submitted that, although the award arguably put an end to the longstanding dispute between India and Italy, the Tribunal's reasoning does not seem to be in line with the conditions for the exercise of jurisdiction over incidental questions as roughly sketched in relevant case law.*

Keywords: Enrica Lexie; award of the arbitral tribunal; immunity claim; compromissory clauses; jurisdiction over incidental questions.

1. INTRODUCTION

It may come as a surprise that, of the many issues addressed by the arbitral tribunal in the *Enrica Lexie* award,[1] the one that has drawn more attention – both within[2] and outside the Tribunal[3] – pertains to an apparently rather peripheral

---

[*] Researcher in International Law, University of Napoli "Federico II".

[1] *The "Enrica Lexie" Incident (The Italian Republic v. The Republic of India)*, Award of 21 May 2020, PCA Case No. 2015-28. For a comprehensive analysis of the award, see RONZITTI, "Il caso della Enrica Lexie e la sentenza arbitrale nella controversia Italia-India", RDI, 2020, p. 937 ff.

[2] See the dissenting opinion of Judge Robinson and the concurring and dissenting opinion of Dr Rao.

[3] METHYMAKI and TAMS, "Immunities and Compromissory Clauses: Making Sense of Enrica Lexie" (Parts I and II), EJIL: Talk!, 27 August 2020, available at: <https://www.ejilt-alk.org/>; RAJU, "The Enrica Lexie Award – Some Thoughts on "Incidental" Jurisdiction" (Parts I and II), Opinio Juris, 22 July 2020, available at: <http://opiniojuris.org/>; SCHATZ, "Incidental jurisdiction in the award in 'The Enrica Lexie Incident (Italy v. India)'" (Parts I and II), Völkerrechtsblog, 23 and 24 July 2020, available at: <https://voelkerrechtsblog.org/>; KUMAR, "Jurisdiction of the Permanent Court of Arbitration over Marines' Immunity in the

IYIL, Vol. 30 (2020), pp. 191-208
ISSN 0391-5107

question: the basis of the Tribunal's jurisdiction over the claim of immunity from criminal jurisdiction of the two marines. Indeed, something highly controversial lies behind such a question and the way the Tribunal approached it. Determining whether an international tribunal facing a multifaceted dispute can exercise its jurisdiction over incidental substantive matters that fall outside the scope of its principal jurisdiction is a much-debated issue in the contemporary practice of international adjudication. This question reflects the more general tension between the consensual paradigm of international jurisdiction and the need to settle disputes in a complete and – to borrow from the language of the *Enrica Lexie* Tribunal – "satisfactory" way.

The *Enrica Lexie* award adds another important piece to the ever-increasing number of recent international judicial decisions dealing with this tension. Moreover, as will be shown, some aspects of the award contribute to making the problem even more controversial, given the opaque reasoning underlying the finding that the arbitral tribunal had jurisdiction to entertain the question of immunity.

The present comment situates the *Enrica Lexie* award's stance on the jurisdiction over the marines' immunity within the broader debate on the scope of jurisdiction of international courts and tribunals over incidental questions. After illustrating the Tribunal's approach to the question at hand (Section 2), this paper discusses the main issues surrounding this kind of jurisdiction. Starting from an appraisal of those instances where an international tribunal with limited jurisdiction can decide issues and apply rules that are "external" to their principal jurisdiction (Section 3), the paper focuses on the jurisdiction over incidental questions, which is the most debated avenue for an international tribunal to engage with external issues (Section 4). Finally, the Tribunal's approach in the *Enrica Lexie* award is critically assessed against the above debate (Section 5).

2. THE TRIBUNAL'S TAKE ON THE EXERCISE OF JURISDICTION OVER THE CLAIM OF IMMUNITY

As a general rule, courts and tribunals referred to in Part XV of the UN Convention on the Law of the Sea (UNCLOS) have jurisdiction limited to any dispute concerning the interpretation and application of the Convention.[4] Quite predictably, since the beginning of the litigation of the *Enrica Lexie* case before UNCLOS tribunals, the question arose as to whether Italy's claim on the immunity of the marines could fall within the limited jurisdiction of such tribunals.[5]

Enrica Lexie Incident: a Critical Evaluation", Cambridge International Law Journal Blog, 12 February 2021, available at: <http://cilj.co.uk/2021/02/12/jurisdiction-of-the-permanent-court-of-arbitration-over-marines-immunity-in-the-enrica-lexie-incident-a-critical-evaluation/>.

    [4] Arts. 286 and 288(1) UNCLOS.

    [5] See RONZITTI, "The *Enrica Lexie* Incident: Law of the Sea and Immunity of State Officials Issues", IYIL, 2012, p. 3 ff., p. 13; MILANO, "Il caso "Marò": alcune considerazioni sull'utilizzo di strumenti internazionali di risoluzione delle controversie", SIDIBlog, 3 April

Because of the ways India framed its objections to the jurisdiction, in the award under consideration the Tribunal addressed the question in two different stages. In the first place, it settled the parties' dispute as to their characterisation of the dispute, meaning whether the dispute as a whole concerned the interpretation and application of the Convention. Indeed, while according to Italy the dispute squarely fell within the scope of Article 288 UNCLOS, being essentially a dispute related to which State is entitled to exercise jurisdiction over the incident, thus involving the interpretation and application of several provisions of the Convention, India argued that the Tribunal should have declined to globally exercise jurisdiction over the dispute. India's argument was that "the core issue, the real subject matter of the dispute" was the question of immunity from criminal jurisdiction of the two marines, a question lying outside the jurisdiction of the Tribunal.[6] The Tribunal ultimately agreed with Italy's characterisation of the dispute. According to the Tribunal, the Parties' dispute was "appropriately characterised as a disagreement as to which State is entitled to exercise jurisdiction over the incident", raising questions of interpretation and application of several provisions of the Convention, in respect of which the Parties had different views.[7] With respect to the question of the immunity of the marines, which constituted a specific claim made by Italy accompanied by a request for a specific declaratory relief on it,[8] the Tribunal noted that Italy's request:

> was but one of several bases upon which Italy substantiated its more general request for a finding that, "by asserting and exercising jurisdiction over the Enrica Lexie and the Italian Marines", India violated the Convention". Indeed, the asserted immunity of the Marines was not the only basis upon which Italy alleges India's exercise of jurisdiction to be contrary to the Convention. On Italy's case, it was conceivable that the dispute between the Parties would be decided without a determination on the question of immunity (such as by a finding by the Arbitral Tribunal that Italy has exclusive jurisdiction over the incident under Articles 87 or 97 of the Convention).[9]

In other words, according to the Tribunal, the dispute as a whole was a dispute concerning the interpretation and application of the Convention which "may raise, but is not limited to, the question of immunity of the Marines".[10]

Having so characterised the dispute, the Tribunal was still left with India's specific objections to jurisdiction with respect to the question of immunity of the marines. Indeed, while India claimed that the Tribunal lacked jurisdiction entire-

---

2013, available at: <http://www.sidiblog.org/2013/04/03/il-caso-maro-alcune-considerazioni-sullutilizzo-di-strumenti-internazionali-di-risoluzione-delle-controversi/>.

[6] Award, para. 226.
[7] Award, para. 243.
[8] Award, para. 75(2)(f).
[9] Award, para. 239.
[10] Award, para. 243.

ly, based on the fact that the dispute related to a question alien to the Convention, it also maintained, in the alternative, its specific objections to jurisdiction over the question of immunity.[11] That is the reason why the Tribunal ended up dealing with the question of its jurisdiction over the immunity of the two marines in a later stage. Having first found that, potentially, the question of immunity might not need to be decided, being "but one of several bases" on which Italy alleged that India violated the Convention, the same question turned out to be a decisive one for the dispute. In fact, after having established that both India and Italy were entitled to exercise jurisdiction over the incident, the Tribunal noted that the finding of concurrent jurisdiction was "without prejudice to the question whether India is precluded from exercising jurisdiction over the Marines because of their status as State officials entitled to immunity in relation to acts performed in the exercise of their official functions".[12]

It should be recalled that Italy's claim on immunity of the two marines was not raised without any reference to the Convention. In its final submission, Italy requested the Tribunal to adjudge and declare that "by asserting and continuing to exercise its criminal jurisdiction over [the two Marines], India is in violation of its obligation to respect the immunity of the Marines as Italian State officials exercising official functions, in breach of Articles 2(3), 56(2), 58(2) and 100 of UNCLOS".[13] The external issue of immunity, in Italy's view, would be imported into the Convention by means of *renvoi* made by several UNCLOS provisions referring to "other rules of international law", "the rights and duties of other States", and "other pertinent rules of international law".[14] The Tribunal, however, found that these provisions were not pertinent and applicable in the present case. Thus, it acknowledged that the question of immunity was not covered by any provision of the Convention, meaning that, in principle, it should not have jurisdiction over the issue.

It is at this point that, crucially, the Tribunal turned to the shaky ground of the jurisdiction over incidental questions. Having found it necessary to assess whether "there is *any other justification* for it to exercise jurisdiction over the issue of the immunity of the Marines",[15] the Tribunal considered whether the issue of the entitlement to exercise jurisdiction over the incident "could be *satisfactorily* answered without addressing the question of the immunity of the Marines".[16] In this respect, the Tribunal found that, since immunity from jurisdiction "operates as an exception to an otherwise-existing right to exercise jurisdiction", such an exception "forms an integral part of the Arbitral Tribunal's task to determine which Party may exercise jurisdiction over the Marines". In the Tribunal's view, it "could not provide *a complete answer* to the question as to which Party may

---

[11] Award, para. 227.

[12] Award, para. 367.

[13] Award, para. 75(2)(f).

[14] As a subsidiary argument, Italy attempted to link the question of immunity also to Art. 297 UNCLOS. See Award, paras. 779 ff.

[15] Award, para. 803 (emphasis added).

[16] Award, para. 805 (emphasis added).

exercise jurisdiction without incidentally examining whether the Marines enjoy immunity". By referring only to one judicial precedent, together with some pieces of scholarship, the Tribunal stated that the issue of immunity "belongs to those 'questions preliminary or incidental to the application' of the Convention".[17] Accordingly, it found that:

> while the Convention may not provide a basis for entertaining an independent immunity claim under general international law, the Arbitral Tribunal's competence extends to the determination of the issue of immunity of the Marines that necessarily arises as an incidental question in the application of the Convention.[18]

As known, the Tribunal then proceeded in analyzing on the merits the question at hand and concluded that, since the two marines enjoyed immunity in relation to the incident, India was precluded from exercising its jurisdiction over the marines.[19] It is thus fair to observe that what was supposed to be a mere incidental question finally turned out to be the crucial question for the case. As has been rightly noted, given that the main question of jurisdiction had been resolved in the sense that both parties had concurrent jurisdiction over the incident, "had the Tribunal bypassed the question of immunity, India would have walked away with a binding award affirming its jurisdiction".[20]

The final outcome of the case, however, rests on murky legal reasoning. It is not by chance that the Tribunal's approach as to its jurisdiction over the question of immunity met with strong dissent by two judges. According to Judge Robinson, the Tribunal should have declined jurisdiction over the whole dispute because the "external" issue of the immunity of the marines was the core element of the dispute, and not an incidental one. The "original error" of the Majority was the mischaracterisation of the dispute, which lead, in judge Robinson's opinion, to a "cascade of errors", including the Majority's failure to properly consider and apply the law relating to incidental questions in light of the relevant case law.[21] Less radically, though still dissenting, Dr Rao argued that, instead of taking a global approach to the dispute, the Tribunal should have characterised the case as one involving "two distinct and separate disputes", one on the entitlement of jurisdiction over the incident and the other concerning the immunity of the two marines. It is only over the first dispute that the Tribunal should have exer-

---

[17] Award, para. 808, referring to *Case Concerning Certain German Interests in Polish Upper Silesia (Germany v. Poland)*, Judgment of 25 August 1925, PCIJ Series A, No. 6, p. 18 ff., and to CHENG, *General Principles of Law as applied by International Courts and Tribunals*, Cambridge, 1987 (first published 1953), p. 266; KOTUBY JR and SABOTA, *General Principles of Law and International Due Process*, Oxford, 2017, pp. 159-160.

[18] Award, para. 809. In a slightly different wording the Tribunal concluded that "examining the issue of the immunity of the Marines is an incidental question that necessarily presents itself in the application of the Convention in respect of the dispute before it" (para. 811).

[19] Award, paras. 838 ff.

[20] METHYMAKI and TAMS, *cit. supra* note 3. In similar terms, RAJU, *cit. supra* note 3.

[21] Dissenting opinion of Judge Robinson, paras. 80-81.

cised its jurisdiction without entertaining a claim that fell outside the scope of the Tribunal's adjudicatory power and could not be considered as "incidental" to the question of the entitlement of jurisdiction over the incident.[22]

3. COMPROMISSORY CLAUSES AND THE OUTSIDE WORLD

Already in themselves, the two dissents convey how controversial is the ground upon which the Tribunal decided to exercise its jurisdiction over the question of immunity. In order to fully appreciate the reasons why the *Enrica Lexie* award stimulates the debate surrounding the question of jurisdiction over matters falling outside the scope of compromissory clauses some preliminary considerations are in order.

It is not unusual for international tribunals whose jurisdiction is based on compromissory clauses to decide issues and apply rules that are external to the scope of the relevant treaty containing the compromissory clause. Even if compromissory clauses limit the exercise of jurisdiction only to a certain set of disputes concerning the interpretation and application of the relevant treaty, an international tribunal should be able to resort to other rules of international law that may come into play in the process of adjudicating a dispute. That is the reason why the law applicable by international tribunals is usually not confined to the treaty whose interpretation and application is disputed. For instance, while under Article 288(1) UNCLOS, courts and tribunals constituted according to the Convention have jurisdiction over "any dispute concerning the interpretation and application of the Convention", Article 293(1) provides that the law applicable by such courts and tribunals shall be the Convention "and other rules of international law not incompatible with the Convention".

There are at least two instances in which it is well-established that international tribunals may decide upon external issues and applying external law. First, *secondary* or *foundational rules* are often applied to settle issues which are not regulated by the disputed treaty.[23] Issues whose settlement in the course of proceedings require the application of general principles of procedure, the law of treaties, the rules on State responsibility or rules on diplomatic protection are often decided by applying these external norms.[24] Second, and relatedly, external *primary rules* can be applied to assist the interpretation and application of the disputed treaty. To assist the *interpretation* of the disputed treaty, external primary

---

[22] Concurring and Dissenting opinion of Dr Rao, conclusions.

[23] *Arctic Sunrise Arbitration* (*Netherlands v. Russia*), Award on the Merits of 14 August 2015, PCA-Case No. 2014-02, para. 190. See also *The Duzgit Integrity Arbitration* (*Malta v. São Tomé and Príncipe*), Award of 5 September 2016, PCA-Case No. 2014-07, para. 208. In both decisions the arbitral tribunals held that "in order properly to interpret and apply particular provisions of the Convention, it may be necessary for a tribunal to resort to foundational or secondary rules of general international law such as the law of treaties or the rules of State responsibility". See further *infra* note 27.

[24] See PAPADAKI, "Compromissory Clauses as the Gatekeepers of the Law to be 'Used' in the ICJ and the PCIJ", Journal of International Dispute Settlement, 2014, p. 560 ff.

rules may be imported through the gate of the principle enshrined in Article 31(3)
(c) of the 1969 Vienna Convention on the Law of Treaties.[25] When it comes to
assisting the *application* of the disputed treaty, external rules may be referred to
if the disputed treaty itself expressly permits this in a so-called "referral clause".[26]
In such cases, the disputed treaty incorporates external rules, meaning that the
disputed provision containing the referral clause will be interpreted and applied
also in light of the external rules referred to by the provision.

Each instance sketched above is well-established in theory but in practice
presents its own hurdles. Consider for instance the application of the secondary rules of State responsibility. No one would deny that, absent special rules
provided by the relevant treaty, an international tribunal is entitled to apply the
general rules concerning, for instance, the attribution of conduct or the issue of
reparation.[27] More controversial is the case of defences based on non-reciprocal
countermeasures. A respondent State may invoke the law on countermeasures to
justify a conduct which the applicant State claims is a violation of a treaty between them. The treaty in question may limit the jurisdiction of any specified adjudicative body to disputes relating to the treaty's interpretation and application.
If so, the question is whether a tribunal can address a countermeasures defence,
which would entail engaging with an assessment of the prior internationally
wrongful act, allegedly committed by the applicant State, in a field partially or
totally alien to the treaty providing for the jurisdictional clause. In the most recent
ICAO Council cases, the International Court of Justice (ICJ) answered this question in the affirmative, holding that such an assessment of external issues upon
which the defence is grounded would be possible "for the exclusive purpose of

---

[25] See e.g. *South China Sea Arbitration (Philippines v. China)*, PCA-Case No. 2013-
19, Award on Jurisdiction and Admissibility of 29 October 2015, para. 176: "[t]he Tribunal
is satisfied that Article 293(1) of the Convention, together with Article 31(3) of the Vienna
Convention on the Law of Treaties, enables it in principle to consider the relevant provisions
of the CBD for the purposes of interpreting the content and standard of Articles 192 and 194 of
the Convention". See also para. 282.

[26] See e.g. *Pulp Mills on the River Uruguay (Argentina v. Uruguay)*, Judgment of 20 April
2010, ICJ Reports 2010, p. 46 ff., para. 63, where the Court excluded that Art. 41 of the 1975
Statute of the River Uruguay constituted a "referral clause": "Consequently the various multilateral conventions relied on by Argentina are not, as such, incorporated in the 1975 Statute.
For that reason, they do not fall within the scope of the compromissory clause and therefore
the Court has no jurisdiction to rule whether Uruguay has complied with its obligations there-
under". See FORTEAU, "Regulating the competition between international courts and tribunals.
The role of *ratione materiae* jurisdiction under Part XV of UNCLOS", The Law and Practice
of International Courts and Tribunals, 2016, p. 195 ff.

[27] *Application of the Convention on the Prevention and Punishment of the Crime of
Genocide (Bosnia and Herzegovina v. Serbia and Montenegro)*, Judgment of 26 February
2007, ICJ Reports 2007, p. 43 ff., para. 149. See more recently, ITLOS, *Request for Advisory
Opinion Submitted by the Sub-Regional Fisheries Commission*, Advisory Opinion of 2 April
2015, where the ITLOS held that, in order to examine the questions submitted, it would have
been "guided by relevant rules of international law on responsibility of States for internationally wrongful acts" (para. 143).

deciding a dispute which falls within its jurisdiction".[28] While the Court referred here to the ICAO Council and its dispute settlement function, its findings may be generalized and considered applicable to any international tribunal.[29] Still, practice remains inconsistent among international adjudicative bodies, with the WTO dispute settlement organs[30] and NAFTA investment tribunals[31] rejecting, for reasons traceable to their limited jurisdiction, the possibility of examining "external" violations even if for the sole purpose of assessing the applicability of a circumstance precluding wrongfulness, that is to say the validity of a defence based on a non-reciprocal counter-measure.[32]

Also, when it comes to those instances where external primary norms are at stake there are a number of issues that are still subject to intense debate. Resort to primary norms through the principle of systemic integration under Article 31(3) (c) of the Vienna Convention should be limited to the purpose of interpreting the treaty over which a tribunal has jurisdiction and cannot constitute a *de facto* application of the external norm. This would have the effect of stretching the boundaries of the jurisdiction, inasmuch as a tribunal may even end up considering issues relating to the correct implementation of an external primary norm. Yet, in practice, the line between interpretation purposes and *de facto* application of external norms has often been subject to diverging approaches by international courts and tribunals.[33]

---

[28] *Appeal Relating to the Jurisdiction of the ICAO Council under Article 84 of the Convention on International Civil Aviation (Bahrain, Egypt, Saudi Arabia and United Arab Emirates v. Qatar)* and *Appeal Relating to the Jurisdiction of the ICAO Council under Article II, Section 2, of the 1944 International Air Services Transit Agreement (Bahrain, Egypt and United Arab Emirates v. Qatar)*, Judgments of 14 July 2020, para. 61. On these judgments, see the contribution by FORLATI in this volume.

[29] See VENTOURATOU, "Defences and Indispensable Incidental Issues: The Limits of Subject-Matter Jurisdiction in View of the Recent ICJ ICAO Council Judgments", EJIL: Talk!, 23 July 2020, available at: <https://www.ejiltalk.org/defences-and-indispensable-inci-dental-issues-the-limits-of-subject-matter-jurisdiction-in-view-of-the-recent-icj-icao-coun-cil-judgments/>; and CANNIZZARO and BONAFÉ, "Fragmenting International Law through Compromissory Clauses? Some Remarks on the Decision of the ICJ in the *Oil Platforms* case", EJIL, 2005, p. 492 ff., with reference to the ICJ. See *contra* the declaration of Judge Gevorgian appended to the judgements in the *ICAO Council* cases.

[30] See most notably the WTO Appellate Body Report of 6 March 2006 in *Mexico – Tax Measures on Soft Drinks and Other Beverages*, WT/DS308/AB/R. The approach taken by WTO dispute settlement organs is discussed, among others, by GRADONI, "'Four Corners' Doctrine", in RUIZ-FABRI (ed.), *Max Planck Encyclopedia of International Procedural Law*, February 2018.

[31] See e.g. *Archer Daniels Midland Co. v. The United Mexican States,* ICSID Case No. ARB(AF)/04/ 05, Award of 26 September 2007; *Corn Products Int'l, Inc. v. The United Mexican States*, ICSID Case No. ARB(AF)/04/01, Decision on Responsibility of 15 January 2008.

[32] A detailed account of the issue is provided by CALAMITA, "Countermeasures and Jurisdiction: Between Effectiveness and Fragmentation", Georgetown Journal of International Law, 2011, p. 233 ff.

[33] For reference to the ICJ practice, see e.g. PAPADAKI, *cit. supra* note 24; see also RACHOVISTA, "The Principle of Systemic Integration in Human Rights Law", ICLQ, 2017, p. 557 ff.

Finally, the case of "referral clauses" may also raise the question of their proper interpretation. In some cases, they can in fact extend the jurisdiction by incorporating external primary norms for purposes of application of the disputed treaty.[34] However, in other cases, they are so broadly formulated that it may be questionable whether they import primary obligations capable of being litigated before a tribunal or simply have the purpose of assisting the interpretation of the relevant provision wherein they are included (being in such cases nothing more than express references to the principle of systemic integration). Apart from the *Enrica Lexie* award, where, as seen, the Tribunal found the alleged *renvoi* provisions invoked by Italy to be inapplicable without really enquiring on their scope,[35] the question recently arose before the ICJ in the *Immunities and Criminal Proceedings* case. In this case, the Court found that the reference to the principle of sovereign equality in Article 4 of the UN Convention against Transnational Organized Crime (Palermo Convention) does not incorporate the customary rules relating to immunities of States and State officials, therefore the dispute between the parties over the immunity did not concern the interpretation and application of the Palermo Convention.[36] The Court arrived at this conclusion after a rather detailed interpretation of the provision but still met with several dissents.[37] This shows how controversial the interpretation of provisions referring to external norms may be when it comes to assessing whether they extend the scope of jurisdiction of a tribunal to claims of violations of external obligations or simply work as interpretative references of the disputed treaty. It is submitted, at any rate, that even when a referral clause is deemed to be capable of sustaining a claim over an external issue, such a claim cannot be an "independent" claim lacking any attachment to the disputed treaty. A claim based on a referral clause should still be framed as a question concerning the interpretation and application of the treaty. As the ICJ recently put it, with respect to an asserted referral clause to immunity rules in the 1955 United States-Iran Treaty of Amity, for the questions of immunities to be relevant, "the breach of international law on immunities would have to be capable of having some impact on compliance with the right guaranteed by [the referral clause]".[38]

---

[34] See e.g. Arts. 19 and 39 UNCLOS; FORTEAU, *cit. supra* note 26, pp. 195-196; TZENG, "Supplemental Jurisdiction under UNCLOS", Houston Journal of International Law, 2016, p. 535 ff.

[35] See the dissenting opinion of Judge Robinson, who elaborated on the issue and found that "[a]s a matter of law, those Articles do not constitute a *renvoi* to customary international law […] the Articles are relevant as part of the applicable law, but they have no relevance for jurisdictional purposes" (para. 31).

[36] *Immunities and Criminal Proceedings (Equatorial Guinea v. France)*, Preliminary Objections, Judgment of 6 June 2018, ICJ Reports 2018, p. 292 ff., para. 102.

[37] Joint Dissenting Opinion of Vice-President Xue, Judges Sebutinde and Robinson and Judge *ad hoc* Kateka.

[38] *Certain Iranian Assets (Islamic Republic of Iran v. United States of America)*, Preliminary Objections, Judgment of 13 February 2019, ICJ Reports 2019, p. 7 ff., para. 70.

Notwithstanding the difficulties that practice shows with respect to each instance of recourse to external primary or secondary rules in order to decide external issues, it seems clear that, in principle, such instances cannot entail an "expansion" of the jurisdiction of an international tribunal. There is no symmetry between the breadth of the law applicable by an international tribunal and its jurisdiction. A "cardinal distinction"[39] between jurisdiction and applicable law has often been emphasized in international jurisprudence, and particularly by UNCLOS tribunals. In *Arctic Sunrise*, an Annex VII Tribunal clearly held that "Article 293(1) does not extend the jurisdiction of a tribunal [...] [It] is not [...] a means to obtain a determination that some treaty other than the Convention has been violated, unless that treaty is otherwise a source of jurisdiction [as in the cases governed by Article 288(2)], or unless the treaty otherwise directly applies pursuant to the Convention".[40] Moreover, as seen, even in the case of referral clauses, which is referred to in the last part of the quoted passage ("unless the treaty [or a customary rule] otherwise directly applies pursuant to the Convention"), a dispute over the external issue will be relevant and fall within the tribunal's jurisdiction only if it is genuinely connected with the dispute over the referral clause, meaning that the dispute may be deemed to be one concerning the interpretation and application of the treaty.

At this point, one may wonder whether there are any other avenues for an international tribunal to decide external issues and apply external law. The question of immunity, as treated by the Tribunal in the *Enrica Lexie* award, clearly does not fall within any of the instances considered thus far. Besides not constituting an issue involving a secondary or foundational norm, the question of immunity was not taken into account for reasons of interpretation, nor because it formed part of a referral clause. The question of immunity was raised by Italy as a claim over an external primary norm whose application in the case at hand was challenged by India. The Tribunal decided the immunity issue and included its findings in the operative part of the award. How was that possible? As seen, the Tribunal relied on a third instance in which it is possible for international tribunals to decide external issues and apply external law.

---

[39] *Mox Plant Case (Ireland v. United Kingdom)*, Suspension of Proceedings on Jurisdiction and Merits and Request for Further Provisional Measures, Order No. 3 of 24 June 2003, para. 19. See also *The Eurotunnel Arbitration*, Partial Award of 30 January 2007, para. 152.

[40] Similarly, but with respect to customary law, ITLOS, *"ARA" Libertad Case (Argentina v. Ghana)*, Order of 15 December 2012, Separate Opinion of Judges Wolfrum and Cot, para. 7. It should be noted that in a much-criticized line of cases some UNCLOS tribunals overstretched the scope of their jurisdiction by resorting to the applicable law clause (Art. 293 UNCLOS) in order to exercise their jurisdiction over non-UNCLOS issues. See ITLOS, *M/V Saiga (No. 2) Case (Saint Vincent and the Grenadines v. Guinea)*, Judgment of 1 July 1999, paras. 155, 159 and 183(9); *Guyana v. Suriname*, Award of 17 September 2007, paras. 406, 487(ii) and 488; ITLOS, *M/V "Virginia G" (Panama/Guinea-Bissau)*, Judgment of 14 April 2014, paras. 350-362 and 452(13). For a discussion, see MAROTTI, "Between Consent and Effectiveness: Incidental Determinations and the Expansion of the Jurisdiction of UNCLOS Tribunals", in DEL VECCHIO and VIRZO (eds.), *Interpretations of the United Nations Convention on the Law of the Sea by International Courts and Tribunals*, Cham, 2019, p. 384 ff.

4.   The Third Way of the Jurisdiction over Incidental Questions

The third potential way for a tribunal to exercise jurisdiction over external issues looks directly at the scope of the compromissory clause and, particularly, at the character of the dispute brought pursuant to it. Here is where the notion of jurisdiction over incidental questions finds its place. In order to understand if and how compromissory clauses might leave some room for jurisdiction over external issues, it is worth starting from the general assumptions underlying the function of compromissory clauses.

States' consent to the jurisdiction of international tribunals given through compromissory clauses often may turn out as a stretch of the reality of international disputes. As acknowledged by the ICJ "[o]ne situation may contain disputes which relate to more than one body of law".[41] States attempt to limit the possible multifaceted character of international disputes through compromissory clauses. Such clauses artificially produce a "compartmentalizing" effect, meaning that they "tend to draw a dividing line between the category of disputes which fall within their scope [...] from those which fall outside their scope".[42] It is the task of international adjudicative bodies to set a balance between the need to preserve such a "compartmentalization", which reflects the consent given by States, and the effective exercise of the judicial function, which cannot be frustrated by the multifaceted character of an international dispute. The ICJ noted that "it cannot decline to take cognizance of one aspect of a dispute merely because that dispute has other aspects, however important".[43] At the same time, States cannot use a compromissory clause "as a vehicle for forcing an unrelated dispute with another State"[44] before an international tribunal. The required balance may be summarized – and generalized – once again with the Court's words whereby it "must not exceed the jurisdiction conferred upon it by the Parties, but it must also exercise that jurisdiction to its full extent".[45]

On these premises, it may be said that the jurisdiction over incidental questions is a tool to exercise jurisdiction "to its full extent". In fact, the notion refers to the capacity of international tribunals to decide external issues, involving the application of external law, which are incidental to the principal dispute and whose determination is necessary for the exercise of the principal jurisdiction

---

[41] *Application of the International Convention on the Elimination of All Forms of Racial Discrimination (Georgia v. Russian Federation)*, Preliminary Objections, Judgment of 1 April 2011, ICJ Reports 2011, p. 70 ff., para. 32. See also *Obligation to Negotiate Access to the Pacific Ocean (Bolivia v. Chile)*, Preliminary Objection, Judgment of 24 September 2015, ICJ Reports 2015, p. 592 ff., para. 32.

[42] CANNIZZARO and BONAFÉ, *cit. supra* note 29, p. 484.

[43] *United States Diplomatic and Consular Staff in Tehran (United States v. Iran)*, Judgment of 24 May 1980, ICJ Reports 1980, p. 3 ff., para. 36.

[44] Separate Opinion of Judge Koroma in *Application of the International Convention on the Elimination of All Forms of Racial Discrimination, cit. supra* note 41, para. 7.

[45] *Continental Shelf (Libya/Malta)*, Judgment of 3 June 1985, ICJ Reports 1985, p. 13 ff., para. 19.

over the main dispute.[46] There seems to be general agreement among scholars as to the power of international tribunals to decide such incidental questions. Judicial practice, however, is rather fragmented.

Recent instances in which the question arose as to the exercise of jurisdiction over incidental questions falling outside the principal jurisdiction relate to questions necessary to establish the *territorial jurisdiction* of the relevant tribunal. The International Criminal Court (ICC) has recently been called upon to determine whether Palestine can be considered "the State on the territory of which the conduct [...] occurred" under Article 12(2)(a) of the Rome Statute.[47] It relied on the interpretation of such provision, and particularly on the fact that it refers to a State Party to the Statute, to conclude that Palestine's accession to the Rome Statute followed the correct and ordinary procedure "regardless of Palestine's status under general international law".[48] In the wake of the Ukraine-Russia strife, investment tribunals have also faced a similar situation when called upon to determine their territorial jurisdiction with respect to allegedly wrongful conduct committed in disputed territories.[49]

These cases, however, seem less controversial than cases where the exercise of jurisdiction over incidental questions affects the jurisdiction *ratione materiae* of an international tribunal. When it comes to decide whether a given conduct has taken place on a given territory (for the sole purpose of establishing the jurisdiction *ratione loci*) and the incidental issue is represented by the determination of whether that territory belongs or not to a State party, the power to make such determinations finds its source in the principle whereby international tribunals have the power to determine their own competence (competence-competence).[50] Moreover, the treaty establishing the jurisdiction (or the tribunal itself) may expressly refer to the notion of *territory* which has to be interpreted by the relevant tribunal. This interpretation, in cases such as that of the ICC, may also benefit from an institutional setting (the accession procedure) which helps the tribunal

---

[46] See among others LOVE, "Jurisdiction over Incidental Questions in International Law", ASIL, 2017, p. 316 ff.; TZENG, "The Implicated Issue Problem: Indispensable Issues and Incidental Jurisdiction", New York University Journal of International Law & Politics, 2018, p. 447 ff.; HARRIS, "Incidental Determinations in Proceedings under Compromissory Clauses", ICLQ, 2021, p. 417 ff. Further references in MAROTTI, *cit. supra* note 40.

[47] ICC, Pre-Trial Chamber I, Decision of 5 February 2021 on the "Prosecution request pursuant to article 19(3) for a ruling on the Court's territorial jurisdiction in Palestine", ICC-01/18-143.

[48] *Ibid.*, para. 102. The Court stated that "[b]ased on the principle of the effectiveness, it would indeed be contradictory to allow an entity to accede to the Statute and become a State Party, but to limit the Statute's inherent effects over it".

[49] See among others ZARRA, "L'applicabilità dei trattati di protezione degli investimenti al caso della Crimea", RDI, 2019, p. 454 ff.; TZENG, "Investment on Disputed Territory: Indispensable Parties and Indispensable Issues", Brazilian Journal of International Law, 2017, p. 122 ff.

[50] See generally CRAWFORD, "Continuity and Discontinuity in International Dispute Settlement: An Inaugural Lecture", Journal of International Dispute Settlement, 2010, p. 15 ff.

in discharging its role in determining the territorial jurisdiction.[51] In the case of investment tribunals the determination of the meaning of territory may require an assessment of the legal and factual reality of the disputed territory. Even in such case, however, there is always a connection between such incidental determinations over external issues and the relevant treaty establishing the jurisdiction. It is the treaty itself that links the territorial jurisdiction of the tribunal to a legal or factual reality that, while "external" to the subject-matter jurisdiction, may be relevant to assess whether an investor of one Contracting Party has made an investment "on the territory of the other Contracting Party".[52]

In the case of jurisdiction over incidental issues that do not fall within the jurisdiction *ratione materiae* of an international tribunal, there is no such a direct treaty link between the potential external issue and the tribunal's jurisdiction as delimited by the jurisdictional clause. When it comes to assessing whether an external issue should be incidentally entertained in order to decide the principal dispute – and not simply the jurisdiction *ratione loci* – the relevant link can only be found between the external issue and the dispute itself. In fact, the treaty is apparently clear in limiting the jurisdiction to disputes concerning its interpretation and application. This makes it much harder to draw general criteria as to the scope and limit of such jurisdiction. There may be an infinite variety of disputes with infinite degrees of connection with external issues that may be or may not be caught by the jurisdiction of international tribunals. It follows therefore that most of the solutions to the issues concerning the extent of jurisdiction over incidental questions are to be found on a case-by-case basis, and that international tribunals enjoy a rather wide discretion in this context. However, the lack of clarity in this area means that the jurisdiction over incidental questions is seldom expressly invoked in judicial practice, and that general statements on its contours are rare.

As seen, in the *Enrica Lexie* award the Tribunal relied only on the Permanent Court of International Justice (PCIJ) statement in the *Case Concerning Certain German Interests in Polish Upper Silesia* whereby:

> It is true that the application of the Geneva Convention is hardly possible without giving an interpretation of Article 256 of the Treaty of Versailles and the other international stipulations cited by Poland. But these matters then constitute merely *questions pre-*

---

[51] As the Court indeed noted, "given the complexity and political nature of statehood under general international law, the Rome Statute insulates the Court from making such a determination, relying instead on the accession procedure and the determination made by the United Nations General Assembly. The Court is not constitutionally competent to determine matters of statehood that would bind the international community. In addition, such a determination is not required for the specific purposes of the present proceedings or the general exercise of the Court's mandate. As discussed, article 12(2)(a) of the Statute requires a determination as to whether or not the relevant conduct occurred on the territory of a *State Party*, for the sole purpose of establishing individual criminal responsibility" (Decision of 5 February 2021, *cit. supra* note 47, para. 108).

[52] Art. 1 of the 1998 Bilateral Investment Treaty between Ukraine and Russia. See ZARRA, *cit. supra* note 49, p. 463.

liminary or incidental to the application of the Geneva Convention. Now the interpretation of other international agreements is indisputably within the competence of the Court if such interpretation must be regarded as incidental to a decision on a point in regard to which it has jurisdiction.[53]

As aptly noted by Judge Robinson in his dissenting opinion, this case does not really help in identifying the conditions for the exercise of the jurisdiction over incidental questions, and particularly whether an external question might be considered as incidental to the principal dispute.[54] In Judge Robinson's view, "[t]he later cases show that since a court or tribunal would normally not have jurisdiction over the incidental question, it is of the greatest importance to ensure that the question is properly characterized as incidental".[55]

Curiously enough, the Tribunal did not make any reference to the most recent case law dealing with the issue, which, by the way, comes precisely from UNCLOS Annex VII tribunals. Suffice it to recall here that in *Chagos Marine Protected Area Arbitration* the arbitral tribunal provided the most elaborated statement on the jurisdiction over incidental questions. Even though only *obiter*, the tribunal admitted the possibility of such jurisdiction but approached it in a more cautious way than the PCIJ.[56] According to the tribunal:

> where a dispute concerns the interpretation or application of the Convention, the jurisdiction of a Court or Tribunal pursuant to Article 288(1) extends to making such findings of fact or ancillary determinations of law as are necessary to resolve the dispute pre-

---

[53] *Case Concerning Certain German Interests in Polish Upper Silesia, cit. supra* note 17, p. 18 (emphasis added).

[54] Dissenting opinion of Judge Robinson, para. 45: "there is noticeably absent from the PCIJ's decision in this case any significant examination of the relationship between the incidental question over which the Court had no jurisdiction and the dispute over which it had jurisdiction; in particular, there is no discussion as to whether the incidental question was the real issue dividing the Parties; if it warranted that description, the Court would have had no jurisdiction over it since it did not relate to the interpretation or application of the Geneva Convention".

[55] *Ibid.*

[56] It should be incidentally noted that in the subsequent *South China Sea Arbitration*, the arbitral tribunal, although again only in an *obiter dictum*, apparently closed the doors on the possibility of a jurisdiction over external "necessary" issues, holding that it "might consider that the Philippines' Submissions could be understood to relate to sovereignty [such as to exclude the jurisdiction] if it were convinced that [...] the resolution of the Philippines' claims would *require the Tribunal to first render a decision on sovereignty*, either expressly or implicitly"; *South China Sea Arbitration, cit. supra* note 25, para. 153 (emphasis added). In a similar vein, Judge Robinson argued that "[i]f the Majority is right that the dispute, as characterized by it, cannot be resolved without examining the issue of the immunity of the marines, then that would suggest that that issue is anything but an incidental question" (Dissenting Opinion of Judge Robinson, para. 41). See TZENG, "Investment on Disputed Territory", *cit. supra* note 49; LOVE, *cit. supra* note 46, pp. 319-320; for a critical view, MAROTTI, *cit. supra* note 40, pp. 397-398.

sented to it [...] The Tribunal does not categorically exclude that in some instances a minor issue of territorial sovereignty could indeed be ancillary to a dispute concerning the interpretation or application of the Convention.[57]

From this passage it may be inferred that in order for the external issue to fall within the tribunal's jurisdiction two conditions should be met.

First, the determination over the external issue must be necessary to settle the main dispute, meaning that the decision over the main dispute cannot be reached without a prior determination over the external issue. This is what the PCIJ arguably had in mind when referring to questions *preliminary or incidental* to the application of the disputed treaty over which it had jurisdiction (the application of the Geneva Convention being "hardly possible" without engaging with the external issue).[58]

Secondly, the external issue must be "ancillary" or "incidental" to the main dispute. This requirement "essentially touches upon that of how the dispute [...] should be characterised".[59] It means that a tribunal should not conflate the incidental issue and the main dispute. In other words, the incidental (external) issue cannot constitute the real issue of the case and the object of the claim. As the *Chagos* tribunal held, "it is for the Tribunal itself 'while giving particular attention to the formulation of the dispute chosen by the Applicant, to determine on an objective basis the dispute dividing the parties, by examining the position of both parties' [...] and in the process 'to isolate the real issue in the case and to identify the object of the claim'".[60] In the process of characterisation of the dispute, the tribunal should in turn identify incidental questions, which can be addressed only to the extent that they are necessary to resolve the main dispute. As a specification of such requirement, the *Chagos* tribunal referred to the "minor" character of the necessary and incidental issue. Indeed it may be argued that when a decision over a "major" external issue turns out to be necessary for the settlement of the dispute, this is a strong hint that the external issue is not really incidental but constitutes the real issue in the case.

As one can easily see, the conceptual framework of the jurisdiction over incidental questions, as provided by the *Chagos* award, appears rather vague. Moreover, the requirements set out therein have never been found to be fulfilled in practice, so it remains quite hard to picture an incidental issue meeting the

---

[57] *Chagos Marine Protected Area Arbitration (Mauritius v. United Kingdom)*, Award of 18 March 2015, PCA Case No. 2011-03, paras. 220-221.

[58] As SCHATZ, *cit. supra* note 3, aptly notes the Court here "equat[ed] the term 'incidental' with 'preliminary'". See also the Dissenting Opinion of Judge Robinson, para. 45.

[59] *Dispute Concerning Coastal State Rights in the Black Sea, Sea of Azov, and Kerch Strait (Ukraine v. The Russian Federation)*, Award Concerning the Preliminary Objections of the Russian Federation, 21 February 2020, PCA Case No. 2017-06, para. 194.

[60] *Chagos Marine Protected Area Arbitration*, *cit. supra* note 57, para. 208, quoting the ICJ in *Fisheries Jurisdiction (Spain v. Canada)*, Judgment of 4 December 1998, ICJ Reports 1998, p. 432 ff., para. 30, and *Nuclear Tests (New Zealand v. France)*, Judgment of 20 December 1974, ICJ Reports 1974, p. 457 ff., para. 30.

conditions for the exercise of jurisdiction pursuant to the *Chagos* scheme.[61] As already noted, a practical application of such test requires a case-by-case approach which is also inevitably discretionary-based. Characterising a dispute or determining whether external issues are "necessary" and "minor" enough to be incidentally decided are all exercises subject to subjective evaluations depending on a number of factors, including the way such issues are framed by the parties to a dispute and the nature of the rights and obligations at stake.[62] In any case, the *Chagos* award provides, so far, the most detailed elaboration of the limits for the exercise of a jurisdiction which, in itself, extends beyond States' consent to international adjudication. Yet this case was completely neglected by the *Enrica Lexie* tribunal.

5. CONCLUSION: THE *ENRICA LEXIE* AWARD BETWEEN FORM AND REALITY

Notwithstanding the uncertainties surrounding the jurisdiction over incidental questions, it may be seriously doubted that the external issue of immunity in the *Enrica Lexie* case met the requirements of such jurisdiction as set out in the *Certain German Interests* judgment and, most notably, in the *Chagos* award described above.[63]

As seen, Judge Robinson basically contested the "ancillary" nature of the issue, claiming that the Tribunal erred in its characterisation of the dispute. The real issue of the case, in Judge Robinson's opinion, was a dispute over the immunity issue. To this, one may also add that since the question of immunity finally turned out as a decisive question for the outcome of the case, it was not properly a mere "minor" issue related to the UNCLOS dispute. In any case, one

---

[61] In the more recent *Ukraine v. Russia* case, *cit. supra* note 59, the Annex VII tribunal endorsed the *Chagos* approach, but found that "the Parties' dispute regarding sovereignty over Crimea is not a minor issue ancillary to the dispute concerning the interpretation or application of the Convention" (paras. 193-195).

[62] See e.g. TALMON, "The Chagos Marine Protected Area Arbitration: Expansion of the Jurisdiction of UNCLOS Part XV Courts and Tribunals", ICLQ, 2016, p. 934 ff., arguing that, even if tribunals often stress the fact that the characterisation of a dispute should be made on an objective basis, this process remains an "inherently subjective exercise". Indeed, to characterise a dispute, tribunals are called to weigh and balance different factors, including the parties' submissions and other contextual elements which may lend themselves to different weighing and balancing. See also CROSATO NEUMANN, "Sovereignty disputes under UNCLOS: some thoughts and remarks on the Chagos Marine Protected Area Dispute", Cambridge International Law Journal Blog, 7 August 2015, available at: <http://cilj.co.uk/2015/08/07/sovereignty-disputes-under-unclos-some-thoughts-and-remarks-on-the-chagos-marine-protected-area-dispute/>, referring to the assessment of the incidental nature of the issue, and particularly of its "minor" character, and arguing that "[t]his determination would not only need to be made on a case-by-case basis, but would also be very subjective, since it would depend on the judge or arbitrator's connection and sensitivities towards a dispute". See generally HARRIS, "Claims with an Ulterior Purpose: Characterising Disputes Concerning the "Interpretation or Application" of a Treaty", The Law and Practice of International Courts and Tribunals, 2019 p. 279 ff.

[63] RONZITTI, *cit. supra* note 1, pp. 947-948; SCHATZ, *cit. supra* note 3; RAJU, *cit. supra* note 3.

may still conclude that the Tribunal was right in characterising the dispute as one concerning the entitlement of jurisdiction over the incident, thus concerning the interpretation and application of the Convention. After all, the process of characterisation of a dispute may be subject to divergent approaches in the weighing and balancing of the relevant elements that a tribunal should take into account to isolate the real issue of the case.

More problematic, in fact, appears the fulfilment of the requirement of "necessity". If the logic underlying the jurisdiction over incidental questions is arguably based on the necessary character of the decision over the external issue, meaning that the exercise of the principal jurisdiction requires a prior determination of the incidental issue, it is evident that the question of immunity was not a "necessary" issue. The determination of what was, in the Tribunal's view, the main dispute, viz. the question of the entitlement of jurisdiction over the incident pursuant to Articles 92 and 97 UNCLOS, was clearly not subject to a necessary prior determination of the question of immunity of the two marines. Indeed, the same Tribunal acknowledged that "it was conceivable that the dispute between the Parties would be decided without a determination on the question of immunity". The finding that the parties have concurrent jurisdiction would have settled the UNCLOS dispute, even without any other findings on non-UNCLOS issues. It is worth recalling in this respect that even if immunity should be construed as a primary rule constituting an exception to the right to exercise jurisdiction,[64] the ICJ made it clear that "jurisdiction does not imply absence of immunity, while absence of immunity does not imply jurisdiction".[65]

At a closer look, it thus seems that the Tribunal misconceived the "necessity" requirement for the exercise of jurisdiction over incidental questions. The decision over the issue of immunity was not necessary for the determination of the main dispute but was considered necessary for rendering a *satisfactory* and *complete* answer to the question as to which Party may exercise jurisdiction over the incident.

The law relating to the jurisdiction over incidental questions, as (imprecisely) defined by the relevant case law, does not provide, in the end, a sound legal basis for the exercise of jurisdiction over the non-UNCLOS dispute relating to immunity. In this sense, the award contributes to watering down the – already in themselves quite murky – conditions for the extension of jurisdiction over external issues. One may also argue that the award simply confirms that the scope and limits of the jurisdiction over incidental questions are also affected by the nature of the rights at stake. The "rule-exception" relation between jurisdiction and immunity might imply that less strict conditions are required for the jurisdiction over incidental questions involving rules that provide for exceptions to the disputed rights. Still, one is left with the impression that, now as much as ever,

---

[64] METHYMAKI and TZANAKOPOULOS, "Freedom With Their Exception: Jurisdiction and Immunity as Rule and Exception", in BARTELS and PADDEU (eds.), *Exceptions and Defences in International Law*, Oxford, 2020, p. 225 ff.

[65] *Arrest Warrant of 11 April 2000 (Democratic Republic of the Congo v. Belgium)*, Judgment of 14 February 2002, ICJ Reports 2002, p. 3 ff., para. 59.

more predictability in this field is needed, not least because the jurisdiction over incidental questions may risk becoming a potentially unlimited avenue for the expansion of the jurisdiction of international tribunals.

Even if the Award's treatment of the issue of immunity does not fit well with the framework of jurisdiction over incidental questions, its rationale may perhaps be found in the realistic, rather than formalistic, approach taken by the Tribunal in handling the dispute. The reference to the need for a *satisfactory* and *complete* answer to the whole dispute reflects the Tribunal's awareness that, without settling the dispute over immunity, the actual controversy between Italy and India would be only partially resolved. Due to the objective limits of its jurisdiction *ratione materiae*, the Tribunal attempted to anchor such a realistic approach to the only potentially available avenue for the exercise of jurisdiction over an external issue, that of incidental questions. But reality in this case did not match well with form, and the effective settlement of a longstanding dispute arguably came at the expense of a possible contribution to a consistent development of the law governing the jurisdiction over incidental questions.

THE ARBITRAL AWARD IN THE *ENRICA LEXIE* CASE AND ITS QUESTIONABLE RECOGNITION OF FUNCTIONAL IMMUNITY TO THE ITALIAN MARINES UNDER CUSTOMARY INTERNATIONAL LAW

Raffaella Nigro[*]

Abstract

The dispute between Italy and India on the Enrica Lexie incident has finally been decided by the Award handed down on 21 May 2020 by the Arbitral Tribunal to which the Parties had referred the case. After having concluded that it had jurisdiction on the issue of the immunity of the two Italian marines involved in the case at hand, the majority judgment (by three votes to two) affirmed that under customary international law the latter enjoyed functional immunity from the criminal jurisdiction of India. This article will argue that the Arbitral Tribunal's conclusions are unconvincing, first and foremost, considering that, based on State practice, it is not possible to affirm without reservations that a settled customary rule exists under international law conferring immunity to all State officials, and regardless of the type of functions they perform. In fact, immunity has often been recognized as applying only to certain categories of State officials, and on the basis of the governmental nature of the functions they perform on behalf of the State. Given the doubtful existence under customary international law of a clear rule establishing the functional immunity of all State officials, for all the acts performed in the exercise of their functions, this article argues that the Arbitral Tribunal should have firstly ascertained the existence of a specific customary rule on the immunity of the military abroad, together with the exact content of such rule and, secondly, whether this was applicable in the case of the Enrica Lexie. As current practice stands, military forces abroad are entitled to immunity only under specific circumstances, which do not seem to occur in the present case. In particular, this article maintains that the Italian marines were not entitled to functional immunity. While the acts they performed did indeed fall within their typical functions, they were exercised on behalf of a private subject and not on behalf of the Italian State.

Keywords: functional immunity; State officials; governmental functions; military forces abroad.

---

[*] Associate Professor of International Law, Magna Græcia University of Catanzaro.

IYIL, Vol. 30 (2020), pp. 209-225
ISSN 0391-5107

1. THE ARBITRAL AWARD IN THE *ENRICA LEXIE* CASE AND THE DIFFERENT
    EXISTING APPROACHES TO THE ISSUE OF THE FUNCTIONAL IMMUNITY OF
    STATE OFFICIALS UNDER CUSTOMARY INTERNATIONAL LAW

The lengthy and complex dispute that arose between Italy and India following the Enrica Lexie incident, which occurred on 15 February 2012 off the coast of India – concerning, as is well-known, the killing of two Indian fishermen on board the Indian vessel St. Antony by shots fired by two Italian marines stationed on the Italian merchant vessel Enrica Lexie[1] – was finally decided by the Award handed down on 21 May 2020 by the Arbitral Tribunal to which the Parties had referred the case.[2] After having concluded that it had jurisdiction on the issue of the immunity of the two marines – considering the issue as an incidental question "that necessarily presents itself in the application" of the United Nations Convention on the Law of the Sea (UNCLOS)[3] – the majority judgment (by three votes to two) affirmed that, under customary international law, the Italian marines enjoyed functional immunity from the criminal jurisdiction of India.[4] However, the narrow majority reached by the Tribunal may reflect uncertainties about the actual existence of an undisputed rule under customary international law granting immunity to *all State officials*, including the military, for *all acts* performed in the exercise of their functions, rather than only to *specific types of State officials*, for *specific types of functions*.

According to a traditional approach, in order to avoid infringing on the sovereignty and independence of a foreign State, immunity should be recognized for all State officials, for all acts carried out on behalf of their State.[5] Other authors,

---

[1] For a reconstruction of the events and an analysis of the relevant legal issues, see RONZITTI, "La difesa contro i pirati e l'imbarco di personale militare armato sui mercantili. Il caso della *Enrica Lexie* e la controversia Italia-India", RDI, 2013, p. 1073 ff. See also the contribution by CATALDI in this Focus.

[2] *The Italian Republic v. The Republic of India concerning the "Enrica Lexie" incident*, PCA Case No. 2015-28, Award of 21 May 2020, available at: <https://pcacases.com/web/sendAttach/16500>. For a comment on the Award, see RONZITTI, "Il caso della *Enrica Lexie* e la sentenza arbitrale nella controversia Italia-India", RDI, 2020, p. 937 ff.; BARBERINI, "Marò: il capitolo conclusivo sul caso della Enrica Lexie", Questione Giustizia, 24 July 2020, available at: <https://www.questionegiustizia.it/articolo/maro-il-capitolo-conclusivo-sul-caso-della-enrica-lexie>; ALEXANDER, "Is Immunity for Killing Two Indian Fishermen Justified? Curious Case of 'Enrica Lexie'", Opinio Juris, 26 October 2020, available at: <http://opiniojuris.org/2020/10/26/is-immunity-for-killing-two-indian-fishermen-justified-curious-case-of-enrica-lexie/>.

[3] Award, paras. 733-811. For an analysis of the issue of the Tribunal's jurisdiction, see the contribution by MAROTTI in this Focus.

[4] Award, paras. 847-862. The Arbitral Tribunal also ruled that the Italian marines cannot be precluded from enjoying immunity *ratione materiae* as a result of the application of the "territorial tort" exception – as it had been rather argued by India – because "to the extent that the 'territorial tort' exception is a customary rule of international law, it would in any event not apply in this case because the Marines were not on Indian territory when they committed the acts at issue"(para. 873).

[5] RONZITTI, "The *Enrica Lexie* Incident: The Law of the Sea and Immunity of States Officials Issue", IYIL, 2012, p. 3 ff.; WEBB, "Comment on 'The Functional Immunity of

however, have argued that under customary international law immunity has a narrower scope.[6] In the most recent relevant practice, in effect, immunity has been granted only to certain types of State officials, and only for certain types of functions. As this author has more extensively discussed elsewhere,[7] it is suggested that this tendency in the practice could be explained on the basis of an evolution in the concept of sovereignty that the norms on immunity are intended to protect. Different interpretations and applications of immunity are indeed, in this author's opinion, the result of the different meaning that the concept of sovereignty has acquired in three different historical phases. When the modern State developed in the 16th and 17th centuries, the idea of sovereignty as an exercise by States of their governmental authority was still closely bound up with the absolute authority and personal interests of the respective sovereign monarchs. In this regard, one may recall the famous expression ascribed to Louis XIV, "*l'Etat, c'est moi!*". This conception of sovereignty necessarily entailed an interpretation and a consequent application of the immunity rule in almost absolute terms.[8] However, in the 18th and 19th centuries, with the consolidation of the European Christian-centric community following the Peace of Westphalia of 1648, sover-

---

State Official from Foreign Jurisdiction: A Critique of the Traditional Theories'", Questions of International Law, Zoom-out 17, 2015, p. 43 ff., available at: <http://www.qil-qdi.org/comment-on-the-functional-immunity-of-state-officials-from-foreign-jurisdiction-a-critique-of-the-traditional-theories/>; BUZZINI, "The enduring validity of immunity ratione materiae: A Reply to Professor Pisillo Mazzeschi", Questions of International Law, Zoom-out 17, 2015, p. 33 ff., available at: <http://www.qil-qdi.org/the-enduring-validity-of-immunity-ratione-materiae-a-reply-to-professor-pisillo-mazzeschi/>. See, recently, VAN ALEBEEK, "Functional Immunity of State Officials from the Criminal Jurisdiction of Foreign National Courts", in RUYS, ANGELET and FERRO (eds.), *The Cambridge Handbook of Immunities and International Law*, Cambridge, 2019, p. 496 ff., who affirms that "foreign state officials do not enjoy immunity from foreign criminal jurisdiction in relation to every act that is related to the exercise of their function or that they have committed under colour of law", but "the exact scope of the exceptions and limitations remains controversial", p. 523.

[6] DE SENA, *Diritto internazionale e immunità funzionale degli organi statali*, Milano, 1996; FRULLI, *Immunità e crimini internazionali. L'esercizio della giurisdizione penale e civile nei confronti degli organi statali sospettati di gravi crimini internazionali*, Torino, 2007; ID., "On the Existence of a Customary Rule Granting Functional Immunity to State Officials and Its Exceptions: Back to Square One", Duke Journal of Comparative & International Law, 2016, p. 479 ff.; PISILLO MAZZESCHI, "The Functional Immunity of State Officials from Foreign Jurisdiction: A Critique of the Traditional Theories", Questions of International Law, Zoom-out 17, 2015, p. 3 ff., available at: <http://www.qil-qdi.org/wp-content/uploads/2015/05/02_Functional-Immunity_PISILLO_FIN.pdf>; ID., "Organi degli Stati stranieri (Immunità giurisdizionale degli)", Enciclopedia del diritto, 2014, Vol. VII, p. 749 ff.; CONFORTI, "In tema di immunità funzionale degli organi statali stranieri", RDI, 2010, p. 5 ff.; AMOROSO, "Sull'(in)esistenza di un regime generale in materia di immunità funzionale degli organi stranieri", Giurisprudenza italiana, 2013, p. 1900 ff.; FOCARELLI, *Trattato di diritto internazionale*, Padova, 2015, p. 870; ID., *International Law*, Cheltenham/Northampton, 2019, p. 349.

[7] NIGRO, *Le immunità giurisdizionali dello Stato e dei suoi organi e l'evoluzione della sovranità nel diritto internazionale*, Padova, 2018, p. 11 ff.

[8] Reservations on the absolute immunity of States since the very beginning of such rule's consolidation under customary international law were expressed in an Italian judgment of 1925 on the cases *Governo Francese v. Serra* and *C v. Ceretti et al.*, RDI, 1936, p. 540 ff.

eignty came to be understood as the exercise of governmental power aimed at pursuing the interests of the State (or a small group of States) understood as an entity in its own right, rather than simply an extension of the sovereign monarch. Consequently, the international norms on immunity evolved towards limiting the application of immunity, in the case of State officials, only to the acts performed by them *in the exercise of their official functions* and, in the case of States, to the acts attributable to them and involving their sovereign prerogatives. Finally, in the 20th century, the characteristics of an increasingly broad and interconnected international community have contributed to the emergence of common needs that transcend the interests of individual States or a small group of them in their *inter se* relationships. Thus, a new concept of sovereignty has emerged, according to which the governmental authority of each State is perceived as being exercised in the common interest of all States of ensuring global order.[9] This entails two consequences for the purposes of immunity. Firstly, the sovereignty that the recognition of immunity is meant to protect no longer concerns the State as such, nor every type of act performed by State officials on its behalf, but rather the State *as part* of an inter-State system in which the States themselves have decided to allocate their governmental authority to ensure global order. Secondly, since only certain functions are related to the exercise of such governmental authority at the international level, *it is these functions* that the rules on immunity are meant to protect.

Of course, governmental authority is also exercised by States at the domestic level through officials who only occasionally operate abroad, and these officials should similarly be protected for the functions they perform on behalf of their States. However, this author would argue that the recognition of immunity for this type of official should be verified on a case-by-case basis and cannot be inferred from an alleged general customary rule recognizing immunity for all State officials, and regardless of the type of functions they perform.

That under international law there exists a distinction between State organs that typically perform governmental functions at the international level, on one side, and State organs that perform their functions on behalf of the State but at an essentially domestic level, is evidenced by the fact that States have conferred only to the former almost absolute immunity *ratione personae*, for the duration of their office. I am referring, in particular, to diplomatic agents, Heads of State and Heads of Government and Ministers of Foreign Affairs, who exercise typical governmental functions towards other States, as they represent their home State in its international relations by virtue of their office.[10] A similar need to protect

---

[9] On the conception of the State in a systemic approach to international law, see FOCARELLI, *International Law*, cit. *supra* note 6, p. 9; ID., *International Law as Social Construct. The Struggle for Global Justice*, Oxford, 2012, p. 153 ff.

[10] In the *Arrest Warrant* case, the International Court of Justice stated that Ministers for Foreign Affairs generally act as the Government's representative "in international negotiations and intergovernmental meetings", also underling that "there is a presumption that a Minister for Foreign Affairs, simply by virtue of that office, has full powers to act on behalf of the State", see *Arrest Warrant of 11 April 2000 (Democratic Republic of the Congo v. Belgium)*, Judgment of 14 February 2002, ICJ Reports 2002, p. 3 ff., para. 53. With regard to the activities

the exercise of State functions during their office has not been called for with respect to other State organs which, although being able to perform functions at the international level and on behalf of their States, essentially operate at the domestic level.

This could be explained by considering that, in the case of organs exercising functions in the context of their home State's relations with other States, the exercise of governmental functions that is deemed worthy of protection through immunity is *presumed*, whereas, in the case of organs operating rather at the domestic level, the recognition of immunity for acts exceptionally performed abroad has to be proved, either on the basis of an *ad hoc* customary rule conferring immunity to specific categories of State officials, or on the basis of specific international instruments.

According to this reading of the functional immunity of State officials, it would have been more appropriate for the Arbitral Tribunal in the *Enrica Lexie* case to verify, first and foremost, the existence of an *ad hoc* customary rule recognizing the immunity of militaries abroad, and, secondly, on the basis of its specific contents, whether such rule applied to the specific case. This article seeks to demonstrate that, as current practice stands, military forces abroad have been deemed entitled to immunity only under specific circumstances, which do not seem to occur in the case of the *Enrica Lexie*. In particular, it is argued that the Italian marines were not entitled to functional immunity. Although the acts they performed did indeed fall within their typical functions, they were exercised on behalf of a private subject, not on behalf of the Italian State. Thus, before focusing on the judgment of the Arbitral Tribunal (Section 4), it seems worth clarifying the existing customary international law on the immunity of State officials from criminal jurisdiction, which is relevant for the case at hand (Section 2), and the specific legal regime applicable to militaries abroad (Section 3).

2. IMMUNITY OF STATE OFFICIALS FROM CRIMINAL JURISDICTION AND THE EXERCISE OF GOVERNMENTAL FUNCTIONS

In order to assess whether the Italian marines enjoyed immunity *ratione materiae* under customary international law, the Arbitral Tribunal firstly ascertained whether they qualified as State officials, before moving on to assessing whether the acts committed by the marines during the incident were "official acts" or "acts performed in an official capacity".[11]

---

of the Ministers of Foreign Affairs, Hernández's Fourth Report of the ILC on the Immunity of State Officials from Foreign Criminal Jurisdiction has underlined that they "derive from the exercise of elements of the governmental authority at the highest level" and "they are examples that must be taken into consideration in determining the criteria for identifying what constitutes an act performed in an official capacity"; See HERNÁNDEZ, Fourth Report to the International Law Commission on the Immunity of State Officials from Foreign Criminal Jurisdiction, UN Doc. A/CN.4/686 (2015), para. 38.

[11] Award, paras. 847 ff.

With regard to the first issue, the Tribunal referred to the Second Report of the International Law Commission (ILC) on the Immunity of State Officials from Foreign Criminal Jurisdiction, where the former Special Rapporteur, Roman Anatolevich Kolodkin, highlighted an "agreement in the doctrine" as to the category of persons entitled to immunity *ratione materiae*. According to Kolodkin, this category covers all State officials, irrespective of their position within the structure of the organs of State power.[12] As to the exercise by the marines of official functions, the Tribunal again mentioned Kolodkin's Report, according to which, on the basis of the imputability test, if the conduct of a State official is attributable to the sending State, "then continuing immunity *ratione materiae* should apply".[13] Affirming that "there exists a presumption under international law that a State is right about the characterisation of the conduct of its official as being official in nature",[14] the majority judgment concluded that the Italian marines qualified as State officials who, during the Enrica Lexie incident, were fulfilling a State function in their official capacity, and consequently enjoyed immunity in relation to the acts of February 2012.

This authors finds this conclusion unconvincing, first and foremost, considering that, based on State practice, it is not possible to unambiguously affirm the existence of a settled customary rule which confers immunity to all State officials and regardless of the type of functions they perform.[15]

Surprisingly, in its reasoning, the Tribunal made no reference to the most recent Fourth Report of the ILC's Special Rapporteur Concepción Escobar Hernández, which, in light of international and national judicial practice, seems to espouse the more restrictive approach referred to above, asserting that, for the purposes of State officials enjoying immunity from foreign criminal jurisdiction, "the attribu.tion of an act to a State is the prerequisite for that act to be considered an 'act performed in an official capacity'", but the fulfilment of such requirement is not enough.[16]

As specified in the Report, the application of an additional, teleological criterion is required, entailing that such act "must also be a manifestation of sovereignty, constituting a form of exercise of the [state's] governmental authority".[17] Although the Special Rapporteur has acknowledged that a clear definition of the concept of "governmental authority" is lacking, she has nonetheless clarified that it may be "ascribed to the variety of scenarios that can exist in practice and that necessitate a case-by-case analysis".[18]

---

[12] KOLODKIN, Second Report to the International Law Commission on the Immunity of State Officials from Foreign Criminal Jurisdiction, UN Doc. A/CN.4/631 (2011), para. 21. See Award, para. 849.

[13] KOLODKIN, *cit. supra* note 12, para. 25. See Award, para. 857.

[14] See Award, para. 858.

[15] For a contrary view, see RONZITTI, "Il caso della *Enrica Lexie*", *cit. supra* note 2, p. 951 ff.

[16] HERNÁNDEZ, *cit. supra* note 10, para. 118.

[17] *Ibid.*

[18] In this regard, the Special Rapporteur also refers to the Report of the International Law Commission on the work of its fifty-third session, UN Doc. A/56/10, and the consideration

The ILC Report's analysis of existing practice begins by acknowledging the variety of approaches followed by national courts with regard to the recognition of immunity of State officials, leading the Special Rapporteur to argue that "it cannot be concluded [...] that a consistent pattern has been uniformly followed".[19] In fact, while the majority of the judicial decisions that have so far granted immunity *ratione materiae* to State officials have been based on the status of the latter, and the attribution of their acts to the State,[20] in other cases, the courts did not only base their decision on the fact that the acts were carried out on behalf of the State, but also ruled on the nature of the acts, emphasizing that they were carried out in the exercise of governmental authority or were sovereign acts, noting that they constituted a performance of public functions.[21] In a number of cases, *a contrario sensu*, national courts have concluded that some acts exceeded the limits of official functions, or functions of the State, and were therefore not covered by immunity[22] as, for example, in cases linked to corruption, underlining that such conduct does not relate to the exercise of sovereignty or governmental authority.[23]

In other cases, courts have denied foreign officials immunity from criminal jurisdiction on the assumption that the attribution to a State of an act carried out by its officials was not sufficient to recognize immunity, as in the *Kovtunenko* case,[24] the *Yusufu* case[25] and the *Khurts Bat* case,[26] all relating to State officials that did not perform typical governmental functions in international relations.

The idea that immunity should only protect specific governmental functions is also evident from State practice that has excluded immunity for the organs that usually operate abroad on behalf of the State, when such organs act outside of their typical functions.

---

on Article 5 of the Draft Articles on Responsibility of States for internationally wrongful acts and the exercise of elements of governmental authority, according to which "[o]f particular importance will be not just the content of the powers, but the way they are conferred[, ...] the purposes for which they are to be exercised and the extent to which the entity is accountable to government for their exercise" (p. 43, para. 6). See HERNÁNDEZ, *cit. supra* note 10, para. 83.

[19] *Ibid.*, para. 51.

[20] *Ibid.*, para. 52.

[21] *Ibid.*, para. 53.

[22] *Ibid.*, para. 55.

[23] See, for example, the case of Teodoro Nguema Obiang Mangue, in which the French courts have ruled on immunity, affirming that the misappropriation of public funds and money-laundering "are distinguishable from the performance of State functions protected by international custom in accordance with the principles of sovereignty and diplomatic immunity", and that the acts Nguema Obiang Mangue is charged with, by their nature, do not relate to the exercise of sovereignty or governmental authority, nor are they in the public interest; cited *ibid.*, para. 58.

[24] Supreme Court of Burma, *Kovtunenko v. U Law Yone*, Judgment of 1 March 1960, 31 ILR 259.

[25] Lambeth Magistrate's Court, *R. v. Lambeth Justices, ex parte Yusufu*, Judgment of 6 February 1985, 88 ILR 323.

[26] High Court, Queen's Bench Division, *Khurts Bat v. Investigating Judge of the Federal Court of Germany*, Judgment of 29 July 2011, 147 ILR 633.

Thus, for example, the most recent practice has tended to specify that diplomatic agents enjoy immunity for acts that concern the performing of their diplomatic functions, not merely on the grounds that their acts are imputable to the State. In the 2009 and 2010 judgments in the *Swarna* case, the New York Court and the United States Court of Appeals respectively stressed that functional immunity is enjoyed by diplomatic agents only for "official acts", i.e. acts related to their functions as defined in Article 3 of the 1961 Vienna Convention on Diplomatic Relations, concluding that, even assuming that, in the specific case, the hiring of a person was an official act carried out on behalf of the State, it did not automatically imply the recognition of the diplomat's immunity.[27]

Likewise, in the ruling on the kidnapping of Imam Abu Omar in Milan, the Italian *Corte di Cassazione* ruled that the advisor and two secretaries of the United States' embassy involved in the Imam's kidnapping did not enjoy diplomatic immunity. The Court stated that the three accused contributed to the kidnapping of Abu Omar not in the exercise of their diplomatic functions, but as high-level officials of the CIA in Italy, and that this did not justify the recognition of diplomatic immunity.[28]

In other cases, the courts have also ruled that consuls are not entitled to immunity for all types of acts that they may perform in the exercise of their functions. In the aforementioned *Abu Omar* case, with respect to one of the defendants, who was a US consul in Milan, the Court of Cassation underlined that functional immunity "is recognised to the consul when an offence is committed *in the exercise of consular functions*".[29] The Court specified that immunity is only available in order to protect the typically administrative functions exercised by consuls, rather than any function performed by them in the interest of their State.[30] This judgment appears to confirm the trend in State practice denying immunity to State officials for acts that *do not* fall within the exercise of governmental functions, regardless of their unlawfulness. A first element supporting this interpretation can be found, with respect to immunity for *ultra vires* acts, in Hernández's Fourth Report where the Commission – recalling a number of cases where US judges explicitly determined that *ultra vires* acts were not subject to sovereign immunity, since the perpetrators acted beyond their authority – pointed out that such *ultra vires* acts should be differentiated from unlawful acts, considering that several courts have concluded that the latter are not exempt from immunity simply because they are unlawful.[31]

A second element that has emerged in ILC deliberations on immunity is whether to consider the denial of immunity for international crimes as an "ex-

---

[27] United States District Court, Southern District of New York, *Swarna v. Al-Awadi*, Judgment of 20 March 2009, 607 F.Supp.2d 509 (2009), and the judgment of the Unites States Court of Appeals, Second Circuit, of 24 September 2010, 152 ILR 617.

[28] *Corte di Cassazione, Criminal proceedings against Medero, Castelli and Russomando*, 25 September 2014, No. 39788, p. 8, IYIL, 2014, p. 465 ff., with a comment by AMOROSO.

[29] *Corte di Cassazione, Criminal proceedings against Adler and others*, 29 November 2012, No. 2099, p. 102, IYIL, 2012, p. 388 ff., with a comment by SERRA.

[30] *Ibid.*, p. 105.

[31] See HERNÁNDEZ, *cit. supra* note 10, para. 55.

ception" to the general rule on immunity, or as a "limit" to the recognition of immunity itself.

In this regard, in its Fifth Report, Special Rapporteur Hernández affirmed that while national courts have almost unanimously acknowledged that no limitations or exceptions are applicable to immunity *ratione personae*, with regard to immunity *ratione materiae*, it can be assumed that the majority trend is to accept the existence of certain "limitations and exceptions" to such immunity.[32] The Report specifies that what is different in this practice is the variety of arguments used by national courts to conclude that immunity *ratione materiae* is not applicable when State officials are charged with international crimes.[33] For example, while some courts have held that immunity should not apply due to the gravity of the acts committed by the State official,[34] in other cases the denial of immunity has been based on the violation of *jus cogens* norms.[35] In some other cases, immunity was denied based on the consideration that the acts in question could not be regarded as acts performed in an official capacity, since the commission of international crimes cannot under any circumstances be considered an ordinary function of the State or of a State official.[36]

Because of these different approaches, the Report of the ILC on the Work of its Sixty-Ninth Session (2017) underlined that some ILC members questioned why the proposed title of Draft Article 7 was referring to situations "in respect of which immunity does not apply", when Hernández's Fifth Report discussed "limitations and exceptions" to immunity, suggesting that the uncertainty over the meaning and scope of the phrase "limitations and exceptions" demonstrated that Draft Article 7 did not reflect settled international law.[37] In particular, a number of members considered that the distinction between limitations and exceptions was useful and should be maintained, because it helped to distinguish situations in which immunity was not at issue (as the relevant conduct could not be considered as an official act or as an act performed in an official capacity) from cases in which immunity was excluded on the basis of exceptional circumstances.[38]

Ultimately, the practice on immunity and international crimes suggests that in some cases the denial of immunity is justified by the absence of any

---

[32] HERNÁNDEZ, Fifth Report to the International Law Commission on the Immunity of State Officials from Foreign Criminal Jurisdiction, UN Doc. A/CN.4/701 (2016), para. 121.

[33] *Ibid.*, para. 115.

[34] Israeli Supreme Court, *Eichmann*, Judgment of 29 May 1962, 36 ILR 309. See also the other cases cited by the ILC in HERNÁNDEZ, Fifth Report, *cit. supra* note 32, para. 115, footnote 234.

[35] The Fifth Report cited in this regard *Corte di Cassazione, Criminal proceedings against Lozano*, 24 July 2008, No. 31171, IYIL, 2008, p. 346 ff., with a comment by SERRA.

[36] Court of First Instance of Brussels, *Pinochet*, Judgment of 6 November 1998, 119 ILR 349; see also the other cases cited by the ILC in HERNÁNDEZ, Fifth Report, *cit. supra* note 32, para. 115, footnote 236.

[37] Report of the International Law Commission on the work of its sixty-ninth session (2017), ILC Report A/72/10, para. 116.

[38] *Ibid.*, para. 117.

connection with the governmental functions that immunity is intended to protect.[39]

3. THE CONTROVERSIAL LEGAL REGIME GOVERNING THE FUNCTIONAL IMMUNITY OF MILITARY FORCES ABROAD

Given the doubtful existence under customary international law of a clear rule establishing the functional immunity of all State officials, for all the acts performed in the exercise of their functions, the Arbitral Tribunal should have firstly ascertained the existence of a specific rule on the immunity of military forces abroad, and the exact content of such rule,[40] and secondly whether such rule was applicable in the case of the *Enrica Lexie*. In this regard, according to existing State practice, immunity has been granted to military forces deployed on the territory of a foreign State, only for specific acts, and providing that the foreign State had consented to their deployment. In any case, the performance by the military of specific functions on behalf of the sending State is a prerequisite for the recognition of immunity. From this perspective, the *Enrica Lexie* case is rather different as, during the incident of February 2012, the two Italian marines involved were on board a private vessel, and they were performing their functions on behalf of the shipowner.

As is well-known, the conduct of military forces abroad is subject to specific agreements, commonly referred to as Status of Forces Agreements (SOFAs), which the sending State usually concludes with the host State, and which allocate State jurisdiction over the acts performed by the foreign military on the territory of the host State which may violate the latter's domestic law.[41]

When States do not conclude an international agreement on their military forces abroad, the applicable customary law is rather uncertain: all that can be inferred from it is the recognition of immunity to visiting forces only for matters concerning discipline and the internal administration of the force, and on the assumption that the receiving State has consented to the deployment on its territory of said foreign armed forces.[42]

---

[39] On the possibility to prosecute State officials in national courts for international crimes without finding an exception to a general rule, see FRULLI, "On the Existence", *cit. supra* note 6, p. 498.

[40] According to some authors, a customary rule on the immunity of the military abroad does not exist, see FRULLI, "On the Existence", *cit. supra* note 6, p. 498; PISILLO MAZZESCHI, "The Functional Immunity", *cit. supra* note 6; FOCARELLI, *International Law*, *cit. supra* note 6, p. 356 ff. In the opinion of others, militaries abroad enjoy functional immunity according to customary international law, see WEBB, *cit. supra* note 5; RONZITTI, "The *Enrica Lexie* Incident", *cit. supra* note 5; SARI, "The Immunities of Visiting Forces", in RUYS, ANGELET and FERRO (eds.), *cit. supra* note 5, p. 558 ff.; VOETELINK, "Status of Forces and Criminal Jurisdiction", NILR, 2013, p. 231 ff.

[41] Reference can be made to the NATO SOFA, the 1951 London Agreement between the States Parties to the North Atlantic Treaty.

[42] FOX and WEBB, *The Law of State Immunity*, 3rd ed., Oxford, 2013, p. 601 ff.

This principle was quite clear in older practice, on the basis of which it was affirmed that "with regard to the criminal jurisdiction of the local courts, it also appears that there is no general recognition of any rule of international law under which members of a foreign visiting force are entitled to absolute immunity".[43] Later, however, the ambiguity of customary international law on the immunity of the military abroad was emphasized, as for instance in the *Bolton* case of 1987, where the High Court of Australia underlined the "uncertain boundaries of international law"[44] on the immunity accorded to members of a visiting force abroad. The Court clearly affirmed that "public international law recognizes that consent by a receiving state to the entry of forces of another state implies a waiver of the receiving state's normal supervisory jurisdiction over those forces, though the extent of immunity may be debatable".[45]

In cases where immunity was granted to the military abroad on the assumption of a customary rule applicable to all State officials, the judges actually followed an unclear reasoning in which the immunity of the State was often confused with the immunity of State officials.

This was for example the argument followed by the Italian *Corte di Cassazione* in the 2008 judgment on the *Lozano* case, concerning the killing of the Italian SISMI agent Nicola Calipari by a US soldier in Iraq.[46] The Court ascertained that the acts carried out by the US military at the checkpoint in Iraq were to be considered as acts *jure imperii*, and that, as such, they could not be subjected to the jurisdiction of Italy. It also ruled that the principle of functional immunity "has found wide and uncontested recognition [...] although in the restrictive or relative notion, that is limited only to activities which, unlike those *iure gestionis*, are direct and immediate expression of the sovereign function of the States", and that "among these activities ontologically fall those carried out in the course of military operations".[47]

This reasoning does not seem sufficiently clear. The distinction between acts *jure imperii* and *jure gestionis* seems to allude to the immunity of the State, as well as the idea that military activities "ontologically" fall into the sovereign functions of the State itself. However, State immunity for acts *jure imperii* carried out by its armed forces does not automatically imply that the latter must also be granted immunity. In fact, these are two distinct rules whose application is independent of each other.

Moreover, even the jurisprudence referred to by the Court of Cassation in support of its conclusions, is not completely relevant for the purposes of affirming the functional immunity of State officials. In fact, such jurisprudence concerned

---

[43] EVATT, "The Visiting Forces Act, 1952", Sidney Law Journal, 1954, p. 225 ff.

[44] High Court of Australia, *R v. Bolton and Another, ex parte Beane*, Judgment of 9 April 1987, 85 ILR 155, para. 6.

[45] *Ibid.*, para. 18.

[46] *Lozano, cit. supra* note 35. See for a comment, CASSESE, "The Italian Court of Cassation Misapprehends the Notion of War Crimes. The Lozano Case", JICJ, 2008, p. 1077 ff.; RONZITTI, "L'immunità funzionale degli organi stranieri dalla giurisdizione penale. Il caso *Calipari*", RDI, 2008, p. 1033 ff.

[47] See para. 5 of the judgment.

international and State practice relating to the immunity of States, or to possible exceptions to State immunity in the case of serious human rights violations.[48]

A few years later, the same Court of Cassation, in the above-mentioned 2012 *Abu Omar* case, denied the existence of a customary rule conferring immunity to all State officials, for all the acts performed in the exercise of their duties. With regard to this change of opinion, a former judge of the same Court, referring specifically to the *Enrica Lexie* case and criticizing the conclusions of the Arbitral Tribunal on the immunity of the Italian marines, recently stated that "this sudden change of position by the Court of Cassation is an example of the strong uncertainty that seems to emerge in international jurisprudential practice, when there is no express provision" on the immunity of the military abroad.[49]

The confusion between immunity of the military and State immunity can also be found in a recent judgment of the Hague District Court of 2020, where functional immunity was accorded to two Israeli commanders for damage claimed by the victims of an Israeli air strike in the Gaza Strip. The Court ruled that immunity of State officials derives from the immunity of States and has the aim of preventing "a situation in which State immunity can be circumvented by holding government officials responsible".[50] This Court's reasoning is not entirely convincing. On the one hand, there is no established practice necessarily extending the functional immunity granted to State officials also to the military. On the other, the assumption that functional immunity prevents State immunity from being circumvented, is once again confusing. This statement seems to ignore that, in the aftermath of the Second World War, the international responsibility of individuals was envisaged alongside the possible distinct responsibility of the State precisely to avoid a situation where the imputability to a State of the acts of its military or other officials could prevent the ascertainment of individual responsibility for serious violations of human rights.

This author agrees that the immunity of State officials originates from the immunity of States, but only in the sense that the former is aimed at protecting certain acts and functions that individuals actually perform on behalf of the State. However, this does not mean that State officials enjoy both immunity as officials and the immunity of States, or that both immunities have the same contents, and thus can be applied indistinctly to States and State officials.

This is all the more evident in the context of immunity from criminal jurisdiction. Suffice it to consider that State immunity in proceedings regarding the alleged commission of international crimes entails the possibility that a State is

---

[48] *Ibid.*

[49] BARBERINI, *cit. supra* note 2.

[50] Hague District Court, Judgment of 29 January 2020, available at: <https://uitspraken.rechtspraak.nl/inziendocument?id=ECLI:NL:RBDHA:2020:667#_3d669af3-966f-40db-ba3a-4a53baab9313>, para. 4.11. For a comment, see RYNGAERT, "Functional Immunity of Foreign State Officials in Respect of International Crimes before the Hague District Court: A Regressive Interpretation of Progressive International Law", EJIL: Talk!, 2 March 2020, available at: <https://www.ejiltalk.org/functional-immunity-of-foreign-state-officials-in-respect-of-international-crimes-before-the-hague-district-court-a-regressive-interpretation-of-progressive-international-law/>.

held liable on a civil basis, but it does not automatically imply that State officials cannot be held accountable for the same acts in separate criminal proceedings.[51] On the other hand, to deny the immunity of State officials does not necessarily entail that State immunity is circumvented, as the latter can still be affirmed in civil proceedings, as has, in fact, happened in well-established national and international practice.[52]

The distinction between the two immunities has been reaffirmed in Hernández's Fourth Report, which has emphasized that "[t]he criminal nature of the act performed by a State official determines an important consequence in that its immunity is distinct from that of the State",[53] and that "when an act is attributable both to the State and to an individual, and both can be held responsible, two types of immunity can be distinguished: immunity of the State, on the one hand, and immunity of the official, on the other".[54] In very clear terms the Report concluded that "the immunity of State officials from foreign criminal jurisdiction *ratione materiae* is individual in nature and distinct from the immunity of the State *stricto sensu*".[55]

To conclude, the existing practice suggests that there is no specific customary rule which accords immunity to military forces abroad for all the functions they perform. On the contrary, their immunity has been recognized only in specific circumstances which did not occur in the case of the Enrica Lexie, considering that the Italian marines were performing security functions on board a private ship and on behalf of a private entity, not on behalf of the Italian State. It is on this aspect that the article will now focus in order to conclude the analysis.

4. THE ITALIAN MARINES AND THEIR FUNCTIONS ON BOARD THE ENRICA LEXIE

As already mentioned, the Arbitral Tribunal concluded that since the Italian marines were State officials and were acting on behalf of the Italian State, they should be granted immunity from India's criminal jurisdiction. The conclusion reached by the Tribunal appears questionable, since, in the case at hand, even admitting that the two marines were State officials, they were nonetheless per-

---

[51] See HERNÁNDEZ, Fourth Report, *cit. supra* note 10, para. 104. See also KEITNER, "Functional Immunity of State Officials before the International Law Commission: The 'Who' and the 'What'", Questions of International Law, Zoom-out 17, 2015, p. 51 ff., available at: <http://www.qil-qdi.org/wp-content/uploads/2015/06/05_Functional-Immunity_KEITNER_FIN.pdf>, affirming that "the notion that state immunity and *ratione materiae* immunity should always be congruent seems puzzling". On the distinction between State immunity and functional immunity, see also VAN ALEBEEK, *cit. supra* note 5, p. 499 ff.

[52] *Jurisdictional Immunities of the State (Germany v. Italy; Greece intervening)*, Judgment of 3 February 2012, ICJ Reports 2012, p. 99 ff., para. 91.

[53] HERNÁNDEZ, Fourth Report, *cit. supra* note 10, para. 97.

[54] *Ibid.*, para. 110.

[55] *Ibid.*, para. 105.

forming their functions on behalf of the shipowner of the Enrica Lexie, rather than the Italian State.

The presence of military personnel on board merchant vessels flying the Italian flag transiting through maritime areas at risk of piracy – known as Vessel Protection Detachments (VPDs) – is regulated under Italian law by Law Decree No. 107/11 of 12 July 2011.[56] Pursuant to Article 5 of the Law Decree, the Ministry of Defence may enter into framework agreements with private Italian shipowners for the employment of VPDs on board merchant vessels. Article 5(2) also provides that the commander of each unit and the staff employed by him acquire the additional status of officers and agents of the judicial police, authorising them, among other things, to arrest pirates and keep them in their custody.

Some scholars have observed that the Italian law entrusting military personnel on board merchant ships with specific functions related to the fight against piracy, raises an issue with regard to the consistency of such national provisions with Article 107 UNCLOS, according to which "a seizure on account of piracy may be carried out only by warships or military aircraft, or other ships or aircraft clearly marked and identifiable as being on government service and authorized to that effect".[57] It seems clear that this definition does not cover merchant ships normally traveling for commercial purposes, even if they have military personnel on board. One could also argue that, even admitting that the Italian marines involved in the present case can be qualified as organs of the Italian State, this does not involve an automatic recognition of their immunity, as the Arbitral Tribunal itself seemed to admit. As mentioned in Section 3, the nature of their functions remains, indeed, to be established. On this question, the Arbitral Tribunal proceeded to verify whether the acts of the Italian marines were indeed acts within the scope of their duties as officials of the Italian State. In its opinion, "as members of Italy's armed forces", the marines were fulfilling a State function.[58] The fact that the marines were stationed on a merchant vessel and not a warship did not, in the Tribunal's view, alter their status and the character of their mission as part of the VPDs, nor the fact that their acts were deemed to be performed in an official capacity attributable to the Italian State.

This author agrees in principle that the military can carry out security functions on board a civilian ship, without this circumstance affecting their status as State officials. Nor can it be doubted that, in the present case, the marines were carrying out their typical functions of defending a ship in areas at risk of piracy. Nonetheless, the decisive issue remains the fact that in the present case the marines were carrying out these functions on behalf of a private subject.

The majority judgment affirmed that the marines had been deployed on board the Enrica Lexie "pursuant to a mandate from the Italian State as provided in the

---

[56] The Law Decree was converted into Law No. 130/11 of 2 August 2011, available at: <https://www.gazzettaufficiale.it/eli/id/2011/08/05/11A10810/sg>.

[57] VILLONI, "La vicenda dei marò italiani in India", Questione Giustizia, 13 March 2013, available at: <https://www.questionegiustizia.it/articolo/la-vicenda-dei-maro-italiani-in-india_13-03-2013.php>. See also BARBERINI, cit. supra note 2.

[58] See Award, para. 859.

Italian law on VPDs", but this law only provides for the possibility that military personnel *is made available* to shipowners, i.e. private subjects, *upon their request and at their expense.*

With regard to the payment of the marines for the activities carried out on board the Enrica Lexie, the Arbitral Tribunal argued that "[a]lthough shipowners contributed to the expense of stationing a VPD on board their ship, such contribution was, as described in the Template Agreement, for the purposes of 'repay[ing] [to the Italian Ministry of Defence] the costs incurred for the employment of the VPD'". The Tribunal added that "[t]his reimbursement to the Italian government, as opposed to a direct payment of salaries by the shipowners, is a standard and common practice designed to simply compensate the Ministry of Defence for the costs incurred by the VPD when stationed on board a vessel", and "[a]s such, it does not detract from the extensive evidence demonstrating that, as part of a VPD [...] the Marines were members of the Italian Navy, and officers and agents of the judicial police".[59]

In this author's opinion, the fact that the shipowners' contribution to the expense of stationing a VPD on board their ship is qualified as a reimbursement to the Italian government rather than a direct payment of the marines' salaries, simply relates to the method of payment, but does not alter the fact that the expenses for the marines' activities on board the Enrica Lexie were in any case borne by the shipowner, and not by the Italian State. Furthermore, the Tribunal's view that the reimbursement of the expenses to the Italian government confirms the status of the marines as members of the Navy and as officers and agents of the judicial police, while certainly correct, has no bearing on the nature of the functions performed by the marines in the present case, nor on the nature of the subject on whose behalf the latter had been performed.

That the VPDs acted autonomously from the Italian State seems, instead, to be confirmed by the Memorandum of Understanding (MoU) concluded on 11 October 2011 between the Ministry of Defence and *Confitarma* (the Italian association of shipowners), in order to make military personnel available to the latter in accordance with the provisions of Law Decree No. 107/2011. The MoU, in fact, provides that "there is a need to complement the actions carried out at sea by military ships to guarantee the defence and safety of national communications lines in risk areas [...] through the use of VPDs specially trained and equipped, able to *independently* ensure the direct protection of national merchant ships from acts of piracy or armed pillage".[60]

Doubts about the relationship between the Ministry of Defence and the marines, as well as on the nature of the latter on board the Enrica Lexie, were also expressed at the Italian Senate by one of its members, who stated that "although the two Marines qualify, in the present case, as members of the Italian Navy, and therefore as an emanation (*emanazione*) of the Italian State, and were thus carry-

---

[59] *Ibid.*, para. 854.
[60] The text of the MoU is available at: <http://www.unife.it/giurisprudenza/giurisprudenza/studiare/diritti-umani-conflitti-armati/materiale-da-archiviare/dudu-2013/salerno/A_101011_Protocollo_Difesa_CONFITARMA_UG.pdf> (emphasis added).

ing out a function that is typical of its armed forces, [...] they were not, in actual fact, obligated towards the Ministry of Defence, but towards the internal hierarchy of a civilian ship, and the choices and decisions made by [such hierarchy]". As a result, the Italian government was asked to "allow a review of the regulatory framework governing the embarkment of VPDs on civilian ships, in order to clarify their rules of engagement and to recognize their mandatory military nature with all the consequences in terms of operation and command discipline".[61]

The foregoing confirms that the mere circumstance that an organ of a State performs an act, even typical of its functions, does not automatically mean that the act is performed on behalf of the State and is attributable to it for the purposes of immunity. Once again, it is necessary to verify whether in this case a governmental function was carried out on behalf of the Italian State, and whether it is a function protected by international law. It is significant that the ILC – in specifying that an act performed in an official capacity is not just any act attributable to the State and performed on behalf of the State, "but [it] must also be a manifestation of sovereignty, constituting a form of exercise of the governmental authority"[62] – considered relevant for the qualification of the functions of State organs "not just the content of the powers, but the way they are conferred [...] the purposes for which they are to be exercised and the extent to which the entity is accountable to government for their exercise".[63]

In the case of the Enrica Lexie, the powers exercised by the marines on board the vessel were conferred by the shipowner and for the purposes of guaranteeing the safety of a private ship. Above all, there are no elements in the Decree Law 107/2011, nor in the MoU suggesting that the marines were accountable to the Italian government for the exercise of their functions on board the Enrica Lexie.

The question raised by Judges Sreenivasa Rao and Patrick Robinson in their dissenting opinion to the majority judgment of the Arbitral Tribunal, on the nature of the agreement between the Ministry of Defence and the Italian shipowners, is a different one. The dissenting judges concluded that the Italian marines could not be granted immunity, since the agreement in question is a commercial one, and therefore an act *jure gestionis* – for which the Italian State itself is not entitled to immunity.[64] The nature of the agreement is relevant, in this author's opinion, solely for the purposes of the possible immunity invoked by Italy, since, as argued above, any conclusions regarding the immunity of the State do not have automatic nor, most importantly, necessarily corresponding implications for the immunity of State officials or the military.

In conclusion, it should be noted that the argument put forward in this article that the marines were not entitled to functional immunity in the present case, does not in any way mean that they should not, in any case, be protected dur-

---

[61] See *Senato della Repubblica*, "Di Biagio, Ordine del giorno n. G5.200 al DDL n. 1248", available at: <http://www.senato.it/japp/bgt/showdoc/print/17/Emend/00763806/00746072/0>.

[62] *Supra* note 17.

[63] *Ibid.*, para. 83.

[64] See the Dissenting Opinion of Judge Rao, p. 432, para. 80 of the Award, and the Dissenting Opinion of Judge Robinson, p. 463, para. 63(ii) of the Award.

ing the exercise of their functions on board commercial vessels, but simply that such protection cannot derive from an alleged rule of customary international law conferring immunity to all State officials, for every type of function performed in an official capacity. Other means of protection may be necessary and more appropriate for marines employed on civilian ships, for example in the form of international agreements. It could be argued that no further instruments are actually necessary, given that the Tribunal has recognized the immunity of the Italian marines. However, it should not be underestimated that (also because of the nature of the adjudicating body) the Arbitral Tribunal appears to have aimed at reaching a compromise solution, by issuing a judgment that could be "satisfactory" for both Parties. In fact, on the one side, despite Italy's submissions on India's violation of the marines' immunity and request for both declaratory and non-declaratory reliefs, the Tribunal limited itself to affirming that India "must take the necessary steps to cease to exercise its criminal jurisdiction over the Marines".[65] On the other side, the Tribunal determined that India is entitled to the payment of compensation in connection with the loss of life, physical harm, material damage to property and moral harm suffered by the captain and the other crew members of the St. Antony, as a consequence of Italy's violation of Articles 87(1)(a) and 90 of the UNCLOS due to the interference by the Enrica Lexie with the navigation of the Indian vessel. For this reason, the Tribunal's conclusions do not seem adequate to support the existence of a customary rule granting immunity to military personnel abroad in any circumstance, on the sole basis of their qualification as State officials.

---

[65] See Award, para. 888.

FUNCTIONAL IMMUNITY OF THE MARINES ON THE ENRICA LEXIE: A REPLY TO RAFFAELLA NIGRO

NATALINO RONZITTI*

Abstract

This article is a short reply to Raffaella Nigro's assessment of the Arbitral Tribunal award in the Enrica Lexie case. Professor Nigro analyzes the rule of functional immunity of State officials from foreign criminal jurisdiction and argues that it cannot be applied to the two marines, even supposing that military personnel are covered by such a rule. Professor Nigro bases this conclusion on the facts that the marines were stationed on a commercial vessel and were servicing the interests of the private shipowner.

In reply, this author reaffirms the existence of a rule of customary international law on functional immunity and argues that military personnel assigned to commercial vessels are carrying out these duties in order to protect Italian interests and contribute to the defeat of piracy. Therefore, the marines on board the Enrica Lexie were (and still remain) under the protection of the rule on immunity from foreign criminal jurisdiction.

Keywords: State officials' immunity from foreign criminal jurisdiction; identification of customary international law; functional immunity of the marines on the Enrica Lexie.

1. INTRODUCTION

The Arbitral Tribunal recognized in its award in the *Enrica Lexie* case the important principle of the functional immunity of State officials from foreign criminal jurisdiction. It stated, albeit with a decision by majority (three votes to two), that the Italian "Marines are entitled to immunity in relation to the acts that they committed during the incident of 15 February 2012 and that India is precluded from exercising its jurisdiction over the Marines".[1]

The Tribunal acknowledged the existence of a norm of customary international law on the immunity *ratione materiae* (or functional immunity) of State officials and, in order to support its finding, it cited the *Blaškić* case, decided by the International Criminal Tribunal for the former Yugoslavia (ICTY), and the International Court of Justice (ICJ) judgment on *Certain Questions of Criminal*

---

* Of the Board of Editors.

[1] *The Italian Republic v. The Republic of India concerning the "Enrica Lexie" Incident*, PCA Case No. 2015-28, Award of 21 May 2020, available at: <https://pcacases.com/web/sendAttach/16500>, para. 1094(B)(2).

Assistance.[2] Interestingly, the Tribunal did not mention the *Arrest Warrant* case, usually also quoted as a precedent by those supporting the existence of the norm in question.[3]

In the *Blaškić* case, the ICTY held as follows:

> The Appeals Chamber dismisses the possibility of the International Tribunal addressing *subpoenas* to State officials acting in their official capacity. Such officials are mere instruments of a State and their official action can only be attributed to the State. They cannot be the subject of sanctions or penalties for conduct that is not private but undertaken on behalf of a State. In other words, State officials cannot suffer the consequences of wrongful acts which are not attributable to them personally but to the State on whose behalf they act: they enjoy so-called 'functional immunity'. This is a well-established rule of customary international law going back to the eighteenth and nineteenth centuries, restated many times since. More recently, France adopted a position based on that rule in the *Rainbow Warrior* case. The rule was also clearly set out by the Supreme Court of Israel in the Eichmann case.[4]

The Arbitral Tribunal also cited the work of the International Law Commission (ILC) on the immunity of State officials, in support of the existence of a norm of customary international law, even though it acknowledged that many aspects of the discussion on State officials' immunity "are in a state of flux".[5] It is also noteworthy that the Tribunal highlighted that neither Italy nor India questioned the existence of the customary rule on functional immunity of State officials.[6] India only questioned the applicability of the rule to the incident and to the two marines. This author has already expressed his positive stance on the Tribunal's findings, in a comment published soon after the publication of the judgment.[7]

---

[2] *Ibid.*, para. 844.

[3] *Arrest Warrant of 11 April 2000 (Democratic Republic of the Congo v. Belgium)*, Judgment of 14 February 2002, ICJ Reports 2002, p. 3 ff. Even if the judgment is related only to the Minister of Foreign Affairs, it contains a passage relevant for fixing the notion of functional immunity (see para. 61).

[4] Appeal Chamber, *Prosecutor v. Tihomir Blaškić*, Case No. IT-95-14-AR108 *bis*, Judgment of 29 October 1997 on the Request of the Republic of Croatia for Review of the Decision of Trial Chamber II of 18 July 1997, para. 38.

[5] Award, *cit. supra* note 1, para. 845.

[6] *Ibid.*, para. 846.

[7] RONZITTI, "Il caso della *Enrica Lexie* e la sentenza arbitrale nella controversia Italia-India", RDI, 2020, p. 937 ff.

2. THE CRITICAL APPROACH BY RAFFAELLA NIGRO

Raffaella Nigro is the author of a valuable book on the immunity of States and their organs, in which she addresses the functional immunity of State officials and concludes that the principle should not be disregarded, but that its application must be carefully circumscribed.[8] Much depends – according to Nigro – on the modern notion of the State and its organs, and of the functions that States now play within an international community that is much more integrated than in the past and much more aimed at co-operation. This article recognizes that the international community has evolved and that much of its evolution depends on the existence of *jus cogens* and *erga omnes* obligations. However, it is submitted that these notions have not eliminated the traditional conception of the State, as a member of the international community. This is proven *inter alia* by the fact that the "national interest" is still an important ingredient of State policy. This is not the place to comment on the rationale of Nigro's notion or on the content of functional immunity. Rather, this article will focus on the last part of Nigro's article where it is argued that the two Italian marines should not be under the shield of functional immunity.

Nigro relies mainly on the following reasons:

a) Military personnel abroad enjoy functional immunity only within the base in which they are located, provided that the host State has given its consent to the stationing of foreign military personnel. However, the marines were operating on the high seas (for the purpose of navigation) at the time of the incident and, if they were to embark/disembark in a foreign port, a Status of Forces Agreement (SOFA) could have been concluded by Italy.

b) A comment by an Italian author is quoted, affirming that Vessel Protection Detachments (VPDs) were behaving illegally, since Article 107 of the United Nations Convention on the Law of the Sea (UNCLOS) entitles only warships to capture pirate vessels.[9] This is correct. However, the VPDs' function was not to "hunt pirates", but only to exercise the right of self-defence in case of pirate attacks.

c) The marines were not serving the interests of the Italian State but those of a private shipowner. This is not true. As evidenced by several documents, the VPDs were complementing the efforts of the Italian warships in fighting piracy, even though they had only a passive role of self-defence. They could operate only on board Italian ships, thus carrying out a role of protection that is a legitimate aim of the armed forces. Moreover, under Article 5 of the Law regulating the institution of VPDs, the marines were to operate under the "directives and rules

---

[8] NIGRO, *Le immunità giurisdizionali dello Stato e dei suoi organi e l'evoluzione della sovranità nel diritto internazionale*, Padova, 2018.

[9] The author quoted is VILLONI, "La vicenda dei marò italiani in India", Questione Giustizia, 13 March 2013, available at: <https://www.questionegiustizia.it/articolo/la-vicenda-dei-maro-italiani-in-india_13-03-2013.php>.

of engagement of the Ministry of Defence".[10] The Master of the ship could not interfere with the conduct chosen by the marines in repelling a pirate attack. The marines had also been given the rank of police officers in relation to the capture and detention of pirates.

d) As for the observation that the shipowner had to compensate the Ministry of Defence for the services given, this is not a sound argument for denying the qualification of the marines as State agents. First of all, because the money was not given directly to the marines, but to the Ministry of Defence. Secondly, and most importantly, because the money could be considered as a kind of taxation for the extra costs incurred by the Ministry of Defence and thus by the Italian State.

3. THE RATIONALE OF THE CUSTOMARY RULE ON FUNCTIONAL IMMUNITY OF STATE OFFICIALS

The rationale of functional immunity is grounded in the attribution to the State of the acts of its organs. The State as a legal person cannot act on its own, but rather does so through its organs. This means that an act performed on official duty is an act that is attributed to the State for which the organ operates and does not remain its own (but for a few exceptions). This simple truth is supported by logic and by State practice, as we shall see.

In preserving functional immunity, the international legal order protects the State's domestic organization, shielding it under the principle of non-interference/non-intervention. A State is entitled under international law to be respected as far as its internal and external structure is concerned (i.e. its organization). Functional immunity (or immunity *ratione materiae*) stems from the fact that the acts performed by an official are attributed to the State to which he/she belongs. Disregarding functional immunity means an infringement of the sovereignty and independence of the foreign State. If the act performed by the State official amounts to an international wrong, only the State is responsible and not the State official (unless an international crime has been committed).[11] The issue of functional immunity has been the subject of a resolution of the Institut de droit international (Naples Session, 2009). Article II, paragraph 1, affirms that:

> Immunities are conferred to ensure an orderly allocation and exercise of jurisdiction in accordance with international law in proceedings concerning States, to respect the sovereign equality of States

---

[10] Law Decree No. 107 of 12 July 2011 (GU No. 160 of 12 July 2011), converted with amendments into Law No. 130 of 2 August 2011 (GU No. 181 of 5 August 2011).

[11] These views have been developed by the author in many of his writings. An English version, from which we draw for the present article, was published in Questions of International Law, Zoom-out 17 (2015), p. 55 ff., under the title "The Immunity of State Organs – A Reply to Pisillo Mazzeschi".

and to permit the effective performance of the functions of persons who act on behalf of States.[12]

4. STATES' VIEWS

The *opinio juris* of States may be drawn from the work of the International Law Commission on the immunity of State officials from foreign criminal jurisdiction and related documents.[13] One important manifestation is the statement contained in the Background Paper on "Immunity of State Officials from Foreign Criminal Jurisdiction", presented at the Inter-sessional Meeting of Legal Experts to Discuss Matters Relating to the International Law Commission, held at the Asian-African Legal Consultative Organization (AALCO) Secretariat in New Delhi on 10 April 2012. It states:

> Unlike immunity *ratione personae*, immunity *ratione materiae* covers only official acts, that is, conduct adopted by a State official in the discharge of his or her functions. This limitation to the scope of immunity *ratione materiae* appears to be undisputed in the legal literature and has been confirmed by domestic courts. In its recent judgment in the *Djibouti v. France* case, the International Court of Justice referred in this context to acts within the scope of [the] duties [of the officials concerned] as organs of State.[14]

Several States have addressed this subject, either in response to the work of the ILC on State officials' immunity, or within the General Assembly 6th Committee. All of them directly or indirectly acknowledged the principle of State officials' functional immunity. For instance, at the 67th session of the ILC, the information submitted by Austria, Cuba, Czech Republic, Finland, France, Germany, Netherlands, Poland, Spain, Switzerland and UK did not question the principle of State officials' immunity. Most of them repeated their comments at the 68th, 69th, 70th, 71st and 72nd sessions. Also Australia, Paraguay (68th session), Mexico (69th session), El Salvador (70th session) and Belarus (72nd session) expressed their views. The main differences of opinion were about the possible exceptions to the principle, i.e. the cases in which the immunity is forfeited because the organ has committed an international crime or has been engaged in an espionage activity. Even among those States admitting that there are exceptions, opinions vary with respect to the legal basis for exceptions, ranging

---

[12] Institut de droit international, "Resolution on the Immunity from Jurisdiction of the State and of Persons Who Act on Behalf of the State in case of International Crime", 2009.

[13] Analytical Guide to the Work of the International Law Commission, Immunity of State officials from foreign criminal jurisdiction, available at: <https://legal.un.org/ilc/guide/4_2.shtml>.

[14] The Background Paper quoted is available at: <http://www.aalco.int/Background%20 Paper%20ILC%2010%20April%202012.pdf>.

from the existence of an *ad hoc* norm to the interpretation of the customary rule, which cannot cover international crimes since they cannot fall under the category of official acts.[15]

5. SCHOLARS' VIEWS

The author of this article supports the existence of a broad rule of functional immunity for State officials. The extensive notion of immunity *ratione materiae* has been endorsed by Pierre d'Argent in his contribution on the matter.[16] Learned authors support this finding, for instance Jean Salmon[17] and Ian Brownlie.[18] Dupuy (P-M), in the 12th edition of his manual, also seems to share the broad notion of functional immunity.[19] Even in the most recent legal literature, the existence of immunity of State officials has been reaffirmed. For instance, Rosanne van Alebeek does not question the principle, but only its exceptions.[20] Very recently, the question of the existence of a customary norm of functional immunity has been examined by Curtis Bradley in the American Journal of International Law.[21] Even though his article is dealing with the problem of applicability of the FSIA to the immunity of foreign officials by US Courts, he recognizes the customary principle of immunity of foreign officials.

There are other learned authors (a few) who share the opposite view and express their doubts about the wider notion of functional immunity. The principal tenant is Benedetto Conforti, whose theoretical approach is followed mainly in Italy by a group of scholars that includes also Raffaella Nigro.[22]

---

[15] See VAN ALEBEEK, "Functional Immunity of State Officials from the Criminal Jurisdiction of Foreign National Courts", in RUYS, ANGELET and FERRO (eds.), *The Cambridge Handbook of Immunities and International Law*, Cambridge, 2019, p. 510 ff.

[16] D'ARGENT, "Immunity of State Officials and the Obligation to Prosecute", in PETERS, LAGRANGE, OETER and TOMUSCHAT (eds.), *Immunities in the Age of Global Constitutionalism*, Leiden/Boston, 2014, p. 244 ff., pp. 248-249.

[17] SALMON, "Representatives of States in International Relations", Max Planck Encyclopedia of Public International Law, 2007, available at: <https://opil.ouplaw.com/>, paras. 32-44.

[18] CRAWFORD, *Brownlie's Principles of Public International Law*, 8th ed., Oxford, 2012, pp. 688-689; ID., *Brownlie's Principles of Public International Law*, 9th ed., Oxford, 2019, pp. 477 and 662.

[19] DUPUY and KERBRAT, *Droit international public*, 12th ed., Paris, 2014, pp. 155-156.

[20] VAN ALEBEEK, *cit. supra* note 15, p. 526.

[21] BRADLEY, "Conflicting Approaches to the U.S. Common Law of Foreign Officials Immunity", AJIL, 2021, p. 1 ff.

[22] CONFORTI, "A Few Remarks on Functional Immunity of the Organs of Foreign States", Questions of International Law, Zoom-out 17 (2015), p. 64 ff. See also the Italian authors quoted in footnote 6 of Nigro's article.

6. CASE LAW

The international case law has already been quoted: the *Blaškić* case by the ICTY and the ICJ judgments concerning the *Arrest Warrant* and *Dijbouti v. France*. A further case is that of *Jones and Others v. United Kingdom*, which was decided in 2014 by the European Court of Human Rights (ECtHR). The Court held that:

> The weight of authority at international and national level therefore appears to support the proposition that State immunity in principle offers individual employees or officers of a foreign State protection in respect of acts undertaken on behalf of the State under the same cloak as protects the State itself.[23]

At the domestic level, we can cite the following cases (only some samples):
– *Jones v. Ministry of Interior Al-Mamlaka Al-Arabiya AS Saudiya (the Kingdom of Saudi Arabia) and Others* (2006). The House of Lords held not only that Saudi Arabia could not be sued, but nor could the individual officials responsible for acts of torture.[24]
– The *Lozano* case (2008). The *Corte di Cassazione* held that Lozano, a soldier belonging to the US military contingent in Iraq, could not be tried in Italy for the killing of an Italian agent since he enjoyed functional immunity.[25]
– In the *Abu Omar* case (2012), the *Corte di Cassazione* stated that the CIA agents responsible for the extraordinary rendition of Abu Omar could be tried in Italy. The result is correct but wrongly motivated. The decision can be reconciled with the other case law by understanding that the CIA's clandestine activity constituted an exception to the rule of functional immunity.[26]
– The case of *Kazemi* (2014). The Supreme Court of Canada held that a civil suit for acts of torture could not be brought against Iran or against the responsible State officials because of immunity of jurisdiction, a rule to be applied not only to foreign States but also to foreign officials.[27]

---

[23] ECtHR, *Jones and Others v. The United Kingdom*, Applications Nos. 34356/06 and 40528/06, 14 January 2014, para. 204.
[24] *Jones v. Ministry of Interior Al-Mamlaka Al-Arabiya AS Saudiya (the Kingdom of Saudi Arabia) and Others*, 14 June 2006, [2006] UKHL 26.
[25] *Corte di Cassazione (Sez. I penale), Criminal proceedings against Lozano* 24 July 2008, No. 31171, IYIL, 2008, p. 346 ff., with a comment by SERRA.
[26] *Corte di Cassazione (Sez. V penale), Criminal proceedings against Adler and others* 20 November 2012, No. 2099, IYIL, 2012, p. 388 ff., with a comment by SERRA.
[27] BATROS and WEBB, "Domesticating the Law of Immunity: The Supreme Court of Canada in Kazemi v. Iran", EJIL: Talk!, 7 November 2014, available at: <https://www.ejiltalk.org/domesticating-the-law-of-immunity-the-supreme-court-of-canada-in-kazemi-v-iran/>.

7. ARMED FORCES AND FUNCTIONAL IMMUNITY

Military forces present unique issues which require special treatment, even in the opinion of those who deny the functional immunity of State officials from foreign criminal jurisdiction.

Peace and wartime/armed conflict need to be kept separate and cannot be dealt with in the same way. The basic feature is that in times of peace, armed forces may only enter foreign territory with the consent of the territorial State, whilst in a situation of wartime/armed conflict this condition is absent, unless a State is intervening with the consent/request of the constituted government in a territory where a civil war is taking place (or in collective self-defence).

In times of peace, the status of foreign forces is usually regulated by a SOFA. This does not mean that, in the absence of a SOFA, a member of a visiting armed force is deprived of immunity *ratione materiae* when performing his/her functions. Usually, a SOFA grants immunities that are wider than those connected with the activity of the armed forces and/or details the allocation of jurisdiction between the visiting and the receiving State.

Completely different is a situation of armed conflict. In such a circumstance, members of armed forces cannot be tried by the enemy unless a war crime has been committed. If captured, they enjoy the status of prisoners of war. A different treatment is granted to spies and saboteurs (war treason), but this point is also regulated by the law of armed conflict.

In a situation of occupation (or similar situations), where there are contingents belonging to different nations, the real problem is the allocation of jurisdiction between the occupying armed forces. As a matter of fact, SOFAs regulate the relationship between the foreign forces and the receiving State (if its authority has been rebuilt), but not between the foreign forces present on the ground. As the *Lozano* case[28] proves, in the absence of such an agreement, the principle to be applied is that of functional immunity.

As far as the *Enrica Lexie* case is concerned, the incident is regulated by the law of peace, since the fight against piracy does not fall within the notion of armed conflict. Moreover, the incident happened in the Indian Exclusive Economic Zone (EEZ), which for the purpose of navigation should be considered as the high seas. In other words, the incident did not happen within Indian territory. Therefore, there is no question of applicability of any SOFA between India and Italy. The marines were on a ship flying the Italian flag and subject to Italian jurisdiction. Moreover, they had the special status of police officers when engaged in fighting piracy. It does not matter that the marines were on a commercial ship. While only warships are entitled to "hunt" pirates, those on board private vessels are entitled to resist and repel pirate attacks. A State has the right to place military personnel on board private vessels flying its flag, since this falls within the State's function of protecting its citizens. Moreover, by using its military personnel to deter pirates and act in self-defence against pirate attacks, the

---

[28] *Cit. supra* note 25.

State is contributing to its obligation to co-operate in the repression of piracy, as set out in Article 100 UNCLOS. Therefore, the placement of VPDs on commercial vessels cannot be viewed as a service provided by the State to the shipowners. For all these reasons, the qualification of the marines as State officials cannot be doubted. As already said, it is not relevant that the shipowner was obliged to pay for the VPDs' services. The contribution was not paid directly to the military personnel but to the Ministry of Defence. The contribution falls within the Italian fiscal policy for extra services rendered to its citizens.

8. FUNCTIONAL IMMUNITY AND HOME STATE JURISDICTION

Functional immunity does not mean that the holders are *legibus soluti*. If they commit a wrongful act, they should be judged by the State on whose behalf they are acting. On this point, the solution of the Arbitral Tribunal is correct. The Italian State, as the national State of the two marines, may and should investigate if they committed any wrongful act by firing bullets when the *St. Anthony* was approaching.

Functional immunity should also be taken into account in relation to the immunity of States from civil jurisdiction. As already stated, the acts of State officials should be attributed to the State for which they perform their activity. The action cannot be attributed to the individual State officials, except for cases of international crimes or clandestine activity. Therefore, the State official cannot be criminally prosecuted by the foreign State and nor can he/she be sued before a foreign tribunal for civil damages. In short, State officials enjoy functional immunity both from criminal and civil proceedings. Since the action is imputed to the State, it bears responsibility for its officials and it may be sued for the wrongful act committed. The customary rules on State immunity from civil jurisdiction determine whether the State was performing an activity *jure imperii* or *jure gestionis*, with the consequence that only in the second case can the State be sued before a domestic foreign tribunal for damages. Obviously, where a State's citizens have suffered damages, that State can intervene via diplomatic protection against the State whose officials have caused the damage. But this is an inter-State action and has nothing to do with the foreign State's sovereign immunity.

9. CONCLUSION

The Arbitral Tribunal Award in the *Enrica Lexie* case may be open to criticism with respect to some of the tribunal's findings. However, the Award should be praised for its sound affirmation of the existence of a customary rule on functional immunity of State officials from foreign criminal jurisdiction. By upholding the rule, the Tribunal has added weight to the existing international jurisprudence and reaffirmed a principle already stated by the ICJ, ICTY and ECtHR. The Award also provides a stimulus for the ILC to conclude its work on the matter.

A number of problems with the Award are still to be discussed. Firstly, in its consideration of the rationale behind the norm of functional immunity, the Tribunal only considered repercussions for individual State officials; whereas, the full explanation of the rule's importance is more complex, as this article has tried to demonstrate. Secondly, it was not necessary for the Tribunal to attempt to enumerate and address the range of possible exceptions to the rule. In particular, the tribunal dedicated a lengthy discussion to the question of tort as an exception to functional immunity, even though this has nothing to do with functional immunity. Thirdly, it was not necessary for the Tribunal to address the question, which was outside the competence of the Tribunal, of the relationship between the immunity of the State from civil jurisdiction and the functional immunity of State officials both from civil and criminal jurisdiction.

ARTICLES

ELECTING JUDGES AND PROSECUTORS
OF THE INTERNATIONAL CRIMINAL COURT:
A REAPPRAISAL OF THE PRACTICE THROUGH THE LENSES
OF TRANSPARENCY AND LEGITIMACY

LUCA POLTRONIERI ROSSETTI*

Abstract

This article – seizing the occasion of the election of six new judges and of the third Prosecutor of the International Criminal Court (ICC) at the Assembly of States Parties' (ASP) 19th session of late 2020 and early 2021 – aims at reassessing the practice of States and of the ASP in the nomination and election of judges and prosecutors, reflecting on its impact on the (perception of) legitimacy of the Court. The article will analyze the trends and changes in this practice over the years in relation to the challenges faced by the Court, including the practical ones posed by the COVID-19 pandemic that have impacted on the last election. Moreover, it shall assess the effectiveness of reforms aimed at establishing a more transparent nomination and election process, which have only partially contributed to strengthening the perception of legitimacy of the institution and have left some States unsatisfied with the screening of candidates carried out by the advisory bodies established by the ASP and the Bureau. The article concludes with a few proposals to enhance the nomination and election process, mainly through non-invasive measures, in the belief that far-reaching reforms of the Statute are unlikely to be adopted in the near future, and that States' interests and political considerations cannot (and probably should not) be entirely eschewed from the process.

Keywords: ICC; nomination and election process; judges; Prosecutor; transparency; legitimacy.

1. INTRODUCTION

A crucial aspect in the institutional design of any judicial organ resides in the rules governing its composition.[1] These rules determine, *inter alia*, the number of individuals composing the court or tribunal, the required qualifications and

---

* PhD, Università di Trento; Postdoctoral Researcher, Scuola Superiore Sant'Anna di Pisa.

[1] On the relationship between the composition of judicial organs and the "constitutional" design of a given legal system, see SHAPIRO, *Courts: A Comparative Political Analysis*, Chicago, 1981; ALTER, "Agents or Trustees? International Courts in their Political Context", European Journal of International Relations, 2008, p. 34 ff., pp. 45-48. With focus on the

IYIL, Vol. 30 (2020), pp. 239-264
ISSN 0391-5107

disqualifications for sitting on the court or tribunal, as well as the procedures and bodies governing nomination, appointment or election to the court or tribunal. The rules governing composition vary significantly, both at the national and international level.[2] In the case of international judicial bodies, aspects such as geographical balance and representation of different legal traditions play a fundamental role in delineating the institutional profile of the court or tribunal under consideration.[3] States have traditionally retained a degree of political control – variable in relation to distinct international dispute settlement mechanisms – over the procedures leading to the nomination and election of members of the international judiciary.[4] This tendency can be traced back to the creation of the Permanent Court of International Justice (PCIJ) and of its successor, the International Court of Justice (ICJ).[5] The discussion on the composition of international judicial organs and the profile of judges grew in parallel with the proliferation of dispute settlement bodies and of international(ized) criminal jurisdictions.[6] Against this background, the case of international(ized) criminal jurisdictions poses additional issues, given the peculiarity of criminal proceedings and the pronounced divergences among legal traditions in the administration of criminal justice.[7]

In the case of the ad hoc Tribunals for the Former Yugoslavia and Rwanda (ICTY and ICTR), relatively little discussion was carried out in relation to the composition of the judicial and prosecutorial bodies, and no elaborate supervision

---

International Court of Justice, see LAUTERPACHT, *Aspects of the Administration of International Justice*, Cambridge, 1991, p. 77 ff.

[2] For a comparative analysis of different models of appointment, see MALLESON and RUSSELL, *Appointing Judges in an Age of Judicial Power: Critical Perspectives from Around the World*, Toronto, 2006. For a comparison between the International Court of Justice and the ICC, see MACKENZIE et al., *Selecting International Judges: Principle, Process, and Politics*, Oxford-New York, 2010.

[3] On this matter, see BERMAN, *Global Legal Pluralism: A Jurisprudence of Law Beyond Borders*, New York, 2012, pp. 171-174. Balanced geographic representation is invariably stipulated in the statutes of international tribunals. See, e.g., Art. 9 of the Statute of the International Court of Justice; Art. 2(2) of the Statute of the International Tribunal for the Law of the Sea; Art. 17(3) of the Dispute Settlement Understanding on the composition of the WTO's Appellate Body; Art. 36(8)(a)(i)-(ii) of the Statute of the International Criminal Court.

[4] On the motivations behind States' decisions on the nomination and election of international judges, see VOETEN, "The Politics of International Judicial Appointments", Chicago Journal of International Law, 2009, p. 387 ff., pp. 390-391.

[5] On the enduring influence of the flexible model of appointment of the PCIJ and ICJ, see MACKENZIE et al., *cit. supra* note 2, pp. 10-19.

[6] On the proliferation of international dispute settlement mechanisms, see HIGGINS, "A Babel of Judicial Voices? Ruminations from the Bench", ICLQ, 2006, p. 791 ff. More specifically on international(ized) criminal jurisdictions, see POCAR, "The Proliferation of International Criminal Courts and Tribunals", JICJ, 2004, p. 304 ff.

[7] On the peculiarity of international criminal courts and tribunals, see VON BOGDANDY and VENZKE, "On the Functions of International Courts: An Appraisal in Light of their Burgeoning Public Authority", Leiden JIL, 2013, p. 49 ff, pp. 54 and 67. With regard to the character of the ICC's jurisdiction and its impact on the choice of judges, see MACKENZIE et al., *cit. supra* note 2, p. 51.

over the appointing mechanism was established.[8] To the contrary, in designing the Statute of the International Criminal Court, the issue of the nomination and election of judges and of the Prosecutor was a highly debated topic both at the preparatory stage and at the Rome Conference.[9] Subsequent practice of the ASP in the interpretation and application of the pertinent treaty provisions contributed to shaping the judicial profile of the institution as we see it today.[10] Said practice, as well as the changes that have occurred over time and their institutional outcomes, shall be analyzed in the following paragraphs with a view to critically reflecting on the relations between the nomination and electoral processes and the legitimacy of the Court. On this basis, the article concludes by putting forward proposals to strengthen the transparency and effectiveness of these processes as a way to reinforce the credibility of the institution.

2. THE NORMATIVE FRAMEWORK FOR THE ELECTION OF JUDGES AND THE PROSECUTOR

The provisions of the Rome Statute concerning the election of judges and of the Prosecutor are the result of a delicate balance between, on the one hand, the need to ensure that nominees possess the necessary qualifications and experience for the job and, on the other hand, States' desire to maintain some degree of (political) control over the process in order to shape the criminal policy goals of the Court.[11]

The rules governing qualifications, nomination and election for judgeship at the Court are mostly found in Article 36 of the Statute, and can be summarized as follows:

---

[8] See Arts. 13 *bis* and *ter* of the ICTY Statute, attached to UN Doc. S/Res/827 (1993) with subsequent amendments, and Arts. 12 *bis* and *ter* of the ICTR Statute, attached to UN Doc. S/Res/955 (1994) with subsequent amendments. Analysis of the verbatim records does not reveal a special attention to the composition of the tribunals, with limited exceptions. See UN Doc. S/PV.3217, pp. 18 and 21 (particularly the position of the UK and Hungary on the necessary criminal law experience of judges); UN Doc. S/PV.3453, pp. 6 (on the position of the UK, analogous to that expressed for the ICTY), 8 (where Argentina suggests that most judges be appointed from "continental legal systems"), and 15 (where Rwanda deems "the composition and structure of the International Tribunal for Rwanda inappropriate and ineffective").

[9] On the position of States, see BOHLANDER, "Pride and Prejudice or Sense and Sensibility? A Pragmatic Proposal for the Recruitment of Judges at the ICC and Other International Criminal Courts", New Criminal Law Review, 2009, p. 529 ff., pp. 533-534; ID., "Article 36 – Qualifications, Nomination and Election of Judges", in TRIFFTERER and AMBOS (eds.), *The Rome Statute of the International Criminal Court: A Commentary*, 3rd ed., Munich/Oxford/Baden-Baden, 2016, p. 1216 ff., pp. 1219-1223. See also INGADOTTIR, "Election of Judges", Max Planck Encyclopedia of International Procedural Law, 2019, available at: <http://www.mpi.lu/mpeipro/>.

[10] Such practice must be taken into account in interpreting the rules laid down by Art. 36 of the Statute, as mandated by Art. 31(3)(b) of the Vienna Convention on the Law of Treaties, 23 May 1969, entered into force 27 January 1980.

[11] See *supra* note 9 for works that have analyzed the preparatory and negotiating phase in this regard.

a) Pre-requisites. Nominees must be "persons of high moral character, impartiality and integrity".[12]

b) Linguistic abilities. Excellent knowledge and fluency in at least one of the working languages of the Court (English or French) are required.[13]

c) Professional competences and qualifications. Candidates must "possess the qualifications in their respective States for the appointment to the highest judicial offices";[14] moreover, they must have either "established competence in criminal law or procedure, and the necessary relevant experience, whether as a judge, prosecutor, advocate or in other similar capacity, in criminal proceedings" (List A);[15] or "have established competence in relevant areas of international law such as international humanitarian law and the law of human rights, and extensive experience in a professional legal capacity which is of relevance to the judicial work of the Court" (List B).[16]

d) Gender balance. The composition of the Court must give a "fair representation" of female and male judges, without fixed quotas.[17]

e) Equitable geographic representation and in respect of the different legal systems of the world.[18]

f) Expertise on specific issues, such as gender violence and crimes against children.[19]

While some of these rules resemble those established for other international judicial organs – in primis the ICJ – others reveal the significantly more recent institution of the Court and its special character as a permanent international criminal jurisdiction (as opposed to a mechanism for the solution of inter-State disputes).[20] In particular, the provision on gender balance and the reference to specific professional experience and competences set the ICC apart from other international courts and tribunals.[21] The provision on the two lists of candidates

---

[12] Rome Statute of the International Criminal Court, 17 July 1998, entered into force on 1 July 2002, Art. 36(3)(a) (hereinafter Statute or ICC Statute).

[13] *Ibid.*, Art. 36(3)(c).

[14] *Ibid.*, Art. 36(3)(a).

[15] *Ibid.*, Art. 36(3)(b)(i).

[16] *Ibid.*, Art. 36(3)(b)(ii). It should be noted that, pursuant to para. 5 of the same article, at the first election, at least nine judges shall be elected from List A and five from List B. Subsequent elections must be organized in order to maintain the equivalent proportion of candidates from the two lists.

[17] *Ibid.*, Art. 36(8)(a)(iii).

[18] *Ibid.*, Art. 36(8)(a)(i)-(ii).

[19] *Ibid.*, Art. 36(8)(b).

[20] On the continuities and discontinuities between the rules on composition of the PCIJ/ICJ and the ICC, see MACKENZIE et al., *cit. supra* note 2, pp. 22-23.

[21] On gender balance in international courts, see VAUCHEZ, "Gender Balance in International Adjudicatory Bodies", Max Planck Encyclopedia of International Procedural Law, 2019, available at: <http://www.mpi.lu/mpeipro/>. With emphasis on the link between gender representation and legitimacy, see GROSSMAN, "Sex Representation on the Bench and the Legitimacy of International Criminal Courts", International Criminal Law Review, 2011, p. 643 ff., p. 652. Besides the ICC, only the African Court on Human and Peoples' Rights requires balanced gender representation. See Arts. 5(2) and 7(5) of the Protocol to the African

is evidence of the drafters' attempt to strike a balance between the differing views of States on the most appropriate composition of the Court.[22]

Given the conceptual and practical distinctions between the nomination and election processes,[23] attention must also be paid to the mechanisms leading to the selection and nomination of the candidates by States. The Rome Statute offers two different avenues in order to select potential nominees. The first is inherited from the PCIJ and ICJ Statutes, consisting in the nomination of candidates by the national groups of the Permanent Court of Arbitration (PCA).[24] The second allows States to follow the domestic procedures for nominating candidates for "appointment to the highest judicial offices in the State in question".[25] Both possibilities are associated with disparate national practices, given the extreme variability in the composition and functioning of PCA national groups (and their relations with, and independence from, governments),[26] and also across national procedures for appointment to the highest judicial posts (ranging from purely political appointment to more transparent and competence-based procedures).[27] Information on practice in this regard can be derived from the statements that States are required to submit in support of nominations, pursuant to Article 36(4)(a) of the Statute. In more recent elections, some States have provided additional information on their own national nomination procedures, pursuant to a non-binding recommendation of the ASP.[28]

Charter on Human And Peoples' Rights on the Establishment of an African Court on Human and Peoples' Rights, 10 June 1988, entered into force 25 January 2004.

[22] According to MACKENZIE et al., *cit. supra* note 2, p. 50, quoting HUDSON, *The Permanent Court of International Justice, 1920-1942: A Treatise*, New York, 1943, para. 138, the inclusion of two main pools of candidates, namely national judges and academics or international law experts, can be explained by the necessity to "accommodate a common law preference for international judges with national judicial experience and a civil law preference for non-judges". See, *ibid.*, pp. 54-60 with regard to the ICC, with reference to the views of judges, diplomats and legal advisers who participated in the negotiations.

[23] These two crucial moments need to be distinguished, in light of the predominantly national component of nomination procedures, and of the differing level of politicization at the two stages.

[24] Art. 36(4)(a)(ii) ICC Statute refers to "the procedure provided for the nomination of candidates for the International Court of Justice in the Statute of that Court", which is established by Art. 4 of the ICJ Statute.

[25] Art. 36(4)(a)(i) ICC Statute.

[26] On PCA national groups, see JORRITSMA, "National Groups: Permanent Court of Arbitration (PCA)", Max Planck Encyclopedia of International Procedural Law, 2019, available at: <http://www.mpi.lu/mpeipro/>; MCWHINNEY, "Law, Politics and 'Regionalism' in the Nomination and Election of World Court Judges", Syracuse Journal of International Law and Commerce, 1986, p. 1 ff; GEORGET, "Article 4", in ZIMMERMAN et al. (eds.), *The Statute of the International Court of Justice. A Commentary*, 3rd ed., Oxford, 2019, p. 314 ff. On "informal" nomination procedures through the PCA groups, see MACKENZIE et al., *cit. supra* note 2, pp. 86-87.

[27] For a comparative analysis of nomination procedures to, for instance, constitutional courts, see HARDING, LEYLAND and GROPPI, "Constitutional Courts: Forms, Functions and Practice in Comparative Perspective", Journal of Comparative Law, 2008, p. 1 ff., pp. 11-15.

[28] The recommendation was formulated in the Report of the Advisory Committee on Nominations of Judges on the work of its third meeting, ICC-ASP/13/22, Annex II, Appendix

Based on these rules and on the experience of other long-standing international courts and tribunals, it should not come as a surprise that the quality and professional profile of candidates at the ICC have varied greatly, particularly along lines of geography and legal tradition.[29]

With regard to the Court's Prosecutor (and Deputy Prosecutors), the Statute strives to establish guarantees of independence akin to those of judges, while at the same time recognizing the "party but not partisan" nature of the prosecution in international criminal proceedings.[30] This independence is reflected in the Prosecutor having the sole authority over the administration of the Office.[31] In other words, the Prosecutor is treated as an integral part of the international judiciary in the broad sense, despite his or her primary responsibility to carry out investigations and bring charges.[32] The rules governing the qualifications, nomination and election of the Prosecutor that are spelled out in Article 42 of the Statute are comparatively more detailed than those found in the Statutes of ad hoc tribunals.[33] This clearly shows the drafters' awareness that the Office of the Prosecutor plays a crucial role in the everyday functioning of the Court and contributes to shaping the Court's profile as a judicial institution in the eyes of States Parties and the international community at large.[34]

The rules for the nomination and election of judges and prosecutors at the ICC are more detailed than those provided for other international courts and tribunals, showing an attempt to mitigate the element of unchecked political bargaining that has been historically endemic in the election practice of other international judicial institutions.[35] In this sense, the Statute also provides for the ASP's power

---

III, 29 September 2014. The ASP further encouraged States to provide such information in its Resolution on the review of the procedure for the nomination and election of judges, ICC-ASP/18/Res.4, 6 December 2019, para. 6. The full list of States that have provided information on national nomination procedures is available at: <https://asp.icc-cpi.int/en_menus/asp/ACN/Pages/2020-National-Procedures.aspx>.

[29] For instance, some States have historically preferred to nominate national judges, while others have preferred academics, diplomats with legal background, former legal advisers to international organizations (mainly at Permanent Missions to the UN), or members of the International Law Commission. See *supra* note 22.

[30] This formula was eloquently expressed in the Separate Opinion of Judge Shahabuddeen, Appeals Chamber, *Prosecutor v. Barayagwiza*, Case No. ICTR-97-19-AR72, Decision of 31 March 2000, para. 68.

[31] Art. 42(2) ICC Statute, referring to the Prosecutor's "full authority over the management and administration of the Office".

[32] *Ibid.*, Art. 42(1), which clearly stipulates that the Prosecutor "shall act independently as a separate organ of the Court", while Art. 54(1)(a) establishes that with a view to assisting the Court in the establishment of the truth, he or she shall "investigate incriminating and exonerating circumstances equally".

[33] Compare Art. 42 of the ICC Statute with Art. 16 of the ICTY Statute and Art. 15 of the ICTR Statute.

[34] CÔTÉ, "Independence and Impartiality", in REYDAMS, WOUTERS and RYNGAERT (eds.), *International Prosecutors*, Oxford, 2012, p. 319 ff, p. 321.

[35] MACKENZIE et al., *cit. supra* note 2, pp. 19, 23, 51, 61 and 65-66, 101. On the prevalence of vote trading, see also ULFSTEIN, "The International Judiciary", in KLABBERS, PETERS and ULFSTEIN (eds.), *The Constitutionalization of International Law*, New York, 2009, p. 126 ff.,

to establish – "if appropriate" – an Advisory Committee on Nominations, to help the Assembly in the assessment of the nominees for judgeship. This subsidiary body was created in 2011.[36]

Pervasive politicization – at least in its more derogatory and arbitrary aspects – was evidently deemed incompatible with the peculiar function of a criminal court, and certainly detrimental to its legitimacy. In any event, the degree to which these rules have succeeded in shielding the institution from an excessive politicization of judicial nominations can only be assessed in light of the actual practice of States and the ASP, to which the following paragraphs are devoted.

3. THE EARLY PRACTICE OF THE ASP: THE INTERNATIONAL LEGAL AND DIPLOMATIC "OFFICIALDOM" FROM ROME TO THE HAGUE

When the first roster of judges was nominated and elected in 2003, the process was based on voting requirements established by the ASP through a resolution adopted by consensus ahead of the election.[37] This resolution established the so-called minimum voting requirement (MVR). Under the MVR, in order for a State's ballot to be valid, it must vote for at least nine candidates from List A and five candidates from List B, and at least three candidates from each of the five regional groups.[38] Moreover, each State must vote for at least six candidates of each gender.[39] Some of the MVR rules (namely those on gender and geographic representation) can be discontinued after a certain number of rounds.[40] Based on these criteria, of the first 18 judges, ten were elected under List A and eight under List B, 11 being males and seven being females.[41] The MVR rules were later

---

pp. 129-130; TERRIS, ROMANO and SWIGART, *The International Judge. An Introduction to the Men and Women who Decide the World's Cases*, Oxford-New York-Hanover, 2007, pp. 15-16.

[36] See Art. 36(4)(c) ICC Statute for the legal basis of such power. On the establishment of the Advisory Committee, see Report of the Bureau on the establishment of an Advisory Committee on the appointment of judges of the International Criminal Court, ICC-ASP/10/36, 30 November 2011 and, for the adoption of the recommendation, Strengthening the International Criminal Court and the Assembly of States Parties, ICC-ASP/10/Res.5, 30 November 2011, para. 19.

[37] Procedure for the election of the judges for the International Criminal Court, ICC-ASP/1/Res.3, 9 September 2002.

[38] *Ibid.*, para. 3(a)-(b).

[39] *Ibid.*, para. 3(c).

[40] *Ibid.*, paras. 4-7.

[41] The current composition is of 11 judges from List A and seven from List B, with nine women and nine men. This is a significant achievement in terms of gender balance, especially compared to other international courts and tribunals. For instance, in the 75 years of activity of the ICJ, only four women have served as judges. Nevertheless, MVR relating to gender can be discontinued if after four ballots it has not been possible to fill all vacant seats. See Procedure for the nomination and election of judges, the Prosecutor and Deputy prosecutors of the International Criminal Court (Consolidated version), ICC-ASP/3/Res.6, 10 September 2004, para. 21.

modified by the ASP in order to maintain the correct proportions according to the statutory criteria and solve additional electoral issues.[42]

Some judges – mainly nominated under List B – were experts and diplomats who had actively participated (sometimes with high-level roles) in the negotiations at the Rome Conference.[43] This choice, probably motivated by States' desire to elect judges already familiar with the Statute and its negotiating history, has since been criticized, in particular in relation to judges with more of a diplomatic than a legal background.[44] At the same time, the initial, almost equal, representation of judges from List A and List B has been identified by some commentators as one of the reasons for the lack of a shared judicial culture, especially in the Court's early jurisprudence.[45] In any event, candidates with a more diplomatic profile have continued to be chosen in recent elections.[46] Another trend, which was especially pronounced in the first elections, relates to the nomination by States and election by the ASP of former or sitting judges of ad hoc or other international(ized) criminal tribunals.[47] Some of these candidates were nominated under List A despite not being judges or prosecutors with criminal law experience in their domestic legal system, under the assumption that previous experience at international criminal tribunals satisfied the requirements for inclusion in that list.[48] In any event, in more recent elections the balance between candidates

---

[42] *Ibid.*, part B.

[43] For instance, the names of future judges Politi, Slade, Kaul, Kirsch, and Kourula can be found in the list of States' delegations at the Rome Conference. Other participants in the Rome negotiations have been elected judges in subsequent elections. This is the case of judges Fernández de Gurmendi, Pangalangan, Perrin de Brichambaut, Prost, and Lordkipanidze. See United Nations Diplomatic Conference of Plenipotentiaries on the Establishment of an International Criminal Court, Official Records, UN Doc. A/CONF.183/13 (Vol. II), p. 5 ff.

[44] In this sense, see MACKENZIE et al., *cit. supra* note 2, pp. 58 and 81-82. For a critique of the inclusion of former diplomats, see Open Society Justice Initiative, "Raising the Bar: Improving the Nomination and Election of Judges to the International Criminal Court", 2019, available at: <https://www.justiceinitiative.org/uploads/7627a69c-dc69-43da-a58c-c66162f1c2b0/raising-the-bar-20191028.pdf>, pp. 4, 21-22 and 35. In this sense, see also, BOHLANDER, *cit. supra* note 9, pp. 534-537. For a more nuanced position on List B judges, see GUILFOYLE, "Of Babies, Bathwater, and List B Judges at the International Criminal Court", EJIL: Talk!, 13 November 2019, available at: <https://www.ejiltalk.org/of-babies-bathwater-and-list-b-judges-at-the-international-criminal-court/>.

[45] *Ibid.* See also *infra* Section 7 for further discussion on List B.

[46] At the last election, three out of six judges were chosen from List B candidates. A number of currently sitting judges have a distinctively more diplomatic than legal background.

[47] For the personal profiles of judges, see the ICC website at: <https://www.icc-cpi.int/former-judges> and <https://www.icc-cpi.int/about/judicial-divisions/biographies/Pages/current-judges.aspx>. The following ICC judges had previously held positions as judge or *ad litem* judge at ad hoc or other tribunals: Van den Wyngaert, Politi, Clark, Jorda, Pillay, Odio Benito, Diarra, Morrison, Mindua, Chung, Bossa, Prost. Among the judges elected in late 2020, Korner (United Kingdom) has been senior trial attorney at the ICTY, while Samba (Sierra Leone) has been judge at the Residual Special Court for Sierra Leone.

[48] The Statute makes no distinction between professional experience in criminal law and procedure at the national or international level, but the practice of the ASP and advisory bodies has attached significant weight to previous international experience.

of List A and List B has at times shifted in favour of the former.[49] As far as geographic representation is concerned, results have been influenced by the contingent majorities at the ASP, considering that nomination and election of judges at the ICC is part of a larger picture of electoral balances, which includes other judicial posts in international courts and tribunals, or high-profile legal roles in UN bodies.[50] It should be noted that a few States have been able so far to secure the uninterrupted presence of one of their nationals in the post of ICC judge.[51]

The practice relating to the election of the Prosecutor, despite some similarities with that of judges,[52] has followed a significantly different path in light of, amongst other factors, the majorities required for election and the monocratic character of this post.[53] More specifically, a trend has developed of identifying a consensus candidate following informal consultations among the States Parties, in order to avoid a potentially divisive vote at the ASP.[54] Such consensus was reached in the case of the election of the first Prosecutor, the Argentinian Moreno-Ocampo,[55] and of his successor, Bensouda of The Gambia, who had previously held the position of Deputy Prosecutor under the tenure of Moreno-Ocampo.[56] Despite the behind-closed-doors character of the consultations that

---

[49] Before the last election, the balance between List A and B judges was 13-5. After the 2020 election, the proportion reverted back to 11-7.

[50] See MACKENZIE et al., *cit. supra* note 2, p. 77, on the relations between elections to different international judicial posts and the "winnability" of an election.

[51] These are France, Germany, Italy, the Republic of Korea, and the United Kingdom. Other States, such as Japan, Canada, Uganda, and Trinidad and Tobago have had two or more nationals at the Court.

[52] See Res. ICC-ASP/3/Res.6, *cit. supra* note 41, parts D and E. Paras. 28-29 establish that the procedure for the nomination of judges shall apply *mutatis mutandis* to the nomination of the Prosecutor, but that the nomination should preferably be made with the support of multiple States.

[53] Art. 42(4) ICC Statute establishes that an absolute majority at the ASP is required for the election of the Prosecutor (and Deputy Prosecutors, who are elected from a list of candidates provided by the Prosecutor). Considerations of geographic representation are certainly not irrelevant in the process and have influenced the consultations leading to a consensus in the election of the first two prosecutors. Alternance between prosecutors from different geographical groups has so far been respected.

[54] See Res. ICC-ASP/3/Res.6, *cit. supra* note 41, para. 33 establishing that "[e]very effort shall be made to elect the Prosecutor by consensus". Only failing such consensus, shall the election take place by secret ballot following the rules of Art. 42(4) of the Statute.

[55] See Election of the Prosecutor of the International Criminal Court, Addendum to Note of the Secretariat, ICC-ASP/1/6/Add.1, 8 April 2003, para. 3 and Proceedings of the first session, ICC-ASP/1/3/Add.1, para. 35.

[56] In the case of the election of Fatou Bensouda, four candidates had been officially nominated by the respective Governments, with the consensus that the Prosecutor should be African. Bensouda's nomination was co-sponsored by 66 States and emerged as the only one after consultations. See Report of the Search Committee for the Position of the Prosecutor of the International Criminal Court, 22 October 2011; Consultations to identify the next Prosecutor of the International Criminal Court, Statement by the President of the Assembly, 1 December 2011; Election of the Prosecutor of the International Criminal Court, Note by the Secretariat, ICC-ASP/10/38, 9 December 2011, para. 10-11 and the Annex for the list of countries supporting Bensouda.

led to the elections of both Prosecutors, it should be noted that the 2011 election of Bensouda was carried out in a more structured and transparent way, in particular thanks to the facilitating role played by the Searching Committee specifically instituted for the task.[57] Nevertheless, these advances fell short of a truly open, competitive, and transparent selection process, with limited public scrutiny of the candidates for one of the most delicate jobs at the Court.

In sociological terms, from the analysis of the nomination and election practice, it emerges that a good percentage of the candidates for judicial and prosecutorial posts at the ICC have been individuals from the "(in)visible college"[58] of international (criminal) lawyers, either with previous experience at ad hoc tribunals or in advising roles for governments in prominent international settings, a select group of people constituting the kind of "legal officialdom" that contributes to shaping the action of international judicial institutions.[59]

4. PROCEDURAL REFORMS. "ACT ONE": THE ADVISORY COMMITTEE ON THE NOMINATION OF JUDGES AND ITS INFLUENCE ON RECENT ELECTIONS

The external perception of the procedures leading to the nomination and election of judges and prosecutors at the ICC has been that of an opaque and politicized process, potentially to the detriment of the quality, credibility and legitimacy of the institution.[60] The practice of States and of the ASP has come under substantial scrutiny by scholars, practitioners, and international civil society at large, and all of these actors have proposed changes to the system.[61] This

---

[57] *Ibid.*, paras. 6-8.

[58] The debate on the concept of the "college" of international lawyers was started by TOMUSCHAT, "The Invisible College of International Lawyers", North Western University Law Review, 1977, p. 217 ff. Anthea Roberts has called into question this concept and has spoken in a recent book of a "divisible college of international lawyers", see ROBERTS, *Is International Law International?*, New York, 2017, p. 1 ff. On the role of legal advisers as a "visible college of international lawyers", see ZIDAR and GAUCI, "Introduction: Legal Advisers as the Visible College of International Lawyers", in ZIDAR and GAUCI (eds.), *The Role of Legal Advisers in International Law*, Leiden, 2017, p. 1 ff. More specifically, on international criminal lawyers, see KRESS, "Towards a Truly Universal Invisible College of International Criminal Lawyers", TOAEP Occasional Paper Series, 2014, p. 1 ff. and CHRISTENSEN, "The Creation of an Ad Hoc Elite and the Value of International Criminal Law Expertise on a Global Market", in HELLER at al. (eds.), *The Oxford Handbook of International Criminal Law*, New York, 2020, p. 89 ff., pp. 95-101.

[59] BURCHARD, "The International Criminal Legal Process: Towards a Realistic Model of International Criminal Law in Action", in STAHN and VAN DEN HERIK (eds.), *Future Perspectives on International Criminal Justice*, Den Haag, 2010, p. 81 ff., pp. 81-87.

[60] See Open Society Initiative's Report, *cit. supra* note 44; MACKENZIE et al., *cit. supra* note 2, pp. 128 and 175; VON BOGDANDY and VENZKE, *In Whose Name?: A Public Law Theory of International Adjudication*, New York, 2014, pp. 163-170.

[61] For critiques from civil society organizations, see Open Society Initiative's Report, *cit. supra* note 44; Coalition for the International Criminal Court, "20 Candidates Under Full Scrutiny: ICC Judges Must Be Elected on Merit Alone", available at: <https://www.fidh.org/en/issues/international-justice/international-criminal-court-icc/20-candidates-under-full-scru-

has prompted procedural reforms, mainly enacted through the self-regulatory and administrative powers of the ASP and its Bureau, aimed at creating a more structured, open and transparent assessment of the candidates.

With regard to the election of judges, it was only in 2011 that the ASP decided to establish the Advisory Committee on Nomination of Judges (ACN).[62] The institution of this consultative body was welcomed by civil society and international organizations supportive of the work of the Court.[63]

According to its Terms of Reference (TOR), the role of the Advisory Committee – which has included over the years former judges of the ICC and of other international tribunals[64] – is to "to facilitate that the highest-qualified individuals are appointed as judges of the International Criminal Court".[65] To this effect, the Committee has developed useful tools to standardize the assessment process, including a model curriculum vitae and a standard questionnaire in which candidates must demonstrate, *inter alia*, their experience and qualifications, the possession of linguistic requirements, and their track record of impartiality and integrity. In addition, the Committee has developed a practice of face-to-face interviews with the candidates in order to better assess their qualifications. The most recent version of the TOR, which was applied for the first time in 2020, extends the supervisory powers of the ACN over the vetting of candidates to checks on references and publicly available information, and introduces a "declaration for all candidates to sign that clarifies whether they are aware of any allegations of misconduct, including sexual harassment, made against them".[66]

This process results in a final report submitted to the Bureau and then circulated to States Parties ahead of the election.[67] The reporting practice of the Committee evolved from the concise style of the first report, issued in 2013, to a more detailed one in recent reports.[68] More specifically, in 2017, the ACN began

---

tiny-icc-judges-must-be-elected-on-merit>; Human Rights Watch, "Nomination of Candidates for the 2009 ICC Judicial Election: Letter to Foreign Affairs Ministers of ICC States Parties", available at: <http://www.hrw.org/en/news/2008/08/19/nomination-candidates-2009-icc-judicial-election>.

[62] See *supra* note 36.

[63] See, e.g., Amnesty International, "Recommendations to the Assembly of States Parties at its Tenth Session", December 2011, available at: <https://www.amnesty.org/download/Documents/32000/ior530092011en.pdf>, p. 6; European Parliament, Resolution of 17 November 2011 on EU support for the ICC: facing challenges and overcoming difficulties, P7_TA(2011)0507, para. 53.

[64] Currently, the ACN includes four former ICC judges, namely Cotte, Fulford, Monageng, and Sang-Hyun Song. In the past, other former ICC judges and one ICJ judge have been members (Kirsch, Nsereko, and Simma).

[65] See para. 5 of the Terms of Reference for the establishment of an Advisory Committee on nominations of judges of the International Criminal Court, ICC-ASP/10/36 – Annex, adopted by the Assembly by resolution ICC-ASP/10/Res.5, and amended by resolutions ICC-ASP/13/Res.5, Annex III and ICC-ASP/18/Res.4, Annex II.

[66] *Ibid.*, para. 5 *bis*(c)-(d).

[67] *Ibid.*, letter (g) and para. 10 *bis*.

[68] See Report of the Advisory Committee on Nominations of Judges on the work of its second meeting, ICC-ASP/12/47 – Annex I, 29 October 2013. The same, not very detailed, style was maintained also for the 2014 and 2015 reports.

the practice of issuing a global evaluation of each candidate, a sort of grading of the nominees, distinguishing between candidates (only) "formally qualified for appointment" and those "particularly well qualified for appointment".[69] In the 2020 report, the ACN established four possible grades, namely "not qualified", "only formally qualified", "qualified", and "highly qualified".[70] Despite the ACN's efforts to make this evaluation more in-depth, it is not always easy to understand why specific candidates receive a certain grading compared to others, and what aspects carry the most weight in the Committee's assessment.[71]

The screening process for the elections that took place in late 2020 posed additional challenges in connection with the COVID-19 pandemic, making it necessary for the ACN to adjust its working methods and to hold virtual interviews with the nominees, which were conducted by three-member sub-committees and recorded in order to allow the individual assessment of candidates by all members of the Committee.[72] Of the 20 candidates in the 2020 elections, none were considered not qualified, seven were considered only formally qualified, three qualified and ten highly qualified.[73]

Despite the positive developments in terms of transparency and the increased public scrutiny allowed by the activity of the ACN, it should be stressed that the assessment of the Committee is certainly not binding upon States, which remain free to decide who to vote for in the election at the ASP, irrespective of the grading of the candidates. This is clearly demonstrated by the fact that in 2017 the ASP elected two nominees judged only "formally qualified",[74] and in 2020 a nominee judged "qualified", notwithstanding the fact that another candidate from the same geographic group had received a better assessment.[75] At the last

---

[69] Report of the Advisory Committee on Nominations of Judges on the work of its sixth meeting, ICC-ASP/16/7 – Annex I, 10 October 2017.

[70] Report of the Advisory Committee on Nominations of Judges on the work of its seventh meeting, ICC-ASP/19/11, 30 September 2020, para. 32.

[71] On these inconsistencies, see the analysis by OWISO and NAKANDHA, "'Grading' the Nominees for the International Criminal Court Judges Election 2021-2030: The Report of the Advisory Committee on Nomination of Judges – Part I", Opinio Juris, 9 October 2020, available at: <http://opiniojuris.org/2020/10/09/grading-the-nominees-for-the-international-criminal-court-judges-election-2021-2030-the-report-of-the-advisory-committee-on-nomination-of-judges-part-i/>; ID., "'Grading' the Nominees for the International Criminal Court Judges Election 2021-2030: The Report of the Advisory Committee on Nomination of Judges – Part II", Opinio Juris, 9 October 2020, available at: <http://opiniojuris.org/2020/10/09/grading-the-nominees-for-the-international-criminal-court-judges-election-2021-2030-the-report-of-the-advisory-committee-on-nomination-of-judges-part-ii/>.

[72] ACN Report 2020, cit. supra note 70, paras. 5-12.

[73] Ibid., Annex II, pp. 11-24. The committee was unable to make a final determination with regard to Mr Milandou (Democratic Republic of the Congo) and Mr Chagdaa (Mongolia), respectively in relation to the possession of the requirements for being appointed to the highest judicial offices, and proficiency in the working languages of the Court. The ACN could have probably concluded with a "not qualified" assessment in these two cases.

[74] These are judge Aitala (Italy) and judge Alapini-Gansou (Benin).

[75] This is the case of judge Lordkipanidze (Georgia), who was preferred over Ćosić Dedović (Bosnia and Herzegovina), despite the latter's "highly qualified" assessment. See ACN Report 2020, cit. supra note 70, pp. 12-13 and 22.

election, roughly one third of the nominees were found only formally qualified, with the Committee seriously questioning in some cases the adequacy of their qualifications, a sign that the current screening procedure is not necessarily pushing States to nominate the best possible candidates.[76]

5. Procedural Reforms. "Act Two": The Committee on the Election of the Prosecutor, the New Vetting Process and the Lack of a Consensus Candidate

The 19th session of the ASP was also tasked with the election of the ICC's third Prosecutor, in light of the approaching expiration of Bensouda's term. Well ahead of the session, the process leading to the nomination of candidates was set in motion with the adoption of the Terms of Reference for the election.[77] This document is a step forward in the direction of transparency, in that it envisages the creation of two subsidiary bodies tasked with facilitating the election of the Prosecutor. These are the Committee on the Election of the Prosecutor (CEP) – composed of five members designated by the Bureau to represent each regional group – and a Panel of five independent experts (one per regional group, but of different nationalities to the CEP's members) to assist the Committee in the assessment of applications, with a view to forming a longlist of candidates for subsequent competence-based interviews.[78] Based on the results of this screening process, the CEP is then to form an unranked shortlist of three to six of the most highly qualified candidates, to be submitted to the ASP for consideration with a view to reaching a consensus.[79] It should be noted that the determinations of the CEP and Panel of experts are not binding upon States.[80]

After the two bodies were formed, the vacancy announcement for the position was issued and applications started to be received and filtered.[81] Out of the over 140 applications received, the CEP formed a longlist of 14 potential candidates, who were then subjected to a full vetting process leading to the formation of a shortlist of four candidates, namely Morris A. Anyah (Nigeria), Fergal Gaynor (Ireland), Susan Okalany (Uganda) and Richard Roy (Canada).

---

[76] See *supra* note 73.

[77] Bureau of the Assembly of States Parties: Election of the Prosecutor – Terms of Reference, ICC-ASP/18/INF.2, 11 April 2019.

[78] *Ibid.*, paras. 4-21 on composition, mandate, and working methods.

[79] *Ibid.*, paras. 15-16.

[80] In this sense, see HELLER, "Why States are Free to Nominate New Candidates for Prosecutor", Opinio Juris, 19 July 2020, available at: <http://opiniojuris.org/2020/07/19/why-states-are-free-to-reject-the-candidates-for-prosecutor/>. A document circulated by the Secretariat of the ASP, Election of the Prosecutor: Background Note, 6 July 2020, clarifies that "[t]he CEP and subsequent consultation process is *supplementary* to the formal procedure set out in the nomination resolution. Any State Party is entitled to submit a nomination during the formal nomination period" (emphasis added).

[81] Report of the Committee on the Election of the Prosecutor, Addendum, Vacancy Announcement, ICC-ASP/19/INF.2/Add.1, 30 June 2020.

It must be emphasized that despite the call for transparency in the Terms of Reference, the CEP decided not to disclose the identities of all of the applicants, including the 14 longlisted ones.[82] Moreover, it decided *proprio motu* to establish a confidential full-fledged vetting process on the longlisted candidates in addition to interviews.[83] The vetting process included "detailed reference checks, checks of publicly sourced information (including candidates' own social media accounts), and security and criminal record checks".[84] This procedure was expressly consented to by all 14 longlisted candidates, a clear indication that the original TOR would not have provided sufficient legal basis for such a process.[85] The shortlisted candidates subsequently underwent a session of public (and recorded) hearings in which States Parties and civil society organizations participated.[86] The consultation process was then opened by the ASP's President with a view to finding a consensus Prosecutor.

Soon after the adoption of the CEP's final report and before the hearings, some States Parties expressed their dissatisfaction with the shortlist (or with particular candidates), thus putting the consultation process on a slippery slope from the start.[87] In particular, Kenya openly rejected the list, allegedly due to the role of two of the candidates in representing victims of post-electoral violence that was formerly the subject of an investigation by the ICC's Prosecutor.[88] In light of the unlikely possibility of reaching a consensus – and despite the calls from civil society to stick to the four shortlisted candidates[89] – the Bureau decided in November 2020 to expand the list of nominees, allowing other longlisted candi-

---

[82] Report of the Committee on the Election of the Prosecutor, ICC-ASP/19/INF.2, 30 June 2020, paras. 19-23. Originally, there were 16 longlisted candidates, but later on two withdrew their candidature.

[83] *Ibid.*, paras. 27-32. The CEP admitted that the establishment of such a vetting process *ex post facto* was not the ideal course of action, and recommended that in future elections such process should be set up from the beginning.

[84] *Ibid.*, para. 29.

[85] See HELLER, *cit. supra* note 80; ID., "Four Thoughts on the Election for ICC Prosecutor", Opinio Juris, 17 November 2020, available at: <http://opiniojuris.org/2020/11/17/four-thoughts-on-the-election-for-icc-prosecutor/>.

[86] The video recordings of all hearings are available at: <https://asp.icc-cpi.int/en_menus/asp/elections/prosecutor/Pages/Prosecutor2020.aspx>.

[87] In particular, Kenya voiced its disapproval of the shortlist, by means of a letter sent by the Kenyan Ambassador in The Hague to the President of the ASP. See "Lack Experience? Kenya Rejects Four Candidates Listed for ICC Prosecutor Post", The Star, 15 July 2020, available at: <https://www.the-star.co.ke/news/2020-07-15-lack-experience-kenya-rejects-four-candidates-listed-for-icc-prosecutor-post/>; and "ICC: Member States Unimpressed With Candidates Shortlisted to Replace Bensouda", The Africa Report, 3 August 2020, available at: <https://www.theafricareport.com/36189/icc-member-states-unimpressed-with-candidates-shortlisted-to-replace-bensouda/>.

[88] Gaynor and Anyah had represented victims in proceedings later discontinued against Uhuru Kenyatta.

[89] Joint Civil Society Statement, "Electing the Next ICC Prosecutor: States Should Respect the Process They Established", 16 July 2020, available at: <https://www.justiceinitiative.org/uploads/f0dfe1c8-181a-43eb-9fcd-0236c612c5b1/joint-civil-society-statement_icc-prosecutor-en.pdf>.

dates who still wished to be considered to be included in the list.[90] At the ASP's session, held in December 2020, nine candidates were heard, before consultations began with the assistance of five focal points appointed by the President.[91] Meanwhile, the deadline for submitting the nominees for election was repeatedly extended and the Presidency reconvened a resumed session of the ASP in early 2021.[92] On 8 February 2021, after four unsuccessful rounds of consultations,[93] a final two-day extension for nominations by States was agreed, and the Assembly was convened for the vote on 12 February.[94] Four individuals were formally nominated by their Governments, namely Carlos Fernández Castresana (Spain), Fergal Gaynor (Ireland), Karim Khan (UK), and Francesco Lo Voi (Italy).[95] At the second round of voting, Khan was elected with 72 votes (62 being the required majority).[96]

It is too early to assess the effects of this wearying electoral process on the relations between the Office of the Prosecutor (and the ICC in general) and certain States, which were already tense in light of some recent contested decisions of the chambers and other challenges to the work of the Office.[97] Certainly, Prosecutor-elect Karim Khan – whose nomination was opposed by some African NGOs and strongly supported by others[98] – will have to work hard to build (or restore) the necessary trust of both States and civil society in the centrality of the work of the Court, as well as to give new momentum and leadership to the work of the Office.

---

[90] Election of the Prosecutor – Way Forward, 13 November 2020.

[91] *Ibid.*, para. 4.

[92] See ICC-ASP/19/SP/45; ICC-ASP/19/SP/50; ICC-ASP/19/SP/65; ICC-ASP/19/SP/78; ICC-ASP/19/SP/79; ICC-ASP/R19/SP/03; ICC-ASP/R19/SP/20; ICC-ASP/R19/SP/21; ICC-ASP/R19/SP/22.

[93] On the consultation process, see Modalities for Consultation and the Focal Points, 11 December 2020.

[94] See ICC-ASP/R19/SP/22, *cit. supra* note 92, and Note from the Secretariat, ICC-ASP/19/19, 11 February 2021.

[95] The documents in support of the candidatures and CVs of the contestants are available at: <https://asp.icc-cpi.int/en_menus/asp/elections/prosecutor/2021Nominations/Pages/default.aspx>.

[96] See Nineteenth Session (first and second resumptions), Official Records, ICC-ASP/19/20/Add.1, pp. 19-20.

[97] Reference can be made, for instance, to the highly sensitive investigation in the Afghanistan situation, or to the recent decision on jurisdiction on Palestine, which has already elicited strong reactions from Israel and the United States, but also from like-minded States such as Germany, Australia, and Canada. On the challenges facing the new Prosecutor, see the insightful discussion carried out in a joint Opinio Juris/Justice in Conflict symposium, available at: <https://justiceinconflict.org/2020/04/08/the-next-icc-prosecutor-a-symposium/>.

[98] Some African NGOs have expressed their negative views on the nominee (see Civil Society Letter to the attention of the ASP Bureau, 7 January 2021, available at: <https://jfjustice.net/wp-content/uploads/2021/02/CivilsocietyLetter_ASPBureau_6Jan2021-2-1-1.pdf>), while others have expressed support (see Letter by African NGOs to the attention of the ASP Bureau, 7 January 2021, available at: <https://jfjustice.net/wp-content/uploads/2021/02/NGO_letter-to-ASP-jan-2021-1.pdf>). Khan replied to critics in a letter to Journalists for Justice, available at: <https://jfjustice.net/wp-content/uploads/2021/02/Journalists-for-Justice-Karim-Khan-QC-2-1.pdf>.

6. THE INELIMINABLE ROLE OF STATES IN SELECTING MEMBERS OF THE
    INTERNATIONAL JUDICIARY: CAN "TOO MUCH" TRANSPARENCY UNDERMINE
    (THE PERCEPTION OF) LEGITIMACY?

In the previous paragraphs, this article has attempted to sketch out the evolution of the practice relating to the nomination and election of judges and of the
Prosecutor of the ICC, underlining the most relevant innovations that have integrated and partially transformed the process in recent years. An additional critical
reflection on these developments seems now warranted in respect of the role of
States in the choice of members of the international judiciary, through the lenses
of transparency and legitimacy.

Vast empirical enquiries on States' practice in the nomination and election of
members of international courts have demonstrated that States – while accepting
certain limited forms of external input, overview or screening – are generally not
willing to relinquish their power to influence the composition of international adjudicative bodies.[99] The degree of politicization of these processes varies in time
and space, depending on the structure and functions of the court under consideration (inter-State dispute settlement bodies, human rights courts, international
criminal tribunals) as well as on the institutional context (universal, regional,
subregional).[100] Based on this empirical evidence, it would be frankly naïve to
foresee, any time in the near future, the removal of States' political considerations from the nomination and electoral process.[101]

Certainly, the case of international criminal tribunals is qualitatively different
from that of traditional inter-State dispute settlement bodies, in that the addressees of their decisions are primarily individuals whose criminal liability must be
ascertained through trial procedures. In the case of inter-State dispute settlement
bodies, States' desire to influence the composition and the jurisprudential trajectory of a court is easier to grasp, since the decisions of such bodies impinge
directly on States' rights and duties under international law, "[shaping] the path
of law".[102] At the same time, decisions of international criminal tribunals cannot
be confined to their effects on the accused or victims and have much wider ramifications. For instance, the complementarity assessment at the ICC, as a precondition to the exercise of jurisdiction, amounts to an indirect negative judgement

---

[99] See, e.g., MACKENZIE et al., *cit. supra* note 2; VOETEN, *cit. supra* note 4; HARLAND,
"International Court of Justice Elections: A Report on the First Fifty Years", CYIL, 1996, p.
303 ff.

[100] At the regional level, especially in the case of full representation courts, it is perhaps
easier to establish less politicized selection procedures.

[101] ROSENNE, *The World Court: What it is and How it Functions*, Dordrecht, 1989, p. 64,
according to whom States are not expected to "exclude political considerations when they come
to perform the very important function of electing the members of the Court"; POLONSKAYA,
"Selecting Candidates to the Bench of the World Court: (Inevitable) Politicization and Its
Consequences", Leiden JIL, 2020, p. 409 ff.

[102] BURCHARD, *cit. supra* note 59, p. 96.

on the conduct of State bodies;[103] the interpretation of provisions on war crimes touches the connection between international criminal law and underlying rules of international humanitarian law directed to States;[104] decisions on matters of cooperation might deal with the normative relations – and potential antinomies – between the Statute and conventional or customary rules outside the "Rome law";[105] etc. Moreover, the very nature of the crimes within the jurisdiction of the Court means that political or military leaders might be the target of investigation and prosecution. Therefore, States are certainly not indifferent to the normative developments of international criminal law and are interested in influencing them, including through the process of nomination and election of judges and prosecutors.

The debate on transparency must therefore be put in perspective, and checked against the practical effects of the more recent practice purportedly inspired by the desire to foster transparency. The creation of screening bodies and new possibilities for engagement with civil society are welcome developments, but they are certainly not a panacea against legitimacy and credibility challenges, and have not been applied in a fully consistent way. For instance, one could ask why the work of advisory bodies has not been itself subject to a rigorous standard of openness and transparency. In the vetting process for the election of the Prosecutor, the CEP and experts not only decided not to make public the names of the applicants and of the longlisted candidates, but also failed to explain in detail the reasons why out of the 14 original candidates only four made it to the shortlist. There should be more effective ways to convey to the public such detailed reasoning – for instance disclosing whether certain candidates failed on grounds of their professional ethics, or due to episodes of harassment, or because of other question marks over their moral character[106] – while still ensuring confidentiali-

---

[103] On "negative" complementarity, see STAHN, "Taking Complementarity Seriously", in STAHN and EL ZEIDY (eds.), *The International Criminal Court and Complementarity: From Theory to Practice*, Cambridge, 2011, p. 233 ff.

[104] An example of how the interpretation of war crimes might transform the content of underlying rules of international humanitarian law is the *Ntaganda* case. See NESI and POLTRONIERI ROSSETTI, "Member-On-Member Sexual and Gender-Based Crimes as War Crimes: Towards the Autonomy of Individual Criminal Responsibility From Underlying Violations of International Humanitarian Law?", CI, 2020, pp. 341 ff.

[105] Reference could be made to the judicial saga on the antinomy between States Parties' duty to cooperate in the arrest of individuals at large and the rule of customary international law on the immunity of Heads of State, stemming from the *Al-Bashir* case. See AKANDE and DE SOUSA DIAS, "Does the ICC Statute Remove Immunities of State Officials in National Proceedings? Some Observations from the Drafting History of Article 27(2) of the Rome Statute", EJIL: Talk!, 12 November 2018, available at: <https://www.ejiltalk.org/does-the-icc-statute-remove-immunities-of-state-officials-in-national-proceedings-some-observations-from-the-drafting-history-of-article-272-of-the-rome-statute/>.

[106] Apparently, this was not the case for the longlisted candidates who did not make it to the shortlist. See "ICC Prosecutor Election: The Wheeling And Dealing is not yet Done", Justice Info, 25 September 2020, available at: <https://www.justiceinfo.net/en/45491-icc-prosecutor-election-wheeling-and-dealing-not-yet-done.html>. The Chairperson has reportedly said that "the vetting process did not disclose any disqualifying information".

ty.[107] In addition to that, one could question whether the kind of public interviews carried out during the last round of elections (also taking into account the technical problems and the less than impeccable direction of the chairpersons) really added anything significant to the assessment of the candidates.[108] Sometimes the questions and answers resulted in a mere duplication of information already available on paper, and did little to shed light on the competence or character of the candidates.[109]

Moreover, the kind of screening that applies to the selection of judges differs on various grounds from that applied to the Prosecutor, and not necessarily in a justified or reasonable manner. For instance, the CEP did not provide a detailed assessment of all candidates in the way that the ACN does with the nominees to the post of judge. The informal character of consultations among States does not seem to require non-disclosure of the applicants' identities or of how the applicants were graded (if there exists grading similar to that used for judges). This *modus operandi* seems premised on the supposition that reaching a consensus is desirable at all costs, and that some opacity and confidentiality might facilitate it; something that the recent election clearly disproved.

However, another observation concerns the potentially detrimental effects of boosting transparency in a situation marked by deep divisions among States on the role of the institution and the best choices for its top judicial and prosecutorial posts. In such conditions, transparency not backed by a shared vision on the future of the organization can be a double-edged sword, because it risks amplifying divisions and giving to third States and international civil society the impression of institutional weakness and lack of legitimacy. Indeed, in the case of the election of the Prosecutor, it cannot be excluded that the way in which the CEP and the expert panel operated was one of the reasons for States' discontent with the results of the screening process.[110] In other words, transparency enhances the credibility and legitimacy of a selection mechanism only if it is equally applied at all stages and if States, which remain the masters of the process, are incentivized by technical and advisory bodies to fully embrace it.

With regard to the effects of procedural reforms, a final observation concerns the (perception of) legitimacy surrounding the elected individuals and the institu-

---

[107] On these issues, see HELLER, "Did the CEP Exclude Prosecutor Candidates Because of Moral Character Issues?", Opinio Juris, 16 October 2020, available at: <https://opiniojuris.org/2020/10/16/did-the-cep-exclude-candidates-because-of-moral-character-issues/>.

[108] Serious connection problems have impaired the possibility for Susan Okalany, the only shortlisted female candidate, to fully participate in the hearing. In addition to that, the Vice-President of the ASP was accused of sexism for requesting the Ugandan candidate to "give [him] a smile", once a disappointed Okalany had finally been able to restore her connection. On this last issue, see ETKIN, "'Give Me a Smile': The Sexism at Play During ICC Prosecutor Proceedings", Justice in Conflict, 5 August 2020, available at: <https://justiceinconflict.org/2020/08/05/give-me-a-smile-the-sexism-at-play-during-icc-prosecutor-proceedings/>.

[109] *Ibid.* See also the video recordings of the hearings, *supra* note 86.

[110] One should not forget that the Bureau – which chose the members of the advisory bodies – is itself an administrative body where only a fraction of the States Parties is represented, being composed of 21 members (18 plus the President and the two Vice-Presidents).

tion as such.[111] It is hard to deny that States choosing to override the assessment of advisory bodies might reduce the external perception of legitimacy of the institution, giving the impression that meritocracy only plays a minor role in these decisions. Nevertheless, the perception of legitimacy of an international court does not depend solely on the nature and results of the electoral process. Certainly, the quality of judges and prosecutors is fundamental, but courts remain collegial bodies that speak to international audiences through their decisions and interpretive choices. Therefore, as various scholars have convincingly argued, it is on the persuasiveness and consistency of these decisions and on the establishment of a reasonably shared judicial culture – as well as on the necessary administrative and procedural reforms – that attention should be concentrated with a view to reinforcing the Court's credibility.[112]

7. PROPOSALS TO ENHANCE THE TRANSPARENCY AND LEGITIMACY OF THE NOMINATION AND ELECTION PROCESS: PRAGMATISM OVER UTOPIAN VOLUNTARISM

The performance of the various mechanisms introduced to increase the transparency and legitimacy of the ICC has been the object of severe criticism in recent years, prompting an open debate on the reforms needed to revitalize trust in the institution and in the international criminal justice project.[113] In 2019, the ASP decided to establish an Independent Expert Review process in order to put forward global reform proposals, which led to the adoption of a Final Report.[114] Interestingly, the topic of nomination and election of judges did not fall under the broad remit of the experts, since the ASP has tasked a dedicated Working Group on Nomination and Election of Judges to deal with the review of these proce-

---

[111] On the issue of legitimacy, see FICHTELBERG, "Democratic Legitimacy and the International Criminal Court: A Liberal Defence", JICJ, 2006, p. 765 ff.; GLASIUS, "Do International Criminal Courts Require Democratic Legitimacy?", EJIL, 2012, p. 43 ff.

[112] On the many aspects in need of reform, see, e.g., GUILFOYLE, "Reforming the International Criminal Court: Is it Time for the Assembly of State Parties to be the Adults in the Room?", EJIL: Talk!, 8 May 2018, available at: <www.ejiltalk.org/reforming-the-international-criminal-court-is-it-time-for-the-assembly-of-state-parties-to-be-the-adults-in-the-room/>; SLUITER, "Key Reforms for the Next Decade of the ICC – Towards a Stronger Judicial Role in the Investigations and a More Robust System of Enforcing State Cooperation", ICC Forum, 2018, available at: <https://iccforum.com/anniversary#Sluiter>. On consistency of judicial decisions, see MCINTYRE, "The Impact of a Lack of Consistency and Coherence: How Key Decisions of the International Criminal Court Have Undermined the Court's Legitimacy", Questions of International Law, Zoom-in 67 (2020), p. 25 ff.

[113] See GUILFOYLE, cit. supra note 112; ID., "Lacking Conviction: Is the International Criminal Court Broken? An Organisational Failure Analysis", Melbourne Journal of International Law, 2019, p. 401 ff., for a detailed analysis of these institutional issues.

[114] Review of the International Criminal Court and the Rome Statute system, ICC-ASP/18/Res.7, 6 December 2019 (including Annex I containing the Terms of Reference for the Expert Review). See also Independent Expert Review of the International Criminal Court and the Rome Statute System, Final Report, 30 September 2020.

dures.[115] Nevertheless, the experts decided to include in their report some considerations and recommendations on the topic.[116] Based on the foregoing analysis, and further developing some of the experts' suggestions, it seems appropriate to formulate additional proposals that might contribute to enhancing the credibility, transparency, and efficacy of the nomination and election procedures for both judges and the Prosecutor.

The first line of action relates to the bodies tasked with assisting the ASP with the assessment of candidates and with providing expert advice on the selection process. The multiplication of such bodies, the frequent changes to their terms of reference, and the sometimes-unreasonable discrepancies between their mandates, have probably weakened their role and the authoritativeness of their reports in the eyes of States. The present unsatisfactory situation might be addressed in various ways by the ASP and the Bureau, resorting to their regulatory and administrative powers, and/or through limited reforms of the Statute. Here are two options that might be considered:

a) Unifying the advisory functions of the ACN and CEP in a single standing organ to be convened ahead of scheduled elections, and whose members would serve for a fixed (non-renewable) term, and whose composition could be slightly extended.[117] This unified organ would then operate on the basis of clear and harmonized terms of reference according to the electoral process under consideration.

b) Maintaining the current non-standing advisory body for the less frequent election of the Prosecutor, and creating an independent Judicial Appointment Commission for the more frequent election of judges, along the lines of other international courts.[118] The Commission would be responsible for the formalization of nominations, upon the proposals made by States pursuant to the two existing mechanisms, and after a full-fledged public assessment of the candidates. This more radical proposal would almost certainly require amendments to the Statute, but could ensure that only candidates considered particularly well qualified would actually be eligible.

The composition of the advisory bodies should be better addressed, possibly requiring that they include a minimum number of former international judges or prosecutors, and provide adequate gender balance and representation of different legal traditions.

Whatever the institutional solution chosen, it could be established that the final reports containing the assessment and grading of the candidates – while

---

[115] Also known as the New York Working Group, established pursuant to the resolution Strengthening the International Criminal Court and the Assembly of States Parties, ICC-ASP/18/Res.6, Annex I, 6 December 2019, para. 6(a)-(b).

[116] Expert Review Final Report, *cit. supra* note 114, paras. 961-977.

[117] The current composition of the two advisory bodies is relatively narrow, and comprises nine individuals for the ACN and five for the CEP (plus five experts in the panel).

[118] See, e.g., the case of the Caribbean Court of Justice, where the nomination procedure is entrusted to an independent non-governmental body called the Regional Judicial and Legal Services Commission. For further examples, see MACKENZIE et al., *cit. supra* note 2, pp. 147-152.

remaining formally non-binding on States – could only be overridden by States through an explicit and motivated resolution of the ASP rejecting in whole or in part the advisory bodies' conclusions. In order to be adopted, such resolution would require the same majority necessary to elect judges or the Prosecutor.[119]

A second line of action that should be explored concerns the working methods, objectives and methodology of the vetting process, and the nature of the final reports issued by the advisory bodies. These procedural adjustments should address the following aspects:

a) Improvements to the transparency and publicity of the assessments, in compliance with confidentiality requirements. In particular, with regard to the candidates for the Prosecutor's post, the relevant advisory body could make public the identity of all applicants (perhaps limited to those who consent to be named), or at least of those who are longlisted. In addition, the ASP could amend the TOR to allow for a longer shortlist, given that the three to six-name list currently envisaged seems too narrow.

b) A more structured approach to interviews and hearings, both the individual ones conducted by the advisory bodies and those conducted at the time of election by States' representatives and civil society. In particular, such interviews should focus more closely on testing the actual experience of the candidates, their judicial philosophy and, particularly in the case of the Prosecutor, on his or her vision for the work of the Office and the Court and for the administrative and managerial changes that the nominee wishes to enact if elected.[120] With regard to judges, the commitment of nominees to encouraging collegiality at the Court should be addressed.

c) With regard to the vetting process proper (i.e., references and security checks, criminal record checks, enquiries into allegations of misconduct or harassment, etc.), the scope and the kind of materials and sources allowed for consideration and the respective weight attributed to them should be made clear and established in advance – preferably by the ASP or at least by the Bureau – and not during the procedure at the discretion of the advisory body. Moreover, findings indicating that particular candidates do not meet the required criteria or have failed the vetting should be made public, to the extent necessary for keeping the public informed, but without disclosing confidential information or damaging the reputation of the nominees.[121]

---

[119] The idea that States should afford maximum consideration to the advisory bodies' assessment has been expressed in the Expert Review Final Report, *cit. supra* note 114, p. 324, recommendation 378.

[120] Hearings should focus on more practical proposals relating, for instance, to prosecutorial policies, prioritization strategies, administrative reforms, performance assessment, communication strategies, etc.

[121] For instance, allegations of harassment or complaints about previous behaviour in work places should be carefully evaluated. On this matter, see "By Failing to Screen ICC Prosecutor Candidates for Sexual Misconduct, States Put Court at Risk", International Justice Monitor, 9 March 2020, available at: <https://www.ijmonitor.org/2020/03/by-failing-to-screen-icc-prosecutor-candidates-for-sexual-misconduct-states-put-court-at-risk/>. Checks on private activities outside the ICC should not stop at the time of election, as the scandal that has damaged

d) With regard to the final reports of the advisory bodies, these documents need to be drafted in a more consistent manner, and to provide sufficiently reasoned explanations for the conclusions reached with regard to the candidates. This includes adopting a more candid assessment of candidates with below-standard qualifications and experience.

To conclude, a few additional remarks could be made with respect to general issues concerning the composition of the Court, with a view to strengthening the institution and making it more effective and representative.

In the first place, all efforts should be made to ensure that a balanced gender representation is maintained at the Court. Despite the fact that the ICC's record on the matter is significantly better than that of other international courts – currently the Court has equal representation of both genders – there are wide discrepancies among regional groups and individual States as to their willingness to take gender into account when putting forward nominations. In this sense, the ASP could modify the minimum voting requirements in relation to gender, for instance by imposing a minimum requirement of gender representation at the stage of nominations, or by extending the gender representation requirement at the election stage to all rounds of voting. Alternatively, the ASP could establish a rule according to which States that submit a nomination in successive elections should at a minimum alternate a male and a female nominee. Of the five States that have had, uninterruptedly, a judge at the Court since 2003, four have presented only male nominees.[122] Others, such as Japan, have only selected female candidates to date.[123] Disappointingly, WEOG States have been significantly less successful in advancing female candidates than other regional groups.[124]

In the second place, the issue of finding the right balance between judges elected under List A and List B should finally be addressed by the ASP, in light of a practice that has gradually reduced the presence of judges of the latter list. Various arguments have been put forward in favour of the elimination of List B, including by experts in their reform proposals, scholars, and former judges.[125] While some of these arguments are not misplaced, it seems excessive to attribute to a minority of academics and international lawyers the problems of consistency and persuasiveness affecting the Court's case law.[126] The debate over

---

former Prosecutor Moreno-Ocampo clearly demonstrates. See BERGSMO et al., "A Prosecutor Falls, Time for the Court to Rise", FICHL Policy Brief Series No. 86, 2017.

[122] Italy, France, Germany, and the Republic of Korea have presented male nominees at all relevant elections, despite being large countries where it is certainly not difficult to find well-qualified female candidates among the ranks of the national judiciary, legal profession, and academia.

[123] Judges Saiga, Ozaki, and Akane.

[124] With regard to elected WEOG candidates, only four have been female (out of 16 judges), a meagre result when compared to the seven (out of 12) from Latin America and the Caribbean and eight (out of 11) from Africa.

[125] See *supra* note 44 on these positions.

[126] Some of the most contentious decisions of the Court have been adopted by chambers mostly or completely composed of List A judges. See MCINTYRE, *cit. supra* note 111, p. 55 and GUILFOYLE, *cit. supra* note 44. The lack of collegiality is clearly exemplified by the excessive

List A/List B judges should be less about preconceived ideas on how previous experience might influence the attitude of a judge and more about the pragmatic administration of justice, particularly as regards the criteria for the formation of divisions and chambers. It seems reasonable that pre-trial and trial divisions and chambers should comprise a majority of judges with strong judicial experience, and/or that the presiding judges should preferably be professional judges, so as to ensure the smooth conduct of proceedings at stages in which the procedural and substantive issues are by and large criminal in nature. At the same time, List B judges could positively contribute to certain aspects of pre-trial proceedings (such as the authorization of investigations and preliminary rulings on jurisdiction) or proceedings relating to State cooperation, where international law issues may be prevalent over criminal law aspects. In addition to this, it can be argued that at the appellate level the presence of at least some judges with public international law expertise could better ensure that final decisions properly coordinate the interpretation of the Court's legal texts with international law outside the Rome system. Obviously, chambers are also under such duty (for instance, to guarantee full respect of internationally recognized human rights), but achieving coherence, if necessary by settling differences among chambers, is a responsibility that falls on the Appeals Chamber. Moreover, at the appellate level, judges are often called upon to decide purely legal issues in predominantly written proceedings in which the principles of orality and immediacy are less relevant than at the confirmation of charges and trial stages. This different procedural setting probably makes the experience and mindset of professional judges – for instance in the management of hearings – less crucial than at other junctures. In any event, given that international and criminal law issues are often inextricably entangled in cases pending before the Court, it is almost impossible to design a flexible system for the allocation of judges based on the specific expertise needed in each situation or case. While it would in principle be possible to create specialized chambers to deal exclusively with certain matters (cooperation, reparation, etc.), this would require major institutional reforms, possibly including an increase in the number of judges and complex administrative adjustments. Considering the current coexistence of List A and List B judges, some degree of rationalization might come from a more "functionalist" practice of the Presidency in the assignment of judges to the different divisions and in the formation of chambers. Taking more closely into account the specificities of situations and cases in making these decisions might ensure a better balance within judicial formations and help to enhance the consistency of the Court's case law.[127]

---

recourse to separate and dissenting opinions, in clear contrast with the duty to attempt to reach unanimity in deliberations, established by Art. 74(3) of the Statute.

[127] Before the last election, the Appeals Division was entirely formed of judges from List A. Pursuant to the re-shuffling of the divisions decided by President Hofmański, the Appeals Division is now formed of three List A and two List B judges (information is available at: <https://www.icc-cpi.int/Pages/item.aspx?name=pr1577>). In favour of a more pragmatic use of presidential powers in the formation of divisions and chambers, see GUILFOYLE, *cit. supra* note 44. Sometimes the fact that a certain situation or case will pose fundamental issues of international law or specific issues of criminal law that could benefit from a particular legal

In the third place, the election of judges by the ASP is but the conclusion of a long journey that begins with the nominations by States. Therefore, more progressive reform efforts should be focused on this crucial first stage, in order to ensure that the most qualified candidates are selected, by exerting a coordinated political, professional and societal pressure on States. In particular, nomination through the national PCA groups offers, in some cases, only limited guarantees of securing the nomination of the best candidates, given the extreme variability in the composition, methods of work, and independence of such organs. Proposals have been advanced to entirely do away with this procedure, in favour of the domestic nomination procedures for the national highest judicial offices.[128] Nevertheless, these procedures also vary greatly between States, and sometimes consist in purely discretionary political appointments. To allow some degree of harmonization, the ASP could issue guidelines on the minimum transparency and independence guarantees that should apply at the national level to satisfy the requirements of the Statute, failing which the nominees could be found unfit for election.[129] In addition to that, the ASP could oblige (and not merely recommend as it has done so far) States to provide in writing a detailed explanation of how the nomination was made at the national level, its legal basis, the organs involved, information on whether other candidates were considered, etc. This would improve the transparency of the process and incentivize States to be less secretive about national procedures leading to a nomination, or even to adopt dedicated legislation, as some States have already done.[130] National and international professional and academic associations could also provide valuable feedback to assist States to select the candidates that best fit the job.[131]

---

expertise is clear from the outset, also in light of the preliminary examination or investigation activities carried out by the Prosecutor.

[128] See Expert Review Final Report, *cit. supra* note 114, para. 967, according to which this procedure "should be discouraged". Another possibility would be that of making the nomination through the PCA national groups less informal. See MACKENZIE et al., *cit. supra* note 2, pp. 87-95. See *ibid.*, pp. 145-152, for proposals to strengthen the nomination process at the national level.

[129] Along these lines, see Expert Review Final Report, *cit. supra* note 114, p. 324, recommendations 375-377.

[130] See MACKENZIE et al., *cit. supra* note 2, p. 65, citing the Slovenian Law on Nomination of Judges from the Republic of Slovenia to International Tribunals/Courts, available at: <https://www.legal-tools.org/doc/09028b/pdf/>. Another example of such legislation is Finland. The Netherlands has recently adopted legislation on the PCA national group, see "Royal Decree concerning the Appointment of a National Group in the Permanent Court of Arbitration", 23 January 2020, available at: <https://asp.icc-cpi.int/iccdocs/asp_docs/Elections/EJ2020/Netherlands-NP.pdf>. Some States, such as Belgium, have introduced rules on nominations for the ICC in national legislation on cooperation with the Court (see Art. 42, Loi concernant la coopération avec la Cour pénale internationale et les tribunaux pénaux internationaux, 29 March 2004). Italy has so far omitted to specify the procedure it follows for nominations, probably in light of its largely informal character. In the Open Society Initiative's Report, *cit. supra* note 44, p. 27, the Italian nomination procedure is described as "one of the poorer selection processes".

[131] For instance, consultation with the International Association of Judges, the International Association of Women Judges, the International Criminal Court Bar Association, the

To conclude with a note on the election of the Prosecutor, one could ask whether the ASP's focus on the primary goal of finding a consensus candidate – something laudable but by no means mandated by the Statute – is necessarily the best strategy to safeguard the election from excessive politicization. Facing deep divisions among States on the future of the Court, an open and competitive application process, with adequate and transparent vetting of candidates, followed by a public and thorough discussion at the ASP and a vote might well bring an element of clarity and an incentive for candidates to be more open and less ecumenical in expressing their views and proposals for the future.

8. CONCLUDING REMARKS

This article has attempted to analyze the almost 20 years of practice on the nomination and election of judges and prosecutors at the ICC, reflecting on trends, as well as on the innovations introduced by the ASP via the Bureau. There has been a gradual attempt to provide correctives to the excessive politicization of the process, which many perceive as a deplorable "horse trading" practice.[132] Nevertheless, the degree to which these efforts have succeeded in satisfying civil society's demands for transparency is open to question. On the one hand, the advisory bodies created to support the ASP have only partially lived up to the expectations, due to their unclear mandates and working methods, and the inconsistencies of their final reports. On the other hand, States have demonstrated their intention to keep a good grip on the electoral process, preserving their autonomy vis-à-vis consultative bodies, whose recommendations are not binding on States under the current legal framework. This is but a manifestation of States' desire to avoid a "Frankenstein problem" with the ICC, a way to reduce the risk of losing control over the goals and functioning of the institution.[133]

The discussion on practices relating to the nomination and election of international judges is not a "modelling" exercise, with a view to determining in the abstract a non-existent ideal formula. To the contrary, it addresses one of the structural features of international adjudication, because the rules on the composition and selection of judges bear a significant influence on the functions of the court under consideration and contribute to shaping its institutional, interpretive, and jurisprudential profile. In this sense, the peculiarity of international criminal justice institutions – and the underlying fundamental interests of the accused and the victims – may well warrant different procedures, capable of assuring a higher degree of insulation from political interference.

International Association of Prosecutors, etc., with national judicial and prosecutorial self-governing bodies, and with relevant academic networks, could provide an additional layer of control and peer pressure to promote high-quality nominations.

[132] Expert Review Final Report, *cit. supra* note 114, para 961.

[133] GUZMAN, "International Organizations and the Frankenstein Problem", EJIL, 2013, p. 999 ff.

Nevertheless, the rules on the composition and election of judges (and prosecutors, in the case of criminal courts) of a particular judicial institution are just one of the concurring elements that determine its authoritativeness and legitimacy. Therefore, particularly in the case of the ICC, this aspect should not be overemphasized or considered in isolation from the many institutional, organizational, and administrative issues that have so far affected the work of the Court and the external perception of its credibility. As scholars and independent experts have demonstrated, much of the discontent over the ICC's achievements (or lack thereof) results from the lack of clear prosecutorial and judicial vision; poor collegiality leading to fragmentation and jurisprudential oscillations; as well as administrative malpractice and bureaucratic inefficiency.[134] It is on these aspects that additional efforts are needed to strengthen the institution and revive the international criminal justice project in times of crisis. Certainly, enhancing the quality of the "raw material" by electing more qualified and experienced judges and prosecutors – as well as keeping high the quality of professionals such as legal officers – will help with reclaiming public confidence in the work of the Court. But completely eschewing States – and their legal and political considerations on the role of an international institution they created out of their free consent – from these processes would not only be technically impossible, given the exclusive competences of governing bodies such as the ASP, but risks further alienating their indispensable support and cooperation.

---

[134] On these aspects, see GUILFOYLE, *cit. supra* note 113. On administrative issues, see Expert Review Final Report, *cit. supra* note 114, part I-IV and, on collegiality and judicial decision-making, part IX (paras. 462-473, recommendations 185-188) and part XI (recommendations 216-225).

LIMITS TO MEASURES OF CONFISCATION OF PROPERTY LINKED TO SERIOUS CRIMINAL OFFENCES IN THE CASE LAW OF THE EUROPEAN COURT OF HUMAN RIGHTS

Roberto Virzo[*]

Abstract

In the past thirty years, a growing number of international agreements and acts of international institutions has resorted to different kinds of confiscation ("direct confiscation", "value confiscation", "enlarged confiscation" or "non-conviction based confiscation") to contrast and suppress international and transnational crimes. It can be considered that the flexibility – in terms of variety of measures and functions – of confiscation, together with the forced and permanent deprivation of property to which it always leads, significantly affect the favor towards this measure by States and international organisations. The European Court of Human Rights (ECtHR), taking into account the aforementioned proliferation of international acts and agreements concerning the fight to criminal activities, maintains that common "European and even universal legal standards" can be said to exist which encourage the confiscation of property linked to serious criminal offences. Moreover, the Court has gone so far as to maintain that, in accordance with such "universal legal standards", States Parties to the European Convention of Human Rights must be given "a wide margin of appreciation with regard to what constitutes the appropriate means of applying measures to control the use of property such as the confiscation of all types of proceeds of crime". However, the implementation of such measures by States authorities must conform with human rights guarantees – inter alia *the principle of legality in criminal matters, due process rights and property rights – provided for in customary and conventional international law. This essay seeks to examine the relevant case law of the ECtHR and to focus on the possibility of reconciling, on the one hand, international obligations on the protection of human rights and, on the other hand, international agreements and acts – concerning the fight against criminal activities – that provide for the various types of confiscation measures.*

Keywords: confiscation; transnational crimes; European Court of Human Rights; presumption of innocence; right to property.

---

[*] Associate Professor of International Law, University of Sannio.

IYIL, Vol. 30 (2020), pp. 265-281
ISSN 0391-5107

1. INTRODUCTION

In the past thirty years, a growing number of international agreements and acts of international institutions has resorted to different kinds of confiscation ("direct confiscation", "value confiscation", "enlarged confiscation" or "non-conviction based confiscation") to contrast and suppress international and transnational crimes[1] as well as crimes in respect of which it is maintained that there is "a special need to combat them on a common basis".[2]

It can be considered that the flexibility – in terms of variety of measures and functions – of confiscation, together with the forced and permanent deprivation of property to which it always leads, significantly affect the *favor* towards this measure by States and international organisations.

The European Court of Human Rights (ECtHR) has derived the existence of international standards from a number of international agreements and recommendations of the Financial Action Task Force (FATF) and other supervisory bodies of the Council of Europe or the Organisation for Economic Cooperation and Development (OECD). Indeed, in *Gogitidze and Others v. Georgia*, *Telbis and Viziteu v. Romania* and *Balsamo v. San Marino*,[3] the Court found that "common European and even universal legal standards can be said to exist which encourage [...] the confiscation of property linked to serious criminal offences such as corruption, money laundering, drug offences and so on". These are types of crime that threaten, as stated in the Preamble of the United Nations Convention Against Corruption (UNCAC),[4] "the stability and security of societies, undermining the institutions and values of democracy, ethical values and justice and jeopardizing sustainable development and the rule of law".

---

[1] For a few examples of older agreements, mention may be made, among those concluded between the two world wars, of the Convention for the Suppression of Counterfeiting Currency, 20 April 1929, entered into force 22 February 1931, and among those from the 1970s, of the Convention on International Trade in Endangered Species of Wild Fauna and Flora (CITES), 3 March 1973, entered into force 1 July 1975.

[2] As per the wording of Article 83(1) TFEU. These conventions require each contracting party to adopt the necessary legislative measures to make given conduct a criminal offence even if it is completely unrelated to its domestic law. Consider the Optional Protocol [to the Convention on the Rights of the Child] on the Sale of Children, Child Prostitution and Child Pornography, 25 May 2000, entered into force 18 January 2002, and the Council of Europe Convention on the Manipulation of Sports Competitions, 18 September 2014, entered into force 1 September 2019. Pursuant to Article 3(1) of the former, "Each State Party shall ensure that, as a minimum, the following acts and activities are fully covered under its criminal or penal law, whether these offences are committed domestically or transnationally or on an individual organized basis". Pursuant to the combined provisions of Articles 1(2) and 15 of the latter, the criminal law provisions that the contracting parties must enact concern the offences of "manipulation of national and international sport competitions".

[3] *Gogitidze and Others v. Georgia*, Application No. 36892/05, Judgment of 12 May 2015, para. 105; *Telbis and Viziteu v. Romania*, Application No. 49711/15, Judgment of 26 June 2018, para. 76; *Balsamo v. San Marino*, Application No. 21414/17, Judgment of 8 October 2019, para. 92.

[4] 31 October 2003, entered into force 14 December 2005.

While it is true that the confiscation measures provided for in international agreements and acts are meant to pursue a general interest, their actual implementation must conform with human rights guarantees provided for in customary and conventional international law.

This essay seeks to examine the relevant case law of the ECtHR on the issue of the application of confiscation measures linked to serious criminal offences and, subsequently, to focus on the possibility of reconciling, on the one hand, international obligations on the protection of human rights and, on the other hand, international agreements and acts – concerning the fight against criminal activities – that provide for the various types of confiscation measures.

2.   THE MAIN TYPES OF CONFISCATION PROVIDED FOR BY INTERNATIONAL AGREEMENTS AND ACTS ON COMBATING CRIMINAL ACTIVITIES

Despite the variety of types of confiscation provided for in agreements, recommendations and other acts of international law (whose general features will be briefly described below[5]), a common effect of each of them is the coercive and permanent deprivation of property or assets in various ways connected to certain criminal activities. For example, the United Nations conventions against illicit traffic in narcotic drugs and psychotropic substances,[6] against transnational organized crime (UNTOC)[7] and against corruption[8] clarify that confiscation, "which includes forfeiture where applicable, shall mean the permanent deprivation of property by order of a court or other competent authority".

The finality of the measure has also been considered decisive in ECtHR case law on confiscation.[9] For instance, the Strasbourg judges in *Air Canada v. United Kingdom*[10] ruled out that temporary restrictions amount to confiscation.

On the other hand, the case law of the ECtHR and the EU Court of Justice shows that asset freezing orders that last for a longer period of time or that result in a transfer of the affected assets to a third party may be classified as "measures having equivalent effect to confiscation".

In this regard, it should be recalled that the same international agreements or acts that contain a definition of confiscation often also provide a definition of "freezing" and "seizure", premised on the temporary nature of such measures,

---

[5] But see, more generally, VIRZO, *La confisca nell'azione internazionale di contrasto ad attività criminali*, Napoli, 2020.

[6] Article 1(f) United Nations Convention against Illicit Traffic in Narcotic Drugs and Psychotropic Substances, 20 December 1988, entered into force 11 November 1990.

[7] Article 2(g) UNTOC, 15 November 2000, entered into force 29 September 2003.

[8] Article 2(g) UNCAC.

[9] See *Yasar v. Romania*, Application No. 64863/13, Judgment of 26 November 2019, para. 49: "The Court notes that the confiscation of the applicant's vessel was a permanent measure which entailed a conclusive transfer of ownership".

[10] *Air Canada v. The United Kingdom*, Application No. 18465/91, Judgment of 26 April 1995, para. 33, "the seizure of the aircraft amounted to a temporary restriction on its use and did not involve a transfer of ownership".

which, as such, do not entail a deprivation of property. Consider the three UN Conventions against drug trafficking, transnational organized crime and corruption, according to which "freezing or seizure shall mean temporarily prohibiting the transfer, conversion, disposition or movement of property or temporarily assuming custody or control of property on the basis of an order issued by a court or other competent authority".[11]

Although renewable,[12] freezing measures must have a limited effect *ratione temporis*. If maintained for an indefinite period of time, freezing would no longer be such[13] and would instead constitute a measure whose effect is equivalent to confiscation. As the EU General Court conceded in one of the rulings in the so-called "Kadi saga", in such a case, "[i]t might even be asked whether – given that nearly 10 years have passed since the applicant's funds were originally frozen – it is not time to call into question the findings of this Court [...], according to which the freezing of funds is a temporary precautionary measure which, unlike confiscation, does not affect the very substance of the right of the person concerned to property in their financial assets but only the use thereof".[14]

As for the ECtHR, in its judgment in *Al-Dulimi and Montana Management INC,* the Grand Chamber classified as confiscation "the impugned measure" which "was ordered pursuant to Resolution 1483 (2003) adopted by the UN Security Council".[15] In fact, although formally labelled as freezing, the measure in question consisted of a coercive deprivation of assets involving their transfer to a third party, namely the Development Fund for Iraq.[16]

That said, the traditional type of confiscation measure is direct confiscation, which does not apply to all of the offender's property but only to certain assets directly related to the commission of the offence. In the statutes of some international criminal courts, it is classified as an accessory penalty. Consider, for example, Article 77(2)(b) of the Statute of the International Criminal Court:[17] "In addition to imprisonment, the Court may order: [...]; (b) A forfeiture of proceeds, property and assets derived directly or indirectly from that crime, without prejudice to the rights of bona fide third parties", where precisely the link of pertinence that must exist between a given international crime and the proceeds, property

---

[11] See, for example, Article 2(f) UNTOC.

[12] According to Spörl, "Article 2: Use of Terms", in Rose, Kubiciel and Landwehr (eds.), *The United Nations Convention Against Corruption. A Commentary*, Oxford, 2019, p. 30 ff., the adverb temporarily contained in Article 2(f) "encompasses the concept of renewability".

[13] As remarked by Bastid Burdeau, "Le gel d'avoirs étrangers", JDI, 1997, p. 12 ff., "un gel qui devient définitif ou débouche sur un transfert de propriété perd son caractère".

[14] General Court, Case T-85/09, *Kadi v. Commission*, 30 September 2010, para. 150.

[15] *Al-Dulimi* e *Montana Management INC. v. Switzerland*, Application No. 5809/08, Grand Chamber, Judgment of 21 June 2016, para. 132.

[16] As Ciampi, *Sanzioni del Consiglio di sicurezza e diritti umani*, Milano, 2007, p. 71, observes, the immediate transfer of frozen assets to the Iraqi Development Fund makes the freezing measure non-reversible.

[17] 17 July 1998, entered into force 1 July 2002.

and assets of the person convicted of having committed it[18] leads without any doubt to considering this additional penalty as a form of special confiscation of property.

A second type of confiscation covered by important international agreements and acts is "value confiscation". It responds to the need to overcome difficulties that often arise in the actual application of confiscation of the direct proceeds of a criminal activity. It can happen that the latter, before the conclusion of the criminal proceedings or the possible adoption of precautionary measures, have been transferred to third parties in good faith, reinvested or re-introduced into the legal economy, or have become untraceable because concealed, squandered or even destroyed. Moreover, it is not always easy to prove the causal link between the asset to be confiscated and the crime committed.

In such cases, confiscation of other assets at the disposal of the offender is allowed for a value corresponding to the profit gained from his or her criminal activity. For instance, Article 12 UNTOC and Article 31 UNCAC provide for that type of confiscation in case of "transformed, converted and intermingled proceeds of the crime [...] income and other benefits derived from such proceeds of the crime".

In any case, value confiscation is only permitted on a subsidiary basis and occurs when direct confiscation is precluded due to the impossibility of securing to the full extent the direct proceeds of the criminal activity.

With reference to confiscation by equivalent, it is clear that the criminal policy choice of the international agreements and acts that contemplate it consists in strengthening the deprivation of assets as a muscular sanction with the aim of repressing and deterring profit-making illegal activities.

That criminal policy choice is even more marked in the instruments that provide also for recourse to "extended confiscation". This measure can target the entire property of the convicted person, including assets which, through a nominee, be it a natural or legal person, are actually at his or her disposal. Here the link between what is confiscated and the specific criminal activity for which the conviction has been handed down is further weakened in that there is nothing to preclude the confiscation of assets that, although having a value exceeding that of the proceeds of crime do not indisputably stem from lawful activities or sources.

In other words, extended confiscation is still anchored to a final criminal conviction for the commission of certain crimes and indeed any such conviction is a prerequisite. However, once confiscation is inflicted, it spreads out among the assets of the offender and, like a sort of invasive and voracious red palm weevil, attacks any property "presumably" stemming from unlawful conduct, i.e. without any conviction having been handed down in relation thereto.[19] As a result the

---

[18] At the same time, the link of pertinence constitutes a necessary condition for the actual application of confiscation. This is confirmed by the Extraordinary African Chamber at first instance, *Ministère Public v. Hissen Habré*, Judgment of 30 May 2016, para. 2329.

[19] VIRZO, *cit. supra* note 5, p. 30.

principles of legality and the presumption of innocence, as well as, in general, the "human rights of bad guys" are often violated.[20]

For example, on the basis of Article 12(7) UNTOC, the onus is on the convicted person to rebut the presumption that certain assets are proceeds of crime: it will not suffice to furnish an adequate justification regarding the source of each of his or her assets, but the offender will be obliged to "demonstrate the lawful origin of the alleged proceeds of the crime".

In other words, not only will the offender have to demonstrate that the property liable to confiscation does not constitute the profit of the specific crime for which he or she has been convicted but that the property in question also has a lawful origin, with the consequence that the presumption to rebut is, in reality, that of unlawful acquisition of the property (and not of "alleged proceeds of the crime"). In short, it is a "controversial provision"[21] that is "difficult to reconcile with the presumption of innocence".[22]

The last category of confiscation measures consists of those that can be imposed even in the absence of any criminal conviction.

In this respect, a further distinction must be drawn depending on whether the measure concerns an asset that can be confiscated as such or an asset that can be confiscated not because of its intrinsic characteristic but because it is directly or indirectly at the disposal of a natural or legal person having a certain degree of involvement in a given transnational criminal activity.

Among the treaty provisions that call for the adoption of the measures of the first type, one can include the longstanding Convention for the Suppression of Counterfeiting Currency (Article 11) and CITES (Article VIII): the imposition of confiscation is not intended, at least primarily, to punish the addressee of the measure but respectively to safeguard one of the vital interests of the State,[23] namely its monetary sovereignty, and to protect natural resources of general interest to the international community.

As regards measures of the second type, an example can be found in Article 54(1)(c) UNCAC, which permits confiscation "in cases in which the offender cannot be prosecuted by reason of death, flight or absence or in other appropriate cases". Another example is in Article 4(2) of Directive 2014/42/EU, which allows Member States that see fit to adopt such measures.[24] Also worth mentioning is a FATF recommendation: "Countries should consider adopting measures that allow such proceeds or instrumentalities to be confiscated without requiring a

---

[20] To quote IVORY, *Corruption, Asset Recovery and the Protection of Property in Public International Law. The Human Rights of Bad Guys*, Cambridge, 2014.

[21] MCCLEAN, *Transnational Organized Crime. A Commentary on the UN Convention and its Protocols*, Oxford, 2007, p. 147.

[22] BOISTER, *An Introduction to Transnational Criminal Law*, 2nd ed., Oxford, 2018, p. 338.

[23] See CARREAU and MARRELLA, *Diritto internazionale*, 2nd ed., Milano, 2018, pp. 381-382.

[24] Directive 2014/42/EU of the European Parliament and of the Council of 3 April 2014 on the freezing and confiscation of the instrumentalities and proceeds of crime in the European Union.

criminal conviction (non-conviction based confiscation), or which require an offender to demonstrate the lawful origin of the property alleged to be liable to the
extent that such a requirement is consistent with the principles of their domestic
law".[25]

None of these three provisions or recommendations outlines the characteristic
features of "non-conviction based confiscations". Therefore, the States to which
these provisions or recommendations are addressed are not only not obliged to
implement them but are also free to opt for the forms of non-conviction based
confiscation that they consider more in line with both their legal traditions and
their contingent criminal policy choices. By way of mere example, it should
be noted that the Italian system makes provision for "preventive confiscation",
which is applied to assets that are directly or indirectly available (if necessary,
including through transfer by succession on death to a third party) to persons
suspected of having been a member of a mafia organisation or having committed
other serious offences specified by law in the past.[26]

The ECtHR, commencing from its judgment in *Raimondo v. Italy*,[27] has substantially endorsed the Italian criminal policy choices underlying preventive confiscation.[28] For example, in *Arcuri and Others v. Italy*, the Court pointed out that
this type of deprivation of property "forms part of a crime-prevention policy" and
"sought to prevent the unlawful use, in a way dangerous to society, of possessions whose lawful origin has not been established. It therefore considers that the
aim of the resulting interferences serves the general interest".[29] This also bearing in mind that "in Italy the problem of organised crime has reached a very
disturbing level. The enormous profits made by these organisations from their
unlawful activities give them a level of power which places in jeopardy the rule
of law within the State".[30] It should be added that in none of these judgments did
the ECtHR classify the Italian concept of preventive confiscation as a penalty,[31]
thereby bringing it within the category "non-conviction based confiscations".

Although reaching the same conclusion as the ECtHR on the non-criminal
nature of the preventive confiscation, in its Judgment No. 24/2019 the Italian
Constitutional Court considers that it serves the different purpose of recover-

---

[25] FATF, *International Standards on Combating Money Laundering and the Financing of
Terrorism and Proliferation* (adopted 16 February 2012), recommendation 4.3.
[26] Currently "preventive confiscation" is governed by Articles 16 ff. of Legislative Decree
No. 159 of 6 September 2011 (Code of Anti-Mafia Laws and Preventive Measures). On this
form of confiscation, see, recently, also for further bibliographical references, TRINCHERA,
*Confiscare senza punire? Uno studio sullo statuto di garanzia della confisca della ricchezza
illecita*, Torino, 2020, pp. 169-215.
[27] *Raimondo v. Italy*, Application No. 12954/87, Judgment of 22 February 1994, para. 30.
[28] MAUGERI, "La legittimità della confisca di prevenzione come modello di "processo" al
patrimonio tra tendenze espansive e sollecitazioni sovrannazionali", Rivista italiana di diritto
e procedura penale, 2018, p. 561 ff.
[29] *Arcuri and Others v. Italy*, Application No. 52024/99, Decision as to the Admissibility
of 5 July 2012.
[30] *Ibid.*
[31] *Capitani and Campanella v. Italy*, Application No. 24920/07, Judgment of 17 May
2011, para. 37.

ing illegally accumulated assets and, therefore, restoration of the situation that would have existed in the absence of their unlawful acquisition.[32] An undoubted advantage of this different rationale consists in overcoming what legal scholars – including the very judge who authored Judgment No. 24/2019 – have defined as the "intolerable fiction"[33] of the preventive nature of the measure in question. In fact, preventive confiscation is not mainly aimed at the need to neutralise situations of present danger and avert the commission of future crimes[34] but to deprive the addressees of the measure of the advantages that they have gained through engaging in unlawful activities.[35]

2. LIMITS TO THE APPLICATION OF CONFISCATION MEASURES IN ECtHR CASE LAW: A) THE PRINCIPLE OF LEGALITY IN CRIMINAL MATTERS

It is not uncommon that confiscation measures applied by Council of Europe Member States in the context of international action against criminal activities and in accordance with conventions and acts of intergovernmental institutions conflict with human rights enshrined in customary international law and the European Convention of Human Rights (ECHR).

In fact, confiscation measures are likely to affect, in a non-superficial manner, not only the right to property but also very important principles such as those of legality and the presumption of innocence.

The question of compliance with the principle of legality arises in particular for non-conviction based confiscations. Called to rule on this matter on numerous occasions, the Strasbourg Court considers that there is a violation of the principle in question, as recognised by Article 7(1) ECHR (which also incorporates the related principle of non-retroactivity of criminal law), only if the national measure is in the nature of a penalty regardless of whether it is labelled as non-conviction based confiscation.

This assessment is carried out by the ECtHR on the basis of three independent criteria, outlined in the well-known judgment of *Engel and Others v. The Netherlands*[36] and clarified in subsequent rulings, namely: 1) classification in do-

---

[32] *Corte Costituzionale*, 24 January 2019, Judgment No. 24, para. 10.4.1. See MAUGERI, PINTO DE ALBURBERQUE, "La confisca di prevenzione nella tutela costituzionale multilivello: tra istanze di tassatività e ragionevolezza, se ne afferma la natura ripristinatoria (C. Cost. 24/2019)", Studi penali, 2019, available at: <https://www.sistemapenale.it/it/articolo/confisca-prevenzione-tutela-costituzionale-multilivello-corte-cost-24-2019>; MAZZACUVA, "L'uno-due dalla Consulta alla disciplina delle misure di prevenzione: punto di arrivo o principio di un ricollocamento sui binari costituzionali", Rivista italiana di diritto e procedura penale, 2019, p. 987 ff.

[33] VIGANÒ, "Riflessioni sullo statuto costituzionale e convenzionale della confisca "di prevenzione" nell'ordinamento italiano", in PALIERO et al. (eds.), *La pena, ancora fra attualità e tradizione*, Milano, 2018, p. 896 ff.

[34] *Ibid.*

[35] TRINCHERA, *cit. supra* note 26, p. 390.

[36] *Engel and Others v. The Netherlands*, Applications Nos. 5100-5102/71, 5354/72 and 5370/72, Judgment of 8 June 1976, para. 82. In the judgment it was necessary to ascertain

mestic law;[37] 2) the very nature of the offence; 3) the degree of severity of the penalty that the person concerned risks incurring. The second and third criteria are alternative and not cumulative; therefore criminal nature in relation to the ECHR may be derived from just one of them.[38]

As one can imagine, the most relevant parameter for our purposes is the nature and severity of the penalty. In particular, since the *Welch v. United Kingdom* judgment of 1995[39] the ECtHR has emphasised the purpose of the measure from time to time scrutinised.

In that judgment, after finding that the confiscation measure provided for in the Drug Trafficking Offences Act 1986 was a penalty (imposed retroactively on the applicant), the Court held that Article 7 ECHR was applicable.[40] In rejecting the United Kingdom's arguments, which sought to show that the measure "did not seek to impose a penalty or a punishment for a criminal offence but was essentially a confiscatory and preventive measure",[41] the Court – consistent with *Engel* case law – reiterated that the classification of the measure complained of must be carried out independently without being constrained by formal national nomenclatures but instead looking "behind appearances at the reality of the situation".[42] The ECtHR thus detected a punitive purpose in the aims pursued by the legislation,[43] which "may be seen as constituent elements of the very notion of punishment".[44]

---

whether the disciplinary sanctions affecting personal liberty imposed on the applicants were of a criminal nature.

[37] *Ibid.*, para. 82: "This however provides no more than a starting point. The indications so afforded have only a formal and relative value [...]".

[38] See MANES, "Articolo 7", in BARTOLE, DE SENA and ZAGREBELSKY (eds.), *Commentario breve alla Convenzione europea dei diritti dell'uomo*, Padova, 2012, p. 260 ff.

[39] *Welch v. The United Kingdom*, Application No. 17440/90, Judgment of 9 February 1995.

[40] *Ibid.*, para. 35.

[41] *Ibid.*, para. 24.

[42] *Ibid.*, para. 34.

[43] *Ibid.*, para. 33: "there are several aspects of the making of an order under the 1986 Act which are in keeping with the idea of a penalty as it is commonly understood [...]. The sweeping statutory assumptions [...] that all property passing through the offender's hands over a six-year period is the fruit of drug trafficking unless he can prove otherwise [...]; the fact that the confiscation order is directed to the proceeds involved in drug dealing and is not limited to actual enrichment or profit [...]; and the possibility of imprisonment in default of payment by the offender [...] – are all elements which, when considered together, provide a strong indication of, inter alia, a regime of punishment".

[44] *Ibid.*, para. 30. In subsequent rulings on non-conviction based confiscations, the Court has confirmed this line of reasoning. For example, has the nature of a penalty the Italian "*confisca urbanistica*". Although its examination is beyond the scope of this paper (as it is not an area covered by international agreements and acts designed to combat criminal activities), it should be noted that *inter alia* in *G.I.E.M. s.r.l. and Others v. Italy*, Applications Nos. 1828/06 and 19029/11, Grand Chamber, Judgment of 28 June 2018, the ECtHR held that that type of confiscation was a penalty and highlighted its punitive nature. On such case law, see, amongst others, CANNONE, "La sentenza della Grande Camera della Corte europea dei diritti dell'uomo nell'affare GIEM srl e altri v. Italia del 28 giugno 2018: brevi osservazioni", Studi sull'integrazione europea, 2019, p. 155 ff.; GIANNELLI, "La confisca urbanistica nel dialogo fra le Corti dopo la sentenza G.I.E.M e altri contro Italia", in DI STASI (ed.), *CEDU e ordinamento italia-*

On the other hand, if the Court considers that a form of non-conviction based confiscation is not characterised by a marked punitive purpose, it will not classify it as a penalty. This is so in the case of national measures complying with the Council of Europe Convention on Laundering, Search, Seizure and Confiscation of the Proceeds of Crime,[45] which, even if applied in the context of the fight against international corruption, serve a reparatory purpose. "There are in fact" – as one can read in *Dassa Foundation and Others v. Liechtenstein* – "several elements which make seizure and forfeiture, in the manner in which these measures are regulated under Liechtenstein law, more comparable to a restitution of unjustified enrichment under civil law than to a fine under criminal law".[46]

Similarly, in *Gogitidze*, the Court emphasised that the *in rem* confiscation in force in Georgia was not intended to be punitive but mainly compensatory.[47] The Strasbourg judges considered that the alleged criminal nature of the Georgian confiscation measure could not be deduced even from its collateral deterrent effect consisting of "sending a clear signal to public officials already involved in corruption or considering so doing".[48] This is because what distinguishes the confiscation in question is precisely its compensatory purpose (even though combined with that of general deterrence) of restoring both the offender and the victim to their economic situation existing before the corruption and the unjustified enrichment occurred.[49]

Moreover, according to the Court, as is the case of a compensatory purpose, a merely special deterrent purpose is irrelevant when it comes to deciding whether a given confiscation measure is to be considered as criminal in nature. Consider the *Balsamo* judgment, where the Court, on the one hand, conceded that in the San Marino legal system recourse to confiscation to combat money laundering is aimed at preventing the illegal use of financial resources and therefore the commission of further offences, and on the other hand, held that "in view of the applicant's acquittal precisely on the basis of the lack of intention, it cannot be said that the measure also included a punitive purpose".[50]

---

no. *La giurisprudenza della Corte europea dei diritti dell'uomo e l'impatto nell'ordinamento italiano (2016-2020)*, Milano, 2020, p. 531 ff.

[45] 8 November 1990, entered into force 1 September 1993.

[46] *Dassa Foundation and Others v. Liechtenstein*, Application No. 696/05, Decision as to the Admissibility of 30 August 2007, para. 17.

[47] *Gogitidze*, *cit. supra* note 3, para. 126 and para. 102, stressing that "[t]he compensatory aspect consisted in the obligation to restore the injured party in civil proceedings to the status which had existed prior to the unjust enrichment of the public official in question, by returning wrongfully acquired property either to its previous lawful owner or, in the absence of such, to the State".

[48] *Ibid.*, para. 102.

[49] MAUGERI, "Il regolamento (UE) 2018/1805 per il reciproco riconoscimento dei provvedimenti di congelamento e di confisca: una pietra angolare per la cooperazione e per l'efficienza", Diritto penale contemporaneo, 2019, available at: <https://archiviodpc.dirittopenaleuomo.org/upload/2944-maugeri2019a-converted.pdf>, p. 21.

[50] *Balsamo*, *cit. supra* note 3, para. 62.

Concerning the case law on Italian preventive confiscation,[51] it has already been observed that the ECtHR denies that preventive confiscation is a penalty.[52] According to the Court, the confiscation of assets of a person suspected of belonging to an organized criminal group is not punitive but serves the purpose of preventing the unlawful use and danger to society of assets whose lawful origin has not been ascertained.[53] It would seem, therefore, that according to the Strasbourg Court, it is this special deterrent function that deprives Italian preventive confiscation of any punitive purpose.[54]

4.   B) The Principle of Presumption of Innocence

Whether a given confiscation measure is classified as criminal in nature is also pertinent to the ECtHR's review of alleged violations of the principle of the presumption of innocence under Article 6(2) ECHR.[55]

Geerings v. The Netherlands is emblematic in this respect. The applicant had been sentenced to a term of imprisonment for the offence of theft. At the end of second criminal proceedings, he was acquitted of other offences for lack of evidence. However, as he had failed to prove the lawful origin of the assets suspected by the prosecution to be the proceeds of previous criminal activities, those assets were confiscated. After reiterating that the presumption of innocence is violated if a penalty is imposed on the basis of conjecture or circumstantial evidence, or before guilt of a given offence has been legally established,[56] the ECtHR considered the confiscation imposed on the applicant to be "inappropriate": "If it is not found beyond a reasonable doubt that the person affected has actually committed a crime, and if it cannot be established as fact that any advantage, illegal or otherwise, was actually obtained such a measure can only be based on a presumption of guilt. This can hardly be considered compatible with Article 6 § 2".[57]

---

[51] See amongst others *Raimondo, cit. supra* note 27; *Prisco v. Italy*, Application No. 38662/97, Decision as to the Admissibility of 15 June 1999; *Arcuri, cit. supra* note 29; *Riela and Others v. Italy*, Application No. 52439/99, Decision as to the Admissibility of 4 September 2001; *Bongiorno and Others v. Italy*, Application No. 4514/07, Judgment of 5 January 2010; *Capitani and Campanella v. Italy, cit. supra* note 31; *Cacucci and Sabatelli v. Italy*, Application No. 29797/09, Judgment of 17 June 2014.

[52] *Capitani and Campanella, cit. supra* note 31, para. 37.

[53] *Ibid.*, para. 32.

[54] However, as underlined by Viganò, *cit. supra* note 33, p. 893, also the punishment serves to prevent the commission of new crimes by the offender (special deterrence) and by third parties (general deterrence). Therefore, recognising that the measure pursues a preventive purpose still does not tell us anything about its nature.

[55] "Everyone charged with a criminal offence shall be presumed innocent until proved guilty according to law". On this issue see Boucht, "Civil Asset Forfeiture and the Presumption of Innocence under Article 6(2) ECHR", New Journal of European Criminal Law, 2014, p. 221 ff.

[56] *Geerings v. The Netherlands*, Application No. 30810/03, Judgment of 1 March 2007, para. 41.

[57] *Ibid.*, para. 47.

The *Geerings* judgment would seem to suggest that also the types of extended confiscation provided for in international agreements and acts on the fight against criminal activities pose problems of compatibility with the principle of presumption of innocence. In fact, the application of an extended confiscation measure requires a final conviction for a criminal offence, but once imposed it spreads out among the offender's assets and attacks any property whose lawful origin cannot be explained. There is, therefore, a rebuttable presumption that the assets belonging to the person affected by the measure (or which are at his or her disposal, including through a nominee), whose value is disproportionate to the declared income or to the legal business activity carried on, constitute the proceeds of crime.

However, the ECtHR has come to a different conclusion. In *Phillips v. United Kingdom* and *Grayson and Barnham v. United Kingdom,* it held that, in applying extended confiscation measures against the applicants on the basis of the Drug Trafficking Act 1994 and the 1988 UN Convention against Illicit Traffic in Narcotic Drugs, the respondent State had not breached Article 6(2) ECHR.

First of all, in line with the *Welch* judgment the Court classified the confiscation in question as a penalty with both punitive and general deterrent purposes.[58] However, although they involved the confiscation of assets accumulated in the six years preceding the commission of the offences for which the convictions were handed down (property whose lawful origin the applicants could not prove), the contested measures were not imposed, as in the *Geerings* case, in the context of different criminal proceedings that ended without new convictions. Precisely for this reason, the Court ruled out any violation of the principle of the presumption of innocence. According to the Court, the purpose of the extended confiscation procedure under the Drug Trafficking Act is not to ascertain whether or not the defendant is guilty of further drug trafficking activities but "to assess the amount at which the confiscation order should properly be fixed".[59]

With regard to the presumptions laid down by the Drug Trafficking Act involving the reversal of the burden of proof, the ECtHR has held that they are not necessarily incompatible with the ECHR.[60] In the two judgments the Court observed that "presumptions of fact or law operate in every criminal law system

---

[58] *Phillips v. The United Kingdom*, Application No. 41087/98, Judgment of 5 July 2001, para. 52. See also, *Butler v. The United Kingdom*, Application No. 41661/98, Decision as to the Admissibility of 27 June 2002.

[59] *Phillips, cit. supra* note 58, para. 34, and *Grayson and Barnham v. The United Kingdom*, Applications Nos. 19955/05 and 15085/06, Judgment of 23 September 2008, para. 37. Therefore, according to SIMONATO, "Confiscation and Fundamental Rights across Criminal and Non-criminal Domains", ERA Forum, 2017, available at: <http://www.os-servatoriomisurediprevenzione.it/wp-content/uploads/2018/12/Simonato2017_Article_ConfiscationAndFundamentalRigh.pdf>, p. 372, in *Phillips*, "the Court considered the reference to other offences only as a criterion to determine the extent of the confiscation, operating in the sentencing phase (for the judged offences) but not representing a new charge for the other non-judged offences allegedly committed by the convicted person".

[60] See also *Aboufadda v. France*, Application No. 28457/10, Judgment of 4 November 2014, para. 28.

and are not prohibited in principle by the Convention, as long as States remain within certain limits, taking into account the importance of what is at stake and maintaining the rights of the defence".[61] Moreover, the presumptions set out in the Drug Trafficking Act are rebuttable. Thus, even if the domestic court having jurisdiction in the *Grayson and Barnham* case "was required by law to assume that the assets derived from drug trafficking, this assumption could have been rebutted if the applicant had shown that he had acquired the property through legitimate means".[62]

5.   C) THE RIGHT TO PROPERTY

Confiscation measures, even when not criminal in nature, can only be imposed taking into account the safeguards that Article 1 of Protocol No. 1 to the ECHR makes the lawfulness of any restriction on the right to property conditional on.

Regarding that article, the ECtHR, for example in its *Markus v. Latvia* judgment concerning extended confiscation for bribery offences, highlighted that it "comprises three distinct rules enunciating the principle of the peaceful enjoyment of possession, regulating the deprivation of possessions and recognising the State's right to control the use of the property".[63] Of course, these three rules are connected. Indeed, "[t]he second and the third rule are concerned with particular instances of interferences with the peaceful enjoyment of property and should therefore be construed in the light of the general principle enunciated in the first rule".[64]

Now, with regard to a State confiscation order leading to a permanent deprivation of the right of ownership of a given asset, the ECtHR will ascertain above all whether it has been imposed in the public interest. In this respect, the Court has found that national legislation providing for confiscation orders in the con-

---

[61] *Phillips, cit. supra* note 58, para. 40.

[62] *Grayson and Barnham, cit. supra* note 59, para. 45.

[63] *Markus v. Latvia*, Application No. 17483/10, Judgment of 11 June 2020, para. 64. See also, amongst previous decisions, *Sporrong and Lönroth v. Sweden*, Application No. 7151/75, Judgment of 23 September 1982, para. 61; *Iatridis v. Greece*, Application No. 31107/96, Judgment of 25 March 1999, para. 55; *Beyeler v. Italy*, Application No. 33202/96, Judgment of 5 January 2000, para. 98; *Jahn and Others v. Germany*, Applications Nos. 46720/99 and 72552/01, Judgment of 30 June 2005, para. 78; *Maggio and Others v. Italy*, Applications Nos. 46286/09 and 56001/08, Judgment of 31 May 2011, para. 56; *G.I.E.M. S.r.l., cit. supra* note 44, para. 289. On the three distinct rules of Article 1 ECHR Protocol, see FRIGO, "Peaceful Enjoyment of Possessions, Expropriation and Control of the Use of Property in the System of the European Convention of Human Rights", IYIL, 2000, p. 45 ff.; CATALDI, "Brevi osservazioni sul diritto di proprietà nella CEDU alla luce della giurisprudenza della Corte di Strasburgo", Studi sull'integrazione europea, 2016, p. 244 ff; PISILLO MAZZESCHI, *Diritto internazionale dei diritti umani. Teoria e prassi*, Torino, 2020, p. 348.

[64] *Maggio, cit. supra* note 63, para. 56.

text of the fight against organised crime,[65] money laundering,[66] international drug trafficking,[67] corruption,[68] transfer of large sums of money[69] or illegal fishing[70] is in the general interest.

Conformity with a general interest cannot, however, be considered sufficient to justify the deprivation of property rights. Indeed, in determining whether a confiscation measure which the State deems *necessary* to control the use of property in accordance with the general interest complies with the Protocol, the ECtHR also assesses its proportionality.[71] According to the ECtHR, the sacrifice that confiscation imposes on the person affected by it is only justified if a reasonable balance is struck between the restrictions on the right to property and the general interest pursued by the State. In other words, "there must [...] exist a reasonable relationship of proportionality between the means employed and the aim sought to be realised".[72]

As a result of the weighted assessment described above, the penalty of confiscation was disproportionate, for example, in *Gyrlyan v. Russia*. The applicant, after selling some lands in the vicinity of Moscow, decided to travel to Odessa taking with him banknotes worth about USD 100,000. At Moscow airport, however, the money was confiscated by the Russian authorities on the grounds of a breach of the obligation to report the transfer abroad of sums of money exceeding USD 10,000. Although the ECtHR considered that the confiscation provided

---

[65] *Raimondo, cit. supra* note 27, para 30, where, regarding the Mafia, the Court stated that "Confiscation [...] is an effective and necessary weapon in the combat against this cancer".

[66] *Veits v. Estonia*, Application No. 12951/11, Judgment of 15 January 2015, para. 71: "confiscation in criminal proceedings is in line with the general interest of the community, because the forfeiture of money or assets obtained through illegal activities or paid for with the proceeds of crime is a necessary and effective means of combating criminal activities".

[67] *Saccoccia v. Austria*, Application No. 69917/01, Judgment of 18 December 2008, para. 88.

[68] *Gogitidze, cit. supra* note 3, para. 110.

[69] *Karapetyan v. Georgia*, Application No. 61233/12, Judgment of 15 October 2020, para. 34: "States have a legitimate interest and also a duty by virtue of various international treaties to implement measures to detect and monitor the movement of cash across their borders, since large amounts of cash may be used for money laundering, drug trafficking, financing terrorism or organised crime, tax evasion or the commission of other serious financial offences [...]. The Court therefore considers that the confiscation measure conformed to the general interest of the community".

[70] *Yasar, cit. supra* note 9, para. 59: "the interference complained of pursued the legitimate aim of preventing offences relating to illegal fishing in the Black Sea: since such activities pose a serious threat to the biological resources in the area, this aim serves the general interest".

[71] EISSEN, "Il principio di proporzionalità nella giurisprudenza della Corte europea dei diritti dell'uomo", Rivista internazionale dei diritti dell'uomo, 1989, p. 31 ff.; CONDORELLI, "Premier Protocol Additionnel, Article 1" in PETTITI, DECAUX and IMBERT (eds.), *La Convention européenne des droits de l'homme, Commentaire Article par Article*, 2nd ed., Paris, 1999, p. 971 ff.; ARAI-TAKAHASHI, *The Margin of Appreciation Doctrine and the Principle of Proportionality in the Jurisprudence of the ECHR*, Antwerp, 2001, pp. 146-161; ÇOBAN, *Protection of Property Rights within the European Convention of Human Rights*, Aldershot, 2014, pp. 171-215; PADELLETTI, "Protocollo n. 1, Articolo 1", in BARTOLE, DE SENA and ZAGREBELSKY (eds.), *cit. supra* note 38, p. 800 ff.; IVORY, *cit. supra* note 20, pp. 219-245.

[72] *Phillips, cit. supra* note 58, para. 52.

for by the Russian legislation was in the general interest of preventing a lack of transparency in the international movement of large sums of money from facilitating the commission of transnational criminal activities,[73] it held that its application to this case did not comply with Article 1 of Protocol No. 1. The Court reiterated that "in order to be proportionate, the interference should correspond to the severity of the infringement, and the sanction to the gravity of the offence it is designated to punish – in the instant case, failure to comply with the declaration requirement – rather than to the gravity of any presumed infringement which has not actually been established".[74] Moreover, "the amount confiscated was undoubtedly substantial for the applicant, for it represented almost the entire proceeds of sale of his property in Russia".[75]

Finally, restrictions on the right to property (which are motivated by a general interest and can only be imposed if they are necessary and proportionate to the achievement of that interest) must be regulated by legislation. According to the ECtHR, the condition is deemed to be fulfilled when the legislative provision[76] is accessible and worded with sufficient precision so as to make the applicability of the measures restricting the right to property foreseeable and to enable each citizen to regulate his or her conduct accordingly. As has been summarised, "[t]he relevant provisions must satisfy the requirements of accessibility, precision and foreseeability".[77]

This issue arose for example in the *Saccoccia* case. The applicant argued that there was no provision for confiscation in Austrian anti-money laundering legislation. However, the ECtHR rejected the applicant's argument, noting that the measure was imposed by Austria on the basis of a bilateral mutual legal assistance agreement with the United States, that the respondent State had enforced a foreign forfeiture order issued by the Rhode Island District Court and that the applicability of forfeiture was foreseeable under US federal law regarding the crime of international money laundering.[78]

On the contrary, in *Markus*, after holding that the confiscation was disproportionate because "applied to all properties owned by the applicant, regardless of the manner of their acquisition and of any relation to any offence",[79] the ECtHR added that the Latvian criminal provision under which the confiscation had been ordered "leaves uncertainty about the scope of the trial court's competence, it cannot be regarded as foreseeable and does not provide protection against arbi-

---

[73] *Gyrlyan v. Russia*, Application No. 35943/15, Judgment of 9 October 2018, para. 23.

[74] *Ibid.*, para. 30.

[75] *Ibid.*, para. 31.

[76] It is understood in a broad sense and therefore includes domestic case law, which must, however, fulfil the same requisites required for the adoption of a law and therefore be of an accessible and predictable nature for the community. See PUSTORINO, *Lezioni di tutela internazionale dei diritti umani*, 2nd ed., Bari, 2020, p. 208.

[77] SCHABAS, *The European Convention on Human Rights. A Commentary*, Oxford, 2015, p. 976.

[78] *Saccoccia*, cit. *supra* note 66, paras. 77 and 87.

[79] *Markus*, cit. *supra* note 63, para. 70.

trariness. It may also seriously impede a person's ability to present his or her case effectively"[80] before a domestic court.

6. FINAL REMARKS

As mentioned above,[81] the ECtHR, taking into account the proliferation of international acts and agreements on combating criminal activities, maintains that "common European and even universal legal standards can be said to exist which encourage [...] the confiscation of property linked to serious criminal offences such as corruption, money laundering, drug offences and so on".

According to the Court, the standards in question concern: 1) the imposition of confiscation measures even in the absence of a criminal conviction; 2) the introduction of mechanisms of reversal of the burden of proof further to which it is the person to whom the measure is addressed who must rebut the presumption of the unlawful acquisition of his or her property; 3) the applicability of confiscation not only to the proceeds of criminal activity but also "to property, including any incomes and other indirect benefits, obtained by converting or transforming the direct proceeds of crime or intermingling them with other, possibly lawful, assets"; and 4) confiscation ordered against third parties "which hold ownership rights without the requisite *bona fide* with a view to disguising their wrongful role in amassing the wealth in question".[82]

Moreover, the Court has gone so far as to maintain that in accordance with the aforementioned "universal legal standards", States Parties to the ECHR "must be given" "a wide margin of appreciation with regard to what constitutes the appropriate means of applying measures to control the use of property such as the confiscation of all types of proceeds of crime".[83]

This is evidence of a significant difference with other "generally recognised international standards",[84] which have not been invoked by the Court to restrict the scope of an article of the Convention or the Protocols but rather

---

[80] *Ibid.*, para. 73.

[81] *Supra* Section 1. See also, ORLOVSKA, STEPANOVA, "Confiscation of Proceeds and Property Related to Crimes: International Standards and the ECHR Practice", Juridical Tribune, 2020, p. 493 ff.

[82] *Gogitidze, cit. supra* note 3, para. 105; *Telbis and Viziteu, cit. supra* note 3, para. 76, *Balsamo, cit. supra* note 3, para. 92. The ECtHR has correctly interpreted the international legal instruments from which they have drawn the "universal legal standards". Indeed, with specific reference to the four types of measures covered by the standards, even the relevant international conventions lay down merely optional rules.

[83] *Balsamo, cit. supra* note 3, para. 93.

[84] According to BENVENISTI, "Margin of Appreciation, Consensus and Universal Standards", New York University Journal of International Law & Policy, 1999, p. 843 ff., "universal legal standards for the protection and promotion of human rights [...] are compromised by the doctrine of margin of appreciation".

to interpret it broadly and guarantee the protection of rights not expressly stated.[85]

For example, with reference to the right not to be forced to incriminate oneself, the ECtHR has clarified that "[a]lthough not specifically mentioned in Article 6 of the Convention, there can be no doubt that the right to remain silent under police questioning and the privilege against self-incrimination are generally recognised international standards which lie at the heart of the notion of a fair procedure under Article 6 [...]. By providing the accused with protection against improper compulsion by the authorities, these immunities contribute to avoiding miscarriages of justice and to securing the aim of Article 6".[86]

Therefore, it does not seem to me that the "wide margin of appreciation" afforded to the State authorities by the ECtHR in the *Balsamo* judgment is to be welcomed. Certainly, confiscation is congenial to incisive action against serious criminal activities, often transnational in dimension, and, in particular, against crime whose "main motive"[87] is the accumulation of wealth. However, the case law of the Court of Strasbourg examined in this work has shown that the instances in which confiscation measures issued by State authorities have been deemed contrary to norms of international law and of many democratic constitutions enshrining the principle of legality in criminal matters, due process rights and property rights are all but rare. On the contrary, it is imperative that confiscation measures do not lead to the infringement of human rights, that they be constantly anchored to the values of the rule of law, and that the ECtHR unhesitatingly rein in any abuse of them.[88]

---

[85] See GAJA, "Does the European Court of Human Rights Use its Stated Methods of Interpretation?", in *Divenire sociale e adeguamento del diritto. Studi in onore di Francesco Capotorti*, Milano, 1999, p. 213 ff.

[86] *John Murray v. The United Kingdom*, Application No. 18731/91, Judgment of 8 February 1996, para. 45.

[87] Directive 2014/42/EU, *cit. supra* note 24, first recital.

[88] Abuses well exposed for example by MANES, "The Last Imperative of Criminal Policy: *Nullum Crimen Sine Confiscatione*", European Criminal Law Review, 2016, p. 143 ff.

THE AGREEMENT BETWEEN GREECE AND ITALY ON THE DELIMITATION OF THEIR RESPECTIVE MARITIME ZONES: AN ITALIAN PERSPECTIVE

Marina Mancini[*]

Abstract

In 2020 Greece and Italy concluded a maritime delimitation agreement, extending the already-established boundary line between their respective continental shelf areas to the other maritime areas to which they are entitled under international law. The Greek authorities hailed the agreement as a great success, stressing that it fully reflects their position vis-à-vis maritime delimitation in the Mediterranean and it meets their national interests in the Ionian Sea. This article critically analyzes the agreement, in the light of various recent events, and it finds that it serves Italian interests too. In particular, the 2020 Italo-Greek agreement furthers Italy's growing interest in delimiting the maritime zones to which it is entitled under international law, so as to prevent its rights and jurisdiction over them being impaired by the proclamation of overlapping zones by its neighbours. It also sets the stage for future proclamation by Italy of an EEZ covering the waters adjacent to its territorial sea in the Ionian Sea.

Keywords: continental shelf; exclusive economic zone; maritime boundary; offshore hydrocarbon activities; submarine pipelines.

1. Introduction

Among the international agreements Italy concluded in 2020, remarkable is the maritime delimitation agreement with Greece. The Italian Minister of Foreign Affairs and International Cooperation, Luigi Di Maio, and the Greek Minister of Foreign Affairs, Nikos Dendias, signed it in Athens on 9 June 2020.[1] Alongside the agreement, they signed a joint declaration on the resources of the Mediterranean and a joint communication to the European Commission, which are not publicly available.[2] Greece soon ratified the agreement, while Italy did it

---

[*] Of the Board of Editors.

[1] The agreement was done in two originals, each in the Greek, Italian and English languages, all texts being equally authentic, with the English text prevailing in case of divergences. The Italian and English texts are attached to Law No. 93 of 1 June 2021 (GU No. 149 of 24 June 2021).

[2] KOKKINIDIS, "Greece, Italy Maritime Deal 'Model of Cooperation' in the Mediterranean", Greek Reporter, 11 June 2020, available at: <https://greekreporter.com/2020/06/11/greece-italy-maritime-deal-model-of-cooperation-in-the-mediterranean/>. On the content of both documents, see MARGHELIS, "The Maritime Delimitation Agreement between Greece and Italy of

IYIL, Vol. 30 (2020), pp. 283-294
ISSN 0391-5107

more than one year later.[3] The President of the Italian Republic was authorized by the Parliament to ratify the agreement by Law No. 93 of 1 June 2021.[4] In accordance with Article 5, paragraph 2, the agreement entered into force on the date of exchange of the instruments of ratification.

The Italo-Greek agreement was hailed as a great success by the Greek authorities. They stressed that it fully reflects the position of Greece vis-à-vis maritime delimitation in the Mediterranean and it meets their national interests in the Ionian Sea.[5] The question arises whether this is also true for Italy. This article thoroughly analyzes the agreement and explores whether it serves Italian interests too.

2.   SINGLE MARITIME BOUNDARY

Greece and Italy agreed to extend the boundary line between their respective continental shelf areas to the other maritime areas to which they are entitled under international law, establishing a single maritime boundary. Article 1 of the 2020 agreement stipulates that

> the boundary line of the maritime zones to which the two countries are entitled to exercise, respectively, their sovereign rights or jurisdiction under international law shall be the continental shelf boundary established under the 1977 Agreement between the Hellenic Republic and the Italian Republic on the delimitation of their respective continental shelves (paragraph 1)

and it lists the WGS-84 coordinates of sixteen points which that line connects (paragraph 2).

It is worth recalling that the agreement on the delimitation of the continental shelf was concluded in Athens on 24 May 1977[6] and it entered into force on

---

9 June 2020: An Analysis in the Light of International Law, National Interest and Regional Politics", Marine Policy, 2021, p. 1 ff., pp. 3-4.

[3] As to Greece's ratification of the agreement at issue, see Law No. 4716 of 28 August 2020, Official Gazette of the Hellenic Republic No. 163 of 28 August 2020.

[4] See *supra* note 1.

[5] See: "Statements of the Minister of Foreign Affairs, Nikos Dendias, following his meeting with the Minister of Foreign Affairs of Italy, Luigi Di Maio", 9 June 2020, available at: <https://www.mfa.gr/en/current-affairs/top-story/statements-of-the-minister-of-foreign-affairs-nikos-dendias-following-his-meeting-with-the-minister-of-foreign-affairs-of-italy-luigi-di-maio-athens-june-2020.html>; "Prime Minister Kyriakos Mitsotakis address to the Parliament during the Debate on the Ratification of the EEZ Delimitation Agreements with Italy and Egypt", 26 August 2020, available at: <https://www.mfa.gr/italy/it/the-embassy/news/prime-minister-kyriakos-mitsotakis-ratification-of-the-eez-delimitation-agreements-with-italy-and-egypt.html>. As to the relevance of the agreement at issue to Greek interests, see also MARGHELIS, *cit. supra* note 2, p. 6 ff.

[6] Agreement between the Hellenic Republic and the Italian Republic on the Delimitation of the Respective Continental Shelf Areas of the Two States, Athens, 24 May 1977, UNTS,

12 November 1980.[7] It adopts the median line, with minor adjustments, as the boundary line between the parties' continental shelf areas. The geographical coordinates of sixteen points in the Ionian Sea are provided (Article 1(1)). The line connecting them runs for 268 nautical miles.[8] The northernmost point of the delimitation line (point 1) is the point of closest approach to the coasts of Greece and Italy and it lies respectively 22.0 and 20.1 nautical miles (nm) from them. The southernmost point (point 16) is located 168.9 nm from the coast of Sicily and 163.4 nm from the Greek island of Stamfani.[9] During negotiations, Greece accepted the use of straight baselines along the relevant Italian coasts, including the Italian-claimed closing line of the Gulf of Taranto, and it did not oppose giving only partial effect to the Greek island of Othonoi, situated in the Strait of Otranto, and to the Strofades, two Greek islets off the coasts of the Peloponnese (Stamfani and Arpia). In compensation, Italy conceded Greece a continental shelf area beyond the median line off the coast of the Greek island of Kefallinia.[10]

The 2020 agreement adopts the aforementioned line as the delimitation line of all the maritime zones which Greece and Italy are entitled to declare under international law. Such zones are not specifically mentioned. However, they certainly include the contiguous zone and the exclusive economic zone (EEZ), that are recognized as distinctive maritime zones in the 1982 UN Convention on the Law of the Sea (UNCLOS), which is binding on both States and is expressly referred to in the preamble of the agreement.[11] The agreed line also applies, without doubt, to the delimitation of the parties' ecological protection zones, where they are entitled to exercise only certain of the rights provided in the EEZ.[12]

Vol. 1275, 1982, p. 426 ff. It was done in two originals in the French language, both texts being equally authentic. The President of the Italian Republic was authorized by the Parliament to ratify the agreement at issue by Law No. 290 of 23 May 1980 (Suppl. to GU No. 181 of 3 July 1980).

[7] Data available in the treaties database of the Italian Ministry of Foreign Affairs and International Cooperation: <http://atrio.esteri.it/>.

[8] See the map annexed to this article.

[9] See United States Department of State, "Continental Shelf Boundary: Greece-Italy", Limits in the Seas No. 96, 6 June 1982, available at: <https://www.state.gov/wp-content/uploads/2019/12/LIS-96.pdf>.

[10] See LEANZA, "The Delimitation of the Continental Shelf of the Mediterranean Sea", International Journal of Marine and Coastal Law, 1993, p. 373 ff., p. 382.

[11] It is worth noting that, under Art. 303(2) UNCLOS, the coastal State may also exercise its jurisdiction to prevent and punish the removal of archaeological and historical objects in a zone extending up to 24 nm from the baselines. On the so-called "archaeological zone", see *inter alia* ŠOŠIĆ, "The 24-Mile Archaeological Zone: Abandoned or Confirmed?", in WOLFRUM, SERŠIĆ and ŠOŠIĆ (eds.), *Contemporary Developments in International Law: Essays in Honour of Budislav Vukas*, Leiden/Boston, 2016, p. 305 ff.

[12] On the ecological protection zones, see *inter alia*: WOLF, "Ecological Protection Zones", Max Planck Encyclopedia of Public International Law, 2013, available at: <https://opil.ouplaw.com/>; ANDREONE and CATALDI, "Sui Generis Zones", in ATTARD, FITZMAURICE and MARTÍNEZ GUTIÉRREZ (eds.), *The IMLI Manual on International Maritime Law*, Oxford, 2014, Vol. I, p. 217 ff.

Up to the time of writing, Greece has not proclaimed any of the above mentioned maritime zones; while Italy has declared only an ecological protection zone (EPZ). That zone, however, is not situated in the Ionian Sea and, consequently, it does not fall within the scope of the agreement at issue. The President of the Italian Republic, acting under Law No. 61 of 8 February 2006,[13] established an EPZ in the North-Western Mediterranean Sea, the Ligurian Sea and the Tyrrehnian Sea, by Decree No. 209 of 27 October 2011.[14]

As regards Italy, Law No. 91 of 14 June 2021 is also worth noting.[15] It authorizes the President of the Italian Republic to declare, by decree, an EEZ covering all or part of the waters adjacent to the territorial sea in accordance with the UNCLOS, subject to decision by the Council of Ministers, on the proposal of the Minister of Foreign Affairs and International Cooperation (Article 1(1) and (2)). As to the outer limits of the EEZ, it is specified that they shall be established by agreement with the opposite or adjacent States (Article 1(3)). An agreement of that kind is undoubtedly the one that Italy concluded with Greece in 2020.

It was indeed in view of a future proclamation of an EEZ that Greece and Italy negotiated the agreement at issue. In this respect, it is to be noted that the agreed delimitation appears to be in accordance with Article 74 UNCLOS, under which the delimitation of the EEZ between opposite or adjacent States must be effected "by agreement on the basis of international law, as referred to in Article 38 of the Statute of the International Court of Justice, in order to achieve an equitable solution".[16] No provision of the UNCLOS forbids a single delimitation line for both the continental shelf and the EEZ, such as the one agreed by Greece and Italy. As a matter of fact, the vast majority of maritime delimitation treaties establish a single boundary line for the continental shelf and the EEZ.[17]

The recent Italo-Greek agreement opportunely requires the parties to inform each other, as soon as possible, of their decision to declare a maritime zone extending up to the agreed boundary line (Article 2). Future extension of such line is also contemplated. It is laid down that, once the parties conclude similar delimitation treaties with their respective neighbours, the aforementioned line shall extend northward beyond point 1 and southward beyond point 16 up to the points of intersection with their respective neighbours' maritime zones (Article 1(3)).

Interestingly, a few months after the signature of the agreement at issue, Greece adopted straight baselines, in place of normal baselines, for measur-

---

[13] Law No. 61 of 8 February 2006, GU No. 52 of 3 March 2006.
[14] Presidential Decree No. 209 of 27 October 2011, GU No. 293 of 17 December 2011.
[15] Law No. 91 of 14 June 2021, GU No. 148 of 23 June 2021. On this law, see DI STASIO, "La zona economica esclusiva italiana: il contesto generale dell'iniziativa legislativa", in LEANDRO (ed.), *La zona economica esclusiva italiana: ragioni, ambito, delimitazioni e sfide*, Bari, 2021, p. 37 ff.
[16] For a comment on this provision, see TANAKA, "Article 74", in PROELSS (ed.), *United Nations Convention on the Law of the Sea. A Commentary*, München/Oxford/Baden-Baden, 2017, p. 563 ff.
[17] *Ibid.*, p. 569.

ing the breadth of its territorial sea in the Ionian, exercising the right granted by Article 7(1) of UNCLOS. By Decree No. 107 of 25 December 2020, the President of the Hellenic Republic ordered the closing of bays and the drawing of straight baselines along the Greek coasts from the northernmost point of the Region of Ionian Islands to Cape Tenaro in the Peloponnese.[18] This decision, however, is of no consequence to the maritime boundary with Italy, which was drawn taking into account the Greek normal baseline, that is to say the low-water line along the coast. For the sake of clarity, the above-mentioned decree specifies that the drawing of straight baselines in the Ionian area does not affect the delimitation of maritime zones effected by international agreement (Article 4). Therefore, should Greece declare a contiguous zone, an EEZ or an EPZ in the Ionian Sea, such zone must be measured from the straight baselines established in the said decree, but it cannot extend beyond the delimitation line already agreed with Italy.

3.   FISHING ACTIVITIES

The 2020 agreement expressly preserves fishing activities carried out in accordance with the relevant European Union (EU) regulations. Article 3(a) stipulates that the maritime delimitation does not affect those activities. EU Regulation No. 1380/2013 on the common fisheries policy comes into consideration in this respect.[19] It grants fishing vessels flying the flag of any EU Member States and registered in the EU "equal access to waters and resources in all Union waters" (Article 5(1)), with the main exception of the waters up to 12 nm from baselines under the EU Member States' sovereignty or jurisdiction. In those waters, until 31 December 2022, each EU Member State may restrict fishing to fishing vessels that traditionally fish there from ports on the adjacent coast, without prejudice to the arrangements with other Member States under existing neighbourhood relations and the arrangements contained in Annex I (Article 5(2)). That Annex establishes, for each EU Member State, the geographical zones within the coastal bands of other Member States where fishing activities are carried out and the species concerned. Measures applicable after the expiry of the aforementioned arrangements are to be adopted no later than 31 December 2022 (Article 5(4)).

When the agreement at issue was concluded, the outer limits of the Greek territorial sea were still fixed at 6 nm from the baselines. In view of Greece's announced intention to expand its territorial waters to 12 nm from the baselines in the Ionian, Italy took care that Italian vessels habitually fishing in international waters close to those limits could keep doing so after such expansion. Greece agreed to let sixty-eight Italian vessels continue fishing within the belt between 6

---

[18] Presidential Decree No. 107 of 25 December 2020, Official Gazette of the Hellenic Republic No. 258 of 27 December 2020.

[19] Regulation (EU) No. 1380/2013 of the European Parliament and of the Council of 11 December 2013, OJ EU L 354 of 28 December 2013, p. 22 ff.

and 12 nm, after its conversion into territorial sea, and to let them catch four species.[20] Accordingly, alongside the maritime delimitation agreement, a joint communication to the European Commission was signed requesting an amendment to Annex I of EU Regulation No. 1380/2013 so as to include the said arrangement.[21] Up to the time of writing, however, no such amendment has been adopted.

On 21 January 2021, a law was passed by the Greek Parliament on the breadth of territorial waters in the maritime zone of the Ionian and the Ionian Islands up to Cape Tenaro in the Peloponnese.[22] It expands the territorial waters to 12 nm from the baselines (Article 2). The above-mentioned communication to the European Commission, however, is taken into account. In fact, it is laid down that, until the adoption of the requested amendment to Annex I of EU Regulation No. 1380/2013, EU fishing vessels may be granted permission to fish within the belt between 6 and 12 nm, on a temporary basis, at the discretion of the Minister of Rural Development and Food (Article 4).

Greece and Italy also addressed the issue of protecting marine biodiversity, while consenting to fishing activities. Together with the maritime delimitation agreement and the aforementioned communication to the European Commission, they signed a joint declaration on the resources of the Mediterranean.[23] Therein they expressed their commitment to a balanced and sustainable management of marine biological resources, in line with the EU common fisheries policy, and their intention to hold consultations focused on the conservation of such resources and the preservation of environmental sustainability, while ensuring the smooth conduct of fishing.

As regards marine environment protection, it is also worth noting that a bilateral cooperation agreement on the protection of the marine environment of the Ionian Sea and the Ionian coastal zones was signed in Rome, on 6 March 1979,[24] and it is in force as from 3 February 1983.[25] Under this agreement, Greece and Italy are bound to establish close cooperation in order to prevent, fight and gradually suppress pollution in the Ionian Sea and the Ionian coastal zones (Article 1). To this end, a joint commission has been established with the task of submitting proposals to both the Governments (Articles 3, 4 and 10).

---

[20] "Greek FM: We will defend Greece from any aggression as outlined by the constitution", Greek City Times, 11 June 2020, available at: <https://greekcitytimes.com/2020/06/11/greek-fm-we-will-defend-greece-from-any-aggression-as-outlined-by-the-constitution/>. See also MARGHELIS, cit. supra note 2, p. 4.

[21] See MARGHELIS, cit. supra note 2, pp. 3-4.

[22] Law No. 4767 of 21 January 2021, Official Gazette of the Hellenic Republic No. 9 of 21 January 2021.

[23] See MARGHELIS, cit. supra note 2, pp. 3-4.

[24] Cooperation Agreement between the Hellenic Republic and the Italian Republic on the Protection of the Marine Environment of the Ionian Sea and the Ionian Coastal Zones, 6 March 1979, available at: <http://atrio.esteri.it/vwPdf/wfrmRenderPdf.aspx?ID=44461>. The President of the Italian Republic was authorized by the Parliament to ratify the agreement at issue by Law No. 563 of 10 July 1982 (Suppl. to GU No. 224 of 16 August 1982).

[25] Data available in the treaties database of the Italian Ministry of Foreign Affairs and International Cooperation: <http://atrio.esteri.it/>.

4. OFFSHORE HYDROCARBON ACTIVITIES

The 2020 agreement does not expressly consider offshore hydrocarbon activities, though the maritime delimitation might impact on them. In the preamble, however, it reaffirms the 1977 Agreement, Article II of which addresses the case of mineral deposits straddling the boundary line between the parties' respective continental shelf areas. If the part of a deposit which is located on one side of the boundary line can be exploited by means of installations situated on the other side, Greece and Italy shall endeavour, together with the holders of mining licenses, if any, to reach an agreement on how to exploit the deposit, so that exploitation is as profitable as possible and each party preserves its full rights over the mineral resources of its respective continental shelf area (Article II, paragraph 1). If a mineral deposit straddling the boundary line has already been exploited, Greece and Italy shall strive, after consulting with the holders of mining licenses, if any, to reach an agreement on equitable compensation (Article II, paragraph 2).

The aforementioned provisions may be applied in the near future. In the last few years, exploration and exploitation of onshore and offshore hydrocarbon resources has become a priority for the Greek authorities. In particular, on 17 March 2017, Greece notified Italy of its proposed programme to license offshore hydrocarbon activities and provided Italy with a copy of the relevant strategic environmental assessment, in accordance with Article 7(1) of the EC Directive 2001/42.[26] Eleven blocks were indicated for licensing, all along the Ionian islands and the coasts of the Peloponnese.[27] As contemplated by Article 7(2) of the said Directive, Italy entered into consultations with Greece concerning the likely transboundary environmental effects of those activities. In its comments on the licensing program, dated 18 May 2017, the Italian Ministry for the Environment, Land and Sea noted, *inter alia*, that "the Blocks 1, 2, 4 and 5 are located on the border with the Italian territorial waters",[28] and it highlighted numerous likely transboundary effects of the planned hydrocarbon activities.[29] Block 2 attracted particular media attention. It is situated 30 kilometers west of Corfu Island and its western limit is adjacent to the Italo-Greek boundary line. It potentially covers a huge gas deposit named "Fortuna Prospect", straddling the said boundary line.[30]

---

[26] Directive 2001/42/EC of the European Parliament and of the Council of 27 June 2001, OJ EC L197 of 21 July 2001, p. 30 ff.

[27] See the 2016 Greek report relating to the strategic environmental assessment of the offshore hydrocarbon activities in the Hellenic continental shelf area of the Ionian Sea, available at: <https://va.minambiente.it/File/Documento/200868>, p. 687.

[28] Comments of the Italian Ministry for the Environment, Land and Sea, annexed to the letter of 18 May 2017, available at: <https://va.minambiente.it/File/Documento/204102>, p. 18 of the English translation.

[29] *Ibid.*, p. 7 ff. of the English translation.

[30] GILBERTO, "Metano, sarà sfruttato dai greci il giacimento davanti alla Puglia", Il Sole 24 Ore, 25 September 2019, available at: <https://www.ilsole24ore.com/art/metano-sara-sfruttato-greci-giacimento-alla-puglia-ACbztem>.

In February 2018, a consortium of energy companies, including the Italian company Edison, was granted authorization for exploration activities in Block 2.[31]

It seems that, when signing the 2020 agreement, Italy was assured that the Blocks 1, 2, 4 and 5 would not extend beyond the agreed boundary line. However, if the above-mentioned deposit is confirmed and the part located on the Italian side can be exploited by means of installations erected on the Greek side, then Greece and Italy should negotiate, in conjunction with the companies holding mining licenses, an agreement on the conditions of exploitation, having due regard to the protection of the marine environment. In this respect it is worth recalling that, under the 1977 Agreement, both States are bound to adopt "all possible measures" to ensure that exploration of their respective continental shelf areas and exploitation of discovered resources do not adversely affect the ecological balance in the Ionian Sea (Article III).[32]

5. SUBMARINE PIPELINES

The recent Italo-Greek agreement safeguards the rights and freedoms of other States in the EEZ that each of the parties is entitled to declare. Article 3(b) expressly recalls the provisions of Article 58 UNCLOS regarding the rights and duties of other States in the EEZ. Among them, the right to lay submarine pipelines is worthy of consideration, because of the strategic importance of such facilities to European countries' energy supplies. Since they are laid on the seafloor, the continental shelf regime is to be applied. Under Article 79 UNCLOS, all States are entitled to lay submarine pipelines on the continental shelf, subject to the consent of the coastal State as to their route (paragraphs 1 and 3). The coastal State may also take measures in order to prevent, reduce and control pollution from submarine pipelines (paragraph 2), and establish conditions for pipelines entering its territory or territorial sea (paragraph 4).[33]

As regards the Ionian Sea, the Poseidon pipeline project must be mentioned. If and when built, this pipeline will transport gas from the Eastern Mediterranean to Italy through Greece and the Ionian Sea. It will consist of two sections, one onshore running from Kipi, at the Greek-Turkish border, to Florovouni (Perdika), on Greece's Ionian coast, and the other offshore crossing the Ionian from Florovouni

---

[31] "Total, Edison get Greek go-ahead for oil and gas exploration", Reuters, 28 February 2018, available at: <https://www.reuters.com/article/us-greece-energy-exploration/total-edison-get-greek-go-ahead-for-oil-and-gas-exploration-idUSKCN1GC2D0>.

[32] On the protection of the marine environment against pollution resulting from offshore hydrocarbon activities in the Adriatic and Ionian Seas, see ROS, "Problems of Marine Pollution resulting from Offshore Activities according to International and European Union Law", in CALIGIURI (ed.), *Offshore Oil and Gas Exploration and Exploitation in the Adriatic and Ionian Seas*, Naples, 2015, p. 34 ff.

[33] For a comment on these provisions, see ENGLENDER, "Article 79", in PROELSS (ed.), *cit. supra* note 16, p. 618 ff.

to Otranto.[34] An agreement for the development of such infrastructure was concluded between Greece and Italy in Lecce, on 4 November 2005, and it entered into force on 11 December 2007.[35] The parties agreed that the offshore section had to be developed jointly by the Greek company DEPA and the Italian company Edison through a special-purpose company. A 50-50% joint venture between DEPA and Edison was consequently constituted under the name IGI Poseidon.[36] Up to the time of writing, however, construction has not started on either of the sections. In March 2021, the deadline for completing construction of the Italian part of the pipeline was postponed to 1 October 2025.[37]

6. SETTLEMENT OF DISPUTES

Like the majority of maritime delimitation agreements, the recent Italo-Greek agreement also contains provisions on the settlement of disputes concerning its interpretation or application. According to Article 4, whenever such a dispute arises, the parties shall endeavour to resolve it through diplomatic means (paragraph 1); if no settlement is reached within four months from the date on which one of the parties notified the other of its intention to settle the dispute through those means, the dispute shall be submitted at the request of either party to the International Court of Justice (ICJ) or to any other international body chosen by agreement between the parties (paragraph 2).

Indeed, Article 4 of the 2020 agreement sets forth the very same procedure laid down in Article IV of the 1977 agreement for the settlement of disputes concerning the interpretation or application of the latter. This solution is certainly the most convenient, as potential disputes on the single maritime boundary agreed in 2020 would inevitably concern also the interpretation or application of the provisions of the 1977 agreement. In particular, the inclusion of a compromissory clause conferring jurisdiction on the ICJ is commendable, since either party is allowed to institute proceedings against the other before the ICJ by filing a unilateral application under Article 40(1) of the ICJ Statute, so as to reach a definitive and binding resolution of the dispute.

---

[34] The projected Poseidon pipeline must not be confused with the Trans Adriatic Pipeline (TAP), which became operational at the end of 2020. TAP runs from Kipi, at the Greek-Turkish border, across Northern Greece, Albania and the Adriatic Sea, to San Foca (Melendugno), on the Italian coast. See the website of TAP: <https://www.tap-ag.com>.

[35] Agreement between the Italian Republic and the Hellenic Republic for the Development of the Interconnection Italy–Greece (IGI) Project, 4 November 2005, available at: <http://atrio.esteri.it/vwPdf/wfrmRenderPdf.aspx?ID=48846>. The President of the Italian Republic was authorized by the Parliament to ratify it by Law No. 210 of 25 October 2007 (GU No. 267 of 12 November 2007).

[36] See the website of IGI Poseidon: <http://www.igi-poseidon.com/en>.

[37] Ministry for Ecological Transition, Directorial Decree of 26 March 2021, available at: <https://www.mise.gov.it/images/stories/normativa/Decreto_proroga_Poseidon_26032021.pdf>.

7. CONCLUSION

The recent agreement with Greece furthers Italy's growing interest in delimiting the maritime zones to which it is entitled under international law, so as to prevent its rights and jurisdiction over them being impaired by the proclamation of overlapping zones by its neighbours. The Italian authorities' intent in concluding the agreement at issue was precisely to prevent the recurrence of situations similar to that which occurred with the proclamation by Algeria of an EEZ off its coasts on 20 March 2018, without any previous agreement with Italy.[38] The zone was legitimately contested by the Rome Government as "it unduly overlaps on zones of legitimate and exclusive national Italian interest".[39]

The 2020 Italo-Greek agreement also sets the stage for future proclamation by Italy of an EEZ covering the waters adjacent to its territorial sea in the Ionian. Indeed, agreements such as this are envisaged by the recent Italian law on the establishment of an EEZ, in order to clearly define the EEZ's outer limits. Moreover, the resulting maritime delimitation appears to be in conformity with Article 74 UNCLOS, being effected by agreement on the basis of international law and substantially achieving an equitable solution. Actually, the choice of adopting a single boundary for the continental shelf and the EEZ deserves praise as it prevents possible divergences between the parties deriving from the different regimes applicable to them.

In this regard, it is to be stressed that the subsequent Greek decision to adopt straight baselines, in place of normal baselines, in the Ionian area does not affect the maritime delimitation with Italy. If and when a contiguous zone, an EEZ or an EPZ is declared by Greece in the Ionian Sea, it shall be measured from the straight baselines established in the said decree, but it shall not extend beyond the delimitation line already agreed with Italy.

The agreement at issue was also opportunely complemented by the joint communication to the European Commission requesting an amendment to Annex I of EU Regulation No. 1380/2013, so that a fixed number of Italian vessels can keep fishing within the belt between 6 and 12 nm from the Greek baselines, notwithstanding the extension of Greek territorial waters to 12 nm. In this way, Italy secured the protection of its fishermen's activities in that area, preventing the recurrence of what happened after the conclusion of the maritime delimitation agreement with France, which was signed at Caen on 21 March 2015.[40] The Caen agreement sparked a storm of protests from the Italian fishermen who accused

---

[38] Décret présidentiel n° 18-96 du 20 mars 2018, Journal officiel de la République algérienne, 21 March 2018.

[39] Note verbale of the Permanent Mission of Italy to the United Nations of 28 November 2018, available at: <https://www.un.org/Depts/los/LEGISLATIONANDTREATIES/PDFFILES/2018_NV_Italy.pdf>. On Algeria's response, see the comment of BROGGINI in the section devoted to diplomatic and parliamentary practice of this Volume.

[40] Agreement between the French Republic and the Italian Republic concerning the delimitation of the territorial seas and of the other zones under national jurisdiction between France and Italy, Caen, 21 March 2015, available in French at: <https://www.marineregions.org/documents/accord_frontiere_maritime_franco_italien.pdf>.

the Government of not having safeguarded their interests and, up to the time of writing, it has not been ratified by Italy. Indeed, owing to the fishermen's protests, the Government did not even submit the draft law authorizing ratification to the Parliament.[41]

As to the offshore hydrocarbon activities carried out by Greece in the Ionian Sea, Italy should remain vigilant for their transboundary environmental effects and should enhance cooperation with Greece in order to prevent them, within the framework of the 1979 agreement on the protection of the marine environment in the Ionian and the Ionian coastal zones. Furthermore, Italy and Greece should agree on the conditions for exploitation of any hydrocarbon deposit that may be discovered straddling the boundary line and falling within the scope of Article II, paragraph 1, of the 1977 agreement, with due regard to protection of the marine environment protection.

All things considered, the 2020 Italo-Greek agreement indubitably meets not only the Athens Government's interests, but also the Rome Government's ones, adding to the already existing bilateral agreements concerning the Ionian Sea. It can also serve as a template for future maritime delimitation agreements between Italy and at least some of its neighbouring States.

---

[41] See RONZITTI, "The Agreement between France and Italy on the Delimitation of Maritime Frontiers", IYIL, 2016, p. 617 ff.

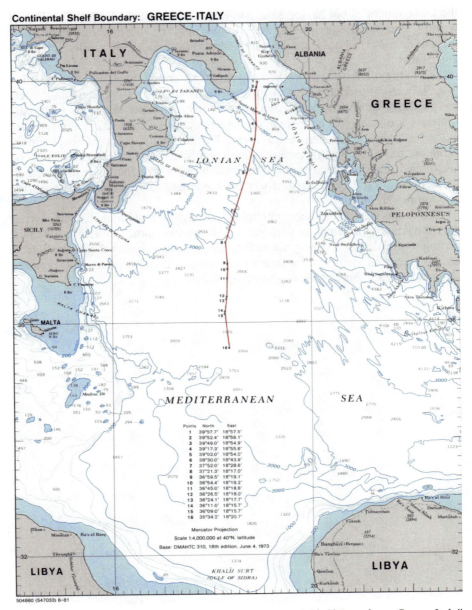

Continental Shelf Boundary: **GREECE-ITALY**

Points	North	East
1	39°57.7'	18°57.5'
2	39°52.4'	18°56.1'
3	39°49.0'	18°54.9'
4	39°17.3'	18°55.6'
5	39°02.0'	18°54.0'
6	38°30.0'	18°43.9'
7	37°52.0'	18°28.6'
8	37°21.3'	18°17.0'
9	36°59.5'	18°19.1'
10	36°54.4'	18°19.2'
11	36°45.0'	18°18.6'
12	36°26.5'	18°18.0'
13	36°24.1'	18°17.7'
14	36°11.0'	18°15.7'
15	36°09.0'	18°15.7'
16	35°34.2'	18°20.7'

Mercator Projection

Scale 1:4,000,000 at 40°N. latitude

Base: DMAHTC 310, 18th edition, June 4, 1973

504860 (547033) 6-81

Source: United States Department of State, "Continental Shelf Boundary: Greece-Italy",
Limits in the Seas No. 96, 6 June 1982, p. 7.

PRACTICE OF INTERNATIONAL COURTS
AND TRIBUNALS

THE JUDICIAL ACTIVITY OF THE INTERNATIONAL COURT OF JUSTICE IN 2020

SERENA FORLATI*

1. THE COURT AND THE DOCKET IN THE YEAR OF THE COVID-19 PANDEMIC

Notwithstanding the COVID-19 crisis, the activity of the International Court of Justice (ICJ) went on fairly smoothly in 2020, which also marked the 100th anniversary of the adoption of the Statute of the Permanent Court of International Justice – and hence of the model of international jurisdiction that is now embodied in the present Court.

The ICJ reacted swiftly to the outbreak of the pandemic, first by postponing hearings and meetings and implementing teleworking,[1] then by relying on hybrid hearings and other forms of remote working in order to resume its judicial activities safely.[2] The Court amended Articles 59 and 94 of its Rules of Court so as to allow for hearings and the reading of judgments with the Parties' participation via video link upon a decision of the Court "for health, security or other compelling reasons".[3]

With these measures in place, the Court was able to pursue its judicial activities without significant hindrances. No new cases were submitted during 2020, probably also due to the impact of the pandemic, but the Court issued four judgments and two particularly significant orders, which are discussed below.

The first of those orders, issued on 23 January 2020 in the case *Application of the Convention on the Prevention and Punishment of the Crime of Genocide (The Gambia v. Myanmar),*[4] resulted in a different kind of procedural innovation, namely in the adoption of a new Article 11 of the Resolution concerning the Internal Judicial Practice of the Court, which establishes a new procedure for monitoring the implementation of provisional measures. Under the new procedure, a Committee of three Judges is entrusted with the task of examining the information supplied by the parties in relation to the implementation of provisional measures and reporting periodically to the Court, which may then take further action. The new provision reads:

---

* Professor of International Law, University of Ferrara.
[1] See ICJ, Press Releases Nos. 2020/8 of 17 March 2020, 2020/9 of 20 March 2020 and 2020/10 of 7 April 2020. When not otherwise indicated, the documents quoted in the survey are available at: <www.icj-cij.org>.
[2] Press Release No. 2020/11 of 23 April 2020. The first virtual hearings were held in the case of the *Arbitral Award of 3 October 1899 (Guyana v. Venezuela)*: see Press Release No. 2020/15.
[3] See Press Release No. 2020/16 of 25 June 2020. See also President Yusuf's Speech on the occasion of the seventy-fifth session of the United Nations General Assembly, 2 November 2020.
[4] ICJ Reports 2020, p. 3 ff.

IYIL, Vol. 30 (2020), pp. 297-319
ISSN 0391-5107

Where the Court indicates provisional measures, it shall elect three judges to form an ad hoc committee which will assist the Court in monitoring the implementation of provisional measures. This committee shall include neither a Member of the Court of the nationality of one of the parties nor any judges ad hoc.

The ad hoc committee shall examine the information supplied by the parties in relation to the implementation of provisional measures. It shall report periodically to the Court, recommending potential options for the Court.

Any decision in this respect shall be taken by the Court.[5]

The year under review also witnessed some changes to the composition of the Court: on 12 November 2020 the General Assembly and the Security Council re-elected Judges Xue Hanqin (China), Peter Tomka (Slovakia), Julia Sebutinde (Uganda) and Yuji Iwasawa (Japan) for another term in office. Moreover, Judge Georg Nolte was elected as a new Member of the Court, replacing Judge Giorgio Gaja who stepped down from office on 5 February 2021.[6]

2. THE COURT'S JUDGMENTS IN 2020

2.1. *The Appeals relating to the Jurisdiction of the ICAO Council*

On 14 July 2020 the Court issued its judgments relating to two of the three cases opposing Qatar to the Gulf countries that were brought before the ICJ in 2018, namely the *Appeal Relating to the Jurisdiction of the ICAO Council under Article 84 of the Convention on International Civil Aviation (Bahrain, Egypt, Saudi Arabia and United Arab Emirates v. Qatar)* (Application A) and the *Appeal Relating to the Jurisdiction of the ICAO Council under Article II, Section 2, of the 1944 International Air Services Transit Agreement (Bahrain, Egypt and United Arab Emirates v. Qatar)* (Application B). The two cases were not joined, since the applicant States were not the same (Saudi Arabia being a Party to the ICAO Convention, which was the object of the first application, but not to the International Air Services Transit Agreement (IASTA, which was the object of the second application) and they objected to joinder;[7] however, they proceeded in parallel and gave rise to virtually identical legal questions. This is reflected in the two virtually identical judgments, in the separate opinions of Judge Cançado Trindade and Judge ad hoc Berman and the Declaration of Judge Gevorgian.[8]

---

[5] See Press Release No. 2020/38 of 21 December 2021.

[6] The warm farewell given by President Yusuf on 8 February 2021 is available at: <https://www.icj-cij.org/en/multimedia/601821ab045e58767b3c8b6b>.

[7] See the Judgment on Application A, paras. 9-10. Quotations below will also be from the Judgment on Application A.

[8] The ICJ recently decided it has no jurisdiction on the merits of the third case, relating to the *Application of the International Convention on the Elimination of All Forms of Racial*

The cases in discussion were part of a more complex dispute, which is in the process of being settled,[9] and touched upon the way in which the ICAO Council exercised its dispute settlement functions under Article 84 ICAO Convention and Article II IASTA, respectively. More specifically, Qatar submitted to the ICAO Council two complaints concerning the measures adopted by the other Gulf Countries affecting air traffic. The latter Countries raised two preliminary objections, contending, firstly, that the ICAO Council had no jurisdiction on "the real issue in dispute between the Parties", namely the lawfulness of the airspace restrictions Qatar complained of, which should be characterized as countermeasures; and, secondly, that the procedural preconditions for bringing the claims to the Council's attention had not been met.[10] The Council rejected the preliminary objections with two Decisions of 29 June 2018. In the second and third grounds of appeal to the ICJ, the Applicants reiterated the contentions put forward in their preliminary objections; they also alleged, in the first ground of appeal, that the ICAO Council had violated "fundamental principles of due process and the right to be heard".[11]

The Court confirmed that it had jurisdiction on the case – something which Qatar had not challenged[12] in light of the ICJ's previous case law[13] – and rejected all grounds of appeal.

While the Gulf Countries contended that "the narrow dispute relating to airspace closures cannot be separated from the broader issues" and that "the legality of the airspace closures cannot be judged in isolation",[14] without taking into consideration issues that fall outside the scope of the ICAO Council's competence *ratione materiae*,[15] the Court considered that the disagreements between the Parties brought before the ICAO Council fell under its jurisdiction pursuant to Article 84 of the ICAO Convention and Article II(2) IASTA, respectively. In this regard, the Judgments reiterated the Court's stance in the *Hostages* case, "whereby legal disputes between sovereign States by their very nature are likely to occur in political contexts, and often form only one element in a wider and long-standing political dispute between the States concerned",[16] positing that

---

Discrimination (Qatar v. United Arab Emirates), in its Judgment of 4 February 2021, which is outside the scope of this review.

[9] See the Statement of the Spokesperson for the UN Secretary General on the Al Ula Declaration, announced at the 41st GCC Summit of 5 January 2021, available at: <un.org/sg/en/content/sg/statement/2021-01-05/statement-attributable-the-spokesperson-for-the-secretary-general-the-al-ula-declaration-announced-the-41st-gcc-summit>.

[10] Judgment on Application A, para. 24.

[11] *Ibid.*, para. 37.

[12] *Ibid.*, paras. 32-33.

[13] ICJ Reports 1972, p. 73 ff.

[14] Judgment in Application A, para. 42.

[15] *Ibid.*, para. 43.

[16] *United States Diplomatic and Consular Staff in Tehran (United States of America v. Iran)*, Judgment of 24 May 1980, ICJ Reports 1980, p. 20 ff., para. 37. The Judgments also refer to the *Certain Iranian Assets (Islamic Republic of Iran v. United States of America)*, Preliminary Objections, Judgment of 13 February 2019, ICJ Reports 2019, p. 23 ff., para. 36.

"[t]he mere fact that this disagreement has arisen in a broader context does not deprive the ICAO Council of its jurisdiction".[17]

Moreover, the possibility for the Applicants to invoke a defence relating to countermeasures was deemed to relate to the merits of the disputes pending before the ICAO Council; therefore, the issue "does not, in and of itself, have any effect on the Council's jurisdiction".[18] This notwithstanding, Judge Cançado Trindade appended to the Judgment a Separate Opinion discussing at length the status of countermeasures in present-day international law, more specifically their purported "lack of legal foundations and their negative effects on the law of nations and on State responsibility" – a testament to Judge Trindade's natural law approach to international law, which, however, does not reflect its current state.

The Court itself did not deal with this issue; it did, however, further clarify that preliminary objections raised before the ICAO Council could in principle address issues of admissibility, if they are purely preliminary in character,[19] but rejected the Applicants' contention that examining the defence would imply a breach of "judicial propriety" by the Council, thus rendering Qatar's applications inadmissible.[20] On the contrary, "the integrity of the Council's dispute settlement function would not be affected if the Council examined issues outside matters of civil aviation for the exclusive purpose of deciding a dispute which falls within its jurisdiction".[21] The Court thus provided an important indication as to the existence of an "incidental" competence of the Council, akin to that of international courts and tribunals. Nonetheless, the Court did not qualify the ICAO Council's dispute settlement function as properly judicial in nature, indirectly confirming that independence is a key requirement of international adjudication.[22] In what is possibly the most interesting part of the Judgments, the Court posited:

> it is difficult to apply the concept of 'judicial propriety' to the ICAO Council. The Council is a permanent organ responsible to the ICAO Assembly, composed of designated representatives of the contracting States elected by the Assembly, rather than of individuals acting independently in their personal capacity as is characteristic of a judicial body. In addition to its executive and administrative functions specified in Articles 54 and 55 of the Chicago Convention, the Council was given in Article 84 the function of settling disagreements between two or more contracting States relating to the interpretation or application of the Convention and its Annexes.

---

[17] Judgment on Application A, para. 48.

[18] *Ibid.*, para. 49.

[19] *Ibid.*, para. 57.

[20] *Ibid.*

[21] *Ibid.*, para. 61.

[22] See FORLATI, "The Judicial Activity of the International Court of Justice in 2018", IYIL, 2018, p. 288 ff., pp. 309-311.

This, however, does not transform the ICAO Council into a judicial institution in the proper sense of that term.[23]

This issue is discussed also by two Judges individually. Judge Gevorgian, in particular, criticized "the Court's expansive view of the ICAO Council's competence to address matters unrelated to civil aviation"[24] in light of the Council's political nature. In his view,

> it is one thing to say that the existence of a broader political dispute should not affect the competence of a body that is composed of 'independent judges', and quite another to apply the same principle to a body made up of States parties to the treaty in question, each of which is likely to have its own political agenda and the potential to be influenced by non-legal considerations.[25]

Also Judge ad hoc Berman observed that

> While [...] Article 84, taken as a whole, can certainly find a place of some kind within the framework of 'dispute settlement' in the broad ecumenical sense of Article 33 of the United Nations Charter with its references to negotiation, enquiry, mediation, conciliation, etc., the language used is not that of *judicial* settlement.[26]

Furthermore, the Court dismissed the allegation that other procedural irregularities rendered the decisions of the ICAO Council "null and void ab initio",[27] as contended by the Applicants in their first ground of appeal. The latter had pointed to procedural irregularities that allegedly "prejudiced in a fundamental way the requirements of a just procedure" before the Council (notably, the lack of reasons in support of the Council's decisions; the lack of deliberations before the vote; the cast of votes by secret ballot; the insufficient amount of time allegedly granted to the Applicants; an error in determining the required majorities for the vote; and the reference to a single preliminary objection, rather than two).[28] The Court deemed that the Council had not erred in determining the "objective question of law" concerning its own jurisdiction, and rejected the ground of appeals. At the same time, some criticism of the Council's management of procedure can be detected in the indication that the Court itself "will be best positioned to act on

---

[23] Judgment on Application A, para. 60. On the debate surrounding the nature of the Council's dispute settlement function see again FORLATI, *cit. supra* note 22. The Court also considered that the procedural preconditions for a decision on the merits, notably a genuine effort by Qatar to settle the dispute out of Court, had been met (see Judgment in Application A, paras. 98 and 105).

[24] See his Declaration appended to the Judgment.

[25] *Ibid.*

[26] Separate Opinion of Judge ad hoc Berman, para. 5.

[27] Judgment on Application A, para. 108.

[28] *Ibid.*, paras. 110 ff.

any future appeal if the decision of the ICAO Council contains the reasons of law and fact that led to the ICAO Council's conclusions".[29] While not taking a stance on whether reasoning is essential to the validity of international judgments and arbitral awards, the Court thus stressed the importance of reasoning also for the purposes of non-judicial dispute settlement.

2.2. The Judgment in the Immunities and Criminal Proceedings Case

On 11 December 2020 the Court rendered its Judgment on the merits of the *Immunities and Criminal Proceedings (Equatorial Guinea v. France)* case. As will be recalled, Equatorial Guinea originally alleged in its application several breaches by France of the Palermo Convention against Transnational Organized Crime and of the Vienna Convention on Diplomatic Relations (VCDR) in the framework of a high-profile criminal investigation against the current First Vice-President of Equatorial Guinea, Theodore Nguema Obiang Mangue.[30] In its Judgment on Preliminary Objections of 6 June 2018, the Court held that the dispute did not fall under the scope of the Palermo Convention *ratione materiae*; in the instance under discussion, therefore, the Court was called upon to ascertain whether France had actually infringed the 1961 Convention as a consequence of law enforcement measures (including seizures) affecting the building at 42 avenue Foch in Paris and valuables present therein. The Court rejected such allegations, mainly on the basis of the conclusion that the building at issue had never acquired the status of "premises of the mission" within the meaning of Article 1(i) of the VCDR, and that, accordingly, France had not breached such Convention, as claimed by Equatorial Guinea.[31] The Court determined, first, how a property acquires such status, considering in particular whether the consent of the host state is necessary for this purpose, as argued by France. The Judgment recalls – and the Parties also acknowledged – that "Article 1 *(i)* is silent as to the respective roles of the sending and receiving States in the designation of mission premises. Article 22 of the Vienna Convention provides no further guidance on this point".[32] The Court therefore decided the issue by taking into account "the context of these provisions as well as the Vienna Convention's object and purpose",[33] concluding that

> the Vienna Convention cannot be interpreted so as to allow a sending State unilaterally to impose its choice of mission premises upon the receiving State where the latter has objected to this choice. In such an event, the receiving State would, against its will, be required to take on the 'special duty' referred to in Article 22, para-

---

[29] *Ibid.*, para. 125.
[30] Judgment of 11 December 2020, paras. 26 ff.
[31] *Ibid.*, para. 27 ff.
[32] *Ibid.*, para. 62.
[33] *Ibid.*

graph 2, of the Convention to protect the chosen premises. A uni-lateral imposition of a sending State's choice of premises would thus clearly not be consistent with the object of developing friendly relations among nations. Moreover, it would leave the receiving State vulnerable to a potential misuse of diplomatic privileges and immunities, which the drafters of the Vienna Convention intended to avoid by specifying, in the preamble, that the purpose of such privileges and immunities is not 'to benefit individuals'.[34]

Moreover, a different interpretation

would allow for the unilateral imposition of a sending State's choice of premises upon the receiving State and require the latter to under-take the weighty obligations contained in Article 22 against its will. [...T]his would be detrimental to the development of friendly rela-tions among nations and would leave receiving States without any appropriate and effective remedy in case of potential abuses.[35]

Finally, the Court also emphasized that the practice of at least some States parties is to the effect that consent of the host is required for the designation of diplomatic premises, noting in this respect:

The Court does not consider that this practice necessarily establish-es 'the agreement of the parties' within the meaning of a rule codi-fied in Article 31, paragraph 3 (b), of the Vienna Convention on the Law of Treaties as regards the existence of a requirement of prior approval, or the modalities through which a receiving State may communicate its objection to the sending State's designation of a building as forming part of the premises of its diplomatic mission. Nevertheless, the practice of several States which clearly requires the prior approval of the receiving State before a building can ac-quire the status of "premises of the mission" – and the lack of any objection to such practice – are factors which weigh against finding a right belonging to the sending State under the Vienna Convention unilaterally to designate the premises of its diplomatic mission.[36]

Although there are no particular modalities that the receiving State should follow in order to object to the sending State's choice, "the receiving State's power to object to a sending State's designation of the premises of its diplomatic mission is not unlimited"[37] and should be exercised

---

[34] Para. 67.
[35] Para. 68.
[36] Para. 69.
[37] Para. 73.

reasonably and in good faith [...]. In light of the above-mentioned requirements, and the Vienna Convention's object and purpose of enabling the development of friendly relations among nations, the Court considers that an objection of a receiving State must be timely and not be arbitrary. Further, in accordance with Article 47 of the Vienna Convention, the receiving State's objection must not be discriminatory in character. In any event, the receiving State remains obliged under Article 21 of the Vienna Convention to facilitate the acquisition on its territory, in accordance with its laws, by the sending State of the premises necessary for its diplomatic mission, or otherwise assist the latter in obtaining accommodation in some other way.[38]

The Court also found that, under the circumstances of the case, "France consistently expressed its objection to the designation of the building at 42 avenue Foch in Paris as part of the premises of Equatorial Guinea's diplomatic mission"[39] and did so in a timely manner.[40] Moreover,

there existed reasonable grounds for France's objection to Equatorial Guinea's designation of the building as premises of Equatorial Guinea's diplomatic mission. These grounds were known, or should have been known, to Equatorial Guinea. In light of these grounds, the Court does not consider that the objection by France was arbitrary in character.[41]

The Court, *inter alia*, deemed the objection non-discriminatory in character[42] and ruled out the existence of an obligation for France to co-ordinate with Equatorial Guinea before raising the objection.[43] On this basis, the Court's majority held that "the building at 42 avenue Foch in Paris has never acquired the status of 'premises of the mission' of the Republic of Equatorial Guinea in the French Republic within the meaning of Article 1 *(i)* of the Vienna Convention on Diplomatic Relations", but seven Judges voted against this part of the *dispositif*.[44]

While Vice-President Xue's Dissenting Opinion was mainly based on her position on the question of jurisdiction,[45] which had already been expressed in re-

---

[38] *Ibid.*
[39] Para. 89.
[40] Para. 92.
[41] Para. 110.
[42] Para. 117.
[43] Para. 111 ff.
[44] Para. 126. Only four Judges (Vice-President Xue, Judges Bhandari and Robinson and Judge ad hoc Kateka) disagreed with the rest of the operative part, notably with the finding that the French Republic had not infringed the 1961 Convention.
[45] Dissenting Opinion of Vice-President Xue, para. 2. Vice-President Xue considered that "three criteria for the manner in which the receiving State raises its objection, i.e. timely, non-

spect of the Judgment on preliminary objections,[46] President Yusuf, Judges Gaja, Sebutinde, Bhandari and Robinson and Judge ad hoc Kateka disagreed with the contention that the designation of diplomatic premises would be subject to the receiving State's approval, or at any rate to a lack of objections on its part.[47] Albeit with different arguments, they all reached the conclusion that the three criteria identified by the Court (timeliness, non-arbitrariness and non-discrimination) did not find a basis either in the 1961 Convention or (as stressed particularly by President Yusuf) in other sources of international law[48] and highlighted that the actual use of the premises for diplomatic functions would be the relevant criterion in this respect.

2.3. The Judgment on Jurisdiction in the Guyana v. Venezuela Case

The third and last judgment issued in the year under review affirmed the Court's jurisdiction in the *Arbitral Award of 3 October 1899 (Guyana v. Venezuela)* case.[49] The submission of the case to the ICJ by Guyana is the last attempt to settle a decades-old dispute over the validity of the Arbitral award, which awarded sovereignty over the territory between the Orinoco and the Essequibo Rivers to what was then British Guyana.[50]

Venezuela did not participate in the proceedings, questioning Guyana's right to unilaterally submit an application to the Court under the Agreement to Resolve the Controversy between Venezuela and the United Kingdom of Great Britain and Northern Ireland over the Frontier between Venezuela and British Guiana, signed at Geneva on 17 February 1966 (Geneva Agreement).[51]

Article IV(2) of the Geneva Agreement, which is the jurisdictional basis invoked by the Plaintiff, ultimately entrusted the United Nations Secretary-General with the task of identifying the appropriate means of settlement of the dispute, among those listed in Article 33 of the United Nations Charter. According to the last part of this provision,

---

arbitrary and non-discriminatory, in principle do not give rise to any questions" (para. 19) but disagreed with the Court's assessment *in concreto* of whether France's objections complied with them, as "undue emphasis on the power of the receiving State to object would upset the delicate balance established by the Vienna Convention between the sending State and the receiving State" (*ibid.*, para. 28). Cf. on this point the Separate Opinion of Judge Sebutinde, para. 22, and the Dissenting Opinion of Judge Bhandari.

[46] *Immunities and Criminal Proceedings (Equatorial Guinea v. France)*, Preliminary Objections, Judgment of 6 June 2018, ICJ Reports 2018, p. 292 ff., Joint Dissenting Opinion of Vice-President Xue, Judges Sebutinde and Robinson and Judge ad hoc Kateka, p. 340.

[47] See the Declaration of Judge Gaja; the Separate Opinions of President Yusuf and of Judge Sebutinde; the Dissenting Opinion of Judges Bhandari and Robinson and of Judge ad hoc Kateka.

[48] Separate Opinion of President Yusuf; Declaration of Judge Gaja.

[49] Judgment of 18 December 2020.

[50] Although Venezuela initially accepted the award (*ibid.*, para. 31) it reversed this stance in 1962 (*ibid.*, para. 35) and thereafter tried to resolve the dispute on different terms.

[51] *Ibid.*, para. 24 ff.

If the means so chosen do not lead to a solution of the controversy, [...] the Secretary-General of the United Nations shall choose another of the means stipulated in Article 33 of the Charter of the United Nations, and so on until the controversy has been resolved or until all the means of peaceful settlement there contemplated have been exhausted.

After several failed attempts to have recourse to diplomatic means of dispute settlement (more specifically, good offices, which are not specifically listed in Article 33 but are included among the "other peaceful means" of dispute settlement mentioned in the provision, as both Parties accepted[52]), Secretary-General Guterres chose the International Court of Justice as the means to settle the dispute.[53] The main issues decided in the Judgment are whether the Secretary-General was entitled to do so and whether his designation could provide a basis for a unilateral application to the Court. The majority of the Court upheld these propositions, relying on the rules on treaty interpretation reflected in Articles 31 and 32 of the Vienna Convention on the Law of Treaties: more specifically, the Court resorted to several interpretative criteria enshrined in Article 31,[54] whereas the customary rules reflected in Article 32 of the Vienna Convention came into play only in order to confirm the conclusion reached on the former basis.[55] The Court confirmed, first, that "the Parties conferred on the Secretary-General the authority to choose, by a decision which is binding on them, the means to be used for the settlement of their controversy".[56] The Court also confirmed that judicial settlement was among the options envisaged by Article IV(2) of the Geneva Agreement[57] and that this conclusion was

not called into question by the phrase 'or until all the means of peaceful settlement there contemplated have been exhausted' at paragraph 2 of that Article, which might suggest that the Parties had contemplated the possibility that the choice, by the Secretary-General, of the means provided for in Article 33 of the Charter, which include judicial settlement, would not lead to a resolution of the controversy. There are various reasons why a judicial decision, which has the force of *res judicata* and clarifies the rights and obligations of the parties, might not in fact lead to the final settlement of a dispute. It suffices for the Court to observe that, in this case, a judicial decision declaring the 1899 Award to be null and void

[52] *Ibid.*, para. 99. The Court also considered that there was no need for the Secretary General to follow any particular order in the choice of means of settlement.
[53] *Ibid.*, para. 59.
[54] In particular, the conclusion that the Parties had agreed to accept also judicial settlement was reached by referring to a joint statement of the Parties and to the Venezuelan law implementing the Geneva Agreement (*ibid.*, para. 87).
[55] *Ibid.*, para. 76.
[56] *Ibid.*, para. 74; cf. para.78.
[57] *Ibid.*, para. 84.

without delimiting the boundary between the Parties might not lead to the definitive resolution of the controversy, which would be contrary to the object and purpose of the Geneva Agreement.[58]

Judge Tomka further elaborated this point in his Declaration, observing that

> should the 1899 Arbitral Award be declared null and void by the Court, as argued by Venezuela, the Court will be in need of further submissions, in the form of evidence and arguments, about the course of the land boundary, in order for it to fully resolve the 'controversy'. Without these submissions, the Court will not be in a position to determine the course of the disputed boundary between the two countries. In such event, the Secretary-General of the United Nations may be called upon once again to exercise his authority under Article IV, paragraph 2, of the Geneva Agreement to choose another of the means of settlement provided in Article 33 of the Charter of the United Nations.[59]

Furthermore, the Court deemed that the Geneva Agreement could as such provide a suitable jurisdictional basis and Guyana had validly seized the Court, since

> the decision taken by the Secretary-General in accordance with the authority conferred upon him under Article IV, paragraph 2, of the Geneva Agreement would not be effective (see paragraphs 74 to 78 above) if it were subject to the further consent of the Parties for its implementation. Moreover, an interpretation of Article IV, paragraph 2, that would subject the implementation of the decision of the Secretary-General to further consent by the Parties would be contrary to this provision and to the object and purpose of the Geneva Agreement, which is to ensure a definitive resolution of the controversy, since it would give either Party the power to delay indefinitely the resolution of the controversy by withholding such consent.[60]

Judge Robinson endorsed this finding, arguing that

> once the Secretary-General chose the International Court of Justice, there was no need for him to have recourse to any of the other means set out in Article 33, because the International Court of Justice as a judicial body would settle the dispute by arriving at a decision that would be binding on the Parties. Intriguing though the questions

---

[58] *Ibid.*, para. 86.
[59] Declaration of Judge Tomka, para. 7.
[60] Judgment, paras. 114 and 120-121. See also the Declaration of Judge Robinson, para. 9.

raised by that argument might be, the phrase 'or until all the means of peaceful settlement there contemplated have been exhausted' having been rendered inoperative, has no practical consequences in the circumstances of this case[61]

and that "[r]eading Article IV (2) as requiring the other Party to agree to the institution of proceedings would run counter to the object and purpose of the Agreement to find a solution for the controversy".[62]

However, other Members of the Court disagreed. Judge Abraham, in particular, argued:

> It is one thing to say that the choice of a means – in this instance, judicial settlement – by the Secretary-General creates obligations for the parties; it is quite another to see in Article IV, paragraph 2, of the Agreement, combined with the Secretary-General's decision, the expression of both parties' consent to the settlement of their dispute by the Court.[63]

Judge Gaja also maintained that, although the choice to resort to judicial settlement of the dispute results from the determination of a third party, the States in dispute "have not yet expressed a common will to submit their dispute to the Court. They are bound to consent to the Court's jurisdiction, whatever form their consent will take".[64] Judge Gevorgian argued:

> The Court in its Judgment ignores this high threshold for finding consent, reaching the unprecedented decision to exercise jurisdiction on the basis of a treaty that does not even mention the Court, let alone contain a compromissory clause. [...] The Geneva Agreement was meant to assist the Parties in achieving an agreed resolution of their dispute, and not to subject the Parties to a particular form of dispute settlement against their will.[65]

In his view,

> Article IV (2) [...] strongly indicates that the Parties, in concluding the Geneva Agreement, did not intend to subject themselves to a binding method of dispute resolution that would guarantee a defini-

---

[61] *Ibid.*, para. 12.

[62] *Ibid.*, para. 9. Judge Robinson also argued that, once the dispute was settled by the ICJ, "the phrase 'or until all the means of peaceful settlement there contemplated have been exhausted' [would be] rendered inoperative" and disagreed with the inclusion of para. 86 in the Judgment (*ibid.*, paras. 12-13).

[63] Separate Opinion of Judge Abraham.

[64] Declaration of Judge Gaja, para. 5.

[65] Dissenting Opinion of Judge Gevorgian, paras. 2-3.

tive resolution of the controversy. If this had been their intent, they could have left out the final portion of Article IV (2), instead ending that provision with the phrase 'and so on until the controversy has been resolved'. Article IV (2) is better interpreted as requiring agreement by the Parties before the Secretary-General's choice of the means of settlement may be implemented.

The way in which the Court assessed the scope of its own jurisdiction under the Geneva Agreement is certainly less controversial. Notably as regards jurisdiction *ratione materiae*, the agreement was deemed to cover both "Guyana's claims concerning the validity of the 1899 Award about the frontier between British Guiana and Venezuela and the related question of the definitive settlement of the land boundary dispute between Guyana and Venezuela".[66] It remains to be seen if Venezuela will be able to accept such settlement, once the Court proceed to the merits phase.

3.   OTHER JUDICIAL PRONOUNCEMENTS

Three Orders issued in 2020 also deserve discussion, as they are probably the most significant and innovative judicial pronouncements of the ICJ in the year under review.

3.1.   *The Order on Provisional Measures in The Gambia v. Myanmar*

The first such pronouncement is the Order on provisional measures in the case relating to the *Application of the Convention on the Prevention and Punishment of the crime of Genocide (The Gambia v. Myanmar)*. The case is of particular significance not only for the seriousness of the allegations raised against Myanmar by The Gambia, which concern multiple violations of the Genocide Convention allegedly committed against the Rohingya minority by Myanmar, in the context of "clearance operations" involving mass atrocities by the Myanmar military and other security forces.[67]

The Order addresses some interesting questions on issues of procedure. Firstly, and notwithstanding Myanmar's objections, the Court concluded that it had sufficient elements "to establish prima facie the existence of a dispute between the Parties" relating to the Genocide Convention.[68] The Court also provisionally rejected Myanmar's objection to its jurisdiction, based on the Respondent's reservation to Article VIII of the Genocide Convention. According to this provision,

---

[66] *Ibid.*, para. 135.
[67] Order of 23 January 2020, para. 21.
[68] Order of 23 January 2020, paras. 30-31.

> Any Contracting Party may call upon the competent organs of the United Nations to take such action under the Charter of the United Nations as they consider appropriate for the prevention and suppression of acts of genocide or any of the other acts enumerated in article III.

The Court considered, however, that the reference to "competent organs of the United Nations" in this provision does not include the ICJ, having regard in particular to the fact that dispute settlement and the Court's role in this regard are addressed in Article IX.[69] While these findings paved the way for affirming the Court's *prima facie* jurisdiction (that is, the first requirement for the adoption of provisional measures),[70] the most interesting procedural issue addressed by the Court relates to the *jus standi* of The Gambia, which Myanmar expressly challenged notwithstanding the *erga omnes* nature of the obligations stemming from the Genocide Convention.[71] Relying on it precedents in the *Reservations to the Convention on the Prevention and Punishment of the Crime of Genocide* and in *Belgium v. Senegal*, the Court confirmed:

> In view of their shared values, all the States parties to the Genocide Convention have a common interest to ensure that acts of genocide are prevented and that, if they occur, their authors do not enjoy impunity. That common interest implies that the obligations in question are owed by any State party to all the other States parties to the Convention [...]. It follows that any State party to the Genocide Convention, and not only a specially affected State, may invoke the responsibility of another State party with a view to ascertaining the alleged failure to comply with its obligations erga omnes partes, and to bring that failure to an end.[72]

This solution is in line with the Court's case law and confirms the possibility for States "not specially affected" by the breach of *erga omnes* obligations to invoke international responsibility also through an application to a judicial body – something that is not expressly set out in the ILC Articles on Responsibility of States for Internationally Wrongful Acts. The matter cannot be deemed entirely settled, in light of the doubts raised in this regard by Vice-President Xue's Separate Opinion;[73] it is however interesting to note that The Gambia is apparently not the only State ready to take an active part in the proceedings against Myanmar.

---

[69] *Ibid.*, paras. 34-35.

[70] *Ibid.*, para. 37.

[71] Order of 23 January 2020, para. 39. According to Myanmar, only Bangladesh would be entitled to bring the dispute before the Court, as a State specifically affected by the alleged breaches of the Genocide Convention.

[72] Order of 23 January 2020, para. 41.

[73] Para. 4 ff.

Other States parties to the Genocide Convention, specifically Maldives,[74] the Netherlands and Canada, made known their intention to intervene in the case. The latter two Countries highlighted the seriousness of the atrocities in Myanmar and their determination to

> assist with the complex legal issues that are expected to arise and will pay special attention to crimes related to sexual and gender-based violence, including rape. States Parties to the Genocide Convention must resolve to prevent genocide but also, critically, to hold perpetrators to account.[75]

Moreover, Canada and the Netherlands called upon "all States Parties to the Genocide Convention to support the Gambia in its efforts to address these violations".[76]

Whether Canada and the Netherlands have already taken any formal steps in this regard, be it in the form of a declaration under Article 63 of the ICJ Statute or of an application under Article 62, is not public knowledge. The former option would make it easier for the intervening States to gain access to the Court but would be limited to issues of interpretation of the Genocide Convention, without any contribution to the assessment of the facts of the case.[77]

The Court deemed the other conditions for the adoption of provisional measures also to be met. Specifically, the plausibility of the rights whose protection was sought was ascertained on the basis of Myanmar's own admission as to the possibile violations of international humanitarian law,[78] the stance taken by the United Nations General Assembly in resolution 73/264 of 22 December 2018[79] and the Report of the International Fact-Finding Mission on Myanmar established by the UN Human Rights Council, to the effect that there were "reasonable grounds to conclude that serious crimes under international law ha[d] been committed that warrant[ed] criminal investigation and prosecution", including the crime of genocide, against the Rohingya in Myanmar.[80]

---

[74] See the Statement of the Foreign Ministry of Maldives of 25 March 2020, available at: <https://foreign.gov.mv/index.php/en/mediacentre/news/5584-foreign-ministers-of-maldives-and-the-gambia-discusses-maldives-decision-to-intervene-in-the-gambia%E2%80%99s-case-against-myanmar-at-the-icj-2>.

[75] See their Joint Diplomatic Note of 2 September 2020, available at: <https://www.government.nl/documents/diplomatic-statements/2020/09/02/joint-statement-of-canada-and-the-kingdom-of-the-netherlands-regarding-intention-to-intervene-in-the-gambia-v.-myanmar-case-at-the-international-court-of-justice>.

[76] *Ibid.*

[77] See GAJA, "Il contributo dello Stato interveniente all'accertamento dei fatti nelle cause dinanzi alla Corte internazionale di giustizia concernenti il rispetto di obblighi *erga omnes*", in *Studi in onore di Francesco Salerno*, Napoli, 2021 (forthcoming).

[78] Order of 23 January 2020, para. 53.

[79] *Ibid.*, para. 54.

[80] *Ibid.*, para. 55, quoting United Nations, Report of the Independent International Fact-Finding Mission on Myanmar, UN Doc. A/HRC/39/64 (2018), paras. 83 and 84-87.

The Court specifically relied on the findings of the Fact-Finding Mission also as regards the plausibility of the *dolus specialis* that is required for the atrocities committed in Myanmar to fall under the scope *ratione materiae* of the Genocide Convention,[81] and did not consider that the standard of proof as regards genocidal intent should be higher than what is usual in the context of provisional measures proceedings. The Order states in this respect:

> In view of the function of provisional measures, which is to protect the respective rights of either party pending its final decision, the Court does not consider that the exceptional gravity of the allegations is a decisive factor warranting, as argued by Myanmar, the determination, at the present stage of the proceedings, of the existence of a genocidal intent. In the Court's view, all the facts and circumstances mentioned above (see paragraphs 53-55) are sufficient to conclude that the rights claimed by The Gambia and for which it is seeking protection – namely the right of the Rohingya group in Myanmar and of its members to be protected from acts of genocide and related prohibited acts mentioned in Article III, and the right of The Gambia to seek compliance by Myanmar with its obligations not to commit, and to prevent and punish genocide in accordance with the Convention – are plausible.[82]

While the risk of irreparable harm was deemed inherent in the rights in question,[83] the Fact-Finding Mission's assessments where also critical to the Court's finding that the requirement of urgency had been met. More specifically,

> the reports of the Fact-Finding Mission [...] have indicated that, since October 2016, the Rohingya in Myanmar have been subjected to acts which are capable of affecting their right of existence as a protected group under the Genocide Convention, such as mass killings, widespread rape and other forms of sexual violence, as well as beatings, the destruction of villages and homes, denial of access to food, shelter and other essentials of life. As indicated in resolution 74/246 adopted by the General Assembly on 27 December 2019, this has caused almost 744,000 Rohingya to flee their homes and take refuge in neighbouring Bangladesh.[84]

---

[81] See the Order, para. 55. The difficulties of giving full proof of the *dolus specialis* in the merits phase is however apparent.

[82] *Ibid.*, para. 56. This approach to the standard of proof was expressly endorsed by Judge ad hoc Kress in his Declaration appended to the Order. Moreover, in discussing the requirement of urgency, the Court further recalled that the provisional measures phase does not require it "to establish the existence of breaches of the Genocide Convention" nor to make "definitive findings of fact" (*ibid.*, para. 66).

[83] Order, para. 70.

[84] *Ibid.*, para. 71.

The Court also noted that "600,000 Rohingya remained in Rakhine State as of September 2019"[85] and that they "remain extremely vulnerable",[86] taking "note of the detailed findings of the Fact-Finding Mission on Myanmar submitted to the Human Rights Council in September 2019, which refer to the risk of violations of the Genocide Convention, and in which it is 'conclude[d] on reasonable grounds that the Rohingya people remain at serious risk of genocide under the terms of the Genocide Convention'".[87]

The Court thus decided that the requirements for the adoption of provisional measures were met, ordering Myanmar to:

> (1) [...] in accordance with its obligations under the Convention on the Prevention and Punishment of the Crime of Genocide, in relation to the members of the Rohingya group in its territory, take all measures within its power to prevent the commission of all acts within the scope of Article II of this Convention [...];
> (2) [...] in relation to the members of the Rohingya group in its territory, ensure that its military, as well as any irregular armed units which may be directed or supported by it and any organizations and persons which may be subject to its control, direction or influence, do not commit any acts described in point (1) above, or of conspiracy to commit genocide, of direct and public incitement to commit genocide, of attempt to commit genocide, or of complicity in genocide;
> (3) [...] take effective measures to prevent the destruction and ensure the preservation of evidence related to allegations of acts within the scope of Article II of the Convention on the Prevention and Punishment of the Crime of Genocide;
> (4) [...] submit a report to the Court on all measures taken to give effect to this Order within four months, as from the date of this Order, and thereafter every six months, until a final decision on the case is rendered by the Court.[88]

These measures are not identical to those requested by The Gambia:[89] notably, the Court did not deem it appropriate to indicate measures aimed at ensuring the non-aggravation of the dispute and the first two measures focus only on the protection of members of the Rohingya minority present in Myanmar's territory, whereas the requests of The Gambia were framed in broader terms. At the same time, The Gambia's core requests were accepted by the Court, as regards the protection of both the substantive rights enshrined in the Genocide

---

[85] *Ibid.*

[86] *Ibid.*, para. 72. Cf. also the Separate Opinions of Vice-President Xue and of Judge Cançado Trindade.

[87] *Ibid.*, para. 72.

[88] Order, operative part.

[89] *Ibid.*, paras. 77-78.

Convention and the integrity of the judicial proceeding. In the former respect, the Order distinguishes between Myanmar's due diligence obligation to prevent acts of genocide by non-State actors and its obligation to avoid directly committing genocidal acts, which is an obligation of result. In the latter perspective, the Order takes a proactive approach, insofar as it seeks to protect evidence but also to monitor compliance with the Order, paving the way for the new monitoring procedure discussed above. It is also noteworthy that the Order was adopted unanimously, although the positions in the Bench were diversified, with Vice-President Xue in particular expressing "serious reservations" about the plausibility of The Gambia's claims.[90]

This new approach to provisional measures, which enhances their preventive function, is particularly important in a context where such serious allegations are at stake; whether this new procedure will actually be sufficient to ensure the correct implementation of the provisional measurers is however doubtful, especially in light of the current political situation in Myanmar.

3.2. The Appointment of Experts in the Armed Activities (Reparations) Case

Two other orders, which the Court adopted respectively on 8 September and 12 October 2020 in the *Armed Activities on the Territory of the Congo (Democratic Republic of the Congo v. Uganda)* case, are also worth discussing. It may be recalled that the Judgment on the merits of this complex and delicate case, issued on 19 December 2005,[91] held Uganda responsible for a number of serious breaches of international law, including international humanitarian law and international human rights law; at the same time, the Democratic Republic of the Congo (DRC) was held responsible for breaching the VCDR of 1961, in light of the mistreatment of Ugandan diplomatic personnel and failure to protect the premises of the Ugandan embassy in Kinshasa. The Court held that each State was under an obligation to make reparation to the other and that, "failing agreement between the Parties, the question of reparation [...] shall be settled by the Court",[92] reserving for this purpose a subsequent procedural phase.

After ten years of fruitless negotiations, the DRC asked the Court to reopen the proceedings "in order to determine the amount of reparation owed by Uganda to the Democratic Republic of the Congo, on the basis of evidence already transmitted to Uganda and which will be made available to the Court".[93] Notwithstanding further efforts to this effect and repeated postponements of the

---

[90] Separate Opinion, para. 2. The Separate Opinion of Judge Cançado Trindade, on the other hand, endorses the Order, stressing the importance of provisional measures in situations where violations of *jus cogens* are at stake.

[91] *Armed Activities on the Territory of the Congo (Democratic Republic of the Congo v. Uganda)*, Judgment of 19 December 2005, ICJ Reports 2005, p. 168 ff.

[92] *Ibid.*, operative part, paras. 6 and 14.

[93] Democratic Republic of the Congo, New Application to the International Court of Justice, filed on 13 May 2015.

hearings, the Parties have not found an agreement on the amount of reparations. The Court itself had highlighted the need to bring the proceeding to a closure, out of consideration for the rights of the victims.[94] As the DRC does not dispute the amount of compensation sought by Uganda in relation to its counter-claim,[95] the main outstanding issue in dispute concerns the amount of compensation due by Uganda to the DRC, which the latter's Counter-Memorial assessed as US$ 13,478,122,950 in principal.[96]

The difficulties for the Congo in proving the exact extent of damage suffered – and therefore for the Court in identifying the appropriate form and quantification of reparations – is apparent. On the one hand, the burden of proving the damage suffered lies in principle with the DRC; on the other hand, the specificities of the case could militate in favour of avoiding a rigid implementation of the principle *onus probandi incumbit actori*. Firstly, part of the heads of damage concern events that took place in the Ituri region, which was deemed to be under belligerent occupation at the time; in this respect, the ICJ may well apply a certain degree of flexibility, since "the respondent may be in a better position to establish certain facts".[97] Moreover, and specifically as regards damage suffered by individuals due to serious violations of international human rights and humanitarian law, a strict application of the principle may be at odds with the requirement to avoid impunity for such breaches and to ensure accountability, if only at the inter-State level. The ICJ case law on this issue is not particularly developed yet and provides little guidance on how the principle of "full reparation" is to be applied in situations such as the one under discussion,[98] and as to whether, for instance, considerations of equity can be applied for the purposes of determining reparation in this respect as well.[99]

The Order of 8 September, whereby the Court called for the appointment of experts to assist it in its task, is a carefully balanced decision in this regard. On the one hand, the Court adopted it notwithstanding Uganda's strong opposition: according to this State,

> to appoint an expert or experts for the stated purpose [...] amount[ed] to relieving the DRC of the primary responsibility to prove her

---

[94] *Armed Activities on the Territory of the Congo (Democratic Republic of the Congo v. Uganda)*, Order of 6 December 2016, ICJ Reports 2016, p. 1135 ff., p. 1136.

[95] See Counter-Memorial of the Democratic Republic of the Congo, February 2018, para. 2.03. The DRC claims, however, that this amount must "be offset against any monetary compensation awarded to the DRC" (*ibid.*, para. 2.04).

[96] *Ibid.*

[97] *Certain Activities Carried Out by Nicaragua in the Border Area (Costa Rica v. Nicaragua)*, Compensation, Judgment, ICJ Reports 2018, p. 15 at 26, para. 33.

[98] On the Court's recent case law see FORLATI, *cit. supra* note 22, p. 291. Regarding the difficulty of applying the principle of full reparation to large-scale breaches of international law, see PAPARINSKIS, "A Case Against Crippling Compensation in International Law of State Responsibility", The Modern Law Review, 2020, p. 1246 ff.

[99] See *Certain Activities (Reparation)*, para. 35, as regards the assessment of environmental damage.

claim (or any particular heads of claim), and assigning that responsibility to third parties, to the prejudice of Uganda and in violation of the relevant principles of international law.[100]

Moreover, in Uganda's opinion

> there is no evidence for the experts to assess or opine on. What remains is for the Court to make the determination as to whether the evidence submitted by the DRC meets the required standard based on its own assessment of the evidence vis-à-vis the applicable principles of international law.

The Court, however, relied on the power to request an expert opinion under Article 50 of the Statute, and on the *Corfu Channel* precedent, recalling that it

> has exercised this power in the past when the circumstances so required [...] including for the assessment of the amount of compensation owed by a party to another, when the estimates and figures submitted by the applicant "raise[d] questions of a technical nature" [...]. The decision to arrange for an expert opinion in no way prejudges the amount of the reparation due by either party to the other, nor any other question relating to the dispute brought before the Court. It leaves intact the parties' right to adduce evidence and submit their arguments on those subjects, in accordance with the Statute and the Rules of Court.

It further posited that in "the circumstances of this case [...] the estimates and figures submitted by the DRC on certain heads of damage raise questions of a technical nature that call for the application of Article 50 of the Court's Statute",[101] reasserting its autonomy vis-à-vis the Parties in the management of procedure, including as regards evidence and proof.[102] At the same time, it took care not to undermine procedural principles it has constantly applied in this regard: firstly, it affirmed that the Parties "will be given the opportunity to comment upon the expert opinion" and "to examine experts in the course of oral hearings under the control of the President".[103] Moreover, and perhaps more significantly, the terms of reference included in the operative part of the order make it clear that the expert opinion is not meant to bring into the Court's file evidence that the Court would not otherwise be in a position to examine: the findings of the experts as regards loss of human life (including the prevailing practice at the time

---

[100] Order of 8 September 2020, para. 10.
[101] Order of 8 September 2020, para. 15.
[102] Ibid., para. 13. On the appointment of experts in the *Maritime Delimitation in the Caribbean Sea and the Pacific Ocean (Costa Rica v. Nicaragua)* case see FORLATI, "The Judicial Activity of the International Court of Justice in 2016", IYIL, 2016, p. 363 ff., p. 381 ff.
[103] Order of 8 September 2020, para. 14.

as to the scale of compensation due for such loss), loss of natural resources (with separate headings for the District of Ituri and other locations in the DRC), and damage to property in that District and in Kisangani (that is, the three heads of damage on which the expert opinion was sought) [104] are to be based only "on the evidence available in the case file and documents publicly available, particularly the United Nations Reports mentioned in the 2005 Judgment".[105] This notwithstanding, Judge Sebutinde strongly criticized the decision to appoint experts and the terms of reference as being unfair and unduly assisting the DRC in discharging their burden of proof. In a Separate Opinion that seems very close to dissent, she argued

> this is not a proper case in which the Court should appoint experts to exercise its powers under Article 50 of the Statute of the Court and Article 67 of the Rules of Court. [...B]oth Parties have had ample opportunity over the last five years to tender whatever evidence they deem necessary or sufficient (including facts, data and methodology) to prove their respective claims. What remains is not for the Court to seek further evidence outside that already submitted by the Parties, but rather to perform its judicial function by examining the evidence already on record and determining the reparations due. [...T]his is not a case involving 'complex issues' that require technical, scientific or specialized knowledge or expertise that is outside the realm of normal judicial expertise. The proposed terms of reference of the experts contained in the Order have the effect of unfairly assisting one of the Parties in buttressing its evidence and discharging its evidentiary burden where that evidence may be wanting, contrary to the principles of a fair hearing and equality of arms. Alternatively, the terms of reference have the effect of inappropriately delegating the judicial function to the experts.[106]

The vote was in any case unanimous, with Judge Cançado Trindade's Separate Opinion further emphasising the relevance of reparations in a natural law perspective, and developing his previous strands of reasoning in the case.

Moreover, in the Order of 12 October the Court appointed four experts, each with different and complementary competences, in line with its previous practice.[107] The Court sought the Parties' opinion before actually appointing the experts; Uganda objected to three out of four names selected by the Court, alleging "in particular [...] preconceived views as reflected in some of the prior publications of two of the potential experts and lack of competence on material issues

---

[104] Order of 12 October 2020.

[105] See *ibid.*, paras. I(a), II(a) and III(a) of the terms of reference.

[106] Separate Opinion of Judge Sebutinde appended to the Order of 8 September 2021, para. 1.

[107] FORLATI, *cit. supra* note 102, p. 382. The Expert Report was submitted on 19 December 2020.

before the Court for two of them".[108] In addressing such objections, the Court once again marked its autonomy from the Parties' wishes in the matter, emphasizing its role as a master of its own procedure. More specifically, the Order notes that

> when exercising its power under Article 50 of the Statute, the Court enjoys some discretion in the designation and appointment of experts called upon to assist it in the assessment of damage caused and the reparation due in a case; [...] in the present case, it is for the Court to ascertain the respective fields of expertise which it finds relevant to the task of providing assistance in determining any reparations due, and, by extension, to satisfy itself of the relevance of the professional qualifications of the individuals to be appointed as experts; [...] the Court considers that Uganda has not shown that any of the prior publications of the potential experts reveal the existence of preconceived views on the subject-matter of the requested expert opinion; [...] consequently Uganda has not demonstrated that the independence of the proposed experts should be called into question; and [...] the Court concludes that none of the experts has expressed any views in their respective publications which would prevent them from examining, with the independence and impartiality required, the documentation from the case file and other publicly available information.

4. CONCLUDING REMARKS

The International Court of Justice swiftly adapted its working methods to the exigencies of the COVID-19 pandemic and managed to keep an almost normal pace in its 2020 judicial activities. The three judgments in the year under review, albeit interesting, were not dealing with the most sensitive and difficult cases on the docket. At the same time, the Court identified particularly innovative solutions in its Order on provisional measures in *The Gambia v. Myanmar* and in those concerning the appointment of experts in *Congo v. Uganda (Reparation)*.

These cases, and the latest modifications to the Rules of Court adopted by the ICJ, confirm that the Court is capable of adapting itself. President Yusuf observed on the occasion of the 100th anniversary of the adoption of the PCIJ Statute:

> One hundred years after its adoption, the Statute has served as the basis for the evolution of international adjudication and has profoundly influenced the formulation of the statutes of other international and regional courts created in the past 70 years. If time is the

---

[108] *Ibid.*

ultimate test of quality, the work of the drafters of the Statute was certainly a masterpiece.[109]

While the State-centered vision of the international legal order embodied in the current Statute is a reflection of the time when the Statute of the PCIJ was adopted, its careful balance allows for innovative solutions tailored to meet the needs and challenges faced by contemporary international society.

---

[109] Speech of H.E. Mr Abdulqawi A. Yusuf, President of the International Court of Justice, on the occasion of the 100th anniversary of the adoption of the Statute of the Permanent Court of International Justice, 10 December 2020, paras. 13-14.

THE INTERNATIONAL TRIBUNAL FOR THE LAW OF THE SEA AND OTHER LAW OF THE SEA JURISDICTIONS (2020)

TULLIO TREVES[*]

1. 2020 saw the handing out of two important awards by Arbitral Tribunals established under Annex VII of the UN Convention on the Law of the Sea (UNCLOS): that of 21 February 2020 on the preliminary objections of the Russian Federation on the *Dispute Concerning Coastal States Rights in the Black Sea, Sea of Azov and Kerch Strait*, and that of 21 May 2020 in the dispute between Italy and India in the dispute concerning *the "Enrica Lexie" Incident*.[1]

Before examining these awards, it seems interesting to mention some developments occurred in 2020 concerning the International Tribunal for the Law of the Sea (ITLOS).

The State Parties held elections for seven seats in the Tribunal. They re-elected Judges Attard (Malta) and Kulyik (Ukraine) and they elected five new judges, namely, Ms Kathy-Ann Brown (Jamaica), Ms Ida Caracciolo (Italy), Mr Jielong Duan (China), Ms Maria Teresa Infante Caffi (Chile), and Mr Maurice Kamga (Cameroon). Their nine year term of office started on 1 October 2020.

Meeting in its renewed composition the Tribunal elected on 2 October 2020 as its new President Judge Albert Hoffmann of South Africa, and as its new vice-president Judge Tomas Heidar of Iceland. On 7 October 2020 the Seabed Disputes Chamber elected as its President Judge Neeru Chadha of India. In 2019 the Tribunal had elected as Registrar the former Deputy Registrar Ms Ximena Hinrichs of Chile, and in 2020 it elected as Deputy Registrar Mr Antoine Olivier of France.

While no judgments or provisional measures orders were issued by the Tribunal in 2020, hearings on preliminary objections were held in the *Dispute concerning delimitation of the marine boundary between Mauritius and the Maldives in the Indian Ocean* before a seven member Chamber of the Tribunal. The judgment was handed out on 28 January 2021 and will be examined in the 2021 instalment of this chronicle.

In 2020 the COVID-19 pandemic had an impact on the activities of ITLOS. The administrative meetings of the Tribunal were held in a hybrid format in which some judges were present and others were connected by video link. Similarly, the above-mentioned hearing in the *Mauritius v. Maldives* case was held in hybrid format combining the physical and virtual participation of the members of the Chamber as well as of the representatives of the Parties.

---

[*] Judge of the International Tribunal for the Law of the Sea (1996-2011), Emeritus Professor of International Law, University of Milano. The views expressed are personal.

[1] Previous instalments of this chronicle (referred to as TREVES, IYIL) were published in the IYIL every year since 2000, the latest being TREVES, "The International Tribunal for the Law of the Sea and Other Law of the Sea Jurisdictions (2019)", IYIL, 2019, p. 271 ff.

IYIL, Vol. 30 (2020), pp. 321-355
ISSN 0391-5107

On 25 September 2020 the Tribunal adopted amendments to its Rules permitting the President to decide "as an exceptional measure, for public health, security or other compelling reasons, to hold meetings entirely or in part by video link" (new paragraph 7 of Article 41). The other amendments of the same date, aimed at implementing such measure, concern: Article 74 (hearings) new paragraph 2 (the previous Article 74 has been renumbered as Article 74, paragraph 1); Article 112, new paragraph 5 (reading of prompt release judgment); Article 124 (reading of judgment), paragraph 3; and Article 135, new paragraph 1 bis (reading of advisory opinion of the Seabed Disputes Chamber).[2]

2. As reported in the 2018 instalment of the present chronicle, the Annex VII Arbitration Tribunal in the *Ukraine v. Russia* case in the *Dispute Concerning Coastal States Rights in the Black Sea, Sea of Azov and Kerch Strait* decided, with Procedural Order No. 3, to accept Russia's request by that the proceedings be bifurcated. The proceedings on the merits were thus suspended and Russia's preliminary objections were considered in a preliminary phase of the proceedings in which Written Observations by Ukraine, a Reply by Russia and a Rejoinder on jurisdiction by Ukraine were filed and a hearing held in the Hague in June 2019. The unanimous Award of 2020[3] thus focuses on the Preliminary Objections submitted by Russia on 21 May 2018.

The characterization of the dispute

The Tribunal notes at the beginning of its reasons that:

> 41. [...] the Parties have chosen an arbitral tribunal constituted in accordance with Annex VII to the Convention as the "principal" or "basic" means for the settlement of disputes concerning the interpretation or application of the Convention. Pursuant to Article 287, paragraph 4, of the Convention, such disputes may be submitted to an arbitral tribunal constituted in accordance with Annex VII. The Arbitral Tribunal consequently finds that the dispute was submitted to it in accordance with the Convention and the declarations made by the Parties.

With its first preliminary Objection Russia submitted that

---

[2] The text of the amendments is in ITLOS, Press Release 306 of 25 September 2020, available at: <www.itlos.org>.

[3] Arbitral Tribunal established under Annex VII of the UN Convention on the Law of the Sea, Award of 21 February 2020 on the preliminary objections of the Russian Federation in the *Dispute Concerning Coastal States Rights in the Black Sea, Sea of Azov and Kerch Strait (Ukraine v. Russian Federation)*, available at: <www.pca-cpa.org>.

43. [...] the Arbitral Tribunal has no jurisdiction over Ukraine's claims because "the dispute in this case concerns Ukraine's claim to sovereignty over Crimea" and a "dispute over territorial sovereignty is not a dispute concerning the 'interpretation or application of the Convention' pursuant to Article 288(1) of UNCLOS."

Ukraine opposed that the Tribunal had jurisdiction, because the dispute concerned the interpretation or application of the Convention (paragraph 44).

The position of the two parties on this issue is well clarified by the answers they submitted to questions put by the Tribunal during the hearing:

146. In response to the first question posed to the Parties by the Arbitral Tribunal at the Hearing (see paragraph 29 of this Award), the Russian Federation submits that the great majority of the claims advanced by Ukraine depend on a prior determination by, or assumption on the part of, the Arbitral Tribunal as to which State is the coastal State in Crimea. The claims that do not so depend, in the Russian Federation's view, are: the submissions advanced at paragraphs 265 (m) and (n) of Ukraine's Memorial with respect to transit passage and navigation and the submissions advanced at paragraphs 265 (o) and (p) of Ukraine's Memorial with respect to a failure to cooperate concerning environmental issues, including the May 2016 oil spill. The Russian Federation states that Ukraine's claim pursuant to Article 92 of the Convention is advanced on the basis that it is the coastal State. Further, according to the Russian Federation, Ukraine's reliance on Article 279, to the extent that it is invoked on the basis that the relevant conduct occurred in maritime areas claimed to be Ukraine's, depends on a prior determination by the Arbitral Tribunal as to which State is the coastal State in Crimea.

147. In response to the second question posed by the Arbitral Tribunal to the Parties, the Russian Federation submits that the Convention does not determine the extent of the rights and duties of the States concerned in circumstances where there is disagreement as to who exercises coastal State rights in respect of a particular maritime area. The Russian Federation maintains that the absence of legal standards in the Convention for the determination of this issue, particularly compared to the fact that the Convention does make provision for steps to be taken when States Parties cannot agree to maritime delimitation under Articles 74 and 83, highlights that disputed issues of land sovereignty do not fall within Article 288 of the Convention.

148. In response to the first question posed to the Parties by the Arbitral Tribunal (see paragraph 29 of this Award), Ukraine submits that the Russian Federation's violations of the following articles of the Convention do not depend on a prior determination by,

or assumption on the part of, the Arbitral Tribunal as to which State is sovereign over Crimea: Articles 38, 43, 44, 92 (which applies to the exclusive economic zone by way of Article 58), 123, 192, 194, 198, 199, 204, 205, 206, 279, and 303. Ukraine clarifies that its argument pursuant to Article 92 is not forwarded on the basis that Ukraine is the coastal State and notes that the violations therefore do not depend on whether they occurred in Ukraine's exclusive economic zone. Ukraine further clarifies that its argument regarding the aggravation of the dispute pursuant to Article 279 does not depend on Ukraine's coastal State rights.

149. In response to the second question posed by the Arbitral Tribunal to the Parties, Ukraine states that the Convention governs the rights and obligations of parties that are in disagreement as to who exercises the coastal State rights in respect of a particular area. If this were not the case, according to Ukraine, the mere existence of an "artificial disagreement" regarding who is entitled to exercise coastal State rights would nullify the rights and obligations under the Convention.

The Tribunal then starts its analysis considering the characterization of the dispute.

151. The first question the Arbitral Tribunal has to address is the nature or character of the dispute brought before it by the Applicant. As the arbitral tribunal in *South China Sea* stated, "[t]he nature of the dispute may have significant jurisdictional implications, including whether the dispute can fairly be said to concern the interpretation or application of the Convention." In addressing this question, the Arbitral Tribunal needs to examine the positions of the Parties, while giving particular attention to the formulation of the dispute chosen by Ukraine as Applicant. However, it is ultimately for the Arbitral Tribunal itself to determine on an objective basis the nature of the dispute dividing the Parties by "[isolating] the real issue in the case and [identifying] the object of the claim."

152. The Arbitral Tribunal notes that, while Ukraine formulates its dispute with the Russian Federation in terms of the alleged violation of its rights under the Convention, thus as a dispute concerning the interpretation or application of the Convention, many of its claims in the Notification and Statement of Claim are based on the premise that Ukraine is sovereign over Crimea, and thus the "coastal State" within the meaning of the various provisions of the Convention it invokes. Ukraine itself acknowledges this and, as will be seen below, submits that this premise must be accepted by the Arbitral Tribunal because the Russian Federation's claim of sovereignty over Crimea is inadmissible and implausible. However, unless the premise that Crimea belongs to Ukraine is to be taken at face value, the claims as

advanced by Ukraine cannot be addressed by the Arbitral Tribunal without first examining and, if necessary, rendering a decision on the question of sovereignty over Crimea. [...]

154. Consequently, if the legal status of Crimea, contrary to Ukraine's assumption, is not settled in the sense that it forms part of Ukraine's territory, but is disputed as the Russian Federation contends, the Arbitral Tribunal would not be able to decide the claims of Ukraine insofar as they are premised on the settled status of Crimea as part of Ukraine without first addressing the question of sovereignty over Crimea. The Arbitral Tribunal therefore considers that the question as to which State is sovereign over Crimea, and thus the "coastal State" within the meaning of several provisions of the Convention invoked by Ukraine, is a prerequisite to the decision of the Arbitral Tribunal on a significant part of the claims of Ukraine. For the purposes of determining the jurisdiction of the Arbitral Tribunal, this characterisation of the dispute before it raises two questions: first, the scope of the jurisdiction of the Arbitral Tribunal under Article 288, paragraph 1, of the Convention; and second, the existence *vel non* of a sovereignty dispute over Crimea. The Arbitral Tribunal will now examine these two questions in turn.

Scope of the Tribunal's jurisdiction

As regards the scope of the Tribunal's jurisdiction under UNCLOS Article 288(1) the Award states:

> 156. [...] The question the Arbitral Tribunal should address is whether a dispute that involves the determination of a question of territorial sovereignty would fall within the jurisdiction of a court or tribunal under Article 288, paragraph 1, of the Convention. While the text of the Convention provides no clear answer to this question, the Arbitral Tribunal is of the view that, in light of Article 297, which carves out certain categories of disputes relating to the exercise of sovereign rights and jurisdiction in the exclusive economic zone, and Article 298, paragraph 1, which allows States to exclude three categories of disputes, such as disputes concerning such sensitive matters as the delimitation of maritime boundaries, from compulsory dispute settlement procedures, a sovereignty dispute, which is mentioned in neither provision, may not be regarded a dispute concerning the interpretation or application of the Convention. The fact that a sovereignty dispute is not included either in the limitations on, or in the optional exceptions to, the applicability of compulsory dispute settlement procedures supports the view that the drafters of the Convention did not consider such a dispute to be "a dispute concerning the interpretation or application of the Convention."

After recalling the views expressed by the Annex VII Arbitral Tribunals in the *Chagos* and in the *South China Sea* cases, the Tribunal states (in paragraph 161) that

> the real issue of contention between the Parties in the present case is whether there exists a sovereignty dispute over Crimea, and if so, whether such dispute is ancillary to the determination of the maritime dispute brought before the Arbitral Tribunal by Ukraine.

The Tribunal than observes in paragraph 165 that

> On the record before the Arbitral Tribunal, however, it is clear that the Parties are in disagreement on various points of law and facts relating to the question as to which State is sovereign over Crimea, and thus who is the "coastal State" within the meaning of various provisions of the Convention invoked by Ukraine.

And that "[t]his finding would seem to be sufficient for a conclusion that a sovereignty dispute exists between the Parties" (paragraph 166).

Before confirming this conclusion, the Tribunal examines in detail and rejects Ukraine's arguments to the effect that Russia's claim to sovereignty is inadmissible and implausible. As regards the inadmissibility claim, Ukraine argues that Russia's claim that the legal status of Crimea has been altered cannot be entertained in the proceedings in light of the principle of non-recognition as reaffirmed with regard to Crimea in resolutions of the UN General Assembly (UNGA) (especially res. 68/262 of 27 March 2014). The Award recalls the jurisprudence of the International Court of Justice (ICJ) to the effect the UNGA resolutions are "not binding but recommendatory in character" (paragraph 172) and that, while in some cases "they can be relevant for ascertaining the existence and contents of a rule of customary law" (paragraph 173), there have been cases "in which the ICJ expressly found that it should not accept determinations made in UNGA resolutions" (paragraph 174). Moreover,

> 175. The Arbitral Tribunal notes that the UNGA resolutions in question are framed in hortatory language. The Arbitral Tribunal further notes that they were not adopted unanimously or by consensus but with many States abstaining or voting against them.
> 176. Regarding the meaning of UNGA resolutions, the Arbitral Tribunal notes that it has the power to interpret the texts of documents of international organisations, including the resolutions of the UNGA. Ukraine's argument that the Arbitral Tribunal must defer to the UNGA resolutions and need only treat Ukraine's sovereignty over Crimea as an internationally recognised background fact is equivalent to asking the Arbitral Tribunal to accept the UNGA resolutions as interpreted by Ukraine. Apart from the question of the legal effect of the UNGA resolutions, if the Arbitral Tribunal were

to accept Ukraine's interpretation of those UNGA resolutions as correct, it would ipso facto imply that the Arbitral Tribunal finds that Crimea is part of Ukraine's territory. However, it has no jurisdiction to do so.

177. Furthermore, the Arbitral Tribunal does not consider that the UNGA resolutions to which Ukraine refers can be read to go as far as prohibiting it from recognising the existence of a dispute over the territorial status of Crimea. In the Arbitral Tribunal's view, such a reading would be incompatible with the proper exercise of its judicial function. Without prejudice to the meaning of the phrase "not to recognize any alteration of the status of the Autonomous Republic of Crimea and the city of Sevastopol," the mere recognition of the objective fact of the existence of a dispute over Crimea in the sense that the claim of one party is positively opposed by the other party cannot be considered to contravene the UNGA resolutions.

The Award further briefly discards the argument that, under the principles of good faith and estoppel, Russia cannot claim sovereignty, specifying that

181. [...] the principles of good faith and estoppel do not operate so as to bar the Russian Federation from maintaining that a dispute concerning sovereignty over Crimea has arisen since March 2014, as the basis of the earlier statements has been substantially and materially changed by developments upon which the Arbitral Tribunal has no jurisdiction to adjudicate.

The Tribunal thus rejects Ukraine's argument that Russia's claim to sovereignty is inadmissible (paragraph 182). It further examines Ukraine's argument that Russia's claim of sovereignty is implausible and rejects it stating that the evidence showed that a dispute between the parties as regards sovereignty clearly existed (paragraphs 185-190).

Lack of jurisdiction on issues presupposing a determination on sovereignty over Crimea

The Tribunal then addresses Ukraine's argument, according to which jurisdiction under UNCLOS could be extended "making any determinations of law as are necessary to resolve the UNCLOS dispute presented to it" (paragraph 191). The award recalls that such possibility was accepted in the *Chagos* award only as regards "ruling upon an ancillary issue of territorial sovereignty" (192-193). It accepts the view that jurisdiction could not be extended under the *Chagos* dictum or otherwise.

195. The Arbitral Tribunal is of the view that, in the present case, the Parties' dispute regarding sovereignty over Crimea is not a

> minor issue ancillary to the dispute concerning the interpretation
> or application of the Convention. On the contrary, the question of
> sovereignty is a prerequisite to the Arbitral Tribunal's decision on
> a number of claims submitted by Ukraine under the Convention.
> Those claims simply cannot be addressed without deciding which
> State is sovereign over Crimea and thus the "coastal State" within
> the meaning of provisions of the Convention invoked by Ukraine.
> 196. The Arbitral Tribunal therefore cannot accept Ukraine's ar-
> gument that even if there exists a predicate territorial sovereignty
> dispute, the Arbitral Tribunal has jurisdiction to address it because
> the relative weight of the dispute lies with the interpretation or ap-
> plication of the Convention.

The Tribunal so accepts, although nuancedly, Russia's first preliminary objection, stating that:

> 197. In light of the foregoing, the Arbitral Tribunal concludes that
> pursuant to Article 288, paragraph 1, of the Convention, it lacks ju-
> risdiction over the dispute as submitted by Ukraine to the extent that
> a ruling of the Arbitral Tribunal on the merits of Ukraine's claims
> necessarily requires it to decide, expressly or implicitly, on the sover-
> eignty of either Party over Crimea. As a result, the Arbitral Tribunal
> cannot rule on any claims of Ukraine presented in its Notification
> and Statement of Claim and its Memorial which are dependent on
> the premise of Ukraine being sovereign over Crimea.
> 198. This conclusion affects many, but not all, of the claims ar-
> ticulated in different forms in Ukraine's Notification and Statement
> of Claim and Ukraine's Memorial. Since the Russian Federation is
> "entitled to know precisely the case advanced against it," it is in the
> interest of procedural fairness and expedition for Ukraine to revise
> its Memorial so as to take full account of the scope of, and limits
> to, the Arbitral Tribunal's jurisdiction as determined in the present
> Award, before the Russian Federation is called upon to respond in
> a Counter-Memorial.

The operative part of the Award, set out in paragraph 492, reflects these findings in two of its points, stating that the Tribunal

> a) Upholds the Russian Federation's objection that the Arbitral
> Tribunal has no jurisdiction over Ukraine's claims, to the extent
> that a ruling of the Arbitral Tribunal on the merits of Ukraine's
> claims necessarily requires it to decide, directly or implicitly, on
> the sovereignty of either Party over Crimea; [...]
> d) Requests Ukraine to file a revised version of its Memorial, which
> shall take full account of the scope of, and limits to, the Arbitral
> Tribunal's jurisdiction as determined in the present Award [...].

Whether the Tribunal lacks jurisdiction on claims pertaining to the Sea of Azov and the Kerch Strait

A second preliminary objection of Russia denied the Tribunal's jurisdiction as regards all of Ukraine's claims pertaining to Sea of Azov and the Kerch Strait.

> 198. The Russian Federation submits that "[i]ndependently of the lack of jurisdiction to decide the question of sovereignty over Crimea, this Tribunal also does not have jurisdiction over any of Ukraine's claims pertaining to the Sea of Azov and the Kerch Strait." The Sea of Azov and the Kerch Strait, according to the Russian Federation, were historically internal waters of the Russian Empire, and later the USSR, and, since 1991, the common internal waters of Ukraine and the Russian Federation. The Russian Federation contends that the Convention does not regulate the regime of internal waters and concludes that issues concerning the Sea of Azov and the Kerch Strait are accordingly not issues concerning the interpretation or application of the Convention pursuant to Article 288, paragraph 1, of the Convention. [...]
>
> 200. Ukraine submits that the Arbitral Tribunal should reject the second preliminary objection of the Russian Federation. According to Ukraine, the Sea of Azov and the Kerch Strait are not internal waters; rather, the Sea of Azov is an enclosed or semi-enclosed sea within the meaning of the Convention, containing a territorial sea and exclusive economic zone, and the Kerch Strait is a strait used for international navigation. Ukraine also argues that the second objection of the Russian Federation does not have an exclusively preliminary character, and should be deferred to the merits phase.

As summarized in the Award, Russia's main arguments were as follows:

> 203. [...] when the USSR ratified the Geneva Convention on the Territorial Sea and the Contiguous Zone [...], on 22 November 1960, the Sea of Azov and the Kerch Strait satisfied the requirements of a bay set out in Article 7 given that the shape of the Sea of Azov met the description of a bay and the opening of the bay, the Kerch Strait, was less than 24 miles wide. Once a closing line was drawn, according to the Russian Federation, the Sea of Azov was considered internal waters pursuant to Article 7, paragraph 4, of the Geneva Convention.
>
> 204. The Russian Federation maintains that "the participation of the USSR in the Geneva Convention and the drawing of baselines across the mouth of the Kerch Strait confirmed the customary internal waters status of the Sea of Azov and the Kerch Strait and established a treaty obligation for the other parties [to that Convention] to recognise such status."

205. The Russian Federation submits that the internal waters status of the Sea of Azov and the Kerch Strait remained unchanged after the dissolution of the USSR and the independence of Ukraine. In the view of the Russian Federation, there is no basis to assume that the Russian Federation and Ukraine intended to change the internal waters status of the Sea of Azov and the Kerch Strait and consequently lose rights that they had formerly enjoyed in those waters.

206. The Russian Federation notes that there has been no waiver on the part of the Russian Federation and Ukraine in respect of their rights. It submits that any waiver or renunciation of a State's rights must either be express or unequivocally implied by the conduct of the State. To the contrary, according to the Russian Federation, Ukraine and the Russian Federation "expressly confirmed that the Sea of Azov and the Kerch Strait retain their internal water status, inter alia, in the State Border Treaty of 28 January 2003 and in the Treaty and Joint Statement of 24 December 2003."

207. The Russian Federation contests Ukraine's argument that a sea surrounded by more than one State generally cannot be claimed as internal waters. It denies the existence of any "strong norm" to this effect. Relying notably on the International Law Commission's commentary to what became Article 7, paragraph 1, of the Geneva Convention, the Russian Federation argues that "Articles 7(1) of the Geneva Convention and 10(1) of UNCLOS do not prohibit the establishment of internal waters in bays with more than one riparian State;" they simply do not address this issue. Accordingly, in the Russian Federation's view, it cannot be said that the Convention "disfavours" pluri-State internal waters. Furthermore, the Russian Federation asserts that it would be contrary to the spirit of the Convention as "a coastal-oriented instrument" to suggest, as Ukraine does, that upon the dissolution of the USSR, the Sea of Azov and the Kerch Strait became "free for all States" without the agreement of the coastal States.

208. The Russian Federation relies on several international cases for the proposition that bays with more than one coastal State can constitute internal waters.

The cases Russia relied upon are the *Gulf of Fonseca* one (*Land, Island and Maritime Frontier Dispute, El Salvador/Honduras: Nicaragua intervening*, ICJ Reports 1992, p. 351 ff., paras. 412 and 432) and the Award of 29 June 2017 in the *Arbitration Between the Republic of Croatia and the Republic of Slovenia (Croatia/Slovenia)*, para. 880. In both cases the waters of a bay with only one riparian state maintained their internal waters character once the riparian States became three in the first case, and two in the second (paragraphs 208 and 209). Russia further relied on treaties between Tanzania and Mozambique, between Brazil and France and between Argentina and Uruguay (paragraph 210).

Answering a question by the Tribunal, it further clarified its position on the Kerch Strait stating that

> 211. [...] "it has been exercising exclusive sovereignty over the waters of the Kerch Strait since it has been exercising its sovereignty on both sides of the strait". Nevertheless, the Russian Federation recognises certain rights of Ukraine related to the Kerch Strait, such as freedom of navigation for Ukrainian ships and a right to free passage for foreign non-military vessels sailing to and from Ukrainian ports, by virtue of the Treaty between the Russian Federation and Ukraine on Cooperation in the Use of the Sea of Azov and the Kerch Strait, 24 December 2003.

Ukraine's opposing view was that

> 212. [...] prior to 1991 the USSR claimed the Sea of Azov and the Kerch Strait as internal waters on the basis that those waters were entirely surrounded by a single State. According to Ukraine, since the dissolution of the USSR, however, these maritime spaces have been bordered by two States, and can no longer qualify as internal waters.
> 213. Ukraine contends that the Sea of Azov is now an "enclosed or semi-enclosed sea" namely "a gulf, basin or sea surrounded by two or more States [the Parties] and connected to another sea or the ocean [the Black Sea] by a narrow outlet [the Kerch Strait] or consisting entirely or primarily of the territorial seas and exclusive economic zones of two or more coastal states," within the meaning of Article 122 of the Convention. Ukraine submits that prior to 1991 the USSR claimed the Sea of Azov and the Kerch Strait as internal waters on the basis that those waters were entirely surrounded by a single State. According to Ukraine, since the dissolution of the USSR, however, these maritime spaces have been bordered by two States, and can no longer qualify as internal waters.

Further Ukraine argues that

> 216. [...] the Convention reflects the "strong and long-standing norm" that a sea surrounded by more than one State cannot be considered internal waters. Ukraine argues that Articles 8 and 10 of the Convention, read together, only contemplate internal waters claims with respect to a single State, not shared claims among two or more States. At a minimum, Ukraine contends that, in light of the way the Convention is written and structured, the notion of pluri-State internal waters should be regarded as "disfavoured and highly exceptional." For Ukraine, the Russian Federation's claim to common internal waters is in tension with the Convention's object and pur-

pose, because pluri-State internal waters claims for which no rule exists in the Convention "may upset th[e] careful balance" established by UNCLOS and undermine the predictability and regularity that it intended to provide.

And that:

> 218. [...] even if the Arbitral Tribunal could recognise that exceptions to the rule against pluri-State bays exist, the conditions for pluri-State internal waters have not been met in this case. Ukraine takes the view that the exceptional status of pluri-State bays has only been recognised where: (a) the body of water is small and not large enough to contain an exclusive economic zone, (b) there is a clear agreement between all bordering States to establish a pluri-State internal waters regime, and (c) third States are not prejudiced by the claim.

The Award then embarks in a detailed analysis of the arguments and practice of both parties in support of their positions, including: those put forward by Russia according to which Ukraine's post-independence general conduct shows – although with one isolated exception – "the treatment of the Sea of Azov and the Kerch Strait as internal waters" (paragraph 230); Ukraine's argument that the Russian vision of the Sea of Azov and the Kerch Strait as common internal waters would prejudice third States" (paragraphs 245-251), as well as the already mentioned Ukrainian argument based on the width of the Sea of Azov set out in paragraph 218 reproduced above (paragraphs 252-261); and the argument of Russia according to which

> 262. [...] the Azov/Kerch Cooperation Treaty and Joint Statement recognise the Sea of Azov and the Kerch Strait as "historically internal" waters. According to the Russian Federation, the claim of historically internal waters should be interpreted also as claims that the rights exercised in the Sea of Azov and the Kerch Strait are based on historic title. The Russian Federation observes that these claims to historic bay status, when published in the *Law of the Sea Bulletin*, did not receive any objections from third States, while the United States elected to protest the Russian Federation's claim to the Peter the Great Bay.

The Award does not take a stand on most of these questions. Instead, it states:

> 291. In the view of the Arbitral Tribunal, the legal regime governing the Sea of Azov and the Kerch Strait depends, to a large extent, on how the Parties have treated them in the period following the independence of Ukraine. The positions of the Parties in respect of

this question can be found or inferred from the subsequent agreements between them, including the Azov/Kerch Cooperation Treaty and the State Border Treaty, as well as their actual practice in those maritime areas. In order to determine whether the Sea of Azov and the Kerch Strait constitute internal waters, therefore, the Arbitral Tribunal must examine not only the subsequent agreements between the Parties but also how the Parties have acted vis-à-vis each other or vis-à-vis third States in the above areas. In particular, this would require the Arbitral Tribunal to scrutinize the conduct of the Parties with respect to such matters as navigation, exploitation of natural resources, and protection of the marine environment in the Sea of Azov and the Kerch Strait.

292. The Arbitral Tribunal further notes that the Russian Federation invokes the concept of historical title as an alternative basis for excluding the application of the Convention to the Sea of Azov and the Kerch Strait. Pursuant to that alternative argument, the Arbitral Tribunal must ascertain whether historic title to the waters in question existed, whether such title continued after 1991, and, if so, what the contents of the regime applicable to such waters has been.

293. The Arbitral Tribunal thus considers that the Russian Federation's objection based on the Sea of Azov and the Kerch Strait having the legal status of internal waters is interwoven with the merits of the present dispute, which have yet to be pleaded by the Parties. In the Arbitral Tribunal's view, this objection may not adequately be addressed without touching upon the questions of the merits, which it should not do at this stage of the proceedings.

This conclusion is repeated in paragraph 297 and confirmed in point b) of the Operative part of the Award:

492. For these reasons, the Arbitral Tribunal unanimously: [...]
    b) Finds that the Russian Federation's objection that the Arbitral Tribunal has no jurisdiction over Ukraine's claims concerning activities in the Sea of Azov and in the Kerch Strait does not possess an exclusively preliminary character, and accordingly decides to reserve this matter for consideration and decision in the proceedings on the merits;

The Tribunal, however, although somehow tentatively, indicates that it "is not entirely convinced" by the Russian argument that UNCLOS does not regulate a regime of internal waters and that, being the Sea of Azov and the Kerch Strait internal waters, "a dispute relating to events that occurred in internal waters cannot concern the interpretation or application of the Convention" and thus does not fall under the jurisdiction of the Arbitral Tribunal (paragraph 294). It further notes that

294. [...] what constitutes internal waters is governed by the Convention. In addition, Article 8, paragraph 2, provides that a right of innocent passage shall exist in internal waters where the establishment of a straight baseline has the effect of enclosing as internal waters areas which had not previously been considered as such.

295. The Arbitral Tribunal also recalls the statement of ITLOS in *Request for Advisory Opinion submitted by the Sub-Regional Fisheries Commission* that the obligation to protect and preserve the marine environment under Article 192 applies to "all maritime areas." Such areas, in the Arbitral Tribunal's view, undoubtedly include internal waters. The Arbitral Tribunal further recalls the observation made by ITLOS in the *ARA Libertad* case that "although article 32 [Immunities of warships and other government ships operated for non-commercial purposes] is included in Part II of the Convention entitled 'Territorial Sea and Contiguous Zone', and most of the provisions in this Part relate to the territorial sea, some of the provisions in this Part may be applicable to all maritime areas, as in the case of the definition of warships provided for in article 29 of the Convention." ITLOS went on to state that "a difference of opinions exists between [the Parties] as to the applicability of article 32 and thus [...] a dispute appears to exist between the Parties concerning the interpretation or application of the Convention".

296. Accordingly, the Arbitral Tribunal is not inclined to accept the proposition that a dispute falls entirely outside the scope of the Convention simply because the underlying events occurred in internal waters. Rather, the relevant question for the Arbitral Tribunal appears to be whether a particular issue raised by the Parties' dispute is regulated by the Convention or whether the particular conduct complained of implicates, or raises questions of the interpretation or application of the Convention.

Other preliminary objections. The "military activities" exception. Alleged jurisdiction of Annex VIII special arbitration tribunals

Other preliminary objections of the Russian Federation were rejected by the Arbitral Tribunal. They were based, inter alia, on the declarations made by both Parties under Article 298(1) UNCLOS (including that the activities considered were "military activities") and on the exception set out in Article 297(3)(a) concerning fisheries activities. Some paragraphs concerning the "military activities" exception are worth recalling:

329. The Arbitral Tribunal notes that it is common ground between the Parties that the events occurring in Crimea in 2014 do not as such form part of the dispute submitted to it. The Arbitral Tribunal further notes that it has upheld the Russian Federation's first pre-

liminary objection to the extent that its ruling on Ukraine's claims necessarily requires it to decide, expressly or implicitly, on the sovereignty of either Party over Crimea. The Arbitral Tribunal accordingly finds that the Russian Federation's global objection has no basis as its premise has not been met.

330. Article 298, paragraph 1, subparagraph (b), of the Convention allows States Parties to exclude from the compulsory jurisdiction of the Convention "disputes concerning military activities." The Arbitral Tribunal notes that the Convention employs the term "concerning," in contrast to other terms, such as "arising out of," "arising from," or "involving," used elsewhere in the Convention to characterise disputes. Compared to such other terms, which are open to a more expansive interpretation, the term "concerning" circumscribes the military activities exception by limiting it to those disputes whose subject matter is military activities. In the Arbitral Tribunal's view, a mere "causal" or historical link between certain alleged military activities and the activities in dispute cannot be sufficient to bar an arbitral tribunal's jurisdiction under Article 298, paragraph 1, subparagraph (b), of the Convention.

331. The Arbitral Tribunal considers that the military activities exception is not triggered in the present case simply because the conduct of the Russian Federation complained of by Ukraine has its origins in, or occurred against the background of, a broader alleged armed conflict. Rather, in the Arbitral Tribunal's view, the relevant question is whether "certain specific acts subject of Ukraine's complaints" constitute military activities.

Finally, it seems worth recalling that the Award is the first and, for the time being, the only decision by an international court of tribunal that considers a claim concerning the jurisdiction of special arbitration tribunals under Annex VIII of UNCLOS. In fact both Russia and Ukraine, while expressing their preference for Annex VII arbitration under Article 287 (1)(c), have also in their declarations stated a preference for a special arbitral tribunal under Annex VIII as regards disputes concerning fisheries, protection and preservation of the marine environment, marine scientific research and navigation, including pollution from vessels and by dumping. Russia argued that the Annex VII Arbitral Tribunal lacked jurisdiction as regards a number of Ukraine's claims which fell under the jurisdiction of special arbitral tribunal established under Annex VIII. The Tribunal rejected this argument stating *inter alia*:

440. The Arbitral Tribunal observes that the dispute before it concerns the maritime rights and obligations of the Parties in the Black Sea, Sea of Azov, and the Kerch Strait. The dispute has many facets, as is evidenced by the claims made by Ukraine in the Notification and Statement of Claim and the Memorial. Ukraine has made allegations regarding inter alia Ukraine's exclusion from access to

and use of its fisheries by the Russian Federation, impediments to navigation introduced by the Russian Federation in the Kerch Strait, and the Russian Federation's failure to cooperate regarding the protection and preservation of the marine environment.

441. The Arbitral Tribunal does not consider each of Ukraine's submissions made in the Notification and Statement of Claim and the Memorial to constitute a distinct and separate dispute, but rather to be part of a single, unified dispute that Ukraine has brought before this Arbitral Tribunal. All aspects of Ukraine's case are, as it were, manifestations of a broader disagreement between the Parties, rather than isolated occurrences that happen to be submitted to arbitration in the same instrument. The fact that the Arbitral Tribunal has decided, above, that it does not have jurisdiction over certain aspects of that dispute does not mean that the remaining aspects should be considered in a piecemeal fashion.

442. Accordingly, in the Arbitral Tribunal's view, it is not possible in the present case to isolate from the broader dispute before it those elements that fall exclusively within the jurisdiction of one or more Annex VIII special arbitral tribunals. Nor would it be in the interest of justice for this Arbitral Tribunal to decline jurisdiction over certain aspects of the dispute before it, as requested by the Russian Federation. The fragmentation of the dispute before the Arbitral Tribunal would risk there being inconsistent outcomes from the various arbitral tribunals that are seised of different aspects of the same dispute. It would also increase the costs and time spent on litigation by the Parties.

3. Previous instalments of the present chronicle have reported on the provisional measures Orders of 2015 by ITLOS and of 2016 by the Annex VII Arbitral Tribunal in the dispute between Italy and India concerning *The "Enrica Lexie" Incident*.[4] These Orders briefly illustrate the facts of this very complex case. The Award of 21 May 2020 settles the dispute pronouncing on jurisdiction as well as on the merits.[5]

A balanced result

As it emerges clearly from a perusal of the operative part, the Award aims at reaching a balanced result. It satisfies Italy in holding (paragraph 1094-B-2) that

---

[4] Respectively in TREVES, IYIL, 2015, p. 369 and TREVES, IYIL, 2016, p. 419.

[5] Arbitral Tribunal constituted under Annex VII to the United Nations Convention on the Law of the Sea, *The Italian Republic v. the Republic of India, concerning the "Enrica Lexie" Incident*, Award of 21 May 2020, PCA Case No. 2015-28. A partial printed text is in RDI, 2020, p. 1123 ff.

"the Marines are entitled to immunity in relation to the acts that they committed during the incident of 15 February 2012, and that India is precluded from exercising its jurisdiction over the Marines", and

> taking note of the commitment expressed by Italy during the proceedings to resume its criminal investigation into the events of 15 February 2012, that India must take the necessary steps to cease to exercise its criminal jurisdiction over the Marines, and that no other remedies are required [...]. (paragraph 1094-B-3)

The Award satisfies India in rejecting all Italy's claims that India had violated Articles 87(1)(a), 92(1) , 97(1) and (3), 100 and, in relation thereto, 300, of UNCLOS (para 1094-B-1); in finding that "by interfering with the navigation of the "St. Antony" Italy has acted in breach of Article 87, paragraph 1, subparagraph (a), and Article 90 of the Convention" (paragraph 1094-B-5); that this latter finding "constitutes adequate satisfaction for the injury of India's non-material interest" (paragraph 1094- B-6a) and is the basis of India's entitlement to payment of compensation in connection with loss of life, physical harm, material damage to property (including to the "St Antony") and moral harm suffered by the captain and other crew members of the "St. Antony", which by its nature cannot be made good through restitution (paragraph 1094-B-6 b).

The Award is in 1094 paragraphs covering over three hundred pages and is accompanied by a joint dissenting Opinion of Arbitrators P.S. Rao and Robinson, by a concurring and dissenting Opinion of Arbitrator P.S. Rao, and by a dissenting Opinion of Arbitrator Robinson. It is not possible to include in this chronicle the passages of the Award concerning all the points of interest, also considering that the Award presents at length the arguments of the Parties reflecting extensive written and oral arguments. I will focus my attention on a selected number of points of procedure and to the main points of substance. I will be very brief on two key issues, namely jurisdiction to consider the question of immunity and immunity of the Italian Marines, in light of the exhaustive and competent treatment by Giuseppe Cataldi, Raffaella Nigro, Natalino Ronzitti and Loris Marotti in the present Volume of the IYIL.[6]

---

[6] CATALDI, "The Enrica Lexie Award Amid Jurisdictional and Law of the Sea Issues"; NIGRO, "The Arbitral Award in the *Enrica Lexie* Case and the Questionable Recognition to the Italian Marines under Customary International Law"; RONZITTI, "Functional Immunity of the Marines on the Enrica Lexie: A Reply to Raffaella Nigro"; and MAROTTI, "A Satisfactory Answer? The *Enrica Lexie* Award and the Jurisdiction over Incidental Questions", in this Volume.

Jurisdiction – Characterization of the dispute

As regards jurisdiction, the Award first characterizes the dispute between the parties as follows:

> 243. [...] the Arbitral Tribunal concludes that the Parties' dispute is appropriately characterised as a disagreement as to which State is entitled to exercise jurisdiction over the incident of 15 February 2012 involving the "Enrica Lexie" and the "St. Antony", which raises questions under several provisions of the Convention, including Articles 56, 58, 59, 87, 92, 97, 100, and 300, the interpretation or application of which the Parties have different views. The dispute may raise, but is not limited to, the question of immunity of the Marines.
> 244. The Arbitral Tribunal thus finds, as it had already concluded on a *prima facie* basis in the proceedings on provisional measures, that there is a dispute between the Parties concerning the interpretation or application of the Convention in the present case.

Incidental jurisdiction to deal with the question of immunity of the Marines

In later developments of the Award, the Arbitral Tribunal envisages the key question whether the immunity of the two Italian marines is covered by the Tribunal's jurisdiction on the dispute as characterized above

> 804. As determined by the Arbitral Tribunal, the dispute between the Parties in the present case concerns which Party is entitled to exercise jurisdiction over the incident of 15 February 2012 involving the "Enrica Lexie" and the "St. Antony" which raises, but is not limited to, the question of the immunity of the Marines.
> 805. The question therefore arises as to whether the issue of the entitlement to exercise jurisdiction over the incident of 15 February 2012 could be satisfactorily answered without addressing the question of the immunity of the Marines. [...]
> 807. The Arbitral Tribunal takes note in this regard that as stated by the counsel for Italy, Sir Michael Wood KCMG, during the Hearing: "in the circumstances of this case, it would make no sense whatsoever for the Tribunal to determine that a state has jurisdiction under the Convention without, at the same time, deciding whether the exercise of such jurisdiction would be lawful under international law. This necessarily requires a decision on immunity."
> 808. Immunity from jurisdiction, by definition, operates as an exception to an otherwise-existing right to exercise jurisdiction. Whether that exception applies in the present case is a question that forms an integral part of the Arbitral Tribunal's task to deter-

mine which Party may exercise jurisdiction over the Marines. The Arbitral Tribunal could not provide a complete answer to the question as to which Party may exercise jurisdiction without incidentally examining whether the Marines enjoy immunity. The issue of immunity of the Marines, in the words of the PCIJ in the *Case Concerning Certain German Interests* belongs to those "questions preliminary or incidental to the application" of the Convention.

809. The Arbitral Tribunal considers that, while the Convention may not provide a basis for entertaining an independent immunity claim under general international law, the Arbitral Tribunal's competence extends to the determination of the issue of immunity of the Marines that necessarily arises as an incidental question in the application of the Convention.

810. The Arbitral Tribunal recalls in this regard Italy's argument that "[t]here is nothing unusual in an international court or tribunal with jurisdiction over a dispute concerning the interpretation or application of a treaty deciding questions of international law that necessarily arise in the resolution of the dispute". India, for its part, has acknowledged that "the very fact that the ITLOS, as well as Annex VII tribunals, are called to apply, besides the UNCLOS itself, 'other rules of international law not incompatible with [the] Convention' confirms the accepted incompleteness of the Convention".

811. The Arbitral Tribunal finds that examining the issue of the immunity of the Marines is an incidental question that necessarily presents itself in the application of the Convention in respect of the dispute before it, namely which Party is entitled to exercise jurisdiction over the incident of 15 February 2012 involving the "Enrica Lexie" and the "St. Antony". The Arbitral Tribunal accordingly concludes that it has jurisdiction to deal with the question of immunity of the Marines in the present dispute.

Admissibility of India's counterclaims

Among the questions of jurisdiction and admissibility dealt with in the Award there is that of the admissibility of India's counter-claims. Although such admissibility was not disputed by Italy, the Tribunal addressed the issue is a few paragraphs that seem of general interest:

254. While the Rules of Procedure adopted by the Arbitral Tribunal in consultation with the Parties at the beginning of the proceedings do not expressly provide for, and regulate, the right to present counter-claims, the Arbitral Tribunal has no doubt that arbitral tribunals established pursuant to Annex VII to the Convention have the inherent power to hear counter-claims. This is consistent with the view previously taken by arbitral tribunals in the Annex VII

arbitrations of *Barbados v. The Republic of Trinidad and Tobago* and *Guyana v. Suriname*.

255. The Arbitral Tribunal recalls in this regard that Annex VII, Article 5, to the Convention empowers an arbitral tribunal to "determine its own procedure, assuring each party a full opportunity to be heard". The Arbitral Tribunal further observes that the rules of procedure in both alternative fora for the compulsory settlement of disputes under the Convention, the ICJ and ITLOS, make express provision for the filing of counter-claims by respondent States, and there is no reason why respondent States should be in any different position in Annex VII arbitrations. Finally, the Arbitral Tribunal notes that all major arbitral rules of procedure, including the PCA Arbitration Rules 2012 and the PCA Optional Rules for Arbitrating Disputes between Two States, envisage the submission of counter-claims.

256. It is a general principle of procedural law, consistently applied by international courts and tribunals, that a counter-claim may be admitted only if it comes within the jurisdiction of the court or tribunal concerned and is directly connected with the subject-matter of the claim of the other party. The Arbitral Tribunal finds that these conditions are met in the present case. India's counter-claims raise questions in respect of several provisions of the Convention – notably Articles 56, 58, 87, 90, and 88 – and therefore concern the interpretation or application of the Convention pursuant to Article 288, paragraph 1, of the Convention. Moreover, the counterclaims arise directly from the incident of 15 February 2012 involving the "Enrica Lexie" and the "St. Antony", which forms the basis of Italy's claims. India's counter-claims are accordingly admissible.

The exercise of jurisdiction over the "Enrica Lexie" and the marines

As regards whether India's exercise of jurisdiction over the "Enrica Lexie" and the marines was compatible with UNCLOS, the Award recalls that India invoked as a basis the "territoriality principle" and the "passive personality principle".

363. The Arbitral Tribunal considers that, to justify India's exercise of jurisdiction in the present case, it would be sufficient for either of the two bases to be compatible with the Convention.

364. The territoriality principle invoked by India denotes the principle that a State may exercise jurisdiction over any offence committed in its territory. According to India, this principle may be extended to a vessel, so that a State may exercise jurisdiction over any offence committed on board its vessel wherever it may be, as if the offence were committed in its territory.

365. The Arbitral Tribunal notes that such an extended territoriality principle is well established, and the domestic criminal legislation of a large number of States confers jurisdiction over offences committed on board national ships or aircraft. In this regard, the Arbitral Tribunal does not consider that this principle amounts to assimilating a vessel with national territory "for all purposes" as if "a ship is a floating part of state territory", as Italy argues.

366. In the view of the Arbitral Tribunal, it is also well established that, where the commission of an offence involves the territories of more than one State (for example, an offence was commenced in the territory of one State and completed in the territory of another State), both the State in whose territory an offence was commenced (subjective territoriality principle) and the State in whose territory it was completed (objective territoriality principle) may exercise jurisdiction over the offence. Likewise, where an offence was commenced on board one vessel and completed on board another vessel, the flag States of both vessels may have concurrent jurisdiction over the offence.

The Award continues as follows, also addressing the basis for Italy's jurisdiction over the vessel and the marines:

367. In the present case, the Marines on board the "Enrica Lexie" fired at the "St. Antony", resulting in the death of two Indian fishermen on board the "St. Antony" and damage to the vessel. The incident thus involves two vessels: the alleged offence was commenced on board the Italian vessel, "Enrica Lexie", and completed on board the Indian vessel, "St. Antony". According to the territoriality principle, both Italy and India are entitled to exercise jurisdiction over the incident. However, this is without prejudice to the question whether India is precluded from exercising jurisdiction over the Marines because of their status as State officials entitled to immunity in relation to acts performed in the exercise of their official functions. This question will be addressed in Part V, Section C, of the Award.

368. Furthermore, in the Arbitral Tribunal's view, India's exercise of jurisdiction over the "Enrica Lexie" incident is not only compatible with the Convention, but justified by Article 92, paragraph 1, of the Convention, which provides for the principle of exclusive flag State jurisdiction. Pursuant to this principle, India, as the flag State, has exclusive jurisdiction over the "St. Antony" and may assert its jurisdiction in respect of the offence that was allegedly completed on board its vessel in the exclusive economic zone, in the same way as Italy, as the flag State, has exclusive jurisdiction over the "Enrica Lexie" and may assert its jurisdiction in respect of the offence that was allegedly commenced on board its vessel.

Right to freedom of navigation

Coming now to the most interesting of the parts of the Award dealing with law of the sea issues, it seems fit to examine first the treatment of the Italian claim that "that India violated Italy's right to freedom of navigation under Articles 87, paragraph 1, subparagraph (a), of the Convention by directing, interdicting, and escorting the Italian-flagged "Enrica Lexie" beyond its territorial waters" (paragraph 435).

> 468. [...] the Arbitral Tribunal notes that the right to freedom of navigation "provides ships of any States with the right to traverse the high seas with no or minimal interference from any other State". Accordingly, as stated by ITLOS in *M/V "Norstar"*, "any act of interference with navigation of foreign ships or any exercise of jurisdiction over such ships on the high seas constitutes a breach of the freedom of navigation, unless justified by the Convention or other international treaties" was found to constitute "a violation of the sovereignty of the country whose flag the vessel flies" [...].
>
> 469. The Arbitral Tribunal observes that interference may take physical or non-physical forms.
>
> 470. As observed by ITLOS in *M/V "Norstar"*, "[i]t goes without saying that physical or material interference with navigation of foreign ships on the high seas violates the freedom of navigation". Interference of a physical nature may include, as stated in the *Arbitration Between the Republic of Croatia and the Republic of Slovenia*, "boarding, arrest, detention, [or] diversion" of a vessel.
>
> 471. However, "even acts which do not involve physical interference or enforcement on the high seas may constitute a breach of the freedom of navigation". The arbitral tribunal in *Guyana v. Suriname* thus considered that a demand by a navy vessel to "leave the area in 12 hours" or "the consequences will be yours", constituted "a threat of the use of force in contravention of the Convention, the UN Charter and general international law". Moreover, as stated by Judge Laing in his separate opinion in *M/V "SAIGA" (No. 2)*, the enjoyment of "freedom of the seas" is dependent on freedom from fear, that is, "security and non-interference, in today's language".
>
> 472. Accordingly, in the Arbitral Tribunal's view, a breach of freedom of navigation may result from acts including physical or material interference with navigation of a foreign vessel, the threat or use of force against a foreign vessel, or non-physical forms of interference whose effect is that of instilling fear in, or causing hindrance to, the exercise of the freedom of navigation.
>
> 473. Additionally, as stated in *M/V "Norstar"*, the exercise of jurisdiction over a foreign ship on the high seas, unless justified by the Convention or other international treaties, is generally agreed to

constitute a breach of freedom of navigation. The Arbitral Tribunal will consider Italy's argument that India exercised jurisdiction over the "Enrica Lexie" primarily in its analysis of Italy's claim pursuant to Article 92, paragraph 1, of the Convention.

As mentioned above, the Tribunal rejects the Italian claim that India had violated Italy's freedom of navigation. It finds, first, that that the Indian authorities' "request for the 'Enrica Lexie' to proceed to Kochi cannot be regarded as constituting interference with navigation of the 'Enrica Lexie', which could amount to a breach of Italy's freedom of navigation" (paragraph 481).

Second, the Tribunal considers that Italy failed to discharge its burden of proof as regards its allegation that "the Indian authorities perpetrated a ruse in order to bring the 'Enrica Lexie' into India's territorial waters" (paragraph 489).

Third, the Tribunal rejects the Italian argument that India's behavior amounted to interdiction of the "Enrica Lexie" in its exclusive economic zone thus violating Italy's freedom of navigation. The Award states the following in this regard:

> 491. In the context of the law of the sea, "interdiction" is generally understood as a State's action of stopping, searching, and arresting foreign flag vessels and crew on the high seas. Interdiction has been taken to denote a "two-step process: first, the boarding, inspection and search of a ship at sea suspected of prohibited conduct; second, where such suspicions prove justified, taking measures including any combination of arresting the vessel, arresting persons aboard or seizing cargo". While a flag State has jurisdiction to interdict vessels flying its flag on the high seas, all other States "may only conduct an interdiction under a permissive rule of international law or with permission from the flag state or the coastal state in whose regulatory zone the vessel is present". [...]
> 494. No boarding or arrest of the "Enrica Lexie" took place when the vessel was in India's exclusive economic zone. The Arbitral Tribunal is not prepared to speculate as to whether the Indian Coast Guard might have used force to compel the "Enrica Lexie" to head to Kochi, or boarded the vessel, had this become necessary. According to the evidence before the Arbitral Tribunal, no such instructions had been given, boarding drills were routine on all missions, and the reason for the presence of police officers in the ICGS "Lakshmibai" was that firing had been reported, thus making the incident a police case.

Fourth, the Tribunal also rejects the Italian claim that "by escorting the 'Enrica Lexie' to Kochi, India breached Italy's freedom of navigation" (paragraph 496) observing *inter alia* that: "[w]ithout sufficient evidence to support Italy's allegation that the purpose of the escort was the apprehension of the 'Enrica Lexie', there is no basis for the Arbitral Tribunal to so conclude" (paragraph 503).

The same notions of freedom of navigation and of interference were resorted to by the Tribunal in addressing in India's argument, set out in the counterclaim, that Italy had violated India's freedom of navigation "when the Marines fired shots at the 'St. Antony' and caused it to change course and veer away in order to avoid further gunfire" (paragraph 1017). After examining Italy's conduct, the Tribunal concludes that:

> 1041. In the Arbitral Tribunal's view, the evidence on the record is clear that it was the act of shooting at the "St. Antony" by the Marines stationed on the "Enrica Lexie" that caused the "St. Antony" to change direction and ultimately head back to shore. The "St. Antony" was, both during and after the incident, prevented from navigating its intended course.
>
> 1042. The shooting at the "St. Antony" amounted to physical interference with the navigation of the "St. Antony". As observed by ITLOS in M/V "Norstar", "[i]t goes without saying that physical or material interference with navigation of foreign ships on the high seas violates the freedom of navigation".
>
> 1043. Accordingly, the Arbitral Tribunal concludes that by interfering with the navigation of the "St. Antony", Italy acted in breach of Article 87, paragraph 1, subparagraph (a), and Article 90 of the Convention.

Exclusive flag State jurisdiction under UNCLOS article 92

The Award also examines, and rejects, Italy's claim that India breached Article 92, paragraph 1, of the Convention by exercising jurisdiction over the "Enrica Lexie" while it was in India's exclusive economic zone. The Award first embarks in defining the notion of "jurisdiction" as utilized in Article 92 of UNCLOS:

> 524. The principle of exclusive flag State jurisdiction has been recognised as an "essential adjunct [...] to the principle of the freedom of the seas" or a "corollary of the open and free status of the high seas".
>
> 525. The concept of "jurisdiction", derived from the Latin *juris dicere* (literally: "to speak the law"), while broadly used in international law, remains largely undefined in the case law of international courts and tribunals.
>
> 526. One may distinguish between prescriptive jurisdiction, adjudicative jurisdiction, and enforcement jurisdiction. Prescriptive jurisdiction is the authority of a State to make laws in relation to persons, property, or conduct; adjudicative jurisdiction is the authority of a State to apply law to persons or things; and enforcement jurisdiction is the authority of a State to exercise its power to com-

pel compliance with law. Under international law, the exercise of jurisdiction by a State entails an element of prescribing laws, rules, or regulations over conduct, or applying or enforcing such laws, rules, or regulations over persons or property.

527. It follows from the above analysis that the principle of exclusive flag State jurisdiction under the Convention is violated when a State other than the flag State seeks to prescribe laws, rules, or regulations over a ship of the flag State, or applies or enforces such laws, rules, or regulations in respect of such a ship. The Arbitral Tribunal also recalls in this respect the observation of ITLOS in *M/V "Norstar"* that the principle of exclusive flag State jurisdiction "prohibits not only the exercise of enforcement jurisdiction on the high seas by States other than the flag State but also the extension of their prescriptive jurisdiction to lawful activities conducted by foreign ships on the high seas".

The Award then examines India's conduct noting *inter alia* that

532. [...] while the Indian Coast Guard deployed an aircraft and naval vessels to "conduct search for suspected vessel between Kollam and Kadungalloor", to "render assistance for apprehension of suspect vessel", and to "interrogate/identify all the merchant vessels in the area" in search of the vessel involved in the firing, the aircraft and vessels did not, in fact, carry out any enforcement measures, such as boarding or detention, while the "Enrica Lexie" was in India's exclusive economic zone. Rather, at 19:20 SMT/19:50 IST, the Dornier aircraft located and arrived above the "Enrica Lexie" and "directed them to amend the course and proceed to Kochi harbour".

And concludes as follows:

534. The Arbitral Tribunal finally recalls that it cannot answer conclusively, on the evidentiary record before it, whether the Indian Coast Guard might have had recourse to force or the threat of force to compel the "Enrica Lexie" to head to Kochi, had it not pursued that course voluntarily.

535. In the view of the Arbitral Tribunal, Italy has not discharged its burden of proving that the Indian Coast Guard, by "interdicting" and "escorting" the "Enrica Lexie", exercised enforcement jurisdiction.

536. In conclusion, the conduct of the Indian authorities while the "Enrica Lexie" was in India's exclusive economic zone did not amount to an exercise of jurisdiction. The Arbitral Tribunal accordingly finds that India did not violate Article 92, paragraph 1, of the Convention.

Authority to institute criminal proceedings under Article 97 UNCLOS.

A further submission by Italy was that

> 576. [...] India breached Article 97, paragraph 1, by instituting penal proceedings against the Marines who, according to Italy, were persons "in the service of the ship" during a "collision or any other incident of navigation". According to Italy, only Italy had the authority to institute penal or disciplinary proceedings pursuant to Article 97, paragraph 1, as either the flag State of the ship or the Marines' State of nationality. In Italy's view, India thus breached Article 97, paragraph 1, by violating Italy's exclusive jurisdiction to prosecute the Marines.

The Tribunal dealt with this submission determining first the meaning of "incident of navigation" in UNCOS Article 97(1).

> 638. The phrase "incident of navigation" is not defined in the Convention. In accordance with Article 31, paragraph 1, of the VCLT, therefore, it must be interpreted "in good faith in accordance with the ordinary meaning to be given to the terms of the treaty in their context and in the light of its object and purpose".
> 639. The dictionary meaning of the term "incident" is a "distinct occurrence or event, esp[ecially] one that attracts general attention or is noteworthy in some way". The term "navigation" refers to the "action or practice of travelling on water; sailing"; the "art or science of directing a ship, boat", and the verb "to navigate" means to "sail, direct, manage, a ship". Thus, based on the ordinary meaning of the phrase, an "incident of navigation" should involve, at least, a distinct or noteworthy event that occurs in relation to the movement and directing or manoeuvring of a ship.
> 640. The term "incident of navigation" appears in two other instances in the Convention.
> 641. First, Article 221, paragraph 2, provides:
>> For the purposes of this article, "maritime casualty" means a collision of vessels, stranding or other incident of navigation, or other occurrence on board a vessel or external to it resulting in material damage or imminent threat of material damage to a vessel or cargo.
> 642. This provision distinguishes between (i) "a collision of vessels"; (ii) "stranding or other incident of navigation"; and (iii) "other occurrence on board a vessel or external to it resulting in material damage or imminent threat of material damage to a vessel or cargo". The first two categories, namely, a collision and a "stranding or other incident of navigation", are but examples of occurrences "on board a vessel or external to it resulting in mate-

rial damage or imminent threat of material damage to a vessel or cargo". Accordingly, "incident of navigation", within the context of the Convention, must be taken to refer to an occurrence on board a vessel or external to it resulting in material damage or imminent threat of material damage to a vessel or cargo.

643. This is corroborated by the further context provided by Article 94, paragraph 7, of the Convention, which addresses "incidents of navigation" "causing loss of life or serious injury to nationals of another State or serious damage to ships or installations of another State or to the marine environment".

Having then discussed the object and purpose of Article 97 as well as its preparatory work, the Tribunal concludes that, in its view:

650. [...] the phrase "incident of navigation" within the meaning of Article 97, paragraph 1, of the Convention, refers to an event that (i) occurs in relation to the movement and manoeuvring of a ship; and (ii) which allegedly causes some form of serious damage or harm, including to the ships involved, their cargo, or the individuals on board.

Applying this definition to the case at hand, the Tribunal states:

651. In order to answer the allegation that India has breached Article 97, paragraph 1, of the Convention, the Arbitral Tribunal must determine whether an "incident of navigation" occurred on 15 February 2012 and, therefore, whether Article 97, paragraph 1, is applicable in the present case. In order to constitute an "incident of navigation", in turn, there must have occurred manoeuvring or movement of a ship that resulted in serious damage or harm, including to the ships involved, their cargo, or the individuals on board.

652. The Arbitral Tribunal observes that it is undisputed between the Parties that no collision occurred between the "Enrica Lexie" and the "St. Antony" on 15 February 2012. In the view of the Arbitral Tribunal, there was a risk of collision. However, no damage resulted from the manoeuvring or movement of a ship. While the "St. Antony" was indeed damaged and two Indian fishermen on board lost their lives during the incident, this damage and mortal harm were not caused by the movement or manoeuvring of either ship. [...]

655. While the acts for which the Marines are being prosecuted, and the harm caused by those acts, took place while two ships were sailing in the exclusive economic zone of India, they are not caused by the movement or maneuvering of those ships and cannot be said to have been part of an "incident of navigation".

656. For the foregoing reasons, no "incident of navigation" has occurred that would trigger the application of Article 97, paragraph 1, of the Convention. While there also is some doubt as to whether the Marines qualify as "other person[s] in service of the ship", given that they are not involved with its navigation or manoeuvring, there is no need for the Arbitral Tribunal to further address this question, since it has already established that Article 97 does not apply in this dispute.

The Award than briefly deals with Italy's contention that India had contravened Article 97(3) UNCLOS according to which "no arrest or detention of the ship, even as a measure of investigation, shall be ordered by any authorities other than those of the flag State":

658. The Parties disagree as to whether Article 97, paragraph 3, prohibits arrest and detention of foreign vessels in the territorial sea in respect of incidents of navigation occurring on the high seas. While Italy submits that such arrest and detention are prohibited, India maintains that such prohibition is only applicable to the high seas.
659. The Arbitral Tribunal observes that it follows from the title of Article 97 that it governs the exercise of penal jurisdiction only in matters of collision or any other incident of navigation. As has been determined by the Arbitral Tribunal in the preceding analysis on a possible applicability of paragraph 1 of Article 97, in the case of the incident that took place on 15 February 2012, there was no collision or any other incident of navigation during that incident. Consequently, Article 97, paragraph 3, is not applicable in the present case as well.

Duty to cooperate in the repression of piracy (Article 100 of UNCLOS). Bad faith and abuse of rights

A further claim by Italy was that, "by failing to recognise and uphold the immunity of the Marines and by asserting jurisdiction over the 'Enrica Lexie' and the Marines in respect of the incident", India had contravened UNCLOS Article 100, stating the obligation of all States to cooperate in the repression of piracy on the high seas, and also breached Article 300 of the Convention by breaching Article 100 in bad faith and that it "abused its right to cooperation in the repression of piracy by using it as a pretext to obtain custody over the 'Enrica Lexie' and the Marines, thereby further breaching its obligations under Article 100, read in conjunction with Article 300" (paragraph 662). The Tribunal rejected this claim with the following argument:

722. The Arbitral Tribunal notes that Article 100 does not stipulate the forms or modalities of cooperation States shall undertake in or-

der fulfil their duty to cooperate in the repression of piracy. In its commentary to Article 38 of the ILC Draft Articles Concerning the Law of the Sea, the forerunner of Article 100 of the Convention, the ILC made the following observation:

> Any state having an opportunity of taking measures against piracy, and neglecting to do so, would be failing in a duty laid upon it by international law. Obviously, the State must be allowed a certain latitude as to the measures it should take to this end in any individual case.

723. The duty to cooperate under Article 100 of the Convention "does not necessarily imply a duty to capture and prosecute pirates". Rather, States' obligations under Article 100 can be implemented, for example, by including "in their national legislation provisions on mutual assistance in criminal matters, extradition and transfer of suspected, detained and convicted pirates" or conclusion of "bilateral and multilateral agreements or arrangements in order to facilitate such cooperation". This is consistent with other provisions of the Convention prescribing a duty to cooperate as "a duty of a continuing nature – an obligation of conduct rather than a one-time commitment or result".

724. In this regard, the Arbitral Tribunal notes that India has provided sufficient information confirming that it has taken and is taking active steps to prevent piracy attempts at sea and plays an active role in this regard within the framework of the ReCAAP [Regional Cooperation Agreement on Combating Piracy and Armed Robbery Against Ships in Asia], launched in November 2006. [...]

727. Further, the Arbitral Tribunal observes that as reflected in the ILC's commentary cited above, the threshold for accusing a State of violating Article 100 of UNCLOS is relatively high, and Italy has not provided sufficient evidence to discharge its burden of proof in this regard. [...]

729. With reference to Italy's allegation of the violation by India of Article 300 of the Convention, the Arbitral Tribunal notes that in the *M/V "Norstar"* case, ITLOS stated:

> article 300 of the Convention cannot be invoked on its own. Therefore, a State Party claiming a breach of article 300 must first identify "the obligations assumed under this Convention" that are not fulfilled in good faith or "the rights, jurisdiction and freedoms recognized in this Convention" that are exercised in an abusive manner. The State Party then has to establish a link between its claim under article 300 and "the obligations assumed under this Convention" or "the rights, jurisdiction and freedoms recognized in this Convention".

730. Consequently, the Arbitral Tribunal finds that, in light of its conclusion that India has not violated Article 100 of the Convention, Article 300 cannot be invoked in the present case.

Immunity of the Marines from jurisdiction of the Indian Courts

The Award then turns to the key aspect of Italy's defence, that India contravened the Italian Marines' immunity by its "assertion and continued exercise of criminal jurisdiction" over them. The most complex and controversial part of the Award on this subject concerns jurisdiction. The passages of the Award establishing that the Tribunal enjoys a form of incidental jurisdiction to treat this matter that is not explicitly regulated by UNCLOS have been presented above and, as already mentioned, are examined in detail in an article by Marotti published in the present Volume of the IYIL. As regards the merits of the claim, also discussed in detail in an article by Nigro and Ronzitti also in this Volume, the Tribunal determined that the Marines are

> 855. […] "State officials of the Italian Republic" for the purpose of determining their entitlement to immunity ratione materiae because they were and remain members of the Italian Navy and officers and agents of the judicial police entrusted with guaranteeing the maritime defence of the State.

And that:

> 862. […] regardless of whether the Marines' acts were ultra vires or unlawful, in the view of the Arbitral Tribunal, the evidence demonstrates that during the incident the Marines were under an apprehension of a piracy threat and engaged in conduct that was in the exercise of their official functions as members of the Italian Navy and of a VPD.

The Tribunal then dismisses the "territorial tort exception" raised by India. The Tribunal does not concede that this exception is provided in customary international law, notwithstanding its inclusion in Article 12 of the UN Convention on Jurisdictional Immunities of States and their Property. The Award states:

> 871. In the present case, it is undisputed that the Marines were on board the "Enrica Lexie", and not on Indian territory, when they committed the acts at issue. As such, there was no situation in which the Indian government's consent for the discharge of the Marines' official functions could have been required or sought, and no intentional breach of India's sovereignty can be imputed to the Marines or the Italian State.

Activities in the exclusive economic zone. Obligation of "due regard" under UNCLOS Articles 56 and 58

In examining India's counterclaims, the Tribunal considers India's argument that Italy's conduct as regards the "St. Antony", a fishing vessel, had contravened

India's sovereign right to fish in its economic zone provided in UNCLOS Article 56. The Tribunal dismisses this argument observing *inter alia*:

> 953. In the view of the Arbitral Tribunal, it is established that the actions by the Marines were not directed at undermining or interfering with India's sovereign rights under Article 56 of the Convention. The Arbitral Tribunal notes, in particular, that the conduct of the Marines in the present case occurred in the context of a singular and isolated incident, which had a merely incidental effect on the ability of a fishing vessel, the "St. Antony", to continue pursuing its fishing activities. Such circumstances do not rise to the level of interference with "sovereign rights for the purposes of exploring and exploiting, conserving and managing the natural resources" of the exclusive economic zone.
>
> 954. In any case, the sovereign rights enjoyed by India in its exclusive economic zone are not unlimited but must be balanced against the rights and duties of other States. This is confirmed by the obligation on the coastal State in Article 56, paragraph 2, of the Convention to have due regard to the rights and duties of other States and the applicability of Article 110 of the Convention.
>
> 955. With respect to the obligation to have due regard to the rights of other States, the Arbitral Tribunal observes that piracy at sea constitutes an international crime. All States have the right and duty to protect their vessels against piracy at sea including in the exclusive economic zone of a coastal State. In the present case, the Marines did not target the "St. Antony" as a fishing vessel, but on the suspicion that it was a pirate vessel intending to board the "Enrica Lexie". The Arbitral Tribunal consequently concludes that the actions taken by the Marines, as Italian State officials, for the discrete purpose of protecting the "Enrica Lexie" against a perceived pirate attack, the domestic law aspects of which will be subject to determination by a competent criminal court, did not result in a violation by Italy of Article 56 of the Convention.

The Award gives a closer look at the notion of "due regard" in discussing India's claim that Italy had violated its duty of due regard set out in Article 58 UNCLOS:

> 973. The notion of "due regard" is not defined by UNCLOS. The ordinary meaning of the phrase "with due regard to" is "with the proper care or concern for". The term "regard" also signifies "[a]ttention, care, or consideration given to a thing or person; concern for, heed of", or "[a] thing or circumstance taken into account in determining action; a consideration, a motive". As a general rule, the ordinary meaning of "due regard" does not contemplate priority for one activity over another.

974. This absence of hierarchy is reflected in the complementarity of Article 56, paragraph 2, and Article 58, paragraph 3, of the Convention. As discussed in the Virginia Commentary, "[t]here is a mutuality in the relationship of the coastal State and other States, and articles 56 and 58 taken together constitute the essence of the regime of the exclusive economic zone".

975. The sovereign rights of the coastal State over the natural resources in the exclusive economic zone coexist with the high seas freedoms enjoyed by other States in that zone. In accordance with Article 56, paragraph 2, the coastal State is required to have "due regard" to the rights and duties of other States in the exclusive economic zone, and correspondingly, under Article 58, paragraph 3, of the Convention, other States shall have "due regard" to the rights and duties of the coastal State in its exclusive economic zone. Thus, the object and purpose of the obligation of "due regard" is to ensure balance between concurrent rights belonging to coastal and other States.

976. In *Chagos Marine Protected Area* Arbitration, the arbitral tribunal defined the notion of "due regard", in the context of Article 56, paragraph 2, of the Convention, as follows:

> In the Tribunal's view, the ordinary meaning of "due regard" calls for the United Kingdom to have such regard for the rights of Mauritius as is called for by the circumstances and by the nature of those rights. The Tribunal declines to find in this formulation any universal rule of conduct. The Convention does not impose a uniform obligation to avoid any impairment of Mauritius' rights; nor does it uniformly permit the United Kingdom to proceed as it wishes, merely noting such rights. Rather, the extent of the regard required by the Convention will depend upon the nature of the rights held by Mauritius, their importance, the extent of the anticipated impairment, the nature and importance of the activities contemplated by the United Kingdom, and the availability of alternative approaches.

977. In the view of the Arbitral Tribunal, the above notion of "due regard" as defined by the arbitral tribunal also applies in the context of Article 58, paragraph 3.

978. It follows from the *Chagos Marine Protected Area* Arbitration award that the extent of the "regard" required by the Convention depends, among others, upon the nature of the rights enjoyed by a State. In other words, Article 56, paragraph 2, and Article 58, paragraph 3, are structured so as to guarantee observance of the concurrent respective rights and duties of coastal and other States. The Virginia Commentary to Article 58, paragraph 3, of the Convention indicates that the Article's significance is "that it balances the rights, jurisdiction and duties of the coastal State with the rights and duties of other States in the exclusive economic zone".

979. The Arbitral Tribunal observes that Article 58, paragraph 2, of the Convention provides that Articles 88 to 115 "apply to the exclusive economic zone". That reference extends specific rights and duties of States as regards the repression of piracy to the exclusive economic zone. The repression of piracy by States in the exclusive economic zone is thus not only sanctioned by the Convention but also, pursuant to Article 100 of the Convention as incorporated into Article 58, paragraph 2, a duty incumbent on all States.

980. It follows that, if protection from and repression of piracy comprise a right and a duty of India and Italy alike, including within India's exclusive economic zone, the conduct of the Marines on board the "Enrica Lexie" in responding to a perceived piracy threat cannot have "unreasonably interfere[d]" with, and thus have failed to show "due regard" to, India's rights as the coastal State. The domestic law aspects of the Marines' response to the putative piracy threat will be subject to determination by a competent criminal court, and it is not for the Arbitral Tribunal to decide on this matter in the present context.

981. In light of the foregoing, the Arbitral Tribunal determines that the actions taken by the Marines, as Italian State officials, to protect the "Enrica Lexie" against an alleged pirate attack did not result in a breach of Italy's obligation of "due regard" for the sovereign rights of India over natural resources in its exclusive economic zone. Consequently, the Arbitral Tribunal concludes that Italy has not violated Article 58, paragraph 3, of the Convention.

Reservation of the high seas for peaceful purposes

A final point of interest of the Award lies in the passages in which it deals with the claim raised by India that Italy infringed Article 88 UNCLOS according to which "the high seas shall be reserved for peaceful purposes". India asserts that:

> 1065. [...] Italy infringed its rights under Article 88 because "the use of force by another State is inconsistent with India's right" under that Article "to have its EEZ reserved for peaceful purposes". India argues that Article 88 should be read together with Article 301 of the Convention, which prohibits the threat or use of force or any other action inconsistent with the Charter of the United Nations.

The Award dismisses India's claim stating that:

> 1069. The Arbitral Tribunal observes that, as pointed out in the Virginia Commentary, Article 88 sets out the general principle that the high seas are to be reserved for peaceful purposes and that this

principle is also confirmed in Article 301 concerning peaceful uses of the seas […].

1070. It is further noted in the Virginia Commentary that there is nothing on the record to connect Article 301 with Article 88. At the same time, Article 301 can be used as an interpretive guide to Article 88.

1071. The Arbitral Tribunal observes that Article 301 of the Convention, which is drawn from Article 2, paragraph 4, of the Charter of the United Nations, is applicable to all activities dealt with by the Convention and would not seem to add anything to the obligations of States that existed prior to the conclusion of the Convention.

1072. Article 2, paragraph 4, of the Charter of the United Nations provides:

> All Members shall refrain in their international relations from the threat or use of force against the territorial integrity or political independence of any state, or in any other manner inconsistent with the Purposes of the United Nations.

1073. Thus, under the Charter of the United Nations, the use of force is not completely prohibited if it is consistent with the Charter and with other rules of international law. This means that pursuant to Article 301 of the Convention, the use of force is not completely excluded on the high seas.

1074. It clearly follows from the articles of the Convention related to the fight against piracy that all States can take the necessary measures, including enforcement measures consistent with the Convention and the Charter of the United Nations, to protect their vessels against pirate attacks. Such measures cannot be viewed as a violation of Article 88 of the Convention or as an infringement on the rights of the coastal State in its exclusive economic zone. This is confirmed by Resolution 2077, which is cited by both Parties.

1075. By that Resolution, the Security Council of the United Nations reaffirmed that international law, as reflected in UNCLOS, sets out the legal framework applicable to combating piracy and armed robbery at sea as well as other ocean activities, and:

> commend[ed] the efforts of flag States for taking appropriate measures to permit vessels sailing under their flag transiting the High Risk Area to embark vessel protection detachments and privately contracted armed security personnel and encouraging States to regulate such activities in accordance with applicable international law and permit charters to favour arrangements that make use of such measures.

1076. It is an established fact that the Italian Marines were on board the "Enrica Lexie" to protect it against potential pirate attacks. As has also been noted in the present Award, the Arbitral Tribunal is of the view, on the basis of information available, that during the incident of 15 February 2012, the Marines acted under the apprehension that the "Enrica Lexie" was under a pirate attack and therefore took actions, the domestic law aspects of which are to be determined by a competent criminal court, to protect the "Enrica Lexie" against a perceived pirate attack.

1077. In light of the foregoing analysis, the Arbitral Tribunal concludes that Italy did not breach Article 88 of the Convention.

INTERNATIONAL CRIMINAL JUSTICE (2020)

RAFFAELLA NIGRO*

1. INTRODUCTION

The present review aims to provide a summary of the most relevant judgments and decisions handed down in 2020 – and early 2021 if particularly significant – by the international criminal tribunals, together with an overview of the main issues arising in their respective activities, in particular the International Criminal Court (ICC) decision on its territorial jurisdiction in Palestine (Section 3.3); and the United States sanctions against the ICC (Section 3.4).

In 2020, the International Residual Mechanism for Criminal Tribunals (MICT), continued its work on the pending judicial cases, a significant portion of which are expected to be completed by the end of May 2021.[1]

As for the ICC, in 2020, the Office of the Prosecutor completed four preliminary examinations with respect to the situations in Palestine, Iraq/UK, Ukraine and Nigeria, while two new preliminary examinations commenced following State Party referrals received from the Government of Venezuela and from the Government of Bolivia, on 13 February 2020 and on 4 September 2020 respectively.[2] Concerning the ICC's case law, noteworthy is the Pre-Trial Chamber's decision of 5 February 2021 on the Court's territorial jurisdiction in Palestine.[3] Other remarkable decisions in 2020 were handed down in relation to the Situation in the Central African Republic,[4] in Comoros,[5] in Côte d'Ivoire,[6] in Libya,[7] and in Mali.[8]

Regarding the Residual Special Court for Sierra Leone (RSCSL), of interest is a decision of 4 September 2020 on the request by Charles Taylor, the former President of Liberia convicted of war crimes and crimes against humanity, to be transferred temporarily from the United Kingdom due to the COVID-19 pandemic to a safe third country.[9]

As regards the Extraordinary Chambers in the Courts of Cambodia (ECCC), on 10 August 2020, the Supreme Court Chamber terminated the case against Ao An, a former senior Khmer Rouge official initially charged with genocide against the Cham people in Kampong Cham province, crimes against humanity,

---

* Associate Professor of International Law, Magna Græcia University of Catanzaro.
[1] See *infra* Section 2.1.
[2] See *infra* Section 3.1.
[3] See *infra* Section 3.2.6.
[4] See *infra* Section 3.2.1.
[5] See *infra* Section 3.2.2.
[6] See *infra* Section 3.2.3.
[7] See *infra* Section 3.2.4.
[8] See *infra* Section 3.2.5.
[9] See *infra* Section 4.1.

IYIL, Vol. 30 (2020), pp. 357-379
ISSN 0391-5107

and violations of the 1956 Cambodian Penal Code.[10] Noting that no agreement had been reached on whether Ao An is subject to the ECCC's jurisdiction after thirteen years of investigation, the Chamber found that there was no definitive and enforceable indictment against him.

With respect to the Special Tribunal for Lebanon (STL), on 25 February 2021, its mandate was extended by the United Nations Secretary General, in accordance with Security Council Resolution 1757 (2007), from 1 March 2021 for a further period of two years, or until the completion of the cases before the STL, if sooner, or the exhaustion of available funds, if sooner.[11]

On 18 August 2020, the Trial Chamber of the STL pronounced its judgment *in absentia* in the *Ayyash et al.* case concerning the attack on the former Lebanese prime minister Rafik Hariri on 14 February 2005 in Beirut.[12]

2. The International Residual Mechanism for Criminal Tribunals (MICT)[13]

2.1. Case law

Since the confirmation of the COVID-19 pandemic in March 2020, the hearings at The Hague and Arusha branches have been postponed until June and August 2020 respectively. The Mechanism's work continued on the pending judicial cases, although no judgment was issued in 2020. On 15 December 2020, President Agius presented the Mechanism's seventeenth progress report to the UN Security Council, informing the Council that a significant portion of the caseload is expected to be completed by the end of May 2021.[14] This is the case for the *Mladić* appeal, whose hearing took place in August 2020, and for the *Stanišić and Simatović* case, whose evidentiary hearing concluded in October 2020. In relation to the ongoing contempt case, in the trial against *Maximilien Turinabo et al.*, which commenced on 22 October 2020, the President noted the conclusion of the presentation of Prosecution witnesses and the anticipated start of the Defence phase in the first part of 2021, with the trial judgment also expected in May 2021.

---

[10] Case No. 004/2-07-9-2019-ECCC/TC/SC (03), Decision on International Co-Prosecutor's Immediate appeal of the Trial Chamber's effective termination of case 004/02, 10 August 2020.

[11] The statement issued by the Spokesperson of UN Secretary-General is available at: <https://www.un.org/press/en/2021/sgsm20600.doc.htm>.

[12] See *infra* Section 5.1.

[13] Judgments and decisions of the MICT are available at: <http://www.irmct.org/en/cases>. On the *ad hoc* Tribunals, see STAHN, AGIUS, BRAMMERTZ and ROHAN (eds.), *Legacies of the International Criminal Tribunal for the Former Yugoslavia. A Multidisciplinary Approach*, Oxford, 2020; RADISAVLJEVIĆ, "The ICTY and the Balancing Act. Reconciliation as Rehabilitation", in PÉREZ-LEÓN ACEVEDO and NICHOLSON (eds.), *Defendants and Victims in International Criminal Justice. Ensuring and Balancing their Rights*, London/New York, 2020, p. 123 ff.

[14] Available at: <https://www.irmct.org/en/news/20-12-15-president-agius-presents-mechanism%E2%80%99s-seventeenth-progress-report-un-security-council>.

Regarding the contempt case against Petar Jojić and Vjerica Radeta, President Agius informed the Member States of a decision, issued on 8 December 2020 by the Single Judge seized of the matter, "reiterating the previous request to Serbia to comply with its obligation to transfer the accused to the seat of the Mechanism in The Hague without delay". Furthermore, the President briefed the Council on the start of the pre-trial proceedings in the *Kabuga* case, in which the accused's initial appearance took place on 11 November 2020, following his transfer to the Mechanism's custody in October.

As to the search for the remaining fugitives indicted by the International Criminal Tribunal for Rwanda, on 14 December 2020, Prosecutor Brammertz briefed the Security Council that Fulgence Kayishema, charged for his role in the 1994 massacre of 2000 Tutsi civilians, remains at large due to South Africa's failure to provide effective cooperation over the last two and a half years. The Prosecutor reported that South Africa is still not providing the cooperation required. He explained that the Office of the Prosecutor recently sent two missions to South Africa to obtain important information to continue the pursuit of Kayishema and that both missions were unsuccessful.[15]

3.   THE INTERNATIONAL CRIMINAL COURT (ICC)[16]

3.1.   Preliminary examinations

In 2020, the Office of the Prosecutor (OTP) completed four preliminary examinations with respect to the situations in Palestine, Iraq/UK, Ukraine and Nigeria.[17]

With respect to Iraq/UK, the Prosecutor closed the preliminary examination and decided not to open an investigation.[18] The Prosecutor confirmed that

---

[15] Available at: <https://www.irmct.org/en/news/20-12-15-prosecutor-brammertz%E2%80%99s-address-un-security-council>.

[16] Judgments and decisions of the ICC are available at: <https://www.icc-cpi.int/>. On the ICC, see STEINBERG (ed.), *The International Criminal Court. Contemporary Challenges and Reform Proposals*, Leiden/Boston, 2020; DE VOS, *Complementarity, Catalysts, Compliance. The International Criminal Court in Uganda, Kenya, and the Democratic Republic of Congo*, Cambridge, 2020; BA, *State of Justice: The Politics of the International Criminal Court*, Cambridge, 2020; CORMIER, *The Jurisdiction of the International Criminal Court over Nationals of Non-State Parties*, Cambridge, 2020; SARKIN, "Reforming the International Criminal Court (ICC) to Achieve Increased State Cooperation in Investigations and Prosecutions of International Crimes", International Human Rights Law Review, 2020, p. 27 ff.

[17] On the preliminary examination in Ukraine see MARCHUK and WANIGASURIYA, "The ICC Concludes its Preliminary Examination in Crimea and Donbas: What's Next for the Situation in Ukraine?", EJIL: Talk!, 16 December 2020, available at: <https://www.ejiltalk.org/the-icc-concludes-its-preliminary-examination-in-crimea-and-donbas-whats-next-for-the-situation-in-ukraine/>.

[18] Situation in Iraq/UK, Final Report, 9 December 2020, available at: <https://www.icc-cpi.int/itemsDocuments/201209-otp-final-report-iraq-uk-eng.pdf>. For a comment, see BALDWIN, "The ICC Prosecutor Office's Cop-Out on UK Military Crimes in Iraq", Opinio

there is a reasonable basis to believe that members of the British armed forces in Iraq committed the war crimes of wilful killing, torture, inhuman/cruel treatment, outrages upon personal dignity, and rape and/or other forms of sexual violence. The Prosecutor further found that the initial response of the British army at the time of the alleged offences was inadequate and vitiated by a lack of genuine effort to carry out relevant investigations independently or impartially, following a detailed inquiry and an evaluation of the totality of the information available. Ultimately, however, the Prosecutor determined that it cannot be concluded that:

> the UK authorities have been unwilling genuinely to carry out relevant investigative inquiries and/or prosecutions, under article 17(1)(a) of the Rome Statute, or that decisions not to prosecute in specific cases resulted from unwillingness genuinely to prosecute, under article 17(1)(b). Specifically, for the purpose of article 17(2) of the ICC Statute, the Office cannot conclude that the relevant investigative inquiries or investigative/prosecutorial decisions were made for the purpose of shielding the person concerned from criminal responsibility for crimes within the jurisdiction of the Court; that there has been an unjustified delay in the proceedings which in the circumstances is inconsistent with an intent to bring the person concerned to justice; or that the proceedings were not or are not being conducted independently or impartially, and they were or are being conducted in a manner which, in the circumstances, is inconsistent with an intent to bring the person concerned to justice.[19]

In 2020, the OTP commenced two new preliminary examinations, following State Party referrals received from the Government of Venezuela and from the Government of Bolivia, on 13 February 2020 and on 4 September 2020 respectively.[20]

As for the Government of Venezuela, pursuant to Article 14(1) of the ICC Statute, the referring State has requested the Prosecutor to initiate an investigation into crimes against humanity allegedly committed on the territory of Venezuela, with the view to determining whether one or more persons should be charged with the commission of such crimes.[21] In particular, the Government of Venezuela alleges that crimes against humanity against the Venezuelan popula-

---

Juris, 18 December 2020, available at: <http://opiniojuris.org/2020/12/18/the-icc-prosecutor-offices-cop-out-on-uk-military-crimes-in-iraq/>; SCHUELLER, "The ICC, British War Crimes in Iraq and a Very British Tradition", Opinio Juris, 11 December 2020, available at: <http://opiniojuris.org/2020/12/11/the-icc-british-war-crimes-in-iraq-and-a-very-british-tradition/>.

[19] See para. 502 of the Report.

[20] For further details on the preliminary examinations before the ICC, see the Report on Preliminary Examinations Activities 2020, 14 December 2020, available at: <https://www.icc-cpi.int/itemsDocuments/2020-PE/2020-pe-report-eng.pdf>.

[21] Available at: <https://www.icc-cpi.int/itemsDocuments/200212-venezuela-referral.pdf>.

tion were committed "as a result of the application of unlawful coercive measures adopted unilaterally by the government of the United States of America against Venezuela, at least since 2014". According to the referral, these measures have contributed to "very significant increases in mortality in children and adults, and negatively affected a range of other human rights, including the right to food, to medical care and to education, thus causing, in turn, a migration phenomenon from the country".[22] The Government of Venezuela emphasizes that "since the measures taken by the US have consequences on the territory of a State Party (Venezuela), the ICC may exercise its territorial jurisdiction with respect to alleged crimes of relevance to the situation occurring on Venezuelan territory".[23] Moreover, according to the referral:

> the economic sanctions imposed by the US Government constitute a widespread or systematic attack upon a civilian population pursuant to article 7(1) of the Rome Statute; that sanctions were imposed by the US for the purpose of promoting regime change and that the consequences of the sanctions can be qualified as crimes against humanity. In particular, the referral alleges that the additional deaths caused by the sanctions constitute killing under article 7(1) of the Rome Statute; the deprivation of access to food and medicine caused were calculated to bring about the destruction of part of the population, constituting extermination under article 7(1); that the unilateral coercive measures created an environment which triggered mass migration from Venezuela, constituting deportation or forced displacement under article 7(1); that the sanctions caused severe deprivations of fundamental rights contrary to international law, including the right to self-determination, and the right to life, food, work, health and medical care, education, and property, constituting persecution under article 7(1); and that the forcible grounding of the entire aircraft fleet of CONVIASA, Venezuela's flag carrier, has inter alia prevented Venezuela from repatriating its citizens, constituting other inhumane acts under article 7(1). The referral further states that Venezuela's inability to punish those responsible for the imposition of these measures, together with their gravity and consequences, would render any potential case admissible.[24]

As for Bolivia, the former Government alleged that in August 2020, "members of political party *Movimiento al Socialismo* and associated organisations engaged in a course of conduct pursuant to an organisational policy to attack the Bolivian population by coordinating hundreds of blockades at various points throughout the country that connected different cities to prevent the passage of

---

[22] See the Report on Preliminary Examinations Activities, *cit. supra* note 20, para. 97.
[23] *Ibid.*, para. 98.
[24] *Ibid.*, paras. 98-99.

convoys, transport and communications".[25] Considering the COVID-19 pandemic, the referral asserted that among the goals of this blockade was "to prevent them [the civilian population in those cities] from accessing public health supplies and services with the direct consequence of causing the death of several people and anxiety in the rest of the population due to the possibility of dying without being able to be treated in public hospitals, or in conditions that allow them to access to medical supplies, treatments and, above all, medical oxygen".[26] The referral further submitted that these actions amount to the crime against humanity of other inhumane acts of a similar character intentionally causing great suffering, or serious injury to body or to mental or physical health under Article 7(1)(k) of the Statute.[27]

On 6 July 2020, the OTP received a communication alleging that genocide and crimes against humanity were being committed by Chinese officials against Uyghurs and members of other Turkic minorities in the context of their detention in mass internment camps in China. It was alleged that the crimes occurred in part on the territories of ICC States Parties Cambodia and Tajikistan as some of the victims were arrested there and deported to China as part of a concerted and widespread campaign of persecution and destruction of the Uyghur community.[28]

Recalling that the Court may assert jurisdiction pursuant to Article 12(2)(a) of the Statute if at least one element of a crime within the jurisdiction of the Court, or part of such a crime, is committed on the territory of a State Party to the Statute, the OTP found that this precondition did not appear to be met with respect to the majority of the crimes alleged in the communication, since the *actus reus* of each of these crimes appears to have been committed solely by nationals of China within the territory of China, a State which is not a party to the Statute.[29]

As regards the crimes for which the part of the *actus reus* appears to have taken place in Cambodia and Tajikistan, in particular alleged acts of deportation, the OTP observed that while the transfers of persons from Cambodia and Tajikistan to China seem to raise concerns with respect to their conformity with national and international law, including international human rights law and international refugee law, it did not appear that such conduct would amount to the

---

[25] ICC, Complaint for Systematics Attacks against the Bolivian people, 31 August 2020, available at: <https://www.icc-cpi.int/itemsDocuments/200909-Bolivia-referral-ICC-Eng.pdf>. See also the Report on Preliminary Examinations Activities, *cit. supra* note 20, para. 82.

[26] *Ibid.*

[27] *Ibid.*, para. 86.

[28] See Report on Preliminary Examinations Activities, *cit. supra* note 20, para. 71. For a comment, see GUILFOYLE, "Is the International Criminal Court Destined to Pick Fights with Non-State Parties?", EJIL: Talk!, 14 July 2020, available at: <https://www.ejiltalk.org/is-the-international-criminal-court-destined-to-pick-fights-with-non-state-parties/>.

[29] See Report on Preliminary Examinations Activities, *cit. supra* note 20, para. 73.

crime against humanity of deportation under Article 7(1)(d) of the Statute within the jurisdiction of the Court.[30]

Therefore, the OTP determined that in the present situation, on the information available, there was no basis to proceed. Finally, the Prosecutor reported that, since issuing the decision, the Office had received a request for reconsideration, pursuant to Article 15(6), on the basis of new facts or evidence.[31]

3.2. Case law

3.2.1. Situation in the Central African Republic

On 18 May 2020, Pre-Trial Chamber II issued its decision on Bemba's claim for compensation and damages.[32] After being convicted by the Trial Chamber in 2016 for crimes against humanity and war crimes under Article 28(3) of the ICC Statute, Bemba was acquitted of all charges by the Appeals Chamber which, by a majority, reversed the Trial Chamber judgment of 8 June 2018. As a result, Bemba submitted two requests to the ICC, one for compensation under Article 85 of the Rome Statute, centred on the allegation that a grave and manifest miscarriage of justice to his detriment had occurred in the case before the Trial Chamber; the other, for compensation as a remedy to the damage allegedly suffered as a result of the Court's failure to properly manage and preserve property and assets that were frozen and seized by order of the Court.

On the first request, the Chamber considered that Bemba failed to establish that he had suffered a grave and manifest miscarriage of justice within the meaning of Article 85 of the Rome Statute, and accordingly, declined to exercise its discretion to award compensation to Bemba. In this regard, the Chamber first observed that:

> The preparatory works leading to article 85(3) of the Statute make it clear that the reference to a grave and manifest miscarriage of justice was never meant to address situations falling within the scope of the dynamics inherent to the natural developments of criminal proceedings. Rather, it was meant to encompass scenarios of an exceptional nature, substantially differing from those that are typical of procedural phases of a trial and for which there are specific opportunities for review.[33]

The Chamber underlined that Article 85 was included in the Statute with a view to providing suspects and accused persons with a full range of guarantees

---

[30] *Ibid.*, para. 74.
[31] *Ibid.*, para. 76.
[32] *In the Case of the Prosecutor v. Jean-Pierre Bemba Gombo*, Case No. ICC-01/05-01/08, Decision on Mr Bemba's claim for compensation and damages, 18 May 2020.
[33] *Ibid.*, para. 33.

against serious violations of their fundamental right to a fair trial, including the possibility for the Court to provide compensation in cases of serious abuse of the judicial process and that this provision "is novel and unprecedented in international criminal law".[34] Then the Chamber affirmed that:

> Both the wording, the drafting history and international human rights law make it clear [...] that the drafters of the Statute never meant to go so far as to vest an acquitted person with a right to benefit from compensation by mere virtue of the fact that the acquittal was preceded by time spent in custody, or of the mere duration of the proceedings, however lengthy either might have been; the duration of the proceedings per se, as long as there is no grave and manifest miscarriage of justice, is not a factor triggering a right to compensation.[35]

After analyzing other relevant international treaties on human rights, as well as national legal systems, the Chamber concluded, on the first request, that Bemba failed to establish that he suffered a grave and manifest miscarriage of justice and that, accordingly, there were no grounds for the Chamber to exercise its discretion to award compensation to Bemba under Article 85(3) of the Statute. The Chamber also affirmed that, in the present case, the restricted scope of Article 85(3) of the Statute as interpreted by the Chamber was consistent with internationally recognized human rights.[36] On the second request, the Chamber found that:

> The wording and drafting history of article 85(3) of the Statute make it apparent that it was never meant to provide a remedy for damages of an economic and financial nature which are not the result of a grave and manifest miscarriage of justice.

Consequently, the Chamber had no jurisdiction over the second request.[37] The Chamber clarified that its determination:

> is without prejudice to Mr Bemba's right to pursue other procedural remedies and avenues which might otherwise be open to him with a view to seeking redress for damages allegedly suffered in connection with his assets targeted by freezing orders and other similar measures undertaken by States in connection with the implementation of the Court's orders.[38]

---

[34] *Ibid.*, para. 34.
[35] *Ibid.*, para. 44.
[36] *Ibid.*, para. 52.
[37] *Ibid.*, para. 61.
[38] *Ibid.*, para. 64.

Interestingly, on the excessive length of the proceedings, the Chamber recognized that the approach ultimately enshrined in Article 85(3) of the Statute is more restrictive than the one followed by several domestic systems, and concluded that:

> it seems unquestionable that the Bemba case provides a case in point as to the seriousness of the consequences entailed by the absence of statutory limits as to the duration either of the proceedings or, even more critically, of custodial detention. The Chamber finds it urgent for the States Parties to embark on a review of the Statute so as to consider addressing those limitations; until then, it will be the Court's own responsibility to be mindful of the expeditiousness of the proceedings as a fundamental tenet of the right to a fair trial and to streamline its own proceedings accordingly.[39]

3.2.2. *Situation in Comoros*

On 16 September 2020, Pre-Trial Chamber I issued a decision in which it rejected the request submitted by the Government of the Comoros seeking a judicial review of the Prosecutor's decision not to proceed with an investigation, under Article 53(1) of the ICC Statute, with respect to crimes allegedly committed in the context of the 31 May 2010 Israeli interception of the Humanitarian Aid Flotilla bound for the Gaza Strip.[40] Although the Chamber found that the Prosecutor committed a series of errors in her assessment of the gravity of the potential cases arising from the situation and did not genuinely reconsider her decision not to initiate an investigation,[41] it decided not to request the Prosecutor to reconsider her decision. The Chamber found that it was unclear, based on the guidance received from the Appeals Chamber in its Judgment of 2 September 2019, whether and to what extent it could request the Prosecutor to correct errors related to questions of law and the application of the law to the facts,[42] and to correct errors related to her assessment of the factors relevant to the gravity requirement.[43] The Chamber further added that:

---

[39] *Ibid.*, para. 69.

[40] *Situation on Registered Vessels of the Union of the Comoros, the Hellenic Republic and the Kingdom of Cambodia*, Case No. ICC 01/13, Decision on the "Application for judicial review by the Government of the Comoros", 16 September 2020.

[41] In particular, the Chamber found that the Prosecutor has: "(i) failed to apply the 'reasonable basis to believe' standard as interpreted by the Chamber; (ii) made premature determinations with regard to the scope of the potential cases and the nature and extent of the victimisation; (iii) failed to take into account factors and/or information relevant to the gravity assessment as instructed by the Chamber; and (iv) relied on considerations that are not relevant to the gravity assessment or to the specific factor concerned", see para. 102 of the Decision.

[42] *Ibid.*, para. 107.

[43] *Ibid.*, para. 110.

the current jurisprudence of the Appeals Chamber does not establish with sufficient clarity the exact distribution of prerogatives between the Prosecutor and the pre-trial chamber in article 53(3)(a)
proceedings. The Chamber notes with concern that in the present
proceedings the Prosecutor has interpreted the Appeals Chamber's
Judgment in a manner that undermines both the Chamber's power
to direct the Prosecutor as to the correct interpretation of the law
and its power to order the Prosecutor to take into account in the
gravity assessment certain factors and/or information, thereby ne-
gating the effectiveness of the procedure under article 53(3)(a) of
the Statute.[44]

3.2.3. Situation in Côte d'Ivoire

On 28 May 2020, the Appeals Chamber issued a decision in the *Gbagbo
and Blé Goudé* case in which it denied Gbagbo's request for reconsideration of a
decision relating to an earlier appeal filed by the Prosecution, and reviewed the
conditions of release for Gbagbo and Blé Goudé.[45] Interestingly, the Decision
indicates that should Gbagbo and Blé Goudé be released from custody, and then
later fail to appear for any future trial hearings, such proceedings could in principle continue without their physical presence. In recalling Article 63(1) of the
Statute, which provides that the accused "shall be present during the trial", the
Appeals Chamber argued that in its view:

> the proper aim of the provision is to deny legality to the trial of a
> person who wants to be present at his or her trial and participate
> in good faith, but was unable to attend due to no fault of his or her
> own. There is a perversion of that legitimate aim, if article 63(1)
> of the Statute is pleaded in aid of an accused person who wants to
> prevent his or her own trial by deliberate absence in circumstances
> of contumacy, following an initial appearance pursuant to article 60
> of the Statute.[46]

In the Chamber's opinion:

---

[44] *Ibid.*, para. 111.

[45] *Situation in the Republic of Côte d'Ivoire*, Case No. ICC-02/11-01/15 OA 14, Decision
on counsel for Mr Gbagbo's request for reconsideration of the "Judgment on the Prosecutor's
appeal against the oral decision of Trial Chamber I pursuant to article 81(3)(c)(i) of the Statute"
and on the review of the conditions on the release of Mr Gbagbo and Mr Blé Goudé, 28 May
2020. For a comment, see WHEELER, "The ICC Appeals Chamber Signals a Possible Change
in Approach to the Permissibility of Trials in Absentia", EJIL: Talk!, 3 July 2020, available at: <https://www.ejiltalk.org/The-Icc-Appeals-Chamber-Signals-A-Possible-Change-In-
Approach-To-The-Permissibility-Of-Trials-In-Absentia/>.

[46] See para. 69 of the Decision.

The continuance of proceedings without the physical presence of the accused in cases of wilful absence is prohibited neither by the Statute properly understood, nor by general principles of law. As long as the right to a fair trial is scrupulously respected, particularly by ensuring proper representation of counsel, such proceedings are permissible in the realms of both international and domestic law.[47]

3.2.4. Situation in Libya

On 9 March 2020, the Appeals Chamber unanimously confirmed the admissibility of the case against Saif Al-Islam Gaddafi before the ICC and rejected his appeal against Pre-Trial Chamber I's decision dismissing his challenge to the admissibility of this case.[48] According to the first ground of appeal, the Pre-Trial Chamber erred in law in holding that Articles 17(1)(c) and 20(3) of the Statute may only be satisfied where a judgment on the merits of a case has acquired *res judicata* effect. In this regard, the Appeals Chamber confirmed the impugned decision, considering that "article 17(1)(c) of the Statute, read together with article 20(3) of the Statute, means that the decision issued by a national jurisdiction must be final before a case can be declared inadmissible on the basis of these provisions".[49] While noting the *sui generis* nature of the complementarity regime in which the Court operates, the Appeals Chamber held that the Pre-Trial Chamber had not erred by "finding the ad hoc tribunal's jurisprudence instructive and finding that that jurisprudence was supported by the interpretation of the *ne bis in idem* principle in international human rights law".[50]

As for the second ground of appeal, counsel for Gaddafi submitted that the Pre-Trial Chamber erred in law and fact, and procedurally, by failing to determine that because Libyan Law No. 6 granted him amnesty, it rendered in practical terms the Libyan proceedings against Ghaddafi final. The Appeals Chamber considered that the Pre-Trial Chamber did not err by relying on the Libyan Government's position in support of its conclusion that Law No. 6 did not apply to Gaddafi.[51] On the issue of the compatibility of Law No. 6 with international law, the Appeals Chamber stated that the Pre-Trial Chamber's holdings were *obiter dicta*.[52] In light of its conclusions on the finality of the Libyan judgment and on the applicability of Law No. 6 to the crimes for which Gaddafi was convicted, the Appeals Chamber did not find it necessary to address the remaining arguments in the second ground of appeal. The Appeals Chamber decided that,

---

[47] See para. 70 of the Decision.

[48] *In the Case of the Prosecutor v. Saif Al-Islam Gaddafi*, Case No. ICC-01/11-01/11, Judgment on the appeal of Mr. Saif-al-Islam Gaddafi against the decision of Pre-Trial Chamber entitled "Decision on the 'Admissibility Challenge by Dr. Saif Al-Islam Gaddafi pursuant to Articles 17(1)(c), 19 and 20(3) of the Rome Statute'" of 5 April 2019, 9 March 2020.

[49] *Ibid.*, para. 63.

[50] *Ibid.*, para. 62.

[51] *Ibid.*, para. 93.

[52] *Ibid.*, para. 96.

for present purposes, it was sufficient to say "only that international law is still in the developmental stage on the question of acceptability of amnesties". The Appeals Chamber affirmed in particular that:

> The Pre-Trial Chamber appears to have accepted this: rather than determining that this question was settled, it found "a strong, growing, universal tendency that grave and systematic human rights violations – which may amount to crimes against humanity by their very nature – are not subject to amnesties or pardons under international law". In these circumstances, the Appeals Chamber will not dwell on the matter further.[53]

3.2.5. Situation in Mali

On 19 February 2020, the Appeals Chamber delivered its judgment rejecting the appeal of Al Hassan and consequently confirming Pre-Trial Chamber I's decision of 27 September 2019, which had considered that the case against Al Hassan is of sufficient gravity to justify further action by the Court.[54] The Appeals Chamber found that:

> the gravity requirement under article 17(1)(d) of the Statute aims at excluding those rather unusual cases where the specific facts of a given case technically qualify as crimes under the jurisdiction of the Court, but are nonetheless not of sufficient gravity to justify further action by the Court. In this regard, the Appeals Chamber agrees with the Pre-Trial Chamber that 'the purpose of article 17(1) (d) of the Statute is not to oblige the Court to choose only the most serious cases, but merely to oblige it not to prosecute cases of marginal gravity'.[55]

In the Appeals Chamber's view,

> the gravity assessment under article 17(1)(d) of the Statute must be made on a case-by-case basis. It involves a holistic evaluation of all relevant quantitative and qualitative criteria, including some of the factors relevant to the determination of the sentence of a convicted person. Quantitative criteria alone, including the

---

[53] *Ibid.*

[54] *In the Case of the Prosecutor v. Al Hassan AG Abdoul Aziz AG Mohamed AG Mahmoud*, Case No. ICC-01/12-01/18 OA, Judgment on the appeal of Mr Assan against the decision of Pre-Trial Chamber I entitled "Décision relative à l'exception d'irrecevabilité pour insuffisance de gravité de l'affaire soulevée par la défense", 19 February 2020.

[55] *Ibid.*, para. 59.

number of victims, are not determinative of the gravity of a given case.[56]

In particular, the Appeals Chamber did not find any error in the Pre-Trial Chamber's consideration, in its gravity assessment, of the nature and scale of the charged crimes, which amount to crimes against humanity and war crimes allegedly committed against the civilian population in Timbuktu and its region,[57] nor in considering the significant role attributed to Al Hassan and the circumstances of the alleged attack, which constituted the contextual elements of the crimes.[58]

3.2.6. Situation in Palestine

On 5 February 2021, Pre-Trial Chamber I decided, by majority, that the Court's territorial jurisdiction in the Situation in Palestine extends to the territories occupied by Israel since 1967, namely Gaza and the West Bank, including East Jerusalem.[59] At the outset, the Chamber discussed the question raised by certain *amici curiae*, States Parties, and representatives of victims that the Prosecutor's Request was of a political nature rather than a legal one. In this regard, the Chamber affirmed that in the situation at hand, the Prosecutor addressed a legal issue to the Chamber, namely whether "the 'territory' over which the Court may exercise its jurisdiction under Article 12(2)(a) comprises the West Bank, including East Jerusalem, and Gaza", and that it is capable of a legal answer based on the provisions of the Statute.[60] In the Chamber's view, the fact that the present decision might entail political consequences shall not prevent the Chamber from exercising its mandate, which is limited to analyzing the relevant facts of which it is seized, in accordance with the Court's applicable legal framework.[61]

After having determined that Article 19(3) of the Rome Statute is applicable in the present proceedings, the Chamber focused on the merits of the Prosecution's request. The first issue was to determine whether Palestine could be considered a "State on the territory of which the conduct in question occurred", within the meaning of Article 12(2)(a) of the ICC Statute. The Chamber found that, in accordance with the ordinary meaning given to its terms in their context and in light of the object and purpose of the Statute, the reference to "the State on the

---

[56] *Ibid.*, para. 94.

[57] *Ibid.*, para. 120.

[58] *Ibid.*, para. 127.

[59] *Situation in the State of Palestine*, Case No. ICC-01/18, Decision on the "Prosecution request pursuant to Article 19(3) for a ruling on the Court's territorial jurisdiction in Palestine", 5 February 2021. On the competence of the ICC to exercise its *ratione loci* jurisdiction over Palestine's territory that comprises the West Bank, including East Jerusalem, and Gaza Strip, on the basis of the armistice agreements that Israel signed with both Jordan and Egypt in 1949, see QAFISHEH, "What is Palestine? The *de jure* Demarcation of Boundaries for the ICC's *ratione loci* Jurisdiction and Beyond", International Criminal Law Review, 2020, p. 908 ff.

[60] *Ibid.*, para. 56.

[61] *Ibid.*, para. 57.

territory of which the conduct in question occurred" in Article 12(2)(a) must be interpreted as a reference to a State Party to the Statute. In this regard, the Chamber affirmed that:

> given the complexity and political nature of statehood under general international law, the Rome Statute insulates the Court from making such a determination, relying instead on the accession procedure and the determination made by the United Nations General Assembly. The Court is not constitutionally competent to determine matters of statehood that would bind the international community. In addition, such a determination is not required for the specific purposes of the present proceedings or the general exercise of the Court's mandate.[62]

As a consequence, according to the Chamber, Article 12(2)(a) of the Statute requires a determination as to whether or not the relevant conduct occurred on the territory of a *State Party*, for the sole purpose of establishing individual criminal responsibility.[63]

The Chamber concluded on this issue that, having acceded to the Rome Statute in accordance with the procedure defined by it, Palestine is a State Party to the Statute and shall have the right to exercise its prerogatives under the Statute and be treated as any other State Party.[64] The Chamber then moved on to consider the second issue, namely the delimitation of the territory of Palestine for the purpose of defining the Court's territorial jurisdiction. In this regard, it noted that:

> in according "non-member observer State status in the United Nations" to Palestine in Resolution 67/19, the United Nations General Assembly "[reaffirmed] the right of the Palestinian people to self-determination and to independence in their State of Palestine on the Palestinian territory occupied since 1967".

In the same Resolution, the United Nations General Assembly recalled other similarly-worded resolutions. On such occasions, it notably: (i) "[affirmed] the need to enable the Palestinian people to exercise their sovereignty over their territory occupied since 1967"; (ii) "[affirmed] that the status of the Palestinian territory occupied since 1967, including East Jerusalem, remains one of military occupation, and [...] that the Palestinian people have the right to self-determination and to sovereignty over their territory"; and (iii) "[stressed] the need for respect for and preservation of the territorial unity, contiguity and integrity of all of the Occupied Palestinian Territory, including East Jerusalem".[65]

---

[62] *Ibid.*, para. 108.
[63] *Ibid.*
[64] *Ibid.*, para. 112.
[65] *Ibid.*, paras. 116-117.

On this basis, the Chamber found that the Court's territorial jurisdiction in the *Situation in Palestine* extends to the territories occupied by Israel since 1967, namely Gaza and the West Bank, including East Jerusalem,[66] emphasizing that this conclusion is consistent with the right to self-determination, explicitly recognized by different international bodies, as an internationally recognized human right within the meaning of Article 21(3) of the Statute.[67]

In his partly dissenting opinion, Judge Péter Kovács considered that the central issue, in the case of Palestine, "relates to the existence or non-existence of the 'territory' or more precisely, the 'territory of the State' as understood under contemporary international law".[68] In his opinion, "the Oslo Accords could be the key to adequately answering the question presented by the Prosecutor concerning the geographical scope of the Court's jurisdiction".[69] In particular, the Judge stated that:

> Given that Palestine's borders are not yet settled under international law, and consequently one cannot say with certainty and authoritative value if a particular parcel of land belongs or not to Palestine, the situation and potential cases cannot be easily matched with the wording of article 12(2)(a) of the Statute, specifically "the State on the territory of which".[70]
>
> Consequently, we find ourselves in an ambiguous and delicate situation where a State (Israel) and a *nasciturus* State (Palestine) – undisputedly recognized by a large number of States as a genuine, real State – exercise different legislative, administrative and judicial competences *ratione personae* and/or *ratione loci* over life in the given territory where – as the ICJ confirmed – the rules of the Geneva Convention IV and of the Hague Convention IV are also to be applied. It is a truly extraordinary, unique and complex situation, as it was rightly qualified in the Request.[71]

On the assumption that "the Prosecutor may exercise her investigative competences under the same circumstances that would allow Palestine, as a State Party, to assert jurisdiction over such crimes under its legal system, namely by duly taking into account the repartition of competences according to the Oslo Accords",[72] the Judge concluded that in his opinion:

---

[66] *Ibid.*, paras. 118.

[67] *Ibid.*, paras. 119-123.

[68] See para. 54 of the Opinion, available at: <https://www.icc-cpi.int/RelatedRecords/CR2021_01167.PDF>.

[69] *Ibid.*, para. 320.

[70] *Ibid.*, para. 322.

[71] *Ibid.*, para. 323.

[72] *Ibid.*, para. 370.

The geographical scope of application of the Prosecutor's competence to investigate covers the territories of the West-Bank, East-
Jerusalem and the Gaza strip but – under the actual legal coordinates and with the exception of the hypothesis of article 13(b) of the
Rome Statute – subject to due consideration of the different legal
regimes applied in areas A, B, C and East Jerusalem according to
the Interim agreement [...] and other subsequent Israeli-Palestinian
agreements adopted on this basis.[73]

3.3. The ICC Decision on the Court's territorial jurisdiction in Palestine

The decision on the ICC's territorial jurisdiction in Palestine has raised several comments in the literature. The main issue concerns the Court's failure to
rule on the statehood of Palestine under international law. During the proceedings, several States, non-governmental organizations, and international law experts submitted written observations on the Prosecutor's request, affirming that
because the Palestinian Territories are currently lacking statehood, the Court did
not have jurisdiction in the specific situation. It has been underlined that in terms
of international law "the original sin was to let an entity which does not meet
the criteria of statehood accede to a treaty which is open for accession only by
'States'", and that once an entity has become a "State Party", there is no basis in
the Rome Statute to deny to it the full application of the Statute.[74] In particular,
"there is no foundation for a two-tier system of State Parties – those which can
transfer their criminal jurisdiction to the Court and those that cannot".[75] In fact,
according to this opinion, the purpose of Article 12(2)(a) of the Statute is to set
out the preconditions for the exercise of jurisdiction by the Court, not to limit the
exercise of jurisdiction to those States Parties that are States in terms of general
international law.

Ambos argued that for the purposes of the ICC decision, an examination of
Palestine's statehood under international law was indispensable and that, in this
regard, the Chamber could have considered the value of the collective recognition of Palestine in connection with the right of peoples to self-determination that
lies in UN General Assembly Resolution 67/19.[76] Moreover, he observed that the
question of the ICC's jurisdiction over the Palestinian Territories has not been

---

[73] *Ibid.*, para. 372.

[74] TALMON, "Germany Publicly Objects to the International Criminal Court's Ruling on
Jurisdiction in Palestine", GPIL-German Practice in International Law, 11 February 2021,
available at: <https://gpil.jura.uni-bonn.de/2021/02/germany-publicly-objects-to-the-interna-
tional-criminal-courts-ruling-on-jurisdiction-in-palestine/>.

[75] *Ibid.*

[76] AMBOS, "'Solid Jurisdiction Basis'? The ICC's Fragile Jurisdiction for Crimes Allegedly
Committed in Palestine", EJIL: Talk!, 2 March 2021, available at: <https://www.ejiltalk.org/
solid-jurisdictional-basis-the-iccs-fragile-jurisdiction-for-crimes-allegedly-committed-in-
palestine/>. For a comment of the ICC Decision, see also HOWSE, "Int'l Criminal Court's
Positive Step on Investigation of Crimes Committed in Palestine", Just Security, 8 February

definitively settled, also because the Chamber majority has explicitly restricted its decision to the "current stage of proceedings", that is, the initiation of formal investigations by the Prosecutor pursuant to Articles 13(a), 14 and 53(1) of the Rome Statute.

Shaw emphasized that the Rome Statute contains no definition of a State, so that there is no authority for the proposition that the Court may exercise jurisdiction with regard to a State defined other than on the accepted basis of international law.[77]

Others wondered if, assuming that Palestine is a State and that the ICC has jurisdiction over crimes committed within its territory, the Court can determine the extent of Palestinian territory in circumstances where some of that territory is also claimed by Israel.[78] The question concerns in particular the competence of the ICC, whose mandate is to ascertain individual criminal responsibility, to determine a territorial dispute between States. In this regard, reference was made to the so-called *Monetary Gold* doctrine according to which, on the basis of the 1954 ICJ judgment in the *Monetary Gold* case (*Italy v. France, United Kingdom and United States*), the principle of consent would require the courts to abstain from deciding a case where the legal interests of a non-consenting third State formed "the very subject matter" of the case itself. It has been argued that although the doctrine does apply to the ICC, as well as to every tribunal established to deal with inter-State disputes, it does not necessarily preclude the exercise of the ICC's jurisdiction over the Palestinian situation. In particular, the Court would not be precluded from applying a legal finding which is already binding or authoritative with respect to the third State on the basis of a determination by a competent body. Therefore, in the context of the situation in Palestine, the question that arises is whether some relevant UN Security Council resolutions determining that the Occupied Palestinian Territory does not constitute a part of the State of Israel, could be regarded as binding and authoritative for the States concerned.

Some authors discussed the 1995 Oslo Agreement which granted Israel exclusive criminal jurisdiction over acts committed by Israelis in parts of the

---

2021, available at: <https://www.justsecurity.org/74601/intl-criminal-courts-positive-step-on-investigation-of-crimes-committed-in-palestine/>.

[77] SHAW, "A State is a State is a State? Some Thoughts on the Prosecutor's Response to Amici Briefs on Territorial Jurisdiction – Part II", EJIL: Talk!, 4 June 2020, available at: <https://www.ejiltalk.org/a-state-is-a-state-is-a-state-some-thoughts-on-the-prosecutors-response-to-amici-briefs-on-territorial-jurisdiction-part-ii/>. Part I is available at: <https://www.ejiltalk.org/a-state-is-a-state-is-a-state-some-thoughts-on-the-prosecutors-response-to-amici-briefs-on-territorial-jurisdiction-part-i/>.

[78] AKANDE, "The Monetary Gold Doctrine and the ICC: Can the ICC Determine the Territorial Boundaries of Israel and Palestine?", EJIL: Talk!, 16 June 2020, available at: <https://www.ejiltalk.org/the-monetary-gold-doctrine-and-the-icc-can-the-icc-determine-the-territorial-boundaries-of-israel-and-palestine/>. For a similar conclusion based on a different reasoning, see RODRÍGUEZ-VILA, "The ICC, The Monetary Gold Principle and the Determination of the Territory of Palestine", Opinio Juris, 2 November 2020, available at: <http://opiniojuris.org/2020/11/02/the-icc-the-monetary-gold-principle-and-the-determination-of-the-territory-of-palestine/>.

Occupied Palestinian Territory. According to one opinion, the provisions of the Oslo Agreement relate only to the Palestinian National Authority's enforcement jurisdiction but do not affect the prescriptive jurisdiction, which entails the capacity of the occupied State to make the law, including the ability to delegate the exercise of its criminal jurisdiction to an international tribunal.[79] Another view, however, holds that, pursuant to the Oslo Agreement, the Palestinian Authority is unable to delegate any jurisdiction concerning Israeli citizens to the ICC.[80]

From a general perspective, one author considered that the case of Palestine in the ICC shows the importance of a normative rather than merely factual approach to the question of statehood, i.e. an approach which emphasizes the right of independence rather than a strict examination of the Montevideo factual criteria.[81]

3.4.   The United States sanctions against the ICC

On 11 June 2020, the President of the United States issued Executive Order 13928 declaring that the investigation by the ICC into possible US crimes against humanity and war crimes associated with the armed conflict in Afghanistan, as well as investigations against non-ICC member allies such as Israel, was an "unusual and extraordinary threat to national security and foreign policy of the United States".[82] The Order authorized restrictions and punishment, including financial sanctions, civil fines and even criminal prosecution/imprisonment of persons and entities that engage with the ICC.[83] The ICC expressed profound regret at the announcement of further threats and coercive actions, including financial measures, against the Court and its officials, affirming that "[t]hese attacks constitute an escalation and an unacceptable attempt to interfere with the rule of law and the Court's judicial proceedings".[84]

On 2 September 2020, the US State and Treasury Departments took their first action on the sanctions program, restricting issuance of visas for ICC

---

[79] ABOFOUL, "The Oslo Accords and the International Criminal Court's Jurisdiction in the Situation in the State of Palestine", Opinio Juris, 28 July 2020, available at: <https://opiniojuris.org/2020/07/28/the-oslo-accords-and-the-international-criminal-courts-jurisdiction-in-the-situation-in-the-state-of-palestine/>.

[80] AMBOS, "'Solid Jurisdiction Basis'?", cit. supra note 76.

[81] GROSS, "Decolonizing the ICC: The Situation in Palestine and Beyond", Just Security, 8 March 2021, available at: <https://www.justsecurity.org/75204/decolonizing-the-icc-the-situation-in-palestine-and-beyond/>.

[82] Available at: <https://www.federalregister.gov/documents/2020/06/15/2020-12953/blocking-property-of-certain-persons-associated-with-the-international-criminal-court>.

[83] On the reactions to the Executive Order at the international level, see SCHAACK, "The Int'l Criminal Court Executive Order: Global Reactions Compiled", Just Security, 1 September 2020, available at: <https://www.justsecurity.org/72256/the-intl-criminal-court-executive-order-global-reactions-compiled/>.

[84] Available at: <https://www.icc-cpi.int/Pages/item.aspx?name=200611-icc-statement>.

Prosecutor Bensouda and the head of the ICC's Jurisdiction, Complementarity and Cooperation Division, Mochochoko.[85]

On 1 October 2020, the Open Society Justice Initiative and four law professors brought an action before the United States District Court, Southern District of New York, to challenge the lawfulness of the Executive Order and its implementing Regulations, under the US Constitution and statutory law.[86] On 4 January 2021, the Court granted the plaintiffs' request for a preliminary injunction in part, thus ordering the Trump administration not to enforce criminal or civil penalties against the plaintiffs for conduct allegedly violating the Executive Order.[87]

On 2 April 2021, the Biden administration, while stressing that the United States continued to object to certain actions by the ICC, revoked the Executive Order and lifted the sanctions against Bensouda and Mochochoko.[88]

Although the Executive Order has now been revoked, it is nonetheless useful to review some of the criticism that it raised.

An argument advanced by a number of scholars was that the Executive Order was incompatible with constitutional rights to freedom of speech, association and due process of law; that "it interferes with the sovereignty of the States parties to the Rome Statute while falsely promoting the notion that the ICC's investigation of American perpetrators of international crimes on foreign soil violates US sovereignty"; and that "it undermines US treaty obligations and legitimate US foreign policy objectives by potentially crippling the ICC's mission to bring the world's worst human rights abusers to justice".[89]

Others underlined that, in attacking the ICC and its staff, and mischaracterizing the ICC as a "threat to national security" that creates a "national emergency," the Order completely ignored that most of the ICC's work is completely aligned with US interests.[90] For example, the crimes allegedly committed in Myanmar, a State against which the US itself has imposed sanctions since 2018, have been

---

[85] Available at: <https://home.treasury.gov/policy-issues/financial-sanctions/recent-actions/20200902>. For a comment, see ANDERSON, "Why Them? On the U.S. Sanctions Against Int'l Criminal Court Officials", Just Security, 2 September 2020, available at: <https://www.justsecurity.org/72275/why-them-on-the-u-s-sanctions-against-intl-criminal-court-officials/>. See also the reaction of the President of the Assembly of States Parties, available at: <https://www.icc-cpi.int/Pages/item.aspx?name=pr1534> and of the Trust Fund for Victims, available at: <https://www.icc-cpi.int/Pages/item.aspx?name=200909-tfv-press-release>.

[86] Available at: <https://www.justiceinitiative.org/uploads/1a2af879-b89c-4c53-8dd2-6c27f403d0ef/osji-et-al.-v.-donald-trump-et-al_Redactedv2.pdf>.

[87] Available at: <https://www.justiceinitiative.org/uploads/ce49dde6-803e-41c0-895e-c99ee00a6402/SDNY-ICC-EO-preliminary-injunction-01042020.pdf>.

[88] See Statement by Secretary of State Antony Blinken, "Ending Sanctions and Visa Restrictions against Personnel of the International Criminal Court", at: <https://www.state.gov/ending-sanctions-and-visa-restrictions-against-personnel-of-the-international-criminal-court/>.

[89] AKRAM and RONA, "Why the Executive Order on the ICC is Unconstitutional and Self-Defeating", Opinio Juris, 13 August 2020, available at: <http://opiniojuris.org/2020/08/13/why-the-executive-order-on-the-icc-is-unconstitutional-and-self-defeating/>.

[90] TRAHAN and FAIRLIE, "The International Criminal Court is Hardly a Threat to US National Security", Opinio Juris, 15 June 2020, available at: <http://opiniojuris.org/2020/06/15/the-international-criminal-court-is-hardly-a-threat-to-us-national-security/>.

referred to the ICC Prosecutor. Another example is the trial before the ICC for crimes against humanity and war crimes allegedly committed in Darfur, a situation that then-US Secretary of State Colin Powell, as well as President George W. Bush, declared as "genocide".

According to another author, a threshold problem with the Executive Order was that the US President did not have the authority to issue it.[91] It was argued in this regard that the protection of war criminals is not a national imperative, and that "it would be remarkable and indeed unprecedented for an American Court to give credence to the notion that it is". Other specific concerns raised by the Order concerned the absence of any identification of the harm that would result from the entry of the ICC personnel into the US, and the fact that the prohibition on providing support to ICC investigators precluded American lawyers and human rights advocates from carrying out activities which are protected by the First amendment, such as advising the ICC or supplying its personnel with legal and factual research.

4. THE RESIDUAL SPECIAL COURT FOR SIERRA LEONE (RSCSL)[92]

4.1. CASE LAW

On 4 September 2020, the Residual Special Court for Sierra Leone denied an application by Charles Taylor, the former President of Liberia convicted of war crimes and crimes against humanity in Sierra Leone, to be transferred temporarily from the UK due to the COVID-19 pandemic to a safe third country.[93] Taylor had argued that, due to the outbreak of COVID-19 in the UK, his continued detention in that country posed "a substantial risk to his right to life". In the decision of 4 September 2020, Justice Teresa Doherty affirmed that, as a result of the plaintiff failing to file an affidavit or other statement, the Court had no direct information on the impact of the COVID-19 prevention regime upon the plaintiff or direct evidence of his physical and mental health,[94] and ruled that there had not been any breach of his human rights.[95] Previously, on 24 August 2020, the Chamber of the RSCSL had rejected a request by Charles Taylor for the recusal of Justice Doherty due to the existence of an appearance of bias.[96] According to the plaintiff,

---

[91] DECELL and JAFFER, "Trump's Executive Order on the ICC is Illegal, Not Just Shameful", Just Security, 13 October 2020, available at: <https://www.justsecurity.org/72835/trumps-executive-order-on-the-icc-is-illegal-not-just-shameful/>.

[92] Judgments and decisions of the RSCSL are available at: <http://www.rscsl.org/RSCSL-Decisions.html>. On the RSCSL, see JALLOH, *The Legal Legacy of the Special Court for Sierra Leone*, Cambridge, 2020.

[93] Case No. RSCSL-03-01-ES-1442, The application of Charles G. Taylor to be temporarily transferred to a safe third country to continue his imprisonment due the massive outbreak of COVID 19 in the UK, Decision of 4 September 2020.

[94] *Ibid.*, para. 43.

[95] *Ibid.*, para. 78.

[96] Case No. RSCSL-03-01-ES, Decision on principal defender's request for the withdrawal and/or recusal of Hon. Justice Teresa Doherty of the United Kingdom (UK) as the duty judge

being a UK citizen, the Judge would have been placed in a position of "passing some form of judgment/assessment of her country's response to COVID-19 especially within that country's prison system".[97] The Chamber concluded that it was "unable to find, looking at all the relevant circumstances and in consideration of the requisite burden of proof, that an independent bystander or reasonable person would have a legitimate reason to fear that Justice Doherty lacks impartiality for the nationality-related grounds advanced by the Applicant".[98]

5.   THE SPECIAL TRIBUNAL FOR LEBANON (STL)[99]

5.1.   Case law

On 18 August 2020, the Trial Chamber of the STL pronounced its judgment *in absentia* in the *Ayyash et al.* case concerning the attack on the former Lebanese prime minister Rafik Hariri on 14 February 2005 in Beirut.[100] The Chamber found Ayyash guilty, pursuant to Articles 2 and 3(1)(a) of the Statute, and Article 212 of the Lebanese Criminal Code, as a co-perpetrator of: i) conspiracy aimed at committing a terrorist act; ii) committing a terrorist act by means of an explosive device; iii) intentional homicide of Rafik Hariri with premeditation by using explosive materials; iv) intentional homicide (of 21 persons in addition to the intentional homicide of Rafik Hariri) with premeditation by using explosive materials; and v) attempted intentional homicide (of 226 persons in addition to the intentional homicide of Rafik Hariri) with premeditation by using explosive materials. The Chamber found the other accused not guilty of all charges.

As to the offence of terrorism, the Chamber had to ascertain whether the motive of the accused is an element of its definition. After determining that there was no clear definition of terrorism under customary international law, the Chamber affirmed that it was unnecessary to consider the international law on the matter and to take it into account in interpreting Article 314 of the Lebanese criminal Code. In this regard, the Chamber held that:

---

on the application of Charles G. Taylor to be temporarily transferred to a safe third country to continue his imprisonment due the massive outbreak of COVID 19 in the UK, Decision of 24 August 2020.

[97] *Ibid.*, para. 3(i).

[98] *Ibid.*, para. 46.

[99] Judgments and decisions of the STL are available at: <https://www.stl-tsl.org/en>. On the STL, see ALKHAWAJA, "In Defense of the Special Tribunal for Lebanon and the Case for International Corporate Accountability", Chicago Journal of International Law, 2020, p. 450 ff.

[100] *The Prosecutor v. Salim Jamil Ayyash, Hassan Abib Merhi, Hussein Hassan Oneissi, Assad Hassan Saba*, Case STL-11-01/T/TC, Judgment of 18 August 2020. For a comment, see FREMUTH and SAUERMOSER, STAVROU, "The Special Tribunal for Lebanon: After the Judgment in Ayyash et al., Justice at Last?", Opinio Juris, 26 October 2020, available at: <http://opiniojuris.org/2020/10/26/the-special-tribunal-for-lebanon-after-the-judgment-in-ayyash-et-al-justice-at-last/>.

nothing in Article 2 of the Statute suggests that the Special Tribunal should examine the law of other nations, the case law of international criminal courts or tribunals or treaties and other international instruments, including those that are not legally binding […] in applying the "provisions of the Lebanese Criminal Code relating to the prosecution and punishment of acts of terrorism".[101]

Referring to the First Interlocutory Decision of the STL Appeals Chamber of 16 February 2011, the Chamber stated that "Despite the Appeals Chamber's lengthy […] *obiter dicta* on the apparent existence of a customary international law definition of terrorism, the Trial Chamber is not convinced that one exists".[102] Although the Appeals Chamber extensively considered the international law that is binding on Lebanon and took it into account in interpreting Article 314 of the Lebanon Code, in the Trial Chamber's view this was unnecessary.[103] In this regard, the Chamber admitted that "this approach may appear at first sight to be paradoxical, because as a matter of international law, Lebanon's customary obligations are part of the law applicable in that country".[104] In the Chamber's view, however, "the clear language of the Statute must take precedence over an unwritten general policy aim of interpreting applicable Lebanese legislation exactly as Lebanese courts should, in theory, interpret them".[105]

In her separate opinion, Judge Janet Nosworthy agreed that a definition of terrorism has not yet "crystallised under customary international law" but stressed that, had such a definition been recognized, it would have been proper to use it to inform the Trial Chamber's interpretation of Article 314. Referring to the *persistent objector* doctrine, Judge Nosworthy affirmed that:

> As there was no evidence of Lebanon entering constant and persistent objections to the potentially emerging definition of terrorism under customary international law – and indeed Lebanon engaged with this emerging area of law by becoming a party to relevant treaties including the Arab Convention on the Suppression of Terrorism – it cannot be said that Lebanon would be excluded from the binding nature of any rule of customary international law which may arise in this area.
> However, full crystallization and maturity are the essential characteristics which any customary international law principle must demonstrate as possessing. After careful consideration, I am not convinced that States' practice in the area of terrorism was sufficiently consistent, or that their acceptance that they were legally

---

[101] *The Prosecutor v. Salim Jamil Ayyash, Hassan Abib Merhi, Hussein Hassan Oneissi, Assad Hassan Saba*, Case STL-11-01/T/TC, Judgment of 18 August 2020, para. 6192.

[102] *Ibid.*, para. 6192.

[103] *Ibid.*

[104] *Ibid.*, para. 6194.

[105] *Ibid.*

bound to follow the same practice – the *opinio juris* – was sufficiently evident, for a customary definition to have clearly crystallised by that time. For that matter, it does not appear to have crystallised by February 2011 when the Appeals Chamber issued its decision, or since the date of that pronouncement.[106]

In its sentencing judgment, delivered on 11 December 2020, the Trial Chamber sentenced Ayyash to life imprisonment.[107] On the same day, it issued an arrest warrant directed to the competent Lebanese authorities,[108] and a new international arrest warrant inviting and authorizing the competent authorities of all States to search for, arrest, detain and ensure the transfer of Ayyash to the Headquarters of the STL.[109]

6. CONCLUSION

Despite the COVID-19 pandemic having slowed down the work of the international criminal tribunals in 2020, some of them achieved significant results in their judicial activity. Of special interest is the decision of the ICC Pre-Trial Chamber affirming that the Court's territorial jurisdiction in the Situation in Palestine extends to the territories occupied by Israel since 1967, namely Gaza and the West Bank, including East Jerusalem. Also of relevance are the new preliminary examinations of the ICC following State Party referrals received from the Government of Venezuela and from the Government of Bolivia, on 13 February 2020 and on 4 September 2020 respectively. As for the case law of the ICC, noteworthy is the decision on Bemba's claim for compensation and damages and the Court's statement on the necessity of a review of the Rome Statute so as to address some limitations on the excessive length of the proceedings. Also of interest are the Appeals Chamber decision of 28 May 2020 in the *Gbagbo and Blé Goudé* case and the Appeals Chamber judgment of 9 March 2020 in the case against Saif Al-Islam Gaddafi, for some noteworthy assertions on the permissibility of trials *in absentia* before the ICC, and on the issue of amnesties for international crimes under international law, respectively.

Finally, worthy of mention is the judgment *in absentia* handed down on 18 August 2020 by the STL in the *Ayyash et al.* case concerning the attack on former Lebanese prime minister Rafik Hariri in Beirut, together with the conclusions on the definition of terrorism under customary international law.

---

[106] See paras. 126-127 of the Opinion.

[107] *The Prosecutor v. Salim Jamil Ayyash*, Case STL-11-01/S/TC, Sentencing Judgment of 11 December 2020.

[108] *The Prosecutor v. Salim Jamil Ayyash*, Case STL-11-01/ES/TC, Warrant for the arrest of Salim Jamil Ayyash of 11 December 2020.

[109] *The Prosecutor v. Salim Jamil Ayyash*, Case STL-11-01/ES/TC, International Warrant for the Arrest of Salim Jamil Ayyash of 11 December 2020.

THE WTO DISPUTE SETTLEMENT SYSTEM IN 2020: FACING THE APPELLATE BODY PARALYSIS

edited by GIORGIO SACERDOTI[*]

1. The COVID-19 economic and trade crisis, which started in early 2020, has hit the WTO at a time when the organization is certainly not in good health. Respect for its rules has reached a low level, due to States' increasing recourse to unilateral restrictive measures of dubious legality (to say the least)[1] and to bilateral agreements that disregard multilateral obligations.[2] The dispute settlement system has been half paralyzed since the demise of the Appellate Body (AB) at the end of 2019. Proposals to update or "modernize" WTO rules, including by negotiating agreements in sectors that are not effectively covered, were put on the multilateral agenda at the last WTO Ministerial Conference (2017) in Buenos

---

[*] Of the Board of Editors, Emeritus Professor of International Law, Bocconi University, Milan; former Chairman of the WTO Appellate Body. This review was carried out within the framework of the PhD programme in International and European Law of the PhD School of Bocconi University in Milan. Professor Giorgio Sacerdoti coordinated the work. Individual reviews of WTO cases were authored by PhD candidates Elena Assenza, Rosalba Famà, Nazlicicek Semercioglu, Diana Wade and PhD alumna Viktoriia Lapa, as indicated at the bottom of each review. The editing was done by Diana Wade and Viktoriia Lapa. Since 2013, yearly reviews of WTO developments and case law have been posted on SSRN, as Bocconi Legal Papers, and in the IYIL.

[1] See the cases brought separately by China, India, the EU, Canada, Mexico, Norway, Russia, Switzerland and Turkey against the US in 2018-2019 (DS 544, 547, 548, 550, 551, 552, 554, 556 and 564, respectively). Some of these WTO Members have adopted trade restrictions against the US as countermeasures under Art. 8 of the Safeguards Agreement, having considered the US measures to be, in reality, disguised safeguards. The US has in turn challenged these countermeasures as unjustified, claiming that its own measures are bona fide and security-based, and starting its own proceedings against Canada, China, the EU, Mexico and Turkey (DS 557, 558, 559, 560 and 561 respectively). The US measures against Mexico and Canada have been lifted, following the conclusion of the USMCA Agreement replacing NAFTA, effective 1 July 2020, and these cases have been withdrawn. All other cases were pending before panels at the end of 2020 with no report yet issued.

[2] We refer to the so-called "phase-1" agreement between the US and China of 15 January 2020, whereby the extra tariffs imposed by the US in 2018 on China's exports to the US were not lifted (but just reduced in part), leaving the tariffs imposed as countermeasures by China on imports from the US untouched. See US-China Economic and Trade Agreement, 15 January 2020, available at: <https://ustr.gov/sites/default/files/files/agreements>. The EU has immediately expressed its reservations as to the WTO-consistency of such a bilateral "mercantilistic" deal, see *EU trade commissioner criticises US-China trade deal*, Financial Times, 17 January 2020. China has challenged the US measures at the WTO, while the US has not impugned China's countermeasures. The Panel in case 543 (commented hereafter), circulated on 15 September 2020, appealed by the US, has affirmed its jurisdiction notwithstanding the agreement of 15 January 2020 and has found the US measures in breach of Articles I and II GATT.

IYIL, Vol. 30 (2020), pp. 381-421
ISSN 0391-5107

Aires, but have gone nowhere in 2020.[3] The cancellation of the Ministerial Conference due to take place in June 2020 in Kazakhstan because of the pandemic has avoided showing publicly that "the emperor has no clothes". The process for the appointment of a successor to Director-General Roberto Azevedo, who had unexpectedly resigned from his post in May 2020, was blocked by the US which alone refused to join the consensus on the candidate who, at the end of a rigorous selection process, enjoyed quasi-universal consensus, Ms Ngozi Okonjo-Iweala of Nigeria.

Among the looming issues facing the WTO is the criticism from the US (and other WTO Members) of China's widespread use (or abuse) of subsidies to and through its State-owned enterprises (SOEs), which distort international competition and are not adequately dealt with by the special provisions of China's Access Protocol to the WTO (a criticism that China of course rejects).[4] Reform of substantive provisions of the WTO Agreement on Subsidies and Countervailing Measures (SCM) was advocated in a joint statement of the United States, the European Union and Japan in January 2020. This proposal includes broadening the concept of State-owned enterprises and overturning the restrictive interpretation of the term "public body" in the ASCM, which was adopted by the AB in several reports – one of the grounds of complaint by the US against the AB jurisprudence.

Even ruling out further liberalization of trade in goods and services, which protectionist and populist sectors of public opinion reject, it is difficult to envisage even modest reforms where consensus is lacking. Majority voting or plurilateral agreements would leave out important players and would defeat the very purpose of the exercise.

Another issue raised by the US that has found some support, but has strongly been rejected by those States which would be affected by it, in primis China, is the proposal to review the privileged self-defined status of "developing country" at the WTO.[5]

Only at the beginning of 2021 has the situation started to improve, although many trade-restrictive measures,[6] officially adopted to ensure medical supplies

---

[3] The sectors proposed for negotiation include e-commerce, data circulation and protection, and outlawing subsidies to illegal fishing. For a selection of proposals see CIGI, "Modernizing the World Trade Organization", May 2020, available at: <https://www.cigionline.org/publications/modernizing-world-trade-organization>.

[4] For an insightful and recent analysis of the problem see BORLINI, "When the Leviathan Goes to the Market: A Critical Evaluation of the Rules Governing State-Owned Enterprises in Trade Agreements", LJIL, 2020, p. 313 ff.

[5] The US has suggested that the participation of a country in the G-20, that is, being a major economic and trading power, should be considered incompatible with developing member status. See Memorandum of 26 July 2019, available at: <https://www.federalregister.gov/documents/2019/07/31/2019-16497/reforming-developing-country-status-in-the-world-trade-organization>. See generally HU, "China as a WTO Developing Member, Is It a Problem?", CEPS Political Insight No 2019/16, November 2019, available at: <https://www.ceps.eu/ceps-publications/china-as-a-wto-developing-member-is-it-a-problem>.

[6] COVID-19 related export restrictions have been notified to the WTO by a number of countries, in accordance with the 2012 "Decision on Notification Procedures for Quantitative

during the first part of the pandemic, remain in force, notwithstanding multiple appeals in favour of international cooperation in facing the crisis.[7] First, trade statistics have shown a more substantial and quick recovery of international commerce than had been anticipated.[8] Secondly, the new US Biden administration joined the consensus on the new director general, allowing Ms Ngozi Okonjo-Iweala to be consensually appointed to the post on 15 February 2021 by the General Council, and hinting at a resumption of multilateral cooperation to reinvigorate the WTO.

2. As to the dispute settlement system (DSS), the effects of the US (Trump Administration) decision to block, from 2018, all appointments to the AB manifested its full impact on the AB in 2020. In December 2019, the AB was left with just one member in office, Ms Hong Zhao, whose term lapsed at the end of November 2020. Not only has the WTO been left without any AB, but also its able secretariat has been dismantled, dispersing a 25-year accumulation of expertise. Moreover, in late 2019, the last three AB members in office (Messrs Ujal Singh Bhatia, Thomas R. Graham and Ms Hong Zhao) decided, after some acrimonious internal debates which were leaked to the public, to go on working after the end of their terms on only the three appeals in which the hearings had already taken place.[9] This has led to the issuance of just three appellate reports in the first part of 2020, which will be reviewed in this paper, leaving 10 other

---

Restrictions". See WTO Information Note on Export Prohibition and Restrictions of 23 April 2020, available at: <https://www.wto.org/english/tratop_e/covid19_e/covid19_e.htm>.

[7] See WTO, "COVID-19: Measures affecting trade in goods", updated as of 4 June 2021, available at: <https://www.wto.org/english/tratop_e/covid19_e/trade_related_goods_measure_e.htm>. For a critical view, see BALDWIN and EVENETT (eds.), *COVID-19 and Trade Policy: Why Turning Inward Won't Work*, London, 2020, available at: <https://voxeu.org/content/covid-19-and-trade-policy-why-turning-inward-won-t-work>. Groups of WTO Members tabled proposals in the same direction at the WTO General Council in April 2020, notably with a view to ensuring open and predictable trade in agricultural and food products (WT/GC/208). As to the legality of those restrictions (what might be admissible under Article XI.2, XX(a) and (b) of GATT), see AATREYA, "Are COVID-19 Related Trade Restrictions WTO-Consistent?", EJIL: Talk!, 25 April 2020, available at: <https://www.ejiltalk.org/are-covid-19-related-trade-restrictions-wto-consistent/>; GLÖCKLE, "Export restrictions under scrutiny – the legal dimensions of export restrictions on personal protective equipment", EJIL: Talk!, 7 April 2020, available at: <https://www.ejiltalk.org/export-restrictions-under-scrutiny-the-legal-dimensions-of-export-restrictions-on-personal-protective-equipment/>.

[8] See WTO, Press release of 6 October 2020, available at: <https://www.wto.org/english/news_e/pres20_e/pr862_e.htm>: "Main points: World merchandise trade volume is forecast to fall 9.2% in 2020. The projected decline is less than the 12.9% drop foreseen in the optimistic scenario from the April trade forecast. Trade volume growth should rebound to 7.2% in 2021 but will remain well below the pre-crisis trend. Global GDP will fall by 4.8% in 2020 before rising by 4.9% in 2021".

[9] See the latest (currently also the last) Appellate Body Annual Report (2019-2020), available at: <https://www.wto.org/english/tratop_e/dispu_e/ab_anrep_2019_e.pdf>. According to Art. 15 of the Working Procedures for Appellate Review, these AB members could have completed the disposition of all pending appeals beyond the end of their terms in office.

appeals indefinitely pending. As a result, since panel reports under appeal cannot be adopted by the Dispute Settlement Body (DSB), these disputes remain for the time being unresolved, and any domestic measure challenged as WTO-inconsistent remains in place, frustrating the very function of the DSS.

As had been widely anticipated, this situation has had a negative impact on the effectiveness of the panel stage, notwithstanding the appearance of "business as usual". Panels have gone on working in 2020: six reports have been issued; seven new panels have been established by the DSB; and, at the end of 2020, 33 panel proceedings were pending. However, all panel reports issued in 2020 have been "appealed in the void", that is to the non-operating AB, leaving also these cases in a limbo with no resolution of these disputes in sight.[10]

3. This situation has shown the limits of the alternative appellate arbitration, which, on the basis of Article 25 of the Dispute Settlement Understanding (DSU), the EU had proposed in order to overcome the stalemate.[11] This elaborate "Multi-party Interim Appellate Arbitration" (MPIA) had been accepted by 22 other WTO Members as of the end of 2020, but none of the appellants against the panel reports issued in this year are party to it.[12] The United States did not hesitate to lodge two such appeals in 2020, evidencing the self-serving scope and effect of its blocking of the AB.[13]

The situation has dealt an enormous blow to States' faith in the ability of the WTO to effectively settle disputes, which has increased the interest in bilateral mechanisms between countries where FTAs are in place with adequate dispute settlement provisions. In fact, in 2020, the EU resorted for the first time to such

---

[10] The cases involved are DS484, *Indonesia – Chicken* (Art. 21.5); DS494, *EU – Cost Adjustment Methodologies and Anti-Dumping Measures* (Second Complaint); DS533, *US – Countervailing Measures on Lumber*; DS543, *US – Tariff Measures on Chinese Goods*; DS553, *Korea – Sunset Review on Stainless Steel Bars* (appeal filed on 22 January 2021); and DS567, *Saudi Arabia – Intellectual Property Rights*. In DS 529, *Australia – Anti-Dumping Measures on A4 Copy Paper*, the panel report, issued on 4 December 2019, was adopted by the DSB on 27 January 2020.

[11] EU, Press release of 27 March 2020, available at: <www.consilium.europa.eu/en/press/press-releases/2020/04/15/council-approves-a-multi-party-interim-appeal-arbitration-arrangement> (with text attached). On 31 July 2020, the participants notified the WTO of the ten arbitrators who will hear appeals of WTO panel reports under the MPIA, marking the final step to make the MPIA operational for disputes between the participants.

[12] The EU has announced that, in the event of a dispute between the EU and an opposing party that is not party to the MPIA, the EU would resort immediately to countermeasures, relying on general international law principles in the area of State responsibility. See "Commission reinforces tools to ensure Europe's interests in international trade", 12 December 2019, available at: <https://trade.ec.europa.eu/doclib/press/index.cfm?id>. Regulation (EU) 2021/167 amending Regulation (EU) No. 654/2014 concerning the exercise of the Union's rights for the application and enforcement of international trade rules entered into force on 12 February 2021.

[13] At the DSB of 14 December 2020, China decried the US appeal in *US – Tariffs on Chinese Goods* (DS 543), labelling it "an abuse of procedural rules", noting that the US had not subscribed to the alternative appeal arbitration (MPIA). See WT/DSB/M/446 p. 12.

a bilateral mechanism to challenge two export bans on timber by Ukraine, under the 2014 Association Agreement (AA). The arbitration panel issued its final report on 11 December 2020, less than 11 months from its establishment, notwithstanding delays due to the COVID-19 pandemic. The report is interesting also for the WTO context, because at issue were an alleged breach of Article XI GATT, referred to by Article 35 of the AA, and Ukraine's defences based on Article XX(b) (accepted by the panel) and Article XX(g) GATT (rejected), made applicable by Article 36 of the AA.[14]

This paper will review the three appellate reports issued in 2020 and two panel reports of special interest: a) the *Saudi Arabia-Intellectual Property* (DS567) report, which is the second panel report on Article XXI GATT following the *Russia-Measures Concerning Traffic in Transit* (DS512) panel report of 2019, and b) the *US-Tariff Measures on Chinese goods* (DS543) report, which is the first panel report issued on the US measures introduced in 2018-2019 that impose additional duties on imports.

GIORGIO SACERDOTI

1. APPELLATE BODY REPORT, *AUSTRALIA – CERTAIN MEASURES CONCERNING TRADEMARKS, GEOGRAPHICAL INDICATIONS AND OTHER PLAIN PACKAGING REQUIREMENTS APPLICABLE TO TOBACCO PRODUCTS AND PACKAGING*[15]

1.1. Introduction and main facts of the dispute

The National Preventative Health Taskforce (NPHT) that was established in Australia in 2008 to provide a blueprint for tackling the burden of chronic diseases caused by, among other things, tobacco, released its final report the following year. It identified 11 "key action areas", including ending all remaining forms of advertising and promotion of tobacco products (which included a specific action to eliminate promotion of tobacco products through packaging design). Thereafter, several legislative measures referred to as Tobacco Plain Packaging (TPP) were passed.[16] Accordingly, the TPP Act of 2011, regulating the retail packaging and appearance of tobacco products, was drafted in order to improve public health and give effect to certain obligations under the World Health

---

[14] See European Commission, "Ukraine wood export ban found illegal in independent panel ruling", 12 December 2020, available at: <https://trade.ec.europa.eu/doclib/press/index.cfm?id=2223>.

[15] Appellate Body Reports, *Australia – Certain Measures Concerning Trademarks, Geographical Indications and Other Plain Packaging Requirements Applicable to Tobacco Products and Packaging*, adopted on 9 June 2020, WT/DS435/AB/R and WT/DS 441/AB/R.

[16] Panel Reports, *Australia – Certain Measures Concerning Trademarks, Geographical Indications and Other Plain Packaging Requirements Applicable to Tobacco Products and Packaging*, circulated on 28 June 2018, WT/DS435/R, WT/DS441/R, WT/DS458/R and WT/DS467/R, paras. 2.6, 2.7 and 2.10.

Organization's Framework Convention on Tobacco Control (WHO FCTC) by discouraging the use of tobacco products.[17]

The TPP measures lay down detailed colour requirements regarding all outer and inner surfaces, specifically prohibiting the appearance of trademarks anywhere on the retail packaging, in conjunction with other legislation such as graphic health warnings (GHW).[18]

1.2. The Panel Report

A single Panel was composed on 5 May 2014 to consider complaints by Honduras, the Dominican Republic, Cuba, Indonesia and Ukraine with respect to certain restrictions imposed by Australia on trademarks, geographical indications (GI) and other plain packaging requirements, applicable to all tobacco products sold, offered for sale, or otherwise supplied in Australia. In their reports, adopted on 28 June 2018, the Panel found that the complainants had not demonstrated that Australia's measures were inconsistent with Article 2.2 of the TBT Agreement, Articles 6-quinquies and 10-bis of the Paris Agreement, Articles 15.4, 16.1, 16.3, 20, 22.2(b) and 24.3 of the TRIPS Agreement, and Article IX:4 of the GATT. No appeals were filed against reports WT/DS458/R and WT/DS467/R. On 19 July 2018 and 23 August 2018 respectively, Honduras and the Dominican Republic filed appeals against reports DS435 and DS441.[19]

1.3. The Appellate Body Report

1.3.1. Article 2.2 of the TBT Agreement

i.   *Whether the Panel erred in its finding with respect to the contribution of the TPP measures to Australia's Objective*

Both of the appellants argued that the TPP measures make no contribution to Australia's objective, nor are they apt to do so. Australia, on the other hand, filed counterclaims demonstrating how such measures do in fact improve public health. The Panel had concluded that, taken as whole, the submitted evidence supports the view that, combined with the comprehensive range of other unchallenged tobacco control measures maintained by Australia, the TPP measures are apt to, and do, make a meaningful contribution to Australia's objective of reducing the use of, and exposure to, tobacco products.[20]

---

[17] The TPP Act of 2011, available at: <https://www.legislation.gov.au/Details/ C2018C00450>.

[18] Panel Reports, *cit. supra* note 16, paras. 2.23, 2.24, 2.25 and 2.32.

[19] Appellate Body Reports, *cit. supra* note 15, pp. 18, 21 and 22.

[20] Appellate Body Reports, *cit. supra* note 15, paras. 6.14-6.18.

a. Whether the Panel erred in its application of Article 2.2

Honduras asserted that despite having set out the correct legal standard, the Panel had failed to apply it to the facts of the case. Australia, however, claimed that this allegation related to the Panel's appreciation of the evidence and pointed to Honduras's failure to develop legal arguments in relation to any of its claims. On this issue, the Appellate Body (AB) concluded that Honduras had not substantiated its claim that the Panel had erred in the application of the article to the facts of the case. Given the complete overlap between arguments made based on Article 2.2 of the TBT and Article 11 of the DSU, the AB addressed all of Honduras's challenges to the Panel's contribution analysis under the rubric of its claims under Article 11 of the DSU.[21]

b. Whether the Panel failed to make an objective assessment of the facts of the case as provided for under Article 11 of the DSU, in its evaluation of the evidence pertaining to the contribution of the TPP measures to Australia's objective

The appellants claimed that the Panel (i) failed to provide a reasoned and adequate explanation of how the facts supported its determination that the imposition of TPP measures led to a reduction in tobacco consumption; (ii) disregarded, misrepresented and distorted material pieces of Honduras's evidence; and (iii) did not respect the basic principles of due process and procedural fairness. Within this context, the AB noted that not every error by a panel amounts to a failure to comply with its duties under Article 11, only those which, taken together or singly, undermine the objectivity of the panel's assessment of the matter before it.[22] In addition, the AB emphasized that it was the complainants, and not the Panel, who bore the burden of adducing credible evidence to prove their proposition that the TPP measures are incapable of contributing to Australia's objective.

The AB, citing its case law, rejected all but two of the allegations. Accordingly, it concluded that the Panel: (i) failed to examine the Dominican Republic's arguments and evidence indicating that Australia's consumption models showed a positive impact of tobacco costliness on cigarette consumption; and (ii) compromised the parties' due process rights by failing to explore the issues of multicollinearity and non-stationarity of the data with the parties prior to the issuance of the interim report. With respect to repercussions of these errors on the Panel's conclusions, the AB held that the second one had no impact on the ulti-

---

[21] *Ibid.*, paras. 6.20-6.26.

[22] Appellate Body Report, *Peru – Agricultural Products*, adopted on 31 July 2015, WT/DS457/AB/R, para. 5.66; Appellate Body Reports, *China – Rare Earths*, adopted on 29 August 2014, WT/DS431/AB/R, WT/DS432/AB/R and WT/DS433/AB/R, para. 5.178; Appellate Body Report, *EC – Fasteners (China)* (Article 21.5 – China), adopted on 12 February 2016, WT/DS397/AB/RW, para. 5.61.

mate finding that "there is econometric evidence suggesting that [the TPP measures] contributed to the reduction in overall smoking prevalence in Australia". However, it opined that the first one fatally undermines the Panel's determination that Australia's evidence was more credible than that of the complainants and consequently vitiates the determination that "there is some econometric evidence suggesting that the TPP measures […] contributed to the reduction in wholesale cigarette sales, and therefore cigarette consumption".

Thereafter, the AB highlighted that of the five different factors the Panel relied on in forming its conclusion that the post-implementation evidence was consistent with the hypothesized impact of the TPP measures (i.e. the pre-implementation evidence regarding the design, structure, and intended operation of the measures), the Appellants demonstrated that the Panel erred with respect to one aspect only, namely, step 3 of the Panel's cigarette consumption analysis. Therefore, the AB concluded the appellants had not demonstrated how any errors by the Panel in its assessment of consumption would also demonstrate that the Panel erred in its assessment of smoking prevalence. Consequently, the AB upheld the Panel's finding since the appellants had not demonstrated that the TPP measures are not apt to make a contribution to Australia's objective of improving public health by reducing the use of, and exposure to, tobacco products.[23]

ii. *Trade restrictiveness of the TPP measures*

a. *Whether the Panel erred in its interpretation of Article 2.2 of the TBT Agreement*

The Panel had first emphasized that "a technical regulation is 'trade-restrictive' within the meaning of Article 2.2 when it has a limiting effect on international trade". Then, it found that the TPP measures limit the opportunity for producers to differentiate their products on the basis of brands, emphasizing the role of brands in engendering consumer loyalty and increasing consumers' willingness to pay. In this respect, the Panel noted that such limitations reduce the opportunities for tobacco manufacturers to compete on the basis of brand differentiation. However, contrary to the claimants' assertions, the Panel concluded that a technical regulation that is applicable to all tobacco products on the entire market (which may in principle increase competition on the market) does not constitute, in itself, a restriction on competitive opportunities for imported products that must be assumed to have a limiting effect on international trade. In this respect, the AB confirmed that the TPP measures equally impact all the goods on the market. Therefore, it concluded that the Panel's determination was consistent with its precedents, according to which a finding that the measures in question are trade restrictive can be reached where they are shown to reduce the competitive

[23] Appellate Body Reports, *cit. supra* note 15, paras. 6.77, 6.260, 6.362, 6.366 and 6.367.

opportunities of imported products as a group, from a Member, vis-à-vis competing domestic products.

The AB concluded that the appellants had not demonstrated that the Panel erred in its interpretation of Article 2.2 of the TBT Agreement.[24]

b. Whether the Panel erred in its application of Article 2.2

The Panel had rejected the argument that the TPP measures raise barriers to entry to the Australian market due to the lack of possibility to create brand awareness and the need to decrease prices to address consumers' reduced willingness to pay. In doing so, it considered that there is significant uncertainty about the strength and relative weight of these effects. However, the Panel noted that the Australian market is supplied entirely through imported tobacco products. Therefore, it concluded that by reducing the use of tobacco products, the TPP measures diminish the volume of imported tobacco products on the Australian market, and thereby have a limiting effect on trade. Yet, in refuting the arguments regarding the decrease in value of trade in tobacco products, the Panel relied on the evidence suggesting that the measures have led to an increase in the price of cigarettes which has more than offset the decrease in the quantity consumed.

On appeal, both appellants claimed that the Panel should have found that a reduction in the opportunity for products to differentiate on the basis of brands sufficed to demonstrate the trade restrictiveness of the TPP measures. In addition, they asserted that the Panel determined the effect of the foregoing on the value of imported products in an inaccurate manner. With respect to the first contention, the AB found that a reduction in the opportunity to differentiate on the basis of brands might impact different products in a diverse manner by harming competitive opportunities for some products while improving the same for others. Therefore, it rejected the argument to that effect. As for the allegation in relation to value, the AB noted that the Panel took into account the qualitative evidence suggesting that the TPP measures may reduce the value of imported products in the future. However, it emphasized that this was not considered sufficient to conclude that they did, or necessarily would, give rise to the occurrence of such an impact. The AB also added that the complainants mistakenly invoked down-trading (consumers shifting from high-end to low-end cigarettes) when claiming that the TPP measures would necessarily lead to a decline in value. Therefore, it refuted the second assertion as well. Lastly, as to the Dominican Republic's argument that the Panel erred by taking into account price increases because a measure does not cease to be trade restrictive just because private actors may be able to adapt their own commercial strategy, the AB noted that if prices had remained constant or declined, the conclusion would have been that a reduction in the value of trade has taken place. The AB concluded that the appellants had

---

[24] *Ibid.*, paras. 6.375, 6.387, 6.378, 6.386, 6.392 and 6.393.

not demonstrated that the Panel erred in its application of Article 2.2 of the TBT Agreement in assessing the trade restrictiveness of the TPP measures.[25]

iii.　Alternative measures

The appellants requested the AB to reverse the Panel's findings that two of the alternative measures that the complainants proposed – namely, an increase in the minimum legal purchasing age (MLPA) for tobacco products and an increase in taxation of tobacco products in Australia – were not reasonably available alternative measures that would be less trade restrictive than the TPP measures while making an equivalent contribution to Australia's legitimate objective.

a.　Whether the Panel erred under Article 2.2 in its assessment of the relative trade restrictiveness of the alternative measures

With respect to the MLPA, the Panel concluded that the complainants had not demonstrated that an increase in the MLPA to 21 years would necessarily be less trade restrictive than the TPP measures. Regarding an increase in taxation, the Panel stated that, to the extent that a taxation increase would be calibrated to have the same degree of contribution as the TPP measures in reducing the use of, and exposure to, tobacco products, and would therefore have an equal impact on overall consumption of such products, it would be as trade restrictive as the TPP measures in terms of its impact on the volume of trade in tobacco products. Accordingly, the Panel similarly concluded that the complainants had not demonstrated that an increase in tobacco taxation would be less trade restrictive than the TPP measures.

Within this context, the AB determined that there was no sufficient basis for finding that the Panel had erred in concluding that neither of the alternative measures would be less trade restrictive than those related to the TPP. The AB highlighted that the complainants had failed to prove that the proposed alternatives would cause adverse impacts to a lesser extent. Therefore, it rejected the appellants' claim to this effect.[26]

b.　Whether the Panel erred under Article 2.2 in its assessment of the relative contribution of the alternative measures

In relation to the objective of reducing smoking, the appellants highlighted that the Panel found that the TPP measures and the two alternatives are similarly apt to make a meaningful contribution. Nonetheless, it found that the contribu-

---

[25] *Ibid.*, paras. 6.397, 6.399-6.401, 6.403, 6.411, 6.422, 6.423, 6.444, 6.448 and 6.450.
[26] *Ibid.*, paras. 6.460, 6. 473, 6.474, 6.478 and 6.479.

tion of each alternative measure would not be equivalent to that of the TPP measures. As the appellants saw it, the Panel erred in its conclusions for two reasons. First, the Panel rejected equivalence on the basis that the alternative measures contribute to Australia's objective through mechanisms different from the TPP measures. Secondly, the Panel failed to make a proper comparison between the contributions of the TPP measures and alternative measures.

The AB found no clear indications in the relevant analysis by the Panel that the overall degree of reduction in the use of, and exposure to, tobacco products achieved by each alternative measure (in addition to any reduction attributable to Australia's other existing tobacco control measures) would be materially smaller than that achieved by the TPP measures. Therefore, it agreed with the appellants that the Panel's reasons for rejecting equivalence did not reflect the correct legal standard under Article 2.2. However, despite finding that the Panel failed to accurately assess the equivalence of the contribution of each alternative, the AB still found that the Panel's findings regarding the complainants' failure to demonstrate that the measures would be less trade restrictive should stand.[27] Accordingly, as noncompliance cannot be established unless it is demonstrated that proposed alternative measures impose limitations to a lesser extent, the appellants' assertions were not upheld.

1.3.2.   Article 16.1 of the TRIPS Agreement

Article 16.1 of the TRIPS Agreement entitles trademark owners to prevent all third parties that do not have their consent from using identical or similar signs in the course of trade, provided that certain conditions such as likeness of goods or services and likelihood of confusion are met. The Panel opined that, in order to show that the TPP measures are inconsistent with Article 16.1, the complainants would have had to demonstrate that, under Australia's domestic law, the trademark owner does not have the right to prevent infringing third-party activities. In this regard, the Panel highlighted that the text of Article 16.1 does not – as the complainants had implied – impose an obligation on Members beyond providing protection to trademark owners against infringing third-party uses. It added that adopting an interpretation so as to require Member States to safeguard a minimum opportunity to use a given trademark would create disharmony with other articles of the agreement, which clearly foresee potential regulatory prevention of utilization. Concluding that the rule in question does not grant a right to use a particular trademark, the Panel did not find the TPP measures to be in violation of Article 16.1 of the TRIPS Agreement. In this regard, the AB confirmed that the provision in question, indeed, does not allow protection of distinctiveness of a trademark through utilization. Therefore, it held that the Panel's conclusion was correct.[28]

---

[27] *Ibid.*, paras. 6.481, 6.490, 6.497, 6.498 and 6.504.
[28] *Ibid.*, paras. 6.545, 6.549, 6.552, 6.558, 6.568, 6.570, 6.588 and 6.619.

1.3.3. Article 20 of the TRIPS Agreement

Article 20 of the TRIPS Agreement prohibits Members from unjustifiably encumbering the use of a trademark in the course of trade by imposing special requirements. The Panel noted that public health is unquestionably among the objectives that may constitute a basis for governmental restrictions, but that the legitimate interest of the trademark owner in using its brand should also be taken into account before reaching a conclusion with respect to justifiability. With respect to the latter, the Panel noted that, while the TPP measures do prevent extraction of economic value from the design features of trademarks, the implications of the TPP's prohibitions are "partly mitigated" by the use of word marks. With respect to the former, the Panel concluded that Australia had sufficient justification for imposing the restrictions since the special requirements under the TPP demonstrably contribute to Australia's objective of improving public health.

The AB refuted the claims that the Panel's conclusion was inaccurate. It noted that reference to the notion of justifiability, rather than necessity, in Article 20, suggests a greater degree of flexibility to impose restrictions. The AB concluded that the Panel did not err in addressing the legitimate interests of the trademark owners by examining their potential to extract monetary value from their brands. In addition, the AB rejected Honduras's claim that the Panel did not undertake any weighing and balancing before reaching its conclusion.

The AB then returned to the complainants' proposed alternative measures. In this regard, the AB highlighted the regulatory autonomy Members enjoy in imposing limitations on the use of trademarks under Article 20. Therefore, the AB ultimately upheld the Panel's conclusion that the complainants had failed to demonstrate the TPP's noncompliance with the provision in question.[29]

1.4. Conclusion

In light of the above, the AB held that the appellants failed to establish that Australia's TPP measures are inconsistent with Article 2.2 of the TBT Agreement and/or Articles 16.1 and 20 of the TRIPS Agreement.

The Panel's report in this dispute is the most extensive ever circulated, since it comprises 888 pages (without the annexes). It also concludes one of the longest WTO disputes, since the first consultations request in this case was submitted on 4 April 2012.

As to the substance, this ruling represents a major milestone for global tobacco control efforts and Australia's actions in the realm of plain packaging. Indeed, with respect to the latter, it finally puts an end to challenges to Australia's TPP measures, brought in several fora (i.e. investment tribunals and local courts). In respect of States where similar measures will soon go into effect, such as

---

[29] *Ibid.*, paras. 6.625, 6.628, 6.630, 6.632, 6.634. 6.647, 6.649, 6.680 6.681, 6.695, 6.697 and 6.707.

Singapore, the recent ruling likely reduces litigation risks, at least vis-à-vis trade obligations. Lastly, the decision reaffirms that international trade and public health goals are not mutually exclusive and States can enact strong, yet evidence-based, tobacco control measures that do not, in principle, go against their obligations on the international plane.[30]

NAZLICICEK SEMERCIOGLU[*]

2. APPELLATE BODY REPORT, *RUSSIA – MEASURES AFFECTING THE IMPORTATION OF RAILWAY EQUIPMENT AND PARTS THEREOF*[31]

2.1. Introduction and main facts of the dispute

By issuing the AB Report on 5 March 2020, the WTO laid down the final ruling in the proceedings of *Russia – Measures Affecting the Importation of Railway Equipment and Parts Thereof*. In the background of this dispute is the confrontation between Ukraine and Russia concerning the latter's annexation of Crimea and support of separatist forces in the Donbass.

This dispute regards certain measures taken by Russia "concerning its conformity assessment procedures for railway products as they relate to suppliers from Ukraine". On 21 October 2015, Ukraine requested consultations with the Russian Federation, challenging certain measures imposed on railway equipment imported from Ukraine. Ukraine raised its claim under the TBT Agreement and the GATT 1994. Ukraine alleged that Russia was impeding access to the Russian market for certain Ukrainian products.

On 10 November 2016, Ukraine requested the establishment of a panel and at its meeting on 16 November 2016, the DSB established a panel, which was composed on 2 March 2017.

Ukraine challenged three categories of measures. Firstly, the suspension of valid conformity assessment certificates for railway products, due to the introduction of new procedures by Customs Union[32] (CU) Decision No. 710 of 2011.[33] Secondly, Russian authorities rejected new applications for conformity assessment certificates, filed by Ukrainian producers pursuant to the newly adopted Technical

---

[30] DIAMOND, "The Final Say on Australia's Plain Packaging Law at the WTO", O'Neill Institute for National & Global Health Law, 8 June 2020, available at: <https://oneill.law.georgetown.edu/the-final-say-on-australias-plain-packaging-law-at-the-wto/>.

[*] Ph.D. candidate in International and European Law, Bocconi University, Milan.

[31] Appellate Body Report, *Russia – Measures Affecting the Importation of Railway Equipment and Parts Thereof*, adopted on 5 March 2020, WT/DS499/AB/R.

[32] Customs Union refers to the Eurasian Customs Union, whose Member States are currently Armenia, Belarus, Kazakhstan, Kyrgyzstan and Russia.

[33] Decision of the Customs Union of 15 July 2011 No. 710 on approval of the technical regulations of the Customs Union "On the security of railway rolling stock", "On high-speed rail safety" and "On the safety of railway infrastructure", also referred to as Technical Regulations (001/2011, 002/2011 and 003/2011).

Regulations[34] of the CU, alleging that it was impossible to carry out inspections in Ukraine or that the applications were incomplete. Thirdly, Russian authorities refused to recognize conformity assessment certificates issued by other CU competent authorities if the certificates covered products made in a non-CU country (non-recognition requirement). Thus, Ukrainian suppliers holding a valid certificate of conformity issued by the Republic of Belarus or the Republic of Kazakhstan were not allowed to export their products to Russia. Finally, Ukraine alleged the systematic prevention of exports of Ukrainian railway products into Russia.

2.2. The Panel Report

The panel findings may be divided as follows:

2.2.1. Measures regarding the suspension instructions

i. Consistency of the suspensions with Article 5.1.1 of the TBT Agreement – National/MFN Treatment (Conformity Assessment) and with Article 5.1.2 of the TBT Agreement – Unnecessary Obstacles to International Trade

Ukraine requested that the Panel find each of the 14 instructions through which the Federal Budgetary Organization (FBO) suspended valid certificates of conformity held by Ukrainian producers of railway products inconsistent with Article 5.1.1[35] and Article 5.1.2[36] of the TBT Agreement. Furthermore, Ukraine submitted that Russia did not carry out the inspections requested, while Russia performed them in other countries. By doing so, Russia granted access to Ukrainian suppliers under conditions less favourable than those granted to suppliers from other countries and Russian suppliers in a comparable situation. Russia contended that due to the security situation in Ukraine, the Ukrainian situation could not be compared to the situation of these other countries.[37]

According to the Panel,[38] Ukraine failed to establish that Russia applied its conformity assessment procedure under less favourable conditions or that it applied the procedure more strictly than necessary.[39] These conclusions were reached considering the risks to life and health of Russian inspectors due to the security situation. Therefore, the situation in Ukraine was not comparable to those of other countries and Russia was justified in not sending its inspectors. Furthermore, Ukraine failed to demonstrate that there were less trade restrictive

---

[34] Technical Regulations (001/2011, 002/2011 and 003/2011).

[35] Panel Report, *Russia – Measures Affecting the Importation of Railway Equipment and Parts Thereof*, adopted on 30 July 2018, WT/DS499/R, para. 7.236.

[36] *Ibid.*, para. 7.396.

[37] *Ibid.*, paras. 7.242-243.

[38] *Ibid.*, paras. 7.389-393.

[39] *Ibid.*, paras. 7.538-543.

means of applying Russia's conformity assessment procedure, such as off-site inspections.

ii.   Consistency of the fourteen instruction suspensions with Article 5.2.2 of the TBT Agreement – Obligation to Transmit the Results of the Conformity Assessment

Ukraine claimed that, regarding the 14 instructions through which the FBO suspended valid certificates of conformity held by Ukrainian producers, Russia violated Article 5.2.2 "by failing to transmit as soon as possible the results of the conformity assessment in a precise and complete manner that would have allowed the applicants to take corrective actions, if necessary".[40]

The Panel concluded that Ukraine was right, except as to one suspension, finding that Russia's certification body had indeed not transmitted the results of the assessments to the applicants, violating the third obligation in Article 5.2.2 of the TBT Agreement.[41]

2.2.2.   Measures regarding the new applications for conformity assessment certificates rejected by the FBO

i.   Consistency of the three rejection decisions under the third obligation of Article 5.2.2 of the TBT Agreement – Obligation to Transmit the Results of the Conformity Assessment in a precise and complete manner to the applicant so that corrective action may be taken if necessary

Ukraine claimed that, in respect of decisions 1 and 2, Russia did not comply with the third obligation of Article 5.2.2 of the TBT Agreement because Russia "failed to transmit in a precise and complete manner the results of the preliminary assessment. Which would have allowed the applicant to take corrective action". As to decision 3, according to Ukraine, Russia did not inform the relevant producer in a precise and complete manner of the results of the FBO's assessment.[42]

The Panel found that the Ukrainian applicants were informed that it was not possible to carry out a certification procedure in full, though the FBO did not make clear which part of the assessment procedure it was referring to in decisions 1 and 2. Furthermore, these decisions did not provide any information about the reasons for the impossibility. Consequently, the applicants had no way to assess whether corrective action could be taken. The Panel upheld Ukraine's claims as to decisions 1 and 2 and ruled that Russia had failed to comply with the third obligation of Article 5.2.2 of the TBT Agreement.[43]

---

[40] *Ibid.*, para. 7.546.
[41] *Ibid.*, para. 7.591.
[42] *Ibid.*, paras. 7.773-774.
[43] *Ibid.*, para. 7.785.

ii.   Consistency of the three rejection decisions under the second obligation of Article 5.2.2 of the TBT Agreement – Obligation to promptly examine the completeness of the documentation and duly to inform the applicant in a precise and complete manner of all deficiencies

Next, the Panel examined Ukraine's claims under the second obligation of Article 5.2.2 of the TBT Agreement. In respect of all three decisions, Ukraine argued that the competent Russian authorities failed to promptly examine the completeness of the application documentation and to inform the relevant producers in a precise and complete manner of all deficiencies (the first and second part of the second obligation of Article 5.2.2). Regarding decisions 1 and 2, the Panel noted that nothing suggested that the FBO had found deficiencies in the applications, nor that it had failed to act promptly in the matter. Thus, the Panel rejected Ukraine's claims regarding the second obligation of Article 5.2.2.[44] In respect of decision 3, the Panel concluded that the FBO had informed the applicant that its application had deficiencies and had provided information about the nature of the deficiencies in a clear and complete manner. Therefore, the Panel rejected Ukraine's challenge.[45]

2.2.3.   Measures concerning non-recognition requirement under Article 2.1 of the TBT Agreement (Preparation, Adoption and Application of Technical Regulations by Central Government Bodies)

Ukraine complained of Russia's non-recognition of CU Technical Regulation certificates issued by other CU countries, under TBT Agreement Article 2.1. The Panel found that the non-recognition requirement does not fall within the scope of Article 2.1 of the TBT Agreement because CU Technical Regulation 001/2011 "serves as the basis" for the non-recognition of the certificates. In other words, the non-recognition requirement concerns conformity assessments that differ from the substantive technical requirements used for the conformity assessment procedure. Thus, the Panel concluded that Ukraine did not establish that the non-recognition requirement falls within the scope of Article 2.1 of the TBT Agreement.[46]

2.2.4.   Claim under GATT Article I:1

Ukraine argued that Russia's decision not to accept in its territory the validity of certificates issued to Ukrainian producers in other CU countries, based on the requirement that only products manufactured in the territory of the CU may be subject to certification, is not compliant with Article I:1. Ukraine claimed

---

[44] *Ibid.*, paras. 7.786-797.
[45] *Ibid.*, paras. 7.798-805.
[46] *Ibid.*, para. 7.885.

that Russia's decision does not grant Ukrainian products the same advantages as those originating within CU territory.[47]

The Panel found that the competent Russian bodies did not recognize the validity of conformity certificates issued for Ukrainian railway products by certification bodies in other CU countries. However, Russia did recognize the validity of certificates issued by the same bodies for railway products manufactured in countries other than Ukraine. Given that all four elements of Article I:1[48] were demonstrated, the Panel ruled that, through the non-recognition requirement, Russia discriminated between railway products from Ukraine and those from other countries, in breach of Article I:1.[49]

2.2.5. Claim under GATT Article III:4

In addition, Ukraine claimed that Russia's non-acceptance of the validity of certificates issued to Ukrainian producers in other CU countries is inconsistent with Article III:4. According to Ukraine, this decision reserves a less favourable treatment to Ukrainian railway products than to products originating in other countries.[50]

The Panel recalled its finding regarding Article I:1, and determined that the non-recognition requirement does apply a less favourable treatment to Ukrainian imported products than to the like domestic ones.[51] Consequently, the Panel concluded that Ukraine had established that Russia discriminated between Ukrainian railway products and like domestic railway products, thus violating GATT Article III:4.[52]

2.2.6. Claims concerning the alleged systematic import prevention – existence of a measure

Ukraine also claimed that Russia had adopted measures that systematically prevent Ukrainian railway products from being imported into Russia, in breach of Articles I:1, XI:1 and XIII:1 GATT.

The Panel rejected this claim since the evidence did not establish that the alleged systematic import prevention measures were designed, structured or op-

---

[47] *Ibid.*, para. 7.887.

[48] The four elements are (a) the measure at issue must fall within the scope of application of Article I:1; (b) the imported products at issue must be like products; (c) the measure at issue grants an advantage, favour, privilege, or immunity to a product originating in the territory of any country; and (d) the advantage, favour, privilege, or immunity is not extended immediately and unconditionally to products originating in the territory of all Members. *Ibid.*, paras. 7.886 and 7.889.

[49] *Ibid.*, para. 7.907.

[50] *Ibid.*, para. 7.909.

[51] *Ibid.*, paras. 7.922-7.926.

[52] *Ibid.*, para. 7.928.

erated in combination to systematically prevent imports of Ukrainian railway products into Russia.[53]

2.3. The Appellate Body Report

Ukraine appealed the report, challenging the Panel's findings under Articles 5.1.1 and 5.1.2 TBT, as well as GATT Articles I:1, XI:1 and XIII:1, claiming also that the Panel failed to make an objective assessment under DSU Article 11. Russia cross-appealed the ruling, alleging errors under DSU Articles 6.2, 7.1 and 11, concerning the Panel's finding on the third measure regarding the non-recognition of certificates issued in CU countries other than Russia.

The AB report included the following key findings:[54]

2.3.1. Russia's claims regarding the Panel's preliminary ruling under Articles 6.2, 7.1 and 11 of the DSU (Identification of Measures/ Legal Basis of Claims/ Terms of Reference)

Russia submitted that the Panel had erred in establishing that Ukraine's panel request correctly linked the contested measures with the appropriate legal basis.[55]

The AB rejected Russia's claims that the Panel erred in its preliminary ruling. The AB confirmed that the Panel correctly analyzed the linkages between the measures challenged by Ukraine and the WTO provisions allegedly infringed, based on the text of the panel request.[56] The AB agreed with the Panel that Ukraine had correctly identified the measures at issue in its panel request. The AB also rejected Russia's claims under DSU Article 11.[57] The AB found that Russia did not establish that Ukraine failed to meet its *prima facie* evidentiary burden to establish the existence of the third measure and, thus, upheld the Panel's finding that the third measure had been demonstrated to exist.[58]

2.3.2. Existence of systematic import prevention

The AB found that the Panel had made an objective and holistic assessment under DSU Article 11 when examining the existence of an alleged systematic import prevention and whether the individual components of the alleged unwritten measures were part of a single plan aimed at impeding imports of Ukrainian

---

[53] *Ibid.*, para. 7.989-995.
[54] Appellate Body Report, *cit. supra* note 31.
[55] *Ibid.*, paras. 5.1 and 5.13.
[56] *Ibid.*, paras. 5.30-35.
[57] *Ibid.*, paras. 5.92-106.
[58] *Ibid.*, paras. 5.76-82.

products into Russia. The AB rejected Ukraine's appeal on the point and upheld the Panel decision.[59]

2.3.3. Ukraine's claims under Article 5.1.1 of the TBT Agreement ("comparable situation")

Ukraine challenged the Panel's interpretation and application of TBT Article 5.1.1, and specifically the interpretation of the phrase "in a comparable situation". Ukraine claimed that the Panel failed to elaborate on what exactly must be compared.

The AB found that the Panel did not err in interpreting the phrase "in a comparable situation" in TBT Article 5.1.1.[60] As to the application of Article 5.1.1, Ukraine complained that the Panel had relied on general considerations about the political and internal security situation in Ukraine, without considering the specific situation relevant to the railway products suppliers. The AB clarified that the factors to be considered should be specific to the suppliers of like products who are claimed to have been granted access under less favourable conditions and the location of the suppliers' facilities.

Consequently, the AB reversed the Panel's decision on the application of Article 5.1.1 to the facts of the present case,[61] since the Panel relied only on information on the record regarding the general security situation in Ukraine and the anti-Russian sentiment.

2.3.4. Ukraine's claims under Article 5.1.2 of the TBT Agreement – Unnecessary Obstacles to Trade ("Less Trade-Restrictive Alternatives")

Ukraine requested the AB to reverse the Panel's ruling as, according to Ukraine, the Panel erred in allocating the burden of proof under Article 5.1.2 by finding that Ukraine had failed to establish that the proposed less trade-restrictive measures were reasonably available.

The AB recalled that it is on the complainant to establish that a challenged measure creates an unnecessary obstacle to international trade. In making its *prima facie* case, the complainant may also seek to identify a less restrictive alternative measure for applying conformity assessment procedures that ensures adequate confidence of conformity. In this respect, Ukraine had put forward four alternative measures.

The AB recalled that, while the complainant must establish that an alternative measure is less trade restrictive, makes an equivalent contribution and is reasonably available, the complainant is not supposed to provide detailed information on how it could be implemented by the respondent. The AB held that, even if

---

[59] *Ibid.*, para. 5.251.
[60] *Ibid.*, paras. 5.129-136.
[61] *Ibid.*, paras. 5.149 and 5.154-156.

the alternative proposed by Ukraine was encompassed by Russian legislation, it was hypothetical in nature, as it remained unapplied. Consequently, according to the AB, the burden of proof placed by the Panel on Ukraine went beyond what Ukraine was required to establish in making a *prima facie* case.[62] In conclusion, the AB faulted the Panel for not having properly allocated the burden of proof and reversed the Panel's finding that Ukraine had failed to establish that Russia acted inconsistently with Article 5.1.2, first and second sentence, for each of the 14 instructions suspending certificates.[63] However, having reversed the Panel finding, the AB declared that it was unable to complete the legal analysis because of insufficient factual findings on the record.[64]

2.4. Concluding remarks

In this highly technical and fact-intensive dispute, certain measures adopted by Russia were challenged under the TBT Agreement and the GATT 1994. The AB reversed the Panel's finding that Ukraine had failed to establish that Russia acted inconsistently with Articles 5.1.1 and 5.1.2 of the TBT Agreement, but it could not complete the assessment of whether Russia was justified in preventing imports of railway products from Ukraine. The question of whether Russia's conformity analysis was consistent with WTO provisions was thus left unanswered because of the lack of sufficient factual findings.[65] Russia commented that concluding with "no decision" could hardly be perceived as satisfactory, after years of litigation.[66]

This ruling was perceived as a "mixed" one, yet one more in favour of Ukraine.[67] Russia informed the DSB on 19 March 2020 that it had already brought all of its measures at issue into conformity with Russia's obligations under WTO Agreements.[68]

This dispute is part of the broader dispute between the Russian Federation and Ukraine stemming from two issues. The first relates to the annexation by Russia of the Crimea peninsula in 2014.[69] The second issue concerns Russian support of a separatist movement in eastern Ukraine since 2014.[70]

---

[62] *Ibid.*, paras. 5.198-200.

[63] *Ibid.*, paras. 5.201-211.

[64] *Ibid.*, paras. 5.205.

[65] SOHLBERG, "Russia – Measures Affecting the Importation of Railway Equipment and Parts Thereof, DS499", World Trade Review, 2020, p. 476 ff.

[66] Available at <https://economy.gov.ru/material/file/6cec657781d71cb25538ada73b880f4e/DS499.pdf>.

[67] FARGE, BLENKINSHOP and ALKOUSAA, "WTO Issues Mixed Ruling in Russia, Ukraine rail Dispute", Reuters, 4 February 2020.

[68] Available at: <https://economy.gov.ru/material/file/6cec657781d71cb25538ada73b880f4e/DS499.pdf>.

[69] Putin Reclaims Crimea for Russia and Bitterly Denounces the West, The New York Times, 18 March 2014.

[70] Russia Steps up Help for Rebels in Ukraine War, The New York Times, 25 July 2014. See *Russia – Measures Affecting the Importation of Railway Equipment and Parts Thereof*, Communication from the Russian Federation, WT/DS499/11.

The present dispute brought by Ukraine against Russia at the WTO must therefore be viewed within the framework of the complex phenomenon named "disaggregation of disputes".[71] This term indicates the separation of complex inter-State disputes into different legal claims introduced before distinct international tribunals under distinct treaties. In this context, the WTO dispute settlement system has necessarily adopted the so-called severability approach, limiting its jurisdiction to the specific claims submitted under the relevant trade agreements.[72] As is well known, in recent years, Ukraine has brought different claims against Russia before various *fora*,[73] thus evidencing the so called "compartmentalization" of broader disputes into discrete legal claims.[74]

In conclusion, considering the critical geo-political situation between Russia and Ukraine, this dispute shows the ability of the WTO dispute settlement system to deal also with politically sensitive disputes, thus ensuring the stability of the multilateral trading system, as far as possible, amidst international tensions.

ROSALBA FAMÀ[*]

3. APPELLATE BODY REPORT, *UNITED STATES – COUNTERVAILING MEASURES ON SUPERCALENDERED PAPER FROM CANADA*[75]

3.1. Introduction and main facts of the dispute

At issue in this dispute is the legality and consistency of certain countervailing duties (CVD), imposed by the US in 2015, with respect to imports of Supercalendered Paper (SC) from Canada.

On 9 June 2016, after unsuccessful consultations with the US, Canada requested the establishment of a Panel to review countervailing measures adopted by the US with respect to SC paper from Canada, as well as the US's "ongoing conduct" of applying adverse facts available (AFA) in respect of information on other forms of financial assistance discovered during a CVD investigation.[76] The Panel was asked to review whether the measures adopted by the US Department of Commerce (USDOC) were consistent with Articles 1.1(a)(1), 1.1(b), 2, 10,

---

[71] CAWTHORNE, "International Litigation and the Disaggregation of Disputes: Ukraine/Russia as a Case Study", ICLQ, 2019, p. 779 ff.

[72] *Ibid.*, pp. 779-815.

[73] Such as the International Court of Justice and the European Court of Human Rights.

[74] The term "compartmentalization" is used by CANNIZZARO and BONAFÉ, "Fragmenting International Law Through Compromissory Clauses? Some Remarks of the ICJ in the Oil Platforms case", EJIL, 2005, p. 481 ff., p. 484.

[*] PhD candidate in European and International Law, Bocconi University, Milan.

[75] Appelate Body Report, United States – *Countervailing Measures on Supercalendered Paper from Canada*, adopted on 5 March 2020, WT/DS505/AB/R.

[76] Panel Report, *United States – Countervailing Measures on Supercalendered Paper from Canada*, circulated on 5 July 2018, WT/DS505/R, para. 1.1.

11.1, 11.2, 11.3, 11.6, 12.1, 12.2, 12.3, 12.7, 12.8, 14, 19.1, 19.3, 19.4 and 32.1 of the SCM Agreement and Article VI:3 of the GATT 1994.[77]

The Panel report was issued to the parties on 15 December 2017 and was then circulated on 5 July 2018.

3.2. The Panel Report

The report is organized in four sections, respectively dealing with: (i) Canada's claims with regards to the USDOC's determination on Port Hawkesbury Paper LP (PHP); (ii) claims with regards to the determination on Resolute FP Canada Inc. (Resolute); (iii) claims concerning the USDOC's determination on Irving Paper Ltd. (Irving) and Catalyst Paper Corporation (Catalyst); (iv) claims with regards to the US's alleged "ongoing conduct" of applying AFA in the context of programmes discovered during CVD investigations that were not reported in response to an "other forms of assistance" (OFA) question, along with the question of whether Canada had provided sufficient evidence of the "ongoing conduct" and the likelihood of future continuance.[78]

3.2.1. Claims concerning the USDOC's determination on PHP

A first set of claims looked at by the Panel with regards to PHP concerned the distribution of electricity to PHP by Nova Scotia power supplier NSPI, which the US had determined constituted a "financial contribution that provides a benefit".[79] According to Canada, the US had mistakenly determined that the provision of electricity "for less than adequate remuneration" had in fact conferred a given benefit to PHP.

After having reviewed the positions of the parties, the Panel held that the USDOC's determination that the provision of electricity by NSPI to PHP conferred a benefit was inconsistent with Article 1.1(a)(1)(iv) of the SCM Agreement, given the failure by the USDOC to exhaustively explain how NSPI was in fact entrusted with responsibility to provide electricity to PHP and how the Government of Nova Scotia "exercised its authority" over the provision of electricity by NSPI to potential customers, including PHP.[80]

The Panel also found the USDOC's determination to be inconsistent with Articles 1.1(b) and 14(d) of the SCM Agreement,[81] which establish the existence of a subsidy "if a benefit is thereby conferred".[82] The Panel considered that the provision of electricity by NSPI to PHP should not have been judged as confer-

---

[77] *Ibid.*, para. 3.1.
[78] *Ibid.*, para. 7.1.
[79] *Ibid.*, para. 7.9.
[80] *Ibid.*, para. 7.59.
[81] *Ibid.*, para. 7.78.
[82] SCM Agreement, Article 1.1(b).

ring a benefit to PHP unless "the provision is made for less than adequate remuneration or the purchase is made for more than adequate remuneration".[83]

3.2.2. Claims concerning the USDOC's determination on Resolute

A second set of claims assessed by the Panel concerned the question of whether the USDOC had acted inconsistently with Articles 11.2, 11.3, 12.1, 12.2, 12.3 and 12.7 of the SCM Agreement, with respect to: (i) the application of adverse facts available (AFA) to Resolute in the context of information discovered at verification; (ii) the failure to provide Canada and Resolute with the relevant findings prior to the final determination; and (iii) the initiation of an investigation into subsidies discovered during Resolute's verification without properly assessing the actual existence of the subsidies in question.[84]

With respect to Article 12.7, the Panel held that the USDOC's application of AFA to Resolute was, indeed, in violation of the relevant provision, given the failure to provide proper explanation for using facts other than those discovered during Resolute's verification,[85] and the failure to establish that information necessary for the USDOC's investigation into the subsidies discovered was in fact missing.[86]

3.2.3. Claims concerning the PPGTP, FSPF, and NIER programmes

The third set of claims brought by Canada required the Panel to assess whether the countervailing duties levied by the US in respect of alleged subsidies given to Supercalendered (SC) Paper, and financial contributions paid to Resolute under the PPGTP,[87] FSPF[88] and NIER[89] programmes, were in violation of Articles 10, 19.1, 19.3 and 19.4 of the SCM Agreement, as well as Article VI:3 of the GATT 1994.[90] The Panel held that the countervailing duties (CVDs) were imposed in violation of Article IV:3 of the GATT and Article 10 of the SCM Agreement.[91]

---

[83] Ibid., Article 14(d).

[84] Panel Report, cit. supra note 75, para. 7.155.

[85] Ibid., para. 7.185.

[86] Ibid., para. 7.186.

[87] According to the USDOC, the purpose of this programme is to improve the environmental performance of Canada's pulp and paper industry: see para. 7.217.

[88] The FSPF programme supports capital investment projects in value-added manufacturing, increased fiber use efficiencies, energy conservation/efficiency and development of electricity co-generation: see para. 7.219.

[89] The purpose of the NIER programme is to assist Northern Ontario's qualifying industrial electricity consumers which commit to developing and implementing an energy management plan: see para. 7.218.

[90] Panel Report, cit. supra note 76, para. 7.215.

[91] Ibid., para. 7.240. A consequentialist approach was adopted by the Appelate Body in a number of cases, inter alia, US – Countervailing and Anti-Dumping Measures (China), adopted on 24 July 2014, WT/DS449/AB/R, paras. 4.19-4.21; US – Anti-Dumping and Countervailing

3.2.4. Claims concerning the USDOC's determination on Irving and Catalyst

Also with respect to SC Paper producers Irving and Catalyst, the Panel found that the USDOC had acted in violation of provisions under the SCM Agreement and the GATT 1994 "by improperly calculating an all-others rate for Irving and Catalyst".[92]

The Panel observed that the fact that the SCM Agreement does not prescribe a methodology for calculating a CVD rate for non-investigated exporters, does not translate into a right of authorities to impose the CVD rate they prefer;[93] rather, Members are required to impose CVDs in accordance with the SCM Agreement and the GATT 1994.[94] Accordingly, the Panel found the USDOC's determination of the all-others rate on the basis of Resolute's rate to be in violation of Articles 19.3 and 19.4 of the SCM Agreement, and Article VI:3 of the GATT 1994.[95]

3.2.5. Claims concerning the "Other Forms of Assistance-AFA measure"

The final set of claims brought by Canada concerned the USDOC's unwritten measure of "applying AFA to subsidy programmes discovered during the course of a CVD investigation that were not reported in response to the 'other forms of assistance' question".[96] Canada considered the measure an "ongoing conduct" repeatedly adopted by the USDOC and evidenced not only in the course of a number of investigations since 2012 but also through changes in US legislation and public policy.[97]

In order to evaluate Canada's claims that the challenged measure amounted to "ongoing conduct", the Panel considered whether Canada had: (i) demonstrated the existence of the ongoing conduct attributed to the United States; (ii) provided enough evidence to establish the content of the conduct; and (iii) established the repeated application of the conduct, as well as the likelihood of its continuation.

With respect to (i), the Panel took into account that "any act or omission attributable to a WTO Member can be a measure of that Member for purposes of dispute settlement proceedings";[98] however, the Panel also recalled the warning by the AB that "a panel must not lightly assume the existence of a 'rule or norm'

Duties (China), adopted on 25 March 2011, WT/DS379/AB/R, para. 358; and *US – Softwood Lumber IV*, adopted on 17 February 2004, WT/DS257/AB/R, para. 143.

[92] Panel Report, *cit. supra* note 76, para. 7.243.

[93] *Ibid.*, para. 7.259.

[94] *Ibid.*

[95] *Ibid.*, paras. 7.274 and 7.275.

[96] *Ibid.*, para. 7.293.

[97] *Ibid.*, para. 7.295.

[98] Appelate Body Report, *US – Corrosion-Resistant Steel Sunset Review*, adopted on 9 January 2004, WT/DS244/AB/R, para. 81. See also Appelate Body Reports, *US – Softwood Lumber IV* (Article 21.5 – Canada), adopted on 20 December 2005, WT/DS257/AB/RW, para. 67; and *US – Anti-Dumping Methodologies (China)*, adopted on 23 May 2017, WT/DS471/AB/R, para. 5.122.

constituting a measure of general and prospective application, especially when it is not expressed in the form of a written document".[99]

To assess (ii), the Panel looked at a number of tables submitted by Canada, concerning the "other forms of assistance" question, included in the USDOC's investigations since 2012, concluding that Canada had in fact provided enough evidence to establish the "precise content" of the unwritten measure.[100]

As to (iii), the Panel examined the USDOC's post-2012 investigations and determinations and held that the US had continued to act "substantially in the same manner when treating information discovered at verification that it considers should have been provided in response to the 'other forms of assistance' question".[101] It therefore concluded that Canada had successfully demonstrated the repeated application of the measure in question. Finally, the Panel found that the evidence also conclusively pointed to the likelihood of continuation of the measure.[102] In particular, the Panel held that "the consistent manner in which the USDOC refers to the measure suggests that the challenged conduct is likely to continue".[103]

Overall, the Panel concluded that the "ongoing conduct" measure adopted by the USDOC was inconsistent with Article 12.7 of the SCM Agreement.

3.3   The Appellate Body Report

The US appealed the following findings of the Panel report: (i) that the OFA-AFA measure amounted to "ongoing conduct"; (ii) the Panel's alleged failure to provide "a basic rationale" for its determination; and (iii) that the OFA-AFA measure was in violation of Article 12.7 of the SCM Agreement.[104] The AB report was circulated on 6 February 2020 and adopted on 5 March 2020.

---

[99] See Appellate Body Report, *US – Zeroing* (EC), adopted on 9 May 2006, WT/DS294/AB/R, para. 196. In para. 197, the AB explains that "when an 'as such' challenge is brought against a 'rule or norm' that is expressed in the form of a written document – such as a law or regulation – there would, in most cases, be no uncertainty as to the existence or content of the measure that has been challenged. The situation is different, however, when a challenge is brought against a 'rule or norm' that is not expressed in the form of a written document. In such cases, the very existence of the challenged 'rule or norm' may be uncertain".

[100] Panel Report, *cit. supra* note 76, para. 7.316. Here the Panel notes that "the variations pointed out by the United States in the wording of the 'other forms of assistance' question, as well as the relevant excerpts of USDOC determinations, do not detract from the fact that substance of the questions and the USDOC's conduct is the same. Variations in the wording of the questions appear to mainly be due to the circumstances of any given investigation while the object of the question remains in essence the same".

[101] *Ibid.*, para. 7.324.

[102] *Ibid.*, para. 7.326.

[103] *Ibid.*, para. 7.328. As to whether the USDOC's conduct amounts to practice under US law, the Panel asserts that such determination is ultimately irrelevant as to the likelihood of the future continuation of the measure in question: "we do not consider that Canada is required to prove the 'certainty' of the future application of the 'Other Forms of Assistance-AFA measure', but rather the likelihood that it will continue to apply".

[104] Appellate Body Report, *cit. supra* note 75, para. 4.1.

3.3.1. Other forms of assistance and "ongoing conduct" as an "unwritten measure"

As to the first finding appealed, the AB found that the Panel was in fact correct in determining the specific content,[105] repeated application[106] and likelihood of continued application[107] of the USDOC's conduct. Specifically with regards to the measure's likelihood of continued application, the AB determined that Canada had provided enough evidence to support the claim that the alleged OFA-AFA measure was likely to continue to be applied by the USDOC, as evidenced by a number of factors analyzed by the Panel.[108]

3.3.2. Article 12.7 of the SCM Agreement and "basic rationale"

The United States appealed the Panel's conclusion that the OFA-AFA measure was in violation of Article 12.7 of the SCM Agreement, claiming the Panel's failure to provide a "basic rationale" for its determination.[109] The AB explained how the "basic rationale" requirement, enshrined in Article 12.7 of the DSU, establishes a minimum standard for the reasoning which must be taken into account by panels when providing their findings and recommendations.[110] In other words, "panels must provide explanations and reasons sufficient to disclose the essential, or fundamental, justification for those findings and recommendations".[111] After reviewing the Panel report in its entirety, the AB concluded that the Panel did not fail to provide a "basic rationale" under Article 12.7 of the DSU when determining that the OFA-AFA measure was in violation of Article 12.7 of the SCM Agreement.[112]

3.3.3. The Panel's finding that the OFA-AFA measure was in violation of Article 12.7 of the SCM Agreement

The final issue appealed by the United States was the Panel's finding that the OFA-AFA measure was inconsistent with Article 12.7 of the SCM Agreement. According to the US, the Panel failed to consider the "significantly impedes"

---

[105] *Ibid.*, para. 5.24.

[106] *Ibid.*, para. 5.41.

[107] *Ibid.*, para 5.47.

[108] The Panel's conclusion in this regard, which was reiterated by the AB, was supported by the "manner in which the USDOC refers to the alleged OFA-AFA measure, the frequent reference to previous applications of the alleged measure in USDOC determinations, the fact that the USDOC refers to the alleged measure as its 'practice', and the USDOC's characterization of a departure from the alleged measure as an 'inadvertent error'".

[109] Appellate Body Report, *cit. supra* note 75, para. 5.50.

[110] *Ibid.*, para. 5.62.

[111] *Ibid.*, para. 5.62.

[112] *Ibid.*, para. 5.68.

ground for application of "facts available" under Article 12.7 of the SCM Agreement. The AB considered the contexts in which "facts available" can be applied under the relevant provision by interested parties or Members,[113] keeping in mind the claim by the United States that failure to answer the OFA question could amount to impedance of an investigation, therefore triggering the application of "facts available". It concluded that the Panel correctly chose not to consider the "significantly impedes" ground for the use of "facts available" under Article 12.7 of the SCM Agreement.[114]

The AB also upheld the Panel's finding that the USDOC's response to the information on assistance it discovered during verification was indeed in violation of Article 12.7.

Finally, the AB concluded that the Panel did not imply that the OFA question could never be a request for "necessary information", since it specifically stated that "the OFA question might pertain to necessary information regarding additional subsidization of the product under investigation".[115]

In conclusion, the AB upheld the Panel's finding that the OFA-AFA measure was inconsistent with Article 12.7 of the SCM Agreement.

3.3.4. Dissenting Opinion of one Appellate Body Division Member

One AB Division member[116] observed that "ongoing conduct" is not a term found in WTO treaty agreements. Rather, it was adopted for the first time by the AB in its *US – Continued Zeroing* report, on the basis of the specific circumstances and facts of that case.[117] The dissenting member, appeared to agree with the US positions. The dissenter considered that in the case at hand, the Panel and the AB majority had gone beyond the reasoning in *US – Continued Zeroing* and had broadened the concept of "ongoing conduct" "into something akin to a 'rule or norm of general and prospective application', only vaguer and less disciplined in its requirements".[118] According to the dissenter, the Panel erred in concluding that the criteria necessary to establish an "ongoing conduct" measure were met in the case of the USDOC asking the OFA question, and further claimed that the Panel assessed such criteria vaguely by relying on inadequate and inappropriate

---

[113] The application of "facts available" under Article 12.7 of the SCM Agreement can be triggered by circumstances when an interested party or interested Member: (i) "refuses access to [...] necessary information within a reasonable period"; (ii) "otherwise does not provide [...] necessary information within a reasonable period"; or (iii) "significantly impedes the investigation".

[114] Appellate Body Report, *cit. supra* note 75, paras. 5.73 and 5.74.

[115] *Ibid.*, para. 5.83.

[116] The AB Division was made up of: Ujal S. Bhatia, Presiding Member; Thomas R. Graham and Hong Zhao, Members.

[117] Appellate Body Report, *cit. supra* note 75, para. 5.86.

[118] *Ibid.*

evidence to identify the content, repeated application and likelihood of continued application of the measure.[119]

Lastly, the dissenting member noted that the 2015 CVD order, in relation to SC Paper from Canada, had been revoked retroactively. Therefore, no dispute between Canada and the United States remained to be resolved and so there was no longer an issue of any "ongoing conduct". The dissenter concluded by expressing the hope that the AB decision's effects would be limited to the specific circumstances of the present case.[120]

3.4. Concluding remarks: the case and its follow-up in the current context of the WTO dispute settlement crisis

The dispute between Canada and the US is particularly significant in light of the current concerns over the WTO dispute settlement system and the ongoing US objections to the AB "precedent doctrine",[121] which was also alluded to in the dissenting opinion circulated with the Appellate Body Report. The US has blocked new appointments to fill vacancies in the AB, alleging the AB's "treatment of its past rulings as binding precedent".[122] In the dissenting opinion, the AB Division member expressed the view that such opinions should be taken into account in future considerations of similar issues,[123] in order to make clear that the AB is not bound by previous decisions.

Along similar lines, upon release of the AB Report, the US declared that "the document [...] heightens the concerns that the United States has been raising about the Appellate Body and its effect on the WTO dispute settlement system", representing "the latest example of its failure to respect WTO rules".[124] The US has pointed to many procedural and substantive issues which, it claims, make the report invalid and thus the US objects to the report's adoption.

Given the novel decision by the United States not to adopt and implement the recommendations made by the DSB, including with respect to its alleged "ongoing conduct" measure, Canada has requested the DSB to authorize it to

---

[119] *Ibid.*, para. 5.89.

[120] *Ibid.*, para. 5.93.

[121] In this respect see SACERDOTI, "The Authority of «Precedent» in International Adjudication: The Contentious Case of the WTO Appellate Body's Practice", The Law & Practice of International Courts and Tribunals, 2020, p. 497 ff.

[122] BACCHUS and LESTER, "The Rule of Precedent and the Role of the Appellate Body", JWT, 2020, p. 183 ff., p. 185.

[123] Appellate Body Report, *cit. supra* note 75, para. 5.95.

[124] *United States – Countervailing Measures on Supercalendered Paper from Canada*, Communication from the United States, WT/DS505/12, available at: <https://docs.wto.org/dol2fe/Pages/SS/directdoc.aspx?filename=q:/WT/DS/505-12.pdf&Open=True>. This has been reiterated also in an official statement by the US Trade Representative released after the circulation of the Panel Report. See Office of the US Trade Representative, "Statement on the WTO Panel Report in Canada's Challenge to U.S. Countervailing Duties on Supercalendered Paper", 6 July 2018, available at: <https://ustr.gov/about-us/policy-offices/press-office/press-releases/2018/july/ustr-robert-lighthizer-statement-wto>.

"suspend concessions or other obligations at an annual level commensurate with the trade effects of any future countervailing duties on Canadian imports of any given good that are attributable to the U.S. 'ongoing conduct' at issue in this dispute".[125]

ELENA ASSENZA*

4. PANEL REPORT, *UNITED STATES – TARIFF MEASURES ON CERTAIN GOODS FROM CHINA*[126]

4.1. *Introduction and main facts of the dispute*

Concerns about forced technology transfer, cybersecurity risks, unfair competition, and loss of business opportunities in connection to trade with and in China have long been raised by the United States Trade Office and US companies.[127] The origins of this dispute result from an investigation under Section 301 of the Trade Act of 1974 into whether "China's law, policies, practices, or actions […] may be unreasonable or discriminatory and […] may be harming American intellectual property rights, innovation, or technology development".[128] The report recommended addressing these matters with "more intensive bilateral engagement, WTO dispute settlement, and/or additional 301 investigations".[129] To "obtain the elimination"[130] of forced technology transfer, intellectual property theft, and cyberattacks on sensitive data, the report proposed imposing additional tariffs on Chinese products, in excess of those in the US's Schedule of Concessions under the GATT 1994.[131]

---

[125] *United States – Countervailing Measures on Supercalendered Paper from Canada*, Recourse to Article 22.2 of the DSU by Canada, 19 June 2020, WT/DS505/13, available at: <https://docs.wto.org/dol2fe/Pages/SS/directdoc.aspx?filename=q:/WT/DS/505-13.pdf&Open=True>.

* PhD candidate in European and International Law, Bocconi University, Milan.

[126] Panel Report, United States – *Tariff Measures on Certain Goods from China*, circulated on 15 September 2020, WT/DS543/R, appealed by the US on 26 October 2020.

[127] Office of the US Trade Representative, "Findings Of The Investigation Into China's Acts, Policies, And Practices Related To Technology Transfer, Intellectual Property, And Innovation Under Section 301 Of The Trade Act Of 1974", 22 March 2018, p. 9, available at: <https://ustr.gov/sites/default/files/Section%20301%20FINAL.PDF>.

[128] *Ibid.*, p. 4.

[129] *Ibid.*, p. 182.

[130] *Ibid.*, p. 5.

[131] The US initiated a dispute at the WTO in 2018 regarding discriminatory licensing technology measures, considering that such measures could be resolved through the WTO's dispute settlement system. A panel was formed, but on 8 June 2020, the US requested that the Panel suspend work and China agreed. Communication from the Panel, *China – Certain Measures Concerning the Protection of Intellectual Property Rights*, 22 June 2020, DS542, available at: <https://docs.wto.org/dol2fe/Pages/SS/directdoc.aspx?filename=q:/WT/DS/542-14.pdf>.

The US imposed additional duties of 25% on products on a list of 818 tariff subheadings[132] (List 1 Measure) on 20 June 2018.[133] On 21 September 2018, it imposed additional duties of 10% on products on a list of 5,745 subheadings and announced the rate would increase to 25% on 1 January 2019 (List 2 Measure). After two postponements, the increase occurred on 9 May 2019.[134] Simultaneously, the US engaged in bilateral negotiations with China with the goal of addressing and preventing forced technology transfer and intellectual property theft.

China, however, sought consultations under the WTO's dispute settlement system on 4 April 2018, thus requiring the US to raise its concerns on alleged forced technology transfer and intellectual property theft by China under the aegis of the WTO. Irrespective of the Economic and Trade Agreement (Phase One Agreement) concluded with the US, China requested the establishment of a panel, on 6 December 2018, on the basis that a mutually satisfactory agreement had not been reached between the two parties. The US responded that the parties had reached a solution by continuing to engage in negotiations, and, thus, the Panel should not make any legal determinations. Further, the US argued that one of the measures at issue in the dispute was outside of the Panel's terms of reference. Finally, the US claimed that any GATT inconsistent measures were justified under the public morals exception of Article XX of the GATT.

The Panel circulated its report on 15 September 2020, and on 26 October 2020, the US notified the DSB of its decision to submit an appeal to the Appellate Body (AB), which currently is unable to review appeals due to ongoing vacancies.

4.2. The Panel Report

4.2.1. Whether the parties had reached a solution within the meaning of Article 12.7 of the DSU

As a preliminary issue, the Panel addressed the US claims that it should only issue a brief statement of the facts and report that a settlement within the meaning of Article 12.7 of the Dispute Settlement Understanding (DSU) had been reached between the two parties by means of bilateral negotiations.[135] The US pointed to the Phase One Agreement as evidence that a solution had been found,[136] arguing that undertaking a bilateral negotiation process amounted to a solution under

---

[132] A tariff heading is a category of goods used to define products based on the World Customs Organization's Harmonized System (HS) code system. A subheading is a more detailed definition of products in that category. World Trade Organization, "HS 6-digit", available at: <https://www.wto.org/english/thewto_e/glossary_e/glossary_e.htm>.

[133] Panel Report, *cit. supra* note 126, para. 2.2.

[134] *Ibid.*

[135] *Ibid.*, para. 7.4.

[136] *Ibid.*

Article 12.7, although negotiations were ongoing.[137] The US also argued that as China had taken retaliatory tariff action against over $100 billion in US exports without first seeking authorization from the DSB, China's request for DSB findings on US tariff measures was an abuse of the dispute settlement system.[138] However, the US had decided not to bring any action against the tariffs imposed by China, as there was "no live WTO matter at issue between the parties".[139] China instead argued that no mutually satisfactory agreement had been reached within the meaning of Article 3.6 of the DSU and that the Phase One Agreement was not legally relevant as it did not address the measures at issue and the additional duties remained in effect.[140] Further, it had not agreed to any process that would constrain the Panel from adjudicating the dispute and issuing findings and recommendations.[141]

The Panel considered that a WTO Member has broad discretion to bring a case whenever the Member believes that proceedings would be fruitful in leading to a solution to the dispute.[142] As the dispute settlement process is compulsory and automatic, WTO Members are "entitled" to a ruling by a WTO panel.[143] Thus, a Panel is required to proceed with its adjudicative responsibilities, unless the parties relinquish their rights by withdrawing the complaint, requesting a suspension which allows for the Panel's jurisdiction to lapse, or reaching a mutually satisfactory solution.[144]

The Panel concluded that China had not relinquished its right to an adjudication of the matter.[145] An engagement to pursue bilateral negotiations is not a mutually satisfactory solution within the meaning of Article 12.7.[146] Under the US' interpretation, which focused on the more general reference to "solution" in the last sentence of the Article, a "solution" would exist even if the bilateral negotiations fail to yield any results and the issues remain unresolved.[147] The Panel rejected such an interpretation, finding that "solution" refers to the phrase "mutually satisfactory solution" in the first sentence of the Article.[148] Thus, a satisfactory solution must be "a shared assessment" by both parties "that they have reached a solution".[149] As China insisted that the issues raised in the panel request remained unresolved, China had not agreed to terminate the dispute nor to seek a resolution outside of the WTO,[150] and, as no written evidence demonstrated that

---

[137] *Ibid.*, para. 7.5.
[138] US, *First Written Submissions: United States – Tariff Measures On Certain Goods From China*, 27 August 2019, DS543, paras. 35-36.
[139] *Ibid.*, para. 35.
[140] Panel Report, *cit. supra* note 126, para. 7.6.
[141] *Ibid.*
[142] *Ibid.*, para. 7.7.
[143] *Ibid.*
[144] *Ibid.*, para. 7.8.
[145] *Ibid.*, para. 7.19.
[146] *Ibid.*, para. 7.12.
[147] *Ibid.*
[148] *Ibid.*
[149] *Ibid.*, para. 7.12.
[150] *Ibid.*, para. 7.14.

a mutually agreed solution had been reached, the Panel determined that such a solution had not yet been found.[151] While negotiations can be pursued in parallel with an ongoing WTO dispute, these negotiations should not be interpreted so as to deny the complainant's right to request findings by the Panel.[152] Finally, as China had not withdrawn its complaint or requested a suspension, it had not relinquished its right to adjudication of the matter by the Panel.[153]

4.2.2.   Whether the Panel's terms of reference covered the tariff increase applied to the List 2 products

The Panel next examined whether the increase of the tariff rate from 10% to 25% on the List 2 products, imposed on 9 May 2019, was covered by the terms of reference China submitted on 6 December 2018. China argued the tariff increase was covered because it was "clearly" a modification of the List 2 Measure identified in the panel request; further, the measure anticipated the increase, and China noted this anticipated increase in its panel request.[154] The US argued that the tariff rate increase was a third measure with "its own, particular rationale" and was imposed after China "made it clear" it would not change its policies, increased duties on US exports, and retreated from specific agreed-upon commitments.[155]

The Panel noted that, generally, the measures in the panel's terms of reference must be in existence at the time of the establishment of the panel. However, amendments to referenced measures enacted after that date may be examined "if the panel request is broad enough to encompass such an amendment and the amendment does not change the 'essence' of the measure".[156] This determination is made on a case-by-case basis and cannot rely on pre-established factors.[157]

The Panel found the 25% rise in duties to be an amendment to the List 2 Measure cited in the terms of reference, covering the same products, and it was appropriate for it to make rulings on the measure as amended. According to the Panel, the rationale behind the increase did not "alter the nature or essence of the measure"; to the contrary, it "seems to confirm that the increase of the additional duties is intrinsically linked to the original measure […]".[158]

---

[151] *Ibid.*, para. 7.20.

[152] *Ibid.*, paras. 7.17 and 7.18.

[153] *Ibid.*, para. 7.19.

[154] *Ibid.*, para. 7.27.

[155] *Ibid.*, para. 7.41.

[156] *Ibid.*, para. 7.35, citing Panel Report, *Thailand — Customs and Fiscal Measures on Cigarettes from the Philippines (Recourse To Article 21.5 Of The DSU By The Philippines)*, circulated on 12 November 2018, WT/DS371/RW, para. 7.808 (currently in compliance proceedings).

[157] Panel Report, *cit. supra* note 126, para. 7.48.

[158] *Ibid.*, para. 7.53. The Panel followed prior WTO adjudicators in finding that broad references authorize a panel to consider legal instruments enacted after the panel's establishment, as "respondents could easily shield measures from scrutiny […] by amending minor aspects during dispute settlement proceedings". *Ibid.*, paras. 7.57 and 7.62.

4.2.3. *Whether the measures are inconsistent with Articles I:1 and II:1(a) and (b) of GATT '94*

i. *Whether China made a* prima facie *case of inconsistency of the List 1 and List 2 measures*

The Panel examined whether China had made a *prima facie* case that List 1 and List 2 measures were inconsistent with Articles I:1 and II:1(a) and (b) of the GATT.[159] Regarding Article I:1, China sufficiently demonstrated the measures were inconsistent:[160] 1) the measures fell within the scope of application of Article I:1 because they were custom duties; 2) the likeness of the List 1 and List 2 products with the products of other Members not subject to additional duties could be presumed, as the measures discriminated only on the basis of origin; 3) applying the additional tariffs only to Chinese products denied China the advantage of equal treatment with all other WTO Members of conformity with the bound tariff rates in the US's Schedule of Concessions; and 4) this advantage was not extended "immediately" or "unconditionally" to China.[161] China also established that the measures were inconsistent with Article II.1(a) and (b): the additional duties were custom duties in excess of the bound rates,[162] and the application of custom duties in excess of those provided for in the US schedule constituted "less favourable" treatment with regards to other contracting parties not subject to the additional duties.[163] As a result, China had established a *prima facie* case that the measures were inconsistent with Articles I:1 and II:1(a) and (b) of the GATT.

ii. *The United States' defence under Article XX of the GATT '94*

The Panel first assessed whether the US measures were provisionally justified under Article XX(a), before considering whether they met the requirements of the *chapeau* of Article XX. Article XX(a) provides an exception to a GATT inconsistent measure if the measure "is necessary to protect public morals".[164] However, a balance must be maintained between the right of a WTO Member to invoke Article XX exceptions and its obligations to respect the rights of other

---

[159] *Ibid.*, paras. 7.75-7.78.

[160] *Ibid.*, para. 7.81.

[161] *Ibid.*, paras. 7.82-7.86.

[162] *Ibid.*, paras. 7.91-7.93.

[163] *Ibid.*, para. 7.95.

[164] *Ibid.*, paras. 7.102 and 7.103. The *Chapeau* of Article XX further requires that the "measures are not applied in a manner which would constitute a means of arbitrary or unjustifiable discrimination between countries where the same conditions prevail, or a disguised restriction on international trade […]": Article XX GATT.

WTO Members.[165] The respondent, in this case the US, must demonstrate that there is "a sufficient nexus between the measure and the interest protected".[166]

The Panel examined whether the measures at issue concerned a public morals objective within the meaning of Article XX(a). The US asserted that the measures protected public morals because they were adopted to eliminate conduct by China that violated US standards of right and wrong, namely the unfair trade acts, policies, and practices outlined in the 301 report.[167] The US submitted several domestic legal instruments, such as state and federal laws, which reflect these standards.[168] China argued that the measures had purely economic objectives and that the term "public morals" in Article XX(a) does not encompass economic policy concerns.[169] The Panel pointed out that WTO Members are given deference in defining the scope of public morals with respect to prevailing societal values,[170] other subparagraphs of Article XX have an economic dimension,[171] and public morals objectives may frequently have inseparable economic aspects, such as measures targeting money laundering or fraud prevention.[172] Thus, the Panel found that the standards of right and wrong invoked by the US in the context of unfair competition and intellectual property theft could, at a conceptual level, be covered by the term "public morals" within the meaning of Article XX(a).[173]

Next the Panel considered whether the measures were designed to protect the public morals objective invoked by the US. China argued that the measures were not designed to apply to goods "embodying" content or conduct offensive to public morals.[174] The US argued that the measures were designed to create a disincentive for China to continue morally objectionable conduct (unfair trade practices).[175] As the design test is a preliminary step that should not be applied too strictly so as to foreclose proceeding with the analysis of an Article XX(a) defence,[176] and as it would have been difficult to assess at a general level whether the US measures were designed to protect public morals, the Panel proceeded to the next step.[177]

In line with prior WTO adjudicators, the Panel assessed whether the measures were necessary by weighing and balancing factors, including 1) the relative importance of the policy objective, 2) the trade restrictiveness of the measures, 3) the extent to which the measures contribute to the realization of the public moral

---

[165] Panel Report, *cit. supra* note 126, para. 7.106.

[166] *Ibid.*, para. 7.109, citing Appellate Body Report, *European Communities – Measures Prohibiting the Importation and Marketing of Seal Products*, adopted 16 June 2014, WT/DS400/AB/R, para. 5.169.

[167] Panel Report, *cit. supra* note 126, para. 7.113.

[168] *Ibid.*, para. 7.127.

[169] *Ibid.*, para. 7.133.

[170] *Ibid.*, para. 7.131.

[171] *Ibid.*, para. 7.136.

[172] *Ibid.*, para. 7.137.

[173] *Ibid.*, para. 7.138.

[174] *Ibid.*, para. 7.143.

[175] *Ibid.*, para. 7.147.

[176] *Ibid.*, paras. 7.151-153.

[177] *Ibid.*, para. 7.151.

objective, and 4) whether a less restrictive alternative proposed by the complainant is reasonably available to the responding Member.[178]

Then the Panel examined the extent to which the measures contributed to the public morals objective by determining whether "a genuine relationship of ends and means between the objective pursued and the measure at issue" existed.[179] The Panel noted that an assertion that a measure contributes to the public morals objective must be supported by evidence demonstrating this contribution.[180] While the US submitted legal instruments that identified a broad range of Chinese products (the initial List 1) and industries that benefited from industrial policies, such as "Made in China 2025", the US did not submit a list of US industries that had allegedly been affected by those practices.[181] The evidence did not demonstrate how the US associated those Chinese industrial policies with specific Chinese products allegedly benefiting from policies considered to violate public morals.[182] Thus, the evidence submitted by the US failed to demonstrate a genuine relationship of ends and means between the imposition of duties on List 1 products and the public morals objective.

Regarding the List 2 products, the Panel concluded that a genuine relationship with a public morals objective could not be derived from the potential existence of a relation to the List 1 Measure; thus, the US failed to adequately demonstrate a genuine relationship between the additional duties imposed on the List 2 products and the invoked public morals objective.[183]

4.2.4. Recommendations by the Panel

In view of its findings summarized above, the Panel recommended that the US bring its measures into conformity with its obligations under the GATT.[184] The Panel also, somewhat surprisingly, encouraged the parties to pursue further efforts to achieve a mutually satisfactory solution to the issues raised in the dispute.[185]

4.3. Concluding remarks

The US submitted its notice to appeal on 26 October 2020. However, as there are currently no sitting members of the AB, due to the US blocking the appoint-

---

[178] *Ibid.*, paras. 7.158-7.159.
[179] *Ibid.*, para. 7.174-175.
[180] *Ibid.*, para. 7.176.
[181] *Ibid.*, para. 7.192.
[182] *Ibid.*, para. 7.194.
[183] *Ibid.*, para. 7.222.
[184] *Ibid.*, para. 8.4.
[185] *Ibid.*, para. 9.5.

ment of new members, this dispute is now left in a judicial limbo.[186] The US Trade Representative was highly critical of the Panel's decision and continues to question whether the WTO is an adequate forum for providing remedies to intellectual property theft in China.[187] The US's decision to appeal may have a strategic purpose – the US is not required to modify the measures until the DSB adopts the decision of the AB, and that date is not in the near future. Outgoing Trade Representative Robert Lighthizer urged President Biden to maintain the tariffs to keep pressure on China to revise the practices and policies of concern to the US.[188] However, it is uncertain to what extent Mr Biden will keep the Trump Administration's tariffs as some of his advisors question whether unilateral action by the US has resulted in significant reforms to Chinese trade and intellectual property policies.

Intellectual property lawyers in the US may not be surprised to learn that the US based its public morals defence on standards of right and wrong regarding competition and economic integrity that preserve US democratic and social institutions, rather than on standards regarding offensive content or conduct.[189] In 2019, the US Supreme Court found a federal trademark law prohibiting the registration of trademarks containing immoral or scandalous terms was a violation of the First Amendment right of freedom of speech (trademarks are a form of speech).[190] Federal registration provides advantages when using the mark in US commerce. As the law allowed examiners broad discretion in determining what is immoral or scandalous, many trademarks could be refused registration based on an examiner's subjective viewpoint and consequently be denied certain benefits for trade in the US. While the Court's decision would not be sufficient evidence in a WTO dispute to demonstrate how a particular measure contributes to a public moral objective,[191] the decision illustrates that "public morals" in the US are not intrinsically linked with concepts of offensive conduct or content (such as China contends), but rather with the preservation of democratic principles, such as freedom of speech, and protection of the economic activity of the US.

DIANA WADE*

---

[186] China decried the US appeal, labelling it "an abuse of procedural rules" at the DSB of 14 December 2020, noting that the US had not subscribed to the alternative appeal arbitration (MPIA) either: see WT/DSB/M/446, p. 12.

[187] Office of the US Trade Representative, "WTO Report on US Action Against China Shows Necessity for Reform", 19 September 2020, available at: <https://ustr.gov/about-us/policy-offices/press-office/press-releases/2020/september/wto-report-us-action-against-china-shows-necessity-reform>.

[188] "Trade Chief Lighthizer Urges Biden to Keep Tariffs on China", Wall Street Journal, 11 January 2021, available at: <https://www.wsj.com/articles/trade-chief-lighthizer-urges-biden-to-keep-tariffs-on-china-11610361001>.

[189] Panel Report, *cit. supra* note 126, para. 7.128.

[190] *Iancu v. Brunetti*, 139 S.Ct. 2294, 2019 WL 2570622 (2019); DONNER, "Supreme Court: Ban on Immoral/Scandalous Trademarks Held Unconstitutional", Manatt, 30 July 2019, available at: <https://www.manatt.com/insights/articles/2019/supreme-court-ban-on-immoral-scandalous-trademarks>.

[191] Panel report, *cit. supra* note 126, para. 7.238.

*PhD candidate in European and International Law, Bocconi University, Milan.

5. Panel Report, *Saudi Arabia – Measures Concerning the Protection of Intellectual Property Rights*[192]

5.1. Introduction and main facts of the dispute

The Gulf diplomatic crisis erupted in 2017 between Qatar and the Arab Quartet (Saudi Arabia, Egypt, United Arab Emirates and Bahrain).[193] To be precise, on 5 June 2017, Saudi Arabia, the UAE, Egypt and Bahrain severed their relations with Qatar, stating that it had been financing terrorism.[194] In particular, the four above-mentioned Gulf States accused Qatar of supporting Islamist groups, such as the Muslim Brotherhood, and disapproved of Qatar's relations with Iran. Yemen, the Maldives and Libya followed with their own restrictions.[195] On 22 June 2017, Qatar was requested to comply with a list of 13 demands presented to it by Saudi Arabia. Qatar refused to comply, asserting that it would not agree to any measures that threaten its sovereignty or violate international law.[196] The Gulf countries responded by imposing an air, sea and land blockade on Qatar.[197] The measures imposed on Qatar had a significant impact on its economy, given its geographically-determined dependence on trade with its neighbours.[198]

Qatar requested consultations with Saudi Arabia, on 9 November 2018, with respect to measures imposed by Saudi Arabia. In short, Qatar identified six types of measures imposed by Saudi Arabia: (1) the 19 June 2017 Circular,

---

[192] Panel Report, *Saudi Arabia – Measures Concerning the Protection of Intellectual Property Rights*, circulated on 16 June 2020, WT/DS567/R.

[193] The Gulf region has been intertwined with many conflicts in the past. See, for example, on the war from 1990-1991, Halliday, "The Gulf War 1990–1991 and the Study of International Relations", Review of International Studies, 1994, p. 109 ff. In 2014, there was another rift between Qatar and three Gulf countries – UAE, Saudi Arabia and Bahrain. See Aboudi et al., "Saudi Arabia, UAE and Bahrain End Rift with Qatar, Return Ambassadors", Reuters, 16 November 2014, available at: <https://www.reuters.com/article/us-gulf-summit-ambassadors/saudi-arabia-uae-and-bahrain-end-rift-with-qatar-return-ambassadors-idUSKC-N0J00Y420141116>.

[194] For a concise overview of the conflict, see "Why Gulf Countries Are Feuding with Qatar", The Economist, 21 June 2018, available at: <https://www.economist.com/special-report/2018/06/21/why-gulf-countries-are-feuding-with-qatar>.

[195] For a timeline of the dispute, see "Qatar-Gulf Crisis: All the Latest Updates", Al Jazeera, 2 August 2018, available at: <https://www.aljazeera.com/news/2017/06/qatar-diplomatic-crisis-latest-updates-170605105550769.html>; and "Qatar Crisis: What You Need to Know", BBC News, 19 July 2017, available at: <https://www.bbc.com/news/world-middle-east-40173757>.

[196] For the demands of the Arab States, see "Arab States Issue 13 Demands to End Qatar-Gulf Crisis", Al Jazeera, 12 July 2017, available at: <https://www.aljazeera.com/news/2017/06/arab-states-issue-list-demands-qatar-crisis-170623022133024.html>.

[197] Mulla, "December 2017 Overview I Qatar Diplomatic Crisis – Where Are We Now?", Baker and McKenzie Client Alert, 15 December 2017.

[198] On economic implications of the Gulf crisis, see Kabbani, "The High Cost of High Stakes: Economic Implications of the 2017 Gulf Crisis", Brookings, 15 June 2017, available at: <https://www.brookings.edu/blog/markaz/2017/06/15/the-high-cost-of-high-stakes-economic-implications-of-the-2017-gulf-crisis/>.

(2) "anti-sympathy" measures (the measures that, directly or indirectly, had the result of preventing beIN (a Media Group headquartered in Qatar) from obtaining Saudi legal counsel to enforce its IP rights through civil enforcement procedures before Saudi courts and tribunals), (3) the travel restrictions, (4) the Ministerial approval requirement, (5) the non-application of criminal procedures and penalties, and (6) the promotion of public gatherings with screenings of the Qatar broadcasting entity beoutQ's unauthorized broadcasts.[199] Qatar claimed that the above-mentioned measures violated Articles 3.1, 4, 9, 14.3, 16.1, 41.1, 42 and 61 of the TRIPS Agreement.[200] Saudi Arabia, on its side, claimed that the Panel should abstain from reviewing Qatar's substantive claims since Saudi's measures could be justified by the security exception of Article 73(b)(iii) TRIPS.[201]

The Panel issued its report to the parties on 27 April 2020 and circulated it on 16 June 2020. Saudi Arabia appealed the report on 28 July 2020. However, following the ongoing crisis at the WTO Appellate Body, there is no Appellate Body division available to deal with this case.[202]

5.2. The Panel Report

It should be mentioned that Saudi Arabia requested that the Panel decline to make any findings or recommendations, since the dispute is not a trade dispute at all, but a political, geopolitical and essential security dispute. That said, Saudi Arabia did not explicitly claim that the Panel had no jurisdiction or that the issue before it was non-justiciable.[203] Following its analysis, the Panel concluded that it could not decline to exercise its jurisdiction over the claims of WTO-inconsistency that fell within its terms of reference and that the matter was justiciable.[204]

As to the order of analysis, the Panel first assessed the inconsistency of the measures with various TRIPS obligations of Saudi Arabia. Then the Panel reviewed whether the invocation of Article 73(b)(iii) of the TRIPS Agreement could justify those inconsistent measures. The Panel explained that "[i]n considering the most appropriate order of analysis in which to address these issues, the Panel has a wide margin of discretion to order and structure its analysis as it sees fit".[205]

---

[199] Panel Report, *cit. supra* note 192, para. 2.47.

[200] *Ibid.*, para. 3.1.

[201] *Ibid.*, para. 3.3.

[202] WTO, "Saudi Arabia Appeals Panel Report Regarding Intellectual Property Measures", 30 July 2020, available at: <https://www.wto.org/english/news_e/news20_e/ds567apl_30jul20_e.htm>.

[203] Panel Report, *cit. supra* note 192, para. 7.8.

[204] *Ibid.*, para. 7.23.

[205] *Ibid.*, para. 7.3.

5.2.1. Measures

The Panel first addressed the existence of the measures in question and whether they were attributable to Saudi Arabia. Upon examination of the evidence, the Panel held that Qatar had not demonstrated that there were formal legal restrictions imposed by Saudi Arabia. However, the Panel established that

> the non-initiation of civil enforcement procedures against beoutQ before Saudi tribunals by beIN, the non-application of criminal procedures or penalties against beoutQ by the Government of Saudi Arabia and the public screening of beoutQ's illegal broadcasts of 2018 World Cup matches in Saudi Arabia are all the result of acts and omissions attributable to Saudi Arabia.[206]

Then the Panel analyzed whether the measures violated the provisions of Articles 41.1 (on civil and administrative procedures and remedies), 42 (general obligations) and 61 of the TRIPS Agreement (on criminal procedures).

As to the general obligations under Article 42 of the TRIPS Agreement, the Panel found that Saudi Arabia had taken measures that directly or indirectly resulted in preventing beIN from obtaining Saudi legal counsel to enforce its IP rights before Saudi courts. Moreover, the Panel stablished that the violation of Article 42 "gives rise to a consequential violation of the obligation under Article 41.1 to 'ensure that enforcement procedures as specified in this Part are available under their law'".[207]

As to the criminal procedures, the Panel concluded that Qatar had made a *prima facie* case that beoutQ was operated by individuals that were subject to the criminal jurisdiction of Saudi Arabia. BeIN and other right holders had informed Saudi Arabia about the alleged piracy by beoutQ. However, Saudi Arabia, on its part, did not take any actions to apply criminal procedures to beoutQ, but, on the contrary, its public authorities promoted public gatherings with screenings of beoutQ's unauthorized broadcasts of the 2018 World Cup matches. In this regard the Panel even analyzed the tweets of the Saudi public officials in order to understand whether those acts were attributable to the State.[208] Consequently, the Panel concluded that Saudi Arabia had acted inconsistently with TRIPS Agreement Article 61.[209]

The Panel exercised judicial economy as to complaints under parts I and II of the TRIPS Agreement.

---

[206] *Ibid.*, para. 7.164.
[207] *Ibid.*, paras. 7.197-199.
[208] *Ibid.*, para. 7.161.
[209] *Ibid.*, paras. 7.214-221.

5.2.2. Justification under Article 73(b)(iii) of the TRIPS Agreement

Upon establishing that the anti-sympathy measures of Saudi Arabia and the non-application of criminal procedures had violated Articles 41.1, 42 and 61 of the TRIPS Agreement, the Panel went on to review whether these violations could be justified by the security exception enshrined in Article 73(b)(iii) of the TRIPS Agreement, which was invoked by Saudi Arabia.

The Panel underlined that Article 73(b)(iii) is identical to Article XXI of the GATT, which was interpreted in the *Russia –Traffic in Transit* case.[210] Moreover, both parties referred to the interpretation developed by the Panel in *Russia – Traffic in Transit*, although with divergent views on certain provisions of Article 73(b)(iii).[211]

The Panel decided that it would be guided by the analytical framework developed in *Russia – Traffic in Transit* (although it did not explicitly state that it would be so guided). In short, in its analysis under Article 73(b)(iii) of the TRIPS Agreement, the Panel followed a four-steps framework based on the *Russia – Traffic in Transit* case:

— whether the existence of a "war or other emergency in international relations" has been established in the sense of subparagraph (iii) to Article 73(b);

— whether the relevant actions were "taken in time of" that war or other emergency in international relations;

— whether the invoking Member has articulated its relevant "essential security interests" sufficiently to enable an assessment of whether there is any link between those actions and the protection of its essential security interests; and

— whether the relevant actions are so remote from, or unrelated to, the "emergency in international relations" as to make it implausible that the invoking Member considers those actions to be necessary for the protection of its essential security interests arising out of the emergency.[212]

The Panel established that a situation of emergency existed in this case, at least starting from 5 June 2017, and that the measures were taken by Saudi Arabia in time of such emergency.[213] The Panel then turned to the assessment of whether Saudi Arabia had provided a sufficient articulation of its essential security interests and whether the measures were too remote from or unrelated to the emergency in international relations. The Panel concluded that Saudi Arabia had sufficiently articulated its essential security interests in protecting itself "from the dangers of terrorism and extremism".[214]

---

[210] As a reminder, Art. 73(b)(iii) provides that: "Nothing in this Agreement shall be construed: […] (b) to prevent a Member from taking any action which it considers necessary for the protection of its essential security interests; […] (iii) taken in time of war or other emergency in international relations".

[211] Panel Report, *cit. supra* note 192, paras. 7.230-7.231.

[212] *Ibid.*, para. 7.242.

[213] *Ibid.*, paras. 7.268 and 7.269.

[214] *Ibid.*, para. 7.280.

Lastly, the Panel decided that the "anti-sympathy" measures adopted by Saudi Arabia against Qatar met the minimum requirement of plausibility, i.e. that they were not implausible as measures protective of essential security interests.[215] Therefore, Saudi Arabia was able to justify its violations under Article 41.1 and 42 of the TRIPS Agreement. The non-application of criminal procedures to the pirate broadcaster, beoutQ, on the contrary, was so remote from the protection of essential security interests that such measures were implausible as measures protective of these interests. Consequently, Saudi Arabia was not able to justify its violations of Article 61 of the TRIPS Agreement.[216]

5.3. Concluding remarks

This was the first case in the history of the WTO to address the security exception in the TRIPS Agreement. As demonstrated above, in its analysis, the Panel referred to the analytical framework under Article XXI of the GATT, adopted in *Russia – Traffic in Transit*. However, the Panel never explicitly stated that it was precisely following the *Russia – Traffic in Transit* framework or, rather, that its own framework was based on *Russia – Traffic in Transit*.[217] Indeed, the Panel reversed the order of analysis under Article 73(b)(iii) of the TRIPS Agreement. Contrary to what the Panel did in *Russia – Traffic in Transit*, here the Panel first reviewed whether the measures violated the TRIPS Agreement and only then went on to review whether such violations could be justified by the security exception under Article 73(b)(iii) of the TRIPS Agreement. It is also worth mentioning that, for the first time in the history of the WTO, the Panel referred to the Twitter posts of public officials as evidence in its report.[218] Last but not least, it must be remembered that there are other active disputes concerning the interpretation of the security exception of the GATT and the interpretation of the security exception is still an ongoing debate.[219]

VIKTORIIA LAPA[*]

---

[215] The Panel referred to various measures adopted by Saudi Arabia against Qatar as "anti-sympathy" measures: *ibid.*, para. 7.59.

[216] *Ibid.*, paras. 7.288 and 7.289.

[217] See on this KREIER, "Saudi Arabia-IP Rights and the Security Exception", International Economic Law and Policy Blog, 14 October 2020, available at: <https://ielp.worldtradelaw.net/2020/10/saudi-arabia-ip-rights-and-the-security-exception.html>.

[218] GLÖCKLE, "The Second Chapter on a National Security Exception in WTO Law: The Panel Report in Saudi Arabia – Protection of IPR", EJIL: Talk!, 22 July 2020, available at: <https://www.ejiltalk.org/the-second-chapter-on-a-national-security-exception-in-wto-law-the-panel-report-in-saudi-arabia-protection-of-ipr/>.

[219] See, for example, *US – Measures on Steel and Aluminium* (DS544, DS547, DS48, DS552, DS554, DS564, DS566).

[*] Academic Fellow, Lecturer, Bocconi University, PhD in Legal studies (Bocconi University).

THE DEVELOPMENT OF INTERNATIONAL INVESTMENT LAW THROUGH 2020 ARBITRAL AND DOMESTIC CASE LAW

GIOVANNI ZARRA[*]

1. INTRODUCTION

International investment law and arbitration are today facing dramatic challenges. From the widely discussed projects of reform concerning this area of the law, to its collocation within the broader framework of public international law, to the relationship of arbitral proceedings with the relevant domestic courts (a topic mainly attracting the attention of private international lawyers), this subject is continuously evolving. Decisions (both arbitral and domestic) issued in 2020 offer quite a broad picture of the current trends. Several *obiter dicta*, indeed, are of particular relevance for the development of both theoretical and practical aspects of international investment law and arbitration, including its relationship with other areas of international law and its place within the wider debate on the fragmentation of international law. The issue of fragmentation applies, especially, to EU law, whose role in the interpretation and application of investment treaties is still subject to debate. Other aspects that featured prominently in 2020 decisions concern the standing of indirect shareholders in investment claims, the impartiality and independence of arbitrators, the confidentiality of arbitral proceedings, as well as the standards of treatment of foreign investors and procedural issues such as the relationship with domestic courts.

This paper will try to give account of the most significant evolutions that took place in 2020 by also focusing on the possible consequences that the case law under scrutiny may have in the wider framework of general international law. Unsurprisingly, the decisions which have been analyzed include awards that directly concern existing rules of general international law, as well as decisions which may evidence trends within the specific area of international investment law but still do not, as of today, affect general international law. An important point raised is that decisions within the specific area of international investment law can also be useful for the resolution of similar legal issues in other areas of law, in particular in light of the fact that in international adjudication there is an increasing tendency to take into account relevant decisions by other courts and tribunals.[1]

The topics and decisions that will be analyzed in the course of this paper will show that, while in several aspects the evolution of international investment law

---

[*] Adjunct Professor of International Law and International Litigation, University of Napoli "Federico II".

[1] On the cross-fertilization between investment law and other areas of international law, see PELLET, "The Case Law of the ICJ in Investment Arbitration", ICSID Review, 2013, p. 223 ff.

IYIL, Vol. 30 (2020), pp. 423-448
ISSN 0391-5107

is coherent with the existing framework of general international law, in dealing with certain particular questions (such as the concept of legitimate expectations) investment arbitrators seem to follow an autonomous path which clearly distinguishes international investment law from the rest of international law.

A significant aspect that will emerge from the analysis of 2020 practice concerns the role of domestic courts in the development of international investment law. Indeed, more than in the past, national judges have agreed on the definitions of principles and standards concerning the international law of foreign investment, both from the substantive and the procedural point of view. In this regard, we will show that domestic judges are – even more than in the past – assuming a favourable attitude towards arbitration and have fostered the recourse to this method of dispute settlement, while avoiding interfering with the smooth prosecution of arbitral proceedings.

2. SYSTEMIC FEATURES OF INTERNATIONAL INVESTMENT LAW AND THE RELATIONSHIP WITH THE DEBATE CONCERNING THE FRAGMENTATION OF INTERNATIONAL LAW

The first significant evolutionary path observed in investment awards issued in 2020 is the existence of systemic features within this area of international law. Indeed, on the one hand, due to the ad hoc nature of all existing investment tribunals, it is still difficult to compare international investment law to a real legal system, i.e.: "a purposeful arrangement or constellation of interrelated elements or components, which cannot accurately be described and understood in isolation from one another".[2]

On the other hand, however, the 2020 case law shows that arbitrators in many circumstances behave *as if* they are in a system.[3] This is mainly based upon the so-called "taking into account approach", according to which tribunals have a duty to consider previous decisions, but may depart from them if the circumstances of the concrete case so require.[4] This attitude is, first of all, compliant with the expectation of the parties in the resolution of disputes, as evidenced by an *obiter dictum* in *Eskosol*:

> [t]he Parties thus implicitly concur that the Tribunal should take the Blusun award into consideration only to the extent it finds the reasoning of that case to be persuasive, a proposition that is no dif-

---

[2] SHANY, *The Competing Jurisdictions of International Courts and Tribunals*, Oxford, 2003, p. 87.

[3] See, for case law predating 2020, ZARRA, *Parallel Proceedings in Investment Arbitration*, Torino/Den Haag, 2017, pp. 25-37.

[4] PALOMBINO, *Fair and Equitable Treatment and the Fabric of General Principles*, Heidelberg, 2018, p. 151 ff.

ferent than the way in which the Tribunal evaluates any other jurisprudence to which its attention has been drawn.[5]

But this is not the only reason for this kind of approach. Taking previous
decisions into account also answers the widely perceived need for harmonious
development of international investment law, as evidenced in the recent *Lee Chin*
award, where the Tribunal affirmed that:

> there is no stare decisis doctrine in international law. Tribunals are
> independent from each other and there is no hierarchic organization
> among them which could make them subject, under certain circum-
> stances, to the decisions of others. However, the Tribunal believes
> it desirable, in general, to foster the development of a jurisprudence
> constante based on previous decisions, not only as a means of pro-
> viding certain predictability to the parties but also as a response to
> *an ongoing demand for more consistency within the international
> investment system, a demand rooted in the need to enhance its le-
> gitimacy.* In fact, typically, the Parties' citations to judicial prec-
> edents are aimed at stating what a good faith interpretation should
> be according to the ordinary meaning of the terms under discussion,
> which is the basic rule of interpretation.[6]

As evidenced by the italicized words in the above quotation, 2020 case law
confirms that tribunals are particularly sensitive to the increasing demand for
consistency among decisions, also in light of the needs to enhance the legitimacy
of arbitration as a valuable method for settling disputes concerning international
investments and to face the still ongoing demands for reform of the system.[7] In
this regard, it is emblematic that, in the cases where tribunals (apparently) did not
pay due attention to these needs, strong dissenting opinions were issued. This is
what happened in *Watkins*, where arbitrator Ruiz Fabri did not consider the majority's decision adequately motivated in light of the existing case law concerning renewable energy in Spain. According to Ruiz Fabri, indeed:

---

[5] *Eskosol S.p.A. in liquidazione v. Italy*, ICSID Case No. ARB/15/50, Award of 4 September
2020 (Tribunal: Jean Kalicki, President, Brigitte Stern, Guido Santiago Tawil), para. 278. See
also *Itisaluna Iraq LLC and others v. Iraq*, ICSID Case No. ARB/17/10, Award of 3 April 2020
(Tribunal: Daniel Bethlehem, President, Wolfgang Peter, Brigitte Stern), para. 65.

[6] *Michael Antony Lee Chin v. Dominican Republic*, ICSID Case No. UNCT/18/3, Partial
Award on Jurisdiction of 15 July 2020 (Tribunal: Diego P. Fernandez Arroyo, President,
Christian Leathley, Marcelo Kohen), para. 80 (emphasis added).

[7] See also *Consutel Group S.p.A. in liquidazione v. Algeria*, PCA Case No. 2017-33, Award
of 3 February 2020 (Tribunal: Alexis Mourre, President, Attila Tanzi, Ahmed Mahiou), para.
290, where it is said: "[l]e Tribunal estime cependant opportun de prendre en considération des
solutions qui ont pu être adoptées de manière constante par d'autres tribunaux sur les questions
de droit soulevées dans le présent arbitrage, afin de contribuer dans la mesure du possible au
développement harmonieux du droit des investissements et de répondre à l'attente légitime de
la communauté des Etats et des investisseurs que les solutions apportées à leurs litiges soient,
autant que faire se peut, cohérentes".

[t]his case is to be located in the broader context of a series of cases
concerning a large number of arbitrations conducted against Spain
for its normative changes in the regulatory framework of the renewable energy sector (sometimes named as the 'Spanish saga'). In a
situation where many different cases stem from the same general
measures and are conducted in parallel, the clarity of the reasoning
is especially important. I fear that the Tribunal in this award is far
from bringing the necessary clarity to the discussion.[8]

Even more explicitly, in *PV*, arbitrator Brower stated that the majority's decision was unsatisfactorily motivated as to why it did not follow previous awards
issued within the same context (again, the dispute concerned incentives for the
renewable energy sector in Spain):

I am of the view that no tribunal should accept an Alternative Claim
over a Primary Claim without justifiable reasons for dismissing the
Primary Claim, *and in the present case I discern no justifiable reason whatsoever for departing from those eleven other tribunals' acceptance of the Primary Claim in like circumstances.* In fact, the
interpretation that my colleagues give to the language of the Old
Regulatory Regime (ORR), allegedly providing such reasons, is
inconsistent with the line of jurisprudence established by the tribunals that considered these very same issues before us.[9]

This line of reasoning is perfectly understandable – from the point of view of
the necessity to adequately justify the departure from a clearly established line of
cases – for two reasons: first, it benefits legal certainty and promotes efficiency
in investment disputes (a well-reasoned award may be a significant benchmark
for future tribunals dealing with similar circumstances); secondly, it increases
the perception that investment awards are based on the rule of law and not on the
subjective perceptions of arbitrators.

What is then to be ascertained is how this alleged investment law system relates to other areas of international law. In this regard, according to the advocates
of the fragmentation of international law, every area of international law (including international investment law) should be considered as a "self-contained
regime", which does not benefit from cross-fertilizations with other areas of international law, with which it lives in parallel.[10] This seems to be the approach

---

[8] *Watkins Holding S.a.r.l. et al. v. Spain*, ICSID Case No. ARB/15/44, Award of 21 January
2020 (Tribunal: Tan Sri Datò Cecil Abraham, President, Michael Pryles, Helene Ruiz Fabri),
Dissent on Liability and Quantum of Helene Ruiz Fabri, para. 3.

[9] *PV Investors v. Spain*, PCA Case No. 2012-14, Final Award of 28 February 2020
(Tribunal: Gabrielle Kaufmann-Kohler, President, Charles N. Brower, Bernardo Sepulveda-
Amor), Concurring and Dissenting Opinion of Charles N. Brower, para. 2 (emphasis added).

[10] This seems to be the approach endorsed by GRADONI, Regime failure *nel diritto internazionale*, Padova, 2009, *passim*.

followed by the majority in *Watkins*, where it was stated that investment law and EU law are two distinct areas of international law which do not communicate with each other. According to this approach:

> [a] last line of argumentation is based on two basic ideas, grounded in public international law: the parallelism of treaties and the distinction between the EU legal order and the international legal order. Some decisions followed a dualist argument distinguishing clearly between the EU legal order and the international legal order. The two legal orders are distinct and should not be seen as working in conflict but in harmony.[11] [...]
>
> The idea of parallelism of treaties is a fundamental principle of public international law [...] [that] can be traced back to the case law of the Permanent Court of International Justice elaborating on this fundamental principle that has since become well-established. [...] Since treaties evolve in parallel, the presumption is the absence of conflict between them, as also clarified in WTO case law.[12]

However, and in compliance with the approach fostered by the International Law Commission,[13] fragmentation does not find significant space in the reasoning of investment tribunals. In the words of the *ad hoc* committee in *InfraRed*:

> [t]he Committee is not persuaded that the ICSID system is 'self-contained', if by that expression it is meant that it exists in isolation from international law. However, it is a system in and of itself, in the sense that it is in the ICSID Convention and the Arbitration Rules (and considering these legal instruments in their entirety) that it is necessary to find the solution for any issue that a committee might face, notably the interpretation of the rules applicable to a given situation.[14] [...] For any decision subject to the ICSID Rules, as is the case, previous decisions issued by ICSID tribunals (and by other international arbitral tribunals) and, even more, by ad hoc

---

[11] *Watkins*, Award, *cit. supra* note 8, para. 215.

[12] *Ibid.*, para. 224. With respect to how the principle has "become well-established" in ICJ case law, the Tribunal referred to the ICJ case of *Aegean Sea Continental Shelf (Greece v. Turkey)*, Judgment of 19 December 1978, ICJ Reports 1978, p. 3 ff., para. 91; as to the reference to "WTO case law", the Tribunal referred to Panel Report, *Indonesia – Certain Measures Affecting the Automobile Industry*, adopted on 23 July 1998, WT/DS54/R, WT/DS55/R, WT/DS59/R and WT/DS64/R, para. 14.28.

[13] See Fragmentation of international law: difficulties arising from the diversification and expansion of international law, Report of the Study Group of the International Law Commission finalized by Koskenniemi, UN Doc. A/CN.4/L.682 (2006).

[14] *InfraRed Environmental Infrastructure GP Limited and others v. Spain*, ICSID Case No. ARB/14/12, Decision on the Continuation of the Stay of Enforcement of the Award (Ad Hoc Committee: Jose-Miguel Jùdice, President, Karim Hafez, Yuejiao Zhang), para. 122.

committees, may be considered as useful guidance, in light of the absence of a system of legal precedents.[15]

This approach is also confirmed by the other awards which discuss the relevance of EU law in international investment arbitration, from which it emerges that a logic of harmonic coexistence between both fields of international law should prevail over the one of complete autonomy. In this regard, in *Adamakopoulos v. Cyprus*, the Tribunal noted that EU law, in particular the rules set out in EU Treaties as interpreted by EU organs, is international law binding on EU Member States. Thus, those rules – like any other rules of international law – can be invoked in investment disputes. Similarly, any decision of the CJEU on the scope, interpretation and application of those rules is equally relevant. However, the Tribunal explained that this does not end the matter, because it is necessary to acknowledge the existence and applicability of another competing set of rules, also rules of international law, those established by investment agreements and by the ICSID Convention.[16]

In establishing which set of rules has to prevail, the Tribunal clarified that, while EU law claims primacy over domestic norms, its relationship with other international norms cannot but be regulated by the 1969 Vienna Convention on the Law of Treaties (VCLT), and namely by Articles 59 and 30(3). It was according to these rules that the Tribunal determined the prevalence of the BIT provisions over EU law.[17] Similarly, and perhaps using a stronger argument against fragmentation, the Tribunal in *Sunreserve* affirmed that:

> [t]he Tribunal is not persuaded by Claimants' characterization of EU law as a regional legal order distinct from public international law. Claimants themselves recognize, at another point in their sub-

---

[15] Para. 125.

[16] ICSID Case No. ARB/15/49, Decision on Jurisdiction of 7 February 2020 (Tribunal: Donald McRae, President, Alejandro Escobar, Marcelo Kohen), para. 160. In this regard, arbitrator Kohen issued a strong dissenting opinion, arguing that on the basis of Arts. 59 and 30(3) VCLT, EU law should prevail over investment law. The subject has already been dealt with (in agreement with the majority's decision) by this author on various occasions (including in the IYIL), to which we hereby refer. See ZARRA, "Investment Arbitration 2018: Back to Basics", IYIL, 2018, p. 413 ff., p. 430 ff.; ZARRA, "The Enforceability of Arbitral Awards Deriving from Intra-EU Investment Agreements. Reflections on Treaty Law Issues and on the EU Unsustainable Position", DCI, 2018, p. 891 ff. The approach followed by the majority in this case has also been followed in all the other intra-EU cases decided in 2020.

[17] Para. 163 ff. Nor have tribunals accepted that the declarations issued by Member States in January 2019 after the CJEU's *Achmea* decision (on which see ZARRA, "The Interface between Investment Arbitration and the 'Outside World': An Analysis through the Prism of 2019 Case Law", IYIL, 2019, p. 395 ff., p. 402), and affirming that investor-State arbitration clauses contained in bilateral investment treaties concluded between Member States are contrary to Union law and thus inapplicable, may be considered as subsequent agreements between EU Member States. See *GPF GP S.a.r.l. v. Poland*, SCC Arbitration V 2014/168, Award of 29 April 2020 (Tribunal: Gabrielle Kaufmann-Kohler, President, David AR Williams, Philippe Sands), para. 351 ff.

missions, that 'EU law is a collection of treaties – nothing more'. To the extent that EU law is comprised of international treaties between sovereign States such as the EU Treaties, i.e., the TEU and the TFEU, it is indisputably a source of international law. In this regard, the Tribunal agrees with the [European Commission] invocation of Article 38 of the Statute of the International Court of Justice [...], which enlists the sources of international law, the primary amongst them being international conventions or treaties.[18]

Having said the above, for the sake of completeness, the Tribunal noted that EU law may also play a role in non-ICSID cases seated in the EU as part of the *lex loci arbitri*. In this regard, however, when the issue emerged before the arbitrators, the latter did not hesitate in affirming that EU law, as incorporated in the legal system of the seat, could not impair the arbitrability of the investment dispute in question, considering that EU law, allegedly, does not regulate disputes arising from investments started before the respondent's accession to the EU.[19]

3.   SHAREHOLDERS' CLAIMS IN INTERNATIONAL INVESTMENT ARBITRATION

A longstanding issue concerning international law is the possibility for shareholders who only suffer indirect damages to bring investment claims against host States. In this regard, starting from the ICJ's ruling in *Barcelona Traction*,[20] international law has evolved to preclude this possibility. In *Barcelona Traction*, the ICJ ruled that the nationality of the shareholders is irrelevant for the purpose of the exercise of diplomatic protection, as diplomatic protection can only be exercised by the State where a company is incorporated because only direct damages are relevant under international law.

While this rule is still purported to be part of customary international law, investment arbitration practice has developed an opposite tendency. This is due to the very broad definition of the concepts of "investments" and "investors" used in BITs, according to which: (i) the mere ownership of shares can certainly be considered as an investment for the purpose of the application of the treaty; and, when the latter's wording so allows, (ii) even the indirect ownership of shares in a company which is the direct investor may be considered as an investment.

2020 case law confirms that investment arbitration very often departs from the *Barcelona Traction* ruling on the entitlement of indirect shareholders to start

---

[18] *Sun Reserve Luxco Holding S.a.r.l. v. Italy*, SCC Arbitration V (2016/32), Award of 25 March 2020 (Tribunal: Albert Jan van den Berg, President, Klaus Sachs, Andrea Giardina), para. 375.

[19] *Sun Reserve, cit. supra* note 18, paras. 426 and 442. In this regard, it is to be noted that the law of the seat (to be joined with the selected procedural rules) is an integrant part of the *lex arbitri*, i.e. the set of procedural norms governing the arbitration. See ZARRA, "La *lex arbitri* e la *lex loci arbitri*: tra verità normative e incertezze dottrinali", DCI, p. 533 ff.

[20] *Barcelona Traction, Light and Power Company, Limited (Belgium v. Spain)*, Judgment of 5 February 1970, ICJ Reports 1970, p. 3 ff.

investment claims. This approach has been clearly confirmed in *Bridgestone v. Panama*, where the arbitrators stated that:

> [i]n an investment treaty arbitration where a chain of companies is involved, indirect interests in an investment are recognized, notwithstanding that this may involve lifting the veil of incorporation. If a direct investor is involved in litigation for the benefit of an investment in which an indirect investor has an interest, and a denial of justice results in damage to that investment, there seems to be no reason in principle why it should not be open to the indirect investor to invoke the denial of justice as a breach of the obligation to accord fair and equitable treatment to the covered investment.[21]

Various cases in 2020 discussed whether it was necessary that foreign investments make a *direct* economic contribution to the activity of the entity that materially carries out the investment. In this regard, all the tribunals confirmed that investments can be operated either directly or indirectly and do not necessarily have to involve a direct activity on the part of the claimant.[22] The Tribunal in *Eyre v. Sri Lanka* explained the rationale for such an approach, by saying that to recognize indirect foreign control through indirect as well as direct share ownership reflects commercial reality. Indeed, according to the Tribunal, in modern international economic relations, chains of closely-held companies are frequently used, without preventing the majority shareholder at the top of a chain from asserting control of or making claims on behalf of a foreign company lower in the chain; for this reason, claims by indirect shareholders are to be accepted in international investment law.[23]

This approach has also been confirmed by a ruling of the Swiss Federal Tribunal, which has recognized that in the presence of clear treaty wording, there is no other possibility than to pragmatically accept that indirect shareholders may bring investment claims.[24]

Overall, it is therefore likely that the only way to preclude claims by indirect shareholders – regardless of the desirability of this solution[25] – is to expressly

---

[21] *Bridgestone Licensing Services Inc. et al v. Panama*, ICSID Case No. ARB/16/34, Award of 14 August 2020 (Tribunal: Nicholas Philips, President, Horacio Grigera-Naon, Christopher Thomas), para. 172.

[22] *Canepa Green Energy Opportunities S.a.r.l. v. Spain*, ICSID Case No. ARB/19/4, Procedural Order No. 3 of 28 August 2020 (Tribunal: Sean Murphy, President, Silvina Sandra Gonzalez Napolitano, Peter Rees), para. 73.

[23] *Raymond Charles Eyre et al v. Sri Lanka*, ICSID Case No. ARB/16/25, Award of 5 March 2020 (Tribunal: Lucy Reed, President, Julian Lew, Brigitte Stern), para. 266.

[24] Swiss Tribunal Federal, *Clorox S.A. v. Venezuela*, Case 4A_306/2019, Decision of 25 March 2020, para. 3.4.2.2. The Tribunal then annulled an arbitral award (issued in Geneva) in which the arbitrators had declined jurisdiction on the basis that the Claimant did not have any investment in Venezuela because it did not pay any amount for its participation in the Venezuelan company that it considered to be its investment.

[25] Something that has been argued in a concept paper of the Academic Forum for ISDS. See ARATO et al., "Reforming Shareholders Claims in ISDS", 2019, available at: <https://papers.ssrn.com/sol3/papers.cfm?abstract_id=3433465>.

draft treaties inserting a qualification in the provision that limits the mechanisms through which loss must be incurred (i.e. refer to direct loss only).[26]

4. IMPARTIALITY AND INDEPENDENCE OF ARBITRATORS

Another important issue analyzed by recent investment awards is the requirement of independence and impartiality of arbitrators. While nobody would deny that these requirements apply to all international adjudicators, the content of these standards is subject to continuous evolution.[27] Over the years, international investment law has elaborated important elements that help to trace the contours of these concepts.

In general terms, it may be argued that independence requires arbitrators to maintain neutrality and an open mind with respect to the issues that they have to decide, while impartiality concerns the possible bias that an arbitrator may have towards one of the parties in dispute. *In concreto*, however, it may become difficult to ascertain whether these standards have been met.

One of the most discussed examples of potential lack of impartiality or independence is the situation where an arbitrator is appointed by several claimants in various cases against the same respondent related to the same factual setting. This is what happened in *VM v. Spain*,[28] where Spain argued that multiple appointments of Prof. Guido Santiago Tawil by claimants in disputes concerning renewable energies involved a double risk: (i) for impartiality, due to the commercial incentive of potential future appointments by investors, and due to the fact that, in some previous cases, Tawil had issued dissenting opinions against Spain, and (ii) for independence, in light of the knowledge acquired by the same arbitrator from similar or identical cases, resulting in the risk of possible preconceptions concerning the outcome of the present dispute. In short, the alleged overlap of factual and legal issues between the previous cases and the current one confirmed – according to Spain – that Tawil lacked the qualities required of an arbitrator. The Chairman of the ICSID Administrative Council, however, reached a different solution. Even in the presence of multiple appointments, arbitrators continue to carry out the same function in an independent way and there is no presumption against this consideration, even more so considering that the case at hand and the previous disputes in which Tawil was involved had various substantive differences. Even in cases where the issues might be similar, the arguments, and the

---

[26] Accordingly see *Daniel W. Kappes et al. v. Guatemala*, ICSID Case No. ARB/18/43, Award of 13 March 2020 (Tribunal: Jean Kalicki, President, John Townsend, Zachary Douglas), para. 130.

[27] SEIBERT-FOHR, "International Judicial Ethics", in ROMANO, ALTER and SHANY (eds.), *The Oxford Handbook of International Adjudication*, Oxford, 2015, p. 757 ff.; IOVANE, *L'influence de la multiplication des juridictions internationales sur l'application du droit international*, RCADI, Vol. 383, 2016, p. 345 ff.

[28] *VM Solar Spain GmbH et al. v. Spain*, ICSID Case No. ARB/19/30, Decision on the Proposal to Disqualify Prof. Dr. Guido Santiago Tawil of 24 July 2020 (Chairman of the Administrative Council: David R. Malpass), para. 91 ff.

manner in which they are presented by different parties could differ depending on the particularities of each case. In these circumstances, a third party undertaking a reasonable evaluation of the facts would not have concluded that Prof. Tawil manifestly appeared to lack the required impartiality and independence to decide the case.[29]

The issue of independence was also discussed in one of the rare cases where the Tribunal's award was annulled according to Article 52 of the ICSID Convention. In *Eiser v. Spain*,[30] the Respondent argued that, after the issuance of the award, it discovered that Arbitrator Alexandrov – appointed by the Claimants – had a long-standing relationship with Mr Lapuerta, the Claimants' expert, and with Mr Lapuerta's employer, the Brattle Group, which he failed to disclose. Such a relationship was developed when Dr Alexandrov worked at Sidley Austin (a well-known law firm established in the US). This generated an improper constitution of the Tribunal and the violation of a fundamental rule of procedure, considering that Brattle's presence might have influenced Alexandrov's neutrality and, hence, manifestly violated Article 14 of the ICSID Convention and ICSID Rule 37, requiring that independence and impartiality are maintained by arbitrators during the entire proceedings.[31] The *Ad Hoc* Committee ruled that:

> [i]t is true that arbitrators, lawyers and experts doing investment arbitrations live on the same planet. Some interaction is, therefore, inevitable. Nevertheless, it is obvious and it is to be expected that the more 'connections' there are between them, across cases and, particularly, in different roles, the more chances there are that these may give rise to conflicts. For the sake of the fair and objective conduct of the arbitral proceedings, these should, therefore, be declared and specifically brought to the attention of the parties and other arbitrators.[32]

The longstanding relationship between Dr Alexandrov and Mr Lapuerta was, therefore, something that should have been disclosed so as to enable a reasonable third party to evaluate whether this was a ground for challenge. Indeed, as stated by General Standard 3(d) of the 2014 IBA Guidelines on Conflict of Interest in International Arbitration, "[a]ny doubt as to whether an arbitrator should disclose certain facts or circumstances should be resolved in favor of disclosure".[33] For this reason, the Committee found that the Tribunal was improperly constituted

---

[29] Paras. 102 and 103.

[30] *Eiser Infrastructure Limited et al. v. Spain*, ICSID Case No. ARB/13/36, Decision on the Kingdom of Spain's Application for Annulment of 11 June 2020 (Ad Hoc Committee: Ricardo Ramirez Hernandez, President, Makhdoom Ali Khan, Dominique Hascher), para. 45.

[31] Para. 168.

[32] Para. 217.

[33] In this regard, at para. 255, the Committee stated that "[a]nnulment committees are guardians of the ICSID system and must set the bar high, with regard to disclosure obligations, in particular, and, in general, with respect to addressing conflict of interest of arbitrators who also choose to act as counsel in investment disputes".

and a fundamental rule of procedure was breached. Accordingly, the award was annulled.

Before concluding this Section, it is worth highlighting that – in compliance with the majority of decisions dealing with the issue – the *Ad Hoc* Committee in *Eiser* treated the IBA Guidelines as the primary standard for addressing the issue of conflict of interest, regardless of the soft law nature of this source. In this regard, as argued by Gabrielle Kaufmann-Kohler[34] and more recently by Fulvio M. Palombino,[35] it is to be noted that, when the recourse to a set of soft law rules is particularly frequent, it is very difficult to draw a distinction between soft and hard law, due to the very common reference to the former to decide certain issues. Hence, it is perhaps surprising to read, in a recent decision, that:

> [i]n the course of its pleadings, the Respondent has referred to the IBA Guidelines on Conflict of Interest in International Arbitration. While these guidelines may serve as a reference, the Unchallenged Arbitrators are bound by the standards set forth in the ICSID Convention. Accordingly, this decision is made based upon the relevant provisions of the ICSID Convention and ICSID Arbitration Rules.[36]

The normative value of the IBA Guidelines on Conflict of Interest thus remains an open issue, even if the vast number of decisions applying these standards justifies concluding that there is, at least, a trend towards the formulation of customary rules of procedure concerning international investment arbitration.[37]

5. THIRD PARTY FUNDING AND CONFLICTS OF INTEREST

Issues concerning possible conflicts of interest in arbitration recently emerged in the context of disputes funded by third parties, a topic which has been subject to significant academic attention but is only recently showing its practical poten-

---

[34] KAUFMANN-KOHLER, "Soft Law in International Arbitration: Codification and Normativity", Journal of International Dispute Settlement, 2010, p. 1 ff.

[35] PALOMBINO, "L'uso della soft law nell'arbitrato sugli investimenti", in MANTUCCI (ed.), *Trattato di diritto dell'arbitrato*, Napoli, 2020, p. 1231 ff.

[36] *Canepa, cit. supra* note 22, Decision on the Second Proposal to Disqualify Mr. Peter Rees QC of 10 February 2020, para. 55.

[37] PALOMBINO, *cit. supra* note 35, pp. 1241-1242. In this regard see ARIAS, "Soft Law Rules in International Arbitration: Positive Effects and Legitimization of IBA as a Rule-Maker", Indian Journal of Arbitration Law, 2018, p. 29 ff., arguing that soft law has contributed to levelling the playing field, increasing certainty and codifying best practices, norms and intelligent guidance on how to tackle recent concerns. The author affirms that the International Bar Association, surely the most active institution when it comes to the creation of soft law at the international arbitration level, is entirely legitimized in its role. This legitimation is given by its experience, its inclusiveness when creating soft law instruments and its reflection of the cultural diversity in the arbitral community.

tial drawbacks, mainly due to the lack of a specific regulation, both in international law and at the level of domestic law systems.

In *Geophysical v. Canada*,[38] the Claimants in a NAFTA arbitration started ancillary domestic proceedings against Canada asking for the removal of Canada's current counsel due to the previous job that one of them (Ms Dosman) had at Vannin Capital, a fund which had been approached by the Claimants for third party funding and which thus had possession of all the Claimants' information concerning the case. The Claimants also asked for an order to restrain the current counsel from communicating the confidential information they acquired to other members of the Canadian Trade Bureau. Hence, Ms Dosman was, allegedly, in a conflict of interests, having received and had access to certain non-public, confidential, and privileged information regarding the claims in the NAFTA proceeding. Unfortunately, the Court avoided ruling on the issue, arguing that this question was to be resolved by the arbitrators and this matter could not be the object of an interim measure ordered by the domestic courts of the seat pursuant to Article 17 of the UNCITRAL Model Law (applied in Canada), which authorizes arbitrators to provisionally rule on this kind of matter and thus rules out a referral to national judges.

Another interesting case concerning interim measures in relation to third party funding has been decided by the London Court of Appeal[39] in relation to an ICSID arbitration involving Turkey.[40] The Appellants were Koza Ltd, an English company, and its sole Director Mr Ipek. The Respondent was Koza Altin AS, a Turkish company (partly publicly owned and partly owned by Mr Ipek and members of his family) which is the immediate parent company of Koza Ltd. The appeal concerned an injunction granted by the Chancery Division, restraining the Appellants from using £3 million of assets belonging to Koza Ltd to fund an arbitration claim against Turkey started by Mr Ipek. The injunction followed an alleged undertaking given by Koza Ltd not to use its assets otherwise than in the ordinary and proper course of business. The dispute between the parties concerned whether the funding fell within that exception. The Court had to determine whether it could grant an injunction which would, in effect, permanently restrain Koza Ltd from allegedly breaching its undertaking, without having first evaluated the nature and effectiveness of the alleged undertaking by Koza Ltd.[41] According to the Court this was not possible precisely because the injunction would have constituted an irremediable prejudice to the Appellants' rights. This

---

[38] Federal Court of Ontario, *Geophysical Service Inc. et al. v. Canada*, Judgment of 20 October 2020, 2020 FC 984, available at: <www.italaw.com>.

[39] *Koza Limited et al. v. Koza Altin Isletmeleri AS*, Judgment of 31 July 2020, [2020] EWCA Civ 1018, available at: <www.italaw.com>.

[40] *Ipek Investment Limited v. Republic of Turkey*, ICSID Case No. ARB/18/18. In this ongoing case, Mr Ipek claims that the Turkish Government has illegally expropriated the Koza Group's assets for political reasons and has pursued a concerted campaign of harassment and oppression against the group and its shareholders and employees, including pursuing criminal proceedings against Mr Ipek and his family on the basis of allegations which Mr Ipek says are spurious.

[41] Para. 138.

is not, however, particularly relevant for our purposes. What is of interest here is that this decision indirectly confirms that, at least in English seated proceedings, the possibility for a private company to fund an arbitration is not precluded. What is perhaps disappointing is that the Court did not discuss the possible implications of the fact that Mr Ipek was Koza's sole director, but this does not come as a surprise when one considers that the subject of third party funding is not regulated (or is poorly regulated, even by soft law instruments) all around the world.

An improvement in this regard would certainly be welcome.

6. CONFIDENTIALITY OF ARBITRAL PROCEEDINGS: WHO DECIDES?

Developments worthy of mention also occurred with regard to the confidential nature of arbitral proceedings and the suitability of arbitrators to address this sensitive matter in investment cases. In this regard, the decision issued by the High Court of Singapore in *India v. Vedanta* is particularly important.[42] In this case, given that Singapore's arbitration law imposes a general obligation on the parties to an arbitration to keep the documents and proceedings in that arbitration confidential, Vinodh Coomaraswamy J had to answer the following questions:

> Does this general obligation of confidentiality extend to all species of arbitration? In particular, does this general obligation extend to an investment-treaty arbitration? And if a party to an arbitration puts this question of law to the tribunal in an investment-treaty arbitration and receives an answer it does not like, can that party put the question again to a Singapore court in an application for declaratory relief?

These are questions which are not only of interest for scholars based in Singapore but that, on the contrary, affect the entire subject of investment arbitration. In this case, India (the Respondent in an arbitration seated in Singapore, started by Vedanta) asked for a court's declaration that the documents concerning the *Vedanta* arbitration and another arbitration started by Vedanta's parent company (Cairn) were not private and confidential. According to India, the obligation of confidentiality in Singapore's arbitration law does not extend to investment-treaty arbitration, due to the public interest involved in this form of dispute settlement.

In order to assess India's request, the Court first clarified that issues of confidentiality are not explicitly addressed by Article 19 of the UNCITRAL Model Law, which governs arbitral procedures seated in Singapore (and which constitutes, jointly with the procedural rules chosen by the parties, the *lex arbitri*).[43] Then, it affirmed that the parties are free to agree on the procedure to be followed

---

[42] *India v. Vedanta*, Decision of 8 October 2020, [2020] SGHC 208, available at: <www.italaw.com>.

[43] Para. 132.

by the arbitral tribunal in conducting the proceedings and that, lacking such agreement, the arbitrators may, subject to the provisions of the law, conduct the arbitration in such manner as they consider appropriate. For this reason, ruling on the matter would not have, in principle, constituted an encroachment upon the arbitral tribunal's competence. Indeed, granting the declaratory relief which the plaintiff sought would not have amounted to a court's intervention in the *Vedanta* arbitration. The question concerned Singapore's substantive law on arbitration and was thus regulated by the ordinary principles which apply to the exercise of the court's declaratory jurisdiction.[44] On this basis, the Court affirmed that:

> [t]his general obligation of confidentiality is, of course, subject to exceptions. Although the list of exceptions is not closed, a number are well-established. These are: (a) where there is express or implied consent to disclosure; (b) where disclosure is permitted by the tribunal order, or with the leave of court; (c) where disclosure is reasonably necessary for the protection of the legitimate interests of a party to the arbitration; and (d) where the interests of justice require disclosure. Disclosure in the public interest is a possible addition to this list of exceptions.[45]

However, the same Court ruled that – provided that arbitrators are fully able to apply the law and develop the common law (as applicable in Singapore):[46]

> [i]n an international commercial arbitration [...], a tribunal may in a sense be said to be obliged to apply Singapore law if it is the law governing the underlying contract. But this obligation does not mean that the tribunal is precluded from considering and deciding a substantive question of law which Singapore's courts have not. Singapore's common law of arbitration – and more specifically, the obligation of confidentiality in arbitration – being situated within Singapore's common law, is and should be no different. It is well within the remit of a tribunal.[47]

Thus, the High Court argued that it is well within the powers of the *Vedanta* Tribunal to decide this issue of Singapore's common law of arbitration in the same way as a judge would have. This case is significant because it confirms that in many systems of law arbitration is perceived as equal to State justice from the perspective of the development of the rule of law (something that will also be discussed under Section 10 below) and that, even in a sensitive matter like the disclosure of information in investment cases (by definition involving the public

---

[44] Para. 111.
[45] Para. 111.
[46] Para. 143, referring to JONES, "Arbitrators as Law-Makers", Indian Journal of Arbitration Law, 2018, p. 18 ff., pp. 19 and 28.
[47] Para. 157.

interest) arbitrators are perceived as perfectly equipped to adequately address the parties' concerns.

7. MANAGEABILITY OF PROCEEDINGS: A NEW PROCEDURAL STANDARD?

The last aspect arising from 2020 case law with regard to arbitral procedure which deserves to be discussed, emerged in *Adamakopoulos v. Cyprus*[48] and concerns the suitability of arbitration to manage mass claims (a topic which has rarely been discussed in the case law).[49] In this case, the Claimants were 951 natural persons and seven companies, who suffered damage as a result of measures adopted by Cyprus in 2012 in response to the economic crisis affecting the banking sector. With the exception of one company incorporated in Luxembourg, the remaining Claimants were Greek nationals. Claims were, therefore, started under the 1993 Greece-Cyprus BIT and the 1999 Belgium-Luxembourg Economic Union-Cyprus BIT. According to Cyprus, neither the provisions of the ICSID Convention nor the provisions of the BITs allowed this kind of mass claim and, therefore, the Tribunal should have declared that it did not have jurisdiction over the claim or, alternatively, that the claim was inadmissible.

As to jurisdiction, the Tribunal argued that the issue of whether there is jurisdiction over a mass claim is not to be resolved simply by concluding that there is jurisdiction over the single individual claims. The first question to be answered is whether those individual claims can be put together as a single "mass claim". In this regard, there must be a "dispute" within the meaning of the relevant BITs and not just a myriad of separate disputes.[50] Therefore, the Tribunal had to determine whether the actual effects of Cyprus's measures on the Claimants were sufficiently similar to constitute a single dispute. The Tribunal argued that there was "substantial unity" or at least similarity in the claims, because the claims arose out of the actions by the Republic of Cyprus in respect of the Laiki Bank and the Bank of Cyprus in 2013 as a consequence of the economic crisis Cyprus faced in the early 2000s. The Claimants were deposit holders or bondholders in one or both of these banks and they all asked for the same kind of relief against Cyprus.

For this reason, according to the Tribunal "the real issue here is not jurisdiction, but rather the Respondent's arguments about the manageability within the ICSID framework of a mass claim with 956 Claimants",[51] something that pertains to the admissibility of the claim. Indeed, a mass claim such as the present one risks "creat[ing] intractable procedural problems". In this regard, the arbitrators

---

[48] *Cit. supra* note 16.

[49] Notable exceptions are: *Abaclat and Others v. Argentine Republic*, ICSID Case No. ARB/07/5 and *Ambiente Ufficio S.p.A. and others v. Argentine Republic*, ICSID Case No. ARB/ 08/9; *Giovanni Alemanni and Others v. The Argentine Republic*, ICSID Case No. ARB/ 07/8.

[50] Para. 205.

[51] Para. 214.

affirmed that it was necessary to make an assessment of the case involving (1) a balancing process concerning the rights of the Claimants to have their claims heard, (2) the capacity of the ICSID framework to manage the claim process, and (3) the due process rights of the Respondent.[52] In this regard, the Tribunal criticized the decision in *Abaclat*, where the majority took the view that it had the authority, deriving from Article 44 of the ICSID Convention and Rule 19 of the ICSID Arbitration Rules, to modify the "normal procedures" for considering claims in order to accommodate the mass claim in that case. In that case, the possible reduction in the protection of the parties' rights was justified on the basis that the alternative of each claimant bringing an individual claim would have been prohibitive for many individual claimants. Contrariwise, the Tribunal in *Adamakopoulos* concluded that "there is no mandate provided for in ICSID for the Tribunal to devise a new procedural framework, outside the existing ICSID framework, to deal with this case".[53] For this reason, the "manageability" of the proceedings was to be determined on the basis of the existing ICSID procedural framework and the need to ensure that the procedural rights of the parties are not affected in the various phases of proceedings. It therefore conducted a prognostic analysis of how the mass claim would impact on, e.g.,[54] document production, length of submissions, length of hearings and quantification of damages, and concluded that, notwithstanding some practical complications, the proceedings were perfectly manageable without any significant impact on the procedural rights of the parties, to whom the full right to be heard and to present their case will be ensured during the entire set of proceedings.

Apart from the solution reached by the Tribunal – which is agreeable but perhaps excessive in criticizing the approach assumed by the majority in *Abaclat*, which seems justifiable in light of the freedom to manage proceedings which the ICSID Convention and Rules grant to arbitrators – this award is noteworthy for having introduced a significant new characterization of the admissibility phase, which, should this decision be followed in the future, may now involve an analysis of the concrete manageability of a case. Should a case be deemed as practically not manageable, this approach would allow arbitrators to refuse to exercise a validly conferred jurisdiction by exercising their inherent power to declare the claim inadmissible.[55]

8.   The Legal Nature and Content of the FET Standard

Moving to substantive standards of treatment of foreign investment, fair and equitable treatment is the one which certainly received the greatest attention in

---

[52] Para. 224.

[53] Para. 246.

[54] Para. 251 ff.

[55] On inherent powers, see MAROTTI, "I poteri inerenti", in MANTUCCI (ed.), *cit. supra* note 35, p. 525 ff.; on admissibility, see FONTANELLI, "L'inammissibilità nell'arbitrato degli investimenti", *ibid.*, p. 363 ff.

2020 case law. In this regard, it is worth starting our discussion from the nature of this standard, which has been defined as a general principle of international law specific to the area of international investment and composed of various sub-principles.[56] This conclusion seems reinforced by recent practice, considering that all the 2020 cases have recognized that FET, within international investment law, responds to a tripartite conception[57] and involves: (i) the protection of legitimate expectations, (ii) the necessity to respect due process, and (iii) the obligation to treat investors in accordance with the principle of proportionality.

In this regard, the only case partially pointing in a different direction is *Interocean Oil Development Company et al. v. Nigeria*,[58] in which the Tribunal did not distinguish between fair and equitable treatment and the international minimum standard and simply equated the latter to customary law (clarifying that an action violates international law when it is "[...] sufficiently egregious and shocking – gross denial of justice, manifest arbitrariness, blatant unfairness, a complete lack of due process, evident discrimination, or a manifest lack of reasons").[59] The case is noteworthy inasmuch as it arose from a contract providing for the application of Nigerian Law but, nevertheless, the Tribunal stated that this entitled the Claimant to bring claims based on customary international law (including the international minimum standard) as enforced in Nigeria. The precedential value of the Tribunal's approach, however, should not be over emphasized (this decision could be seen as an isolated precedent), as the alleged equivalence between FET and the international minimum standard is a problem which emerged in the last decade in relation to the particular wording of Article 1105 of NAFTA and has been today settled in the sense that FET is a self-standing principle of international law.[60]

As to the related consideration that FET is not a principle of customary law, the ICJ decided in the case on the *Obligation to Negotiate Access to the Pacific Ocean* that:

> references to legitimate expectations may be found in arbitral awards concerning disputes between a foreign investor and the host State that apply treaty clauses providing for fair and equitable treatment. It does not follow from such references that there exists in general international law a principle that would give rise to an obligation on the basis of what could be considered a legitimate expectation. Bolivia's argument based on legitimate expectations thus cannot be sustained.[61]

---

[56] PALOMBINO, *Fair and Equitable Treatment, cit. supra* note 4, p. 38 ff.

[57] *Ibid.*, p. 57 ff.

[58] ICSID Case No. ARB/13/20, Award of 6 October 2020 (Tribunal: Willian Park, President, Julian Lew, Eduard Torgbor).

[59] Para. 354.

[60] Please refer to PALOMBINO, *cit. supra* note 4, p. 27 ff.

[61] *Obligation to Negotiate Access to the Pacific Ocean (Bolivia v. Chile)*, Judgment of 1 October 2018, ICJ Reports 2018, p. 507 ff., para. 162.

While this statement excludes that the principle of legitimate expectations is a general international law source – something that has also been denied in scholarship[62] – it certainly does not exclude that, within the context of investment law, the constant reference to fair and equitable treatment in all treaties may have generated a general principle specific to that area of the law providing, inter alia, for legitimate expectations.

Moving to the content of the obligation to respect legitimate expectations, case law shows that legitimate expectations can certainly arise from direct commitments assumed by a State towards foreign investors (e.g. through promise, contract or also administrative acts),[63] but it has sometimes been doubted that they can arise from legislative acts. This contestation will probably be resolved by the *ESPF Beteiligungs GmbH et al. v. Italy* decision,[64] which expressly recognized that a national law can create legitimate expectations and also explained how this phenomenon may take place. This case concerned certain Italian legislative decrees, as well as the relevant implementing acts (so called *Conto Energia* decrees), which guaranteed foreign investors a certain return for a certain period of time (20 years) in relation to investments made in the renewable energy sector. The question before arbitrators was whether these advantages had to be granted without any possibility for future limitation by the State, or could the advantages be reviewed and/or rescheduled by the State (as actually happened through the so-called *Spalma-incentivi* decree) in light of changing economic conditions. The balance, again, is to be struck between the investors' rights and the State's sovereign rights. In this regard, the Tribunal noted that:

> [i]t is undisputed in this case that the object and purpose of Italy's Conto Energia regime was to induce investment in its developing PV sector ahead of when that investment would otherwise occur in light of the high cost of investment prevalent at the time. Italy had complete control over how it designed its scheme and opted for a regime that provided numerous incentives and support for these investments. The main defining feature was the incentive tariff scheme, which provided a constant income stream over the expected life of the investment. The scheme was designed to attract early investment, as it reduced the amount of these tariffs in each successive Conto Energia Decree. Each Conto Energia Decree provided for very specific dates by which a plant needed to be operational in order to benefit from the FITs. There were also limits on the overall

---

[62] PALOMBINO, *Introduzione al diritto internazionale*, Roma/Bari, 2019, p. 55.

[63] See, in this last regard, *Steag GmbH v. Spain*, ICSID Case No. ARB/15/4, Decisión sobre jurisdicción, responsabilidad e instrucciones sobre cuantificación de daños of 8 October 2020 (Tribunal: Eduardo Zuleta, President, Pierre-Marie Dupuy, Guido Santiago Tawil), para. 509.

[64] ICSID Case No. ARB/16/5, Award of 14 September 2020 (Tribunal: Henri Alvarez, President, Michael Pryles, Laurence Boisson de Chazournes), p. 445 ff.

capacity that would receive the incentives. Italy designed its FIT system in a way that allowed it to understand the overall cost and phase out the system once that cost had been reached. Italy later decided that its scheme was too costly for certain consumers and reduced the FIT rates it had been paying.[65]

For this reason:

> in the majority's view, there is no reason in principle why such a commitment of the requisite clarity and specificity cannot be made in the regulation itself where (as here) such a commitment is made for the purpose of inducing investment, which succeeded in attracting the Claimants' investments and, once made, resulted in losses to the Claimants. In these circumstances, there is no principled reason to deny that the investor's expectations of performance by the state are legitimate. The clear and specific guarantee in the Conto Energia Decrees satisfies the requisite degree of specificity needed in order for legitimate expectations to arise from legislation.[66]

On this basis, where an investor's expectations are based on an objective understanding of the legal framework within which the investor made its investment (e.g. a framework providing specific incentives to investors who met specific requirements) or, in other words, what a reasonable investor at the time would have expected,[67] such expectations are to be considered as legitimate. The rescheduling and review of the incentives originally granted to investors in the present case was therefore a violation of FET.

This conclusion is, as to the existence of legitimate expectations arising from legislation, agreeable. What may be subject to criticism is, however, the statement at paragraph 581, according to which: "[i]n the majority's view, where an investor's expectations are found to be legitimate and the Respondent's measures

---

[65] Para. 510.

[66] Para. 512.

[67] In this regard, it is to be noted that the evaluation of the legitimacy of the investor's expectations shall also take into account the investor's behaviour and the accuracy of its evaluation of the so-called "country risk". See *Lidercon SL v. Peru*, ICSID Case No. ARB/17/9, Award of 6 March 2020 (Tribunal: Francisco Gonzalez de Cossio, President, Hugo Perezcano, Jan Paulsson), para. 186, affirming that "[b]efore wondering about the meaning to attribute to the word *legitimate*, however, one needs to consider not only the State's conduct, but also that of the investor in order to ascertain whether there were any *expectations* at all, including with regard to matters of legal security. The Tribunal proceeds on the basis of a notionally objective standard, namely what an ordinarily prudent investor would have been looking at when weighing the risks [of making its investment]". In this regard, it is worth highlighting the words of Pierre-Marie Dupuy in his dissenting opinion in *Steag, cit. supra* note 63, Dissenting Opinion, para. 26: "[e]s la legislación española la que designa y contiene los *hechos jurídicos pertinentes* para definir tales expectativas. Esto es, además, la razón de ser del deber de diligencia del inversor, destinado precisamente a hacerle conocer todas las implicaciones del marco normativo nacional en el que se propone invertir".

violate that expectation, the concepts of reasonableness and proportionality are not relevant". On this point:

> Arbitrator L. Boisson de Chazournes disagrees with the manner according to which the extent of the investors' legitimate expectations have been appraised by the majority. *A balancing and weighing exercise should have been conducted in light of the specific circumstances and facts of the present case.* She does not consider that the applicable regulation in Italy can be construed as "specific assurances" of immutability. The Conto Energia Decrees could not create the legitimate expectation that the tariffs and the payment terms would remain "constant" for the duration of the 20-year term.[68]

The latter kind of approach seems intrinsic to the assessment of FET evaluations, which will necessarily be holistic and include an evaluation of the proportionality of the measures adopted by States, as well as a balancing between the rights of the investors and the sovereign rights of the State. There may be circumstances where a State is mandated, in order to safeguard the public interest, to make certain choices prejudicing investors. The level of liability of States cannot disregard these circumstances and the damages awarded to investors may need to be quantified taking into account such circumstances.[69] This type of reasoning is also reinforced by Dupuy's dissenting opinion in *Steag*:

> [l]as expectativas pueden tener un efecto decisivo cuando se basan en promesas precisas y tangibles hechas por la autoridad competente en un contexto bien determinado, *pero no tienen el poder básico de alterar el poder normativo del Estado* (lo que, además, la presente Decisión no afirma en modo alguno). En otras palabras, las expectativas legítimas deben evaluarse con todo el cuidado debido y tienen que interpretarse de manera restrictiva y, por lo tanto, no invasiva.[70]

Even more explicitly, in *PV*, the Tribunal affirmed that:

---

[68] Para. 645 (emphasis added).

[69] ZARRA, "Right to Regulate, Margin of Appreciation and Proportionality: Current Status in Investment Arbitration in Light of *Philip Morris v. Uruguay*", Brazilian Journal of International Law, 2017, p. 96 ff.

[70] Emphasis added. In English language (own translation): "expectations may assume legal significance when they are based on precise statements or unequivocal facts put into place by the competent [state] authority and within a surrounding context conferring them a certain significance, but the existence of such expectations does not consist in an alteration of the normative power of States (something that is not affirmed in the present decision). In other words, the existence of legitimate expectations shall be evaluated with due caution and adopting a restrictive approach which, by definition, cannot expand the investors' grievances". *Cit. supra* note 63, para. 28.

the Parties to the ECT aimed at realizing a balance between the sovereign rights of the State over energy resources and the creation of a climate favorable to the flow of investments on the basis of market principles. In other words, while the purpose of 'promot[ing] long-term cooperation in the energy field' which is stipulated in Article 2 of the Treaty may be facilitated by stability of the investment framework, the requirement of stability is not absolute; it must be balanced with other principles, including those that are directly derived from 'State sovereignty', e.g. the State's right to regulate and to adapt the regulatory framework to changed circumstances. More generally, the protection of investments and the right to regulate operate in a balanced way under the ECT as in all other investment treaties.[71]

In conclusion, 2020 awards seem to confirm that tribunals privilege a holistic approach to the FET standard, which involves – from the perspective of the investor – an evaluation of all the kinds of commitments assumed by the host State and – from the perspective of the State – the due consideration of the sovereign right to protect the public interest. Such an approach seems to represent an adequate balance between the rights of the parties involved and it is not by chance that, as the abovementioned decisions show, we are facing a crystallization of it within the practice of arbitral tribunals; something that helps to clarify the content of the FET general principle.

9. THE MOST FAVOURED NATION CLAUSE

The scope of application of most favoured nation clauses – treaty clauses allowing investors to benefit from more advantageous clauses contained in other investment treaties – has been the subject of debate for a long time. While some authors and decisions support a wide interpretation of these clauses (allowing even for the importation of arbitration clauses), others favour a stricter approach, according to which MFN clauses may only apply in order to improve the protection concerning standards included in the relevant BIT. In other words, accord-

---

[71] *Cit. supra* note 9, para. 570. Similarly, see *Eskosol, cit. supra* note 5, para. 397 ff. In this regard, see also *Watkins, cit. supra* note 8, para. 601, affirming that proportionality is a FET element (even if, in that case, the Tribunal found that Spain's measures were disproportionate; *contra* see para. 14 of Ruiz Fabri's Dissenting Opinion, affirming: "I regret that no proper exercise of weighing and balancing was conducted and that the context of the economic crisis was not even acknowledged. Other awards have not hesitated to borrow from other courts or tribunals which have developed a framework for proportionality control be it the WTO Appellate Body or the European Court of Human Rights"). See, finally, for a summary of the State's powers concerning foreign investment *Hydro Energy 1 S.a.r.l. et al. v. Spain*, ICSID Case No. ARB/15/42, Decision on jurisdiction, liability and directions on quantum of 9 March 2020 (Tribunal: Lord Collins of Mapesbury, President, Rolf Knieper, Peter Rees), para. 676.

ing to the stricter approach, should a treaty contain, e.g., an MFN clause and a full protection and security clause narrowly worded, the former would allow the tribunal to import wider interpretation of the latter but not to import standards which are completely lacking in the treaty.[72] Strong arguments can be advanced in favour of both approaches: those who support a wide interpretation of MFN clauses base this approach on the wording of investment treaties, which generally do not contain specific limitations to the scope of application of MFN clauses; the strict interpretation, on the contrary, finds support in policy considerations, according to which MFN clauses cannot be seen as a "Pandora's box" allowing the importation of any kind of standard of protection within the system of an investment treaty, even against the will of the drafters.

The tension between these different opinions is also found in the decisions issued in 2020. *Consultel v. Algeria*[73] is certainly a decision favouring a very broad interpretation of MFN clauses. In this case, the Claimant asked to import – on the basis of the MFN clause contained in Article 3 of the Italy-Algeria BIT – the umbrella clause contained in Article 10(2) of the Swiss-Algeria BIT. The effect of this process would have been to import, through an MFN clause, a clause according to which all commitments assumed by Algeria towards Italian investors may constitute the legal basis of a treaty claim. While this result may seem disappointing for its broadness, the Tribunal did not hesitate in stating that it:

> estime à cet égard infondé l'argument de la Défenderesse selon lequel la clause MFN ne pourrait porter sur une clause de respect des engagements en raison de sa nature procédurale. En effet, la clause de respect des engagements a une nature matérielle et non procédurale.[74] [...] Le Tribunal conclut donc que la clause MFN de l'article 3 du Traité permet à la Demanderesse d'invoquer la clause de respect des engagements contenue à l'article 10(2) du traité conclu entre l'Algérie et la Suisse. Le Tribunal abordera maintenant les effets qu'il convient d'attacher à ladite clause dans le cas d'espèce.[75]

In *Itisaluna v. Iraq*,[76] however, the Claimant wanted to import the consent to ICSID arbitration contained in the 2014 Iraq-Japan BIT into a jurisdictional clause which did not refer to it (i.e. Article 17 of the Agreement on Promotion and Protection and Guarantee of Investments among Member States of the Organization of the Islamic Conference: hereinafter "OIC Agreement") through

---

[72] For a detailed analysis of the topic, see LAMPO, "La clausola della nazione più favorita come strumento per l'estensione degli obblighi pattizi in materia di investimenti: il caso *Tatneft v. Ukraine*", Rivista dell'arbitrato, 2019, p. 555 ff., p. 568 ff.

[73] *Consutel Group S.p.A. in Liquidazione v. Algeria*, PCA Case N. 2017-33, Award of 3 February 2020 (Tribunal: Alexis Mourre, President, Attila Tanzi, Ahmed Mahiou).

[74] Para. 357.

[75] Para. 359. In concreto, however, the Tribunal did not apply the umbrella clause in this case because the commitments entered into by Algeria were not specifically directed to the Claimant but to another legal entity.

[76] *Cit. supra* note 5.

the operation of the MFN clause contained in article 8 of the latter agreement. The operation of the MFN clause to incorporate into the OIC Agreement from another treaty "consent in writing to submit [the dispute in question] to the Centre", as required by Article 25(1) of the ICSID Convention, was "the essential bridge that the Claimants must cross if they are to succeed".[77] The Claimants relied on the *Garanti Koza*[78] award, where the majority read consent to ICSID arbitration into a BIT on the basis that the Respondent in that case had consented to ICSID in two other bilateral treaties and in a multilateral treaty to which the Respondent was a party (the Energy Charter Treaty). Contrariwise, in this case, the Tribunal was asked to construe a multilateral treaty by reference to the unrelated bilateral treaty practice of one of its parties. While not excluding that MFN clauses may exceptionally apply to dispute settlement provisions,[79] the arbitrators noted that MFN clauses are not a customary international law principle which is applicable even if not expressly stated. The Tribunal observed that MFN clauses are, rather, an instrument of treaty law that must be expressly stated and which is amenable to limitation, whether expressly or implicitly, having regard to the terms in which the principle is expressed and its purpose in the context of the instrument in which it is found. As a consequence, what had to be ascertained was not whether MFN clauses in the abstract are capable of applying to dispute settlement as a matter of principle but rather whether the particular MFN clause in issue in this case could properly be construed as incorporating into the OIC Agreement written consent to ICSID arbitration. In this regard, referring to *Maffezzini*,[80] the Tribunal noted that if the agreement provides for a particular arbitration forum, such as ICSID, this option cannot be changed by invoking the clause, in order to refer the dispute to a different system of arbitration. For this reason, the arbitrators noted that:

> the OIC Agreement thus establishes a clearly defined and particular dispute settlement regime with institutional elements that include an arbitration forum with bespoke characteristics. It nowhere provides for ICSID arbitration, although it very easily could have done so. The necessary implication is that this omission was a matter of conscious decision.[81]

According to the Tribunal:

---

[77] Para. 146.

[78] *Garanti Koza LLP v. Turkmenistan*, ICSID Case No. ARB/11/20.

[79] Para. 195. In this regard, Arbitrator Stern wanted to be more precise, considering indeed that it is not entirely excluded that an MFN clause could apply to dispute settlement provisions, but only when so indicated in the treaty containing the MFN clause. She considers that there is a "presumption that dispute-resolution provisions do never fall within the scope of an MFN provision in a BIT, unless the contrary is plainly demonstrated".

[80] *Emilio Agustín Maffezini v. The Kingdom of Spain*, ICSID Case No. ARB/97/7, Award of 13 November 2000, para. 63.

[81] Para. 216. This interpretation has been criticized and considered as an unjustified limitation by Arbitrator Rees in his dissenting opinion at para. 226 ff.

there are manifest public policy considerations going to issues of systemic overreach that compel a conclusion that the MFN clause in the OIC Agreement cannot be relied upon to incorporate into the OIC Agreement an ICSID consent to arbitration clause from an unrelated bilateral investment treaty concluded by one of the OIC Contracting Parties alone. In the words of the Maffezini tribunal, with which this Tribunal is happy to agree, 'a distinction has to be made between the legitimate extension of rights and benefits by means of the operation of the clause, on the one hand, and disruptive treaty-shopping that would play havoc with the policy objectives of underlying specific treaty provisions, on the other hand'.[82]

This decision seems to confirm the idea that MFN clauses can be considered as an autonomous cause of action (which can function as a way to even import standards which are extraneous to the relevant treaty) but may not autonomously found an arbitral tribunal's jurisdiction.[83] This is because the assumption of jurisdiction by a tribunal is the logical precursor to the functioning of MFN clauses. Hence, the former process shall necessarily be founded on the wording of the relevant BIT. However, while this approach does not have any drawbacks from the point of view of treaty interpretation, it is to be noted that it ends up justifying approaches such as the one in *Consultel* and therefore significantly altering the content of investment treaties and fostering criticisms against the allegedly excessively pro-investor approaches of investment arbitrators.

10. Relationship between Arbitration and National Courts

Before concluding this analysis, it is necessary to highlight how the decisions issued in 2020 influenced the debate concerning the relationship between investment arbitration and domestic courts. This debate, which should arguably be inspired by a collaborative attitude and by a reciprocal recognition of the adequacy of both avenues for resolving business disputes, may be observed in the 2020 cases both from the perspective of arbitrators and from the perspective of national judges. Surprisingly, we will find that, while domestic courts seem to increasingly encourage the recourse to arbitration and take care to reduce their "invasions" into the arbitration jurisdiction, arbitrators sometimes look with diffidence at domestic jurisdiction.

From the point of view of the arbitrators, a decision which deserves to be mentioned as an example of bad functioning of the dialogue between arbitration and domestic courts is certainly *Michael Antony Lee Chin v. Dominican Republic*.[84] In

---

[82] Para. 220, referring to *Maffezini*, *cit. supra* note 80, para. 63.
[83] LAMPO, *cit. supra* note 72, pp. 574-575 and 580.
[84] ICSID Case No. UNCT/18/3, Partial Award on Jurisdiction of 15 July 2020 (Tribunal: Diego Fernandez Arroyo, President, Christian Leathley, Marcelo Kohen).

this case, arbitrators had to face a murky arbitration clause (Article XIII of the DR-CARICOM Free Trade Agreement), according to which:

> 1. Disputes between an investor of one Party and the other Party concerning an obligation of the latter under this Agreement in relation to an investment of the former which have not been amicably settled *shall*, after a period of three months from written notification of a claim, *be submitted to the courts of that Party or to national or international arbitration.*
>
> 2. *Where the dispute is referred to international arbitration*, the investor and the Party concerned in the dispute *may agree to refer the dispute to an international arbitrator or ad hoc arbitration tribunal* to be appointed by a special agreement or established under the Arbitration Rules of the United Nations Commission on International Trade Law. [...]
>
> 4. The awards of the arbitrator shall be definitive, compulsory and without appeal for the Contracting Party and the investor. [emphases added]

It is evident that the way in which this clause has been drafted leaves it open to differing interpretations. It is not by chance, indeed, that the majority of the arbitrators valorized the phrase "shall refer to arbitration" and considered it sufficient to found their jurisdiction, while dissenting arbitrator Kohen stated that, according to the treaty wording, referring to arbitration was not a possibility for the Claimant.[85] In the opinion of the present author, both these opinions are unsatisfactory.[86] Indeed, while the first and the fourth paragraphs of the dispute settlement provision clearly state that arbitration is a possibility for claimants that has already been accepted by the treaty parties (as evidenced by the binding nature of arbitral awards set forth in paragraph 4), the second paragraph is a clear example of a pathological arbitration clause. The arbitration clause, due to its structural defects, is ineffective and incapable of being performed, considering that the parties had not already (i.e. at the time the dispute arose) expressed the preference for a sole arbitrator or for a panel of three arbitrators and had not not chosen a seat of arbitration. While it might be argued that these missing

---

[85] Arbitrator Kohen, at para. 10 of his dissenting opinion, reached the conclusion that should the clause be interpreted in the sense that the Claimant – and only the Claimant – may start investment proceedings, this would violate the fundamental principle of equality of the parties (which is an essential prong of the due process principle). This interpretation is, however, shocking, considering that, should this reasoning be followed in other cases, the well-established mechanism of arbitration without privity (which founds the entire investment arbitration system and considers BIT dispute settlement clauses as offers to arbitrate that may be activated by investors only) would be entirely ruled out.

[86] Similarly, see LAMPO and MINERVINI, "The First (Tricky) Interpretation of the Consent to Arbitrate in CARICOM-DR FTA: The *Lee-Chin v Dominican Republic* Award", Kluwer Arbitration Blog, 26 October 2020, available at: <http://arbitrationblog.kluwerarbitration.com/2020/10/26/the-first-tricky-interpretation-of-the-consent-to-arbitrate-in-caricom-dr-fta-the-lee-chin-v-dominican-republic-award/>.

elements of the arbitration clause could be filled in by the tribunal by applying the default provisions of the UNCITRAL arbitration rules (which, at Article 7, provide for a panel of three arbitrators that, on the basis of Article 18, may select the seat of arbitration on the basis of the circumstances of the case), this approach might seem an excessive stretching of the wording of paragraph 2. For this reason, the most balanced approach seems to be that the parties should have been referred to arbitration by the national courts of the Respondent (the only domestic courts which are certainly entitled to hear the claim), which should have applied the widely-held attitude of *favor arbitrati* and offered a plausible interpretation of the arbitration clause, starting from the clearly expressed intention to accept arbitration as a method of dispute settlement.[87] The immediate assumption of jurisdiction by the majority might seem, as already stated, a stretch of the wording of Article XIII, testifying to a lack of trust in the possibility of a collaborative attitude being adopted by the courts of the Respondent.

A similar approach has been applied – perhaps more convincingly – in *Strabag SE v. Libya*,[88] where, in the context of a dispute over the violation of an umbrella clause, Libya argued that the Claimant should have privileged dispute settlement provisions of the relevant contracts, which provide for the jurisdiction of Libyan courts. The Tribunal, however, observed that the legal system in Libya after the 2011 revolution was in a state of total uncertainty and this circumstance rendered concretely useless a recourse to Libyan courts.[89]

On the contrary, a collaborative approach between courts and arbitration was assumed, as already noted, in *India v. Vedanta*[90] where the High Court of Singapore avoided any undue interference with the autonomy of the arbitrators in deciding matters concerning the confidentiality of the proceedings and stated that "the Court's supervisory role is to be exercised with a light hand and that arbitrators' discretionary powers should be circumscribed only by the law and by the parties' agreement".[91] In doing so, the High Court recognized a role for the arbitrators in the development of the rule of law and their full capacity to adequately solve investment disputes.[92] This approach is certainly to be welcomed in order to foster a harmonious development of international investment law.

---

[87] This is the approach followed in several jurisdictions throughout the world. See ZARRA, "Il principio del *favor arbitrati* e le convenzioni arbitrali patologiche nei contratti commerciali internazionali", Rivista dell'arbitrato, 2015, p. 138 ff.

[88] ICSID Case No. ARB/(AF)15/1, Award of 29 June 2020 (Tribunal: John Crook, President, Antonio Crivellaro, Nassib Ziadé).

[89] See para. 202: "due to poor security conditions, the courts are not regularly operating in Libya since the Revolution of 2011. Their oral evidence was that some judges were killed, others are impeded from going to office or, in most cases, impeded from exercising their judicial function, inter alia, due to lack of personnel employed by courts to provide clerk services".

[90] *Cit. supra* nota 42, paras. 34 and 143.

[91] Para. 37, citing Supreme Court of Singapore, *Anwar Siraj and another v. Ting Kang Chung and another*, Decision of 24 March 2003, [2003] 2 SLR(R) 28, available at: <https://www.supremecourt.gov.sg/docs/default-source/module-document/judgement/2003-sghc-64.pdf>, para. 42.

[92] See also para. 143.

ITALIAN PRACTICE
RELATING TO INTERNATIONAL LAW

Classification Scheme

© KONINKLIJKE BRILL NV, LEIDEN, 2021 | DOI:10.1163/22116133-03001022

JUDICIAL DECISIONS

(edited by *Daniele Amoroso* and *Andrea Caligiuri*)

VII.   LAW OF THE SEA

Duty to Rescue and Entry into Port: The *Carola Rackete* Decision

Duty to rescue – Law of the Sea – Ports – Jurisdiction – Personal freedom –
Non-refoulement – Article 19(2)(g) of the United Nations Convention on the Law
of the Sea (UNCLOS) – International Convention for the Safety of Life at Sea
(SOLAS) – International Convention on Search and Rescue (SAR)

Corte di Cassazione (Sez. III Penale), 20 February 2020, No. 6626
Criminal proceedings against Carola Rackete

The decision by the Italian *Corte di Cassazione* of 20 February 2020 in the
case concerning Carola Rackete addressed a number of issues relevant for public
international law, in particular law of the sea and human rights law (for an early
commentary on the decision, see PITEA and ZIRULIA, "L'obbligo di sbarcare i
naufraghi in un luogo sicuro: prove di dialogo tra Diritto penale e Diritto internazionale a margine del caso Sea Watch", DUDI, 2020, p. 659 ff.). First and
foremost, it clarified the content of the duty to rescue, a cornerstone of the international law of the sea. Second, it illustrated the distinction between "military
vessels" and "warships" according to the Italian domestic legal order. Third and
last, but not least, it elaborated upon the restriction to personal freedom and the
safeguards that surround derogations from this freedom.

The decision finds it origins in the well-known June 2019 events relating to
Sea Watch 3, a vessel run by the humanitarian NGO Sea Watch for the purpose
of rescuing irregular migrants in distress at sea. On 12 June 2019, *Sea Watch*
3, which operates in the central Mediterranean Sea, rescued some 50 irregular
migrants in distress off the coasts of Libya. On 15 June 2019, Italy's Minister
of the Interior prohibited *Sea Watch 3* from entering into Italian ports. The decision was taken in accordance with Legislative Decree No. 53/2019, which had
been adopted a few days earlier and which allowed the Ministry of the Interior
to refuse entry of specific vessels into the Italian territorial sea for reasons of
public order and security or when the vessel in question had violated the requirements for innocent passage mentioned in Article 19(2)(g) of the United Nations
Convention on the Law of the Sea (UNCLOS) (on the position of Italy vis-à-vis
NGOs operating in the Mediterranean see, among others, BEVILACQUA, "Italy
Versus NGOs: The Controversial Interpretation and Implementation of Search and
Rescue Obligations in the Context of Migration at Sea", IYIL, 2018, p. 11 ff).

Over the following days, *Sea Watch 3* remained just outside the outer limit of
the Italian territorial sea, waiting for Italy to identify the place where the persons

© KONINKLIJKE BRILL NV, LEIDEN, 2021 | DOI:10.1163/22116133-03001023

rescued should be disembarked. Italy however did not indicate any such place and, as the situation on board the vessel was getting worse and worse, on 26 June *Sea Watch 3* entered into the Italian territorial sea and headed towards the island of Lampedusa. On 29 June, after a couple of days of waiting just outside the port of Lampedusa, Carola Rackete, the captain of *Sea Watch 3* decided to force her way into port. During its entrance into Port, *Sea Watch 3* collided with a patrol boat of the Italian *Guardia di Finanza* which was manoeuvring so as to prevent the vessel from reaching the port.

As soon as *Sea Watch 3* was docked, the rescued migrants were disembarked and Captain Rackete was arrested by the *Guardia di Finanza in flagrante delicto* on charges of resistance to public officials and committing an act of violence against a warship. She was, however, soon freed, as the *Giudice per le indagini preliminari* (GIP) *di Agrigento*, with competence for confirming arrests *in flagrante delicto* within 48 hours, did not confirm this arrest. According to the GIP, the arrest was unlawful for two reasons. First, the vessel of the *Guardia di Finanza* could not be considered as a warship, according to Italian law. Second, the acts of Captain Rackete had to be excused on the basis of the defence of "compliance with a duty" – in this case the duty to rescue people in distress at sea – and did not constitute criminal conduct.

The Italian government contested this decision and the case ended up at the *Corte di Cassazione*. The appeal of the Italian government was based on three grounds. First, the GIP had exceeded its powers to evaluate the legitimacy of the arrest. According to Article 385 of the Code of Criminal Procedure, an arrest is unlawful when it "appears" that the facts on which the arrest is based have been carried out in the fulfilment of a duty. Since the GIP had taken ten pages to explain why the acts of Captain Rackete constituted the fulfilment of a duty, this fact was evidently not immediately apparent and thus the arrest was not unlawful. Second, according to the Italian government, the vessels of the *Guardia di Finanza* are warships according to the Italian legislation. Third, the GIP erred in considering that entry into port was justified as part of the fulfilment of the duty to rescue, because this duty is limited to taking people in distress on board a vessel, and does not include the subsequent phase of disembarkation. As a consequence, since the entry into port took place after the duty to rescue had been completed, the duty could not operate as an excuse for the criminal conduct of the Captain of *Sea Watch 3*.

In its decision, the *Corte di Cassazione* dismissed all three grounds of appeal, addressing on the merits the arguments made in relation to the first two grounds. The third ground was considered inadmissible, but the Court did discuss the legal argument at its core – whether rescue also involves disembarkation – in relation to the first ground.

The *Corte di Cassazione* started by assessing the lawfulness of the GIP's evaluation, in accordance with Italian criminal procedural law. The Court clarified that the GIP's powers of judicial review concern only the reasonableness of the arrest evaluated *ex ante*, that is, on the basis of the elements that the police knew or should have known at the time of the arrest. The Court considered that the GIP, in order to evaluate the presence of the defence of fulfilling a duty, correctly considered that the rescue operation carried out by *Sea Watch 3* was a single operation, which included both the collection of the people on board the *Sea Watch 3* and the subsequent conduct up to the moment when the rescued people were disembarked in a place of safety, in the instant case, the port of Lampedusa. The decision, in fact, refers to an "overall, and not parcelled out, evaluation of all the factual elements relevant for understanding the situation" as the right approach for evaluating whether a defence may operate.

As to the existence of a duty to rescue, the *Corte di Cassazione* recalled how this duty is mandated both by international treaties – the judgment refers to the International Convention for the Safety of Life at Sea (SOLAS), the International Convention on Search and Rescue (SAR) and the UNCLOS – and by customary international law. The latter point is of particular importance in the Italian domestic legal order, which allows for the immediate introduction of customary international law through a provision in Article 10 of the Constitution, without the need for any further legislative act. In this respect, the Court made the point that such a duty is "well known by those who operate rescue at sea, but also by those who, because of duty, operate at sea carrying out maritime police activities". This is a point clearly aimed not only at the officers of the *Guardia di Finanza* on duty on the night of 29 June 2019, but also at all other police forces who operate in the context of migration control. The duty, as the Court confirmed, applies not only to States, but also to the masters of vessels (on this issue see STARITA, "Il dovere di soccorso in mare e il 'diritto di obbedire al diritto' (internazionale) del comandante della nave privata", DUDI, 2019, p. 5 ff.; BRIOZZO, "Il ruolo del comandante di nave in relazione ad ipotesi di soccorso in mare nel diritto nazionale ed internazionale", Il Diritto Marittimo, 2019, p. 715 ff.).

Turning to the content of the duty to rescue, the *Corte di Cassazione* stated that it "does not finish with the act of preventing the shipwrecked from getting lost at sea, but entails the accessory and subsequent duty of disembarking them in a place of safety". This introduces the findings of the Court in what is probably the most debated issue concerning the application of the duty to rescue, that is, the identification of a place of safety and disembarkation (see, among others, TURRINI, "Between A "Go Back!" and A Hard (To Find) Place (of Safety): On The Rules and Standards of Disembarkation of People Rescued At Sea", IYIL, 2018, p. 29 ff; NERI, "The Missing Obligation to Disembark Persons Rescued At Sea", IYIL, 2018, p. 47 ff.). In determining the place of safety, the Court referred not only to the IMO Guidelines (MSC Res. 167(78)), but also to Council of Europe Resolution No. 1821 of 21 June 2011, which, "although not being a direct source of law, constitutes an essential interpretative criterion of the concept of 'place of safety' in international law". Based on these documents, the Court made two important findings. First, that a vessel cannot be considered as a place of safety, not only because it is at the mercy of adverse meteorological events, but also because it does not allow the respect of the fundamental rights of the people rescued. Second, and relatedly, that among the fundamental rights which cannot be exercised while on board the vessel there is the right to claim asylum, according to the relevant provisions of the 1951 Convention Relating to the Status of Refugees.

In conclusion, according to the *Corte di Cassazione*, international law includes a duty to rescue people in distress at sea. Rescue consists in saving people from the immediate risk of being lost at sea *and* subsequently disembarking them in a place of safety, where the rescued people may enjoy their fundamental human rights, including the right to claim asylum. This duty has been introduced into the Italian domestic legal system and is well-known, or should be, to all maritime police officials. As a consequence, since Captain Rackete had kept the Italian police informed of all her actions, the police should have known that the entry into port of *Sea Watch 3* constituted the last part of a rescue operation, mandated by a duty, and as such entailed a valid excuse for not complying with the Italian legislation banning entry into port.

Turning to the issue of the status of the *Guardia di Finanza* vessel, the Court distinguished, on the basis of Italian legislation, between military vessels ("*navi militari*") and warships ("*navi da guerra*"). The former category, which is broader and encompasses the latter, certainly includes vessels of the *Guardia di Finanza*. In fact, a vessel is a military vessel if it is registered in a naval role; it is commanded and crewed by military personnel, subject to military discipline; and it bears the markings of the Navy, other military corps or a police force subject to a military order – such as the *Guardia di Finanza*. However, in order for a vessel to be a warship, it must also belong to the armed forces of a State; it must bear the external distinctive markings of military vessels; its crew must be subject to military discipline; and, finally, it must be under the command of a naval officer at the service of the State and registered in the specific role of officials. The latter condition, according to the *Corte di Cassazione*, was not demonstrated with respect to the vessel of the *Guardia di Finanza* involved in the case, which was under the command of a "*maresciallo*", rather than a naval officer.

The findings of the Court relate to an issue which has sometimes puzzled law of the sea scholars: the need to distinguish between military vessels and warships. The UNCLOS, in fact, generally refers to either "warships" or other State-owned vessels, while it uses the word "military" when describing aircraft alongside warships. While the Court's discussion of "warships" and "military vessels" relates to the Italian legal system, it is nonetheless confirmation of the fact that States in general distinguish between (at least) two types of State vessels.

The main contribution of this decision, however, is the clarification of the content of the duty to rescue at sea. Although the case did not directly concern this general rule of international law, the defence of compliance with a duty was based on it and therefore justified the (relatively) lengthy treatment of this duty by the *Corte di Cassazione*. The three main findings of the Court concern the nature of this duty, in international law and in the Italian legal system; the temporal limits of this duty; and the content of the duty itself.

As to the nature of the duty to save life at sea, the *Corte di Cassazione* clearly illustrated how, under international law, this is a duty that is mandated by both treaty law and customary international law. This conclusion accords with an overwhelming and well-established consensus of opinion among international lawyers. As early as 1956, the International Law Commission considered that its draft Article 36 on the duty to rescue codified custom (ILC, Articles concerning the Law of the Sea with Commentaries, 1956, p. 281) and scholars have since consistently confirmed this statement (see, among many others, BARNES, "The International Law of the Sea and Migration Control", in RYAN and MITSILEGAS (eds.), *Extraterritorial Immigration Control: Legal Challenges*, Leiden/Boston, 2010, p. 134; OXMAN, "Human Rights and the United Nations Convention on the Law of the Sea", Columbia JTL, 1998, p. 415 ff.; NORDQUIST, NANDAN and ROSENNE (eds.), *The United Nations Convention on the Law of the Sea 1982: A Commentary*, Den Haag/London/Boston, 1985, Vol. 3; SCOVAZZI, "Human Rights and Immigration at Sea", in RUBIO-MARÍN (ed.), *Human Rights and Immigration*, Oxford, 2014, p. 225 ff.). As a rule of customary international law, furthermore, the duty to rescue becomes automatically part of the Italian legal system, according to Article 10 of the Italian Constitution.

Turning to the temporal limits of this duty, the *Corte di Cassazione* recognized that the GIP of Agrigento correctly evaluated the different events, from the rescue carried out by the *Sea Watch 3* to the moments following the entry into the port of Lampedusa and the arrest of the master of the vessel, as parts of a single operation. The Court pointedly affirmed that the duty to rescue starts when the master of a vessel is informed that there are persons in distress at sea, continues while the master contacts relevant authorities in the effort to find a place to disembark the people rescued, and terminates only when the vessel reaches port and the people are actually disembarked. All acts in between need to be evaluated as part of this duty, and it is not possible, as the Italian government tried to argue, to parcel out different parts. This finding by the *Corte di Cassazione* is of particular relevance for other cases in which States, including Italy, have tried to distinguish between the rescue itself – i.e. the moment when the people in distress are taken onboard the rescuing vessel – and the later moments, when the vessel tries to find a port up until the moment when the vessel actually enters the port and the people disembark.

The search for a place of safety where the rescued people can disembark, therefore, is considered as part and parcel of the duty to rescue. This, in itself, is already a significant finding, as it has sometimes been contested whether this is part of the duty. However, the *Corte di Cassazione* went beyond this and clarified other aspects relating to the content of the duty to rescue, and in particular to the identification of the place of safety, making two significant points. First, a vessel is not a place of safety, not only because it is subject to adverse meteorological conditions, but also – and this is highly innovative – because it cannot grant the people rescued the enjoyment of their fundamental rights. Second, a place, to be considered safe, must allow for the protection of fundamental human rights, including the right to present a request for international protection according to the 1951 Convention on the Status of Refugees. This second finding, which can indeed be considered as subsuming the first finding, applies not only to vessels, but also to any land territory where human rights cannot be protected.

The latter conclusion is certainly innovative and goes beyond what have traditionally been considered as the characteristics of a place of safety. In support of its findings, the *Corte di Cassazione* referred to two soft law instruments: the 2004 IMO Guidelines, mentioned above, and the 2011 Council of Europe Resolution 1821. Reference to soft law instruments could be seen as diminishing the strength of the arguments advanced in the decision. Nonetheless, in the absence of precise indications in hard law concerning the characteristics of the place of safety, it seems not only reasonable, but also convincing to refer to soft law instruments which adhere to the object and purpose of hard law provisions and do not go against the latter's content.

In conclusion, the 2020 decision by the *Corte di Cassazione* in the *Carola Rackete* case confirms and strengthens the attitude of Italian courts to apply the duty to rescue in its entirety. The Court refused to be swayed by shifting political considerations which, unfortunately, too often lead the executive branch of States to disapply international obligations they have themselves created, including the fundamental duty to save life at sea. The Court's reprimand of the *Guardia di Finanza* for twisting legal rules to suit political convenience was clearly expressed when the *Corte di Cassazione*, in referring to the treaty and customary provisions on the duty to save life at sea, noted that they are "all provisions well-known to those who operate salvage at sea, *but also to those who, because of service, operate at sea carrying out maritime police activities*" (emphasis added). In other words, the *Corte di Cassazione* concluded that the very officials who should have been the most acutely aware of the duty to save life at sea, were the ones who ignored this duty in their efforts to arrest a master for acting in compliance with it. This is a precious example of State practice and an example of a teleologically correct application of the international law obligations stemming from the duty to save life at sea.

IRINI PAPANICOLOPULU

VIII. ENVIRONMENT

A POSSIBLE BASIS FOR GRANTING HUMANITARIAN PROTECTION TO "ENVIRONMENTAL MIGRANTS" IN ITALY?

Environmental migrants – Residence Permit for Calamity – Right to health – Subsidiary protection – Right to life – Inhuman and degrading treatment – Non-refoulement principle

Corte di Cassazione (Sez. III Civile), 15 July 2020, No. 25143
M.S. v. Ministero dell'Interno

In the decision under scrutiny, the *Corte di Cassazione* set out the criteria for assessing entitlement to a residence permit on humanitarian grounds when the applicant's condition of "vulnerability" is linked to climatic changes in the country of origin that affect the enjoyment of the right to health.

A Bangladeshi citizen appealed to the *Corte di Cassazione* after the *Tribunale di Caltanissetta* rejected his claim against the Territorial Commission for the Recognition of International Protection for refusing him international protection in the form of subsidiary protection or, alternatively, a residence permit on humanitarian grounds.

© KONINKLIJKE BRILL NV, LEIDEN, 2021 | DOI:10.1163/22116133-03001024

The applicant reported that he fled his country for political reasons, for being a member of a political party in opposition to that of the Mayor of his village, who unjustly accused him of killing his cousin in retaliation for refusing to sell him a property. He stated that the escape was also due to the poverty situation in his village caused by recurrent natural disasters.

The *Corte di Cassazione* rejected two out of the applicant's three contentions. The third one, concerning the denial of humanitarian protection, was declared admissible on the grounds of that there had been "a complete lack of assessment of the level of integration achieved by the applicant in reference to all the conditions, including climatic conditions, of his country of origin, characterized by frequent natural disasters, with repercussions on the fundamental right to health" (para. 6.1). In particular, the Supreme Court, in accordance with Article 360(4) of the Code of Civil Procedure, quashed the decision of the *Tribunale di Caltanisetta* on the ground of lack of reasons.

In this regard, the *Corte* asked the *Tribunale di Caltanisetta* (in a different formation) to rule on the case again in light of the following principle of law:

> with regard to the granting of a residence permit on humanitarian grounds, the applicant's 'condition of vulnerability' must be verified on a case-by-case basis, at the outcome of an individual assessment of his private life in Italy, compared with the personal situation he experienced before his departure and to which he would be exposed in the event of repatriation, since it is not possible to typify the subjective categories deserving of such protection, which is atypical and residual instead. (para. 7)

Therefore, the *Corte* instructed the trial judges to observe a specific line of reasoning: a) to link the norm on humanitarian protection with the fundamental rights that nourish it; b) to appreciate the concept of horizontality of fundamental human rights, with the support of Article 8 of the European Convention on Human Rights (ECHR), to promote the evolution of the norm on humanitarian protection into "a general system clause", capable of fostering human rights and entrenching their implementation; c) to give central importance to a comparative appraisal, under Article 8 ECHR, of the degree of effective integration in Italy and the subjective and objective situation of the applicant in the country of origin, in order to verify whether the return might result in the deprivation of the right to exercise human rights, below the ineliminable and constitutive core of personal dignity, which must include the fundamental right to health, also in relation to climatic conditions.

It should be noted that the *Corte di Cassazione* related the situation of the applicant requesting a residence permit on humanitarian grounds, after emigrating as a result of calamitous events in his country of origin, to Article 20 *bis* of Legislative Decree No. 286/98 (Italian Immigration Law) (para. 6.5).

Article 20 *bis* has introduced a new type of residence permit called "Residence Permit for Calamity". According to this provision, when the country to which the foreigner should return is in a situation of unpredictable and exceptional calamity that does not allow for a safe return and stay, the *Questore* issues a temporary residence permit for calamity. This residence permit is valid for six months and it is renewable; although it authorizes the holder to work, it cannot be converted into a work permit for a longer stay.

Based on a literal wording of this provision and in the absence of specific interpretative case law, Article 20 *bis* seems to offer only a temporary protection against expulsion, suitable for foreign citizens already present in Italy in a situation of irregularity, who find themselves unable to return to their country of origin as a result of unsafe, unpredictable and exceptionally serious conditions.

In the present decision, therefore, the *Corte* seems open to an evolutive interpretation of Article 20 *bis* in compliance with Article 8 ECHR to protect the applicant's right to health.

It would seem reasonable to assume that the *Corte di Cassazione* referred to the ECHR as a means for interpreting national law on the grounds that, at present, only these conventional provisions (and more recently those of the European Social Charter) have been regarded as "interposed norms", according to Article 117(1) of the Italian Constitution. As such, while the ECHR is an interposed parameter of the judicial review of legislation by the Constitutional Court, ordinary (and administrative) courts have the duty to provide an interpretation of domestic laws consistent with the relevant ECHR provisions.

However, the *Corte di Cassazione* does not clearly state which ECtHR case law it is taking as a reference; in fact, the European Court of Human Rights (ECtHR) has not pronounced itself on the protection of environmental migrants yet.

Some limited indications can be gleaned from the case of *Sufi and Elmi v. The United Kingdom* (Applications Nos. 8319/07 and 11449/07, Judgment of 28 June 2011), concerning two Somali nationals being held in detention in the United Kingdom pending deportation to Somalia due to their criminal behaviour. In its judgment, the ECtHR resolved that the return of the two Somali nationals to Mogadishu would amount to inhuman and degrading treatment in breach of Article 3 ECHR because of the situation of general violence there. The ECtHR distinguished between two scenarios in which the provision may be breached, where the occurrence of a particular natural phenomenon could be relevant.

According to the ECtHR, if the humanitarian conditions in Somalia "were solely or even predominantly attributable to poverty or to the State's lack of resources to deal with a naturally occurring phenomenon, such as a drought", a breach of Article 3 ECHR could be argued where such conditions constitute "very exceptional cases" in conformity with the threshold test established in *N. v. The United Kingdom* (Application No. 26565/05, Judgment of 28 May 2008, see para. 43) (para. 283 of the Judgment). However, in the Court's assessment, the conditions in Somalia, although exacerbated by the natural phenomenon of drought, were predominantly due to the direct or indirect actions of the parties to the conflict and al-Shabaab's refusal to allow international agencies to operate in areas under its control. In this case, the Court applied the approach adopted in *M.S.S. v. Belgium and Greece*, which emphasized the following requirements for determining a breach of Article 3: the "applicant's ability to cater for his most basic needs, such as food, hygiene and shelter, his vulnerability to ill-treatment and the prospect of his situation improving within a reasonable time-frame" (*ibid.*). Considering the reports on the situation in the camps for displaced people in Somalia and in the Dadaab refugee camps in Kenya, and the fact that these camps were becoming increasingly overcrowded, the ECtHR concluded that any person seeking internal protection in one of these camps would be at risk of treatment contrary to Article 3 ECHR on account of the dire humanitarian conditions (para. 292 of the Judgment).

This case seems to create an opportunity for change in the relevant case law of the ECtHR because it could imply that the recognition of subsidiary protection from the risk of suffering serious harm in the form of inhuman and degrading treatment must also be granted in a situation of displacement due to climate change. In particular, this would occur in situations of active or omissive conduct by state authorities or non-state agents able to control a given territory and when the deteriorating consequences of climate change or a given environmental change for a portion or the entirety of the population is predominantly due to such active or omissive conduct.

Recently, another human rights conventional system, the International Covenant on Civil and Political Rights (ICCPR), proved offer more room for protection of environmental migrants, as revealed by views adopted by the UN Human Rights Committee (HRC) in the case of *Ioane Teitiota v. New Zealand* (CCPR/C/127/D/2728/2016), on 7 January 2020 (see MALETTO, "Non-refoulement e cambiamento climatico: il caso Teitiota c. Nuova Zelanda", SIDIBlog, 23 March 2020, available at: <www.sidiblog.org/2020/03/23/non-refoulement-e-cambia-mento-climatico-il-caso-teitiota-c-nuova-zelanda>; SOMMARIO, "When Climate Change and Human Rights Meet: A Brief Comment on the UN Human Rights Committee's Teitiota Decision", Questions of International Law, Zoom-in 77 (2021), p. 51 ff.).

In the *Teitiota* case, the HRC rendered its opinion concerning a Kiribati national, who alleged that New Zealand had violated his right to life under Article 6 ICCPR by returning him to Kiribati in September 2015. For the first time, the HRC recognized that, in principle, climate change can pose a "real risk" of irreparable harm to the right to life of an individual in his State of origin.

In its decision, the HRC stated that "the right to life cannot be properly understood if it is interpreted in a restrictive manner, and that the protection of that right requires States parties to adopt positive measures" (para. 9.4 of the views). Thus, not only does the normative content of the human right to life require States to refrain from creating intentional harm or injury to life, it also establishes the positive obligation to protect the population from "reasonably foreseeable threats and life-threatening situations that can result in loss of life" (*ibid.*). The principle that emerges is that a State can be liable for violating the human right to life (Art. 6 ICCPR) when, although it has not intentionally engaged in any conduct likely to provoke a reasonably foreseeable event, it cannot demonstrate that it has taken all possible measures to safeguard the lives of those under its jurisdiction (such as ensuring the right to food, water and shelter) in the face of general conditions that may pose a serious threat to the ability to enjoy the right to life, such as environmental degradation, climate change and unsustainable development, or has failed to take measures to minimize the effects and risks of an unexpected and violent natural phenomenon. It follows that the reasonable foreseeability of a natural event threatening the right to life, including the right of individuals to enjoy a life with dignity, coupled with the inability of the applicant's State of origin to fulfil its positive obligations to protect the right, results in third States having the negative obligation of non-refoulement to the country in question. Finally, it is worth noting that the HRC recognized that the negative effects of climate change can also lead to inhuman and degrading treatment (Art. 7 ICCPR).

In light of the *Teitiota* decision, Italian judges may adopt a reasoning similar to that of the HRC, developing an evolutive interpretation of the ECHR, in accordance with classic international rules on the interpretation of treaties, and giving rise to non-refoulement obligations for Italy under ECHR Articles 2 (right to life) and/or 3 (prohibition of inhuman and degrading treatment), when individuals face removal to their home countries where they risk life-threatening conditions due to climate change. Moreover, it should not be forgotten that the ECtHR itself has emphasized that the ECHR cannot be interpreted in isolation and that, so far as possible, its provisions should be read in a manner that is consistent with other rules of public international law (see *Al-Adsani v. The United Kingdom*, Application No. 35763/97, Grand Chamber, 21 November 2001, para. 55; *Bosphorus Hava Yollari Turizm ve Ticaret Anonim Sirket v. Ireland*, Application No. 45036/98, Grand Chamber, 30 June 2005, para. 150).

Finally, consideration should be given to the *Corte di Cassazione*'s decision to choose the special protection for calamity under Article 20 *bis* of Legislative Decree No. 286/98 as the legal basis for protecting environmental migrants. The limitations of this provision are quite evident as the exceptional nature of the calamity and the absence of safety in case of return are set as conditions for issuing the permit; thus, sudden-onset natural events but of a non-exceptional nature, and slow-onset natural events with a predictable progression, which do not affect safety but rather the minimum conditions of existence, would be deemed irrelevant.

Therefore, it might seem more reasonable for Italian judges to base their assessments on the recognition of subsidiary protection to those who flee from the effects of climate change or from disastrous events on Article 14(b) Legislative Decree No. 251/07 (see BRAMBILLA and CASTIGLIONE, "Migranti ambientali e divieto di respingimento di respingimento", Questione giustizia, 14 February 2020, available at: <https://www.questionegiustizia.it/articolo/migranti-ambi-entali-e-divieto-di-respingimento_14-02-2020.php>). This provision explicitly refers to "torture or any other form of inhuman or degrading treatment or punishment of the applicant in his or her country of origin" as evidence of the "serious damage" threshold required to obtain subsidiary protection in Italy. Thus, if the environmental migrants' situation of "serious damage" in their country of origin is found to have been predominantly caused by an intentional act or a conscious omission otherwise avoidable by that State, they would have a right to enjoy subsidiary protection in the territory of the Italian Republic.

ANDREA CALIGIURI

XI. TREATMENT OF ALIENS AND NATIONALITY

FONDO PER L'AFRICA: RIGHT OF ACCESS TO DOCUMENTATION AND LEGITIMACY OF THE ALLOCATION OF RESOURCES BEFORE THE ITALIAN *CONSIGLIO DI STATO*

Migration – Fondo per l'Africa – Partnership Agreement between Italy and the IOM – Italian Freedom of Information Act – Protection of international relations – Immunities of international organizations – Decree No. 4110/47 – Articles 10(3) and 117(1) of the Italian Constitution – Articles 2 and 3 of the European Convention on Human Rights – Article 4 of Protocol No. 4 to the European Convention on Human Rights

Consiglio di Stato (Sez. IV), 13 May 2020, No. 3012
Lucia Gennari v. Ministero degli affari esteri e della cooperazione internazionale and International Organization for Migration

Consiglio di Stato (Sez. IV), 15 July 2020, No. 4569
Associazione per gli Studi Giuridici sull'Immigrazione et al. v. Ministero degli Affari Esteri e della Cooperazione Internazionale and others

The judgments under scrutiny concern the allocation of resources from the so-called "Africa Fund", established by the Budget Law for 2017 (*Fondo per l'Africa*, Article 1(621) of Law No. 232/2016). The fund, managed by the Ministry of Foreign Affairs, was aimed at financing "extraordinary measures to renew dialogue and cooperation with key African partners on migration". Such measures have been implemented both through agreements with African countries (see in general SPAGNOLO, "The Conclusion of Bilateral Agreements and Technical Arrangements for the Management of Migration Flows: An Overview of the Italian Practice", IYIL, 2019, p. 209 ff.) and through cooperation with international organizations (an overview by the *Associazione per gli Studi Giuridici sull'Immigrazione* (ASGI) is available at: <https://sciabacaoruka.asgi. it/wp-content/uploads/2020/01/Microsoft-Word-ENG-scheda-accessi-OI.docx. pdf>). In particular, the first judgment (No. 3012 of 13 May 2020) addresses the right of access to documents issued by the International Organization for Migration (IOM) concerning activities financed through the *Fondo per l'Africa*, whilst the second decision (No. 4569 of 15 July 2020) examines the legitimacy of the earmarking of resources for the Libyan General Administration for Coastal Security (GACS).

In Judgment No. 3012 of 13 May 2020, the *Consiglio di Stato* ruled on the lawfulness of the refusal by the Ministry of Foreign Affairs to grant access to documents detailing the implementation and financing of a project aimed at facilitating the "voluntary return" of stranded migrants in Libya (the project – "Humanitarian return and reintegration of vulnerable and stranded migrants in Libya" – was outlined in the "Partnership Agreement" of 4 August 2017 between Italy and the IOM and renewed in 2019; on its contested legitimacy, see FILL and MORESCO, "I rimpatri volontari dalla Libia nella strategia di esternalizzazione dell'UE", ASGI, available at: <https://sciabacaoruka.asgi.it/oim-ripatri-volon-tari-contenzioso-strategico/>). In particular, the applicant sought the disclosure of a report that had been issued by the IOM and subsequently transmitted to the Ministry of Foreign Affairs. The Ministry consulted with the IOM, which opposed the disclosure of the document. Accordingly, the authorities rejected the applicant's request on the ground of the "protection of international relations" under Article 5-*bis* of Legislative Decree No. 33/2013 (as amended by Legislative Decree No. 97/2016, known as the Italian "Freedom of Information Act" – FOIA), which sets forth the regime of exceptions to the general right of access to documents (*accesso civico generalizzato*; see ROSSI, "Government Transparency and the Right of Access to Information: Evolving International and European Standards and Their Implementation in the Italian Legal System", IYIL, 2018, p. 181 ff.). The Ministry asserted that the disclosure would have damaged the relationship between Italy and the IOM and caused a "substantial and immediate decrease of the influence of Italy in the countries where it operates in partnership with the IOM, and especially in Libya".

The applicant claimed that, by rejecting the request, the Ministry violated Article 5-*bis*. Indeed, in the applicant's view, the protection of international relations under the Article should be interpreted as excluding the duty to grant access only to information detailing *specific* actions of *identified* individuals, while the *general* structure and financing of operations should always be disclosed. Therefore, the Ministry should have granted the request after having removed the personal data of the individuals mentioned in the document.

On the contrary, in the trial of first instance (*Tribunale Amministratico Regionale per il Lazio, Sez. III ter*, 28 October 2019, No. 12349), the *Tribunale Amministrativo Regionale* (TAR), relying on a previous decision (*Consiglio di Stato*, 2 September 2019, No. 6028, IYIL, 2019, p. 440 ff., with a comment by MINERVINI), asserted that the evaluation of the danger posed to Italy's international relations by the disclosure of a certain document is "highly discretionary, if not even political in nature". Therefore, the scope of the review by administrative courts is limited to assessing if it is "completely implausible" that the publication of the requested documents would damage the country's international relations. Consequently, the TAR ruled in favour of the Ministry of Foreign Affairs.

The *Consiglio di Stato* rejected the interpretation offered by the TAR on the ground that such a narrow scope of the judicial review would *de facto* force administrative courts to passively accept the decisions of public administrations, unreasonably extending a regime similar to State secrets to documents which have not been formally declared as classified. However, the *Consiglio di Stato* did not embrace the interpretation proposed by the applicant either. On the contrary, it ruled that the legitimacy of the refusal to grant access to a document on the ground of the protection of international relations must be ascertained on a case-by-case basis, taking into consideration the specific factual circumstances and the motivation provided for the refusal. The report at issue did not seem to contain any information that, if made public, could have represented a threat to Italy's international relations. Moreover, the arguments for the refusal failed to substantiate any public interest against the disclosure of the document. Therefore, the *Consiglio di Stato* granted access to the report, provided that the personal data was removed.

In light of the reasoning of the Court, two issues are noteworthy.

Firstly, the *Consiglio di Stato* addressed the question of the scope of the judicial review in matters of access to documents under Legislative Decree No. 33/2013. The approach adopted by the Court is consistent with the rationale of the "balancing of the interests" which is core to the Italian FOIA (see *Autorità Nazionale Anticorruzione* (ANAC), Determinazione No. 1309 of 28 December 2016; FILICE, "I limiti all'accesso civico generalizzato: tecniche e problemi applicativi", Diritto Amministrativo, 2019, p. 861 ff.). Indeed, public authorities, when requested to disclose a document, must ascertain whether said disclosure could potentially be harmful to the public interests listed in Article 5-*bis* of Legislative Decree No. 33/2013 (the so-called "harm test"). If there is such a risk, the administration must then proceed to carefully evaluate, on a case-by-case basis, whether the reasons against the disclosure prevail over the public interest in transparency and accountability (see FILICE, *cit. supra*). According to the Judgment under scrutiny, when the motivation for the refusal to grant access reveals that said careful evaluation has not taken place, administrative courts have the power to perform the "balancing" between the conflicting interests themselves and are not limited to a mere *prima facie* review over the abstract legitimacy of the decision taken by the administration (similarly, see TAR *Lazio, Sez. III*, 1 August 2019, No. 10202). This broader interpretation of the scope of the judicial review ensures that citizens have access to an effective remedy when public administrations illegitimately refuse to comply with their obligations under the FOIA.

Secondly, it must be noted that the *Consiglio di Stato* granted access to the report even though the document had been issued by the IOM and the Organization had requested the Ministry of Foreign Affairs not to disclose it. This decision may prove relevant vis-à-vis two issues. First, the Judgment shows that, when a document is transmitted by an international organization to a State, the international organization's opposition to the disclosure does not constitute *per se* a legitimate reason to reject a FOIA request on the ground of the protection of international relations. Second, the *Consiglio di Stato* – by not explicitly considering the matter – aligned itself with the view that documents issued by international organizations cease to benefit from the inviolability of their "archives" once they are transmitted to States within the framework of the organizations' external relations (see AMERASINGHE, *Principles of the Institutional Law of International Organizations*, Cambridge, 2005, p. 315 ff.; for the immunities granted by Italy to the IOM, see Article VII of the 1967 Agreement between the Italian Government and the Intergovernmental Committee for European Migration, approved and executed under Law No. 441/1968). Indeed, according to the aforementioned Italy-IOM Partnership Agreement, Italy received the report as a "donor" to the IOM. In this regard, the Judgment may have a strategic importance for future litigation on FOIA requests concerning operations carried out by international organizations and financed through Italian funds.

The resources of the *Fondo per l'Africa* are also central to the second decision under scrutiny. Indeed, in Judgment No. 4569 of 15 July 2020 (for the first instance decision, see TAR *Lazio, Sez. III*, 1 July 2019, No. 176, IYIL, 2019, p. 440 ff., with a comment by MINERVINI), the *Consiglio di Stato* assessed the legitimacy of Decree No. 4110/47, through which the Ministry of Foreign Affairs assigned 2.5 million euros to the GACS, a department of the Libyan Ministry of Interior. In particular, the funds were earmarked for the repair and maintenance of four patrol boats and a training course for 22 crew members.

The applicant claimed that the assistance provided to the Libyan border authorities constituted an aggravation of the conditions of migrants and asylum seekers, who, having fewer possibilities to leave Libya, were exposed to systematic violations of their fundamental rights. Therefore, the Decree could not possibly be consistent with the purpose of the *Fondo per l'Africa*, thus resulting in a misuse of power. In the alternative, the applicant alleged that Article 1(621) of Law No. 232/2016 instituting the *Fondo per l'Africa* was in breach of Articles 10(3) and 117(1) of the Italian Constitution, which respectively recognize the right to asylum and set forth the duty for the legislative power to be exercised in compliance with international obligations. In the applicant's view, Article 1(621) of Law No. 232/2016 violated Articles 2 and 3 of the European Convention on Human Rights (ECHR) and Article 4 of Protocol No. 4 to the ECHR.

The *Consiglio di Stato* asserted the legitimacy of Decree No. 4110/47, rejecting both claims.

First, by making reference to the guidelines provided by Decree No. 1002/200 of the Ministry of Foreign Affairs, the *Consiglio di Stato* determined that the funding under its scrutiny was aimed at fostering cooperation with a key African partner on migration and was, therefore, consistent with the purpose of the *Fondo per l'Africa*. Then, the Court emphasized "the difference between an intervention having a legitimate purpose [...] and its potential consequences, that, albeit somehow connected to it, are caused by agents that are extraneous and beyond the control of the Italian authorities". Said consequences were reduced to mere "context", that was deemed to fall outside the scope of the judicial review. As for the Decree's usefulness and appropriateness in pursuing the purpose of the *Fondo per l'Africa*, the *Consiglio di Stato* ruled that the choices made by the Government were also outside the scope of the judicial review, given that they fell within the discretionary powers of the administration.

With respect to the alleged inconsistency with the Constitution, the *Consiglio di Stato* found that Italy did not bear any responsibility for the contested human rights violations. First, because Italy does not have effective control over the Libyan territory and authorities. Second, because the funding at issue was earmarked with the stated purpose, among others, of aligning the conduct of the Libyan authorities with the respect of human rights. Moreover, there was no proof that the intervention was intended to support the commission of internationally wrongful acts. With specific regard to the right of asylum, the *Consiglio di Stato* affirmed that the aims of the funding had nothing to do with the procedure for granting refugee status, which presupposes the presence of the applicant in the Italian territory or at the border. In addition, it was emphasized that, although Libya is not a party to the 1951 Refugee Convention, the United Nations High

Commissioner for Refugees (UNHCR) and the IOM have managed to create "a solid framework of assistance" in the country.

In this judgment, the *Consiglio di Stato* evidently adopted a formalistic approach, limiting its review to the declared purposes of the *Fondo per l'Africa* and disregarding its consequences. This approach is hardly acceptable, because it neglects the fundamental matter of the protection of migrants' human rights in Libya, which are undeniably impacted by measures like the one at issue. The judgment also plays into the hands of policies aimed at the externalization of migration and border controls in Libya, that have allowed Italy and the EU to reduce the number of migrants arriving while avoiding any possible responsibility under international law (see DE VITTOR, "Responsabilità degli Stati e dell'Unione europea nella conclusione e nell'esecuzione di 'accordi' per il controllo extraterritoriale della migrazione", DUDI, 2018, p. 5 ff.; GIUFFRÉ and MORENO-LAX, "The Rise of Consensual Containment: From 'Contactless Control' to 'Contactless Responsibility' for Migratory Flows", in JUSS (ed.), *Research Handbook on International Refugee Law*, Cheltenham, 2019, p. 82 ff.).

In this regard, the issue of State jurisdiction is crucial. It must be noted that, in various instances, the European Court of Human Rights (ECtHR) and other international tribunals and Treaty bodies went beyond the standard of effective control, adopted by the *Consiglio di Stato*, to assess the exercise of extraterritorial jurisdiction. In short, it was found that the extraterritorial jurisdiction of States is engaged when their actions have a direct and foreseeable impact on the rights of individuals, when they exercise a decisive influence over a third actor, or when they have an operative involvement in another State's functions (see MORENO-LAX, "The Architecture of Functional Jurisdiction: Unpacking Contactless Control – On Public Powers, *S.S. and Others v. Italy*, and the 'Operational Model'", German Law Journal, 2020, p. 385 ff.). The assistance provided by Italy to Libya could arguably fit into all the aforementioned situations.

Moreover, with respect to Italy's alleged human rights violations, the *Consiglio di Stato* did not address at least two possible grounds of responsibility: complicity under Article 16 of the 2001 Draft Articles on Responsibility of States for Internationally Wrongful Acts (see PASCALE, "Is Italy Internationally Responsible for the Gross Human Rights Violations against Migrants in Libya?", Questions of International Law, Zoom-in 56, 2019, p. 35 ff.) and failure to comply with due diligence obligations (see FERSTMAN, "Human Rights Due Diligence Policies Applied to Extraterritorial Cooperation to Prevent 'Irregular' Migration: European Union and United Kingdom Support to Libya", German Law Journal, 2020, p. 459 ff.).

Lastly, the Court's assessment of the right to asylum deserves particular consideration. On the one hand, it is far from certain that Italy's duties are only engaged when an individual is within the territory of the State or at the border. Indeed, Italian courts held in at least two instances (*Corte di Cassazione, Sez. I Civile*, 25 November 2005, No. 25028; *Tribunale di Roma, Sez. I Civile*, 28 November 2019, No. 22917) that the right to asylum under Article 10(3) of the Constitution entails the right to enter the State's territory, in order to apply for the recognition of the status of refugee (see GIUFFRÉ, "Esternalizzazione delle frontiere e *non-refoulement*: accesso al territorio e alla procedura di asilo alla luce della sentenza n. 22917/2019", Questione Giustizia, 2020, p. 190 ff.). Said component of the right to asylum is symmetrical to the duty of *non-refoulement*, that "encompasses any measure attributable to a State which could have the effect of returning an asylum-seeker or refugee to the frontiers of territories where his or her life or freedom would be threatened, or where he or she would risk persecution" (UNHCR, "Note on International Protection", UN Doc. No. A/AC.96/951 (2001), para. 16; see also *Hirsi Jamaa and Others v. Italy*, Application No. 27765/09, Grand Chamber, Judgment of 23 February 2012, where the ECtHR upheld the extraterritorial scope of the obligation not to *refouler*, that applies wherever a State exercises jurisdiction). On the other hand, the assistance provided to asylum seekers by the UNHCR and IOM in Libya cannot possibly be considered, as the *Consiglio di Stato* seemingly implied, as a valid and legitimate replacement for the *de facto* denial of the right to asylum caused by the externalization of borders (see ASGI, "L'attività delle organizzazioni internazionali in Libia e le problematiche ripercussioni sull'esternalizzazione del diritto di asilo", Questione Giustizia, 2020, p. 178 ff.).

GIACOMO BRUNO and COSTANZA CERNUSCO

ALLEGED WAR CRIMINALS SEEKING ASYLUM: HOW SERIOUS DO THE REASONS FOR EXCLUSION FROM INTERNATIONAL PROTECTION NEED TO BE?

War crimes – Refugee status – Subsidiary protection – Exclusion – United Nations Convention Relating to the Status of Refugees and its 1967 Protocol – Humanitarian protection

Corte di Cassazione (Sez. I Civile), 19 November 2020, No. 26376 (Order)
Jeff Nathanael Gouet v. Ministero dell'Interno

The relationship between international refugee law and international criminal law has been the object of scholarly analysis for quite a while (see LAFONTAINE, RIKHOF and BAIG (guest eds.), "Special Issue. The Interaction Between Refugee Law and International Criminal Justice", JICJ, 2014, p. 1 ff.). The commission of an international crime is, in fact, one of the three grounds envisaged under Article 1F of the 1951 Refugee Convention for excluding unworthy or underserving individuals from the protection of the Convention and of refugee status. Article 1F reads as follows:

> The provisions of this Convention shall not apply to any person with respect to whom there are serious reasons for considering that:
> a) he has committed a crime against peace, a war crime, or a crime against humanity, as defined in the international instruments drawn up to make provision in respect of such crimes;
> b) he has committed a serious non-political crime outside the country of refuge prior to his admission to that country as a refugee;

c) he has been guilty of acts contrary to the purposes and principles of the United Nations.

(for a thorough examination of the provision and its legislative history, see ZIMMERMANN, WENNHOLZ, "Article 1 F", in ZIMMERMANN (ed.), *The 1951 Convention Relating to the Status of Refugees and its 1967 Protocol*, Oxford, 2011, p. 579 ff.). It is interesting to point out that the ultimate rationale underlying the provision is the concern that a country of refuge could become a safe haven, harbouring individuals responsible for international atrocities. Avoiding such a situation is a prominent goal under international criminal law, so deeply entrenched as to be eventually embraced in EU law as well, both with reference to exclusion from the refugee status itself and with reference to exclusion from subsidiary protection. Subsidiary protection is a somewhat lesser status applicable to individuals not meeting the criteria of refugee, and may also be withdrawn in the same cases as set out in Article 1F (see Directive 2011/95/EU of the European Parliament and of the Council of 13 December 2011 on standards for the qualification of third-country nationals or stateless persons as beneficiaries of international protection, for a uniform status for refugees or for persons eligible for subsidiary protection, and for the content of the protection granted (recast), OJ L 337/9, 20 November 2011, hereinafter "qualification directive", Art. 12(2)(a) and Art. 17(1)(a) respectively for exclusion from refugee status and subsidiary protection). Excluded asylum seekers may be extradited, provided that this does not expose them to any risk of persecution, in the case of exclusion from refugee status, or to risks to life and physical integrity, in the case of exclusion from subsidiary protection. They may also be prosecuted by the host State (SANTALLA, "Universal Jurisdiction and the Prosecution of Excluded Asylum-Seekers", in STAHN and VAN DEN HERIK (eds.), *Future Perspectives on International Criminal Justice*, Den Haag, 2012, p. 289 ff.), an avenue which is becoming more and more common. In the last few years, in fact, a significant number of excluded asylum seekers, mainly individuals allegedly responsible for international crimes committed in the context of the ongoing Syrian armed conflict, were indicted or actually prosecuted in States throughout Europe, mostly under the universal jurisdiction principle (SCHARF, STERIO and WILLIAMS, *The Syrian Conflict's Impact on International Law*, Cambridge, 2020, p. 110 ff.; VAN SCHAAK, *Imagining Justice for Syria*, Oxford, 2020, p. 265 ff.). All that taken into account, the overlap and the fruitful cross-fertilization between international refugee law, on the one hand, and international criminal law, on the other, should not come as a surprise; nor, for that matter, should the order by the *Corte di Cassazione* under comment, in which the notion of war crimes proved to be pivotal for the purposes of deciding whether to apply international protection.

In the case under scrutiny, Mr Gouet, an Ivorian asylum-seeker, contested before the *Corte di Cassazione* a decree of the *Tribunale di Napoli* upholding the assessment previously performed by the competent Territorial Commission, whereby he had been denied international protection, both in the form of refugee status and in the form of subsidiary protection (both being provided for under domestic legislation which brings the Italian legal order in line with relevant EU Law provisions;

see D. Lgs. 19 November 2007, No. 251, Arts. 10 and 16, respectively). Mr Gouet had, however, been awarded a temporary permit on humanitarian grounds. The main point underlying the reasoning of the Tribunal, which justified the exclusion of the applicant from being granted international protection, was the existence of a significant impediment, namely the commission of an international crime, albeit in the less serious mode of aiding and abetting. As the applicant (whom the Tribunal deemed to be sufficiently credible and reliable) himself admitted throughout the proceedings, he had indeed taken part in the non-international armed conflict that had raged in Ivory Coast following the post-election outburst of violence between the supporters of the newly elected President Alassane Ouattara (whose victory had been certified by an independent commission) and the acolytes of the Popular Front led by the former President Laurent Gbagbo, who refused to concede the victory. However, far from hurting or killing anyone, he had only been charged with the logistics of the defence of his neighborhood. Mr Gouet claimed, in fact, to have only prepared barricades and patrolled the gates, in order to prevent the access of the presidential forces to his hometown. The Tribunal, however, had qualified such conduct as a war crime, thus confirming the exclusion of the applicant from the benefit of international protection.

The applicant challenged the decision of the Tribunal on the grounds of a violation of Article 3 of D.Lgs. No. 251/2007, alleging a misevaluation of his application, and substantiated his claim through a multifaceted argument, both fact-based and legal-based. Not only did he claim that a tribunal sitting in the context of a status ascertainment hearing lacked the competence to rule on criminal conduct, let alone war crimes, but he also claimed that, in doing so, the Tribunal had mischaracterized his conduct. The latter contention was based on two grounds: first, the installation of barricades was not foreseen as a war crime under Article 8 of the Rome Statute of the International Criminal Court; second, no functional nexus between such conduct and an armed conflict could actually be envisaged. Accordingly, he concluded that, far from having to be excluded from international protection, he was instead fully entitled to it.

The *Corte di Cassazione* addressed and endorsed Mr Gouet's argument. It upheld the twofold merit-based argumentation concerning the wrongful qualification of the applicant's conduct, confirming that the mere construction of barricades could not possibly amount to any of the acts expressly criminalized under the category of war crimes by the Rome Statute (nor to the conduct envisaged under Articles 12-17 Qualification directive), and further confirming the absence of a functional link between the applicant's conduct and the armed conflict. The latter element is, in fact, the quintessential feature of a war crime, envisaged by case law and scholars alike, and a decisive factor for the purposes of clarifying whether an act may amount to a war crime or not. The requirement of a nexus with an armed conflict does not have a mere geographical and temporal scope, but is instead *functional* in nature, meaning that the conduct must be performed for the purposes of furthering the military effort (more thoroughly on the nexus requirement, see WERLE and JESSBERGER, *Principles of International Criminal Law*, 4th ed., Oxford, 2020, p. 473 ff.). An interesting element in the decision is the reference made by the *Corte* to the values of the international community. More precisely, the Court considered the conduct not to be serious enough to amount to a war crime, despite it having been performed in the context of a non-international armed conflict, because it did not affect the "essential values of the international community" (para. 5.2). Having pointed this out, the *Corte* quashed the impugned decision and sent the matter right back to the *Tribunale di Napoli*, for the latter to reassess it in light of the clarifications (para. 8). The solution adopted by the *Corte* is convincing and technically sound; it makes a lot of sense to interpret exclusion clauses in a restrictive manner in order to minimise the scope of exclusion, and reinforce the humanitarian aspirations underlying international refugee law instruments (commentators emphasize this policy goal especially in the context of asylum-seeking child soldiers; see MAYSTRE, "The Interaction between International Refugee Law and International Criminal Law with respect to Child Soldiers", JICJ, 2014, p. 975 ff., p. 986).

Besides the specific consequences of the order under scrutiny on the applicant's personal situation, the Court's examination of the relevance of war crimes for the purposes of international protection (i.e. which definition of "war crime" may legitimately influence the decision on the award of protection) is likely to have an impact on the practice of all tribunals competent to evaluate applications for international protection, as well as a much broader relevance, in systemic terms, on the theoretical and normative assumptions concerning the scope and nature of such evaluation as well as the elements it is premised upon. While addressing the actual scope and meaning of the notion of war crimes, i.e. what conduct is susceptible of amounting to a war crime, what are the main sources under international law and the main tenets of the discipline (paras. 4-6), the *Corte* not only mentioned substantive conventions (e.g. the 1949 Geneva Conventions and the 1977 Additional Protocols) and the statutes of international criminal tribunals (e.g. ICTY Statute, ICTR Statute, Rome Statute), but also the case law of international tribunals. This international case law is often very progressive in nature (suffice to mention the *Tadić* jurisprudence of the ICTY); thus, by relying on it, the *Corte* has contributed to the dynamic and evolutive interpretation of war crimes law. The *Corte* also focused, albeit very briefly and almost in an implicit fashion, on two other important issues: whether and, if so, up to what extent can the task of ruling on war crimes be incidentally performed by tribunals competent to ascertain the status of asylum seekers (para. 2). What can be gathered from the cursory analysis of those issues performed in the decision (paras. 7-8) is that tribunals competent under Article 35-*bis* D.Lgs. 25/2008 in matters of status ascertainment, are also incidentally competent to make findings as to the commission of international crimes qua impediments to recognizing either refugee status or subsidiary protection. In making such an assessment, tribunals need to refer to relevant provisions under international law and to apply them in a proper and correct manner, in order to correctly qualify conduct as likely amounting to an international crime.

However, the *Corte* arguably should have clarified a few related issues, such as the evidentiary standard to be used by tribunals for the purposes of establishing the existence of one or more impediments – especially international crimes – to the granting of international protection. The threshold is not, in fact, easily inferred from relevant provisions, nor is State practice on the matter un-ambiguous (BOND, "Principled Exclusion: A Revised Approach to Article 1(F) (a) of the Refugee Convention", Michigan Journal of International Law, 2013, p. 15 ff., pp. 38-39). The actual meaning of the expression "serious reasons" (see also Art. 10(2), D.Lgs. No. 251/2007, referring to the notion of "*fondati motivi*") and, thus, the nature and scope of the assessment of a potentially rel-evant act for the purposes of exclusion, is, thus, not entirely beyond dispute. One may in fact question whether the very stringent standards dictated by crim-inal law should have to be applied by authorities deciding on the exclusion of asylum-seekers. In other words, was the *Tribunale di Napoli*, sitting in a status ascertainment formation, really expected to perform as thorough an evaluation as a court in the context of criminal proceedings? The only reference to this is-sue in the whole decision is to be found in a very preliminary statement, where the *Corte* established that the applicant's recollection of the facts should have been duly taken into account by the Tribunal, thus triggering the presumption in favour of asylum seekers' declarations under Article 3 D.Lgs. No. 251/2007 (para. 1) and putting the burden of proof onto the country of refuge. This stance can be interpreted as an implicit reference to evidentiary issues, whereby it would appear that, for the purposes of denying international protection, compe-tent authorities would need sufficient elements, so as to rebut a presumption in favour of asylum-seekers. However, commentators emphasize that the position of the United Nations High Commissioner for Refugees (UNHCR) on the mat-ter is ambiguous to say the least, because while it affirms that "exclusion does not require a determination of guilt in the criminal justice sense" (UNHCR, "Background note on the Application of Exclusion Clauses: Article 1F of the 1951 Convention relating to the Status of Refugees", 2003, para. 107), at the same time it refers to quite a number of criminal justice standards and features, e.g. *mens rea* and individual criminal responsibility (for a thorough examina-tion of the discrepancy, see also MAYSTRE, *cit. supra*, pp. 987-988). This is why some commentators speak with regret of a "mismatch of thresholds" (VAN SLIEDREGT, "International Outlaws", Leiden JIL, 2020, p. 535 ff., p. 537). The identification of the actual threshold may, thus, not be self-evident, though it is safe to say that it has to be located between two extremes: on the one hand, an automatic bar, whereby simple undocumented suspicion, unsupported by grounded reasons will trigger exclusion; on the other, the fully-fledged criminal law standard justifying a finding of guilty.

The objective of the refugee system may offer a way out of the conundrum. If the purpose of international protection mechanisms is to protect individuals from persecution and harm, thus maximizing the chances for successful appli-cations and excluding from the system truly undeserving applicants only, then exclusion clauses should be resorted to very carefully. The last thing the draft-ers of the Convention would have wanted is for asylum-seekers to be denied protection by virtue of mere, unsubstantiated suspicions of their unworthiness. Extreme care must thus be taken before rejecting an asylum application on grounds that there are any impediments to the granting of international protec-tion, considering the high risk of serious consequences for an individual whose application is rejected incorrectly. Also, being an exception to the otherwise applicable refugee regime, exclusion clauses should be interpreted in a restrictive manner, admitting disqualification from the benefits of international protection only in case of adamant and crystal-clear impediments. The evidentiary standard requested should thus be found at the very least half-way in between the two ends of the spectrum, and, possibly, closer to the "beyond any reasonable doubt" standard. In other words, the "serious reasons" standard should approach the "beyond any reasonable doubt" threshold, i.e. the typical standard for conviction in most legal orders as well as under international criminal law. Therefore, the contention that the "serious reasons" standard should be equal to the amount of evidence and degree of certainty sufficient for *indicting* (HOLVOET, "Harmonizing Exclusion under the Refugee Convention by References to the Evidentiary Standards of International Criminal Law", JICJ, 2014, p. 1039 ff.) appears to be convincing as well as coherent with the goal of procedural fairness in exclusion.

Still, from a practical point of view, one has to admit that it would be difficult to apply criminal law evidentiary standards and have criminal-style hearings for asylum applications in a "bureaucratic" context like status ascertainment hearings (in this sense NYINAH, "Exclusion under Article 1F: Some Reflections on Context, Principles and Practice", International Journal of Refugee Law, 2000, p. 295 ff., pp. 298-299). The exact nature of the assessment of relevant criminal conduct for the purposes of disqualifying undeserving asylum-seekers from international protection will, thus, continue puzzling scholars and practitioners; hopefully, the *Corte* will clarify the issue sooner rather than later. In policy terms, the matter is urgent and it is paramount that States (and all the more so EU Member States) adopt a coherent and consistent interpretation and application of the exclusion clauses, and give the same responses to asylum applications, lest the trend of forum shopping becomes an actual problem in asylum-seeking.

MARIANGELA LA MANNA

XII.   HUMAN RIGHTS

THE DUTY TO PUNISH RACIAL HATE V. FREEDOM OF EXPRESSION: LOOKING FOR A FAIR BALANCE IN THE DOMESTIC IMPLEMENTATION OF CERD OBLIGATIONS

Relationship between the Italian legal order and the CERD – Domestic implementation of human rights treaties – Hate speech – Racial discrimination – Freedom of expression – Balancing of rights

Corte di Cassazione (Sez. I Penale), 13 December 2019, No. 1602
Criminal proceedings against Rosa Osvaldo and Rosa Mirko

In Judgment No. 1602/2020, adopted on 13 December 2019, and published on 16 January 2020, the *Corte di Cassazione* ruled on the interpretation of Article 3(1)(a) of Law No. 654 of 1975, and subsequent amendments, concerning the criminal offence of racial hate speech and racist propaganda, as well as on the balance between the need to punish those crimes and the right to freedom of expression. The domestic statute at issue incorporated into Italian law the UN Convention on the Elimination of All Forms of Racial Discrimination (CERD), adopted in New York by the UN General Assembly on 21 December of 1965 and entered into force on 4 January 1969.

A short summary of the facts is needed. The defendants were convicted of the offence of racial hate speech and racist propaganda for having displayed two advertising posters stating "illegal migrant kills three Italians with a pick-axe – death penalty immediately!!!" ("*clandestino uccide tre italiani a picconate – pena di morte subito!!!*") in public, more precisely on a commercial truck parked outside their store. In addition, the posters displayed a guillotine stained with blood and, beside it, the severed head of a person of colour, as well as the picture of one of the applicants and the name of their store. The *Corte d'Appello di Milano* considered that the criminal offence had been committed since, in its view, the posters described the suspect as an "enemy" by reason of his race and not on the basis of the crimes (at that time, allegedly) committed. In particular, the *Corte d'Appello* drew this conclusion from the following elements: the emphasis the posters put on the opposition between the "illegal migrant" status of the suspect and the victims' (Italian) nationality; the violent images which showed the head of a person of colour, coupled with the invocation of the death penalty. The defendants appealed the judgment, on point of law, to the *Corte di Cassazione*, arguing, in particular, that the *Corte d'Appello* had erred in law and violated their right to freedom of expression. They argued that the posters had merely expressed their opinion concerning the need to bring back the death penalty for crimes such as those that had been (allegedly) committed, while the expression "illegal migrant" was not based on the colour of the suspect's skin, but on the objective fact that he did not have a permit for staying in Italy. The *Corte di Cassazione,* therefore, had to establish the scope of the offence of racist propaganda and its relationship with freedom of expression.

It upheld the appeal on point of law and quashed the judgment, having found an error in the qualification of the facts as racist propaganda and hate speech and a lack of motivation concerning the *context* of the relevant facts. Therefore, the *Corte di Cassazione* asked (a different Section of) the *Corte d'Appello* to rule again on the case, in light of the following considerations.

As for the formal qualification of the conduct as racist propaganda, the *Corte* did not accept the appeal judges' reasoning, according to which the invocation of the death penalty, coupled with the reference to the accused's race (the head of a person of colour) and the bloody images displayed in the post, was in itself a manifestation of racial discrimination or hate. The *Corte* recalled its previous case law (in particular, *Corte di Cassazione (Sez. V Penale)*, 7 May 2019, No. 32862), stating that the abovementioned criminal provision codifies three different offences: (i) the *propaganda of racist ideas*, which consists in the spread of racist opinions aimed at influencing on a large scale the behaviour or ideas of others; (ii) *racial or ethnic hate,* defined as a feeling capable of creating a concrete danger of discriminatory acts; (iii) *racial discrimination,* which is based on personal and inherent qualities of the targeted individual, and not on his/her behaviour. In the *Corte*'s view, therefore, the *Corte d'Appello* erred in its interpretation of the term *racial discrimination*, by considering that hate based on the targeted individual's behaviour (the crimes, actually or allegedly, committed) could be criminally punished. In this regard, indeed, a specific threshold must be reached, and expressing a generic attitude of dislike, irritation or non-acceptance, even if based on racial, national or ethnic reasons, does not suffice (see also, in this regard, *Corte di Cassazione (Sez. III Penale)*, 14 September 2015, No. 36906, according to which discrimination on the basis of crimes and behaviours is not prohibited under criminal law). The appeal judges, by contrast, had given relevance to the indication of the targeted individual as an "illegal migrant", without properly assessing the context of the relevant facts and, in particular, the reasons on which the "hate" was based (on the need to assess the context of the alleged discriminatory speech, see *Corte di Cassazione (Sez. I Penale)*, 13 December 2007, No. 13234).

Moreover, the *Corte* stated that in order to strike a fair balance between, on the one hand, the principle of equal dignity of individuals and the prohibition of (racial) discrimination and, on the other hand, freedom of expression, it is necessary for the court to determine that the expression of the discriminatory ideas gives rise to a concrete danger. This concrete danger could not be presumed, in the present case, from the mere public display of the posters (as the appeal judges had done). The offence of racist propaganda is a crime of danger (*reato di pericolo*): while it does not require the danger to actually result in discriminatory or violent acts, it does require that a concrete danger of such acts exists (*Corte di Cassazione, (Sez. I Penale)*, 22 May 2015, No. 42727).

It remains to be seen whether the *Corte di Cassazione*'s reasoning is in line with international human rights law. And indeed, although the *Corte* did not even mention the CERD (but only the title of the domestic statute which refers to it), domestic (judicial) institutions are, under the CERD, required to ensure "that the facts and legal qualifications of individual cases are assessed consistently with international standards of human rights" (CERD Committee, General recommendation No. 35, Combating racist hate speech, 26 September 2013, CERD/C/GC/35, para. 18). In order to assess whether the judgment complied with Italy's international obligations it is therefore necessary to identify the relevant international legal framework, as applied by international courts and monitoring bodies.

The domestic provision at issue, Article 3(1)(a) of Law No. 654/1975, used to punish the spread of ideas of racial superiority and racist hate, the public incitement to discrimination, acts of violence and incitement to violence against members of national, ethnic or racial groups, as well as the creation of, or participation in, organizations and associations aimed at committing these crimes. Two reforms (pursuant to Decree Law No. 122/1993 – confirmed by the *legge di conversione* No. 205/1993 – and Law No. 85/2006) lessened the severity of the penalties, although the offences remained unchanged (except for the inclusion of religious discrimination under Law No. 101/1989). Later, pursuant to Law No. 115/2016, the severity of the penalties was increased. Most recently, under Decree Law No. 21/2018, the offences were incorporated within the Italian Criminal Code, under Articles 604-*bis* (propaganda and instigation to commit crimes for reasons of racial, ethnic or religious discrimination) and 604-*ter* (which introduced an aggravating circumstance, according to which the sanction for "ordinary" crimes is more severe when they are committed for reasons of racial, national, ethnic or religious discrimination). The last two reforms, however, were not applicable in the case at hand, because they entered into force after the impugned facts.

The domestic provisions implemented the international obligation enshrined in Article 4(1)(a) CERD, according to which States Parties are required to:

> declare an offence punishable by law all dissemination of ideas based on racial superiority or hatred, incitement to racial discrimination, as well as acts of violence or incitement to such acts against any race or group of persons of another colour or ethnic origin [...].

The monitoring body created pursuant to Article 8 CERD has clarified that Article 4 CERD has a mandatory (although not self-executing) character (CERD Committee, General Recommendation No. 7 Relating to the Implementation of Article 4 Legislation to Eradicate Racial Discrimination, 23 August 1985, A/40/18), and establishes a *duty to criminalize* four different acts – namely: (i) the dissemination of ideas based on racial superiority or hatred; (ii) the incitement to racial hatred; (iii) acts of violence against any race or group of persons of another colour or ethnic origin; and (iv) the incitement to such acts – as well as *positive obligations* of effective enforcement of the adopted legislative provisions (CERD Committee, *General Recommendation No. 15 on Article 4 of the Convention*, 1993, para. 2). Although the CERD Committee stated in 1993 that Article 4 CERD "is compatible with the right to freedom of opinion and expression" (*ibid.*, para. 3), concern persisted that the requirement in Article 4 that its obligations must be implemented "with due regard to the principles embodied in the Universal Declaration of Human Rights" (UDHR), arguably "[...] created a potential conflict between the duty to incriminate hate speech and the freedom of expression, without providing much guidance as to how the conflict can be resolved" (MILANOVIC, "CERD and Hate Speech", EJIL: Talk!, 19 April 2013, available at: <https://www.ejiltalk.org/cerd-and-hate-speech/>). Thus, the CERD Committee has further clarified that Article 4 merely requires that "in the creation and application of offences [...] the principles of the [UDHR] [...] must be given appropriate weight in decision-making processes" (CERD Committee, General recommendation No. 35, para. 19).

The Committee also made clear that the CERD is a living instrument, included in "the wider human rights environment" (*ibid.*, para. 4). Therefore, it is instructive to study several other international instruments that enshrine obligations concerning racial hate and discrimination and to shed light on the relationship of those obligations with freedom of expression (DE SENA and CASTELLANETA, "La libertà di espressione e le norme internazionali, ed europee, prese sul serio:

sempre su Casapound c. Facebook", SIDIBlog, 20 January 2020, available at: <http://www.sidiblog.org/2020/01/20/la-liberta-di-espressione-e-le-norme-internazionali-ed-europee-prese-sul-serio-sempre-su-casapound-c-facebook/>).

First of all, the UDHR itself recognized, in its Article 1, the principle of equality of every human being and, in Article 7, the right to equal protection against discrimination and incitement to discrimination. And while Article 19 UDHR enshrines the right to freedom of opinion and expression, Article 29 establishes that individual rights and freedoms may be limited "for the purpose of securing due recognition and respect for the rights and freedoms of others" (para. 2) and "may in no case be exercised contrary to the purposes and principles of the United Nations" (para. 3). In this regard, the principle of equality of every human being is expressly mentioned in the Preamble of the UN Charter, while Article 1, which enumerates the purposes of that treaty, embodies in its paragraph 3 the principle of non-discrimination on racial grounds.

Secondly, Article 26 of the 1966 International Covenant on Civil and Political Rights (ICCPR) prohibits discrimination and recognizes the right to equal protection by the law. Article 19 guarantees freedom of expression but, under its paragraph 3, restrictions (provided by the law and in keeping with the principles of necessity and proportionality) are admissible for protecting the rights and reputation of others, such as "individual members of a community defined by its [...] ethnicity" (Human Rights Committee (HRC), General Comment No. 34. Article 19: freedom of opinion and expression, 12 September 2011, CCPR/C/GC/34, para. 28). Moreover, Article 20(2) stipulates that, in the exercise of freedom of expression, "[a]ny advocacy of national, racial or religious hatred that constitutes incitement to discrimination, hostility or violence shall be prohibited by law". The HRC has stated that such prohibitions derive from the duties and responsibilities freedom of expression carries with it (HRC, General Comment No. 1: Article 20, 1983, para. 2). More recently, it has clarified that Article 20(2) complements Article 19(3) by requiring that national, racial or religious hate must be expressly prohibited by the law, and not by other (less severe) legal means (HRC, General Comment No. 34, para. 51).

The European Convention on Human Rights (ECHR), for its part, does not (expressly) establish duties to criminalize (but they might arise as positive obligations aimed at protecting human dignity; see CHENAL, "Obblighi di criminalizzazione tra sistema penale italiano e Corte EDU", Legislazione Penale, 2006, p. 172 ff.). However, Article 14 ECHR stipulates the right not to be discriminated against in the exercise of the rights and freedoms guaranteed under the ECHR, while Article 1 of Protocol No.12 – not yet ratified by Italy – establishes a *general* prohibition of discrimination. It is true that the European Court of Human Rights (ECtHR) has stated that Article 10 (freedom of expression) "is applicable not only to 'information' or 'ideas' that are favourably received or regarded as inoffensive [...] but also to those that offend, shock or disturb the State or any sector of the population" (ECtHR, *Handyside v. The United Kingdom,* Application No. 5493/72, 7 December 1976, para. 49). Nevertheless, the ECtHR has also recognized that measures adopted for punishing "hate speech and the glorification of violence" are proportionate measures justified by a pressing social need

(ECtHR, *Sürek v. Turkey (No. 1)*, Application No. 26682/95, 8 July 1999, paras. 61 and 64) and, therefore, do not violate freedom of expression. Moreover, when measures have been adopted by the State against *explicit and direct* forms of hate speech, applications against these measures under Article 10 have been declared inadmissible as an abuse of right pursuant to Article 17 ECHR (ECtHR, *Seurot v. France*, Application No. 57383/00, 18 May 2004).

We shall now apply the legal framework to the facts of the case at hand. As for the legal qualification of the facts, the term *hate speech* is not explicitly mentioned in the CERD, but it was developed in the context of its interpretation (CERD Committee, General Comment No. 35, para. 5). In 1997, the Committee of Ministers of the Council of Europe stipulated that hate speech covers "all forms of expression which spread, incite, promote or justify racial hatred, xenophobia [...] including intolerance expressed by aggressive nationalism and ethnocentrism, discrimination and hostility against minorities, migrants and people of migrant origins" (Recommendation No. R (97) 20 of the Committee of Minister to Member States on "hate speech", 30 October 1997). More recently, an exhaustive definition was provided in the United Nations' Strategy and Plan of Action on Hate Speech, Detailed Guidance on Implementation for United Nations Field Presence, according to which the notion embraces:

> [a]ny kind of communication in speech, writing or behaviour, that attacks or uses pejorative or discriminatory language with reference to a person or a group *on the basis of who they are*, in other words, based on their religion, ethnicity, nationality, race, colour, descent, gender or other identity factor. (emphasis added; September 2020, p. 8)

Therefore, the *material conduct* at issue (the display of an advertising poster) might be considered, at least in principle, as hate speech. Indeed, in the CERD Committee's opinion, the term "speech" embraces different manifestations, whether expressed "orally or in print, or disseminated through electronic media [...] as well as non-verbal forms of expression, such as the display of racist symbols, images and behaviours at public gatherings [...]" (CERD Committee, General Recommendation No. 35, para. 7).

As for the *ground of discrimination*, the *Corte di Cassazione*'s view, according to which discrimination must be based on inherent characteristics of the victims, is in line with the (rather restrictive) interpretation the International Court of Justice (ICJ) recently issued. In particular, when stipulating that Article 1, paragraph 1, CERD does not cover discrimination based on current "nationality" but only on "national origin", the ICJ considered that the Convention only prohibits discrimination based on "characteristics that are inherent at birth" (ICJ, *Application of the International Convention on the Elimination of All Forms of Racial Discrimination (Qatar v. United Arab Emirates)*, Preliminary Objections, Judgment of 4 February 2021, para. 81). The CERD Committee, by contrast, has held that nationality is a ground of discrimination covered by the Convention (CERD Committee, *Admissibility of Inter-State communication submitted by*

Qatar against the United Arab Emirates, CERD/C/99/4, 30 August 2019, para. 62). The (alleged) discriminatory ground in the case at hand was ethnicity (which is an inherent quality of the targeted individual), but, as we have already seen, the *Corte di Cassazione* found that the impugned acts seemed rather to be based on the crimes allegedly committed by the targeted individual.

As for the effective need to punish the (allegedly discriminatory) acts, the *Corte di Cassazione*'s view is in line with the CERD Committee's approach, which recommended that:

> the criminalization of forms of racist expression should be reserved for serious cases, to be proven beyond reasonable doubt, while less serious cases should be addressed by means other than criminal law, taking into account, inter alia, the nature and the extent of the impact on targeted persons and groups (CERD Committee, General Recommendation No. 35, para. 13).

And indeed, the Committee indicated some *contextual factors* to be taken into account in order to identify those forms of racist hate speech that must be considered as criminal offences: (i) the content and form of speech; (ii) the economic, social and political context at the time of the speech, including the possible existence "of patterns of discrimination against ethnic and other groups"; (iii) the position or status of the speaker in society and the audience to which the speech is directed; (iv) the reach of the speech, including the nature of the audience and the means of transmission; (v) the objectives of the speech, as well as "the imminent risk or likelihood that the conduct desired or intended by the speaker will result from the speech in question" (*ibid.*, para. 16).

The ECtHR gave similar indications when considering whether a criminal conviction for hate speech is a disproportionate interference with freedom of expression. The Court has held that due regard has to be given to the manner in which the opinions are expressed, the context and purpose of the expressions, and, in particular, if, "when considered as a whole, [the speech] appeared from an objective point of view to have had as its purpose the propagation of racist views and ideas" (*Jersid v. Denmark*, Application No. 15890/89, 23 September 1994, para. 31). In particular, racist expressions in the context of public and political debate, or in election campaigns (*Féret v. Belgium*, Application No. 15615/07, 16 July 2009), are more easily considered to be punishable under criminal law (*Erbakan v. Turkey*, Application No. 59405/00, 6 July 2006, para. 55). Other relevant factors are the intention of the author as well as their ability to convince, direct and incite a wide audience to commit specific acts (*Gündüz v. Turkey*, Application No. 35071/97, 4 December 2003, paras. 43-44), the status of the perpetrator (*Sürek (no. 1) v. Turkey, cit. supra*, para. 62) and the form and impact of the speech (*Alinak v. Turkey*, Application No. 40287/98, 29 March 2005, para. 45). The ECtHR also assesses the historic, demographic and cultural context in the country, such as the possible existence of an actual problem concerning social integration of migrants (*Soulas and Others v. France*, Application No. 15948/03, 10 July 2008).

Moreover, the ECtHR has ruled on (at least partially) analogous cases to the one being analyzed here. In the *Noorwood* case, a member of the British National Party had displayed in the window of their flat a poster with a photograph of the Twin Towers in flames, with the words "Islam out of Britain – Protect the British People" and the symbol of a crescent and a star in a prohibition sign. The ECtHR considered that:

> the words and images on the poster amounted to a public expression of attack on all Muslims in the United Kingdom. Such a general, vehement attack against a religious group, linking the group as a whole with a grave act of terrorism is incompatible with the values proclaimed and guaranteed by the Convention [...] (*Mark Anthony Norwood v. The United Kingdom*, Application No. 23131/03, 16 November 2004).

The Court concluded that the applicant's acts constituted an abuse of right under Article 17 ECHR, not protected under Article 10 ECHR, and declared the application inadmissible. Similarly, the inadmissibility decision in the *Ivanov* case concerned the editor of a newspaper who had portrayed in his articles the Jews as a source of evil in Russia, calling for their exclusion from social life (*Pavel Ivanov v. Russia*, Application No. 35222/04, 20 February 2007). The differences between these cases, where the group was targeted *as such* and irrespective of the actual conduct of members of the group, and the case decided by the *Corte di Cassazione*, are patent. Moreover, in these cases the authors were, respectively, a politician and a journalist, and were in a position to reach a wider public and to actually influence the behaviour of others.

In light of the international legal framework depicted above, freedom of expression may be limited by punishing hate speech and racial discrimination. However, certain conditions must be fulfilled and in the case at hand, the *Corte di Cassazione*, in line with the relevant international human rights standards, implicitly considered that the conditions were not fulfilled. And indeed, on the basis of similar observations to those highlighted above, one author considered that the *Corte* correctly implemented the relevant international instruments and, in particular, struck a fair balance between the prohibition of racial discrimination and the right to freedom of expression, perhaps also aiming at avoiding a ruling against Italy by the ECtHR (CASTELLANETA, "Discriminazione razziale e propaganda, obblighi di valutazione del contesto e critica politica tra diritto interno e diritto internazionale", MediaLaws – Rivista di diritto dei media, 2020, p. 245 ff.). In general, human rights lawyers agree that "before one can conclude with (relative) certainty that such activities [hate speech] took or will take place, all factual and legally relevant elements of the specific case, such as content, context, intention, impact and the proportionality of the interference, should be taken into consideration" (CANNIE and VOORHOOF, "The Abuse Clause and Freedom of Expression in the European Human Rights Convention: An Added Value for Democracy and Human Rights Protection?", Netherlands Quarterly of Human Rights, 2011, p. 83 ff.).

To conclude, it can be said that, in general, international human rights law and, in particular, Article 4 CERD, "do […] not require the criminal prosecution of all bigoted and offensive statements" (CERD Committee, TBB v. Germany, Communication No. 48/2010, Individual Opinion of Committee Member Mr Caralos Manuel Vazquez, dissenting, para. 2), but domestic authorities have "to gauge the likely impact of the statements in the social context prevailing in the State party" (*ibid.*, para. 3). In determining whether the impugned conduct amounts to racist hate and propaganda and whether a concrete danger might arise from the defendants' conduct, the *Corte d'Appello* will have to follow the principles established by the *Corte di Cassazione*. In particular, it will have to adequately motivate its reasoning in order to strike a fair balance between the protection of human dignity and equality, on the one hand, and the right to freedom of expression, on the other.

LORENZO ACCONCIAMESSA

XIII. INTERNATIONAL CRIMINAL LAW

(Cf. *supra* XI, *Corte di Cassazione (Sez. I Civile)*, 19 November 2020, No. 26376 (Order), *Jeff Nathanael Gouet v. Ministero dell'Interno*)

XVII. RELATIONSHIP BETWEEN MUNICIPAL AND INTERNATIONAL LAW

AN ONLY CHILD WITHOUT "YOUNGER BROTHERS": *CONTRADA V. ITALY (NO. 3)* AND THE NEVER-ENDING SAGA OF THE RELATIONSHIP BETWEEN ITALIAN COURTS AND THE ECtHR

Relationship between the Italian legal order and the ECtHR – Erga alios effects of ECtHR Rulings – Dialogue between courts – Effective remedy – Foreseeability of criminal conviction

Corte di Cassazione (Sezioni Unite Penali), 3 March 2020, No. 8544
Criminal proceedings against Stefano Genco

In the everlasting saga of domestic judgments concerning the impact of the European Court of Human Rights' (ECtHR) case law on the Italian legal order, the ruling under review stands as a not-to-be-missed episode. The judgment revolves around the issue of whether individuals who find themselves in situations that are identical, or at least very similar, to those of applicants who have already obtained a favourable judgment from the ECtHR, may rely on the ECtHR judgment in the domestic courts without needing to apply to the ECtHR themselves. Italian scholarship commonly refers to those individuals as "younger brothers" (*fratelli minori*) to successful applicants to the ECtHR, implying that there is a sort of relationship of kinship between the two categories – both children of

© KONINKLIJKE BRILL NV, LEIDEN, 2021 | DOI:10.1163/22116133-03001028

the same parent (ideally, the violation of a right protected by the ECHR; see ROMEO, "L'orizzonte dei giuristi e i figli di un dio minore", Diritto penale contemporaneo, 16 April 2012, available at: <https://archiviodpc.dirittopenaleuomo. org/upload/1334557367Romeo%20orizzonte%20giuristi.pdf>; VIGANÒ, "Una prima pronuncia delle Sezioni Unite sui 'fratelli minori' di Scoppola: resta fermo l'ergastolo per chi abbia chiesto il rito abbreviato dopo il 24 novembre 2000", Diritto penale contemporaneo, 10 September 2012, available at: <https://archiviodpc.dirittopenaleuomo.org/d/1695-una-prima-pronuncia-delle-sezioni-unite-sui-fratelli-minori-di-scoppola-resta-fermo-l-ergastolo-per>).

The facts underlying the case can be summarized as follows. On 15 February 1999, Stefano Genco was sentenced to four years in prison for aiding and abetting a mafia-type organization from the outside (*concorso esterno in associazione di stampo mafioso*, hereinafter also only *concorso esterno*), pursuant to Articles 110 and 416-*bis* of the Italian Criminal Code. He was accused of multiple acts aimed at supporting a local mafia organization, including conducting agricultural business and committing illegal acts (such as extortion) on behalf and for the benefit of the organization, all taking place until February 1994 (the chronological detail will come in handy later). The judgment became final on 13 June 2000, and from then on Genco began to serve his sentence.

Genco's most famous sibling is Bruno Contrada, former agent of the Italian secret service (SISDE). Contrada was accused of having systematically contributed to the activities of the *Cosa Nostra*, by supplying the organization with information about ongoing police investigations into its members, and was ultimately sentenced to ten years' imprisonment for the same crime as Genco, that is *concorso esterno*. Following his final conviction, Contrada applied to the ECtHR. In the case of *Contrada v. Italy (No. 3)* (Application No. 66655/13, Judgment of 14 April 2015), the ECtHR held that Contrada's conviction for acts amounting to *concorso esterno* which occurred before 1994 was in breach of Article 7 of the ECHR. The Court found that the offence in question had resulted from developments in Italian case law which began in the second half of the 1980s and consolidated only in 1994 (*Corte di Cassazione (Sezioni Unite Penali), Criminal proceedings against Giuseppe Demitry*, 5 October 1994, No. 16). As a result, the ECtHR concluded that the law had not been sufficiently clear and foreseeable to Contrada at the time of the events.

Learning about the success of Contrada, and realizing that he found himself in a very similar situation (he had been convicted for the same offence and for events that had occurred before 1994), Genco filed a petition to the *Corte di Appello di Caltanissetta* seeking a review of his sentence pursuant to Article 630 of the Code of Criminal Procedure, as amended by *Corte costituzionale, Paolo Dorigo*, 7 April 2011, No. 113 (IYIL, 2011, p. 375 ff., with a comment by PALOMBINO). As is known, in the *Dorigo* case, the *Corte costituzionale* found Article 630 to be unconstitutional as it did not provide for retrial where necessary to ensure compliance with the final rulings of the ECtHR, under Article 46 of the ECHR.

The *Corte di Appello* dismissed Genco's petition, finding that *Contrada* was not applicable to his case as that ECtHR judgment contained a flawed appraisal of the foreseeability of the *concorso esterno* offence. Genco filed an appeal on points of law before the *Corte di Cassazione*, arguing that the *Corte di Appello* had erred by ignoring the fact that the ECtHR had found a systemic violation in the Italian legal order in *Contrada*. In spite of its not being a *stricto sensu* "pilot judgment", that judgment was nonetheless applicable beyond the particular case, irrespective of whether the legal reasoning sounded convincing to domestic courts. The breach identified by the ECtHR consisted in the lack of foreseeability of an offence (*concorso esterno*) before a certain date (when the *Demitry* judgment was delivered). Thus, akin to Contrada, an indefinite number of individuals (including Genco) could not foresee a conviction for *concorso esterno* before 1994. The *Sesta Sezione* of the *Corte di Cassazione*, to which the appeal had been allocated, relinquished the case to the *Sezioni Unite* on account of the existing conflict in the case law pertaining to the remedy available – if any – for those individuals who found themselves in a situation identical or similar to Contrada's, but who had not applied to the ECtHR.

Thus, the *Sezioni Unite* were requested to settle the following questions: (i) whether *Contrada* was general in scope and could be extended to identical or similar cases, i.e. *erga alios*; and (ii) in the affirmative, through which domestic remedy should such "extended" implementation of ECtHR's judgments take place. To begin with, the *Sezioni Unite* recapitulated Contrada's judiciary saga. In that case, the ECtHR concluded that there had been a violation of Article 7 ECHR because the Italian courts had failed to demonstrate that Contrada could have been aware of the offence at the time of the impugned events: Contrada's conviction had been based exclusively on the *Corte di Cassazione*'s subsequent rulings. Following the ECtHR's judgment, Contrada eventually had his sentence declared unenforceable pursuant to Article 673 of the Code of Criminal Procedure, which regulates objection to execution following the repeal of an offence.

Turning then to Genco, the *Sezioni Unite* held that he could not invoke Article 46 ECHR as the legal basis for having his sentence reviewed in accordance with *Contrada*, neither on the basis of Article 630 nor on the basis of Article 673 of the Code of Criminal Procedure. The *Sezioni Unite* explained that, as a matter of fact, Article 46 ECHR can be invoked before domestic courts only by individuals who have directly obtained an ECtHR judgment in their favour. Individuals in situations identical or similar to those of the applicants in an ECtHR judgment, can benefit from the relevant ECtHR ruling rendered to their older siblings, but only if the ruling qualifies as a "pilot judgment" or "any other judgment in which the Court draws attention to the existence of a structural or systemic problem" of the domestic legal order, pursuant to Article 61 of the ECtHR's Rules of Court (last modified on 1 January 2020). Only in these cases does the Article 46 ECHR obligation to conform to a final judgment transcend the individual dimension and require that the judgment be extended to any individuals finding themselves in identical or similar situations. As is evident from a cursory reading of the ECtHR's judgment in *Contrada*, this was neither a "pilot judgment" nor a judgment exposing a structural or systemic problem in the Italian legal order. As further evidence, no general statement, such as a request for the adoption of general measures by the Italian government, could be found in the ECtHR's ruling. This sufficed to conclude that Genco could not invoke *Contrada* for the purpose of having his sentence reviewed or declared unenforceable.

After denying the existence of any obligation to conform to *Contrada* in the case under scrutiny, the *Sezioni Unite* somehow felt the need to indulge in further arguments which were apparently unconnected with the issues submitted to their scrutiny. In particular, the *Sezioni Unite* wondered whether, at a more general level, Italian courts were obliged to "take into account" the ECtHR's case law (including the *Contrada* judgment).

When framed within the terms of the general duty to conform to ECtHR rulings, in addition to the classic 2007 "twin judgments" (*Corte costituzionale, R.A. v. Comune di Torre Annunziata; Comune di Montello v. A.C.; M.T.G. v. Comune di Ceprano* and *E.P. et al. v. Comune di Avellino et al.; A.G. et al. v. Comune di Leonforte et al.*, 24 October 2007, Nos. 348 and 349, IYIL, 2007, p. 292 ff., with a comment by CATALDI), the judgment rendered by the *Corte costituzionale* in *Carlo Gurgone et al.*, 26 March 2015, No. 49 (IYIL, 2015, p. 536 ff., with a comment by TERRASI) had to be taken into account. According to this judgment, Italian courts have to conform solely to pilot judgments or to judgments amounting to "well-established European jurisprudence" on a given provision of the ECHR (RUSSO, "Ancora sul rapporto tra Costituzione e Convenzione europea dei diritti dell'uomo: brevi note sulla sentenza della Corte costituzionale n. 49 del 2015", Osservatorio sulle fonti, 2/2015, p. 1 ff.; see also ROSSI, "L'interpretazione conforme alla giurisprudenza della Corte EDU: quale vincolo per il giudice italiano?", Osservatorio sulle fonti, 1/2018, p. 1 ff.). According to the *Sezioni Unite*, this holds true in spite of the findings contained in *G.I.E.M. s.r.l. and Others v. Italy* (Applications Nos. 1828/06 and 2 others, Judgment of 28 June 2018, on which see RENGHINI, "La sentenza *G.I.E.M.* e il confronto tra la Corte europea dei diritti umani e le corti nazionali", DUDI, 2018, p. 702 ff.), in which the ECtHR affirmed that its judgments all had the same legal value.

On this basis, the *Sezioni Unite* argued that a further reason militating against the *erga alios* extension of *Contrada* was that the ECtHR's findings in that case could hardly be said to amount to "well-established European jurisprudence" as per Judgment No. 49/2015, with respect to the requirement of the "foreseeability" of a criminal law provision (Article 7 ECHR). Indeed, previously the ECtHR had, at times, interpreted the requirement from a *subjective* viewpoint – ie having regard to the personal expertise and knowledge of the accused – and at other times from a more *objective* one – ie focusing on the quality of the criminal law provision and its interpretation by the judiciary. In *Contrada*, the ECtHR had displayed an "unprecedented harshness", in that it completely overlooked the role of judicial interpretation as an inevitable tool for clarifying legal rules, including criminal law provisions, and jumped to the conclusion that the *concorso esterno* was totally unforeseeable by the applicant, without inquiring into his awareness of the criminal nature of his conduct. The ECtHR finding was based on factual grounds – namely, the interpretive contrast around Articles 110 and 416-*bis* of the Criminal Code – but these had been wrongly assessed by the ECtHR. As a result, the findings contained in *Contrada* could not be extended to identical or similar cases on account of their being (i) inconsistent vis-à-vis "well-established European jurisprudence" and (ii) in all cases, inherently flawed.

If that was not enough, the *Sezioni Unite* devoted energy to dismantling the ECtHR's very understanding of "foreseeability", and argued that *Contrada* had also erred in relation to the following considerations: (i) it held that the *concorso esterno* amounted to a judge-made offence; (ii) it failed to correctly appraise the relevant case law of the *Corte di Cassazione*; (iii) it considered the *Demitry* judgment as "overruling" previous judgments, which it did not; (iv) it failed to consider that its findings contradicted the prerogative of the *Corte di Cassazione* as guarantor of the correct interpretation of the law; and (v) it overlooked that, in case of doubt as to the criminal relevance of particular conduct, it was a well known principle of criminal law enshrined in Article 5 of the Criminal Code that individuals were expected to refrain from that conduct.

Eventually, Genco's appeal on the points of law was thus declared unfounded, given that *Contrada* could not be extended to Genco's case as it was neither a "pilot judgment" nor could it be considered as amounting to "well-established European jurisprudence".

As stated at the very beginning of this contribution, the judgment at hand tackles a legal conundrum that both Italian jurisprudence and scholarship have been dealing with for a considerable amount of time, namely the scope of the duty to conform to ECtHR rulings beyond a particular case. Scholarship traces this (alleged) duty back to Articles 1, 19, and 32 of the ECHR (see ARNARDÓTTIR, "Res Interpretata, Erga Omnes Effect and the Role of the Margin of Appreciation in Giving Domestic Effect to the Judgments of the European Court of Human Rights", EJIL, 2017, p. 819 ff.) with respect to individuals in similar or identical situations to those of a successful applicant to the ECtHR. Generally speaking, the issue of the *erga alios* scope of ECtHR judgments is strictly connected to the existence of a "structural or systemic problem" in the domestic legal order. A judgment in which the ECtHR finds a violation of the ECHR imposes on the respondent State a legal obligation not only to ensure just satisfaction pursuant to Article 41 ECHR, but also "to choose, subject to supervision by the Committee of Ministers, the general and/or, if appropriate, individual measures to be adopted in its domestic legal order to put an end to the violation found by the Court and make all feasible reparation for its consequences in such a way as to restore as far as possible the situation existing before the breach" (*Scozzari and Giunta v. Italy*, Applications Nos. 39221/98 and 41963/98, Judgment of 13 July 2000, para. 249) as per Article 46 ECHR (COLANDREA, "On the Power of the European Court of Human Rights to Order Specific Non-monetary Measures: Some Remarks in Light of the Assanidze, Broniowski and Sejdovic Cases", Human Rights Law Review, 2007, p. 396 ff.). In tackling this topical issue, however, the *Sezioni Unite* adopted an approach that leaves much to be desired, at least for three reasons.

First, the *Sezioni Unite* contented themselves with noting that no general measures had been explicitly ordered or at least indicated by the ECtHR in *Contrada*, references to Article 46 ECHR being absent altogether. By doing so, however, they ruled out the possibility of inferring the existence of a structural problem from that judgment, a possibility which had been convincingly outlined by the *Sesta Sezione* when relinquishing the case to the *Sezioni Unite*. For the *Sesta Sezione*, the ECtHR had implicitly acknowledged that conviction for *concorso esterno* was not foreseeable for individuals other than Contrada, which resulted in the need for judicial authorities to ascertain which domestic remedies should be activated in such cases. In spite of this, the *Sezioni Unite* adopted a purely *formalistic* approach, which, on closer inspection, contrasted sharply with the jurisprudence of none less than the *Corte costituzionale* (see *Criminal proceedings against Salvatore Ercolano*, 3 July 2013, No. 210, which affirmed that general measures, while discretionary in content, had to be adopted by domestic authorities, if necessary *proprio motu*, that is even though the ECtHR had ordered none in a particular case). At the end of the day, a *substantive* approach dealing with the nature and scope of the violation under scrutiny seemed preferable; unfortunately, the *Sezioni Unite* failed to adequately explain the reasons why they chose to discard such an approach.

Secondly, one may easily notice the "alchemical transformation" the questions addressed to the *Sezioni Unite* underwent during the proceedings: the case was relinquished by the *Sesta Sezione* so that the *Sezioni Unite* could answer the question of whether *Contrada* was a "pilot judgment" or a judgment exposing "the existence of a structural or systemic problem" of the domestic legal order. However, the *Sezioni Unite* ended up replying that the ECtHR's ruling was neither a "pilot judgment" (so far, so good) nor… "well-established European jurisprudence". Would one receive an "asked and answered" objection, if one asked that question again? It is hard to respond in the affirmative, given that the two issues remain conceptually discrete. To argue that a particular judgment of the ECtHR detected a structural problem does not automatically imply that that judgment amounted to "well-established European jurisprudence": "isolated" judgments could also make such a finding. To put it differently, the fact that *Contrada* did not amount to "well-established European jurisprudence" had per se nothing to do with its general scope. The *Sezioni Unite* failed to keep those issues duly distinct; however, it must be admitted that the topic itself – the relationship between the general duty to take into account ECtHR jurisprudence when interpreting the ECHR and the specific duty to conform to a ruling beyond a particular case – has not attracted adequate attention by scholars (with some remarkable exceptions: RANDAZZO, "Interpretazione delle sentenze della Corte europea dei diritti ai fini dell'esecuzione (giudiziaria) e interpretazione della sua giurisprudenza ai fini dell'applicazione della CEDU", Rivista AIC, 2/2015, p. 1 ff.).

Thirdly, another aspect worth mentioning was the – strikingly disproportionate – focus on the issue of whether *Contrada* amounted to "well-established European jurisprudence" as per Judgment No. 49/2015, which appears to have been employed as a tool for (partially, but firmly) "resisting" unwelcome judgments by the ECtHR in this field (AMOROSO, "Italy", in PALOMBINO (ed.), *Duelling for Supremacy: International Law vs. National Fundamental Principles*, Cambridge, 2019, p. 184 ff.). It has already been argued that in fact this was a merely supplementary argument, as the *Sezioni Unite* did respond – negatively – to the question of whether to extend *Contrada* to Genco's case. Nonetheless, the *Sezioni Unite* engaged in a meticulous refutation of the ECtHR's findings in that judgment, with a view to showing that it had resorted to a notion of "foreseeability" that was inconsistent with its previous (and subsequent) case law. One could argue that the *Sezioni Unite*'s main intention was to engage in a "dialogue" with the ECtHR as to the foreseeability of *concorso esterno* for the purposes of Article 7 ECHR in order to adjust some defects displayed by the ECtHR's understanding of the matter (a point which has been correctly highlighted by some Italian scholars: BARTOLI, "Chiusa la saga Contrada: in caso di contrasto giurisprudenziale opera la colpevolezza", Diritto penale e processo, 2020, p. 775 ff.). In sum, Italy was obliged by Article 46 ECHR to comply with the (admittedly flawed) ECtHR judgment, but only as far as Contrada was concerned. No extension whatsoever to "younger brothers" was acceptable: the secret service agent had to remain an only child... an illegitimate one, indeed!

However, the fact that the *Sezioni Unite* decided to tackle and "rebut" the arguments that had led to *Contrada* does not sound so unreasonable when one considers that the ECtHR is expected to rule on the "foreseeability" of *concorso esterno* again in the near future. Two applications concerning the same matter have recently been communicated to the Italian government (*Dell'Utri v. Italy*, Communicated case, Application No. 3800/15, 16 November 2017; *Lo Sicco v. Italy*, Communicated case, Application No. 14417/09, 5 July 2016). Time will tell if the ECtHR will engage in a "dialogue" with the *Sezioni Unite* and revisit its ruling accordingly, or rather it will reaffirm its appraisal of *concorso esterno*. Yet there is an additional reason for anticipating the ECtHR's rulings, particularly the one in *Dell'Utri v. Italy*. Interestingly enough, Dell'Utri applied to the ECtHR, *inter alia*, precisely because of his being denied the status of Contrada's "younger brother", and invoked Article 13 ECHR on the basis that he could not have his sentence reviewed by Italian courts. Incidentally, the issue of which domestic remedy "younger brothers" have to use in order to seek reparation for the violation of their ECHR rights was left totally unexplored by the judgment under review, as a consequence of the *Sezioni Unite*'s denial of *Contrada*'s *erga alios* effects. *Dell'Utri v. Italy* will provide the ECtHR with the opportunity to rule, for the first time, on the issue of "younger brothers" and its relevance under the ECHR (whether via Article 13, or a broad interpretation of Article 46 ECHR, or other provisions). In conclusion, the *saga* of the relationship between the Italian legal order and the ECtHR's rulings seems far from being over: new and compelling episodes are in store for its fans.

DIEGO MAURI

IMPLEMENTING INTERNATIONAL TREATIES INTO THE ITALIAN LEGAL ORDER: DIVERGING VIEWS ON THE IDENTIFICATION OF SELF-EXECUTING PROVISIONS

Relationship between international and domestic law – Dualism – Order of execution – Implementation of international treaty provisions – United Nations Convention against Corruption – International cooperation – United Nations Convention against Transnational Organized Crime – Adjudicative jurisdiction of States

Consiglio di Stato (Sez. IV), 7 May 2020, No. 2868
Anonymous v. Ministero della Giustizia

Corte di Cassazione (Sez. I Penale), 1 July 2020, No. 19762
Criminal proceedings against Tartoussi Youssef

In the cases under scrutiny, the *Consiglio di Stato* and the *Corte di Cassazione* were confronted with the application of international rules contained in treaties that were implemented into the Italian legal order by way of an "order of execution" (*ordine di esecuzione*). The courts adopted different approaches when determining whether the relevant treaty provisions were self-executing – hence applicable by Italian State organs –, thereby confirming the diverging views that characterize both Italian legal scholarship and jurisprudence.

In a preliminary fashion, it is worth recalling that the relationship between international law and the Italian legal order is framed in dualist terms (see MORELLI, *Nozioni di diritto internazionale*, 7th ed., Milano, 1967, p. 76). This entails that, whenever the State binds itself to international obligations that have a bearing on its domestic legal order, it must adapt the latter accordingly through an exercise of its norm-making powers. In doing so, it allows international conventions – that would otherwise display effects solely at the inter-State level – to be applied by State organs as set out in the municipal act (CONDORELLI, *Il giudice italiano e i trattati internazionali*, Milano, 1974, pp. 20-21).

The so-called "ordinary way" to implement treaties in the domestic legal order is through the enactment of a piece of domestic legislation (usually, but not necessarily, adopted by the Parliament) which implements the content of the international rule. From a formal point of view, the municipal act is in no way different from any other equally ranked domestic source and differs solely in its *occasio legis*, namely the aim of effectively discharging the State's treaty-derived obligations.

However, the Italian legislature usually follows a different procedure, known as the "special" one, in which a domestic piece of legislation called an order of execution provides that "full and entire application is given to the treaty", and often reproduces the treaty text to be followed. Once again, the municipal act is the formal source through which the domestic legal order implements the international rule. Its content is, however, determined through a *renvoi* to the international text and is to be ascertained by the relevant State organ on a case-by-case basis. Under the special procedure, a treaty provision can be applied only if it provides sufficient elements for the identification of the corresponding domestic rules (see FABOZZI, *L'attuazione dei trattati internazionali mediante ordine di esecuzione*, Milano, 1961, p. 121) or is – borrowing the North-American nomenclature – *self-executing*. Conversely, should the treaty provision not allow this operation, it will be unsuitable to be applied through the special procedure and will require an ordinary exercise of legislative powers instead.

If the above-mentioned scheme has found widespread acceptance among Italian legal scholarship, a certain disagreement must be registered with regard to the identification of self-executing provisions. To this end, a stream of legal scholarship requires the international text to provide *all the elements* that allow the relevant State organ to determine the content of the domestic rules that are necessary for its implementation (*ex multis*, TREVES, *Diritto internazionale*, Milano, 2005, p. 698). Another stream of scholarship, though not entirely departing from this view, adopts a restrictive approach and identifies a minimum threshold with the imposition of *obligations* on the State by the international rule. Accordingly, treaty clauses cannot be considered self-executing whenever they do not contain obligations but merely endow the State with an option, or when, even in the presence of mandatory wording, the domestic legal order lacks the necessary elements to allow their application (see CONFORTI and IOVANE, *Diritto internazionale*, 12th ed., Napoli, 2021, pp. 352-353).

This doctrinal contrast finds correspondence – though not in identical terms – in the jurisprudence of Italian courts, as also confirmed by the two cases under scrutiny. In the first judgment, the *Consiglio di Stato* was called upon to determine whether a Note issued by the Italian Ministry of Justice was duly reasoned under Article 46(21) of the United Nations Convention against Corruption (UNCAC). The case dealt with the notification of a summons to the legal representative of an anonymous Italian company, indicted for international corruption in criminal proceedings in India. The Italian Minister of Justice followed up on the Indian court's request for judicial assistance and forwarded it to the competent prosecutor by means of a Ministerial Note, the legality of which was later confirmed by the relevant administrative tribunal (*Tribunale Amministrativo Regionale per il Lazio*).

The Italian company filed an appeal before the *Consiglio di Stato* seeking the annulment of the Note for violating, among other things, the duty to provide reasons, which is required for all administrative acts by Law No. 241 of 7 August 1990 (Law No. 241/90). The appellant's view was shared by the *Consiglio di Stato*, which annulled the Ministerial Note because it failed to explain why the case did not fall within the scope of Article 46(21) UNCAC.

The UNCAC was incorporated into the Italian legal order through an order of execution contained in Law No. 116 of 3 August 2009. Therefore, the *Consiglio di Stato* had to make a preliminary determination of the self-executing nature of Article 46(21), which states that "[m]utual legal assistance *may be refused*" (emphasis added) in the listed circumstances. The question of whether such circumstances existed was not specifically addressed in the judgment, which dealt with Article 46(21) solely when framing the content of the duty to state reasons under Law No. 241/90. However, by expecting the Minister to justify the non-application of Article 46(21), the *Consiglio di Stato* considered the provision capable of displaying effects within the domestic legal order and therefore as being self-executing.

In order to understand the reasoning of the *Consiglio di Stato*, it is necessary to examine the domestic legal framework that regulates international requests for mutual legal assistance. Article 696 of the Italian Code of Criminal Procedure (CCP) mandates the primacy of international conventions over Italian law, which is assigned a subsidiary role. Whenever international conventions indicate the Minister of Justice as the competent State organ, Article 723(2) CCP entrusts the

Minister with ample discretion over the acceptance of the foreign request, exception made for the hypothetical scenarios provided in Article 723(5) CCP, in the event of which the request must be denied.

Against this background, Article 46(21) UNCAC lists some specific grounds on which a request for legal assistance may be refused, leaving such determination at the discretion of the "competent authority" of the requested State, namely the Italian Minister of Justice. In doing so, it triggers the application of Article 723(2) CCP. At the same time, it does not affect the situations listed in Article 723(5) in which a request must be rejected.

The *Consiglio di Stato* thus considered applicable (hence self-executing) a provision that provided sufficient elements to identify the relevant existing domestic legal framework, and gave no relevance to its clearly non-mandatory wording (CHRYSIKOS, "Art. 46: Mutual Legal Assistance", in ROSE, KUBICIEL, LANDWEHR (eds.), *The United Nations Convention Against Corruption: A Commentary*, Oxford, 2019, p. 462 ff.). This was made possible by the presence in domestic legislation of specific rules that regulate requests for mutual legal assistance in detail, thus allowing the judges to identify the domestic rules that were necessary for the implementation of the international rule.

In doing so, the *Consiglio di Stato* seemed to conform to a long-standing line of jurisprudence of the Italian Court of Cassation, which identifies self-executing provisions with those that offer a sufficient degree of specificity to infer the corresponding domestic rules, regardless of their mandatory (or non-mandatory) wording. This was the approach adopted by the *Sezioni Unite* of the Court of Cassation in 1973 with regard to the applicability of Article VIII of the GATT 1947 (*Corte di Cassazione (Sezioni Unite)*, Judgment No. 1455 of 21 May 1973). The Court determined the self-executing nature of Article VIII by focusing on the presence of "specific elements, from which one could derive complete domestic rules". The judgment was later recalled on various occasions by the Court's subsequent jurisprudence, and in particular in two cases that dealt with the applicability of Article 3 of the ILO Seafarers' Annual Leave with Pay Convention No. 146 of 1976. In the case *Armenio and others v. CAREMAR* (*Corte di Cassazione*, Judgment No. 9459 of 10 September 1993), the Court maintained that "in order for a treaty to be implemented within the domestic legal order, without the need of further legislative action, it must display the specific elements that allow one to deduce [domestic] rules that are complete". Similarly, in the case *Iacomino v. Tirrenia di Navigazione* (*Corte di Cassazione*, Final Appeal Judgment No. 1062 of 6 February 1999) the Court stated that "in order to be applied, the rules of an international convention must be complete and specific in their content".

Although these courts required self-executing provisions to contain all the *specific* elements needed to deduce the corresponding domestic rules, their view seems not to differ, in substance, from that of the first stream of legal scholarship depicted above, according to which self-executing rules must provide *all the necessary* elements to carry out the same hermeneutic endeavor.

A different approach was adopted in the second case under scrutiny, in which the *Corte di Cassazione* was called upon to determine whether Italian courts had jurisdiction over arms trafficking activities carried out by a foreign national on the high seas. The case concerned the arrest of a Lebanese national who was the captain of a ship that had exported mixed weaponry and soldiers from Turkey to Libya in violation of an arms embargo imposed by the UN Security Council, finally docking in an Italian port.

The preliminary investigations judge retained jurisdiction under Article 7(1) (5) of the Italian Criminal Code, which lists the exceptions to the principle of territorial jurisdiction. These exceptions include, among other things, the existence of international conventions that specifically confer jurisdiction to Italian courts. The relevant international rule identified was Article 15(4) of the United Nations Convention against Transnational Organized Crime (UNTOC), which provides that "[e]ach State Party *may* also adopt such measures as may be necessary to establish its jurisdiction over the offences covered by this Convention when the alleged offender is present in its territory and it does not extradite him or her" (emphasis added). These conclusions were later confirmed by the competent Review Court (*Tribunale del Riesame*).

The accused Lebanese national sought the annulment of the Review Court's decision before the Italian Court of Cassation because, among other grounds, Article 15(4) UNTOC was not self-executing and thus was not applicable in the absence of specific enacting legislation.

Since the UNTOC had been implemented through an order of execution contained in Law No. 146 of 16 March 2006, Article 15(4) was subject by the *Corte di Cassazione* to a preliminary screening of its self-executing nature. The Court defined self-executing provisions, in a rather circular fashion, as those which "are immediately applicable, *impose obligations*, do not require any intermediate actions" (emphasis added). What stood out from such definition was the requirement of the mandatory nature of the international rule, which was the sole focus of the Court's subsequent analysis. The *Corte di Cassazione* found that Article 15(4) did not impose any obligation on the State but merely endowed it with the option of adopting measures to establish jurisdiction and therefore concluded that it was not self-executing.

The approach seemed to conform to a rival line of jurisprudence of the Italian Constitutional Court and of the Court of Cassation. In the *Di Lazzaro* case (*Corte Costituzionale*, No. 183 of 16 May 1994), the Constitutional Court rejected the applicability of Article 6(1) of the European Convention on the Adoption of Children, which provided that "[t]he law shall not permit a child to be adopted except by *either* two persons married to each other, whether they adopt simultaneously or successively, *or* by one person" (emphasis added). In the Court's view, the self-executing nature of the rule was to be excluded due to the latter's non-mandatory content, as it gave the legislature the option to either admit both alternatives (adoption by two persons married to each other or by one person) or to pursue only one of them. This line of reasoning was later replicated by the Court of Cassation when confronted with the same international provision (*Corte di Cassazione*, No. 7950 of 21 July 1995). Another relevant example is the Constitutional Court's decision in the *Priebke* case (*Corte Costituzionale*, No. 58 of 3 March 1997), which dealt with the application of Article 8 of the European Convention on Extradition. The provision established that "[t]he requested Party *may* refuse to extradite the person claimed" (emphasis added) should the circumstances indicated therein occur. The Court decided that, in the presence of a mere option, it was not possible to deduce the necessary domestic rules for the application of the international text and applied Article 705(1) of the Italian Code of Criminal Procedure instead. This line of jurisprudence frames the identification of self-executing provisions in similar terms to the second stream of Italian scholarship recalled above.

However, the reasoning of the *Corte di Cassazione* in the case under scrutiny was not free from inconsistencies. The Court supported its conclusion regarding the non-applicability of Article 15(4) UNTOC by opposing it to Articles 15(1) and 15(2) of the same convention, which were brought as examples of self-executing provisions instead.

Although Article 15(1) displayed mandatory wording by stating that "[e]ach State Party shall adopt measures as may be necessary to establish its jurisdiction", mandatory language is not in itself sufficient to determine the self-executing nature of a provision, as explained by the corresponding line of legal scholarship. It represents a minimum threshold that must be followed by the presence, in the domestic legal order, of the necessary elements that allow the application of the international rule. What follows is that, if the absence of mandatory language will automatically lead to the non-applicability of the international rule, its presence in the treaty text does not entail the opposite conclusion, namely the self-executing nature of the provision. In the case of Article 15(1) UNTOC, the clause is directed to the national legislature and requires an exercise of norm-making activity to display effects in the Italian legal order. In the absence (as in the case at hand) of a specific effort by the Italian legislature to establish jurisdiction, the international provision does not seem to allow the Italian judge to deduce the corresponding domestic legal rules without exceeding the boundaries of interpretation. Consequently, following the approach adopted by the *Corte di Cassazione*, even in the presence of mandatory wording, Article 15(1) should not be considered suitable to be applied through the special procedure.

Equally questionable is the use of Article 15(2) as an example of a self-executing provision. The article reads that "a State Party *may* also establish its jurisdiction" (emphasis added) when the specific conditions laid out in its subsections are met. Under the approach followed by the Court of Cassation, this clearly non-mandatory provision (MCCLEAN, *Transnational Organized Crime – A Commentary on the UN Convention and its Protocols*, Oxford, 2007, p. 168) should have been considered non-self-executing and therefore not applicable. However, not only did the Court conclude differently, but it recalled several occasions in which its previous jurisprudence applied Article 15(2) UNTOC (*ex multis*, *Corte di Cassazione*, Judgment No. 14510 of 27 March 2014).

In conclusion, even though the non-applicability of Article 15(4) UNTOC does not seem questionable under the approach followed by the *Corte di Cassazione*, the arguments it brought in support of such conclusion still do not seem consistent with the Court's reasoning and ultimately cast a shadow on its logic.

In light of the above, the cases under scrutiny highlight how the identification of self-executing treaty provisions is still a troublesome aspect of the implementation of international treaties into the Italian legal order by way of an order of execution. The judgments carry on the long-standing division that characterizes both Italian jurisprudence and legal scholarship and confirm that the disagreement over the identifying elements of self-executing provisions is, so far, yet to be settled.

NICCOLÒ ZUGLIANI

ITALIAN JURISPRUDENCE ON THE BOUNDARIES OF STATE IMMUNITY FROM JURISDICTION AND EXECUTION: WAITING FOR THE NEXT EPISODE

State immunity from civil jurisdiction – State immunity from measures of constraints – Judgment No. 238 of 2014 of the Italian Constitutional Court – Relationship between international and domestic law – ICJ judgment in Jurisdictional Immunities of the State (Germany v. Italy: Greece intervening)

Corte di Cassazione (Sezioni Unite Civili), 28 September 2020, No. 20442
Toldo v. Germany

The judgment under review is the last episode in the saga concerning the interpretation by Italian tribunals of the customary international law principle on the jurisdictional immunity of States for acts amounting to international crimes.

This judgment arose out of another civil case relating to serious violations of human rights and humanitarian law committed by the Third Reich during the Second World War. Specifically, the plaintiff, Paolo Toldo, had instituted civil proceedings before the Tribunal of Florence in his capacity as heir of Michele Toldo, his father, against Germany, claiming damages for war crimes. The plaintiff alleged that Michele Toldo was arrested in August 1944 and subsequently deported to Germany by the Third Reich army, where he was subjected to forced labour and was eventually killed at Gröditz concentration camp.

In the face of this sadly typical factual context, the Tribunal of Florence (Judgment of 14 March 2012, No. 1086) and the Court of Appeal of Florence (Judgment of 17 December 2018, No. 2945) rejected Paolo Toldo's claims in order to abide by the customary international law rule affording jurisdictional immunity to States for acts *jure imperii* amounting to war crimes committed on the forum State territory, as ascertained by the International Court of Justice (ICJ) with the 2012 judgment in the case *Jurisdictional Immunities of the State (Germany v. Italy)*.

The Court of Appeal justified its decision with the following arguments. First, it pointed out that, following the enactment of Law No. 5 of 14 January 2013 on the ratification of the United Nations Convention on Jurisdictional Immunities of States and Their Property, numerous Italian tribunals – including the Court of Cassation – have declined jurisdiction over actions for compensation against Germany for international crimes committed by the Third Reich (see e.g. *Federal Republic of Germany v Heirs of Luigi Ferrini*, 21 January 2014, No. 1136, IYIL, 2013, p. 436 ff., with a comment by CATALDI). As is well know, Law No. 5/2013 was passed by the Italian Parliament to ensure the implementation of the ICJ judgment in *Jurisdictional Immunities of the State* in Italy. In effect, its Article 3(1) compels Italian judges to decline jurisdiction in any case where the ICJ has excluded the possibility of subjecting specific conduct of a foreign State to civil jurisdiction, whereas its Article 3(2) provides that a final judgment could be challenged when it clashes with the ICJ judgment, even when that domestic decision preceded the ruling of the ICJ. Secondly, the Court of Appeal contested the arguments with which the Florence Tribunal challenged the constitutionality of Article 3 of Law 5/2013 – and which led to the Constitutional Court's judgment 238/2014 (*Corte Costituzionale, Simoncioni, Alessi and Bergamini v. Federal Republic of Germany and Presidency of the Council of Ministers*, 22 October 2014, No. 238; IYIL, 2014, p. 1 ff., with comments by FRANCIONI, PISILLO, BOTHE, CATALDI and PALCHETTI). The Court of Appeal did so on the grounds that the Court of Cassation had affirmed that restrictions to the rights of access to justice and to reparation for war crimes were allowed by Article 11 of the Italian Constitution, which states that "Italy agrees [...] to the limitations of sovereignty that may be necessary to a world order ensuring peace and justice among Nations" (*Corte di Cassazione*, Judgment No. 1136/2014, *cit. supra*; *Corte di Cassazione (Sez. I penale), Criminal proceedings against Albers and others*, 9 August 2012, No. 32139). Thirdly, the Court of Appeal upheld the customary international law principle on the jurisdictional immunity of States for acts *jure imperii* because legal actions against sovereign States – including those brought by Nazi victims or their heirs – might negatively impact on the peaceful relations among States, which is one the interests that the principle of immunity seeks to protect.

Incidentally, it should be mentioned that both the Florence Tribunal and the Court of Appeal disregarded the order with which the Court of Cassation had decided on the petition for a preliminary ruling on jurisdiction brought by Germany, holding that the Tribunal had jurisdiction in the civil proceedings instituted by Paolo Toldo (Order of 29 May 2008, No. 14202).

Paolo Toldo challenged the judgment of the Court of Appeal before the *Corte di Cassazione*, which eventually quashed the Court of Appeal's judgment and referred back the underlying case to the Florence Tribunal.

The reason why the judgment under scrutiny is worth examining is that the manner with which the Court of Cassation reversed the judgment of the Court of Appeal differs considerably from previous decisions in cases involving victims (or their heirs) of war crimes and crimes against humanity.

On the one hand, the Supreme Court took the appeal as an occasion to point the way for all Italian judges in order to avoid future miscarriages of justice. Indeed, the *Corte di Cassazione* urged Italian courts in general (and the Court of Appeal of Florence in particular) to affirm jurisdiction in all cases in which damages were sought for international crimes committed by the Third Reich on Italian territory during the Second World War, regardless of the customary rule on the jurisdictional immunity of States as ascertained by the ICJ in the judgment *Jurisdictional Immunities of the State*, and hence in accordance with the relevant Italian jurisprudence. In connection with the latter point, the Court of Cassation did not merely hold that the Court of Appeal had erred in deciding the case at stake without taking into account the existing case law on the jurisdictional immunity of States. More importantly, it actually retraced the evolution of Italian jurisprudence on this issue – from *Ferrini* (*Corte di Cassazione, Ferrini v. Federal Republic of Germany*, 11 March 2004, No. 5044), to the 2012 ICJ judgment *Jurisdictional Immunities of the State*, in the wake of which the *Ferrini* precedent was discontinued, to the Constitutional Court's Judgment No. 238/2014 – in order to confirm that the principles established by *Ferrini* and Judgment No. 238/2014 were still good law. In other words, the Court of Cassation reiterated that international customs violating fundamental rights enshrined in the Italian Constitution could not enter the Italian legal order (the 'counter-limits' doctrine).

On the other hand, the Court of Cassation capitalized the appeal under consideration by pointing out that Italian judges were bound by the Constitutional Court's Judgment No. 238/2014 despite it being an "interpretative judgment of dismissal" ("*sentenza interpretativa di rigetto*"). Pursuant to Italian constitutional law, interpretative judgments of dismissal are in principle binding only on the referring judge *a quo*, that is, the judge that raised the question of constitutionality (in this case the Tribunal of Florence). However, the Court of Cassation recalled its judgment of 16 December 2013, No. 27986, where it established that the interpretative judgments of dismissal of the Constitutional Court provide for a negative constraint for the judge *a quo* and any other judge, that is, the obligation to disregard any rule deemed not in conformity with the Constitution, as ascertained by the Constitutional Court itself.

In other respects, however, the judgment under review is similar to the other judgments whereby the Court of Cassation refused to apply the principle of State immunity to cases involving war crimes and crimes against humanity. In effect, the *Corte di Cassazione* did not dwell on the question of the responsibility of the Italian state for its failure to comply with the ICJ judgment. Moreover, the *Corte di Cassazione* did not deal with the fact that Germany had never paid damages to the winning parties in the cases brought against it in relation to the international crimes committed by the Third Reich during the Second World War. In other words, it did not acknowledge that the approach endorsed by the Italian judiciary since *Ferrini* has not translated into a truly effective remedy for plaintiffs as a result of the customary international law rule on States immunity from execution. Finally, the Court did not acknowledge that Italian judges are still alone in denying State immunity for international crimes amounting to violations of constitutionally guaranteed human rights.

In conclusion, it appears that the Italian judiciary is still stuck in a stalled revolution. On the one hand, it can be praised for the principled approach with which it aims at reconciling State immunity with the protection of constitutionally guaranteed human rights – though this is achieved through multiple breaches of international law. On the other hand, it seems unable or unwilling to challenge the constitutionality of the domestic norms upholding the customary international law rule on States immunity from execution in order to push the restrictive interpretation of immunity from measures of constraints beyond existing limits and hence to render effective the remedies granted to plaintiffs.

ALESSANDRO CHECHI

DIPLOMATIC AND PARLIAMENTARY PRACTICE

(edited by *Pietro Gargiulo*, *Marco Pertile* and *Paolo Turrini*)

VI. TERRITORY

THE DISPUTE WITH FRANCE OVER THE TERRITORIAL BOUNDARY IN THE MONT BLANC AREA

The boundary between Italy and France in the Alpine region is set by the treaty signed in Turin, on 24 March 1860, by the Kingdom of Sardinia and the French Empire concerning the cession to the latter of the Duchy of Savoy and the County of Nice, as well as by the actual delimitation agreements – implementing the 1860 Treaty – signed by the same parties on 27 June and 25 November 1860, 7 March 1861, and 26 September 1862.[1] The border line was primarily drawn in adherence to the principle of the watershed. The line was later modified in four areas by the 1947 Treaty of Peace between Italy and the Allied Powers at the end of the Second World War.[2]

In the 1990s,[3] a dispute between the two States arose due to the French official cartography differing from the Italian one in three points, namely the

---

[1] Respectively, Traité conclu à Turin, le 24 mars 1860, entre la France et la Sardaigne, pour la réunion de la Savoie et de l'arrondissement de Nice à la France, Art. 3 (the text of the convention can be found in DE CLERQ (ed.), *Recueil des traités de la France*, Vol. 8, Paris, 1880, p. 32 ff.); Protocole dressé à Paris, le 27 juin 1860, pour régler les bases de la délimitation entre la France et la Sardeigne, en exécution de l'art. 3 du traité conclu à Turin le 24 mars 1860, Art. 1 (*ibid.*, pp. 59-60); Protocole dressé à Nice le 25 novembre 1860 pour fixer la délimitation entre la France et la Sardeigne, Art. 1 (*ibid.*, p. 150 ff.); Convention de délimitation, signée à Turin le 7 mars 1861 entre la France et la Sardaigne, Art. 1 (*ibid.*, p. 185 ff.); and Procès-verbal N. 2 d'abornement de la frontière entre la France et l'Italie, dressé à Turin le 26 septembre 1862, d'après la convention signée à Turin le 7 mars 1861 par les plénipotentiaires des deux pays et ratifiée par les deux gouvernements (available in ADAMI, *Storia documentata dei confini del Regno d'Italia*, Vol. 1, Confine italo-francese, Roma, 1919, p. 374 ff.). The treaties of June and November 1860 and that of March 1861 draw the boundary along the "current border" (*limite actuelle*) between the Duchy of Savoy and Piedmont, whereas the more recent 1862 agreement seems to revive the "ancient border" (*ancienne limite*) – the latter line being an ambiguous reference but possibly favoring France.

[2] Treaty of Peace with Italy, 10 February 1947, Art. 2. These areas, however, do not cover the boundary segments currently disputed. As a curious side note, in the final months of the Second World War, some French actors promoted the annexation of the Aosta Valley to France, with a move known as *mission Mont-Blanc*: see NICCO, "La questione valdostana e la Conferenza di Parigi", in DEL BOCA (ed.), *Confini contesi: la Repubblica italiana e il Trattato di pace di Parigi*, Torino, 1998, p. 75 ff., p. 78 (this chapter and those by Giovana and Panicacci shed light on the events, related to the boundary between Italy and France and having some legal relevance, that led to the Treaty of Paris).

[3] The issue was first raised in the Italian Parliament at the turn of the century with questions no. 4-00019 (1996) and no. 4-23419 (1999), which were answered in writing by two Undersecretaries for Foreign Affairs, Mr Piero Fassino and Mr Umberto Ranieri, respectively.

IYIL, Vol. 30 (2020), pp. 497-539
ISSN 0391-5107

Mont Blanc summit, the Dôme du Goûter and the Col du Géant. While France reportedly frames the issue in terms of the existence of "diverging interpretations", thus seemingly implying the equal legitimacy of both stances, Italian Governments have more than once deemed the French counterpart as providing a "unilateral interpretation" of the 1861 Convention – which appears to be a euphemism for non-compliance with treaty obligations. A written reply (dated 22 October 2015) by the Undersecretary of State for Foreign Affairs and International Cooperation, Mr Benedetto Della Vedova, to parliamentary question no. 4-04473 maintained that the French "unilateral interpretation [...] ignores the general approach of the [1861] treaty and the constant practice on the field" (the latter clearly being *effectivités* carried on by Italy). Indeed, he remarked that

> The treaty and the practice show, in a clear and continuous way, the actual respect of the criterion of the watershed in the areas, also by means of the uninterrupted exercise of full Italian sovereignty over them (rescue operations, levying of taxes owed for *in situ* real estate, such as the Torino Hut, policing activities).

More recently,[4] the Italian Government qualified the French position as resting on factually flawed historical rights dating back to the 19th century rather than on a treaty. This may be a misrepresentation of the French position, which is in fact a legitimate way of untying a complex legal knot – for sure, too complex to be dealt with here.[5]

Be that as it may, since the mid-2010s the territorial dispute has been fueled by no less than three episodes[6] – occurred in September 2015, June 2019 and October 2020 – that saw France trying to put in place some *effectivités* in

---

[4] I.e., in Mr Scalfarotto's reply quoted *infra* at length.

[5] A summary of the legal and factual events is proposed in ALIPRANDI and ALIPRANDI, *La découverte du Mont-Blanc par les cartographes: 1515-1925*, Ivrea, 2000, pp. 136–137, and in greater detail in ID., *Le grandi Alpi nella cartografia: 1482-1885*, Vol. 2, Ivrea, 2005, pp. 93–168, especially p. 159 ff. The authors side with Italy, but they repeatedly remark the country's acquiescence to certain French claims since the 19th century, despite these were perhaps known to the Italian authorities (should this be the case, such an aware acquiescence might be legally relied on by France). There is merit, however, in saying that acquiescence is to be excluded due to the fact that Italian cartography has never endorsed Mieulet's map, which expresses the French point of view: see STARITA, "La questione del confine italo-francese sul Monte Bianco", RDI, 2020, p. 167 ff., p. 173 (this author, too, supports the idea that the boundary in the Mont Blanc area follows the watershed, with legal arguments different from the principled position espoused by Aliprandi and Aliprandi).

[6] The three cases here briefly presented are those officially addressed by Italian authorities and cannot be understood as an exhaustive list of all relevant episodes. For instance, in 2014, near the Little St Bernard Pass (some kilometers from the Mont Blanc), a French bulldozer moved a boundary marker 150 meters into the Italian territory: "Aiuto, la Francia ci 'ruba' un pezzo del Monte Bianco", La Stampa, 25 June 2015, available at: <www.lastampa.it/montagna/2015/06/25/news/aiuto-la-francia-ci-ruba-un-pezzo-del-monte-bianco-1.35255305>.

the region and were met with Italy's opposition. The first such events triggered the abovementioned response by Mr Della Vedova, which in the remaining part continues as follows:

> The episode of 4 September 2015, when the mayor of Chamonix decided the deployment on Italian soil of a fence and chains and locks applied to otherwise movable barriers, was not echoed by the French Government. Should this episode not remain isolated, the Italian Government is ready to formally remind its counterpart of its well-known national positions on this matter and their legal bases, with the hope that this could work as a general clarification. In the same period, at the beginning of September, the joint study mission carried out on the Mont Blanc massif by the *Istituto Geografico Militare* and the French national geographic agency could not arrive at shared conclusions about the areas of the Dôme du Goûter, the Mont Blanc summit and the Col du Géant, since the French geographers refused, upon instruction, to ratify the watershed criterion for these areas.
>
> Should diverging readings officially endorsed by Paris remain in the future, the Italian Government is willing to demonstrate once more, as it has always done in the past, its openness to deal with the issue at a diplomatic level, through ad hoc delegations comprising experts in legal history and cartographers. By the way, such a working group had been proposed to our counterpart in August 2000. The Italian Government had, on its part, promptly notified the selection of its delegation, but the group could not meet as France never appointed its own representatives.
>
> As Italy holds its stance on the tracing of the State border, should further actions by [French] local authorities and their endorsement by Paris make clear that the watershed criterion is formally put into question, the Government will not refrain from restating once more the Italian points of view, if needed through an accurate survey of the international accords that set the boundary or a joint analysis of the parties' conduct on the field.

Mr Della Vedova's final words – which called for "compliance with the peremptory norm of international law that dictates the inviolability of international frontiers" – voiced the Government's readiness to intervene should analogous events have happened. The occasion came a few years later, when a similar move by France became the object, in the Italian Senate, of parliamentary question no. 4-02207. The new Undersecretary of State for Foreign Affairs and International Cooperation, Mr Ivan Scalfarotto, replied in writing to the interrogating MP with an answer dated 5 June 2020 (an identical communiqué was delivered on 12 October 2020 to the proponents of question no. 4-03541, during the 406th Meeting of the Chamber of Deputies, XVIII Legislature). The text of the reply is as follows:

The issue revolves around a historical boundary dispute between Italy and France, that do not recognize the same border line on the Mont Blanc massif. The Italian official cartography, which is also used by NATO forces and recognized at the global level, is based on the 1861 delimitation convention [...] that, according to the existing historical-legal studies, appears to be the only authentic treaty instrument on the matter. On the contrary, French cartography, that would draw the Mont Blanc border 82 hectares further into the Italian territory, does not rest on a treaty instrument, but it would seem to stem from a unilateral interpretation by Paris and from alleged "historical rights" that can be traced back to the erroneous reproduction of maps over the years, starting from the 19th century. These rights are in disagreement both with the border line set by the 1861 convention and with the consistent practice on the field, which shows a full and continuous exercise of sovereignty by Italy over the areas "claimed" by France.

The issue is back in the news due to the adoption, in late June 2019, of a local measure by the French municipalities of Chamonix and Saint Gervais to temporarily ban, following a deadly accident, paragliding activities in the proximity of Mont Blanc, thus including, however, parts of the Italian territory – such as the whole peak of Mont Blanc – in the area covered by the measure. This was adopted with no prior consultation with, nor prior notification to, Italian local authorities, in contrast with what had been agreed to in 2016 and 2018 at a technical level by the mixed Italo-French commission for the maintenance of the boundary line.

As a consequence, this Ministry, through the [Italian] embassy in Paris, immediately and formally manifested to the French authorities, with firmness, the traditional Italian position on the border line, both as a reaction to the "violation of boundaries and national sovereignty" symbolically carried out by means of the administrative measure of the French local authorities, and with the aim of avoiding that an alleged Italian acquiescence to the French claims may be invoked in the future, with the effect of undermining our position.

In addition to expressing Italy's displeasure at the violation of the boundary, the note verbale sent to the French authorities recalled that in the past, on multiple occasions, Italy has shown its availability to initiate bilateral consultations with France to examine the divergences in the respective maps of Mont Blanc. At the same time, we restated our openness to dialogue with the French authorities with a view to coming to a joint solution to the dispute.

For Italy, at stake is not only an economic interest, but also a symbolic one, which must be protected, as Paris's claims would assign to France the whole summit of Mont Blanc (the highest peak in Europe) and the Torino Hut.

Lastly, it must be noted that the French authorities replied to the Italian request by stating that the administrative measure adopted in June 2019 by local authorities concerns "a geographical area that has been for many decades the object of a dispute between France and Italy". In this regard, French authorities declared their availability to address the question within the mixed commission for the maintenance of the boundary line.

Mr Scalfarotto then concluded by reaffirming the Government's commitment to tackle the issue with France at both a political and a technical level. Along the same lines, in a press release by the Farnesina dated 21 October 2020,[7] an official note by the Minister of Foreign Affairs and International Cooperation, Mr Luigi Di Maio, was said to have been sent to French authorities, reminding them of their express availability to handle the controversy through the abovementioned mixed Italo-French commission, as well as of the common intention to "avoid all unilateral actions by local authorities" in the disputed area.

In his message, Mr Di Maio also asked the French Government to prevent the Haute-Savoie Prefecture from including "in official local measures the Italian territorial areas beyond the border, which, as such, are under Italy's national sovereignty". At any rate, "such unilateral measures, which cannot and must not impinge on the Italian territory, will be devoid of any effect and will not be recognized by Italy". This request originated from a further French deed, this time undertaken on 1 October 2020 by said prefecture in order to protect the natural site around Mont Blanc. The incident was also addressed by the Deputy Minister of Foreign Affairs and International Cooperation, Ms Emanuela Del Re, in her written reply – dated 2 February 2021 – to parliamentary question no. 4-04272. Recalling the two countries' understanding on the need to avoid unilateral actions, and referring to a recent note verbale by the Quai d'Orsay expressing France's availability to solve the dispute within the mixed commission, she reiterated the idea that Italy's contestation of French measures,

> from the standpoint of international law, is capable of avoiding the formation of acquiescence, on Italy's part, toward any hypothetical invocation of a *de facto* change in the State's border caused by the unilateral measures carried out by the Haute-Savoie Prefecture.

Ms Del Re went on by writing that

> The issue of unilateral measures over the disputed areas was most recently debated during the annual meeting of the mixed commission, on 19 November 2020. Our French counterpart, in recognizing the continuous validity of the 1861 convention and the attached

---

[7] Ministry of Foreign Affairs and International Cooperation, "Nota Farnesina – Monte Bianco", available at: <www.esteri.it/mae/en/sala_stampa/archivionotizie/comunicati/nota-farnesina-monte-bianco.html>.

cartographic materials, noted that the problem would descend from a diverging interpretation by the two States. On our part, however, we restated the importance of avoiding misunderstandings on a highly sensitive question for our Government that might be engendered by the adoption of unilateral measures encroaching upon the sovereignty of the Country, pending the carrying out of in-depth analyses of cartographic materials and the smoothing out, as much as possible, of the differences on the border line.

In October 2020, two Italian members of the European Parliament (MEPs) queried the European Commission about the dispute (questions nos. E-005668/2020 and E-005844/2020). On 26 February and 29 March 2021, respectively, both questions were answered in analogous terms by Ms Ylva Johansson on behalf of the institution. The replies reminded the interrogating MEPs that it is for each Member State to determine the extent and limits of its own territory, a matter in which the European Union (EU) has no competence to act.

PAOLO TURRINI

THE PROPOSED ISRAELI ANNEXATION OF PARTS OF THE WEST BANK

On 20 April 2020, the Prime Minister of Israel, Mr Benjamin Netanyahu, and the leader of the White and Blue political alliance, Mr Benjamin Gantz, signed the coalition agreement that ended the political stalemate resulting from the inconclusive results of three consecutive Israeli legislative elections, which had been held in April 2019, September 2019, and March 2020. Under the terms of this agreement, it was decided that Mr Netanyahu would have been authorized to put forward a proposal to annex parts of the West Bank starting from 1 July 2020. The formal annexation would have been subjected to approval by both the Knesset's Foreign Affairs and Defense Committee and, then, the full Knesset. The plan would have been undertaken in close coordination with the United States.[8]

Such a proposal has attracted widespread criticism from the international community.[9] As for Italy, on 22 April 2020, the Deputy Minister for Foreign

---

[8] On the coalition agreement and the annexation plan, see "Netanyahu, Gantz Agree on West Bank Annexation Proposal as Unity Deal Nears", Haaretz, 6 April 2020, available at: <www.haaretz.com/israel-news...bank-annexation-as-unity-deal-nears-1.8745742>. See also "Netanyahu, Gantz Sign Coalition Deal to Form Government", Haaretz, 20 April 2020, available at: <www.haaretz.com/israel-news...gn-coalition-deal-on-monday-evening-1.8783533>.

[9] See the remarks by the Secretary-General and by the Special Coordinator for the Middle East Peace Process, which were echoed by many members of the Security Council, "Annexing Parts of West Bank Will 'Grievously Harm' Two-State Solution, Secretary-General Says, Addressing Security Council on Israeli-Palestinian Conflict", 24 June 2020, available at: <www.un.org/press/en/2020/sc14225.doc.htm#_ftn1>; the remarks by the European Union High Representative Borrell on the possible Israeli annexation in the West Bank, "European Parliament: Remarks by the HR/VP Josep Borrell on the Foreign policy consequences of the COVID-19 crisis, on the PRC national security law for Hong Kong and on the possible Israeli

Affairs and International Cooperation, Ms Marina Sereni, treated the annexation plan as a "serious matter". Ms Sereni further elaborated as follows:

> Italy [...] will work together with its European partners while seeking a convergence on this point also with the American Administration. Keeping the dialogue between the parties open and relaunching bilateral negotiations remains the only option on which the Italian Government is working, in agreement with the other EU countries, with a view to a two-State solution. On the contrary, unilateral acts risk undermining all efforts at dialogue and negotiation for peace.[10]

Subsequently, on 5 May 2020, some members of the Italian Parliament posed a question to the Minister for Foreign Affairs and International Cooperation regarding this political development. More specifically, the interrogating members of the Parliament, recalling the above-mentioned remark by the Deputy Minister, asked whether the Minister intended to undertake any diplomatic initiative to prevent the implementation of the annexation plan. The question was answered by Ms Sereni on 20 October 2020, at the 412nd Meeting (XVIII Legislature) of the Chamber of Deputies. She said:

> Since the formation of the Netanyahu–Gantz Government, Italy has expressed its opposition to Israel's plan to annex parts of the West Bank and of the Jordan Valley. We have reiterated this position many times both at a bilateral level, beginning with the phone call on 1 July between Minister for Foreign Affairs and International Cooperation Di Maio and his Israeli counterpart Ashkenazi, and at a multilateral level, most recently on the occasion of the meeting with the same Israeli Minister on the side-lines of the informal meeting of European Ministers for Foreign Affairs held in Berlin on 28 August.

---

annexation in the West Bank", 18 June 2020, available at: <https://eeas.europa.eu/headquarters/headquarters-homepage_en/81104>; and Resolution no. 8522 adopted by the Council of the League of Arab States on 30 April 2020, enclosed to the Annex to the Letter dated 1 May 2020 from the Permanent Representative of Oman to the United Nations addressed to the Secretary-General, 12 May 2020, UN Doc. A/74/835–S/2020/356.

[10] Italian Ministry for Foreign Affairs and International Cooperation, "Middle East; Ms Sereni's phone call with Palestinian chief negotiator Erekat", 22 April 2020, available at: <www.esteri.it/mae/en/sala_stampa/archivionotizie/comunicati/2020/04/medio-oriente-telefonata-sereni-con-capo-negoziatore-palestinese-erekat.html>. See also Italian Ministry for Foreign Affairs and International Cooperation, "Sereni to the Arab League delegation: working together to prevent the prospect of Israeli annexation", 23 June 2020, available at: <www.esteri.it/mae/en/sala_stampa/archivionotizie/comunicati/2020/06/sereni-alla-delegazione-della-lega-araba-lavorare-insieme-per-prevenire-prospettiva-di-annessioni-israeliane.html>.

The Deputy Minister then clarified the grounds on which Italy's stance is based and, more specifically, she reaffirmed the traditional Italian position that such an annexation is problematic from both a legal and a political viewpoint.[11] Ms Sereni said:

> Our message, in line with the European position, has always been very clear: any annexation of territories by Israel would not be acceptable because it would be in flagrant violation of international law and it would further complicate the prospects for a two-State solution, which Italy firmly supports.

The Deputy Minister then expressed her belief that eventually Israel had refrained from proceeding presumably also due to this joint EU reaction. In any case, she conceded that the annexation plan had been suspended in exchange for the normalization agreements (collectively known as the Abraham Accords) between Israel and, respectively, the United Arab Emirates and the Kingdom of Bahrein. As regards these accords, Ms Sereni continued her reasoning as follows:

> The Abraham Accords mark a major step, which we have welcomed together with our European partners, because by bringing Israel closer to the Arab world they could contribute not only to the stability of the Middle East, but also to its development by promoting economic, health, scientific, technological, and cultural cooperation. Potentially this is a paradigm shift for the balance in the region and thus for a new political environment where the legitimate existence of the State of Israel and its right to live in peace and security are finally recognized. Certainly, to achieve lasting peace in the Middle East, the peace process between Israel and Palestine must be revived through direct negotiations between the parties, so to achieve a two-State solution that is just, viable, and that takes in due consideration the legitimate aspirations of both peoples, in accordance with international law and UN resolutions. Thus, in this regard, our commitment remains firm and we do not miss the opportunity to encourage the parties to return to the negotiating table, with a realistic approach and a constructive spirit.

Even if the Deputy Minister observed that the Abraham Accords cannot by themselves lead to peace in the Middle East, her words clearly described them as a welcome political development inasmuch as they could contribute positively to the peace process.[12] This is noteworthy because these agreements were brokered

---

[11] MOINET, "Territorial Issues Concerning the Arab-Israeli Conflict", IYIL, 2019, p. 470 ff.

[12] Admittedly, this is not an isolated position, so much that, apparently, even the Biden Administration has soon taken the very same position. See the remarks by the United States

by the Trump Administration and are part of a wider diplomatic effort,[13] which however had been criticized by a previous Italian cabinet.[14]

It is equally worth noting that the expressions "realistic approach" and "constructive spirit" arguably convey a specific message to the Palestinians, in that such wording seems to conceal behind euphemisms the demand that they make some compromises on matters of international law. The problem is that international law might be a factor that narrows down the scope of negotiations on final status issues whenever a certain outcome is legally mandated.[15] It is therefore not clear to what extent it would be lawful for the two parties to agree on such compromises, especially when these regard *jus cogens* norms. Admittedly, expressions similar to those used by Ms Sereni are routinely used when it comes to the conflict in question, thus the statement cited above does not particularly stand out. The Permanent Representative of Italy to the United Nations (UN), Ms Maria Angela Zappia, on 5 November 2020, before the Commission on Foreign and European Affairs (III) of the Chamber of Deputies at its 23rd Meeting, was more explicit on the tension between the alleged pragmatic nature of the negotiation process and international legality. In this regard, she observed that:

> Today, after the Abraham Accords, the peace process in the Middle East has the chance to be resumed thanks to a structural change in the dynamics of the region that can revitalize the direct negotiations between Israelis and Palestinians with a view to arriving at a just and viable two-State solution. More specifically, we have to help the Palestinian leadership to somehow draw upon its courage and deal with this new reality with foresight and pragmatism, without having to renounce to principled positions that are absolutely legitimate.

Some members of the Commission asked Ms Zappia her opinion as to the consequences of a hypothetical victory of Mr Joe Biden for the peace process in the Middle East. Ms Zappia, after noting that the candidate of the Democratic

---

Secretary of State, Mr Blinken, in "Secretary Antony J. Blinken with Wolf Blitzer of CNN's The Situation Room", 8 February 2021, available at: <www.state.gov/secretary-antony-j-blinken-with-wolf-blitzer-of-cnns-the-situation-room>.

[13] Indeed, both the agreement between Israel and Bahrain and the one between Israel and the United Arab Emirates mention the Israeli-Palestinian conflict and the latter also reaffirms the peace plan proposed by former United States President Trump. The texts of the agreements (both signed on 15 September 2020) are available respectively at: <www.state.gov/wp-content/uploads/2020/09/Bahrain_Israel-Agreement-signed-FINAL-15-Sept-2020-508.pdf> and <www.state.gov/wp-content/uploads/2020/09/UAE_Israel-treaty-signed-FINAL-15-Sept-2020-508.pdf>. See in general EICHENSER (ed.), "Trump Administration Brokers Accords to Normalize Relations Between Israel and Six Countries", AJIL, 2021, p. 116 ff.

[14] For a comment on the Italian position on the previous stances adopted by the Trump Administration, see TURRINI, "The Status of Jerusalem", IYIL, 2017, p. 468 ff., and MOINET, *cit. supra* note 11.

[15] For such an argument, see DAJANI, "Shadow or Shade? The Roles of International Law in Palestinian-Israeli Peace Talks", Yale JIL, 2007, p. 61 ff.

Party had already expressed his support for the Abraham Accords as well as for the United States diplomatic effort in that area, deemed it unlikely that those agreements would be challenged by a Democrat-led administration. She also stressed that by accepting the agreements Israel is renouncing annexation as a concrete option, and that it is this development that should be encouraged in view of a two-State solution. It remains to be seen to what extent the Biden Administration will ensure continuity with its approach to the Israeli–Palestinian conflict and how third States will react.

JEAN PAUL MOINET

VII.   LAW OF THE SEA

MARITIME DELIMITATION IN THE CENTRAL MEDITERRANEAN SEA AND ALGERIA'S PROCLAMATION OF AN EXCLUSIVE ECONOMIC ZONE

With Presidential Decree no. 18-96 of 20 March 2018, Algeria officially proclaimed an exclusive economic zone (EEZ) in the Mediterranean Sea so as to exercise therein its sovereign rights and jurisdiction in accordance with Part V of the 1982 UN Convention on the Law of the Sea (UNCLOS). The act included a list of 63 geographical coordinates delineating the extension of the maritime claim but envisaged that the outer limits of the EEZ could be modified through bilateral agreements with neighboring States, where necessary.[16]

This move sparked an almost immediate reaction from both Italy and Spain. These countries, through their Permanent Missions to the UN, addressed two separate official communications to the Secretary-General, Mr António Guterres, whereby they brought to notice their disagreement with the geographical coordinates established by Algeria in the Presidential Decree.

In its communication, Italy expressed its opposition to the definition of the Algerian EEZ because it "unduly overlaps on zones of legitimate and exclusive national Italian interest".[17] Italy also referred to Article 74 UNCLOS on the delimitation of the EEZ between States with opposite or adjacent coasts, recalling the legal framework thereby envisaged to regulate the conduct of the parties to a dispute during the transitional period preceding the achievement of a final delimitation agreement. Finally, Italy expressed its readiness to enter negotiations with the counterpart.

The Spanish Government expressed its opposition to the unilateral Algerian act by claiming that some portions of the EEZ "are clearly disproportionate in relation to the equidistant median line between the Algerian and Spanish coasts".

---

[16] Presidential Decree no. 18-96 of 2 Rajab A.H. 1439, corresponding to 20 March A.D. 2018, establishing an exclusive economic zone off the coast of Algeria, 20 March 2018, available at: <www.un.org/Depts/los/LEGISLATIONANDTREATIES/PDFFILES/DZA_2018_Decree_1896_en.pdf>.

[17] Communication from Italy dated 28 November 2018, available at: <www.un.org/Depts/los/LEGISLATIONANDTREATIES/PDFFILES/2018_NV_Italy.pdf>.

It also reaffirmed that, in accordance with Article 74 UNCLOS, "the equidistant line between the baselines from which the breadth of the territorial sea is measured is the most equitable solution for delimiting, by mutual agreement, the exclusive economic zones between States with opposite or adjacent coasts".[18]

On 29 June 2019, Algeria replied to both Italy and Spain by means of two notes verbales. As to the dispute with Rome, the Algerian Ministry for Foreign Affairs stated that the extension of the claimed EEZ was determined by taking into due consideration the "objective rules and relevant principles of international law", in compliance with Article 74 UNCLOS.[19] Nonetheless, the Ministry assured Italy of Algeria's readiness to negotiate an equitable and mutually acceptable solution.[20]

The answer to the Spanish counterpart was more articulated. This is probably due to the fact that Spain, unlike Italy, had already proclaimed an EEZ of its own in April 2013.[21] Algeria, in the note verbale addressed to the Spanish Government, recognized that their respective EEZs effectively overlapped in certain maritime areas. In light of this consideration, Algeria included the following statement:

> Algeria and Spain are required, in accordance with international case law and State practice, to refrain, at this stage, from engaging in activities in that area in connection with their sovereign rights, including exploration and exploitation, and conservation and management of natural resources, whether living or non-living, as set forth in article 56 of the United Nations Convention on the Law of the Sea.[22]

This is an important declaration from the perspective of the law of the sea. Indeed, it appears that Algeria recognizes the existence of an obligation for a coastal State, pending a final delimitation, not to engage in unilateral activities related to the exercise of sovereign rights in disputed sea areas. This is not an obvious recognition, since the precise content of the two separate obligations included in Article 74(3) UNCLOS (and of the analogous obligations for continental shelf disputes included in Article 83(3) UNCLOS) has not been definitively

---

[18] Letter from Spain to the Secretary-General of 27 July 2018, available at: <www.un.org/Depts/los/LEGISLATIONANDTREATIES/PDFFILES/DEPOSIT/communicationsredeposit/mzn94_2013_esp_e.pdf>.

[19] Communication from Algeria addressed to Italy dated 20 June 2019, available at: <www.un.org/Depts/los/LEGISLATIONANDTREATIES/PDFFILES/AlgItaly.pdf>.

[20] Ibid.

[21] Royal Decree No. 236/2013, of 5 April 2013, establishing the Exclusive Economic Zone of Spain in the Northwest Mediterranean, 17 April 2013, available at: <www.un.org/Depts/los/LEGISLATIONANDTREATIES/PDFFILES/ESP_2013_Decree_eng.pdf>.

[22] Communication from Algeria addressed to Spain dated 20 June 2019, available at: <www.un.org/Depts/los/LEGISLATIONANDTREATIES/PDFFILES/AlgSpain.pdf>.

settled under international law. This is widely noted by scholarly contributions on the subject.[23]

As regards the Italian position, one could take the view that the terminology adopted by Italy in its official communication is not the one traditionally used by States when defending their position in maritime delimitation disputes. Italy, instead of framing the Algerian unilateral act as an encroachment on its sovereign rights over certain maritime areas, preferred to qualify it as an interference in maritime zones of "legitimate and exclusive" national interest.[24] On 22 May 2020, in delivering to the Senate of the Republic a written answer to two parliamentary questions (nos. 4-02850 and 4-02860) that had called on the Government to clarify the state of play in the bilateral negotiations with Algeria on the issue of EEZ delimitation, the Undersecretary of State for Foreign Affairs and International Cooperation, Mr Manlio Di Stefano, reiterated that the Algerian EEZ "includes portions of the sea of exclusive Italian interest, even though Italy has not yet established an EEZ or [ecological protection zone] (EPZ) of its own nor claimed sovereign rights".[25]

However, this stance may be deemed incomplete from a law of the sea perspective. It is surprising that the Italian representatives never referred to the legal regime of the continental shelf. It is well known that the sovereign rights of a coastal State over this maritime zone, under customary international law, do not depend on any effective occupation or declaration but exist *ipso facto* and *ab initio*. It is true that the spatial ambit of the sovereign rights of a coastal State in the EEZ and in the continental shelf differs in that, whereas sovereign rights in the former extend to the waters above the seabed, in the latter the legal status of the water column is not affected. This notwithstanding, one may argue that Italy, at least with reference to the seabed and subsoil, could have more convincingly framed the unilateral act carried out by Algeria as an attempt to create a *fait accompli* aimed at preventing Italy from claiming a portion of its continental shelf.

It seems also noteworthy that Algeria, in its note verbale to Italy, did not include a statement analogous to the one included in its reply to the Spanish Government with reference to the obligation of restraint in disputed maritime areas. This is probably attributable to the way in which Italy framed its position. Indeed, as seen above, in its communication to the UN Secretary-General, Italy objected to the coordinates set out by Algeria exclusively on the grounds that the resulting EEZ "unduly overlaps on zones of legitimate and exclusive national Italian interest". It has already been noted that Italy could have mentioned the

---

[23] See MILANO and PAPANICOLOPULU, "State Responsibility in Disputed Areas on Land and at Sea", ZaöRV, 2011, p. 587 ff.; VAN LOGCHEM, "The Scope for Unilateralism in Disputed Maritime Areas", in SCHOFIELD, LEE and KWON (eds.), *The Limits of Maritime Jurisdiction*, Leiden/Boston, 2014, p. 291 ff.; DE HERDT, "Meaningful Responses to Unilateralism in Undelimited Maritime Areas", Journal of Territorial and Maritime Studies, 2019, p. 5 ff.

[24] See *supra* note 17.

[25] Only at a later stage the Italian Parliament adopted a piece of legislation (Law No. 91 of 14 June 2021) authorizing the Government to establish an EEZ "to be notified to the States whose territory is adjacent to the territory of Italy or faces it".

legal regime of the continental shelf. Moreover, one may wonder why Italy did not explicitly mention in its initial protest the fact that the Algerian EEZ partially overlaps with an EPZ proclaimed by Rome in 2011.[26] A reference to this issue, as will be shown below, was made during a parliamentary debate. True, unlike in the case of the EEZ, in an EPZ a coastal State does not exercise sovereign rights for the purpose of exploring and exploiting natural resources; nonetheless, mentioning the establishment of an EPZ, coupled with a reference to the notion of continental shelf, would have probably strengthened the Italian stance and, in turn, prompted a different reaction from Algeria.[27]

On 5 February 2020, the maritime dispute with Algeria resurfaced in the Italian political debate at the 300th Meeting (XVIII Legislature) of the Chamber of Deputies. On that occasion, speaking on behalf of the Minister of Foreign Affairs, the Minister for Parliamentary Relations, Mr Federico D'Incà, addressed a parliamentary question on the matter. The relevant parts of his statement read as follows:

> The [Algerian] decision, taken without a preliminary agreement with neighboring coastal States, creates an EEZ that overlaps, west of Sardinia, with the ecological protection zone (EPZ) established by Italy in 2011 and with an analogous EEZ established by Spain in 2013. The Algerian EEZ laps for 70 nautical miles at the Italian territorial waters to the south-west of Sardinia. By declaring an EEZ of this extension, Algeria has disregarded Article 74 of the UN Convention on the Law of the Sea, which requires States, pending a delimitation agreement, to cooperate in good faith with neighboring States and not to hamper or jeopardize the reaching of a final agreement by engaging in acts that might prejudice the interests of other States.

First of all, one could see that, unlike in Italy's initial protest, in this official stance a specific reference was made to the fact that the Algerian EEZ overlaps with the Italian EPZ. This reference was certainly pertinent, as was pertinent the reference to Article 74 UNCLOS. However, it should be noted that no mention was made of Article 121 UNCLOS on the regime of islands. The EEZ proclaimed by the Algerian Government, as specified by the Minister, also extends to areas immediately beyond the territorial sea around the Italian island of Sardinia. Therefore, in this and in all other official documents here analyzed, Rome could have claimed that the Algerian act deprived the said island, and thus Italy, of its

---

[26] Presidential Decree no. 209 of 27 October 2011, 17 December 2011, available at: <www.un.org/Depts/los/LEGISLATIONANDTREATIES/PDFFILES/ITA_2011_Decree.pdf>.

[27] In fact, it should be specified that the precise content of EPZ regimes tends to vary. For example, the EPZ proclaimed by France in 2003, now replaced by an EEZ, reserved to France also exclusive jurisdiction with respect to the establishment and use of artificial islands, installations and structures. PAPANICOLOPULU, "The Mediterranean Sea", in ROTHWELL et al. (eds.), *The Oxford Handbook of the Law of the Sea*, Oxford, 2015, p. 610 ff.

legitimate entitlement to maritime zones beyond the territorial sea in breach of Article 121(2). It is not possible to cast a doubt on Sardinia's status of island for the purpose of Article 121 UNCLOS, a convention that both Italy and Algeria have ratified. Therefore, during the negotiation of an EEZ delimitation, one could safely assume that the status of Sardinia will not be contested.

In his answer, D'Incà also specified that Italy had proposed the establishment of a joint committee that could lead to the definition of a delimitation agreement between the parties to the dispute. Finally, the Minister recalled that a legislative proposal had been deposited with the Chamber of Deputies on the establishment of an Italian EEZ, a move that would "provide a better framework for negotiations" with the Algerian Government.

On the establishment of a joint committee, it is worth noting that, on 2 March 2020, the Italian Undersecretary of State for Foreign Affairs Mr Di Stefano and the Algerian Minister of Foreign Affairs, Mr Sabri Boukadoum, reached an agreement on the establishment of a Bilateral Technical Commission for the delimitation of their respective maritime areas.[28]

At its 423rd Meeting (XVIII Legislature) held on 5 November 2020, the Chamber of Deputies eventually approved a legislative proposal (Bill No. S.2007), whose text is now under scrutiny of the Senate of the Republic, for the establishment of an EEZ beyond the outer limit of the territorial sea.

Overall, Italy could have been more assertive in defending its position under international law, by making explicit reference to the sovereign rights of a coastal State over the continental shelf and to the legal regime of islands, as shaped by UNCLOS and now embodied in customary international law. Yet, Italy decided to protest against Algeria's unilateral act only by resorting to the notion of "national interest" and calling upon Algeria to respect the provisions included in Article 74 UNCLOS. However, Italy's readiness to enter into negotiations and its active role in the establishment of a Joint Delimitation Committee may be praised.

ENRICO BROGGINI

THE LIBYAN FISHERIES PROTECTION ZONE AND THE POWERS OF ENFORCEMENT OF A LOCAL *DE FACTO* GOVERNMENT DURING THE LIBYAN CIVIL WAR

On 1 September 2020, two Italian fishing vessels from Mazara del Vallo, Sicily, were seized by Libyan forces operating under the authority of the Benghazi unrecognized government. The seizure took place approximately 38 miles off the coast of Cyrenaica. The fishermen of the two boats – eight Italians, six Tunisians, two Indonesians, and two Senegalese – were accused of fishing in Libyan waters and were transferred to Libyan soil where they began a period of detention that

---

[28] Ministry of Foreign Affairs and International Cooperation, "Undersecretary Di Stefano visits Algiers: agreement on the delimitation of maritime areas and the sustainable management of sea resources", 3 June 2020, available at: <www.esteri.it/mae/en/sala_stampa/archivionotizie/comunicati/2020/03/il-sottosegretario-di-stefano-ad-algeri-intesa-su-delimitazione-zone-marittime-e-gestione-sostenibile-delle-risorse-del-mare.html>.

would last 108 days.[29] The fishing vessels were also seized by the Libyan militia.

According to unofficial Libyan sources, during secret negotiations with the Italian intelligence, General Haftar, the strongman of Cyrenaica, had initially conditioned the release of the fishermen on the release of four Libyan boatmen who were serving a sentence in Italy for human trafficking.[30] The detention of the fishermen was ended only on 18 December of the same year, when the President of the Council of Ministers, Mr Giuseppe Conte, and the Minister of Foreign Affairs and International Cooperation, Mr Luigi Di Maio, personally travelled to Benghazi to meet General Haftar. The meeting, which led to the unblocking of the situation, took place without media coverage and without any detailed statement about its content. At the end of it, the Minister of Foreign Affairs merely declared:

> The Government continues to firmly support the stabilization process in Libya. This is what President Giuseppe Conte and I reiterated to Haftar today during our talks in Benghazi.[31]

Politically, the case of the Mazara fishermen represented one of the thorniest issues addressed by the second Conte Government. The case was the object of numerous parliamentary questions portraying it as evidence of Italy's progressive loss of influence in Libya in favor of other foreign actors such as Turkey, Egypt and the Russian Federation.[32] The Italian Government entered into lengthy confidential negotiations but was pressed by the opposition and was accused of inexperience and inertia.

The episode is interrelated not only with the civil war ongoing in Libya, but also with the decade-long "red prawn war" during which the Libyan authorities have been repeatedly obstructing the fishing activities of Italian boats in an area of the Mediterranean where they claim jurisdiction.[33] In this respect, it is worth recalling that Libya has claimed the entire Gulf of Sidra as a historic bay since 1973[34] and that in 2005 the Libyan authorities established a 62 nautical miles

---

[29] "Libia, liberi i pescatori italiani dopo 108 giorni di sequestro. Hanno lasciato Bengasi", ANSA, 18 December 2020, available at: <www.ansa.it/sito/notizie/mondo/2020/12/17/libia-conte-e-di-maio-in-volo-per-bengasi_991904a1-4105-4a45-9486-58a625405812.html>.

[30] "Italy PM flies in as Libya frees Sicilian fishermen", France24, 17 December 2020, available at: <www.france24.com/en/live-news/20201217-italy-pm-flies-in-as-libya-frees-sicilian-fishermen-1>.

[31] See *supra* note 29.

[32] See, for instance, parliamentary questions no. 3-01978 of 14 October 2020 and no. 4-04388 of 10 November 2020. Parliamentary questions were raised also by Italian MEPs. See priority question no. P-005620/2020 to the Commission of 14 October 2020, available at: <www.europarl.europa.eu/doceo/document/P-9-2020-005620_EN.html>.

[33] "Red prawn war fuels anti-EU feeling among Italian fishing crews", The Guardian, 19 November 2019, available at: <www.theguardian.com/world/2019/nov/19/red-prawn-war-fuels-anti-eu-feeling-among-italian-fishing-crews>.

[34] "Information concerning the jurisdiction of the Gulf of Surt, 1973", available at: <www.un.org/Depts/los/LEGISLATIONANDTREATIES/PDFFILES/LBY_1973_Information.pdf>.

fisheries protection zone calculated from the external limit of the territorial waters.[35] Considering the 12 miles of territorial waters, the breadth of the Libyan
fisheries protection zone is thus 74 miles from the baselines, the Gulf of Sidra
being qualified as internal waters. Subsequently, in 2009, Libya also instituted an
EEZ whose outer limits remain undefined as they "shall be established together
with neighboring States in accordance with instruments concluded on the basis
of international law".[36] It is also worth noting that the 2008 Treaty of Friendship
between Italy and Libya envisaged *inter alia* the establishment of some form of
economic cooperation between the parties in the field of fishing activities.[37] On
the Italian side, however, the stipulation of treaties on this matter falls within
the competence of the EU, which, as of now, has negotiated no agreement with
Libya.

From a legal standpoint, the interest of this case is twofold. Firstly, the Italian
Government was called on to take a position on the legality of the Libyan claims
to some areas of the Mediterranean under the applicable rules of the law of the
sea. Secondly, it is of note that on this occasion the enforcement action by the
Libyan side was not carried out by the internationally recognized Government of
Tripoli, but by the local *de facto* government controlling the eastern territories
in the context of a civil war. The case of the fishermen is therefore an important
opportunity to know whether, in the view of Italy, an unrecognized insurgent
government is legally entitled to carry out enforcement action in the areas of the
sea under their control.

With regard to the first point of interest, one should consider that, in its declarations before Parliament, the Italian Government did not contest explicitly the
lawfulness of the Libyan fisheries protection zone. In particular, on 18 October
2020, answering a parliamentary question before the Senate of the Republic
(XVIII Legislature, 266th Meeting), the Minister of Foreign Affairs stated:

> The Libyan intervention [...] seems to have stemmed from the al-
> leged violation of the self-proclaimed fishing protection zone. The
> stretch of sea where the vessels were seized is said to be considered
> a military zone on the eastern Libyan side. Beyond the war situation
> that characterizes the Libyan scenario and the evaluations of the legal-

---

[35] General People's Committee Decision No. 37 of 1373 from the death of the Prophet (AD
2005) concerning the declaration of a Libyan fisheries protection zone in the Mediterranean Sea,
available at: <https://www.un.org/Depts/los/LEGISLATIONANDTREATIES/STATEFILES/
LBY.htm>.

[36] General People's Committee Decision No. 260 of A.J. 1377 (A.D. 2009) concern-
ing the declaration of the exclusive economic zone of the Great Socialist People's Libyan
Arab Jamahiriya, available at: <www.un.org/Depts/los/LEGISLATIONANDTREATIES/
PDFFILES/lby_2009_declaration_e.pdf>.

[37] Trattato di amicizia, partenariato e cooperazione tra la Repubblica italiana e la Grande
Giamahiria araba libica popolare socialista, 30 August 2008, ratified by Law no. 7 of 6 February
2009, Article 17. See RONZITTI, "Italia-Libia: il Trattato di Bengasi e la sua effettiva rilevan-
za", Affari internazionali, 14 July 2018, available at: <www.affarinternazionali.it/2018/07/
italia-libia-trattato-bengasi>.

international profile, in May 2019, the Interministerial Coordination Committee for the Safety of Transport and Infrastructure (Cocist) [*Comitato di Coordinamento Interministeriale per la Sicurezza dei Trasporti e delle Infrastrutture*], declared the area of the Libyan fishing protection zone at high risk for all vessels flying the Italian flag, without distinction. On several occasions in the past, the Farnesina [i.e. the Ministry for Foreign Affairs], together with the General Command of the Coast Guard and the Ministry of Agricultural Policies, has recommended that Italian fishing vessels avoid the waters off the Libyan coast. In accordance with the Cocist's decisions, Navy units navigating in the area are inviting Italian fishing vessels located there to leave. A state of detention for someone who violates a self-proclaimed zone – I want to say it – is unacceptable, but that remains a risk zone – this is a message I am sending to all the fishing communities – just as it would be unacceptable if someone were to tell us: "If you free ours, we will give you the Italians".

The analysis of this statement reveals that the position of the Italian Government on the lawfulness of the Libyan fisheries protection zone is somewhat ambiguous. On the one hand, the fishing protection zone is qualified as "self-proclaimed", with language leading to the conclusion that such zone has not been established in agreement with the Italian authorities and is not recognized by them. On the other, it is clarified that, for reasons of security, the Navy invites Italian fishing vessels to avoid those waters. In essence, therefore, by using the term "self-proclaimed" the Italian authorities do not explicitly qualify the Libyan claim as unlawful because under the law of the sea the establishment of protection zones can be unilaterally made. In addition, it is noteworthy that the Italian Navy refrains from physically protecting the Italian vessels operating in the area.

The additional clarification by Minister Di Maio affirming that detention for violating "a self-proclaimed zone" is "unacceptable" is equally inconclusive as it might refer not only to the potential illegality of the fisheries protection zone but also, arguably, to that of the sanction adopted by the Libyan authorities.[38]

This nuanced position, which refrains from qualifying the Libyan fisheries protection zone as unlawful, is probably motivated by the fact that the breadth of the Libyan zone is below the 200 nautical miles that States can claim as their

---

[38] Art. 73(2) UNCLOS provides that "[a]rrested vessels and their crews shall be promptly released upon the posting of reasonable bond or other security", and the ensuing paragraph clarifies that "[c]oastal State penalties for violations of fisheries laws and regulations in the exclusive economic zone may not include imprisonment, in the absence of agreements to the contrary by the States concerned, or any other form of corporal punishment". The customary status of this rule, however, is dubious. See RONZITTI, "La tormentata vicenda della pesca nelle acque libiche", Affari internazionali, 11 November 2020, available at: <www.affarinternazionali.it/2020/11/la-tormentata-vicenda-della-pesca-nelle-acque-libiche>.

EEZ under UNCLOS and customary law.[39] Furthermore, the Libyan claim falls short of a hypothetical median line from the Italian coasts, that is, the default criterion in delimitation agreements and judicial decisions.[40] In the Mediterranean, the proclamation of a reduced fisheries protection zone is generally a deliberate choice of States aimed at avoiding issues of delimitation with other coastal States.[41] Among the measures adopted by Libyan authorities, the most problematic one is thus the closure of the Gulf of Sidra on the grounds of its alleged status as historic bay.[42] In this respect, it should be noted, however, that Italy adopted a similar position in the case of the Gulf of Taranto.[43]

In conclusion, the cautious approach of the Italian Government seems to be justified in light of the absence of strong legal arguments in favor of a right to fish in the area where the vessels were seized. The Italian authorities could perhaps have invoked the potential existence of historic rights on the part of Sicilian fishermen in the waters under consideration and the qualification of the Mediterranean as semi-enclosed sea. It should be acknowledged, however, that reference to historic rights has not been made in the articles of UNCLOS related to maritime delimitation and that the existence of a self-standing role for historic rights detached from delimitation has not been firmly established in international practice.[44] Under UNCLOS, moreover, the qualification of the Mediterranean as semi-enclosed sea does not bring about a modification of the legal regime on maritime delimitation, but only encourages States to cooperate on a number of matters, including the management of living resources.[45]

Turning now to the second element of legal interest in the case at hand, that is, the position of Italy with regard to the exercise of powers of administration by the government of eastern Libya, a written answer by the Deputy Minister of Foreign Affairs and International Cooperation, Ms Marina Sereni, must be considered. On 20 October 2020, Ms Sereni answered in writing parliamentary question no. 4-04252 of 15 October 2020. She affirmed:

> A state of detention for someone violating a self-proclaimed zone is unacceptable, especially considering that it is issued by an entity

[39] Libya has signed but not ratified UNCLOS, which sanctioned the legal concept of the EEZ. However, it is widely held that such concept has been recognized by customary law as well. See *Continental Shelf (Libyan Arab Jamahiriya/Malta)*, Judgment of 21 March 1984, ICJ Reports, 1985, p. 3 ff., para. 44.

[40] RONZITTI, *cit. supra* note 38.

[41] PAPANICOLOPULU, "Mediterranean Sea", Max Planck Encyclopedia of Public International Law, 2012, available at: <https://opil.ouplaw.com/>.

[42] On the issue, see FRANCIONI, "The Status of the Gulf of Sirte under International Law", Syracuse Journal of International Law and Commerce, 1984, p. 311 ff. The author argues for a "relative approach" to historic bays, emphasizing the role of reciprocity.

[43] *Ibid.*, pp. 323-324.

[44] BERNARD, "The Effect of Historic Fishing Rights in Maritime Boundaries Delimitation" in SCHEIBER and SANG KWON (eds.), *Securing the Ocean for the Next Generation*, Papers from the Law of the Sea Institute, UC Berkeley– Korea Institute of Ocean Science and Technology, Seoul, 2012, p. 2 ff.

[45] See Arts. 122-123 UNCLOS.

that neither Italy nor the international community recognizes as a legitimate government. Italy does not accept blackmail. This does not alter the fact that this remains a risk zone.

The Deputy Minister also underlined the need for a bilateral agreement of delimitation with Libya:

In recent years, a growing number of States have proclaimed their own maritime zones to exercise exclusive rights of sovereignty. Italy has concluded agreements with some of these, such as Algeria and Greece.[46] It is obviously impossible, at this stage, to envisage similar agreements with Libya, which is unfortunately the scene of armed clashes and disputes between several factions.

The first part of this declaration clearly militates against the thesis according to which insurgents, especially when they establish a local *de facto* government, may exercise limited powers of administration, including the closure of ports, opposable to third parties.[47] To the contrary, in the view of the Italian Government, emerging from this case is that the exercise of enforcement action at sea by an unrecognized government is unacceptable. The second part of the answer is also interesting as it clarifies that stipulating a delimitation agreement with a country ravaged by a civil war would be "impossible". As this part of the statement does not differentiate between the position of the recognized government and that of other factions in the civil war, one could argue that even delimitation agreements with the internationally recognized government, such as the one recently stipulated by Turkey and Libya for the delimitation of the EEZ, would be precluded pending a final settlement of the internal conflict.[48]

---

[46] [Translator's note] The ratification of the delimitation agreement was authorized in June 2021 by the Italian Parliament, which also provided for its domestic implementation. See Law No. 93 of 1 June 2021 on the "Ratification and implementation of the Agreement between the Italian Republic and the Hellenic Republic on the delimitation of their respective maritime zones, done at Athens on 9 June 2020". On this topic see also, in this Volume, MANCINI, "The Agreement between Greece and Italy on the Delimitation of their Respective Maritime Zones: An Italian Perspective".

[47] Based on some elements of the arbitral and State practice of the 19th and 20th centuries, a number of scholars have argued that local *de facto* governments during civil wars may exercise powers of administration on the territory and the sea areas under their control. See, for instance, JENNINGS and WATTS (eds.), *Oppenheim's International Law (Peace)*, Vol. I, 9th ed., London, 1993, pp. 167-168; DICKINSON, "The Closure of Ports in Control of Insurgents", AJIL, 1930, p. 69 ff., pp. 73-74. For a review of the debate, see PERTILE, *Diritto internazionale e rapporti economici nelle guerre civili*, Napoli, 2020, pp. 278-287. With direct reference to the present case, arguing that the insurgent government has the right to claim the "exercise of rights" on behalf of Libya, see RONZITTI, *cit. supra* note 38.

[48] See Memorandum of Understanding between the Government of the Republic of Turkey and the Government of National Accord-State of Libya on Delimitation of the Maritime Jurisdiction Areas in the Mediterranean, available at: <www.un.org/Depts/los/LEGISLATIONANDTREATIES/PDFFILES/TREATIES/Turkey_11122019_(HC)_MoU_Libya-Delimitation-areas-Mediterranean.pdf>. With regard to the wider issue of the powers

As a final comment, it is worth noting that, if, on the one hand, it is clear that Italy does not recognize the insurgents of the eastern territories as the government of Libya, on the other, the official interaction with them, which culminated in the visit of the President of the Council of Ministers and the Minister of Foreign Affairs to Benghazi, certainly amounts to a form of recognition of insurgency.

MARCO PERTILE

XI. TREATMENT OF ALIENS AND NATIONALITY

THE CLASSIFICATION OF ITALY'S PORTS AS PLACES UNSAFE FOR MIGRANTS RESCUED BY FOREIGN VESSELS OUTSIDE THE COUNTRY'S SAR AREA

Even though greatly reduced compared to the peaks of the previous years, migratory flows across the Mediterranean Sea towards Italy's coasts continued in 2020 – as did the tragic deaths of migrants, compounded by the inaction of Southern European States, in particular Italy and Malta. This was the premise of the parliamentary question that Mr Erasmo Palazzotto addressed to the Italian Government on 16 April 2020, at the 327th Meeting (XVIII Legislature) of the Chamber of Deputies. Mr Palazzotto expressed his hope that the assistance that in those very same hours Italy was providing to the migrants rescued by the *Alan Kurdi* vessel could mark a *de facto* superseding of Interministerial Decree No. 150 of the Minister of Infrastructure and Transport, the Minister of Foreign Affairs and International Cooperation, the Minister of the Interior and the Minister of Health of 7 April 2020. According to Article 1 of the Decree,

> For the whole duration of the national health emergency due to the COVID-19 pandemic, Italian ports do not meet the necessary requirements to be classified and defined as "places of safety" pursuant to the Hamburg Convention on Maritime Search and Rescue [SAR Convention], as far as rescues carried out outside the Italian SAR area by naval units flying a foreign flag are concerned.

In his question, the MP leveled a twofold criticism against Decree No. 150. First of all, he stressed the impossibility for the Government to neutralize its international obligations by means of a ministerial decree, as the hierarchy of sources sets the former source higher than the latter. Moreover, a legal instrument to release Italy from its duties under the SAR Convention was not even needed, as the country was equipped with the necessary structures to allow for the safe landing of migrants – as demonstrated by the continuing inflow of people by sea through Italian ports. Indeed – this was the second objection – the decree was discriminatory in two respects: on the one hand, commercial vessels of any

---

of disposition of the incumbent government during a civil war, see PERTILE, *cit. supra* note 47, pp. 133-141.

nationality were still allowed to put into port and, on the other, migrants saved by Italian ships or in the country's SAR area could be disembarked. But, as Mr Palazzotto stated, "in the definition of a place of safety, no flag-based discretion is admissible": after all, if a place is unsafe for rescuees, it is so for all of them.

The Undersecretary of State for Infrastructure and Transport, Mr Salvatore Margiotta, replied on the part of the Government to the question, clarifying from the start that he could not express a view on the revision of a decree signed by four different ministers.[49] Having briefly recalled the duties of a State in matters of rescue and assistance of people in distress at sea, Mr Margiotta added that

> as early as 17 March 2020, the President of the Council of Ministers notified his European partners of the impossibility of ensuring, also with respect to the rescue operations that are not coordinated by Italy, a port for the disembarkation of migrants crossing the Mediterranean Sea, as the Italian operative structures, from health offices to police, have been at all times adjusting their activities to tackle the evolution of the COVID-19 health emergency. Thus, Italy stressed the need to share with the flag States the responsibility of the management of rescue operations carried out by private vessels, so as to avoid the creation of search and rescue mechanisms that are distinct from, and parallel to, the institutional structures set up by international conventions, as well as to prevent conducts that may encourage, even indirectly, irregular migration towards Italy and the European Union, especially in light of the *de facto* suspension of all instruments aimed at an orderly and joint management of migration at the European level, due to the relentless spread of the virus.

The Undersecretary went on to highlight that Decree No. 150 was not at odds with Italy's obligations under the relevant international norms. He summarized two of them:

> The first is that of the essential cooperation of the signatories to the [SAR] Convention, which also entails the duty of the flag States of rescuing units to take charge themselves of the assistance to and relocation of migrants, including the identification of a place of safety for disembarking them.[50]

---

[49] Interestingly, the Undersecretary of State said he was representing only one such ministries, although one may argue that he was in fact representing the whole Government, to which the question was addressed.

[50] In the case of the *Alan Kurdi*, a German-flagged ship, such a responsibility would rest with Germany – as explicitly affirmed by the Italian Government: Ministry of Sustainable Infrastructures and Mobility, "Alan Kurdi: porti italiani privi dei requisiti di sicurezza richiesti da convenzione Amburgo", 9 April 2020, available at: <www.mit.gov.it/comunicazione/news/migranti-porti/alan-kurdi-porti-italiani-privi-dei-requisiti-di-sicurezza>.

If, as it is reasonable on both logical and contextual grounds, this sentence must be understood to mean that such an identification of a place of safety should occur in the territory of the flag State, then this would be a misrepresentation of the obligations alluded to. It must be said that the Italian authorities have already put forth such a distorted view in the second half of the 2010s[51] (though only after having taken the opposite stance just a few years before).[52] However, the truth is that the flag State is just one of the countries involved in the choice of the place of safety where rescued people can finally go ashore,[53] no one of them being, as a matter of (legal) principle, required to a greater extent than the others to provide for such a place. Therefore, the State coordinating the rescue operation – that is, the State in whose SAR area the rescue occurred – is not compelled to open its ports merely by virtue of its role, even though it is that State (rather than the flag State of the rescuing ship) that has a last-resort responsibility in this respect.[54]

The second obligation referred to by Mr Margiotta concerned the definition of the place of safety as one where the primary needs of rescuees, including health necessities, can be satisfied. Therefore,

---

[51] See TURRINI, "Between a 'Go Back!' and a Hard (to Find) Place (of Safety): On the Rules and Standards of Disembarkation of People Rescued at Sea", IYIL, 2018, p. 29 ff.

[52] In sharp contrast with what was stated by Mr Margiotta in his reply, in 2009 Italy and Spain lamented that "in the majority of the operations where Spanish- or Italian-flagged ships have been involved, the Governments responsible for the SAR regions, where persons have been rescued, have failed to provide a safe place for their disembarkation": International Maritime Organization (IMO), Measures to Protect the Safety of Persons Rescued at Sea: Compulsory Guidelines for the Treatment of Persons Rescued at Sea, FSI 17/15/1 (2009), quoted in TREVISANUT, "Which Borders for the EU Immigration Policy? Yardsticks of International Protection for EU Joint Borders Management", in AZOULAI and DE VRIES (eds.), *EU Migration Law: Legal Complexities and Political Rationales*, Oxford, 2014, p. 106 ff., p. 132.

[53] IMO, Principles Relating to Administrative Procedures for Disembarking Persons Rescued at Sea, FAL.3/Circ.194 (2009), para. 2.3. See also, along similar lines, the Model Framework for Cooperation following Rescue at Sea Operations involving Refugees and Asylum-Seekers prepared by the UNHCR, that can be found in International Journal of Refugee Law, 2012, p. 485 ff., pp. 492-494. The negotiation by some European States, including Italy, of a Regional memorandum of understanding on concerted actions and procedures relating to the disembarkation of persons rescued at Sea, under the aegis of IMO, appears to have been on hold since 2014; seemingly, the same cooperative approach was taken in the memorandum, with the State supervising the SAR area where the rescue was carried out having only a "primary responsibility" in matters of disembarkation (see *infra* note 54): HESSE, "Persons Rescued at Sea", November 2011, pp. 11-14, available at: <www.unhcr.org/4ef3061c9.pdf>.

[54] Note that such responsibility does not translate into an obligation, because the government responsible for the SAR area merely "should" accept disembarkation on its territory: IMO, cit. *supra* note 53, para. 2.3. Italy, together with Spain, proposed to amend the SAR Convention so that "[t]he Contracting Government responsible for the search and rescue region, where the rescue operation takes place, *shall* exercise primary responsibility for ensuring that […] the persons rescued at sea are disembarked from the vessel involved in the rescued operation and delivered to a place of safety under its control" (IMO, cit. *supra* note 52, emphasis added), but the move was stopped by Malta's counter-proposal, which wanted disembarkation to happen at the "port closest to the location of the rescue".

in a wholly legitimate way, the interministerial decree qualifies the emergency stemming from the spread of the coronavirus as a situation that makes it impossible to ensure such safe places on the Italian territory, without undermining the functionality of the national health, logistical and security structures devoted to containing the spread of the pandemic and to assisting and treating COVID-19 patients.

In these words, an undue switch between subject and object in the causal relationship can be noticed. Even though the protection of health in the place of disembarkation is a reasonable objective, such a place is not eligible for landing people if it is not safe for them, rather than the other way around. That is, ineligibility cannot be established based on the risk that disembarked people may pose to those living in the place of safety. It is true that, should the rescuees actually imperil the health system of the host country, then that State would become unsafe also for them; however, the argument according to which a small number of people could have such a deleterious effect on a whole country should be supported by evidence. The Undersecretary's line of reasoning is even more problematic as said harmful effect, apparently, is only considered under certain circumstances:

> This would be limited to the cases where Italy did not play any coordination role in the search and rescue operations and, therefore, did not take on any of the obligations stemming from said coordination. At the same time, I have already recalled the responsibility of the rescuing unit's flag State, which, by virtue of the aforementioned principle of cooperation provided for by the SAR Convention, is called upon to cooperate with Italy in identifying a shared solution to the management of shipwrecked people. Whenever, on the contrary, the rescue is carried out in the Italian SAR area with the help of the Country's naval units, Italy is obliged, even in the face of the current emergency, to take charge of the devising of every appropriate solution to save migrants and the identification of suitable places where these can be disembarked and hosted. This provides a partial answer to your [i.e., the interrogating MP's] query on the difference that objectively exists between different cases: a ship flying the Italian flag or that carried out a rescue in Italy's SAR area and cases where such conditions are not met.

Mr Margiotta's defense of the measure at issue or the measure itself appear to be flawed in at least three respects. Firstly, there is a problem with the purported legal basis of the policy, and a potential misalignment between such a justification and the policy itself. Indeed, if the duty of a State to allow for the disembarkation of people rescued at sea rests on the fact that the rescue took place in the SAR area of that State (which is also required to take on the coordination of the operation), then it seems illogical to conclude that the ports of the State must be open also to people saved by vessels flying its flag outside its SAR zone and even, perhaps, in the SAR zone of another country. Conversely, if the abovementioned duty is to be attributed to the State of the flag of the rescuing ship, the State supervising the SAR area where the operation was carried out is not required to open its ports. The only way to reconcile the two stances is by merging the respective legal bases, so that both the State of the flag and the State responsible for the SAR area are obliged to permit disembarkation. To ascertain what the position embraced by Italy is, however, would be both hard and pointless, as all three options are ill-founded, the duty to allow for disembarkation resting on a completely different ground.[55]

A second issue is the internal inconsistency of the measure, whose promulgation is allegedly premised on both the preservation of Italy's safety and the protection of the rescuees' health (as stated in the preamble of the Decree). As to the latter point, one may wonder how refusing admittance of migrants – who are often fleeing from persecution and other disastrous conditions – may be deemed to be more beneficial to them than welcoming them into the Country, albeit plagued by COVID-19.[56] True, this does not necessarily amount to *refoulement*, as Italy expects the flag State to take responsibility for these people. But this is an unwarranted expectation: if COVID-19 is a reason for labelling one's own ports as unfit, then, already in April 2020, most European countries could have legitimately done the same, since – as recalled in the preamble of Decree No. 150 itself – the pandemic has a global reach.

The third flaw has already been mentioned and concerns the discriminatory approach taken by Italy. Indeed, the criterion of the "safe place" is an objective one that cannot be made dependent on the circumstances of the rescue operation. All migrants must be treated equally, and the same principle of non-discrimination must guide the treatment of migrants, on the one hand, and other sea travelers, on the other. In patent disregard of such principle, the Government considered the Italian territory as safe for most people coming from abroad, by land, by air and by sea.

The COVID-19 emergency was first addressed by the Italian authorities with Decree-Law No. 6 of 23 February 2020, which *inter alia* provided for the possibility of restricting or suspending transport services, including maritime transport. These were effectively halted, also in the territorial sea and with a few exceptions, by means of the Decree of the President of the Council of Ministers of 1 March 2020, which also introduced a mere notification requirement for people

---

[55] That is, on a customary norm that requires each State in the position to do so to welcome people risking their life and health at sea, irrespective of all other circumstances. See, again, TURRINI, *cit. supra* note 51.

[56] As noted by ALGOSTINO, "Lo stato di emergenza sanitaria e la chiusura dei porti: sommersi e salvati", ASGI, 21 April 2020, available at: <www.asgi.it/notizie/lo-stato-di-emergenza-sanitaria-e-la-chiusura-dei-porti-sommersi-e-salvati/>. Unsurprisingly, Interministerial Decree No. 150 has been unanimously criticized by doctrine, based on a number of grounds: see, e.g., ZAMUNER, "Convenzione SAR e luogo sicuro alla prova dell'emergenza Covid-19: i limiti del decreto interministeriale del 7 aprile 2020", RDI, 2020, p. 838 ff., and the writings quoted therein.

entering the Country after having visited areas "at epidemiological risk", possibly leading to quarantine. The very same measure was reiterated by two subsequent Decrees of the President of the Council of Ministers, of 4 March and 8 March 2020 respectively (the latter decree repealing the former one and the 1 March decree). Another Decree of the President of the Council of Ministers, dated 11 March 2020, entrusted the Minister of Infrastructure and Transport and the Minister of Health with the power to regulate, limit and suppress transports for health reasons. Such power was exercised by the two ministers on multiple occasions.

With Interministerial Decree No. 120 of 17 March 2020, the duty of notification to health authorities was extended to all travelers arriving to Italy by any means, who necessarily had to quarantine. The subsequent day, the few exceptions set forth by said provision were enriched by Interministerial Decree No. 122, which excluded cross-border workers and healthcare personnel from the abovementioned obligation. On 19 March 2020, a new decree of the same kind (No. 125) prohibited cruise ships flying a foreign flag from landing at an Italian port, whereas the service of Italian cruise ships was suspended and travelling vessels were required to disembark all passengers, irrespective of their nationality, at the respective (Italian)[57] final ports of call; foreign passengers had to be immediately transferred abroad. Finally, with an Ordinance of 28 March 2020, the Minister of Infrastructure and Transport and the Minister of Health set the modalities to be followed for the entry into the Country. More specifically, each person crossing the border had to notify the reasons for their travel and state both the place where the period of quarantine would be completed and the private means of transportation that would be used to reach that place; in case, upon arrival, such a place could not be effectively reached, the Civil Protection would indicate one. Transport services, including maritime ones, had to ensure safety conditions aimed at preventing infections and collect the previously mentioned information. The Ordinance confirmed and expanded the class of people exempted from this regulatory framework, adding the staff of freight services.[58] These limitations, together with their exceptions, were later repeatedly prolonged, with the Decrees of the President of the Council of Ministers of 1, 10 and 26 April and 17 May.

Even though, beginning with the Decree of the President of the Council of Ministers of 22 March 2020, the severe restrictions to free movement previously enforced at a local level were extended to the whole Italian territory, and despite Decree-Law No. 19 of 25 March 2020 provided for the possibility – "based on the principles of adequacy and proportionality with respect to the actual [health]

---

[57] Even though not specified, this must be presumed.

[58] Consistently with the idea that trade flows had to be preserved, in the same period, Italy joined other States in "reaffirm[ing] the need for critical infrastructure such as [...] seaports to remain open to support the flow of essential goods" (Joint statement on "Open markets, flow of essential goods and supply chain connectivity" promoted by Italy, Canada, Chile, Egypt, Guyana, Malawi, New Zealand, Singapore, Sweden and Rwanda, 21 May 2021, available at: <https://italyun.esteri.it/rappresentanza_onu/en/comunicazione/archivio-news/2020/05/comunicato-congiunto-su-open-markets.html>).

risk" – of restraining or barring access to Italy, from February to mid-May[59] no generalized, absolute limitation was ever imposed. Moreover, people travelling for work or health reasons or other cogent needs were exempted from abiding by the restrictions to internal movement, whereas the norms concerning the entry into the country could be exceptionally waived by the Government in order to comply with European and international rules (thus including, in principle, those relating to migration and asylum).

All in all, this picture proves that, notwithstanding the strict limitations enacted in the Spring 2020 to curb the pandemic, Italy still permitted the inflow of a potentially large number of people, thanks to the exemption of certain categories of travelers or the carving out of exceptions arguably based on need.

Since the validity of the measure taken by Interministerial Decree No. 150 was tied to the duration of the health emergency, which has been repeatedly extended by the Italian Government, as of 30 June 2021 this norm is still officially in force. On 12 April 2020, and thus only a few days after the enactment of said decree, the Head of the Civil Protection Department issued Decree No. 1287, which laid down the procedures to be followed with respect to two categories of migrants. Those who reach the Italian shores autonomously may be hosted on the Italian territory in dedicated areas and buildings – therefore, not directly in the pre-existing reception facilities for immigrants, which have been the object of detailed rules to prevent the spread of COVID-19[60] – where they are provisionally quarantined. Those who are rescued at sea and cannot be attributed a place of safety pursuant to Decree No. 150 are instead isolated on ships docked at Italian ports. This was the fate of the people rescued by the *Alan Kurdi* and *Aita Mari* vessels in April 2020 and of many thousands of other migrants in the subsequent months. This raises issues relating, *inter alia*, to the right to health of the people spending quarantine aboard and their right to apply for asylum, which has often been impeded.[61]

PAOLO TURRINI

XII.   HUMAN RIGHTS

THE ARREST AND CONTINUOUS DETENTION OF EGYPTIAN RESEARCHER PATRICK ZAKI

On 7 February 2020, Patrick Zaki, an Egyptian researcher, was arbitrarily arrested by the Egyptian authorities at Cairo airport. He was returning home from Italy for a family visit. Since August 2019, he had been on leave from his job at the

---

[59] A general ban to access Italy was enforced, for a very short period of time, only by means of Decree-Law No. 33 of 16 May 2020, and again, subject to some exceptions.

[60] See, e.g., the circulars issued by the Ministry of the Interior on 26 March and 1 April 2020.

[61] "Criticità del sistema navi-quarantena per persone migranti: analisi e richieste", 10 December 2020, available at: <www.meltingpot.org/IMG/pdf/criticita_del_sistema_navi-quarantena_per_persone_migranti-_analisi_e_richieste.pdf>.

Egyptian Initiative for Personal Rights (EIPR) to study for a postgraduate degree at the University of Bologna. Upon his arrival at Cairo airport, Zaki was disappeared for 24 hours. He was transferred to a National Security Investigations facility in Cairo where, according to his lawyers, he was tortured and interrogated about his work and activism. On 8 February, Zaki appeared before a public prosecutor in Mansoura and was presented with a list of charges, including "publishing rumors and false news that aim to disturb social peace and sow chaos", "incitement to protest without permission from the relevant authorities with the aim of undermining state authority", "calling for the overthrow of the state, managing a social media account that aims to undermine the social order and public safety" and "incitement to commit violence and terrorist crimes".[62] The Prosecutor denied allegations of police torture. Since then, Zaki's pre-trial detention has been extended several times.

Zaki's detention prompted the immediate response of several actors. Two parliamentary enquiries were immediately tabled at the European Parliament, asking the High Representative of the Union for Foreign Affairs and Security Policy to raise the case with the Egyptian authorities as a matter of urgency, demand his immediate release,[63] and conduct a review of the EU relations with Egypt that could potentially "involve a suspension of the free trade agreement with Egypt until Zaki and all other activists who are unfairly tried and detained are released".[64] In December 2020, the European Parliament, following the arrest and subsequent release of three EIPR staff members, passed a resolution calling *inter alia* "for Patrick George Zaki's immediate and unconditional release and for all charges against him to be dropped".[65] Moreover, civil society organizations, including Amnesty International[66] and Scholars at Risk,[67] issued statements condemning the Egyptian authorities.

---

[62] Egyptian Initiative for Personal Rights (EIPR), "An Egyptian Human Rights defender disappeared and tortured: EIPR Gender & Rights Researcher Patrick Zaki, arrested at Cairo airport, tortured and sent to Prosecutors after 24 hours of incommunicado detention. Prosecution ordered his detention for 15 days", 8 February 2020, available at: <https://eipr. org/en/press/2020/02/egyptian-human-rights-defender-disappeared-and-tortured-eipr-gender-rights-0>.

[63] European Parliament, Question for written answer E-000803/2020 to the Vice-President of the Commission/High Representative of the Union for Foreign Affairs and Security Policy, 10 February 2020, available at: <www.europarl.europa.eu/doceo/document/E-9-2020-000803_EN.html>.

[64] European Parliament, Question for written answer E-000855/2020 to the Vice-President of the Commission/High Representative of the Union for Foreign Affairs and Security Policy, 12 February 2020, available at: <www.europarl.europa.eu/doceo/document/E-9-2020-000855_EN.html>.

[65] European Parliament, Resolution on the deteriorating situation of human rights in Egypt, in particular the case of the activists of the Egyptian Initiative for Personal Rights (EIPR), 16 December 2020, 2020/2912(RSP), available at: <www.europarl.europa.eu/doceo/document/RC-9-2020-0426_EN.html>.

[66] Amnesty International, "Egypt: Arbitrary arrest and torture of researcher studying gender in Italy", 10 February 2020, available at: <www.amnesty.org/en/latest/news/2020/02/egypt-arbitrary-arrest-and-torture-of-researcher-studying-gender-in-italy/>.

[67] Scholars at Risk, "Patrick George Zaki, Egypt", available at: <www.scholarsatrisk.org/actions/patrick-george-zaki-egypt/>.

The Italian Government started to monitor Zaki's detention shortly after his arrest. On 12 February 2020, at the Chamber of Deputies (303rd Meeting, XVIII Legislature), in response to parliamentary question no. 3-01294, the Minister for Parliamentary Relations, Mr Federico D'Incà, assured that the case had been raised with the informal human rights coordination group of Western embassies, and that the Government had requested that the case be included in the EU trial observation program. Furthermore, he added that the Italian embassy in Cairo had raised the issue with the Egyptian National Council for Human Rights, an independent body entrusted with the protection of human rights in Egypt, expecting that Zaki would be afforded "a treatment consistent with international treaty standards". The Minister further added that

> The Government, reiterating its commitment to monitor all issues concerning the protection of human rights with the utmost attention, will continue, from this perspective, to prioritize the case of Zaki, including in relation to his detention conditions and the need to ensure swift judicial proceedings, with a view preferably to his prompt release.

The outbreak of the COVID-19 pandemic hindered the possibility of the Italian (and European) diplomatic personnel to observe Zaki's trial, due to the restrictions imposed by the Egyptian Government. On 19 November 2020, following the arrest of three staff members of the EIPR, with whom the Italian authorities were in regular contact in relation to Zaki's detention, the Deputy Minister of Foreign Affairs, Ms Marina Sereni, before the Commission on Foreign and European Affairs (III) of the Chamber of Deputies, conveyed the "grave concern" of the Italian Government for the multiple arrests and the forthcoming hearing in the case of Zaki. She informed that the Director General for Political Affairs and Security had raised the Italian authorities' concerns in relation to the situation of human rights defenders in Egypt with the Head of the Egyptian diplomatic mission in Rome.

On 18 June 2020, Motion no. 1-00247 was presented at the Senate of the Republic (231st Meeting, XVIII Legislature) to the effect that the Government would commit to stop an arms trade agreement with Egypt that had been authorized by the Council of Ministers on 11 June. Among the reasons that would justify the termination of the agreement, the signatories of the motion mentioned the prolonged detention of Patrick Zaki. During the same session, several Senators queried the Ministers of Foreign Affairs and International Cooperation, of Economic Development and of Defense with parliamentary question no. 3-01699. They stated that, in light of Egypt's persistence "in refusing any form of political or judicial cooperation with [Italy] in relation to the murder of Giulio Regeni and, more recently, the forced arrest of young student Patrick Zaki", they believed "that supporting such a sizable arms sale to [Egypt] constitutes a grave mistake".

Since Zaki's arrest, the Italian Government has maintained that, while the researcher is a foreign national, this does not preclude Italy from monitoring the developments of the case. In an interview with *Corriere della Sera*, in February 2020, the Italian Minister of Foreign Affairs and International Cooperation, Mr Luigi Di Maio, further reiterated the Government's commitment to monitoring the proceedings against Zaki, despite the fact that he is an Egyptian citizen. Mr Di Maio commented that "beyond nationality, Italy is always committed to the respect of human rights".[68] In contrast to this, on 14 July 2020 (239th Meeting, XVIII Legislature), in response to an MP's question addressed to the Minister of Foreign Affairs regarding the continued diplomatic dialogue between Italy and Egypt despite the latter's continued human rights violations, the President of the Senate, Ms Maria Elisabetta Alberti Casellati, stated the following: "You know that there are international relations and [Patrick Zaki] is not an Italian citizen".

On 14 December 2020, with Motion no. 1-00305 tabled at the Senate (281st Session, XVIII Legislature), the signatories, expressing concern for Patrick Zaki's mental and physical health, asked the Italian Government to urge the Egyptian authorities to promptly release the student. The text of the motion – which was not approved – clarified that:

> The fact that Patrick Zaki is a foreign national does not preclude Italy from undertaking the same actions that it would undertake in favor of its own nationals abroad. This power is justified by the existence, in the international community, of human rights obligations that have been codified since the end of the Second World War.

As Zaki's detention continued, a number of Italian municipalities adhered to the *#100CittàConPatrick* campaign, launched by a civil society organization known as GoFair, and granted him honorary citizenship. Since the launch of the campaign, 41 municipalities have taken this step.[69] In January 2021, a public petition[70] was launched asking the Italian authorities to grant Patrick Zaki Italian citizenship for "eminent services to Italy", pursuant to Article 9(2) of Law No. 91 of 5 February 1992, which states that:

> By an Order of the President of the Republic made following consultation of the Council of State and consideration by the Council of Ministers, upon the recommendation of the Minister of the Interior and in agreement with the Minister of Foreign Affairs, citizenship may be granted to an alien who has rendered eminent services to Italy, or where its granting is in the special interest of the State.

---

[68] Italian Ministry of Foreign Affairs and International Cooperation, "Di Maio: 'Rome will follow the proceedings. To do a dialogue with Cairo is essential' (Corriere della Sera)", 12 February 2020, available at: <www.esteri.it/mae/en/sala_stampa/interviste/2020/02/di-maio-roma-seguira-il-processo-per-farlo-serve-il-dialogo-col-cairo-corriere-della-sera.html>.

[69] A list of all the municipalities that have conferred honorary citizenship onto Patrick Zaki is available at: <www.facebook.com/gofairorganization/?ref=page_internal>.

[70] Station to Station, "Cittadinanza Italiana a Patrick Zaki", available at: <www.change.org/p/ministero-degli-affari-esteri-cittadinanza-italiana-onoraria-a-patrick-zaki>.

On 17 February 2021, Motion no. 1-00421 was tabled at the Chamber of Deputies (458th Meeting, XVIII Legislature), which sought to commit the Government "to adopt, within its competences, the initiative to grant Patrick Zaki the Italian citizenship". The motion – again, not approved – expounded that:

> the conferral of Italian citizenship, despite its lengthy process, would represent a very strong signal to both Egypt and the European allies who support Zaki's release, and it would allow Italy and Europe to exert a heightened pressure on Cairo. Our law provides that citizenship may be granted to a foreign national "who has rendered eminent services to Italy, or where its granting is in the special interest of the State", which Italian citizens and institutions are loudly demonstrating.

Similarly, on 24 March 2021, Motion no. 1-00329 was tabled at the Senate (307th Meeting, XVIII Legislature), which asked the Government "to urgently undertake all due initiatives to ensure that Zaki is granted Italian citizenship pursuant to Article 9, Paragraph 2 of Law no. 91 of 1992". The motion was premised *inter alia* on the following observation:

> Zaki's dramatic conditions and his detention in the Tora maximum security prison, known for the inhumane treatments and continued abuses against detainees, as repeatedly exposed by several international organizations, coupled with [...] systematic human rights violations against political dissidents, clearly constitute an exceptional interest of our country to promptly grant Italian citizenship to the Egyptian researcher.

On 14 April 2021, the Senate (315th Meeting, XVIII Legislature) debated Motion no. 1-00329. In response to the debate, the Deputy Minister for Foreign Affairs and International Cooperation, Ms Marina Sereni, stated the following:

> With regard to potentially granting Italian citizenship to Zaki, [the Government] acknowledges the ideal, symbolic and humanitarian value of this move [...]. Nonetheless, I wish to underline that the motion being discussed today, in its latest version – whose text I wish to stress the Government approves of – refers also to the need to verify that all requirements for the conferral of citizenship are met. I wish to draw your attention to the need to meticulously assess the circumstances of the context in which such conferral would take place. I urge you and myself to reflect, in particular, on two points. Preliminarily, we need to consider that granting Zaki with Italian citizenship would constitute a symbolic measure, with no practical effect for the grantee's protection. In light of international law and principles, among other things, Italy would meet significant challenges in providing [Zaki] with consular protection, given

his Egyptian citizenship, which would prevail being his primary citizenship, a principle that is strictly applied by the Egyptian authorities. Even more importantly, we need to assess the risk that such move may have on the objective that we most have at heart: to obtain Patrick's release. In this sense, granting him with citizenship may – I say "may" and for this reason we ask and accept the idea of an assessment – even prove counterproductive and it is our shared responsibility to reflect on this.

The Senate ultimately approved the motion. Two days later, on 16 April 2021, during a press conference, the President of the Council of Minister, Mr Mario Draghi, curtly commented that "[this] is a parliamentary initiative, which, at present, does not involve the Government".[71] Nonetheless, on 19 April 2021, the Undersecretary of State for Foreign Affairs and International Cooperation, Mr Benedetto Della Vedova, stated that the Government would start assessing whether the conditions for granting Zaki Italian citizenship exist.[72]

Both the notions of "eminent services to Italy" and "in the special interest of the State", which justify the conferral of Italian citizenship onto foreign nationals pursuant to Article 9(2) of Law No. 91/1992, require the identification of a special link between the individual and the State. In the past, Italian citizenship has been granted to athletes who had taken part in important sport competitions wearing Italy's colors, or individuals who had distinguished themselves for their charitable efforts in support of Italian citizens or, rarely, their humanitarian work for the benefit of non-Italians abroad, which furthers the country's foreign policy on international cooperation and human rights promotion.

Zaki's personal link with Italy can be established in light of his studies at the University of Bologna. Moreover, elements that may justify the conferral of Italian citizenship onto him may be his commitment to the promotion and protection of human rights in Egypt, which aligns with the Italian strategy in the Mediterranean and more generally with the objectives of Italy's international cooperation. Moreover, a "special interest" of the Government has been clearly outlined in Motion no. 1-00329 – i.e., Zaki's detention conditions and the systematic human rights violations against political dissidents in Egypt. The notion of "special interest" enshrined in Article 9(2) of Law No. 91/1992 would thus be read in light of Italy's constitutional commitment to the internationally recognized human rights, in particular through Article 10 of the Constitution.

Those who support granting Patrick Zaki Italian citizenship believe this would provide the Italian authorities with the right to exercise diplomatic protection in respect of the researcher, including by directly communicating with

---

[71] Italian Presidency of the Council of Ministers, "Conferenza stampa del Presidente Draghi e del Ministro Speranza", 16 April 2021, available at: <www.governo.it/it/articolo/conferenza-stampa-del-presidente-draghi-e-del-ministro-speranza/16652>.

[72] "Da oggi verifiche del Governo per dare la cittadinanza a Zaki", ANSA, 19 April 2021, available at: <www.ansa.it/sito/notizie/flash/2021/04/19/-della-vedova-da-oggi-verifiche-per-cittadinanza-a-zaki-_ea4dc897-7336-456c-9353-f02bbc8b28b4.html>.

him, visiting him in prison and arranging for his legal representation, pursuant to Article 36 of the Vienna Convention on Consular Relations. Nonetheless, the Egyptian authorities could question the genuineness of the link between Patrick Zaki and Italy by virtue of the customary principle according to which "[a] State of nationality may not exercise diplomatic protection in respect of a person against a State of which that person is also a national unless the nationality of the former State is predominant, both at the date of injury and at the date of the official presentation of the claim".[73] Establishing the predominance of the Italian nationality in regards to Patrick Zaki would likely prove a daunting task, in light of the International Law Commission's directions as to what factors would have to be taken into account for such determination:

> The authorities indicate that such factors include habitual residence, the amount of time spent in each country of nationality, date of naturalization (i.e., the length of the period spent as a national of the protecting State before the claim arose); place, curricula and language of education; employment and financial interests; place of family life; family ties in each country; participation in social and public life; use of language; taxation, bank account, social security insurance; visits to the other State of nationality; possession and use of passport of the other State; and military service.[74]

In light of this, it is unlikely that granting Italian citizenship to Patrick Zaki will per se have any noticeable impact on his continuous detention. However, coupled with other initiatives, especially if coordinated at the European level, it may bolster pressures on the Egyptian authorities to release him, as recognized in Motion no. 1-00338, approved on 14 April 2021.

PIERGIUSEPPE PARISI

XIV. CO-OPERATION IN JUDICIAL, LEGAL, SECURITY, AND SOCIO-ECONOMIC MATTERS

RESPONSIBILITY FOR THE SPREAD OF COVID-19 AND SOCIO-ECONOMIC CONCERNS IN THE FIGHT AGAINST THE PANDEMIC

The year 2020 was marked by COVID-19, which was declared a pandemic on 11 March 2020 by the World Health Organization (WHO).[75] COVID-19 not

---

[73] International Law Commission, Draft Articles on Diplomatic Protection, 2006, Art. 7.

[74] International Law Commission, Report of the International Law Commission to the General Assembly, 1 May-9 June and 3 July-11 August 2006, UN Doc A/61/10, p. 46, para. 5.

[75] WHO, "WHO Director-General's opening remarks at the media briefing on COVID-19", 11 March 2020, available at: <www.who.int/director-general/speeches/detail/who-director-general-s-opening-remarks-at-the-media-briefing-on-covid-19---11-march-2020>.

only caused millions of deaths around the world, but it impacted almost every aspect of human life, from the world economy to personal freedoms and the right to healthcare.

The Italian Government expressed its stance on several issues related to the pandemic. Firstly, the consequences of COVID-19 have been so serious that it has been speculated that China – the country where the virus originated from – could be held accountable for not having contained the spreading of the disease and timely warned the international community. Secondly, the implementation of measures restrictive of citizens' liberties in order to limit the spread of the virus has had repercussions on individual rights, especially of vulnerable people. Finally, the development of a vaccine underlined the necessity of a world alliance for its research, production, and distribution in light of the universal value of this medical treatment.

China's Responsibility Under International Law

On 19 May 2020, a few months after the COVID-19 pandemic's outbreak, the 73rd World Health Assembly adopted the "COVID-19 response" Resolution, calling for the timely sharing of detailed information and for a joint effort to tackle the spreading of the virus.[76] The EU, including Italy, strongly advocated for committing the WHO to "investigate the origins of the virus and its transmission to humans".[77] As underlined by the Italian Undersecretary of State for Foreign Affairs and International Cooperation, Mr Manlio Di Stefano, in replying to parliamentary question no. 5-04146 on 11 June 2020 before the Chamber of Deputies,

> The Italian Government has expressed, in all appropriate international fora and on all occasions, its position in favor of maximum transparency and sharing of information about the management of the epidemic.

On 17 June 2020, in addressing another question (no. 4-03498) presented at the Senate, Mr Di Stefano welcomed the abovementioned WHO Resolution, which "expressly recognize[d] the need to launch within a reasonable timeframe a transparent, independent and in-depth analysis of the lessons learnt from the crisis". The Resolution also requested the WHO Director-General to continue to work closely with international organizations and countries "to identify the zoonotic source of the virus and the route of introduction to the human population [...] including through efforts such as scientific and collaborative field mis-

---

[76] 73th World Health Assembly, COVID-19 response, WHA73.1, 19 May 2020, available at: <https://apps.who.int/gb/ebwha/pdf_files/WHA73/A73_R1-en.pdf>.

[77] As reported by the Deputy Minister for Foreign Affairs and International Cooperation, Ms Emanuela Del Re, on 6 May 2020 before the Commission on Foreign and European Affairs (III) of the Chamber of Deputies.

sions". Only on 7 July 2020 the Organization announced that a team of ten WHO experts would have travelled to China to investigate the zoonotic origins of the virus.[78]

One might argue in this respect that even though the aim of the WHO field mission was purely scientific, its findings could possibly be used to invoke China's responsibility under international law, most likely as a consequence of the country's delay in sharing information about the disease with other WHO members and its supposed negligence in containing the spread of the pandemic.[79] On this point, Mr Di Stefano, in the abovementioned reply of 11 June 2020, stated that

> In contrast to what is argued by some about China having breached its international obligations under the World Health Organization to promptly notify and share information, although this argument can be supported and may be well-founded, some authoritative scholars point out that it may not be possible to find a solid legal basis on which to bring China before an international court, while arbitration would only be an option if China agreed.

As for a possible action taken by Italy in this regard, the Undersecretary added that

> the Italian action, as always in these cases, must be in line with the coordinated action by Europe and the World Health Organization, which is the only viable way of – possibly – confronting China with its own responsibilities for its management of the pandemic.

The Discriminatory Impact of Restrictive Measures on Vulnerable Persons

Since the very beginning of the COVID-19 pandemic, the Italian Government has considered the compatibility of restrictive measures with human rights. The Minister of Health, Mr Roberto Speranza, as well as the Undersecretary of State for Health, Ms Sandra Zampa, before the Senate of the Republic (30 January 2020, 186th Meeting, XVIII Legislature) and the Chamber of Deputies (5 March 2020, 316th Meeting, XVIII Legislature), respectively, justified the enforcement of limitations by referring to the principle of precaution, based on the measures' proportionality to the gravity of the situation acknowledged by the WHO. The same concept was restated by Italy – albeit primarily referred to markets – also through a joint statement at the UN, which maintained that "measures designed to tackle COVID-19, if deemed necessary, must be targeted, proportionate, trans-

---

[78] WHO, "WHO experts to travel to China", 7 July 2020, available at: <www.who.int/news/item/07-07-2020-who-experts-to-travel-to-china>.

[79] On this issue see, in general, PAPARINSKIS, "COVID-19 Claims and the Law of International Responsibility", Journal of International Humanitarian Legal Studies, 2020, p. 311 ff.

parent, and temporary".[80] In May 2020,[81] the Italian delegation at the UN remarked that

> Emergency responses, or measures, must be made in accordance with international law, including human rights law and should be guided by the principles of democracy, rule of law, gender equality, inclusivity and equity. When we come out of this crisis, we must ensure that our standards have not shifted in a negative direction. [...]
> Governments must ensure that international human rights are at the center of all COVID-19 responses and that no one is left behind. Response plans must identify and put in place targeted measures to address the disproportionate impact of the virus on marginalized groups.

Thus, according to Italy, vulnerable categories ought to be taken into account when conceiving and implementing restrictive measures, also bearing in mind that the pandemic engenders a "particular and unique effect on those who face multiple and intersecting forms of discrimination".[82] Based on governmental statements delivered in multiple fora, such categories include women, migrants, and, more generally, people in conflict situations,[83] but also LGBTI+ persons and persons with disabilities. These people's needs must be addressed with special care, as restrictions might impede access to necessary medical treatments and have socio-economic consequences which might be *de facto* discriminatory.

Specifically in relation to persons with disabilities, Italy remarked on multiple occasions that special attention should be paid to their needs in the critical COVID-19 context, and welcomed international political commitments in this regard,[84] such as the UN Secretary-General's Policy Brief on "A Disability-

---

[80] Joint statement, *cit. supra* note 58.

[81] Permanent Mission of Italy to the UN, "Italy joins the Statement on the Occasion of the International Day against homophobia, biphobia, interphobia and transphobia", 18 May 2020, available at: <https://italyun.esteri.it/rappresentanza_onu/en/comunicazione/archivio-news/2020/05/l-italia-partecipa-al-comunicato.html>.

[82] *Ibid.*

[83] As stated by the Italian President of the Council of Ministers, Mr Giuseppe Conte, at the UN General Assembly on 25 September 2020 (the text of the speech is available at: <https://estatements.unmeetings.org/estatements/10.0010/20200925/3Yf6QppA2NrI/eOpfBeKL-Rz5J_en.pdf>). Women had already been defined by Italy a vulnerable group at the Security Council on 17 July 2020 (the text of the statement is available at: <https://italyun.esteri.it/rappresentanza_onu/en/comunicazione/archivio-news/2020/07/consiglio-di-sicurezza-dibatti-to_58.html>).

[84] Permanent Mission of Italy to the UN, "Italy joins the statement on 'Disability-inclusive response to COVID-19 – Towards a better future for all' – A response to the Secretary-General's Policy Brief", 18 May 2020, available at: <https://italyun.esteri.it/rappresentanza_onu/en/comunicazione/archivio-news/2020/05/l-italia-partecipa-al-comunicato_0.html>.

Inclusive Response to COVID-19"[85] as well as other UN relevant guidance by the WHO[86] or the UN High Commissioner for Human Rights.[87] Moreover, when implementing measures involving this category, Italy stressed the importance of "[m]eaningful consultation [with] and active participation of persons with disabilities and their representative organizations in all stages of the COVID-19 response"[88] – as further remarked by the President of the Italian Republic, Mr Sergio Mattarella, on the International Day of Disabled Persons, on 3 December 2020.[89]

Vaccines as a Universal Good and Their Accessibility

The seriousness of the pandemic made governments soon realize that only world-scale vaccination could eventually stop the spread of the virus and prevent further disastrous consequences on the human and economic levels. The Italian Government has advocated for a global alliance to advance the research of COVID-19 vaccines and guarantee their rapid production and equitable distribution since the very beginning of the pandemic, as recalled at the UN Security Council on 2 July 2020 during the Open Debate on "Pandemics and Security"[90] and on 11 August 2020 during the High Level Open Debate.[91] In particular, Italy has been especially concerned that, once entered into the production stage, the vaccine be accessible also to developing countries and that the EU take the initiative to ensure its large-scale distribution also outside Europe, as underlined by the President of the Council of Ministers, Mr Giuseppe Conte, before the Chamber of Deputies on 14 October 2020 (408th Meeting, XVIII Legislature).

In fact, securing a fair distribution of life-saving vaccines to countries in need had been on the agenda of Italian Governments for several years even before the COVID-19 emergency. For instance, Italy has been financially supporting the Global Alliance for Vaccines and Immunization since 2006[92] and the Coalition

---

[85] UN, Policy Brief: A Disability-Inclusive Response to COVID-19, May 2020, available at: <www.un.org/sites/un2.un.org/files/sg_policy_brief_on_persons_with_disabilities_final. pdf>.

[86] WHO, Disability considerations during the COVID-19 outbreak, 2020, available at: <www.who.int/publications/i/item/WHO-2019-nCoV-Disability-2020-1>.

[87] OHCHR, COVID-19 and the Rights of Personas with Disabilities: Guidance, 19 April 2020, available at: <www.ohchr.org/Documents/Issues/Disability/COVID-19_and_The_ Rights_of_Persons_with_Disabilities.pdf>.

[88] See *supra* note 84.

[89] The full text of the statement is available at: <https://italyun.esteri.it/rappresentanza_ onu/en/comunicazione/archivio-news/2020/12/dichiarazione-del-presidente-mattarella.html>.

[90] The full text of the statement is available at: <https://italyun.esteri.it/rappresentanza_ onu/en/comunicazione/archivio-news/2020/07/youth4climate-una-serie-di-incontri.html>.

[91] The full text of the statement is available at: <https://italyun.esteri.it/rappresentanza_ onu/en/comunicazione/archivio-news/2020/08/consiglio-di-sicurezza-dibattito_61.html>.

[92] More information on GAVI is available at: <www.gavi.org/investing-gavi/funding/ donor-profiles/italy>.

for Epidemic Preparedness Innovations since its launch in 2017.[93] Together with the WHO and UNICEF, these two projects established in April 2020 the COVID-19 Vaccines Global Access (COVAX) alliance to buy doses for distribution to developing countries.[94]

The purchase of vaccines and their free supply to low-income States is one option available to industrialized countries to ensure that access to these and other life-saving treatments be "fair",[95] "universal" and "equitable",[96] as Italy has repeatedly affirmed it must be. This conviction may find its basis in the qualification – whose legal nature and consequences are unclear – of vaccines as a global public good. This was affirmed by the Italian Parliament with Motion no. 1-00353, approved by the Chamber of Deputies on 5 August 2020 (387th Meeting, XVIII Legislature), which

> commits the government: […] to support, also in the competent international fora, the need to pool research for the development of a safe and effective vaccine against COVID-19, to be considered as a global public good and accessible to all.

In September 2020, the President of the Council of Ministers declared before the UN General Assembly[97] that

> Italy considers these [vaccines] to be global public goods, with the objective of leaving no one behind. […] [H]ealth is a common, inalienable good, and as such, it must be guaranteed for every woman and every man on the Planet.

Mr Conte also said that

> Italy now pursues an approach inspired by the "ethics of vulnerability", which calls on all members of the international community to assume their share of collective responsibility for "global public

---

[93] More information on CEPI is available at: <https://cepi.net/about/whoweare/>.

[94] More information on COVAX is available at <www.gavi.org/vaccineswork/covax-explained>.

[95] Permanent Mission of Italy to the UN, "18 African and European Leaders, among them Prime Minister Giuseppe Conte, signed an article published on Financial Times", 15 April 2020, available at: <https://italyun.esteri.it/rappresentanza_onu/en/comunicazione/archivio-news/2020/04/18-leaders-africani-e-europei-tra.html>.

[96] As affirmed during the High Level Open Debate in August 2020 (see *supra* note 91) and the Virtual Event on "Shaping a Better World for All: G20 Efforts Under the Presidency of Saudi Arabia During the COVID-19 Pandemic", 5 November 2020, available at: <https://italyun.esteri.it/rappresentanza_onu/en/comunicazione/archivio-news/2020/11/evento-virtuale-su-shaping-a-better.html>.

[97] Statement by the President of the Council of Ministers of Italy at the 75th Session of the United Nations General Assembly, 25 September 2020, available at: <https://estatements.unmeetings.org/estatements/10.0010/20200925/3Yf6QppA2NrI/eOpfBeKLRz5J_en.pdf>.

goods", such as fundamental human rights, health, education, sustainability, social and institutional resilience.

When it comes to understanding the meaning of the qualification of vaccines as global public goods, the Italian position appears fluctuating. Still on 10-11 March 2021, Italy had refused to endorse – along with many other developed countries – the temporary waiver[98] of patent rights for vaccines tabled by India and South Africa at the World Trade Organization (WTO) in October 2020 and supported by over 80 developing countries.[99] Waiving the rules of the WTO-covered Agreement on Trade-Related Aspects of Intellectual Property would have brought, according to the proponents, to an increased production of vaccines by allowing generic manufacturers to enter the market. However, after the United States' U-turn of 5 May 2021, when the Biden Administration declared to support the waiver, the Italian Government appeared to follow suit. On 6 May, the new President of the Council of Ministers, Mr Mario Draghi, reiterated that "vaccines are a global common good" and labelled "the striking down of obstacles hindering vaccination campaigns" a priority. The same day, the Minister of Health welcomed President Biden's move on "free access for everyone to vaccine patents", defining it "an important step forward".[100] Yet, in the subsequent few days Mr Draghi reportedly took inconsistent stances, by both expressly approving the US Administration's move and, soon thereafter, showing a more tepid attitude.[101]

BEATRICE BONO

XIX. ARMED CONFLICT, NEUTRALITY, AND DISARMAMENT

ARMS EXPORT TO SOME NEAR- AND MIDDLE-EASTERN COUNTRIES

In 2020, the interest – from a legal viewpoint – in Italy's position on arms export stemmed from what the Country's representatives omitted to say rather than from the explicit content of their declarations.

By way of introduction, it is worth recalling the legal framework applicable to arms exports in the Italian legal system. In line with all other EU Member States, Italy is subject to the obligations deriving from the Arms Trade Treaty

---

[98] "Rich countries block push by developing nations to waive COVID vaccine patents", EURACTIV, 11 March 2021, available at: <www.euractiv.com/section/economy-jobs/news/rich-countries-block-push-by-developing-nations-to-waive-covid-vaccine-patents-rights/>.

[99] The full text of the proposal is available at: <https://docs.wto.org/dol2fe/Pages/SS/directdoc.aspx?filename=q:/IP/C/W669.pdf&Open=True>.

[100] "Joe Biden 'libera' i vaccini. Ue pronta a dialogo, Draghi: 'Abbattere ostacoli'", Huffington Post, 6 May 2021, available at: <www.huffingtonpost.it/entry/joe-biden-libera-i-vaccini-oms-svolta-storica-deluse-le-big-pharma_it_60939b33e4b05af50dcbeb36>.

[101] "Brevetti vaccini, Ue aperta alla discussione ma senza entusiasmi. Draghi: 'Posizione Usa da capire. Questione complessa'", Il Fatto Quotidiano, available at: <www.ilfattoquotidiano.it/2021/05/08/brevetti-vaccino-leuropa-spaccata-tra-merkel-e-biden-macron-fa-retromarcia-sulla-liberalizzazione-draghi-appoggia-washington/6191203/>.

(ATT), which was ratified by means of Law No. 118 of 4 October 2013, and from Council Common Position 2008/944/CFSP (hereinafter, CCP944), as recently amended.[102] There is a high degree of complementarity between the ATT and the CCP944: the latter is explicit when it demands in its Article 2(1)(bb) that "[a]n export licence shall be denied if approval would be inconsistent with, inter alia: [...] the international obligations of Member States under the Arms Trade Treaty". In similar terms, Article 6(2) of the former foresees that a "State Party shall not authorize any transfer of conventional arms [...] if the transfer would violate its relevant international obligations under international agreements to which it is a Party, in particular those relating to the transfer of, or illicit trafficking in, conventional arms". In addition to the supranational framework, Italian arms export is governed by a national law – Law No. 185 of 9 July 1990 – as subsequently amended.[103]

A trait common to these three legal acts is the existence of criteria that an export shall satisfy to be authorized. The two criteria that are of main relevance for the purpose of this commentary are the respect for human rights law and the respect for international humanitarian law. In this regard, both the ATT and the CCP944 provide for a similar, although not identical, wording and require national authorities to perform a risk assessment as to the possibility that the exported arms could be used to commit (or even to facilitate, in the case of the ATT) a serious violation of human rights law and/or humanitarian law. In contrast, in the Italian legal order, the domestic criterion on human rights law diverges from this forward-looking perspective and mandates an assessment of the past conduct of the recipient country. More specifically, Article 1(6)(d) of Law No. 185 provides that "the export shall be denied to countries whose governments are responsible for serious violations of international human rights conventions, ascertained by the competent bodies of the United Nations, the European Union or the Council of Europe". As to the criterion on international humanitarian law, the ATT and the CCP944 are to a large extent similar, in that the relevant provisions of both acts require an assessment of the possibility that the arms could be used to commit a serious violation of international humanitarian law in the future. Conversely, Law No. 185[104] focuses on already existing situations when it requires to deny authorizations to export to "countries in a state of armed conflict, contrary to the principles of Article 51 of the Charter of the United Nations" or

---

[102] Council Common Position 2008/944/CFSP of 8 December 2008 defining common rules governing control of exports of military technology and equipment. The last amendment was enacted through Council Decision (CFSP) 2019/1560 of 16 September 2019 amending Common Position 2008/944/CFSP defining common rules governing control of exports of military technology and equipment.

[103] Law No. 185 was amended by: Law No. 222 of 27 February 1992, Decree of the President of the Republic No. 373 of 20 April 1994, Law No. 148 of 17 June 2003, Legislative Decree No. 66 of 15 March 2010, Legislative Decree No. 105 of 22 June 2012, and Decree-Law No. 114 of 10 October 2013.

[104] Respectively, paras. 6(a) and 6(b) of Art. 1.

to "countries whose policies are in contrast with the principles of Article 11 of the Constitution".[105]

This premise allows us to better understand the problematic approach that emerges from the written response of the Undersecretary of State for Foreign Affairs and International Cooperation, Mr Manlio Di Stefano, to the questions raised at the Senate of the Republic on the arms export to Egypt, also in connection with the death of the Italian student Giulio Regeni and Egypt's insufficient cooperation on that matter. In his reply dated 24 July 2020 to parliamentary questions nos. 4-02924 and 4-03750, Mr Di Stefano stated that

> The issue of arms sales to Egypt must be approached bearing in mind two assessments, both important: the rules and political sensitivity. On the basis of Law No. 185 of 1990, the Government, through the national authority UAMA, examines case by case the requests of Italian companies for authorization to negotiate supply contracts and then to export. In addition to national legislation, the deliberations of the European Union concerning relations with Egypt are naturally looked at. The Government evaluates the specific nature of materials, the recipient, the user, their possible use. The control is carried out also through the contribution of technical-military opinions. The granting of authorizations is subject to the strict application of these criteria. The inexistence of impediments is also ascertained, both with regard to the companies involved, and with reference to possible declarations of total or partial embargo of war supplies by the UN, the European Union and the OSCE.[106]

---

[105] According to Art. 11 of the Italian Constitution, "Italy rejects war as an instrument of aggression against the freedom of other peoples and as a means for the settlement of international disputes. Italy shall agree, on conditions of equality with other States, to such limitations of sovereignty as may be necessary to ensure peace and justice among Nations. Italy shall promote and encourage international organizations pursuing such a goal".

[106] Although the Undersecretary clarified that, under Law No. 185, the authorization to negotiate is distinct from the authorization to export, the fact that the assessment is conducted against the same parameters implies that a denial of export after the negotiations have been authorized will only occur because of a change in the conditions of legal or political relevance during the period of the negotiations. As to these political conditions, Mr Di Stefano mentioned the importance of Egypt for the Lybian conflict, for the fight against terrorism and trafficking, for the management of migration flows and for cooperation in energy matters. Answers along the very same lines were given by the Government on other occasions, in 2020. However, on 16 July, in his reply before the Senate (241st Meeting, XVIII Legislature) to an analogous parliamentary question, the Minister for Parliamentary Relations, Mr Federico D'Incà, added an obscure sentence whose meaning may be debated but whose potential wrongness from a legal point of view deserves to be noted. Indeed, Mr D'Incà stated that "no other European country has adopted restrictive measures on this kind of armaments so far, as any reference to possible violations committed during law-and-order activities is missing" (in the relevant legal framework – it might be presumed). Unsurprisingly, in her rejoinder, the interrogating MP remarked that violating human rights is not a matter of domestic law and order.

Three comments are warranted vis-à-vis the above statement. Firstly, the legal framework referred to by the Undersecretary of State is *prima facie* incomplete. If it is true that the notion of "national legislation" also encompasses Law No. 118 of 4 October 2013, through which Italy incorporated by reference the ATT, it is still questionable whether Mr Di Stefano actually meant to include in its reply such an international treaty, as he only quoted explicitly Law No. 185. Secondly, the European legal framework is missing – at least in part – from the statement, as reference is made only to the "deliberations" of the EU. It is also unclear in this regard whether the generic term "deliberations" alludes to restrictive measures adopted by the Council or to a more general political evaluation. A third point, which logically follows the previous ones, is the incomplete enumeration of the criteria. In this respect, it must be recalled that under both the ATT and the CCP944, national authorities must also consider, *inter alia*, the impact that the exported arms would have on peace and security,[107] regional stability,[108] as well as the internal situation of the country of destination.[109] In addition, as seen above, the assessment required under national and supranational rules differ as to the nature of the evaluation requested. On the one hand, Law No. 185 mandates an enquire into the past behavior of the recipient country and, in the field of human rights, further necessitates a formal ascertainment of grave violations by the competent organs of the UN, the EU or the Council of Europe. On the other hand, the ATT and the CCP944 center on the danger that the arms would be used to commit serious violations and the evaluation represents, therefore, a prognostic risk assessment where the past conduct of the recipient is only one of the elements to be considered. Both approaches present shortfalls but, taken together, they can be read as mutually reinforcing. The strength of the domestic criterion lies in the fact that a past grave violation is sufficient in itself to block an export, even if the attitude of the recipient has changed. In other words, a past violation already implies an overriding risk that grave human rights violations may be committed again. The strength of the supranational rules is apparent if viewed from the opposite angle: the fact that grave violations have not been committed so far is not sufficient per se to authorize an export, but a broader evaluation is warranted.

As seen, the above statement by Mr Di Stefano was issued in the context of a case centered on respect for human rights, but a similar position was taken in relation to situations that involve the respect for international humanitarian law. In replying to a question on the authorization for arms exports to Turkey, Saudi Arabia and the United Arab Emirates, Mr Di Stefano failed to mention the existence of EU and international rules applicable to Italy. On 11 June 2020, before the Commission on Foreign and European Affairs (III) (386th Meeting, XVIII Legislature) of the Chamber of Deputies, the Undersecretary of State replied as follows:

---

[107] Art. 7(1)(a) ATT.
[108] Art. 2(4) CCP944.
[109] Art. 2(3) CCP944.

> The Government, through the National Authority-UAMA, scrupulously applies Law No. 185 of 1990 and examines the requests of Italian companies following all the indications provided by the regulation currently in force.

Differently from the statement analyzed above, in this reply, the only reference made is to Law No. 185, and the Government failed to mention both the broader concept of "national legislation", which, as seen, would formally include Law No. 118, and EU rules. As has been seen, with regard to international humanitarian law, the omission can be troublesome. A clear-cut reference to the need to respect humanitarian law is missing in Law No. 185, even if, according to its Article 1(5), arms export shall be denied if contrary to Italy's international commitments. Given that humanitarian law forms part of these commitments, the view can be taken that an authorization must be denied if it undermines the performance of the obligations under common Article 1 of the four Geneva Conventions.[110] The other two criteria of Law No. 185 that specifically apply to exports to States in situations of conflict are those provided for by Article 6(1)(a)-(b). Yet, in fact, these criteria deal with questions of *jus ad bellum* rather than *jus in bello*, as underlined by the reference to Article 51 of the UN Charter and Article 11 of the Italian Constitution. This implies that, set aside the indirect reference to international commitments, Law No. 185 lacks a criterion devoted to compliance with humanitarian law. In contrast with the case of respect for human rights law examined earlier, where the evaluation is limited to the past track record of the recipient, in this case there is no specific assessment to be performed. It is, therefore, surprising that the Undersecretary of State omitted any references to the supranational rules, as these are filling a void left by domestic legislation. In particular, both Article 7(1)(b)(i) ATT and Article 2(2) CCP944 require national authorities to assess the risk that the arms would be used to commit a serious violation of humanitarian law. Moreover, Criterion 6 of the CCP944 also imposes to assess the recipient's "compliance with its international commitments, in particular on the non-use of force, and with international humanitarian law".[111]

As seen throughout this commentary, the position of Italy vis-à-vis arms export and the criteria for authorization sparks interest more for its omissions than for what it actually states. In the two excerpts analyzed, the legal references made by the Government are limited to domestic legislation and, within this remit, to Law No. 185. Not only is Law No. 118, which incorporates the ATT, not mentioned, but the EU legal framework is entirely missing, save for a vague reference to EU "deliberations". The legal significance of the omission lies in the fact that

---

[110] Art. 1 reads: "The High Contracting Parties undertake to respect and to ensure respect for the present Convention in all circumstances". On the relationship between this provision and arms export, see BREHM, "The Arms Trade and States' Duty to Ensure Respect for Humanitarian and Human Rights Law", Journal of Conflict and Security Law, 2007, p. 359 ff.

[111] Art. 2(6)(b) CCP944.

the criteria included in both the ATT and the CCP944 should always form part of the assessment performed by every EU Member State's national authority for the authorization of arms export. In the case of Italy, Law No. 185 alone does not account for all relevant supranational criteria and this incompleteness is reflected in the position taken by the Government.

IOTAM LERER

BIBLIOGRAPHIES

ITALIAN BIBLIOGRAPHICAL INDEX
OF INTERNATIONAL LAW 2020

(edited by *Giulio Bartolini* and *Alessandro Chechi*)

This bibliography includes books and articles published during the year 2020, with some exceptions going back to 2019.

Items are listed only once, under their most appropriate heading. Headings correspond to the Classification Scheme adopted for the Italian practice relating to international law.

Unless otherwise specified, texts are in the same language as corresponding entries in the bibliography. When available, translations of titles have been reproduced from the original source.

The bibliography includes only works on public international law. Works considered as belonging to European Union law and to private international law are generally omitted.

Any indication of items inadvertently omitted will be appreciated with a view to publication in the next volume of the *Yearbook*.

I. INTERNATIONAL LAW IN GENERAL

BARTOLINI G. (ed.), *A History of International Law in Italy*, Oxford, 2020, pp. 562.

BARTOLINI G., "Italian Legal Scholarship of International Law in the Early Decades of the Twentieth Century", in BARTOLINI G. (ed.), *A History of International Law in Italy*, Oxford, 2020, p. 127 ff.

BARTOLINI G., "Italy between the Two World Wars: International Law Issues", in BARTOLINI G. (ed.), *A History of International Law in Italy*, Oxford, 2020, p. 359 ff.

BARTOLINI G., "What Is a History of International Law in Italy for? International Law through the Prism of National Perspectives", in BARTOLINI G. (ed.), *A History of International Law in Italy*, Oxford, 2020, p. 3 ff.

CANNIZZARO V., "Diritto Internazionale" (International Law), 5th ed., Torino, 2020, pp. 576.

CARCANO A., "The Challenges of Populism: What Role for International Law Scholars?", DUDI, 2020, p. 5 ff.

CATALDI G., "Disobbedienza e diritto nell'ottica dell'internazionalista" (Disobedience and Law from an Internationalist Perspective), DUDI, 2020, p. 159 ff.

CONFORTI B. and FOCARELLI C., *Le Nazioni Unite* (United Nations), 12th ed., Milano, 2020, pp. 573.

DI RUZZA T., "The 'Roman Question': The Dissolution of the Papal State, the Creation of the Vatican City State, and the Debate on the International Legal

IYIL, Vol. 30 (2020), pp. 543-580
ISSN 0391-5107

Personality of the Holy See", in BARTOLINI G. (ed.), *A History of International Law in Italy*, Oxford, 2020, p. 310 ff.

DISTEFANO G. and KOLB R., "Some Contributions from and Influence of the Italian Doctrine of International Law", in BARTOLINI G. (ed.), *A History of International Law in Italy*, Oxford, 2020, p. 433 ff.

FOCARELLI C., "International Law in the Twentieth Century", in ORAKHELASHVILI A. (ed.), *Research Handbook on the Theory and History of International Law*, 2nd ed., Cheltenham, 2020, p. 394 ff.

FRANZINA P., "The Integrated Approach to Private and Public International Law. A Distinctive Feature of Italian Legal Thinking", in BARTOLINI G. (ed.), *A History of International Law in Italy*, Oxford, 2020, p. 262 ff.

GAETA P., ZAPPALÁ S. and VIÑUALES J.E., *Cassese's International Law*, Oxford, 2020, pp. 616.

GRADONI L., "Burn Out and Fade Away: Marxism in Italian International Legal Scholarship", in BARTOLINI G. (ed.), *A History of International Law in Italy*, Oxford, 2020, p. 234 ff.

GREPPI E., "The Risorgimento and the 'Birth' of International Law in Italy", in BARTOLINI G. (ed.), *A History of International Law in Italy*, Oxford, 2020, p. 79 ff.

INGRAVALLO I., "The Formation of International Law Journals in Italy: Their Role in the Discipline", in BARTOLINI G. (ed.), *A History of International Law in Italy*, Oxford, 2020, p. 190 ff.

MARCHISIO S., "The Unification of Italy and International Law", in BARTOLINI G. (ed.), *A History of International Law in Italy*, Oxford, 2020, p. 285 ff.

MILANO E., "The Main International Law Issues Arising in the Aftermath of World War II", in BARTOLINI G. (ed.), *A History of International Law in Italy*, Oxford, 2020, p. 406 ff.

MURA E., "The Construction of the International Law Discipline in Italy between the Mancinian and Positive Schools", in BARTOLINI G. (ed.), *A History of International Law in Italy*, Oxford, 2020, p. 109 ff.

NESI G., "Diritto internazionale, diritto comparato e *comparative international law*: riflessioni sul metodo comparato" (International Law, Comparative Law and Comparative International Law: Reflections on the Comparative Method), *Blog per i 70 anni di Roberto Toniatti*, Trento, 2020, available at: <www.robertotoniatti.eu/contributi/diritto-internazionale-diritto-comparato-e-comparative-international-law>.

PALCHETTI P., "The Italian Doctrine over Recent Decades", in BARTOLINI G. (ed.), *A History of International Law in Italy*, Oxford, 2020, p. 468 ff.

PAVONI R., "Italian Yearbook of International Law: Genesis, Development and Prospects", NYIL, Vol. 50, 2019, p. 195 ff.

SCOVAZZI T., "The Italian Approach to Colonialism: The First Experiences in Eritrea and Somalia", in BARTOLINI G. (ed.), *A History of International Law in Italy*, Oxford, 2020, p. 334 ff.

SOSSAI M., "Catholicism and the Evolution of International Law Studies in Italy", in BARTOLINI G. (ed.), *A History of International Law in Italy*, Oxford, 2020, p. 215 ff.

STORTI C., "Early 'Italian' Scholars of *Ius Gentium*", in BARTOLINI G. (ed.), *A History of International Law in Italy*, Oxford, 2020, p. 19 ff.

TANCREDI A., "The (Immediate) Post-World War II Period", in BARTOLINI G. (ed.), *A History of International Law in Italy*, Oxford, 2020, p. 168 ff.

VIOLI F., "The Function of the Triad 'Territory', 'Jurisdiction', and 'Control' in Due Diligence Obligations", in KRIEGER H., PETERS A. and KREUZER L. (eds.), *Due Diligence in the International Legal Order*, Oxford, 2020, p. 75 ff.

VIRZO R., "The Influence of Italian International Law Scholars on the Crafting of the 1948 Constitution", in BARTOLINI G. (ed.), *A History of International Law in Italy*, Oxford, 2020, p. 390 ff.

II. INTERNATIONAL CUSTOM, LAW OF TREATIES AND OTHER SOURCES OF INTERNATIONAL LAW

BUSCEMI M., LAZZERINI N., MAGI L. and RUSSO D. (eds.), *Legal Sources in Business and Human Rights. Evolving Dynamics in International and European Law*, Leiden, 2020, pp. xiv-339.

CALIGIURI A. (ed.), *Legal Technology Transformation. A Practical Assessment*, Napoli, 2020, pp. 279.

CALIGIURI A., "A New International Legal Framework for Unmanned Maritime Vehicles?", in CALIGIURI A. (ed.), *Legal Technology Transformation. A Practical Assessment*, Napoli, 2020, p. 99 ff.

CALIGIURI A., "Limiti alla efficacia di norme internazionali generali in materia penale nell'ordinamento italiano" (Limits to the Effectiveness of Rules of General International Law in Criminal Matters in the Italian Legal Order), in PUMA G. (ed.), *Diritto internazionale e sistema delle fonti. Tra modello accentrato e modello diffuso del controllo di costituzionalità*, Bari, 2020, p. 53 ff.

CANZIO G., "The Dialogue between the Courts and the Coordination Best Practices", Ars interpretandi, 2020, p. 85 ff.

CHECHI A., "The Case of the Crimean Art Treasure and the Question of the Application of the UNESCO Convention of 1970", RDI, 2020, p. 469 ff.

CHIUSSI L., "Corporate Human Rights Due Diligence: From the Process to the Principle", in BUSCEMI M., LAZZERINI N., MAGI L. and RUSSO D. (eds.), *Legal Sources in Business and Human Rights. Evolving Dynamics in International and European Law*, Leiden, 2020, p. 11 ff.

CREMA L., "The Unity of International Law in Legal Reasoning", Ars interpretandi, 2020, p. 101 ff.

DE VIVO M.C., "Digital Humanism between Ethics, Law and New Technologies", in CALIGIURI A. (ed.), *Legal Technology Transformation. A Practical Assessment*, Napoli, 2020, p. 65 ff.

FARAGUNA P., "Identità costituzionale e diritto internazionale generale" (Constitutional Identity and General International Law), in PUMA G. (ed.), *Diritto internazionale e sistema delle fonti. Tra modello accentrato e modello diffuso del controllo di costituzionalità*, Bari, 2020, p. 39 ff.

FASCIGLIONE M., "A Binding Instrument on Business and Human Rights as a Source of International Obligations for Private Companies: Utopia or Reality?", in BUSCEMI M., LAZZERINI N., MAGI L. and RUSSO D. (eds.), *Legal Sources in Business and Human Rights. Evolving Dynamics in International and European Law*, Leiden, 2020, p. 31 ff.

FORLATI S., "Judicial Interpretation and the Development of International Law", Ars interpretandi, 2020, p. 51 ff.

FORLATI S., "The Relationship between the Law of Treaties and the Law of International Responsibility", in FORLATI S., MBENGUE M.M. and McGARRY B. (eds.), *The* Gabčíkovo-Nagymaros *Judgment and Its Contribution to the Development of International Law*, Leiden, 2020, p. 109 ff.

FORLATI S., MBENGUE M.M. and McGARRY B. (eds.), *The* Gabčíkovo-Nagymaros *Judgment and Its Contribution to the Development of International Law*, Leiden, 2020, pp. 263.

LUGATO M., "La libertà di culto tra Costituzione e Convenzione europea dei diritti umani: pluralismo religioso, pacifica convivenza e *vivre ensemble*" (Freedom of Religion between the Constitution and the European Convention on Human Rights: Religious Pluralism, Peaceful Coexistence and *Vivre Ensemble*), in PUMA G. (ed.), *Diritto internazionale e sistema delle fonti. Tra modello accentrato e modello diffuso del controllo di costituzionalità*, Bari, 2020, p. 93 ff.

MARGIOTTA C., "Codifying Rules of Interpretation: The Specificity of the International Legal Order", Ars interpretandi, 2020, p. ff.

MAURI D., "Direct and Indirect Involvement of Companies in the Development of Business and Human Rights Law: Insights from Practice", in BUSCEMI M., LAZZERINI N., MAGI L. and RUSSO D. (eds.), *Legal Sources in Business and Human Rights. Evolving Dynamics in International and European Law*, Leiden, 2020, p. 123 ff.

NINATTI S., "Domesticating the Convention? Diritto interno e Convenzione europea di fronte al giudice costituzionale" (Domesticating the Convention? National Law and European Convention before the Constitutional Court), in PUMA G. (ed.), *Diritto internazionale e sistema delle fonti. Tra modello accentrato e modello diffuso del controllo di costituzionalità*, Bari, 2020, p. 71 ff.

PERRINI F., "Sviluppi attuali in materia di stipulazione di accordi in forma semplificata nell'ordinamento italiano" (Recent Developments on the Conclusion of Executive Agreements in the Italian Legal System), OIDU, 2020, p. 67 ff.

PIETROBON A., "Withdrawal from Disarmament and Non-Proliferation Agreements", RDI, 2020, p. 85 ff.

PUMA G. (ed.), *Diritto internazionale e sistema delle fonti. Tra modello accentrato e modello diffuso del controllo di costituzionalità* (International Law and Sources of Law. Centralized and Decentralized Models of Constitutional Control), Bari, 2020, pp. 155.

PUMA G., "Il diritto internazionale nel sistema delle fonti dell'ordinamento italiano: l'attualità di un dibattito" (International Law in the System of Sources of the Italian Legal Order: On the Relevance of a Debate), in PUMA G. (ed.), *Diritto internazionale e sistema delle fonti. Tra modello accentrato e modello diffuso del controllo di costituzionalità*, Bari, 2020, p. 3 ff.

RAGNI C., *Scienza, diritto e giustizia internazionale* (Science, Law and International Justice), Milano, 2020, pp. xvi-255.

RASI A., "Lo sviluppo dei principi generali di diritto nel tempo" (The Development of General Principles of Law over Time), RDI, 2020, p. 959 ff.

SALERNO F., "Le norme di diritto internazionale 'generalmente riconosciute' nella prospettiva della Corte costituzionale" (The 'Generally Recognised' Principles of International Law from the Perspective of the Constitutional Court), in PUMA G. (ed.), *Diritto internazionale e sistema delle fonti. Tra modello accentrato e modello diffuso del controllo di costituzionalità*, Bari, 2020, p. 11 ff.

SALERNO F., "Le norme di diritto internazionale 'generalmente riconosciute' nella prospettiva della Corte costituzionale" (The 'Generally Recognised' Principles of International Law from the Perspective of the Constitutional Court), RDI, 2020, p. 291 ff.

SPAGNOLO A., "To What Extent Does International Law Matter in the Field of Business and Human Rights?", in BUSCEMI M., LAZZERINI N., MAGI L. and RUSSO D. (eds.), *Legal Sources in Business and Human Rights. Evolving Dynamics in International and European Law*, Leiden, 2020, p. 74 ff.

TANZI A., "Concluding Remarks: The Legacy of a Landmark Case", in FORLATI S., MBENGUE M.M. and MCGARRY B. (eds.), *The* Gabčíkovo-Nagymaros *Judgment and Its Contribution to the Development of International Law*, Leiden, 2020, p. 229 ff.

TINO E., "Riflessioni sulla natura consuetudinaria delle regole enunciate nell'art. 56 della Convenzione di Vienna sul diritto dei trattati" (Remarks on the Customary Nature of the Rules Stated in Article 56 of the Vienna Convention on the Law of Treaties), RDI, 2020, p. 321 ff.

TRAMONTANA E., "Multi-Stakeholder Initiatives and New Models of Co-Regulation in the Field of Business and Human Rights", in BUSCEMI M., LAZZERINI N., MAGI L. and RUSSO D. (eds.), *Legal Sources in Business and Human Rights. Evolving Dynamics in International and European Law*, Leiden, 2020, p. 145 ff.

VILLANI U., "Brevi note sul valore dei 'principi supremi' nei confronti di norme esterne" (Some Remarks on the Value of the 'Supreme Principles' in Relation to External Rules), in PUMA G. (ed.), *Diritto internazionale e sistema delle fonti. Tra modello accentrato e modello diffuso del controllo di costituzionalità*, Bari, 2020, p. 143 ff.

VITALE A., "Il recesso dai trattati multilaterali: tra buona fede e principio di non riconoscimento" (Withdrawal from Multilateral Treaties: Between Good Faith and Non-Recognition), CI, 2020, p. 653 ff.

III. STATES AND OTHER INTERNATIONAL ENTITIES

CANNIZZARO V., *La sovranità oltre lo Stato* (Sovereignty beyond the State), Bologna, 2020, pp. 127.

CARACCIOLO I. and LEANZA U., *Il diritto internazionale: diritto per gli Stati e diritto per gli individui* (International Law: The Law for States and for Individuals), 3rd ed., Torino, 2020, pp. 528.

MANCINI M., *Statualità e non riconoscimento nel diritto internazionale* (Statehood and Non-Recognition in International Law), Torino, 2020, pp. xii-276.

NESI G., "Frontiere, confini e diritto internazionale nel mondo contemporaneo" (Boundaries and International Law in Contemporary World), Gnosis, 2020 (2), p. 142 ff.

NINO M., "The Evolution of the Concept of Territorial Sovereignty. From the Traditional Westphalian System to the State-Peoples Binomial", CI, 2020, p. 561 ff.

IV. DIPLOMATIC AND CONSULAR RELATIONS

CURTI GIALDINO C., *Diritto diplomatico-consolare internazionale ed europeo* (International and European Diplomatic and Consular Law), 5th ed., Torino, 2020, pp. 768.

PUMA G., "Riconoscimento di Governi, rottura delle relazioni diplomatiche e trattamento della sede della missione: il caso della crisi costituzionale venezuelana" (Recognition of Governments, Severance of Diplomatic Relations and Treatment of the Premises of the Diplomatic Mission: The Case of the Constitutional Crisis in Venezuela), RDI, 2020, p. 453 ff.

V. IMMUNITIES

CHECHI A. and RENOLD M.-A., "Staatliche Immunität" (State Immunity), *Kultur Kunst Recht*, Basel, 2020, p. 641 ff.

PAVONI R., "Cultural Heritage and State Immunity", in FRANCIONI F. and VRDOLJAK A.F. (eds.), *The Oxford Handbook of International Cultural Heritage Law*, Oxford, 2020, p. 551 ff.

VENTURINI C., "Ancora un conflitto tra immunità personale dell'agente diplomatico ed obblighi di protezione dei diritti umani: il caso A Local Authority v. AG" (Another Conflict between a Diplomatic Agent's Personal Immunity and the Obligation to Protect Human Rights: The Case A Local Authority v. AG), RDI, 2020, p. 1098 ff.

VI. TERRITORY

CINELLI C., *La disciplina degli spazi internazionali e le sfide poste dal progresso tecnico-scientifico* (The Regulation of International Spaces and the Challenges Posed by Technical-Scientific Progress), Torino, 2020, pp. 208.

DE VERGOTTINI G., *Osimo, un trattato che fa ancora discutere* (The Treaty of Osimo, Still a Contentious Treaty), Milano, 2020, pp. 84.

STARITA M., "La questione del confine italo-francese sul Monte Bianco" (The Question of the Border between France and Italy on the Mont Blanc), RDI, 2020, p. 167 ff.

TREVES T., "Freedoms in Common Areas', in VIÑUALES J. (ed.), *The UN Friendly Relations Declaration at 50*, Oxford, 2020, p. 314 ff.

VII LAW OF THE SEA

CALIGIURI A., "Clarifying Freedom of Navigation through Straits Used for International Navigation: A Study on the Major Straits in Asia", QIL, Zoom-in 76, 2020, p. 1 ff.

CATALDI G., "Introduction", in CHANTAL RIBEIRO M., LOUREIRO BASTOS F. and HENRIKSEN T. (eds.), *Global Challenges and the Law of the Sea*, 2020, p. 1 ff.

CATALDI G., "Quelques problèmes actuels de délimitation des espaces maritimes dans les mers fermées et semi-fermées", in CHANTAL RIBEIRO M. and MENEZES W. (eds.), *Direito do Mar Regulamentação normativa dos espaços marítimos*, Belo Horizonte, 2020, p. 129 ff.

CATALDI G., "Search and Rescue of Migrants at Sea in Recent Italian Law and Practice", in CATALDI G., DEL GUERCIO A. and LIGUORI A. (eds.), *Migration and Asylum Policies Systems. Challenges and Perspectives*, Napoli, 2020, p. 11 ff.

CATALDI G., "The Strait of Hormuz", QIL, Zoom-in 76, 2020, p. 5 ff.

CATALDI G., DEL GUERCIO A. and LIGUORI A. (eds.), *Migration and Asylum Policies Systems. Challenges and Perspectives*, Napoli, 2020, p. 11 ff.

CATALDI G., "Búsqueda y rescate: la necesidad de equilibrar el control de fronteras con las obligaciones en materia de derecho del mar y de los derechos humanos" (Search and Rescue: The Need to Balance Border Control with Law of the Sea and Human Rights Obligations), Revista Española de Derecho Internacional, 2020, p. 197 ff.

CINELLI C., "La disciplina della ricerca scientifica in mare alla luce della recente prassi internazionale" (The Legal Regime of Scientific Research at Sea in the Light of Recent International Practice), RDI, 2020, p. 103 ff.

CORLETO M., "The Protection of Unaccompanied Foreign Minors through the Lens of Italian Asylum Procedures", in CATALDI G., DEL GUERCIO A. and LIGUORI A. (eds.), *Migration and Asylum Policies Systems. Challenges and Perspectives*, Napoli, 2020, p. 55 ff.

DEL GUERCIO A., "The Right to Asylum in Italy", in CATALDI G., DEL GUERCIO A. and LIGUORI A. (eds.), *Migration and Asylum Policies Systems. Challenges and Perspectives*, Napoli, 2020, p. 27 ff.

FAZZINI A., "The Protection of Migrants against Collective Expulsions between Restriction and Uncertainty: Reading the ECtHR's *ND and NT v. Spain*

Judgment", in CATALDI G., DEL GUERCIO A. and LIGUORI A. (eds.), *Migration and Asylum Policies Systems. Challenges and Perspectives*, Napoli, 2020, p. 271 ff.

FERRARA M., "Looking Behind the *Teitiota v. New Zealand* Case: Further Alternatives of Safeguard for 'Climate Change Refugees' under the ICCPR and the ECHR?", in CATALDI G., DEL GUERCIO A. and LIGUORI A. (eds.), *Migration and Asylum Policies Systems. Challenges and Perspectives*, Napoli, 2020, p. 291 ff.

LIGUORI A., "Two Courts but a Similar Outcome – No Humanitarian Visas", in CATALDI G., DEL GUERCIO A. and LIGUORI A. (eds.), *Migration and Asylum Policies Systems. Challenges and Perspectives*, Napoli, 2020, p. 159 ff.

MAGI L., "L'obbligo internazionale del comandante di soccorrere i naufraghi e il diritto ad un porto di rifugio" (The International Obligation of the Shipmaster to Rescue Shipwreckeds and the Right to a Port of Safety), RDI, 2020, p. 691 ff.

TANI I., *Le baie storiche: un'anomalia nel rapporto tra terra e mare* (Historic Bays: An Anomaly in the Relationship between Land and Sea), Torino, 2020, pp. 288.

VEZZANI S., *Jurisdiction in International Fisheries Law: Evolving Trends and New Challenges*, Milano, 2020, pp. 473.

VIII. ENVIRONMENT

CELENTANO F.E., "Il sistema internazionale di contrasto al cambiamento climatico tra inefficacia e astrattezza. Il necessario coinvolgimento dei privati" (The International Legal Framework in the Field of Climate Change: Too Weak, Too Generic. The Importance of the Involvement of the Private Sector), CI, 2020, p. 43 ff.

MORGERA E., PARKS L. and SCHROEDER M., "Methodological Challenges of Transnational Environmental Law", in HEYVAERT V. and DUVIC-PAOLI L.-A. (eds.), *Research Handbook on Transnational Environmental Law*, Cheltenham, 2020, pp. 416.

PAPANICOLOPULU I. and ROCHA A., "Oceans, Climate Change and Non-State Actors", in MCDONALD J., MCGEE J. and BARNES R. (eds.), *Research Handbook on Climate Change, Oceans and Coasts*, Cheltenham, 2020, pp. 544.

SAVARESI A. and HARTMANN J., "Using Human Rights Law to Address the Impacts of Climate Change: Early Reflections on the Carbon Majors Inquiry", in LIN J. and KYSAR S.D.A. (eds.), *Climate Change Litigation in the Asia Pacific*, Cambridge, 2020, p. 73 ff.

SINDICO F., *International Law and Transboundary Aquifers*, Cheltenham, 2020, pp. 208.

TIGNINO M. and IRMAKKESEN Ö., *The Geneva List of Principles on the Protection of Water Infrastructure*, Leiden, 2020, pp. 104.

IX. CULTURAL HERITAGE

BARTOLINI G., "Cultural Heritage and Disasters", in FRANCIONI F. and VRDOLJAK A.F. (eds.), *The Oxford Handbook of International Cultural Heritage Law*, Oxford, 2020, p. 145 ff.

BORTOLOTTO C. and NEYRINCK J., "Article 9: Accreditation of Advisory Organizations", in BLAKE J. and LIXINSKI L. (eds.), *The 2003 UNESCO Intangible Heritage Convention: A Commentary*, Oxford, 2020, p. 153 ff.

CANNONE A., "La Convenzione UNESCO del 1972 sulla tutela del patrimonio mondiale culturale e naturale" (The 1972 UNESCO Convention concerning the Protection of the World Cultural and Natural Heritage), in CATANI E., CONTALDI G. and MARONGIU BUONAIUTI F. (eds.), *La tutela dei beni culturali nell'ordinamento internazionale e nell'Unione europea*, Macerata, 2020, p. 83 ff.

CARDUCCI G., "Article 11: Role of States Parties", in BLAKE J. and LIXINSKI L. (eds.), *The 2003 UNESCO Intangible Heritage Convention: A Commentary*, Oxford, 2020, p. 173 ff.

CARDUCCI G., "Articles 4-8: Organs of the Convention", in BLAKE J. and LIXINSKI L. (eds.), *The 2003 UNESCO Intangible Heritage Convention: A Commentary*, Oxford, 2020, p. 134 ff.

CARDUCCI G., "The Role of UNESCO in the Elaboration and Implementation of International Art, Cultural Property, and Heritage Law", in CARSTENS A.-M. and VARNER E. (eds.), *Intersections in International Cultural Heritage Law*, Oxford, 2020, p. 183 ff.

CATANI E., CONTALDI G. and MARONGIU BUONAIUTI F. (eds.), *La tutela dei beni culturali nell'ordinamento internazionale e nell'Unione europea* (The Protection of Cultural Objects in the International Legal Order and in the European Union), Macerata, 2020, pp. 210.

CHECHI A. and RENOLD M.-A., "Der rechtliche Schutz von Kulturgütern in bewaffneten Konflikten" (The Legal Protection of Cultural Objects in the Event of Armed Conflict), *Kultur Kunst Recht*, Basel, 2020, p. 359 ff.

CHECHI A., "Article 19: Cooperation", in BLAKE J. and LIXINSKI L. (eds.), *The 2003 UNESCO Intangible Heritage Convention: A Commentary*, Oxford, 2020, p. 349 ff.

CHECHI A., "Traffici illeciti di beni culturali e diritto internazionale" (Illicit Trade in Cultural Objects and International Law), in JUCKER D. (ed.), *Le buone pratiche del collezionismo*, Napoli, 2020, p. 123 ff.

FRANCIONI F., "Article 2(1): Defining Intangible Cultural Heritage", in BLAKE J. and LIXINSKI L. (eds.), *The 2003 UNESCO Intangible Heritage Convention: A Commentary*, Oxford, 2020, p. 48 ff.

FRANCIONI F., "Custom and General Principles of International Cultural Heritage Law", in FRANCIONI F. and VRDOLJAK A.F. (eds.), *The Oxford Handbook of International Cultural Heritage Law*, Oxford, 2020, p. 531 ff.

FRANCIONI F., "World Cultural Heritage", in FRANCIONI F. and VRDOLJAK A.F. (eds.), *The Oxford Handbook of International Cultural Heritage Law*, Oxford, 2020, p. 250 ff.

FRIGO M., "Codes of Ethics", in FRANCIONI F. and VRDOLJAK A.F. (eds.), *The Oxford Handbook of International Cultural Heritage Law*, Oxford, 2020, p. 787 ff.

FRULLI M., "International Criminal Law and the Protection of Cultural Heritage", in FRANCIONI F. and VRDOLJAK A.F. (eds.), *The Oxford Handbook of International Cultural Heritage Law*, Oxford, 2020, p. 100 ff.

LENZERINI F., "Articles 16-17: Listing Intangible Cultural Heritage", in BLAKE J. and LIXINSKI L. (eds.), *The 2003 UNESCO Intangible Heritage Convention: A Commentary*, Oxford, 2020, p. 306 ff.

LENZERINI F., "Intentional Destruction of Cultural Heritage", in FRANCIONI F. and VRDOLJAK A.F. (eds.), *The Oxford Handbook of International Cultural Heritage Law*, Oxford, 2020, p. 75 ff.

MUCCI F., "From Clash of Diversities to Protection of Pluralism During and After Conflicts, Through the Respect of the World Cultural Heritage", in CARACCIOLO I. and MONTUORO U. (eds.), *Protection of Cultural and Religious Minorities. Leadership for International Peace and Security*, Torino, 2019, p. 241 ff.

PAVONI R., "International Legal Protection of Cultural Heritage in Armed Conflict: Achievements and Developments", Studi Senesi, Vol. 132, 2020, p. 335 ff.

PETRILLO P.L., "La tutela giuridica del patrimonio culturale immateriale" (The Legal Protection of Intangible Cultural Heritage), in CATANI E., CONTALDI G. and MARONGIU BUONAIUTI F. (eds.), *La tutela dei beni culturali nell'ordinamento internazionale e nell'Unione europea*, Macerata, 2020, p. 117 ff.

QUIRICO O., "Nested Boxes: Tangible Cultural Heritage and Environmental Protection in Light of Climate Change", in CARSTENS A.-M. and VARNER E. (eds.), *Intersections in International Cultural Heritage Law*, Oxford, 2020, p. 267 ff.

SCOVAZZI T., "International Cultural Heritage Law: The Institutional Aspects", in FRANCIONI F. and VRDOLJAK A.F. (eds.), *The Oxford Handbook of International Cultural Heritage Law*, Oxford, 2020, p. 737 ff.

SCOVAZZI T., "Questioni aperte in tema di protezione del patrimonio culturale subacqueo" (Open Questions regarding the Protection of Underwater Cultural Heritage), in CATANI E., CONTALDI G. and MARONGIU BUONAIUTI F. (eds.), *La tutela dei beni culturali nell'ordinamento internazionale e nell'Unione europea*, Macerata, 2020, p. 97 ff.

UBERTAZZI B., "Article 2(2): Manifesting Intangible Cultural Heritage", in BLAKE J. and LIXINSKI L. (eds.), *The 2003 UNESCO Intangible Heritage Convention: A Commentary*, Oxford, 2020, p. 58 ff.

VADI V., "Cultural Heritage in International Investment Law", in FRANCIONI F. and VRDOLJAK A.F. (eds.), *The Oxford Handbook of International Cultural Heritage Law*, Oxford, 2020, p. 483 ff.

VIDETTA C., "Protection of Cultural Heritage as a Pillar of Sustainable Development: An Additional Tool for Peace?", in CARACCIOLO I. and MONTUORO U. (eds.), *Protection of Cultural and Religious Minorities. Leadership for International Peace and Security*, Torino, 2019, p. 283 ff.

XI. TREATMENT OF ALIENS AND NATIONALITY

BORELLI S. and M.C. VITUCCI, "The Italian Response to Exploitation of Migrant Workers in the Agricultural Sector: Between Criminalization and Prevention", IYIL, Vol. XXIX-2019, 2020, p. 165 ff.

FARINELLI F., "Syrian Refugees in Europe: Assessing Challenges, Practices and Integration Policies", in MOODRICK-EVEN H., BOMS N.T. and ASHRAPH S. (eds.), *The Syrian War*, Cambridge, 2020, p. 217 ff.

GARGIULO P., "La cittadinanza sociale nel diritto trasnazionale" (Social Citizenship in Transnational Law), in POMPEJANO D., PANELLA L. and VILLANI A. (eds.), *Cittadinanze trasversali*, Milano, 2020, p. 37 ff.

IPPOLITO F., BORZONI G. and CASOLARI F. (eds.), *Bilateral Relations in the Mediterranean. Prospects for Migration Issues*, Cheltenham, 2020, pp. 368.

PERRINI F., "Il difficile cammino verso nuove forme di cittadinanza di rifugia-ti e di titolari di protezione sussidiaria" (The Difficult Path towards New Forms of Citizenship for Refugees and Holders of Subsidiary Protection), in POMPEJANO D., PANELLA L. and VILLANI A. (eds.), *Cittadinanze trasversali*, Milano, 2020, p. 69 ff.

POMPEJANO D., "Una *Silent Revolution* contro la cittadinanza" (A Silent Revolution against Citizenship), in POMPEJANO D., PANELLA L. and VILLANI A. (eds.), *Cittadinanze trasversali*, Milano, 2020, p. 13 ff.

SCIACCALUGA G., *International Law and the Protection of "Climate Refugees"*, 2020, pp. 217.

VILLANI A., "'Towards a Newer World'? Il contributo delle campagne del-le Nazioni Unite in tema di cittadinanza" (The Contribution of the UN Campaigns on Citizenship), in POMPEJANO D., PANELLA L. and VILLANI A. (eds.), *Cittadinanze trasversali*, Milano, 2020, p. 49 ff.

XII. HUMAN RIGHTS

ANGIOI S., "Ethnicity, Race and Minorities in International Law", in CARACCIOLO I. and MONTUORO U. (eds.), *Protection of Cultural and Religious Minorities. Leadership for International Peace and Security*, Torino, 2019, p. 3 ff.

ANTONIAZZI C.T., "Articolo 4" (Article 4), in BERTÒ E. and MARCANTONI M. (eds.), *30 voci per 30 diritti. Liberi commenti agli articoli della Dichiarazione Universale dei Diritti Umani*, Trento, 2020, p. 46 ff.

ANTONIAZZI C.T., "Flash mob, libertà di riunione e 'pregiudizio importante'" (Flash Mob, Freedom of Assembly and "Significant Disadvantage"), Giur. It., 2020, Vol. 172(1), p. 33 ff.

ANTONIAZZI C.T., "Il rapporto della *Fundamental Rights Agency* sulle istituzioni nazionali per i diritti umani e le prospettive per un'istituzione italiana" (The Fundamental Rights Agency Report on National Human Rights Institutions and the Prospects for an Italian Institution), in *Osservatorio sulle attività del-le organizzazioni internazionali e sovranazionali, universali e regionali, sui temi di interesse della politica estera italiana*, Working Paper II-2020, Napoli, p. 77 ff.

ANTONIAZZI C.T., "Sotto esame: l'Italia e il terzo ciclo della Revisione periodica universale" (Under Scrutiny: Italy and the Third Cycle of the Universal Periodic Review), in *Osservatorio sulle attività delle organizzazioni internazionali e sovranazionali, universali e regionali, sui temi di interesse della politica estera italiana*, Working Paper I-2020, Napoli, p. 32 ff.

ANTONIAZZI C.T., DE GUTTRY A. and CAPONE F., "Il Rapporto indipendente di valutazione dell'attuazione degli impegni OSCE in materia di diritti umani" (The Independent Evaluation Report on the Implementation of Selected OSCE Commitments on Human Rights in Italy), in AZZONI A. (ed.), *Ricostruire il dialogo: La Presidenza italiana dell'OSCE nel 2018*, Pisa, 2020, p. 153 ff.

ASTA G., "Il contributo della Dichiarazione universale dei diritti umani alla lotta contro la schiavitù e le altre gravi forme di sfruttamento umano" (The Contribution of the Universal Declaration of Human Rights to the Fight against Slavery and other Serious Forms of Human Exploitation), in TONOLO S. and PASCALE G. (eds.), *La Dichiarazione universale dei diritti umani nel diritto internazionale contemporaneo*, Torino, 2020, p. 215 ff.

BERGAMINI E., "La Dichiarazione universale dei diritti umani nella giurisprudenza della Corte di giustizia dell'Unione europea" (The Universal Declaration of Human Rights in the Case Law of the Court of Justice of the European Union), in TONOLO S. and PASCALE G. (eds.), *La Dichiarazione universale dei diritti umani nel diritto internazionale contemporaneo*, Torino, 2020, p. 109 ff.

BERTÒ E. and MARCANTONI M. (eds.), *30 voci per 30 diritti. Liberi commenti agli articoli della Dichiarazione Universale dei Diritti Umani*, Trento, 2020, pp. 232.

BIAGIONI G., "The Convention on the Rights of the Child and the EU Judicial Cooperation in Civil Matters", DUDI, 2020, p. 365 ff.

BORLINI L. and CREMA L., "The Legal Status of Decisions by Human Rights Treaty Bodies: Authoritative Interpretations or Mission Éducatrice?", Global Community Yearbook of International Law and Jurisprudence, 2020, p. 129 ff.

BOSCO G., "The Protection of the Rohingya Population", in CARACCIOLO I. and MONTUORO U. (eds.), *Protection of Cultural and Religious Minorities. Leadership for International Peace and Security*, Torino, 2019, p. 143 ff.

BUONOMENNA F., "L'influenza della Dichiarazione universale dei diritti umani sul diritto ad avere una cittadinanza e brevi considerazioni sull'apolidia nel diritto internazionale" (The Influence of the Universal Declaration of Human Rights on the Right to Citizenship and Some Remarks on Statelessness in International Law), in TONOLO S. and PASCALE G. (eds.), *La Dichiarazione universale dei diritti umani nel diritto internazionale contemporaneo*, Torino, 2020, p. 437 ff.

CADONNA M., "Il diritto di voto nell'interpretazione del Comitato per i diritti delle persone con disabilità: oltre la prassi del Comitato per i diritti umani e della Corte europea dei diritti dell'uomo" (The Right to Vote in the Interpretation of the Committee on the Rights of Persons with Disabilities: Beyond the Practice of the Human Rights Committee and the European Court of Human Rights), CI, 2020, p. 625 ff.

CALIGIURI A., "La 'corporate civil liability' nell'ordinamento giuridico canadese" (The "Corporate Civil Liability" in the Canadian Legal System), DUDI, 2020, p. 607 ff.

CARACCIOLO I. and MONTUORO U. (eds.), *Protection of Cultural and Religious Minorities. Leadership for International Peace and Security*, Torino, 2019, pp. 344.

CARACCIOLO I., "Protecting Religious and Cultural Minorities in the Perspective of International Criminal Law", in CARACCIOLO I. and MONTUORO U. (eds.), *Protection of Cultural and Religious Minorities. Leadership for International Peace and Security*, Torino, 2019, p. 69 ff.

CARCANO A., *Notable Cases of the European Court of Human Rights on the Right to Life. Materials and Analysis*, Torino, 2020, pp. 304.

CARLI E., "Trattenimento di migranti a bordo di navi, divieto di detenzione arbitraria e responsabilità internazionale dell'Italia" (International Responsibility of Italy for Arbitrary Detention of Migrants on Ships), DUDI, 2020, p. 689 ff.

CARPANELLI E., "La Dichiarazione universale dei diritti umani e il divieto di tortura" (The Universal Declaration of Human Rights and the Prohibition of Torture), in TONOLO S. and PASCALE G. (eds.), *La Dichiarazione universale dei diritti umani nel diritto internazionale contemporaneo*, Torino, 2020, p. 237 ff.

CARTA M.C., "Le incognite della nuova competenza consultiva della Corte EDU ispirata al rinvio pregiudiziale alla Corte di giustizia UE" (The Unknowns of the New Advisory Jurisdiction of the ECHR Inspired by the Preliminary Ruling Procedure to the EU Court of Justice), OIDU, 2020, p. 559 ff.

CASTELLANETA M., "La revisione della normativa italiana sulla sanzione del carcere nei casi di diffamazione a mezzo stampa dopo l'ordinanza n. 132/2020 della Corte costituzionale" (The Reform of Italian Legislation Providing for Custodial Sentences in the Event of Defamation through the Press after the Constitutional Court's Order No. 132/2020), RDI, 2020, p. 1043 ff.

CATALDI G., "Reflections on the Right of Property under the ECHR in the Light of the Jurisprudence of the Court of Strasbourg concerning Italy", in *Enjeux et Perspectives. Droit international, droit de la mer, droits de l'homme. Melanges en l'honneur de la Professeure Haritini Dipla*, Paris, 2020, p. 271 ff.

CERETTI A. and CORNELLI R. (eds.), *Milano-Bogotà. Percorsi di giustizia nella Colombia dopo l'Accordo di pace* (Milan-Bogotà. Pathways to justice in Colombia after the Peace Agreement), Torino, 2020, pp. 224.

CHECHI A., "When Culture and Human Rights Collide: The Long Road to the Elimination of Gender-Based Harmful Traditional Practices", OIDU, 2020, p. 839 ff.

CHIUSSI CURZI L., *General Principles for Business and Human Rights in International Law*, Leiden, 2020, pp. 356.

CILIBERTO G., "La Dichiarazione universale dei diritti umani e l'evoluzione della tutela internazionale della libertà religiosa" (The Universal Declaration of

Human Rights and the Evolution of the International Protection of Religious Freedom), in TONOLO S. and PASCALE G. (eds.), *La Dichiarazione universale dei diritti umani nel diritto internazionale contemporaneo*, Torino, 2020, p. 261 ff.

CITRONI G., "The Indigenous Peoples' Right to Lands and Natural Resources in the Inter-American Human Rights System: Preserving Cultural Identity while Ensuring Development", in DI BLASE A. and VADI V. (eds.), *The Inherent Rights of Indigenous Peoples in International Law*, Roma, 2020, p. 123 ff.

CREMA L., "The Convention on the Rights of the Child Before the UN Treaty Bodies and the ICJ: 'Taking into Account' or Ignoring?", DUDI, 2020, p. 79 ff.

DANISI C., "La tutela della vita privata e familiare nella Dichiarazione universale dei diritti umani: standard superati o ancora potenziali?" (The Protection of Private and Family Life in the Universal Declaration of Human Rights: Outdated or Still Effective Standards?), in TONOLO S. and PASCALE G. (eds.), *La Dichiarazione universale dei diritti umani nel diritto internazionale contemporaneo*, Torino, 2020, p. 287 ff.

DE SENA P., "Slaveries and New Slaveries: Which Role for Human Dignity?", in GATTINI A., GARCIANDIA R. and WEBB P. (eds.), *Human Dignity and International Law*, Leiden, 2020, p. 113 ff.

DE VIDO S., "Violence against Women's Health through the Law of the UN Security Council: A Critical International Feminist Law Analysis of Resolutions 2467 (2019) and 2493 (2019) within the WPS agenda", QIL, Zoom-in 74, 2020, p. 3 ff.

DEANA F., "L'incidenza della Dichiarazione universale dei diritti umani sulla libertà di opinione e di espressione nell'era dell'odio online" (The Impact of the Universal Declaration of Human Rights on the Freedom of Opinion and Expression in the Era of Hate Online), in TONOLO S. and PASCALE G. (eds.), *La Dichiarazione universale dei diritti umani nel diritto internazionale contemporaneo*, Torino, 2020, p. 321 ff.

DELLA MORTE G., "Quanto *Immuni*? Luci, ombre e penombre dell'app selezionata dal Governo italiano" (How Much Immune? Lights, Shadows and Penumbra of the App Selected by the Italian Government), DUDI, 2020, p. 303 ff.

DI BLASE A. and VADI V. (eds.), *The Inherent Rights of Indigenous Peoples in International Law*, Roma, 2020, pp. 327.

DI BLASE A. and VADI V., "Introducing the Inherent Rights of Indigenous Peoples", in DI BLASE A. and VADI V. (eds.), *The Inherent Rights of Indigenous Peoples in International Law*, Roma, 2020, p. 19 ff.

DI BLASE A., "The Self-Determination of Indigenous Peoples", in DI BLASE A. and VADI V. (eds.), *The Inherent Rights of Indigenous Peoples in International Law*, Roma, 2020, p. 47 ff.

DI FILIPPO M., "Walking the (Barbed) Wire of the Prohibition of Collective Expulsion: An Assessment of the Strasbourg Case Law", DUDI, 2020, p. 479 ff.

DI GIANNI F., "Note sulla tutela della salute dei migranti in condizione irregolare" (Notes on the Protection of the Health of Migrants in Irregular Condition), CI, 2020, p. 681 ff.

DI STASI A., "La Dichiarazione universale dei diritti umani nella giurisprudenza della Corte interamericana" (The Universal Declaration of Human Rights in the Case Law of the Inter-American Court), in TONOLO S. and PASCALE G. (eds.), *La Dichiarazione universale dei diritti umani nel diritto internazionale contemporaneo*, Torino, 2020, p. 67 ff.

ERRICO S., "ILO Convention No. 169 in Asia: Progress and Challenges", International Journal of Human Rights, 2020, p. 156 ff.

FARNELLI G.M., "Proporzionalità ed emergenza sanitaria da COVID-19 nei parametri CEDU" (Proportionality and COVID-19 Health Emergency within the European Convention on Human Rights), CI, 2020, p. 97 ff.

FASCIGLIONE M., *I Principi Guida su Imprese e Diritti Umani* (Guiding Principles on Business and Human Rights), Roma, 2020, pp. xiv-68.

FAVUZZA F., "Il rilievo della Dichiarazione universale dei diritti umani nella definizione del diritto alla libertà e alla sicurezza personale" (The Importance of the Universal Declaration of Human Rights in Defining the Right to Liberty and Personal Security), in TONOLO S. and PASCALE G. (eds.), *La Dichiarazione universale dei diritti umani nel diritto internazionale contemporaneo*, Torino, 2020, p. 185 ff.

FERRARA M., "L'ordinanza cautelare della Corte internazionale di giustizia nel caso Gambia c. Myanmar: la prova dell'intento genocidario tra giurisdizione prima facie e test di plausibilità della pretesa" (The Order on Provisional Measures of the International Court of Justice in The Gambia v. Myanmar Case: The Evidence of the Genocidal Intent Between Prima Facie Jurisdiction and Plausibility Test of the Claim), DUDI, 2020, p. 551 ff.

FOCARELLI C., "Indigenous Peoples' Rights in International Law: The *Ogiek* Decision by the African Court of Human and Peoples' Rights", in DI BLASE A. and VADI V. (eds.), *The Inherent Rights of Indigenous Peoples in International Law*, Roma, 2020, p. 175 ff.

FORLATI S., "The Role of the European Court of Human Rights in the Development of Rules on Universal Civil Jurisdiction: Naït-Liman v Switzerland in the Transition between the Chamber and the Grand Chamber", in FORLATI S., FRANZINA P. and LA MANNA M. (eds.), *Universal Civil Jurisdiction – Which Way Forward?*, Leiden, 2020, p. 38 ff.

FORLATI S., FRANZINA P. and LA MANNA M. (eds.), *Universal Civil Jurisdiction – Which Way Forward?*, Leiden, 2020, pp. 219.

FRANCIONI F., "Pluralism, Universality and the Challenge of Global Public Goods", in CARACCIOLO I. and MONTUORO U. (eds.), *Protection of Cultural and Religious Minorities. Leadership for International Peace and Security*, Torino, 2019, p. 175 ff.

FRANZINA P., "The Changing Face of Adjudicatory Jurisdiction", in FORLATI S., FRANZINA P. and LA MANNA M. (eds.), *Universal Civil Jurisdiction – Which Way Forward?*, Leiden, 2020, p. 170 ff.

FRULLI M., "The Promise of International Criminal Justice: Achievements and Failures in Protecting Human Dignity", in GATTINI A., GARCIANDIA R. and WEBB P. (eds.), *Human Dignity and International Law*, Leiden, 2020, p. 52 ff.

GAGLIARDI S., *Minority Rights, Feminism and International Law*, London, 2020, pp. 202.

GATTINI A., "Pure Theory of Law Amidst the Tempest: Hans Kelsen, Democracy and Human Rights", in GATTINI A., GARCIANDIA R. and WEBB P. (eds.), *Human Dignity and International Law*, Leiden, 2020, p. 22 ff.

GATTINI A., "Setting the Scene: 100 Years of Human Dignity", in GATTINI A., GARCIANDIA R. and WEBB P. (eds.), *Human Dignity and International Law*, Leiden, 2020, p. 1 ff.

GATTINI A., GARCIANDIA R. and WEBB P. (eds.), *Human Dignity and International Law*, Leiden, 2020, pp. 235.

GRAZIANI F., "The *Molla Sali* Case before the ECtHR: Religious Pluralism v. Right to Self-Identification as a Minority's Member", in CARACCIOLO I. and MONTUORO U. (eds.), *Protection of Cultural and Religious Minorities. Leadership for International Peace and Security*, Torino, 2019, p. 195 ff.

IPPOLITO F., "Adjudicating Human Dignity of Irregular Migrants", in GATTINI A., GARCIANDIA R. and WEBB P. (eds.), *Human Dignity and International Law*, Leiden, 2020, p. 194 ff.

IPPOLITO F., "The Convention on the Rights of the Child in Litigation before the European Social Charter Committee and the European Court of Human Rights: 'Why Then, Can One Desire Too Much of a Good Thing?'", DUDI, 2020, p. 93 ff.

IPPOLITO F., *Understanding Vulnerability in International Human Rights Law*, Napoli, 2020, pp. xiv-452.

LA MANNA M., "Residual Jurisdiction under the Brussels I bis Regulation: An Unexpected Avenue to Address Extraterritorial Corporate Human Rights Violations", in FORLATI S., FRANZINA P. and LA MANNA M. (eds.), *Universal Civil Jurisdiction – Which Way Forward?*, Leiden, 2020, p. 140 ff.

LENZERINI F., "International Human Rights Law and Self-Determination of Peoples Related to the United States Occupation of the Hawaiian Kingdom", in SAI D.K. (ed.), *The Royal Commission of Inquiry: Investigating War Crimes and Human Rights Violations in the Hawaiian Kingdom*, Honolulu, 2020, p. 174 ff.

LENZERINI F., "Practice and Ontology of Implied Human Rights in International Law", Intercultural Human Rights Law Review, 2020, p. 73 ff.

LO JACONO C., "The Religious Tolerance between Islam and Christianity", in CARACCIOLO I. and MONTUORO U. (eds.), *Protection of Cultural and Religious Minorities. Leadership for International Peace and Security*, Torino, 2019, p. 231 ff.

MACERATINI A., "New Technologies, Big Data and Human Rights: An Overview", in CALIGIURI A. (ed.), *Legal Technology Transformation. A Practical Assessment*, Napoli, 2020, p. 11 ff.

MANCA L., "Il fenomeno corruttivo nella prassi degli organi di controllo delle Nazioni Unite sulla tutela dei diritti umani" (The Corruptive Phenomenon in the Practice of the UN Human Rights Monitoring Bodies), OIDU, 2020, p. 609 ff.

MARCHEGIANI P., MORGERA E. and PARKS L., "Indigenous Peoples' Rights to Natural Resources in Argentina: The Challenges of Impact Assessment, Consent and Fair and Equitable Benefit-Sharing in cases of Lithium Mining", International Journal of Human Rights, 2020, p. 224 ff.

MARONGIU BONAIUTI F., "Limitations to the Exercise of Civil Jurisdiction in Areas Other Than Reparation for International Crimes", in FORLATI S., FRANZINA P. and LA MANNA M. (eds.), Universal Civil Jurisdiction – Which Way Forward?, Leiden, 2020, p. 120 ff.

MARRANI D., "Genetic Information, Artificial Intelligence (AI) and Human Rights: Balancing Individual and Collective Interest", OIDU, 2020, p. 626 ff.

MINERVINI G., "Viola v. Italy: A First Step towards the End of Life Imprisonment in Italy", IYIL, Vol. XXIX-2019, 2020, p. 217 ff.

MONTINI M., "Verso una giustizia climatica basata sulla tutela dei diritti umani" (Towards a Climate Justice Based on Human Rights Protection), OIDU, 2020, p. 506 ff.

MONTUORO U., "The Suppression of Religious and Cultural Identities: An Evil as Old as Athens", in CARACCIOLO I. and MONTUORO U. (eds.), Protection of Cultural and Religious Minorities. Leadership for International Peace and Security, Torino, 2019, p. 319 ff.

MOTTESE A., "Ergastolo e diritti umani nella prospettiva del diritto internazionale ed europeo" (Life Imprisonment and Human Rights: An International and European Law Perspective), DUDI, 2020, p. 55 ff.

MUSSI F., "Articolo 14" (Article 14), in BERTÒ E. and MARCANTONI M. (eds.), 30 voci per 30 diritti. Liberi commenti agli articoli della Dichiarazione Universale dei Diritti Umani, Trento, 2020, p. 92 ff.

MUSSI F., "Cambiamento climatico, migrazioni e diritto alla vita: le considerazioni del Comitato dei diritti umani delle Nazioni Unite nel caso Teitiota c. Nuova Zelanda" (Climate Change, Migration and Right to Life: The Views Rendered by the Human Rights Committee in the Teitiota v. New Zealand Case), RDI, 2020, p. 827 ff.

MUSSI F., "La Dichiarazione universale dei diritti umani e i diritti 'di movimento' dei migranti: il diritto di ciascuno di lasciare ogni Paese, incluso il proprio, e il diritto di cercare e godere di asilo dalla persecuzione" (The Universal Declaration of Human Rights and the Migrant's Rights of Movement: The Right to Leave Any Country Including One's Own, and the Right to Seek and Enjoy Asylum), in TONOLO S. and PASCALE G. (eds.), La Dichiarazione universale dei diritti umani nel diritto internazionale contemporaneo, Torino, 2020, p. 413 ff.

MUSSI F., "La sentenza N.D. e N.T. della Corte europea dei diritti umani: uno 'schiaffo' ai diritti dei migranti alle frontiere terrestri?" (The ECtHR's Judgment in the Case of N.D. and N.T.: A "Slap" to Migrants' Rights at the Land Borders?), SIDIBlog, 19 marzo 2020.

NALIN E., "COVID-19 e deroghe e restrizioni alla Convenzione europea dei diritti dell'uomo" (COVID-19, Derogations and Limitations under the European Convention on Human Rights), Studi sull'integrazione europea, 2020, p. 629 ff.

NESI G., "Articolo 9" (Article 9), in BERTÒ E. and MARCANTONI M. (eds.), *30 voci per 30 diritti. Liberi commenti agli articoli della Dichiarazione Universale dei Diritti Umani*, Trento, 2020, p. 69 ff.

PADELLETTI M.L., "La riforma della prescrizione tra diritti dell'imputato e della persona offesa: riflessioni dal punto di vista della Convenzione europea dei diritti dell'uomo" (The Reform of the Statute of Limitations and Possible Effects on the Rights of the Accused and the Offended Person: Some Reflections in Light of the European Convention on Human Rights), DUDI, 2020, p. 461 ff.

PANELLA L., "La Dichiarazione universale dei diritti umani e i diritti delle donne" (The Universal Declaration of Human Rights and Women's Rights), in TONOLO S. and PASCALE G. (eds.), *La Dichiarazione universale dei diritti umani nel diritto internazionale contemporaneo*, Torino, 2020, p. 367 ff.

PAPA M., "The Hazara of Afghanistan. The Most Neglected Minority in a Country of Minorities", in CARACCIOLO I. and MONTUORO U. (eds.), *Protection of Cultural and Religious Minorities. Leadership for International Peace and Security*, Torino, 2019, p. 257 ff.

PAPA M.I., "La Dichiarazione universale dei diritti umani nella giurisprudenza della Corte internazionale di giustizia" (The Universal Declaration of Human Rights in the Case Law of the International Court of Justice), in TONOLO S. and PASCALE G. (eds.), *La Dichiarazione universale dei diritti umani nel diritto internazionale contemporaneo*, Torino, 2020, p. 3 ff.

PASCALE G., "La Dichiarazione universale dei diritti umani nella prassi della Commissione africana e nella giurisprudenza della Corte africana dei diritti umani e dei popoli" (The Universal Declaration of Human Rights in the Practice of the African Commission and in the Jurisprudence of the African Court of Human and Peoples' Rights), in TONOLO S. and PASCALE G. (eds.), *La Dichiarazione universale dei diritti umani nel diritto internazionale contemporaneo*, Torino, 2020, p. 85 ff.

PIETROBON A., "State Negationism and the Rule of Law", in GATTINI A., GARCIANDIA R. and WEBB P. (eds.), *Human Dignity and International Law*, Leiden, 2020, p. 164 ff.

PIRRONE P., "I primi pareri pregiudiziali della Corte europea dei diritti umani: aspetti procedurali" (The First Preliminary Advisory Opinions of the European Court of Human Rights: Procedural Aspects), 2020, DUDI, p. 531 ff.

PIRRONE P., "La Convenzione sui diritti del fanciullo nell'ordinamento italiano a trent' anni dalla sua adozione" (The Effects of the Convention on the Rights of the Child in the Italian Legal System Thirty Years after Its Adoption), RDI, 2020, p. 389 ff.

PISILLO MAZZESCHI R., *Diritto internazionale dei diritti umani. Teoria e prassi* (International Human Rights Law. Theory and Practice), Torino, 2020, pp. xlvi-412.

PITEA C. and ZIRULIA S., "L'obbligo di sbarcare i naufraghi in un luogo sicuro: prove di dialogo tra diritto penale e diritto internazionale a margine del caso Sea Watch" (The Duty to Disembark Rescued Migrants in a Safe Place: A Dialogue Between Criminal Law and International Law Around the Sea-Watch Case), DUDI, 2020, p. 569 ff.

POLEGRI F., "Ergastolo ostativo e Corte europea dei diritti dell'uomo: riflessioni a margine della sentenza resa nel caso Marcello Viola c. Italia (n. 2)" (Life Imprisonment and the European Court of Human Rights: Reflections on the Judgment in the Case Marcello Viola v. Italy (No. 2)), RDI, 2020, p. 174 ff.

POLI L., "Equilibri istituzionali alla prova nella prima procedura d'infrazione di fronte alla Corte europea dei diritti umani" (Testing Institutional Equilibrium in the First Infringement Procedure before the ECtHR), DUDI, 2020, p. 761 ff.

POLLICINO O., "Metaphors and Judicial Frame: Why Legal Imagination (also) Matters in the Protection of Fundamental Rights in the Digital Age", in PETKOVA B. and OJANEN T. (eds.), *Fundamental Rights Protection Online. The Future Regulation of Intermediaries*, Cheltenham, 2020, pp. 352.

PONTECORVO C.M., "Il diritto internazionale ai tempi del (nuovo) Coronavirus: prime considerazioni sulla recente epidemia di 'COVID-19'" (International Law at the Time of (New) Coronavirus: First Remarks on the Recent "COVID-19" Pandemics), DUDI, 2020, p. 195 ff.

PUSTORINO P., "La Dichiarazione universale dei diritti umani nella giurisprudenza della Corte europea dei diritti umani" (The Universal Declaration of Human Rights in the Case Law of the European Court of Human Rights), in TONOLO S. and PASCALE G. (eds.), *La Dichiarazione universale dei diritti umani nel diritto internazionale contemporaneo*, Torino, 2020, p. 55 ff.

PUSTORINO P., *Lezioni di tutela internazionale dei diritti umani* (Course on the International Protection of Human Rights), 2nd ed., Bari, 2020, pp. 270.

RICCARDI A., "Alla ricerca di una via legale di fuga. Note a margine di M.N. e al. c. Belgio di fronte alla Corte europea dei diritti umani" (In Search of a Legal Escape Route. Some Preliminary Thoughts on M.N. et al. v. Belgium before the European Court of Human Rights), Studi sull'integrazione europea, 2020, p. 693 ff.

RICCARDI A., "La Dichiarazione universale dei diritti umani nella giurisprudenza della Corte penale internazionale" (The Universal Declaration of Human Rights in the Jurisprudence of the International Criminal Court), in TONOLO S. and PASCALE G. (eds.), *La Dichiarazione universale dei diritti umani nel diritto internazionale contemporaneo*, Torino, 2020, p. 33 ff.

RUOPPO R., "L'inammissibilità della rinuncia abdicativa al diritto di proprietà: un esempio di dialogo costruttivo tra Corte europea dei diritti dell'uomo e giurisprudenza nazionale" (The Inadmissibility of Extinguishing the Right to Property through Renounciation: An Example of Constructive Dialogue between the European Court of Human Rights and National Courts), RDI, 2020, p. 1106 ff.

RUOTOLO G.M., "A Little Hate, Worldwide! Di libertà d'opinione e discorsi politici d'odio on-line nel diritto internazionale ed europeo" (A Little Hate, Worldwide! On Freedom of Opinion and On-line Political Hate Speech in International and European Law), DUDI, 2020, p. 549 ff.

RUSSO D. and PARODI M., "The Implementation of the Convention on the Rights of the Child in the Italian Legal Order: A Provisional Balance", DUDI, 2020, p. 141 ff.

SACCUCCI A., "The Case of Näit-Liman before the European Court of Human Rights: A Forum Non Conveniens for Asserting the Right of Access to a Court in Relation to Civil Claims for Torture Committed Abroad?", in FORLATI S., FRANZINA P. and LA MANNA M. (eds.), *Universal Civil Jurisdiction – Which Way Forward?*, Leiden, 2020, p. 3 ff.

SARZO M., "Human Dignity in International Labour Rights", in GATTINI A., GARCIANDIA R. and WEBB P. (eds.), *Human Dignity and International Law*, Leiden, 2020, p. 71 ff.

SAVARESE E., "'What Is Done, Is Done': come non espugnare la filiazione internazionalprivatistica, ma armonizzarla con i diritti umani" ('What Is Done, Is Done': How not to Storm Parent-Child in Private International Law, but to Harmonize It with Human Rights Law), DUDI, 2020, p. 265 ff.

SAVARESE E., "L'espansività del diritto alla vita a partire dalla Dichiarazione universale dei diritti umani" (The Right to Life Starting from the Universal Declaration of Human Rights), in TONOLO S. and PASCALE G. (eds.), *La Dichiarazione universale dei diritti umani nel diritto internazionale contemporaneo*, Torino, 2020, p. 157 ff.

SINAGRA A., "Protection of Cultural and Historical Majority", in CARACCIOLO I. and MONTUORO U. (eds.), *Protection of Cultural and Religious Minorities. Leadership for International Peace and Security*, Torino, 2019, p. 309 ff.

STIANO A., "Il diritto alla privacy alla prova della sorveglianza di massa e dell'intelligence sharing: la prospettiva della Corte europea dei diritti dell'uomo (Right to Privacy at the Test of Mass Surveillance and Intelligence Sharing: The Approach of the European Court of Human Rights), RDI, 2020, p. 591 ff.

SULLO P., "Transitional Justice in the Libyan Constitutional Transition", DUDI, 2020, p. 709 ff.

TERRASI A., "Protection of Personal Data and Human Rights between the ECHR and the EU Legal Order", in CALIGIURI A. (ed.), *Legal Technology Transformation. A Practical Assessment*, Napoli, 2020, p. 21 ff.

TONOLO S. and PASCALE G. (eds.), *La Dichiarazione universale dei diritti umani nel diritto internazionale contemporaneo* (The Universal Declaration of Human Rights in Contemporary International Law), Torino, 2020, pp. xx-496.

TRAMONTANA E., "The UN Convention on the Rights of the Child's Role in Litigation before the Committee of Experts of the African Children's Charter", DUDI, 2020, p. 121 ff.

TREVES T., "Italian International Lawyers Facing Racial Laws: The Fate of Angelo Piero Sereni and Edoardo Vitta", in GATTINI A., GARCIANDIA R. and WEBB P. (eds.), *Human Dignity and International Law*, Leiden, 2020, p. 9 ff.

VADI V., "The Spatio-Temporal Dimensions of Indigenous Peoples Sovereignty in International Law", in DI BLASE A. and VADI V. (eds.), *The Inherent Rights of Indigenous Peoples in International Law*, Roma, 2020, p. 91 ff.

VILLANI U., "Le misure italiane di contrasto al COVID-19 e il rispetto dei diritti umani" (Italian Measures to Combat COVID-19 and the Respect for Human Rights), CI, 2020, p. 165 ff.

ZANOBETTI A., "La Dichiarazione universale dei diritti umani e la protezione e promozione dei diritti dei minori" (The Universal Declaration of Human Rights and the Protection and Promotion of the Rights of the Child), in TONOLO S. and PASCALE G. (eds.), *La Dichiarazione universale dei diritti umani nel diritto internazionale contemporaneo*, Torino, 2020, p. 397 ff.

ZARRA G., "Sulla compatibilità di misure restrittive, adottate in Italia e nella Regione Campania per contenere l'epidemia di COVID-19, con gli articoli 5 e 2 del Protocollo n. 4 CEDU" (The Compatibility with Articles 5 and 2, Protocol No. 4, ECHR of the Restrictive Measures Adopted by the Italian Government and the Campania Region to Face the Coronavirus Pandemic), DUDI, 2020, p. 581 ff.

XIII. INTERNATIONAL CRIMINAL LAW

ACQUAROLI R., "Blockchain and Criminal Risk", in CALIGIURI A. (ed.), *Legal Technology Transformation. A Practical Assessment*, Napoli, 2020, p. 189 ff.

ANNONI A., "International Cooperation for the Repression of Core Crimes. What Role for the UNTOC?", in FORLATI S. (ed.), *The Palermo Convention at 20. Institutional and Substantive Challenges*, Leiden, 2020, p. 22 ff.

CARCANO A., "On the Exercise of the Judicial Function at the International Criminal Court: Issues of Credibility and Structural Design", QIL, Zoom-in 67, 2020, p. 3 ff.

COLACINO N., "'Sfruttamento e abuso sessuale' nelle operazioni di pace. Le fattispecie di illecito, le misure internazionali di contrasto e i profili di responsabilità" ("Exploitation and sexual abuse" in Peacekeeping Operations. Offenses, International Legal Repressive Measures and Cases of Liability), Napoli, 2020, pp. 321.

FORLATI S. (ed.), *The Palermo Convention at 20. Institutional and Substantive Challenges*, Leiden, 2020, pp. 90.

FORLATI S., "Droit à la vie, à la liberté, à la sûreté (et aux autres droits humains) en mer: quel rôle dans le cadre de la lutte contre la criminalité?", in RASPAIL H. (ed.), *Les droits de l'homme et la mer*, Paris, 2020, p. 91 ff.

LA MANNA M., *La giurisdizione penale universale nel diritto internazionale* (Universal Criminal Jurisdiction in International Law), Napoli, 2020, pp. xii-272.

LATINO A., "Il diritto alla memoria" (The Right to Memory), in LATTANZI F. (ed.), *Genocidio. Conoscere e ricordare per prevenire*, Roma, 2020, p. 83 ff.

LATTANZI F. (ed.), *Genocidio. Conoscere e ricordare per prevenire* (Genocide. Acknowledging and Remembering in Order to Prevent), Roma, 2020, pp. 144.

LATTANZI F., "La pulizia etnica come genocidio" (Ethnic Cleansing as Genocide), in LATTANZI F. (ed.), *Genocidio. Conoscere e ricordare per prevenire*, Roma, 2020, p. 39 ff.

MARCHESI A., "Crimini contro l'umanità e genocidio, protezione degli individui e protezione dei gruppi" (Crimes against Humanity and Genocide, Protecting

Individuals and Groups), in LATTANZI F. (ed.), *Genocidio. Conoscere e ricordare per prevenire*, Roma, 2020, p. 29 ff.

MOTTESE E., *La lotta contro il danneggiamento e il traffico illecito di beni culturali nel diritto internazionale. La Convenzione di Nicosia del Consiglio d'Europa* (The Fight against the Damaging and Illicit Trafficking in Cultural Objects in International Law. The Nicosia Convention of the Council of Europe), Torino, 2020, pp. 240.

MUSSI F., "Exercising Criminal Jurisdiction over Migrant Smugglers in International Waters: Some Remarks on the Recent Case-Law of Italian Courts", in LIROLA DELGADO I. and GARCÍA PÉREZ R. (eds.), *Seguridad y Fronteras en el Mar*, Valencia, 2020, p. 265 ff.

NESI G. and POLTRONIERI ROSSETTI L., "Member-on-Member Sexual and Gender-Based Crimes as War Crimes: Towards the Progressive Autonomy of International Criminal Responsibility from International Humanitarian Law?", CI, 2020, p. 341 ff.

ODELLO M. and ŁUBIŃSKI P. (eds.), *The Concept of Genocide in International Criminal Law. Developments after Lemkin*, London, 2020, pp. 306.

ODELLO M., "Genocide and Culture: Revisiting their Relationship 70 years after the Genocide Convention", in ODELLO M. and ŁUBIŃSKI P. (eds.), *The Concept of Genocide in International Criminal Law. Developments after Lemkin*, London, 2020, p. 236 ff.

PERTILE M., "The Borders of the Occupied Palestinian Territory are Determined by Customary Law: A Comment on the Prosecutor's Position on the Territorial Jurisdiction of the ICC in the Situation Concerning Palestine", JICJ, 2020, p. 967 ff.

POLTRONIERI ROSSETTI L., "Commentary on Four Decisions of the ICC on matters of Criminal Procedure", in KLIP A. and FREELAND S. (eds.), *Annotated Leading Cases of International Criminal Tribunals*, Cambridge, 2020, p. 50 ff.

POLTRONIERI ROSSETTI L., "Equo processo ed esercizio della giurisdizione penale militare nei confronti di civili" (Due Process and the Exercise of Military Criminal Jurisdiction on Civilians), Giur. It., 2020, vol. 172(1), p. 31 ff.

POLTRONIERI ROSSETTI L., "Le sanzioni dell'amministrazione USA nei confronti della Corte penale internazionale: un nuovo capitolo di una burrascosa relazione" (US Sanctions against the ICC: A New Chapter in a Stormy Relationship), in *Osservatorio sulle attività delle organizzazioni internazionali e sovranazionali, universali e regionali, sui temi di interesse della politica estera italiana*, II-2020, Napoli, p. 19 ff.

PONTI C., "The Review Mechanism of the United Nations Convention against Transnational Organized Crime and Its Protocols. An Analysis Based on Peer Review Methodology", in FORLATI S. (ed.), *The Palermo Convention at 20. Institutional and Substantive Challenges*, Leiden, 2020, p. 22 ff.

SACERDOTI G., "Criminalizing Holocaust Denial: From International Standards to Domestic Implementation. The Case of Italy", in GATTINI A., GARCIANDIA R. and WEBB P., (eds.), *Human Dignity and International Law*, Leiden, 2020, p. 154 ff.

SALERNO F., "Emergenza, delimitazione e implicazioni degli obblighi di natura solidale in tema di prevenzione e repressione del genocidio" (Emergence, Delimitation and Implications of the Obligations of Solidarity in matters of Prevention and Repression of Genocide), in LATTANZI F. (ed.), *Genocidio. Conoscere e ricordare per prevenire*, Roma, 2020, p. 61 ff.

VIRZO R., *La confisca nell'azione internazionale di contrasto ad attività criminali* (Confiscation in the International Fight against Criminal Activities), Napoli, 2020, pp. xiv-250.

XIV. CO-OPERATION IN JUDICIAL, LEGAL, SECURITY, AND SOCIO-ECONOMIC MATTERS

CALIGIURI A., "The Legal Basis of the Principle of *Ne Bis In Idem* in the Italian Criminal System", IYIL, Vol. XXIX-2019, 2020, p. 456 ff.

DIMETTO M., "La punibilità dei giudici internazionali corrotti secondo l'ordinamento italiano" (Criminal Prosecution of Corrupt International Judges According to Italian Law), RDI, 2020, p. 487 ff.

FRIGESSI DI RATTALMA M. (eds.), *La pandemia da COVID-19. Profili di diritto nazionale, dell'Unione europea ed internazionale* (The COVID-19 Pandemic. Aspects of National, European Union and International Law), Torino, 2020, pp. 206.

FRIGESSI DI RATTALMA M. and LAZZARONI M., "Le misure di contenimento della pandemia da Covid-19 e i contratti commerciali internazionali" (Measures to Contain the COVID-19 Pandemic and International Commercial Contracts), in FRIGESSI DI RATTALMA M. (eds.), *La pandemia da COVID-19. Profili di diritto nazionale, dell'Unione europea ed internazionale*, Torino, 2020, p. 39 ff.

GARGIULO P., "Recenti tendenze della cooperazione internazionale in materia di migrazioni. Contenuto, potenzialità e limiti del Global Compact on Migration" (Recent Trends in the Field of International Cooperation on Migration. Content, Strengths and Limits of the Global Compact on Migration), OIDU, 2020, n.1 (Supplemento), p. 1 ff.

GRECO D., "Diritto internazionale e salute pubblica: l'Organizzazione mondiale della sanità alla prova della pandemia di COVID-19" (International Law and Public Health: The World Health Organization in the Time of COVID-19 Pandemic), CI, 2020, p. 203 ff.

MAURO M.R., "'National Security', Foreign Investments and National Screening Procedures: The Italian Regime", IYIL, Vol. XXIX-2019, 2020, p. 199 ff.

ROMANIN JACUR F., "Diritto internazionale e risposta alla pandemia da Covid-19" (International Law and Response to the COVID-19 Pandemic), in FRIGESSI DI RATTALMA M. (eds.), *La pandemia da COVID-19. Profili di diritto nazionale, dell'Unione europea ed internazionale*, Torino, 2020, p. 144 ff.

RONZITTI N., "The Agreement between Italy and Niger on Defence Cooperation", IYIL, Vol. XXIX-2019, 2020, p. 193 ff.

SOSSAI M., "'The Dynamic of Action and Reaction' and the Implementation of the Iran Nuclear Deal", QIL, Zoom-in 66 (2020), p. 5 ff.

VISMARA F., "Redistribuzione della ricchezza, fiscalità e ordinamento internazionale" (Redistribution of Wealth, Taxation and International Law), CI, 2020, p. 189 ff.

ZORZI GIUSTINIANI F., *International Law in Disaster Scenarios. Applicable Rules and Principles*, 2020, pp. 209.

XV.   INTERNATIONAL ECONOMIC LAW

ACCONCI P. and BARONCINI E. (eds.), *Gli effetti dell'emergenza Covid-19 su commercio, investimenti e occupazione. Una prospettiva italiana* (The Effects of the Covid-19 Emergency on Trade, Investment and Employment. An Italian Perspective), Bologna, 2020, pp. xix-442, http://amsacta.unibo. it/6440/#.

ACCONCI P., "The Safeguard of Indigenous Peoples within International and EU Law on Investment. An Overview", in DI BLASE A. and VADI V. (eds.), *The Inherent Rights of Indigenous Peoples in International Law*, Roma, 2020, p. 253 ff.

ACCONCI P., "La promozione della condotta socialmente responsabile delle imprese nel quadro del diritto internazionale e dell'Unione europea in materia di investimenti" (The Promotion of Socially Responsible Business Conduct in the Framework of the International and European Union Law on Investments), in CATERINO D. and INGRAVALLO I. (eds.), *L'impresa sostenibile alla prova del dialogo dei saperi*, Lecce, 2020, p. 427 ff.

ADINOLFI G., "A Tale of Two Crises: quali risposte dell'Organizzazione Mondiale del Commercio alla pandemia da Covid-19?" (A Tale of Two Crises: What Responses to the Covid-19 Pandemic from the World Trade Organizations?), in ACCONCI P. and BARONCINI E. (eds.), *Gli effetti dell'emergenza Covid-19 su commercio, investimenti e occupazione. Una prospettiva italiana*, Bologna, 2020, p. 63 ff.

ARCURI A., "Global Food Safety Standards: The Evolving Regulatory Epistemology at the Intersection of the SPS Agreement and the Codex Alimentarius Commission", in DELIMATSIS P. (ed.), *The Law, Economics and Politics of International Standardisation*, Cambridge, 2020, p. 79 ff.

BORLINI L. and CLARKE P., "International Contestability of Markets and the Visible Hand. Trade Regulation of State-owned Enterprises between Multilateral Impasse and New Free Trade Agreements", Columbia Journal of European Law, 2019/20, p. 84 ff.

BORLINI L. and LONATI S., "Compliance and Privatization of Law Enforcement. A Study of the Italian Legislation in the Light of the US experience", in MAKINWA A. and SØREIDE T. (eds.), *Negotiated Settlements in Bribery Cases: A Principled Approach*, Cheltenham, 2020, p. 278 ff.

BORLINI L. and SILIGARDI S., "Enforcement of International Arbitration Awards", in CHAISSE J., CHOUKROUNE L. and JUSOH S. (eds.), *Handbook of International Investment Law and Policy*, Singapore, 2020, p. 1 ff.

BORLINI L., "On Financial Nationalism and International Law. Sovereignty, Cooperation and Hard/Soft Governance in International Finance", EJIL, 2020, p. 1123 ff.

BORLINI L., "The International Rule of Law and the Role of Transparency in the International Trading System", in LEAL-ARCAS R. (ed.), *The Future of International Economic Law and the Rule of Law*, Chisinau, 2020, p. 25 ff.

BORLINI L., "When the Leviathan Goes to the Market: A Critical Evaluation of the Rules Governing State-Owned Enterprises in Trade Agreements", Leiden JIL, 2020, p. 313 ff.

CAZZINI F., "L'incidenza del Covid-19 sul settore agroalimentare nel quadro dell'OMC e dei controlli sugli investimenti esteri diretti" (The Impact of Covid-19 on the Agri-Food Sector in the Framework of the WTO and on the Controls on Foreign Direct Investments), in ACCONCI P. and BARONCINI E. (eds.), *Gli effetti dell'emergenza Covid-19 su commercio, investimenti e occupazione. Una prospettiva italiana*, Bologna, 2020, p. 135 ff.

COSTAGGIU C., "The Evolution of BITs: Toward Reconciling Foreign Investment Protection and Socio-Economic Human Rights", IYIL, Vol. XXIX-2019, 2020, p. 111 ff.

ESPA I., "Sicurezza alimentare e commercio internazionale ai tempi del Covid-19" (Food Security and International Trade in the Time of Covid-19), in ACCONCI P. and BARONCINI E. (eds.), *Gli effetti dell'emergenza Covid-19 su commercio, investimenti e occupazione. Una prospettiva italiana*, Bologna, 2020, p. 123 ff.

FACCIO S., "Sviluppo sostenibile e investimenti diretti esteri dopo l'emergenza Covid-19: quale ruolo per i contratti di investimento?" (Sustainable Development and Foreign Direct Investments after the Covid-19 Emergency: What Role for Investment Contracts?), in ACCONCI P. and BARONCINI E. (eds.), *Gli effetti dell'emergenza Covid-19 su commercio, investimenti e occupazione. Una prospettiva italiana*, Bologna, 2020, p. 293 ff.

FACCIO S., "The Assessment of the FET Standard between Legitimate Expectations and Economic Impact in the Italian Solar Energy Investment Case Law", QIL, Zoom-in 71, 2020, p. 3 ff.

FACCIO S., *Indirect Expropriation in International Investment Law. Between State Regulatory Powers and Investor Protection*, Napoli, 2020, pp. xii-348.

FARNELLI G.M., "Obblighi positivi dello Stato nell'emergenza sanitaria e diritto internazionale degli investimenti" (Positive Obligations of the State in the Health Emergency and International Investment Law), in ACCONCI P. and BARONCINI E. (eds.), *Gli effetti dell'emergenza Covid-19 su commercio, investimenti e occupazione. Una prospettiva italiana*, Bologna, 2020, p. 225 ff.

GRECO D., "Covid-19 e restrizioni al commercio internazionale: il dialogo (soft) tra OMS e OMC" (Covid-19 and Restrictions to International Trade: The (Soft) Dialogue between WHO and WTO), in ACCONCI P. and BARONCINI E. (eds.), *Gli effetti dell'emergenza Covid-19 su commercio, investimenti e occupazione. Una prospettiva italiana*, Bologna, 2020, p. 23 ff.

GRECO R., *The Human Right to Water and International Economic Law*, Torino, 2020, pp. 288.

LAMPO G., "L'impatto del Covid-19 sui diritti degli investitori stranieri: le misure di contenimento dell'epidemia come espressione del 'power to regulate' dello Stato ospite" (The Impact of Covid-19 on the Rights of Foreign Investors: The Measures of the Host State to Contain the Epidemic as an Expression of the "Power to Regulate"), in ACCONCI P. and BARONCINI E. (eds.), *Gli effetti dell'emergenza Covid-19 su commercio, investimenti e occupazione. Una prospettiva italiana*, Bologna, 2020, p. 239 ff.

LATINO A., "L'impatto del Covid-19 sui contratti commerciali transnazionali alla luce delle 'force majeure' e 'hardship clauses'" (The Impact of Covid-19 on Transnational Commercial Contracts in the light of the "Force Majeure" and "Hardship Clauses"), in ACCONCI P. and BARONCINI E. (eds.), *Gli effetti dell'emergenza Covid-19 su commercio, investimenti e occupazione. Una prospettiva italiana*, Bologna, 2020, p. 265 ff.

MARRELLA F., *Manuale di diritto del commercio internazionale* (Handbook of International Trade Law), 2nd ed., Milano, 2020, pp. xliii-837.

MAURO M.R., "L'effetto del Covid-19 sull'accesso degli investimenti stranieri: le recenti modifiche introdotte nel regime di 'golden power'" (The Impact of Covid-19 on Access of Foreign Investments: Recent Development following the Introduction of the "Golden Power" Regime), in ACCONCI P. and BARONCINI E. (eds.), *Gli effetti dell'emergenza Covid-19 su commercio, investimenti e occupazione. Una prospettiva italiana*, Bologna, 2020, p. 193 ff.

MOLA L. and SALUZZO S., "Temporal Limits to Trade and Investment Measures Coping with a Sanitary Emergency under International Law", in ACCONCI P. and BARONCINI E. (eds.), *Gli effetti dell'emergenza Covid-19 su commercio, investimenti e occupazione. Una prospettiva italiana*, Bologna, 2020, p. 153 ff.

MUCCIONE A., "Le misure di contrasto all'epidemia globale del tabacco alla prova del diritto OMC. Il caso Australia - Tobacco Plain Packaging" (Measures Combatting the Global Epidemy of Tobacco Tested against WTO Law. The Case Australia - Tobacco Plain Packaging), RDI, 2020, p. 143 ff.

PERONI G., *Stabilità economica e sostenibilità nel diritto internazionale* (Economic Stability and Sustainability in International Law), Milano, 2020, pp. xvi-416.

RENGHINI C., "Protection and Trade of Non-Personal Data", in CALIGIURI A. (ed.), *Legal Technology Transformation. A Practical Assessment*, Napoli, 2020, p. 40 ff.

RUSSO D., "The Attribution to States of the Conduct of Public Enterprises in the Fields of Investment and Human Rights Law", IYIL, Vol. XXIX-2019, 2020, p. 93 ff.

SACERDOTI G. and MARIANI P., "The Negotiations on the Future Trade Relations", in FABBRINI F. (ed.), *The Law & Politics of Brexit: Volume II: The Withdrawal Agreement*, Oxford, 2020, p. 212 ff.

SACERDOTI G., "Is USMCA Really 'The New Gold Standard' of Investment Protection?", Columbia FDI Perspectives on Topical Foreign Direct Investment Issues, No. 281, 2020.

SACERDOTI G., "L'adieu au multilatéralisme? Quel avenir pour la mondialisation du droit?", in JOURDAIN-FORTIER C. (ed.), *Sources du droit, commerce inter-*

national, éthique et marchés, 50 ans de travaux de l'école de Dijon, vol.53, Paris, 2020, p. 93 ff.

SACERDOTI G., "Multilateralism and the WTO in the Post Covid-19 World", IYIL, Vol. XXIX-2019, 2020, p. 3 ff.

SACERDOTI G., "Quo Vadis WTO After Covid-19?", in ACCONCI P. and BARONCINI E. (eds.), *Gli effetti dell'emergenza Covid-19 su commercio, investimenti e occupazione. Una prospettiva italiana*, Bologna, 2020, p. 47 ff.

TIGNINO M., "Human Rights Standards in International Finance and Development: The Challenges Ahead", in MCINTYRE O. and NANWANI S. (eds.), *The Practice of Independent Accountability Mechanisms (IAMs). Towards Good Governance in Development Finance*, Leiden, 2019, p. 105 ff.

VADI V., "The Protection of Indigenous Cultural Heritage in International Investment Law and Arbitration", in DI BLASE A. and VADI V. (eds.), *The Inherent Rights of Indigenous Peoples in International Law*, Roma, 2020, p. 203 ff.

VEZZANI S., "The Protection of Traditional Knowledge of Agricultural Interest in International Law", in DI BLASE A. and VADI V. (eds.), *The Inherent Rights of Indigenous Peoples in International Law*, Roma, 2020, p. 279 ff.

VITERBO A., *Sovereign Debt Restructuring: The Role and Limits of Public International Law*, Torino, 2020, pp. 288.

ZAMBRANO V., "Il diritto a godere dei benefici del progresso scientifico: profili problematici di un diritto ancora in cerca di effettività" (The Right to Enjoy Benefits of Scientific Progress: Problematic Aspects of a Right Still Looking to be Fulfilled), CI, 2020, p. 415 ff.

ZANIBONI E., *Sovranità responsabile e processi redistributivi della ricchezza nel diritto internazionale* (Responsible Sovereignty and Processes for the Redistribution of Wealth in International Law), Torino, 2020, pp. 256.

ZARRA G., "International Investment Treaties as a Source of Human Rights Obligations for Investors", in BUSCEMI M., LAZZERINI N., MAGI L. and RUSSO D. (eds.), *Legal Sources in Business and Human Rights. Evolving Dynamics in International and European Law*, Leiden, 2020, p. 52 ff.

XVI. INTERNATIONAL ORGANIZATIONS

ACCONCI P., "Editoriale sull'Organizzazione mondiale della sanità alla prova dell'emergenza sanitaria Covid-19" (Editorial on the World Health Organization Facing the Health Emergency Due to the Covid-19), DPCE online, 2020/2, p. xv ff.

ACCONCI P., "La crisi economica al tempo dell'emergenza sanitaria Covid-19. Le reazioni delle organizzazioni internazionali" (The Economic Crisis at the Time of the Covid-19 Health emergency. The Reactions of International Organizations), in *Osservatorio sulle attività delle organizzazioni internazionali e sovranazionali, universali e regionali, sui temi di interesse della politica estera italiana*, Working Paper II-2020, Napoli, p. 9 ff.

ACCONCI P., "The Responses of International Organizations to the Health Emergency Due to the Covid-19. A First Impression", RDI, 2020, p. 415 ff.

ANEMONI V., "Il conflitto in Nagorno-Karabakh e le risposte della Comunità internazionale" (The Conflict in Nagorno-Karabakh and the Reactions of the International Community), in *Osservatorio sulle attività delle organizzazioni internazionali e sovranazionali, universali e regionali, sui temi di interesse della politica estera italiana*, Working Paper II-2020, Napoli, p. 117 ff.

ARCARI M., "Some thoughts in the aftermath of Security Council Resolution 2532 (2020) on Covid-19", QIL, Zoom-out 70, 2020, p. 59 ff.

BARTOLINI G., "Le misure di preparazione alle pandemie previste nei regolamenti sanitari internazionali e la loro (mancata) attuazione" (Preparedness Measures to Pandemics Provided by the International Health Regulations and Their (Failed) Implementation), CI, 2020, p. 367 ff.

BUSCEMI M., *Illeciti delle Nazioni Unite e tutela dell'individuo* (Wrongful Acts of the United Nations and Protection of the Individual), Napoli, 2020, pp. ix-386.

DI TURI C., "The Association of Southeast Asian Nations (ASEAN) under Scrutiny: A New Regional Organization for the Protection of Human Rights and the Peaceful Settlement of Disputes?", OIDU, 2020, p. 225 ff.

DRAETTA U., *Principi di diritto delle organizzazioni internazionali* (Principles of Law of International Organizations), 4th ed., Milano, 2020, pp. xviii-242.

FASOLI E., "La 25a Conferenza delle Parti della Convenzione quadro delle Nazioni Unite sul cambiamento climatico (Madrid, 2019): molti rinvii e qualche speranza" (The 25th Conference of the Parties to the United Nations Framework Convention on Climate Change (Madrid, 2019): Several Postponements and Some Hope), in *Osservatorio sulle attività delle organizzazioni internazionali e sovranazionali, universali e regionali, sui temi di interesse della politica estera italiana*, Working Paper I-2020, Napoli, p. 27 ff.

FASOLI E., "ONU e attività di contrasto al cambiamento climatico: (ulteriore) rallentamento o accelerazione a fronte della pandemia?" (The UN and the Fight against Climate Change: Further Delay or Acceleration in Light of the Pandemic?), in *Osservatorio sulle attività delle organizzazioni internazionali e sovranazionali, universali e regionali, sui temi di interesse della politica esterna italiana*, Working Paper I-2020, Napoli, p. 129 ff.

FUCCI V., *Evolution and Reform of the United Nations System*, Torino, 2020, pp. 128.

GARGIULO P., "Le organizzazioni internazionali tra crisi del multilateralismo e iniziative di neo-protezionismo: conclusioni generali" (International Organizations between the Crisis of Multilateralism and Neo-Protectionism: General Conclusions), OIDU, 2020, n. 3 (Supplemento), p. 182 ff.

GAUDIOSI F., "Le tensioni marittime tra Grecia e Turchia: un ruolo per la NATO?" (Maritime Frictions between Greece and Turkey: A Role for NATO?), in *Osservatorio sulle attività delle organizzazioni internazionali e sovranazionali, universali e regionali, sui temi di interesse della politica estera italiana*, Working Paper II-2020, Napoli, p. 83 ff.

GERACI A., "Il piano strategico di risposta dell'OIM: assistere i migranti e cooperare con i partner internazionali, regionali e nazionali per contrastare il Covid-19. Le priorità promosse e i primi risultati raggiunti" (IOM's Strategic Response Plan: Assisting Migrants and Cooperating with International, Regional and National Partners to Combat Covid-19. The Priorities and the First Results), in *Osservatorio sulle attività delle organizzazioni internazionali e sovranazionali, universali e regionali, sui temi di interesse della politica estera italiana*, Working Paper II-2020, Napoli, p. 91 ff.

GESTRI M., "La risposta delle organizzazioni internazionali alla pandemia e profili di responsabilità dello Stato d'origine" (The Response of International Organizations to the Pandemic and Some Thoughts on the Alleged International Responsibility of China), Rivista italiana di diritto del turismo, Special Issue 2020, p. 19 ff.

LAZZARONI M., *L'aviation safety nel diritto internazionale ed europeo* (Aviation Safety in International and European Union Law), Roma, 2020, pp. 184.

NESI G., "The United Nations Principal Political Organs and the Universal Pandemic: How to Meet, Negotiate and Deliberate under 'New, Extraordinary and Exceptional Circumstances'?", QIL, Zoom-out 70, 2020, p. 5 ff.

PENNETTA P., "Brevi note sul Trattato istitutivo dell'Organization of the African, Caribbean and Pacific States" (A Brief Note about the Treaty Establishing the Organization of African, Caribbean and Pacific States), CI, 2020, p. 477 ff.

SOSSAI M., *Sanzioni delle Nazioni Unite e organizzazioni regionali* (Sanctions of the United Nations and Regional Organizations), Roma, 2020, pp. 196.

TARANTINO L., "La Banca Asiatica d'Investimento per le Infrastrutture: profili giuridico-istituzionali e standard sulla tutela delle persone e dell'ambiente" (The Asian Infrastructure Investment Bank (AIIB): Legal-Institutional Aspects and Standard on the Protection of People and Environment), OIDU, 2020, p. 330 ff.

TOSCANO-RIVALTA M., "Disaster Risk Reduction in Light of the COVID-19 Crisis: Policy and Legal Considerations", QIL, Zoom-out 70, 2020, p. 37 ff.

TREVES R.T., "The Health of International Cooperation and UNGA Resolution 74/274", QIL, Zoom-out 70, 2020, p. 21 ff.

XVII. RELATIONSHIP BETWEEN MUNICIPAL AND INTERNATIONAL LAW

ALÌ A., "L'utilizzo del diritto per il conseguimento di obiettivi politico-strategici" (The Use of Law for the Attainment of Politico-Strategic Objectives), Gnosis, 2020 (2), p. 173 ff.

AMOROSO D., "*Inutiliter data*? La Convenzione delle Nazioni Unite sui diritti delle persone con disabilità nella giurisprudenza italiana" (*Inutiliter data*? The UN Convention on the Rights of Persons with Disabilities in the Italian Case Law), Quaderni di SIDIBlog, 2020, p. 228 ff.

BARATTA R., "L'effetto diretto delle disposizioni internazionali self-executing" (The Direct Effect of Self-Executing Provisions of International Law), RDI, 2020, p. 5 ff.

CARACCIOLO I., "Protratta inesecuzione di un provvedimento giurisdizionale di sgombero (art. 6, par. 1, CEDU; art. 1, Protocollo addizionale)" (Protracted Non-Execution of an Eviction Order (Article 6, para. 1, ECHR; Article 1, Additional Protocol)), in DI STASI A. (ed.), CEDU e ordinamento italiano. La giurisprudenza della Corte europea dei diritti dell'uomo e l'impatto nell'ordinamento interno (2016-2020), Milano, 2020, p. 475 ff.

CARDAMONE D., "Il diritto ad un ricorso giurisdizionale effettivo nei confronti delle misure privative della libertà (art. 5, par. 4, CEDU)" (The Right to an Effective Judicial Remedy against Measures Involving the Deprivation of Liberty (Article 5, para. 4, ECHR)), in DI STASI A. (ed.), CEDU e ordinamento italiano. La giurisprudenza della Corte europea dei diritti dell'uomo e l'impatto nell'ordinamento interno (2016-2020), Milano, 2020, p. 213 ff.

CASSETTI L. and VANNUCCINI S., "Il diritto al rispetto dell'integrità psichica e fisica dei minori di età in condizioni di 'particolare vulnerabilità' (artt. 3 e 8 CEDU)" (The Right to Respect for the Mental and Physical Integrity of Minors in "Particularly Vulnerable" Conditions (Articles 3 and 8 ECHR)), in DI STASI A. (ed.), CEDU e ordinamento italiano. La giurisprudenza della Corte europea dei diritti dell'uomo e l'impatto nell'ordinamento interno (2016-2020), Milano, 2020, p. 131 ff.

COLUCCI V., "Il diritto di visita del minore nella giurisprudenza della Corte europea dei diritti dell'uomo (art. 8 CEDU)" (The Right to Visit of the Minor in the Case law of the European Court of Human Rights), in DI STASI A. (ed.), CEDU e ordinamento italiano. La giurisprudenza della Corte europea dei diritti dell'uomo e l'impatto nell'ordinamento interno (2016-2020), Milano, 2020, p. 591 ff.

D'AVINO G., "La tutela ambientale tra interessi industriali strategici e preminenti diritti fondamentali (art. 8 CEDU)" (Environmental Protection between Strategic Industrial Interests and Preeminent Fundamental Rights (Article 8 ECHR)), in DI STASI A. (ed.), CEDU e ordinamento italiano. La giurisprudenza della Corte europea dei diritti dell'uomo e l'impatto nell'ordinamento interno (2016-2020), Milano, 2020, p. 709 ff.

DE MARZO G., "Legge di interpretazione autentica ed equo processo (art. 6, par. 1, CEDU)" (Law of Authentic Interpretation and Fair Trial (Article 6, para. 1, ECHR)), in DI STASI A. (ed.), CEDU e ordinamento italiano. La giurisprudenza della Corte europea dei diritti dell'uomo e l'impatto nell'ordinamento interno (2016-2020), Milano, 2020, p. 329 ff.

DI STASI A. (ed.), CEDU e ordinamento italiano. La giurisprudenza della Corte europea dei diritti dell'uomo e l'impatto nell'ordinamento interno (2016-2020) (ECHR and Italian Legal Order. The Case Law of the European Court of Human Rights and Its Impact on the Domestic Legal Order (2016-2020)), Milano, 2020, pp. 941.

DI STASI A. and RUSSO I., "La violazione dell'obbligo di motivazione come fattore di iniquità del processo (art. 6, par. 1, CEDU)" (The Violation of the

Obligation to Provide Reasons as a Factor of Unfairness of the Process (Article 6, para. 1, ECHR)), in DI STASI A. (ed.), *CEDU e ordinamento italiano. La giurisprudenza della Corte europea dei diritti dell'uomo e l'impatto nell'ordinamento interno (2016-2020)*, Milano, 2020, p. 404 ff.

DI STASI A., "Il diritto alla vita e all'integrità della persona con particolare riferimento alla violenza domestica (artt. 2 e 3 CEDU)" (The Right to Life and the Integrity of the Person with particular Reference to Domestic Violence (Articles 2 and 3 ECHR)), in DI STASI A. (ed.), *CEDU e ordinamento italiano. La giurisprudenza della Corte europea dei diritti dell'uomo e l'impatto nell'ordinamento interno (2016-2020)*, Milano, 2020, p. 1 ff.

DIDONE A. and DIDONE A., "La ragionevole durata del processo e la legge Pinto (art. 6, par. 1, CEDU)" (The Reasonable Length of the Trial and the Pinto Law (Article 6, para. 1, ECHR)), in DI STASI A. (ed.), *CEDU e ordinamento italiano. La giurisprudenza della Corte europea dei diritti dell'uomo e l'impatto nell'ordinamento interno (2016-2020)*, Milano, 2020, p. 268 ff.

DIOTALLEVI G., "Il giusto processo e la garanzia del diritto di difesa nel sistema multilivello del diritto europeo (art. 6, parr. 1 e 3, CEDU)" (Due Process and the Right of Defense in the European Multilevel System (Article 6, paras. 1 and 3, ECHR)), in DI STASI A. (ed.), *CEDU e ordinamento italiano. La giurisprudenza della Corte europea dei diritti dell'uomo e l'impatto nell'ordinamento interno (2016-2020)*, Milano, 2020, p. 343 ff.

FIORENTIN F. and GALLIANI D., "La dignità umana e le motivazioni della detenzione (art. 3 CEDU)" (Human Dignity and the Reasons for Detention (Article 3 ECHR)), in DI STASI A. (ed.), *CEDU e ordinamento italiano. La giurisprudenza della Corte europea dei diritti dell'uomo e l'impatto nell'ordinamento interno (2016-2020)*, Milano, 2020, p. 57 ff.

FIORENTIN F., "L'ergastolo ostativo e la tutela della dignità umana" (Life Imprisonment and the Protection of Human Dignity), in DI STASI A. (ed.), *CEDU e ordinamento italiano. La giurisprudenza della Corte europea dei diritti dell'uomo e l'impatto nell'ordinamento interno (2016-2020)*, Milano, 2020, p. 60 ff.

GIANNELLI A., "La confisca urbanistica nel dialogo fra le corti dopo la sentenza G.I.E.M. e altri contro Italia (art. 7 CEDU; art. 1, Protocollo addizionale)" (Confiscation in the Dialogue between the Courts after the Judgment in G.I.E.M. and others versus Italy (Article 7 ECHR, Article 1 Additional Protocol)), in DI STASI A. (ed.), *CEDU e ordinamento italiano. La giurisprudenza della Corte europea dei diritti dell'uomo e l'impatto nell'ordinamento interno (2016-2020)*, Milano, 2020, p. 531 ff.

LANA A.G., "Migranti irregolari e Corte di Strasburgo: verso un affievolimento delle tutele? (artt. 5 e 8 CEDU)" (Irregular Migrants and the Strasbourg Court: Towards a Weakening of Protections?), in DI STASI A. (ed.), *CEDU e ordinamento italiano. La giurisprudenza della Corte europea dei diritti dell'uomo e l'impatto nell'ordinamento interno (2016-2020)*, Milano, 2020, p. 235 ff.

MACCHI C. and BRIGHT C., "Hardening Soft Law: The Implementation of Human Rights Due Diligence Requirements in Domestic Legislation", in BUSCEMI M., LAZZERINI N., MAGI L. and RUSSO D. (eds.), *Legal Sources in Business and Human Rights. Evolving Dynamics in International and European Law*, Leiden, 2020, p. 218 ff.

MARRANI D., "Il diritto al rispetto della vita privata nel contesto di trattamenti e cure mediche: la negligenza medica (art. 8 CEDU)" (The Right to Respect for Privacy in the Context of Medical Treatment and Care: Medical Negligence (Article 8 ECHR)), in DI STASI A. (ed.), *CEDU e ordinamento italiano. La giurisprudenza della Corte europea dei diritti dell'uomo e l'impatto nell'ordinamento interno (2016-2020)*, Milano, 2020, p. 693 ff.

MONEGO D., "La Dichiarazione universale dei diritti umani nella giurisprudenza della Corte costituzionale italiana" (The Universal Declaration of Human Rights in the Case Law of the Italian Constitutional Court), in TONOLO S. and PASCALE G. (eds.), *La Dichiarazione universale dei diritti umani nel diritto internazionale contemporaneo*, Torino, 2020, p. 127 ff.

NIGRO R., "La responsabilità oggettiva di Amazon per danni provocati da prodotti difettosi: aspetti problematici della responsabilità dei *marketplace* nel caso *Bolger*" (The Strict Liability of Amazon for Injuries Caused by Defective Products: Controversial Aspects of the Marketplace Liability in the *Bolger* case), Diritto di Internet, 2020, p. 589 ff.

NINO M., "La problematica della compatibilità delle *extraordinary renditions* e del segreto di stato italiano con la Convenzione europea dei diritti umani (artt. 3, 5, 8 e 13 CEDU)" (The Compatibility of Extraordinary Renditions and State Secret under Italian Law with the European Convention of Human Rights (Articles 3, 5, 8 and 13 ECHR)), in DI STASI A. (ed.), *CEDU e ordinamento italiano. La giurisprudenza della Corte europea dei diritti dell'uomo e l'impatto nell'ordinamento interno (2016-2020)*, Milano, 2020, p. 174 ff.

ORIOLO A., "Equo processo e rinnovazione in appello dell'istruttoria dibattimentale (art. 6, par. 1, CEDU)" (Fair Trial and Renewal on Appeal of the Trial Investigation (Article 6, para. 1, ECHR)), in DI STASI A. (ed.), *CEDU e ordinamento italiano. La giurisprudenza della Corte europea dei diritti dell'uomo e l'impatto nell'ordinamento interno (2016-2020)*, Milano, 2020, p. 431 ff.

PALLADINO R., "Comportamenti delle forze dell'ordine contrari al divieto di tortura o di trattamenti inumani o degradanti (art. 3 CEDU)" (Behavior of Law Enforcement Bodies Contrary to the Prohibition of Torture or Inhuman or Degrading Treatment (Article 3 ECHR)), DI STASI A. (ed.), *CEDU e ordinamento italiano. La giurisprudenza della Corte europea dei diritti dell'uomo e l'impatto nell'ordinamento interno (2016-2020)*, Milano, 2020, p. 33 ff.

PALMISANO G. (ed.), *Il diritto internazionale ed europeo nei giudizi interni* (International and European Union Law in Domestic Proceedings), Napoli, 2020, pp. 568.

PALOMBINO F.M., "La Dichiarazione universale dei diritti umani nella giurisprudenza dei tribunali italiani" (The Universal Declaration of Human Rights in the Case Law of the Italian Courts), in TONOLO S. and PASCALE G. (eds.), *La Dichiarazione universale dei diritti umani nel diritto internazionale contemporaneo*, Torino, 2020, p. 149 ff.

PANELLA L., "La Carta sociale europea come parametro interposto nei giudizi di legittimità costituzionale ex art. 117, co. 1 Cost. Revirement della corte costituzionale o ambigui progressi in materia di parità tra fonti internazionali?" (The European Social Charter as an Interposed Parameter in the Constitutional Legitimacy Judgments pursuant to Article 117, para. 1, of the Italian Constitution. A Revirement from the Constitutional Court or an Ambiguous Progress towards Equality between International Sources?), OIDU, 2020, p. 26 ss.

PARISI N. and RINOLDI D., "Misure di prevenzione personale e libertà di movimento (art. 2, Protocollo n. 4; artt. 6, parr. 1, 13 e 41 CEDU)" (Personal Prevention Measures and Freedom of Movement (Article 2, Protocol No. 4; Article 6, para. 1, Articles 13 and 41 ECHR)), in DI STASI A. (ed.), *CEDU e ordinamento italiano. La giurisprudenza della Corte europea dei diritti dell'uomo e l'impatto nell'ordinamento interno (2016-2020)*, Milano, 2020, p. 848 ff.

PICCONE V., "Tutela familiare e interesse alla conservazione dei rapporti di affettività (art. 8 CEDU)" (Family Protection and Interest in the Preservation of Emotional Relationships (Article 8 ECHR)), in DI STASI A. (ed.), *CEDU e ordinamento italiano. La giurisprudenza della Corte europea dei diritti dell'uomo e l'impatto nell'ordinamento interno (2016-2020)*, Milano, 2020, p. 561 ff.

PUSTORINO P., "Il diritto alla vita privata e familiare in relazione alle questioni di orientamento sessuale (artt. 8 e 14 CEDU)" (The Right to Private and Family Life in relation to Issues of Sexual Orientation (Articles 8 and 14 ECHR)), in DI STASI A. (ed.), *CEDU e ordinamento italiano. La giurisprudenza della Corte europea dei diritti dell'uomo e l'impatto nell'ordinamento interno (2016-2020)*, Milano, 2020, p. 679 ff.

ROSSI P., "The Role of National Courts for the International Rule of Law: Insights from the Field of Migration", European Journal of Legal Studies, 2020, p. 195 ff.

ROSSI P., "Using International Law for Construing Domestic Law: A Study of Consistent Interpretation", AVR, 2020, p. 279 ff.

RUSSO T., "Il diritto di accesso ad un giudice e il c.d. 'filtro' in cassazione (art. 6, par. 1, CEDU)" (The Right of Access to a Judge and the so-called "Filter" in Cassation (Article 6, para. 1, ECHR)), in DI STASI A. (ed.), *CEDU e ordinamento italiano. La giurisprudenza della Corte europea dei diritti dell'uomo e l'impatto nell'ordinamento interno (2016-2020)*, Milano, 2020, p. 455 ff.

SALERNO F., "La politica giudiziaria della Corte costituzionale rispetto alle norme costituzionali di garanzia del diritto internazionale" (The Constitutional Court's Judicial Policy with Regard to Constitutional Rules Guaranteeing Compliance with International Law), RDI, 2020, p. 1095 ff.

SAPIENZA R., "Libertà di espressione e limiti convenzionali: il difficile bilanciamento (art. 10, par. 2, CEDU)" (Freedom of Expression and Treaty Limits: The Difficult Balance (Article 10, para. 2, ECHR)), in DI STASI A. (ed.), *CEDU e ordinamento italiano. La giurisprudenza della Corte europea dei diritti dell'uomo e l'impatto nell'ordinamento interno (2016-2020)*, Milano, 2020, p. 767 ff.

SCARPA A., "Diritto di proprietà, espropriazione, occupazione *sine titulo* (art. 1, Protocollo addizionale CEDU)" (Property Right, Expropriation, Occupation *sine titulo*), in DI STASI A. (ed.), *CEDU e ordinamento italiano. La giurisprudenza della Corte europea dei diritti dell'uomo e l'impatto nell'ordinamento interno (2016-2020)*, Milano, 2020, p. 785 ff.

XVIII. USE OF FORCE AND PEACE-KEEPING

CELLAMARE G., "In tema di cooperazione tra Nazioni Unite, Unione africana e Unione europea in materia di mantenimento della pace e della sicurezza internazionale" (Remarks on the Cooperation Between the United Nations, the African Union and the European Union in the Field of the Maintenance of International Peace and Security), CI, 2020, p. 537 ff.

LONGOBARDO M., *The Use of Armed Force in Occupied Territory*, Cambridge, 2020, pp. xxix-335.

MAURI D., "The Political Question Doctrine vis-à-vis Drones' 'Outsized Power': Antithetical Approaches in Recent Case-Law", QIL, Zoom-in 68, 2020, p. 3 ff.

PERTILE M. and FACCIO S., "What We Talk about When We Talk about Jerusalem: The Duty of Non-Recognition and the Prospects for Peace after the US Embassy's Relocation to the Holy City", Leiden JIL, 2020, p. 621 ff.

PERTILE M., "Mettere in discussione la stabilità delle situazioni territoriali illecite: l'obbligo di non riconoscimento nella prospettiva dello *jus post bellum*" (Calling into Question the Stability of Unlawful Territorial Situations: The Duty of Non-Recognition in the Light of *Jus Post Bellum*), in LACCHÈ L. and LAVENIA V. (eds.), *Alberico Gentili e lo jus post bellum. Prospettive tra diritto e storia. Atti del Convegno della XVIII Giornata Gentiliana, San Ginesio, 21-22 settembre 2018*, Macerata, 2020, p. 117 ff.

XIX. ARMED CONFLICT, NEUTRALITY, AND DISARMAMENT

AMOROSO D. and TAMBURRINI G., "Autonomous Weapons Systems and Meaningful Human Control: Ethical and Legal Issues", Current Robotics Reports, 2020, p. 187 ff.

AMOROSO D., *Autonomous Weapons Systems and International Law. A Study on Human-Machine Interactions in Ethically and Legally Sensitive Domains*, Napoli/Baden-Baden, 2020, pp. xii-288.

BORGIA F., "Osservazioni sulla (il)liceità delle operazioni mirate con i droni nella lotta al terrorismo: sistemi di norme a confronto" (Remarks on the (Un)Lawfulness of Armed Drones Operations under International Law: Comparing Systems of Rules), CI, 2020, p. 391 ff.

PASCALE G., "Programma nucleare iraniano, Consiglio di sicurezza e unilateralismo statunitense" (Iranian Nuclear Plan, the Security Council and US Unilateralism), RDI, 2020, p. 757 ff.

PERTILE M., *Diritto internazionale e rapporti economici nelle guerre civili* (International Law and Economic Relations in Civil Wars), Napoli, 2020, pp. 332.

VADI V., "Perfect War: Gentili on the Use of Force, and the Early Modern Law of Nations", Grotiana, 2020, p. 263 ff.

VADI V., *War and Peace. Alberico Gentili and the Early Modern Law of Nations*, Leiden, 2020, pp. 592.

VENTURINI G., "The Legal Regime of the Use of Nuclear Power Sources in Space Missions", in BLACK-BRANCH J.L. and FLECK D. (eds.), *Nuclear Non-Proliferation in International Law. Legal Challenges for Nuclear Security and Deterrence*, 2020, p. 73 ff.

XX. INTERNATIONAL RESPONSIBILITY

BARTOLINI G., "The Historical Roots of the Due Diligence Standard", in KRIEGER H., PETERS A. and KREUZER L. (eds.), *Due Diligence in the International Legal Order*, Oxford, 2020, p. 23 ff.

GASBARRI L., "The European Union is not a State: International Responsibility for Illegal, Unreported and Unregulated Fishing Activities", Maritime Safety and Security Law Journal, 2019-2020, p. 54 ff.

PUSTORINO P., "Diritto internazionale e complicità fra Stati: considerazioni sull'elemento soggettivo dell'illecito" (International Law and Complicity between States: Remarks on the Subjective Element of Wrongful Acts), RDI, 2020, p. ff.

VIGNI P., "Cultural Heritage and State Responsibility", in FRANCIONI F. and VRDOLJAK A.F. (eds.), *The Oxford Handbook of International Cultural Heritage Law*, Oxford, 2020, p. 605 ff.

XXI. INTERNATIONAL DISPUTE SETTLEMENT

ALÌ A., "National Security and Trade Wars: Legal Implications for Multilateralism", IYIL, Vol. XXIX-2019, 2020, p. 77 ff.

BARONCINI E., "Preserving the Appellate Stage in the WTO Dispute Settlement Mechanism: The EU and the Multi-Party Interim Appeal Arbitration Arrangement", IYIL, Vol. XXIX-2019, 2020, p. 33 ff.

BONAFÈ I.B., "Universal Civil Jurisdiction and Reparation for International Crimes", in FORLATI S., FRANZINA P. and LA MANNA M. (eds.), *Universal Civil Jurisdiction – Which Way Forward?*, Leiden, 2020, p. 99 ff.

BUSCEMI M., "The Non-Justiciability of Third-Party Claims before UN Internal Dispute Settlement Mechanisms. The 'Politicization' of (Financially) Burdensome Questions", QIL, Zoom-in 68, 2020, p. 23 ff.

CANTONI S. and FOIS E. (eds.), *Giurisprudenza della Corte Internazionale di Giustizia: casi scelti* (The Case Law of the International Court of Justice. Selected Cases), 2nd ed., Torino, 2020, pp. 320.

CASERTA S., *International Courts in Latin America and the Caribbean. Foundations and Authority*, Oxford, 2020, pp. 320.

CHECHI A., "Alternative Dispute Settlement Mechanisms", in FRANCIONI F. and VRDOLJAK A.F. (eds.), *The Oxford Handbook of International Cultural Heritage Law*, Oxford, 2020, p. 718 ff.

DE STEFANO C., "From Arbitrators to Judges? Reflections on the Reform of Investor-State Dispute Settlement", IYIL, Vol. XXIX-2019, 2020, p. 137 ff.

DE STEFANO C., *Attribution in International Law and Arbitration*, Oxford, 2020, pp. xliv-211.

FORLATI S., "Confidentiality of Conciliation Proceedings and Their Outcome. A Reflection in Light of the Experience of the Timor-Leste/Australia Conciliation Commission", in TOMUSCHAT C. and KOHEN M. (eds.), *Flexibility in International Dispute Settlement Flexibility in International Dispute Settlement. Conciliation Revisited*, Leiden, 2020, p. 181 ff.

FORLATI S., "Infra petita", in RUIZ FABRI H. (ed.), *Max Planck Encyclopedia of International Procedural Law*, Oxford, 2020 (on-line).

FORLATI S., "O papel do juiz ad hoc no proceso perante a Corte internacional de justiça" (The Role of the Judge ad hoc in Contentious Proceedings before the International Court of Justice), in DAL RI A. and LIMA L.C. (eds.), *A jurisprudência da Corte internacional de justiça. História e influência no Direito Internacional*, Belo Horizonte, 2020, p. 371 ff.

FORLATI S., "The Judicial Activity of the International Court of Justice in 2019", IYIL, Vol. XXIX-2019, 2020, p. 247 ff.

FORLATI S., "Revision (ICJ)", in RUIZ FABRI H. (ed.), *Max Planck Encyclopedia of International Procedural Law*, Oxford, 2020 (on-line).

GAGLIANI G., "The International Court of Justice and Cultural Heritage: International Cultural Heritage Law Through the Lens of World Court Jurisprudence?", in CARSTENS A.-M. and VARNER E. (eds.), *Intersections in International Cultural Heritage Law*, Oxford, 2020, p. 223 ff.

GIACALONE M., *Alternative dispute resolution e garanzia di accesso alla giustizia* (Alternative Dispute Resolution and Right to Access to Justice), Napoli, 2020, pp. 182.

GRAZIANI F., "*Iura novit curia* e riqualificazione giuridica del fatto: una breve riflessione sulla giurisprudenza della Corte internazionale di giustizia" (*Iura Novit Curia* and Legal Re-Qualification of the Alleged Facts: Some Reflections on the Jurisprudence of the International Court of Justice), CI, 2020, p. 501 ff.

GRAZIANI F., *Giudice e amministrazione della prova nel contenzioso internazionale. Il ruolo della Corte internazionale di giustizia* (Judge and Rules of Evidence in International Litigation. The Role of the International Court of Justice), Napoli, 2020, pp. 392.

MAGI L., "The Effect of the WTO Dispute Settlement Crisis on the Development of Case Law on National Security Exceptions: A Critical Scenario", QIL, Zoom-in 69, 2020, p. 29 ff.

MARASSI S., "International Framework Agreements and Management of Global Supply Chain: Extra-Judicial Mechanisms to Enforce International Labour Standards", QIL, Zoom-out 73, 2020, p. 53 ff.

MAROTTI L. and PALCHETTI P., "Of Restoring Compliance, *Lex Specialis* and Intersecting Wrongs: the Question of 'Remedies' in Gabčikovo-Nagymaros", in FORLATI S., MBENGUE M.M. and McGARRY B. (eds.), *The* Gabčíkovo-Nagymaros *Judgment and Its Contribution to the Development of International Law*, Leiden, 2020, p. 145 ff.

MUSSI F., "From the Campbell Case to a Recent Ruling of the Constitutional Court of South Africa: Is There Any Hope to Revive the Tribunal of the Southern African Development Community?", African Journal of International and Comparative Law, 2020, p. 110 ff.

NIGRO R., "International Criminal Justice (2019)", IYIL, Vol. XXIX-2019, 2020, p. 305 ff.

PALMIERI G., "Il ruolo dell'Avvocatura dello Stato nella difesa dello stato italiano nei giudizi davanti alla Corte di Strasburgo" (The Role of the Avvocatura dello Stato in the Defense of the Italian State in Proceedings before the Strasbourg Court), in DI STASI A. (ed.), *CEDU e ordinamento italiano. La giurisprudenza della Corte europea dei diritti dell'uomo e l'impatto nell'ordinamento interno (2016-2020)*, Milano, 2020, p. 875 ff.

PANTALEO L., "The Future of Investment Arbitration in the light of Opinion 1/17", QIL, Zoom-out 73, 2020, p. 21 ff.

PAPA M.I., "La tutela degli interessi collettivi nell'ordinanza sulle misure provvisorie nel caso Gambia c. Myanmar" (The Protection of Collective Interests in the Order on Provisional Measures in the case Gambia v. Myanmar), RDI, 2020, p. 729 ff.

PISILLO MAZZESCHI R. and CARLI E., "The Conciliation Procedure of the OSCE Court: Problems and Prospects", in TOMUSCHAT C. and KOHEN M. (eds.), *Flexibility in International Dispute Settlement Conciliation Revisited*, Leiden, 2020, p. 205 ff.

RONZITTI N., "Il caso della Enrica Lexie e la sentenza arbitrale nella controversia Italia-India" (The Enrica Lexie Case and the Arbitral Award in the Dispute between Italy and India), RDI, 2020, p. 937 ff.

SACERDOTI G. (ed.), "The WTO Dispute Settlement System in 2019: The Case Law of the Appellate Body before Its Demise", IYIL, Vol. XXIX-2019, 2020, p. 331 ff.

SACERDOTI G., "After the US-Orchestrated Demise of the WTO Appellate Body: Any Way Out?", in LEAL-ARCAS R. (ed.), *The Future of International Economic Law and the Rule of Law*, Chisinau, 2020, p. 11 ff.

SACERDOTI G., "Alternative all'arbitrato degli investimenti: protezione diplomatica e arbitrato interstatale" (Alternatives to Investment Arbitration: Diplomatic Protection and Inter-State Arbitration), in *Trattato di Diritto dell'Arbitrato*, vol. XIII, Napoli, 2020, p. 1 ff.

SACERDOTI G., "International Trade Disputes", in RUIZ FABRI H. (ed.), *Max Planck Encyclopedia of International Procedural Law*, Oxford, 2020 (on-line).

SACERDOTI G., "The Authority of 'Precedent' in International Adjudication: The Contentious Case of the WTO Appellate Body's Practice", The Law & Practice of International Courts and Tribunals, 2020, p. 497 ff.

SACERDOTI G., "The Challenge of Re-Establishing a Functioning WTO Dispute Settlement System", in *Modernizing the WTO*, CIGI Essay Series, 20 April 2020, https://www.cigionline.org/on-line

SOAVE T., "Who Controls WTO Dispute Settlement? Socio-Professional Practices and the Crisis of the Appellate Body", IYIL, Vol. XXIX-2019, 2020, p. 13 ff.

TANZI A., "Substantialising the Procedural Obligations of International Water Law between Compensatory and Distributive Justice", in RUIZ-FABRI H., FRANCKX E, BENATAR M. and MESHEL T., (eds.), *A Bridge over Troubled Waters. Dispute Resolution in the Law of International Watercourses and the Law of the Sea*, Leiden/Boston, 2020, p. 351 ff.

TREVES T., "The International Tribunal for the Law of the Sea and Other Law of the Sea Jurisdictions (2019)", IYIL, Vol. XXIX-2019, 2020, p. 271 ff.

ZARRA G., "The Interface between Investment Arbitration and the 'Outside World': An Analysis through the Prism of the 2019 Case Law", IYIL, Vol. XXIX-2019, 2020, p. 395 ff.

BOOK REVIEWS

(edited by *Marco Gestri*)

GIULIO BARTOLINI (ed.), *A History of International Law in Italy*, Oxford, Oxford University Press, 2020, pp. 491.

This is an impressive scholarly work, featuring, as it does in almost 500 pages, 19 chapters by 17 authors (without counting the editor who has contributed three pieces), covering Italian doctrine and scholarship from the time of Alberico Gentili (1552-1608) to living and still active scholars.

The editor, associate professor of international law at Roma-Tre University, has taken upon himself the daunting task of presenting to the international public the evolution of the Italian scholarship in the field (for previous analysis, SERENI, *The Italian Conception of International Law*, New York, 1943 – the author was a Jewish academic, at the time in the US as a refugee; MESSINEO, "Is There an Italian Conception of International Law?", Cambridge Journal of International and Comparative Law, 2013, p. 879 ff.). Thanks to the wise choice of competent authors, he has been able to present Italian international lawyers' key contributions to international law doctrine, through both a historical and a systematic perspective. Thus, after Bartolini's Introduction, in Part II of the volume ("The Development of International Law Scholarship in Italy"), the reader is guided through natural law doctrines, the nationality and idealistic schools of the mid XIX century (Pasquale Stanislao Mancini and Pasquale Fiore), the subsequent prevailing adherence to German positivist doctrines (with original contributions by such authors as Donato Donati and Santi Romano), to contemporary humanistic and universalistic human rights visions (without ignoring those authors who have inclined towards Marxism and the persistence of the dualistic approach). The work takes into account in Part III the most notable historical and political events which have impacted on Italian scholarship, from the unification of Italy in the XIX century, to colonialism and fascism in the first part of the XX century, to the return to democracy in the former Soviet States and thereafter the context of progressive European integration.

There is an open debate among international lawyers on the extent to which international law is truly international (see ROBERTS, *Is International Law International?*, Oxford, 2017 and the review of the book by ASTERITI, IYIL, 2018, 583 ff.).

Observing that international law academics in different countries are subject to different influences, from the local legal tradition to the political context, which affect how they understand and approach international law is not new. Until recently, it was fully accepted that there were different national "schools" of international law based on different legal traditions and education and on the position and influence of the countries of origin in the international arena, as well as their domestic political set up. As well as these factors, differences in the languages

IYIL, Vol. 30 (2020), pp. 581-601
ISSN 0391-5107

used by international law scholars help to explain why it was common to refer to the British, French, German, Italian, Spanish, Latin American, Japanese, etc. "schools" of international law (at the University of Milan, established in 1925, the rich international law library, organized by Roberto Ago when he taught there after WWII, still presents treatises of international law subdivided by the nationality of their authors). This view is also reflected in the formulation of Article 38(1)(d) of the ICJ Statute where it refers to the "teachings of the most highly qualified publicists of the various nations". Of course, with respect to language, the situation is now different given the current dominance of English as a *lingua franca* – which by the way was the reason for launching this Yearbook in English almost 50 years ago (see PAVONI, "Thirty Volumes On: Genesis, Development and Prospects of the Italian Yearbook of International Law", in this Volume) – with young scholars of any nationality publishing even their PhD thesis in English with accredited "international" (mostly UK-based) publishers.

This work thus enables non-Italian scholars, who happen not to be familiar with Dante Alighieri's idiom, to get acquainted with the long history of continuous original contributions by Italian international lawyers. These contributions concern both general doctrines (notably effective sovereignty being an inherent element of States as subjects of international law; the theory of international organizations and their constitutive elements; State responsibility; the relationship between domestic and international law; the role of national courts in developing international law; and the concept of an international community as distinct from its constituent States entities) and specific fields.

It is of course not possible within the present analysis to review the many interesting contributions included in the volume. I would highlight Bartolini's own contribution on the League of Nations and Fascism period, when Italy had a prominent international role as one of the winners of WWI (as evidenced also by the prominent role of Dionisio Anzilotti, notably at the PCIJ). He points out how Italian international law professors were mostly able to escape "fascistization" by retreating to theoretical work (compare with the Nazification of international law in Germany: VAGTS, "International Law in the Third Reich", AJIL, 1990, p. 661 ff.). Some of them developed in this period a solid scholarly basis for the future, such as Roberto Ago with his seminal Hague course of 1939 on "Le délit international". He notably distinguished there primary from secondary obligations, paving the way to his innovative and successful contribution as rapporteur to the ILC on the codification of State responsibility.

Another notable feature of the Italian tradition is duly noted in the volume (Chapter 11 by Pietro Franzina): the integrated approach to private and public international law. This dual background has allowed most Italian international lawyers to navigate both fields, an ability that shows its usefulness in the present time of globalization characterized by the blurring of the distinction between public and private actors and between the instruments (contracts, treaties) available for their respective or common activities.

In his piece with Giovanni di Stefano on the influence of Italian doctrine notwithstanding the language barrier, Robert Kolb, the only non-Italian contributor, highlights especially the Italian contribution to the development and codification of the law of State responsibility thanks to the work of Anzilotti, Ago and Arangio-Ruiz (later followed by Giorgio Gaja as rapporteur on the responsibility of international organizations): "[t]he rejection of the distinction between tortious and contractual responsibility, as well as the upholding of a unitary system of international responsibility of States, must be highlighted as distinctive contributions of the Italian school". This, notwithstanding the fact that Ago's innovative distinction between "international delicts" and "international crimes" (Article 19 of the 1996 draft) was subsequently dropped due to widespread opposition from States.

Italian doctrine has also had an influence through the role of Italian law professors as members of international courts where they have been appointed thanks to the uncommon propensity of the Italian Ministry of Foreign Affairs to support professors for such posts. The list of such distinguished international lawyers turned judges includes, first of all, Dionisio Anzilotti (member of the PCIJ from 1921 to 1939 and President from 1928 to 1930); Gaetano Morelli, Roberto Ago, Luigi Ferrari Bravo and Giorgio Gaja at the ICJ; Giorgio Balladore Pallieri and Benedetto Conforti at the ECtHR; Riccardo Monaco and Francesco Capotorti at the ECJ; as well as, more recently, Antonio Cassese and Fausto Pocar (ICTY) and Tullio Treves (ITLOS).

I will share the conclusions of Di Stefano and Kolb (p. 466) as they summarize the main take-aways from reading Bartolini's notable work: "[f]irst, the Italian tradition forms one of the great legal schools of international law. It has distinctive features and brings to the fore a pedigreed type of analysis of international law. It cannot be confused with the German, French, English, or Spanish contributions. Second, the Italian school has its own areas and tools of predilection. Its influence has been especially marked regarding questions such as State responsibility, the conception of the State (as well as unions of States and subjects of the law), and the sources of law. Its method is particular, since it has long privileged conceptual analysis. In this context, it has exerted a certain influence in the areas of legal precision and the mastery of various tools of systematization of the law. Third, the reception of Italian legal thinking has not been as significant as it could and should have been, mainly due to language barriers […]. Fourth, the modern tendency of Italian authors is to adopt tools of analysis more akin to the general trend and to publish more extensively in English. This naturally leads to a spread of Italian doctrine but also, to some extent, to a dilution of its very distinctive features".

In the concluding essay, Paolo Palchetti highlights some of the contemporary trends in Italian doctrine which are bringing it closer to the evolutions occurring in other countries, while still maintaining its own distinct tradition. In Palchetti's view, contemporary trends confirm Antonio Cassese's evaluation of Italian international law doctrine as of 1990 (CASSESE, "Diritto internazionale", in BONANATE (ed.), Studi internazionali, Torino, 1990, p. 113 ff.). While Italian scholarship was characterized by a rather theoretical approach to international law until the 1960s, a shift in the methodology subsequently took place, with the emphasis moving from theory and logical analysis to a practice-oriented analysis. Cassese had also noted that, in selecting topics and issues, Italian scholarship had progressively moved away from abstract and theoretical problems regarding the foundations of the discipline and toward problems which reflected a greater interest in the living reality of international relations. This evolution has been encouraged by the increasing use of the English language in publications and by the academic mobility of Italian scholars abroad (in 2014, approximately 45 percent of publications by Italian scholars were published in non-Italian periodicals or by non-Italian publishers based on an analysis of the "Italian bibliographical index of international law", published in this Yearbook, 2014 issue). Moreover, many of the youngest generation of Italian scholars have research experience, or even gained part of their education, outside Italy.

However "despite the increasing use of English in scholarly works, it would be premature to say that Italian scholars have totally abandoned Italian as their working language. In fact, a conspicuous part of the scientific debate continues to take place in Italian. The great majority of articles in Italian international law journals, from the oldest and still most authoritative, are still written in Italian" as are most monographs by Italian authors, including the youngest ones (Palchetti, "The Italian Doctrine over Recent Decades", p. 468 ff., pp. 470-471). The use of Italian is supported by an ample domestic market and the fact that the teaching of international law, from which European law has emancipated itself as a distinct field, is compulsory in Italian law schools' curricula (cf. the success of prof. Benedetto Conforti's handbook *Diritto internazionale* – 12th edition by Massimo Iovane after the author's death, Naples, 2021 – which is the standard textbook for those taking the diplomatic service entrance exam).

Fidelity to tradition is evidenced, according to Palchetti, by the following features (a judgment that I share): "[f]irst, a rule-oriented approach dominates the international legal discourse in Italian scholarship: its focus is on the determination, interpretation, and application of international rules. Within this strictly legal analysis, formal sources continue to play a key role, in that they permit a distinction between law and non-law". The second point relates to the important role attributed to international practice in the analysis of international law problems: "[o]ne may even wonder whether the importance placed upon international practice in international legal analysis has not come at the expense of a systematic vision of international law, once a hallmark of Italian scholarship" (p. 473).

The last point concerns the role of scholarship in critically appraising the rules and fostering their development. While the distinction between *lex lata* and *lex ferenda* – between the law in force and mere aspirations and proposals – remains one of the pillars of the positivistic legal analysis practised by Italian scholars, the idea that legal analysis also involves criticizing existing law and promoting the development of new law now appears to be widely accepted. Palchetti notes (p. 474) that, in any case, neither of these elements – a greater awareness of the indeterminacy of the law and increasing attention toward the extra-legal context of the law – has led Italian scholarship to reconsider the basic postulates of the positivistic method. The Italian approach to international legal problems continues to be characterized by a sharp distinction between determining what the existing law is, and criticizing that law or making proposals for innovations. There is also a clear distinction between strictly legal considerations and political or ethical ones. Finally, Italian doctrine has to be lauded (in my judgment) for upholding the conception of international law as a unitary system, notwithstanding widespread inevitable specialization.

While different methods with which to address the problems of international law flourish nowadays, especially in American academia, Italian scholarship tends to stick to a strictly juridical, rules-based, positivistic approach. A connected feature that distinguishes Italian scholarship is, in Palchetti's view, the limited attention devoted by Italian scholarship to theoretical reflection on the methods and techniques of international law. The same can be said as to the lack of inclination towards empirical analysis in Italian scholarship, considered to be rather a field for sociologists of the law, as with all other quantitative analysis.

To conclude. The quality of most contributions, with their detailed examination of the relations between different trends in scholarship, considered also in an international context, and between different theories in a historical perspective, makes reading this volume a must for all those who wish to understand the origins and developments of current theories and scholarly approaches to international law generally. By the way, nothing comparable exists in the Italian language!

GIORGIO SACERDOTI[*]

GABRIELA A. OANTA, *La sucesión de Estados en las Organizaciones internacionales: Examen de la práctica internacional*, Barcelona, J.M. Bosch editor, 2020, pp. 379.

In this book (written in Spanish), the author addresses the issue of State succession to membership in international organizations, providing a careful and up-to-date analysis of a large body of international practice. Under international public law, there are three main types of State succession, namely, State succession in respect of treaties; succession in respect of matters other than treaties; and succession in respect of membership of international organizations. The latter is a subject of increasing interest in contemporary international law. This recently published volume by Gabriela Oanta aims to shed light on this important intersection between States and international organizations, a subject which has been neglected by the process of codification of the law on succession of States elaborated by the International Law Commission (ILC).

Interestingly, and contrary to previous contributions in this field, which adopted a State-focused approach and described the situation with reference to single States that experienced a succession and their attitude towards "inheriting" the seat of their predecessor within the organizations concerned (see e.g. BIIHLER, *State Succession and Membership in International Organizations. Legal Theories versus Political Pragmatism*, Den Haag/London/Boston, 2001) or contributions that followed a chronological perspective and examined practice in relation to

---

[*] Of the Board of Editors.

successive historical periods (i.e. post-WW2, the period of decolonization, the 90s, etc.), the methodology behind the partition of topics adopted in this book aims to assess the regime of State succession in the membership of international organizations with a global approach. The author achieves this by making a distinction between organizations whose membership is on a world-wide scale and organizations operating on a regional or sub-regional basis. The author does not try to construct a general theory on the issue because, as the author herself puts it, *"la irreductible individualidad de las Organizaciones internacionales hace vano, en nuestra opinión, qualquier intento de construir una teoría general de una práctica tan diversa"* (p. 30). Thus, given that "the irreducible individuality of each organization renders vain any attempt to construct a general theory of such a diverse practice", the author's strategy is to highlight for the reader the most outstanding points and the coincidences that occur in the practice of international organizations on this matter.

In line with the whole perspective of the volume, and rather than trying to elaborate a general theory, attention is given to the practice of succession in the membership of different types of intergovernmental organizations: organizations of a universal character with general and sectoral aims, respectively (Chapter II); organizations that operate within one continent (Chapter III); regional and sub-regional organizations (Chapter IV). The last part (Chapter V) is devoted to commenting on the peculiar situation of whether the withdrawal of a State from an international organization affects the membership of both the State and organization vis à vis their respective participation in another intergovernmental organization.

To begin with, in the first Chapter, a general survey is made of the discipline of State succession in international organizations. The starting point is the assumption that every organization constitutes a *sui generis* legal entity and that, therefore, in order to understand the mechanism of State succession in the membership, one has to consider the rules of each organization separately, on a case-by-case basis. The author argues that since every organization possesses its own characteristics that distinguish it from the others, the practice of admission/succession is not the same and does not always have the same relevance in every organization's constitution (p. 36). Consequently, succession must be assessed in accordance with the rules and constituent instruments of the specific organization concerned. When it comes to the identification of such rules, the author relies on the definition used in the Draft Articles on the Responsibility of International Organizations, adopted by the ILC in 2011, which notably enlarges the notion so as to encompass not only the organization's constituent instruments, but also "decisions, resolutions and other acts of the international organization adopted in accordance with those instruments, and established practice of the organization" (as specified under Article 2(b) ILC Draft). Then, the author also takes note of the useful references contained in the Draft Articles on the Representation of States in their Relations with International Organizations (1971) and the 1986 Vienna Convention on the Law of Treaties between States and International Organizations or between International Organizations.

Starting from the assumption that a question of State succession usually arises when one State is absorbed by another (incorporation); breaks into parts (dissolution); or loses part of its territory (by secession in breach of the pre-existing State's constitution or peacefully via a negotiated separation) (CHIU, "Succession in International Organisations", ICLQ, 1965, p. 88 ff.), this volume analyzes the different positions of the pre-existing State and the successor State under general international law. This brings about two different scenarios depending on whether the predecessor State maintains its legal personality or not. In the first case, each State has its own international legal personality, whereas in the second case the successor State replaces the predecessor. Obviously, the scenario in which the successor State can carry on with the legal rights and obligations of the former largely unaffected and without having to reapply for membership of international organizations is one which is attractive to States. It clearly explains why certain entities, such as the Russian Federation or the Federal Republic of Yugoslavia, have in the past gone to great lengths to argue that, despite a rupture in their international legal personality, they should be considered the continuator State (DEVANEY, "What Happens Next? The Law of State Succession", GCILS Working Paper Series no. 6, Glasgow, 2020). An overview of key case studies on this issue is the necessary starting point for the analysis that follows.

The second assumption is that the constituent instrument of an international organization is obviously a treaty. Thus, a succession may give rise to questions concerning the law of treaties that are governed by the relevant rules of international law. The author finds some guidance in Article 4 of the 1978 Vienna Convention on Succession of States in respect of Treaties. This provision is relevant to the issue at hand since it seems to exclude the automatic acquisition of membership by the successor State (pp. 40 and 86). Consequently – Oanta notes – "new States can become members of a specific organization only in accordance with the organization's own rules and not through succession" (p. 87). It follows that, when the constitutive treaty establishes rules for the acquisition of membership status, the candidate State must submit to the relevant rules and procedures provided for admission by the legal system of said organization.

The problem, however, remains open for those universal organizations with a sectoral scope that have not adopted specific rules on admission. The issue is examined in the second part of Chapter II, with particular regard to economic and financial institutions. In the latter institutions – the author notes – admission is mainly a political issue, so the candidate country is not guaranteed future membership based on the treaty. Through an attentive analysis of the practice, the book demonstrates that the position of the IMF and World Bank is basically based on a case-by-case evaluation, calibrated to meet the political and economic exigencies of the moment.

The third Chapter focuses on the position of those organizations that operate at continental and inter-continental levels. They are the expression of the so called *"fenomeno del regionalismo istituzionalizado"* that regulates inter-State cooperation. "Institutionalized regionalism" is indeed a very wide and heterogeneous phenomenon that encompasses over 300 institutions worldwide. They vary considerably from one another with respect to their membership requirements because each one has set forth its own objective and subjective conditions for becoming a member. From the African Bank of Development to the Arab League, from NATO to OCSE, among many others. Each one has established rules on admission and this has generated a rich and diversified praxis in the five Continents, which is analyzed following a geographical order. In Africa, the most important case study is that of the African Union (AU). The fact that, in recent years, secessionist movements have become active in several of its member States, such as Angola, Senegal, the Congo and Somalia, leads the author to consider that the AU may have to face problems related to the admission of new States in the future, despite the fact that AU members are fierce supporters of the maintenance of the status quo. However, considering the tumultuous history and geopolitical complexity that characterize the African continent, the AU can count on a rich practice on the formation of new States by way of secession, that is widely described in the book. In her examination of the position of States that originated from the decolonization process within the many continental intergovernmental organizations, Oanta also considers the organizations operating in the Pacific area. The Pacific Community, for example, is composed of States from the Pacific Islands and Oceania. Its peculiarity lies in the circumstance that among its members there are also overseas territories which, at the moment of their admission, were not yet independent States. The author notes that the subsequent transformation of those territories into sovereign States has not affected their membership in the organization, but the author does not further explore the extent to which an entity which has not yet achieved statehood can legally bind itself to an international agreement.

In Chapter IV, the volume pays particularly appreciable attention to the numerous organizations operating at the regional level *strictu senso*, and at the subregional level. It is quite surprising to learn how many there are. The thorough analysis of the statutes and rules governing the various regional organizations testifies to the accuracy of the research.

Finally, taking its cue from Brexit, Chapter V addresses a problem that has been largely overlooked by legal doctrine, namely that of the consequences of the withdrawal of a State from an international organization (Organization B) on the membership in another organization (Organization A) of that State and of the first organization itself (Organization B).

The EU is currently the effective member of 40 intergovernmental organizations (FRID DE VRIES, "European Union, Membership in International Organizations or Institutions", Max Planck Encyclopaedia of Public International Law, 2019, available at: <https://opil.ouplaw.com/home/mpil>) and has acquired observer status in several other global institutions, such as the UN, the WHO and the IMO.

Indeed, the European Union's membership in international organizations is an important issue, considering that the EU has a major role in regional integration and in global cooperation. On this point, the author observes that when the field of action of the organization concerned is within the exclusive competence of the EU, a joint participation of both the Union and its Member States is somewhat paradoxical, unless the competence of that organization is wider than that of the EU (p. 275). Oanta's book notes that the participation of the European Community first and then of the Union at the FAO is particularly problematic. Here, the EU has more restricted rights and obligations than States, but it must take into account the standards established by the FAO when adopting normative texts and external action policies (p. 291).

The final section of Chapter V is particularly remarkable, and presents a thoughtful discussion on the situation of ex-EU Member State succession in those organizations of which only the European Union is a party and not its Member States. This scenario is likely to become all the more urgent following Brexit. The author succeeds in illustrating the peculiar position of the UK with respect to the various sectoral organizations dealing with conservation and management of the living resources of the seas to which only the EU has acceded so far, due to its exclusive competence in this domain.

In conclusion, Oanta's book has identified a useful taxonomy that will help us to critically examine issues relating to State succession in international organizations in its various forms. In general terms, the work of the ILC to codify the law of State succession has largely failed to do so, making it even more difficult to find a general rule on membership succession. The various types of organizations appear to favour *ad hoc* solutions which, as this study demonstrates, cannot be reduced to a unitary outcome.

The multifaceted practice of State succession in international organizations in its manifold forms unavoidably dominates a regime that seems governed more by pragmatism than by law. Faced with an international practice that is fragmented and often context-specific, the question remains open: will the solutions that such a multifaceted practice has provided in order to meet concrete issues eventually reveal some underlying precepts of general application? Certainly this original and timely contribution to the scholarship may serve as a first stepping stone for further developments of a doctrine of succession in this field.

ALESSANDRA LANCIOTTI*

SERENA FORLATI, MAKANE MOÏSE MBENGUE and BRIAN MCGARRY (eds.), *The Gabčíkovo-Nagymaros Judgment and Its Contribution to the Development of International Law*, Leiden/Boston, Brill Nijhoff, 2020, pp. 263.

The judgment of the International Court of Justice (ICJ) in the *Gabčíkovo-Nagymaros* case, which was rendered in 1997 in the context of a dispute between Slovakia and Hungary over the construction and operation of a large barrage project on the Danube river, is widely considered to be one of the most influential pronouncements given by the Court over the last three decades. It would perhaps be an understatement to say that the judges' treatment of the delicate legal (and real-world) problems arising from the case has captured the imagination of more than one generation of international lawyers. From Judge Weeramantry's oft-

---

* Professor of International Law, University of Perugia.

celebrated exploration of the "principle" of sustainable development in his separate opinion, to the Court's clarification of the relationship between the termination and suspension of treaties and the circumstances precluding wrongfulness,
Gabčíkovo-Nagymaros is essentially a "gift that keeps on giving", its treasure
trove of insights continuing to appeal to a variety of different audiences and at
turns generating both praise and critical reflections.

The body of academic scholarship relating to the dispute is equally impressive
– spanning from case notes published in the immediate aftermath of the judgment
to deeper analyses of the Court's treatment of, and influence on, specific international legal principles and rules. The multiple interweaving claims advanced by
Hungary and Slovakia during the proceedings, as well as the complex social-ec-
ological issues raised by a dam infrastructure project of this magnitude, have also
continued to inform research outside the boundaries of international law, for example in the realms of international relations (e.g. DEETS, "Constituting Interests
and Identities in a Two-Level Game: Understanding the Gabčíkovo-Nagymaros
Dam Conflict", Foreign Policy Analysis, 2009, p. 37 ff.), political science (e.g.
FITZMAURICE, *Damming the Danube: Gabčíkovo and Post-Communist Politics
in Europe*, Abingdon, 1998) and ecosystem ecology. What is, in this context, the
added value of dedicating a new volume to the dispute, and can such an effort
reveal something new about the present (and future) of our discipline? In order
to answer such questions, it is first and foremost necessary to discuss the content
of this thought-provoking collective endeavour, which has been skilfully edited
by Serena Forlati (University of Ferrara), Makane Moïse Mbengue (University
of Geneva) and Brian McGarry (Leiden University).

As illustrated by the title of the volume itself, the task that the editors took
upon themselves is fairly linear, and largely builds on the authors' contributions
to a 2017 seminar held in Ferrara, Italy, to commemorate the 20th anniversary
of the judgment. In essence, the volume aims to unpack the multiple legal issues
that are discussed and addressed by the Court in its decision, while simultaneously exploring the contribution that the "solutions" provided by the judges have
since made to the development of international law. To fulfil these two interweaving tasks, the editors organize the volume around four parts, with Part 1 aiming
to discuss the background and facts of the case and the following three parts each
focusing on a key area of international law whose development the judgment has
purportedly contributed to – namely the law of treaties (Part 2), the law of international responsibility (Part 3), and what the editors call "the law of sustainable
development" (Part 4).

Part 1 consists of three contributions. In Chapter 1, Alain Pellet provides a
personal recollection of the dispute, in which he successively acted as counsel
for both Hungary and Slovakia, offering an interesting perspective on the significant novelty and implications of the on-site visit conducted by the Court in April
1997. Chapter 2, by Malgosia Fitzmaurice, is the only one that actually deals
with the facts of the case, presenting in rich detail the historical background of
the dispute and the realities of the barrage project on the ground. For his part,
Jean d'Aspremont (Chapter 3) focuses on the dynamics of cross-referencing that
characterized the judgment of the Court and the simultaneous drafting of the

International Law Commission's (ILC) Articles on the Responsibility of States for Internationally Wrongful Acts, suggesting that the resulting "reflecting mirrors effect" played an important role in universalizing a certain mode of legal reasoning with respect to the issue of international responsibility.

As mentioned above, Part 2 of the volume is dedicated to the influence of *Gabčíkovo-Nagymaros* on the development of the law of treaties. It opens with a contribution from Laura Pineschi (Chapter 4), who analyzes the interface between the general rules of treaty interpretation, as applied by the Court, and the need to incorporate emerging principles of international environmental law into the solution of international environmental disputes. Her conclusion aptly notes that "while the methods of systemic, evolutionary and teleological interpretation can play a major role [...], unfortunately the ICJ refrained from adopting a thorough integrated approach in the present case" (p. 55). In Chapter 5, Christina Binder and Jane A. Hofbauer devote their attention to the Court's treatment of two treaty interpretation techniques, namely those of "approximate application" and "evolutionary interpretation", and focus particularly on the impact that the latter had on the judges' efforts to uphold the principle of *pacta sunt servanda* and the stability of treaty relations. Closing Part II, Panos Merkouris (Chapter 6) focuses on the Court's response to Hungary's invocation of multiple grounds for treaty termination, while simultaneously offering some thoughts on the "fuzzy borders" between the law of treaties and the law of State responsibility. In contrast to the other two chapters in this Part, Merkouris deals less with the judges' reasoning as such and more with its relationship to the Vienna Convention on the Law of Treaties, arguing that the judgment served to clarify or solidify the normative status of several of the Convention's provisions on the termination of treaties.

Part 3 zooms in on the law of State responsibility. Alessandra Gianelli (Chapter 7) introduces this Part by situating the judgment's treatment of State responsibility issues within the wider legal developments that were already shaping the field at the time of the Court's pronouncement – and particularly the work of the ILC and the *Rainbow Warrior* arbitral award. In Chapter 8, Serena Forlati delves deeper into one of the most celebrated aspects of the judgment, namely its clarification of the relationship between the law of treaties and the law of State responsibility, which are treated as autonomous but necessarily "complementary and convergent" regimes (p. 114). At the same time, Forlati also explores the several questions left open by the Court and taken up in subsequent disputes, with a focus on the complex interactions between the rules on treaty termination and circumstances precluding wrongfulness. The latter are then extensively explored in Chapter 9, by Pierre Bodeau-Livinec. The chapter illustrates both the importance of *Gabčíkovo-Nagymaros* in the crystallization – through a "creative legal dialogue" (p. 133) – of the circumstances precluding wrongfulness that are contained in the ILC's Articles on State Responsibility, as well as the legacy that the judgment has had on the Articles themselves and on the modes of reasoning used by other international courts and tribunals. Finally, Chapter 10 (by Loris Marotti and Paolo Palchetti) explores the innovative (and partly controversial) response provided by the Court to the remedies sought by the Parties, especially in terms of its "flexible" application of the secondary rules on responsibility codified by the ILC in the areas of restitution and compensation.

Part 4 completes the volume by focusing on what, in 1997, was perceived as a truly landmark aspect of the judgment, namely the willingness of the Court to engage with questions of international environmental law and refer to the concept of sustainable development in its reasoning. In Chapter 11, Laurence Boisson de Chazournes briefly introduces this Part by noting that the judgment, while certainly timid in its treatment of these questions, nonetheless opened a series of doors that the Court later revisited in its subsequent jurisprudence. Chapter 12, by Makane Mbengue, goes on to argue that *Gabčíkovo-Nagymaros* represents "the first sustainable development dispute to ever be settled by an international court" (p. 166), rather than an environmental case *per se*. Mbengue describes how the concept of sustainable development, although *prima facie* not central in the dispute, was to a certain extent behind the Court's findings regarding the validity of the 1977 Treaty between Hungary and Slovakia. Although he recognizes that the Court broke new ground in this respect, he criticizes its lack of precision in discussing the supposedly far-reaching origins of the concept, which in 1997 was still only emerging, as well as its failure to recognize that sustainable development is more than "a mere principle of reconciliation" (p. 187). Leslie-Anne Duvic-Paoli (Chapter 13) focuses on the contribution of the judgment to the development of the principle of prevention in international environmental law, highlighting how the judges' reference to the principle did not lead to prevention playing an actual role in their reasoning. On the contrary, Duvic-Paoli dissects the problems raised by the pronouncement on the matter (for example, in terms of the Court's reluctance to engage with scientific data), concluding, in sync with the volume's general sentiment, that the ICJ paved the way, rather than charted a clear course, for its subsequent environmental jurisprudence. In his contribution (Chapter 14), Brian McGarry then frames *Gabčíkovo-Nagymaros* against the normative evolution that predated and continued around the same time as the judgment, problematizing the Court's uncertain treatment of this evolution, as exemplified in its elusive reference to "new norms and standards". According to McGarry, who engages extensively with the case law that has since elucidated some of the decision's obscure points, "the terminologies of the *Gabčíkovo–Nagymaros* judgment have – if not slowed – then at least failed to accelerate the clarification of general international environmental law" (p. 227). Concluding the volume, Attila Tanzi (Chapter 15) draws on the preceding chapters to offer some reflections on the various functions that could be ascribed to the judgment, including the distributive justice approach endorsed by the Court in the declaratory and prescriptive parts of the judgment; its contribution to the adaptation of international water law to emerging environmental norms; and its interface with the work of the ILC in areas ranging from State responsibility to the law of international watercourses.

Overall, the volume largely does what it sets out to achieve, dissecting the multiple dimensions of *Gabčíkovo–Nagymaros* with meticulous precision, while successfully illuminating those underlying normative developments that first made the Court's judgment possible and then significantly advanced its findings, with an emphasis on the progressive expansion of international environmental disputes that occurred around the turn of the century. There is certainly no other source which provides such an overarching and holistic view of the legal aspects of the case. However, the breadth of the project also results in certain (perhaps inevitable) drawbacks. From this standpoint, there are two minor sets of observations that could be raised. The first one of these relates to the structure of the volume. On the one hand, Part I could have done more to lay the groundwork for the rest of the contributions, for example through a more extensive introductory chapter (a function that is left to a short preface, in contrast with the other parts of the volume) or by presenting the facts at hand in greater detail. It is true that Fitzmaurice's chapter deals entirely with the real-world background of the case, but it would have perhaps been relevant to include additional insights on how the judgment affected the situation on the ground *after* 1997 (including with respect to the longer-term environmental impacts of the barrage project) – a task that is left to some passing observations about the ongoing "ossification" of the dispute. On the other hand, the fact that many aspects of the Court's judgment are so strictly interrelated creates a number of overlaps between discussions situated in different sections of the volume, giving a sense of déjà vu that slightly affects the flow of the chapters.

The second set of observations relates to a certain lack of imagination with respect to the forward-looking implications (or lack thereof) of *Gabčíkovo-Nagymaros* on matters of international environmental law and sustainable development, almost as if the editors decided to stop right on the threshold of current debates in this area. The problem is certainly not the quality of the contributions contained in Part 4, which are arguably the most forward-looking of the volume and offer a wide range of stimulating observations on the topic. No matter the innovative character it had at the time it was pronounced, the ICJ judgment simply cannot be stretched out so far as to accommodate or explain the rapid changes and emerging challenges facing international environmental law. In her chapter, Malgosia Fitzmaurice briefly nods to the idea, as she ponders "[…] whether the Judgment of the Court would today be slightly different and less timid over environmental questions" (p. 21). I felt that this consideration could have provided the scope to look afresh at a number of issues touched upon by the ICJ. For example, it could have prompted the editors to analyze the judges' treatment of the principles of precaution and prevention in the light of subsequent assessments of the ecological status of the Danube river, as well as to discuss the potential future relevance of the concept of "state of ecological necessity", especially as the interconnected crises facing the global environment might call for a rethink of how we approach the notion of "grave and imminent peril" contained in Article 25 of the Articles on the Responsibility of States. However, pursuing this line of inquiry would have certainly affected the overall balance and goals of the volume, which remains remarkably coherent in its intentions and precise in its execution.

DARIO PISELLI*

---

* PhD Candidate, Department of International Law, Graduate Institute of Geneva; Affiliated Researcher, Centre for International Environmental Studies, Graduate Institute of Geneva.

EMMANUEL H.D. DE GROOF, *State Renaissance for Peace: Transitional Governance under International Law*, Cambridge, Cambridge University Press, 2020, pp. 395; EMMANUEL H.D. DE GROOF and MICHA WIEBUSCH (eds.), *International Law and Transitional Governance: Critical Perspectives*, Abingdon, Routledge, 2020, pp. 165.

Ten years ago, the civil war in Syria began; the following year the UN General Assembly endorsed the Arab League's decision "to facilitate a Syrian-led political transition to a democratic, pluralistic political system" (UN Doc A/Res/253 (2012)). While, at present, the conflict remains ongoing, the UN continues to facilitate talks on constitutional reform; the EU and others meanwhile continue to call for the transition to begin. Across the continental divide, in Africa, political transitions *have* recently begun in Sudan, South Sudan and Libya, with the UN and IGAD supporting "transitional" governments. A common component of internationally-facilitated political transitions after civil war, transitional governments are generally selected undemocratically from among the elite of opposing parties so as to serve as a bridge between conflict and peace, and dysfunctional and effective government. Aside from exercising day-to-day rule, transitional governments are to steward the transition, generally culminating in elections and the adoption of a new or reformed constitution.

While a transition in Syria is yet to start, a transition in Yemen was recently restarted and Somalia remains in a permanent state of unfinished "transition". Though one may rightly question the effectiveness of transitional governance as a generic response to war and political upheaval, it is a practice that is clearly favoured – and, indeed, actively promoted and facilitated – by many States and international organizations. It is therefore surprising that the topic has received little international legal attention. This is all the more so given that the practice poses questions of central relevance to international law. Should transitional governments be recognized as the legitimate representatives of the State and its people and if so, on what basis? What legal rules, if any, guide such governments during the transitional period? And what legal rules, if any, guide States and international organizations in initiating and facilitating political transitions?

In responding to such questions, *State Renaissance for Peace: Transitional Governance under International Law*, by Emmanuel H.D. De Groof, and *International Law and Transitional Governance: Critical Perspectives*, edited by De Groof and Micha Wiebsuch, have taken the lead. Together they suggest that transitional governance does not operate in an international legal vacuum: there *are* (evolving) international legal norms that delineate the powers and duties of transitional governments as well as affect their legitimacy. There are also international legal rules that limit and influence the nature of international engagement with transitional governments. Whereas in *State Renaissance for Peace*, De Groof argues that international law increasingly recognizes that political transitions must be progressively inclusive of the broader society as well as "locally-owned", contributors to *International Law and Transitional Governance* suggest that in practice international actors, and by implication international law, may be contributing to transitions which are to the contrary: exclusionary and externally

© KONINKLIJKE BRILL NV, LEIDEN, 2021 | DOI:10.1163/22116133-03001042

imposed. Together, the two books make for compelling and complementary reading.

In *State Renaissance for Peace*, De Groof begins by tracing the history of interim governance arrangements. He notes that the notion of the "interregnum", a temporary interruption in the ordinary constitutional order between two political regimes, has a long history dating back to ancient times (p. 1). In the modern era, and especially since the end of the Cold War, however, transitional governance has become increasingly internationalized, institutionalized and associated with peacebuilding through State transformation: what De Groof calls the "peace-through-transition paradigm" (p. 6).

Drawing on practice relating to more than 20 States in transition, as well as a (re-)examination of established international legal principles, De Groof argues that an international legal framework for transitional governance has begun to emerge. It includes recognition that the authority of transitional governments is limited in both time and scope: extending to security and basic administration during the transition, but not to determining the future (post-transition) constitutional order (pp. 207-221). Transitional governments are also increasingly understood to be required to progressively open up both the process of constitutional change, and government itself, to be "inclusive" of the broader society (pp. 253-254). External actors who engage with States in transition must respect the obligations and limits of transitional governments (p. 283). External involvement must be based on consent and cannot extend to imposing particular governments or constitutional frameworks (pp. 286-292). Except under very limited circumstances involving the breach of a *jus cogens* norm, external involvement also cannot extend to coercively inducing opposition-led transitions (pp. 364-367). In other words, transitional governance must be genuinely "nationally-owned".

This is the first major work to consider the international legal aspects of transitional governance as an integrated phenomenon combining interim administration with constitution-making in an internationalized (post-)conflict setting. The book provides detailed analysis and findings of significant value to scholars and practitioners, not only of international law but also comparative constitutional law and peace and conflict studies. Following the introductory chapters, the second part of the book draws on rigorous analysis to develop a typology of transitional governance that will be invaluable to future researchers. By identifying new (evolving) international legal norms and clarifying the application of established international legal norms, subsequent parts of the book show that there is no legal "black hole" during political transitions. Of particular note, the book suggests that self-determination should be considered an "umbrella principle" guiding political transitions (p. 232), and that "inclusion" can be understood as an (evolving) obligation of progressive realization towards achieving this (p. 259). The book is especially strong on the limits of external engagement: it offers a thorough analysis of the principle of non-intervention and the law on countermeasures in relation to the (un)lawfulness of external inducement of opposition-led transitions (p. 333). It further makes the case that external actors closely engaged in supporting transitional governments may be held indirectly liable for the acts of such governments exceeding their authority (p. 276).

De Groof positions himself as a "witness" to the development of international law, rather than a norm entrepreneur or advocate (p. 196). Nevertheless, the book straddles the line between arguing what the law is (becoming) and what it should be. De Groof rightly sees the potential for international law to serve a positive and much needed function: promoting the rule of law in a time of legal uncertainty, encouraging greater societal inclusion, and curbing the excesses of international interventionism. In light of the terrible consequences of externally-imposed political transitions, these are worthy aims, and De Groof's call for a "revival" of the principle of self-determination in the transitional context (p. 258) seems a good place to start. While the book itself does not set out to address the question of effectiveness, one cannot help, however, but wonder how effective the legal framework set out in *State Renaissance* is (or could be). As De Groof notes (p. 315), those who initiate the transition and form the transitional government invariably define the rules of the game, thereby exercising significant influence over the transition. The capacity of other societal groups to shape the transition's outcomes may therefore remain limited, even if they are subsequently and progressively "included" in the process.

Such issues are picked up in *International Law and Transitional Governance*. Contributors to the edited volume come from a range of academic and practitioner backgrounds with the aim to "dig deeper and identify possible pitfalls" of transitional governance, and in so doing, "signal a number of key biases and challenges" (p. 154). While the topics addressed by the authors are varied, the book's central contribution is to highlight the agendas that frequently lie behind international engagement in political transitions. The first two chapters, by the editors, describe the phenomenon of transitional governance in line with the typology offered in *State Renaissance*, and argue for greater international legal research (pp. 1 and 14-15). In the third chapter, Adam Day and David M. Malone place transitional governance in its historical context, explaining how the difficult and costly experiences of international territorial administration in Kosovo and East Timor in the 1990s led to "domestically-driven internationally-supported transitional governance as the preferred response to major conflicts" (p. 19). They suggest that, given this history, "Western agendas in post-conflict transitions can be deeply problematic, but remain crucial to understanding the context of post-conflict transitions" (p. 20).

Having set the scene, subsequent chapters delve deeper into the potentially problematic role of external actors in political transitions. Sumit Bisarya describes the expansive range of international organizations heavily engaged in supporting constitution-making during transitions. Citing examples from Kenya and Tunisia, he suggests that, contrary to the ideal of neutral and unbiased advice-giving, many of these actors are constrained or otherwise influenced by the domestic and international legal frameworks within which they operate. Zinaida Miller challenges the notion of transitional governance as "temporary, transitional and exceptional" (p. 123) and in so doing explores how international actors have come to define the ends, and therefore the aims, of transitions (pp. 123-124). Vasuki Nesiah goes one step further to argue that transitional governance has allowed external actors to pursue (neo-)colonial aims under the guise of "local-

ownership": through transitional governance, she suggests, "local ownership becomes a dimension of global governance" (p. 141). On a separate note, Christine
Bell and Robert A. Forster address the political and legal factors that influence the
formal manner in which political transitions are constituted. Noam Wiener argues
that there is no requirement in international law for transitional governments to
be democratically elected, and Matthew Saul suggests that a commitment to self-
determination through "develop[ing] an environment suitable for elections" (p.
104) may serve as a more appropriate, if as yet underdeveloped, yardstick.

   The edited volume is particularly effective at highlighting the practical di-
lemmas and contradictions concerning the role of international actors, and international law, in transitional governance. As with De Groof in *State Renaissance*,
Saul sees the potential for self-determination to serve as a guiding norm towards
inclusive and nationally-owned political transitions. He rightly points out, however, that determining who can validly give consent to international intervention
may be difficult, and suggests that international recognition may help to determine whether a transitional government can validly do so (pp. 99-102). This
author wonders, however, whether such an approach may place ultimate power
back in the hands of international actors, thereby defeating the rule's purpose.
States and international organizations often play a significant role in legitimizing,
if not determining, the composition of transitional governments: to what extent
can the "consent" of such governments be truly genuine, representative and free?
Notably, Saul acknowledges that "the individuals chosen to form the transitional
government may have little claim to be an embodiment of the will of the people" and that "[i]n such circumstances, consent from the transitional authority to
international involvement may maintain consistency with the legal right to self-
determination, but this will be largely without substance" (pp. 101-102). Other
contributors are much more sceptical as to the positive role of international law.
Miller suggests that even the principle of self-determination, forged through the
struggles of decolonization, does not live up to its emancipatory expectations (p.
124) and calls for far more attention to be paid "to the ways in which transitional
governance itself distributes power and allocates resources" (p. 126).

   Ultimately, the two books make for interesting, informative and contrasting reading. While *State Renaissance* highlights the potential for international
law to serve as a framework for inclusive and locally-owned political transitions, contributors to *International Law and Transitional Governance* caution
that, in practice, the in-built biases of international law may undermine these
very aims. In the introductory chapters of *State Renaissance*, De Groof identifies the contradiction inherent in a form of governance which is both ostensibly
"locally-owned" and yet is often internationally initiated and facilitated (see in
particular p. 36). If the international legal framework for transitional governance
evolves through the practice of States that support it, one may query the extent to
which that framework can be effective in restraining it. Given, however, the legal
uncertainty which clouds most political transitions and the importance of restoring effective government in conflict-affected States, it is hard not to accept that
greater regulation could be useful. Is international law as it currently stands part
of the problem? And even if it is, can it be part of the solution? By posing such

questions, *State Renaissance: Transitional Governance under International Law* and *International Law and Transitional Governance: Critical Perspectives* have begun an important conversation.

WILLIAM UNDERWOOD[*]

ROBERTO VIRZO, *La confisca nell'azione internazionale di contrasto ad attività criminali* (Confiscation in International Action Against Crime), Napoli, Edizioni Scientifiche Italiane, 2020, pp. XIV-250.

Roberto Virzo's book is a welcome addition to the growing body of Italian and international scholarship addressing confiscation as a tool in the fight against crime. Some of these works have focused on the domestic legal framework and the significant developments occurring at the EU level, which often build upon, or are at any rate connected to, international obligations or recommendations to enact different forms of confiscation (see for instance LIGETI and SIMONATO (eds.), *Chasing Criminal Money: Challenges and Perspectives on Asset Recovery in the EU*, Oxford, 2017, or more recently CASTRONUOVO and GRANDI (eds.), *Confische e sanzioni patrimoniali nella dimensione interna ed europea* ("Confiscations and sanctions targeting assets in the domestic and European dimensions"), Napoli, 2021); other recent studies deal with specific international instruments or with international obligations relating to confiscation as part of a broader analysis of those instruments (see e.g. ROSE, KUBICIEL and LANDWEHR (eds.), *The United Nations Convention Against Corruption – A Commentary*, Oxford, 2019; BALSAMO, MATTARELLA and TARTAGLIA (eds.), *La Convenzione di Palermo: il futuro della lotta alla criminalità organizzata transnazionale* ("The Palermo Convention: the future of the fight against transnational organized crime"), Torino, 2021, in chapter 7 of which Antonio Balsamo addresses asset recovery). Virzo's monograph offers instead an all-round analysis of confiscation from the perspective of international law, discussing the various purposes it may serve – and the multifarious international legal instruments that regulate it – as a means of preventing and repressing criminal activities; it also discusses the difficulties that may arise in the implementation of confiscation measures, particularly insofar as they impact on internationally protected human rights.

The book divides into three chapters and a Conclusion. Chapter I sets out the framework for the analysis, providing a concise historical outline of international regulation of confiscation – from limitations envisaged by the Jay Treaty and instruments of international humanitarian law (p. 2 ff.) to the different approach adopted by modern instruments, where asset recovery is considered as a key tool in effectively combating crime. Furthermore, Virzo specifies the notion of confiscation he accepts for the purposes of the book as one based on the permanent effects of deprivation of property in some way connected to criminal activities:

---

[*] Doctoral Candidate in International Law, Stockholm University.

this approach is in line with that followed by several international treaties and by the European Court of Human Rights and allows a distinction to be drawn between confiscation and other similar measures (notably seizure) (pp. 8-9). This Chapter also discusses the different typologies and functions of confiscation: the analysis addresses examples of domestic legislation – from examples of complete dispossession that are not of exclusively historical interest (pp. 2 and 17) to the Italian "*confisca di prevenzione*" (preventive confiscation) (p. 41 ff.) – but chiefly focuses on confiscation under international law. It is from this perspective that the author discusses confiscation of the instrumentalities and proceeds of crime (p. 20 ff.), value confiscation (p. 25 ff.), extended confiscation (p. 29 ff.) and forms of non-conviction-based confiscation (p. 34 ff.), addressing the distinct problems originated by the latter type of confiscation in a human rights context, specifically in the light of ECtHR case law. As this case law confirms, confiscation measures are usually thought of as either a form of (accessory) punishment or as functional to deterring crime, in terms of both specific and general prevention, or as compensatory measures. Virzo's analysis shows that the function of confiscation is usually hybrid, combining one or more of the above aims, as well as protecting other interests of States and of the international community as a whole. For instance, confiscation as a measure implementing the CITES convention (also) serves the interest of preserving biodiversity for future generations (p. 36), whereas confiscation under the Statute of the International Criminal Court is functional to obtaining reparation for victims of international crimes (p. 167 ff.).

These functions are at times furthered and developed through domestic implementing practice, as is the case with the CITES itself (p. 117 ff.) as well as other instruments, such as those currently in force in the field of the protection of cultural heritage (p. 122 ff.), which do not impose the adoption of confiscation measures on participating States but are in this respect complemented through domestic implementing legislation. Chapter II discusses these aspects in the context of a systematic analysis of the role of confiscation in addressing a wide range of criminal activities – from drug trafficking to human trafficking and corruption, from trafficking in protected species to the financing of terrorism and international crimes *stricto sensu*, and more. Relevant international instruments are examined in the light of international and domestic case law: besides considering numerous "transnational criminal law" treaties – including the Palermo Convention and its Supplementing Protocols, the United Nations Convention against Corruption, the United Nations Convention against the Illicit Traffic in Narcotic Drugs and Psychotropic Substances, the International Convention for the Suppression of the Financing of Terrorism, the Council of Europe Convention on Action against Trafficking in Human Beings and other regional regimes, including but not limited to EU Law – Chapter II also discusses the statutes of international criminal tribunals, notably of the International Criminal Court (ICC) mentioned above, and of hybrid tribunals such as the Extraordinary African Chambers in Senegal; conventions that are not primarily focused on criminal matters, such as the CITES Convention, and treaties relating to the protection of cultural heritage discussed above; resolutions of the Security Council and non-binding instruments such as, for instance, the Financial Action Task Force's recommendations, which underpin the case law of the European Court of Human Rights in the framework of its systemic interpretation of the European Convention on Human Rights.

This comprehensive analysis confirms that confiscation is perceived as particularly useful in the fight against very different forms of crime; bearing this in mind, Chapter III considers the limitations to States' discretion in adopting confiscation measures stemming from international human rights law. Virzo convincingly suggests a systemic approach to the interpretation of international norms relating to confiscations, which should be read in the light of international human rights guarantees (p. 175 ff.). The most relevant problems in this respect are discussed by focusing mainly on the case law of the European Court of Human Rights, in particular on the compatibility between confiscation and, respectively, the principle of legality (Article 7 ECHR), the right to a fair trial (Article 6 ECHR) and the right to property (Article 1 of Protocol No. 1) (p. 178 ff.). This emphasis is not surprising since other regional human rights courts have not had many opportunities to address the topic so far, but the focus on the regional European experience nonetheless means that some questions relating to universal human rights standards are not explicitly addressed in this context. In particular, the author assumes that the right to property is protected by universally applicable standards, and here some elaboration might have been welcome since neither the Covenant on Civil and Political Rights nor the Covenant on Economic, Social and Cultural Rights enshrine it. Be that as it may, relevant universal legal standards are identified and discussed by reference to developments in other contexts, notably the case law of the Special Tribunal for Lebanon (p. 179 on the principle of legality), the International Court of Justice and the ICC (e.g. at p. 186 ff. as regards fair trial), the International Tribunal on the Law of the Sea and other law of the sea jurisdictions (p. 193 on fair trial, p. 197 ff. on the right to property).

While fully aware of the widespread perception that confiscation is as an effective tool to combat different forms of crime, the author maintains that customary international law does not presently set forth any obligations in this regard: he reaches this conclusion on the basis of a critical analysis of international practice, *opinio juris* and case law, carefully appraising developments and stances which might point to a different outcome (p. 206 ff.).

Moreover, the Conclusion restates that whenever obligations to enact confiscation are envisaged by treaties and other international instruments, they should be implemented with full respect of international and domestic human rights guarantees. Also in this respect, which is crucial to the correct implementation of international obligations relating to the fight against crime more broadly, the book offers a balanced justification, which considers not only the consistent body of case law of the Strasbourg court but also universal treaty practice and case law of other international jurisdictions. More generally, the main value of the book lies in the author's ability to address its topic from an inter-systemic and general international law perspective, taking account of developments in very different areas of international (and EU) law and with full consideration of their impact on domestic legal orders. This will engage the interest of both international and domestic lawyers, and not only those with a specific interest in confiscations or in the international legal framework relating to the fight against crime.

SERENA FORLATI[*]

---

[*] Professor of International Law, University of Ferrara.

INDEX

MAGNETIC CONFINEMENT FUSION:
ENERGY THAT IMITATES THE STARS

Magnetic fusion works well in the Sun, where gravitational forces and dizzying temperatures force hydrogen atoms to join together to form helium and release energy. Reproducing similar conditions on earth requires an enormous effort. Being aware of the strategic importance of contributing to addressing this challenge, Eni is working with its partners to create a reactor prototype, SPARC, which will be able to manage and confine the mixture of deuterium and tritium brought to ultra-high temperatures by electromagnetic wave beams to create the conditions for controlled fusion [...]

Read more
on
eni.com